A. Randall.

Oxfd.

1965.

ILLUSTRIOUS FRIENDS

JOSEPH SEVERN
Drawing by Seymour Kirkup, Rome 1822

SHEILA BIRKENHEAD

ILLUSTRIOUS
FRIENDS

THE STORY OF JOSEPH SEVERN
AND HIS SON ARTHUR

HAMISH HAMILTON

LONDON

Printed in Great Britain
in the City of Oxford
AT THE ALDEN PRESS

To Lady B
grand-daughter of Joseph Severn and niece of Arthur
in admiration and affection

CONTENTS

LIST OF ILLUSTRATIONS

INTRODUCTION

IT IS A CURIOUS COINCIDENCE that a father and his son should each have left his name to posterity because of his friendship with a great man. Joseph Severn's name is known not, as he had hoped, as a celebrated painter, but as the friend who nursed John Keats, almost single-handed, through the terrible weeks of his fatal illness in Rome, far from all other friends.

Arthur Severn, Joseph's youngest son, is remembered — again, not as he had hoped, as a famous artist — but as having, with his wife, cared for her cousin, John Ruskin. His case was very different. His father's friendship for the poet was between two young men of the same generation, but Ruskin was twenty-three years Arthur's senior; and while Joseph's unselfish care of Keats helped him to success as an artist, Arthur's involvement with Ruskin, though it made his life easier, in the end probably worked against the full development of his gifts.

Following early success, with a picture accepted for the Royal Academy before his twenty-first birthday, he married Joan Ruskin Agnew, Ruskin's cousin, after being made by him to wait three years for her. She adored her cousin, to whom, as one of his friends said, she was both sister and daughter. Ruskin would call upon her whenever he needed comfort or reassurance, and though she was devoted to Arthur and to her children, she always responded without hesitation; so that as Ruskin's health deteriorated Arthur's life was constantly liable to sudden disruption, when Joan would leave home at a moment's notice to fly to her cousin, and later, as Ruskin's attacks became more severe, he would have to abandon whatever he was doing to accompany her. The increasing amount of time that they spent with Ruskin at Brantwood, where Arthur could indulge his passion for sailing, on Coniston Water, and where he had no financial responsibilities, may have been comfortable, but it blunted his ambition and discouraged the hard work and dedication to a painter's life with which he had started out as a young man.

Incidentally it is not true, as almost all biographers of Ruskin have said, and as Joan Severn at the end of her life came to imply, that she and Arthur went to live permanently with her cousin soon after he bought Brantwood. The truth is that they went to stay with him then for a few weeks and returned to their own house at Herne Hill (the lease of which had been given to Joan as a wedding present by Ruskin). Herne Hill was, and continued to be, their home. Ruskin would stay with them there when he was in London, but every summer he would urge them to come to Brantwood, and later to bring their children with them. When he had a mental breakdown they had to be there, to take responsibility for him, and in any case Joan was so devoted to him that she could not have borne to be away from him when he was ill. As the danger of such collapses became more frequent they had to spend more and more time there, but it was not until Ruskin's last attack, from which his brain never recovered, that it became their home, although he had made it over to them several years before. Arthur renewed the lease of the Herne Hill house for 21 years when it ended, and after that bought another house in London. He was never really a country man.

I have been struck when reading Leonard Woolf's tragic description of his wife's illness, how exactly Virginia Woolf's symptoms and mental processes paralleled those of Ruskin. Both were in the same pitiful dilemma – though Ruskin did not come to it until the middle of his life, while she lived with its menace from childhood. If they could be content to live the life of vegetables, never tiring themselves mentally or physically, they could remain well. But if they were subjected to any severe physical, mental or emotional strain, symptoms at once appeared which, if ignored, would be followed by mental breakdowns, at their worst passing into temporary insanity. Ruskin in his romance with Rose La Touche was submitted to intense emotional pressure and to him, as to Virginia Woolf, a life without concentrated work and flights of brilliant creative imagination was inconceivable. 'As well try to prevent the sea coming in as keep him from working,' Joan said of her cousin in despair. By giving full rein to their genius both sealed their own fate.

I have already told Joseph Severn's story in a book entitled *Against Oblivion* which was published during the war. But I have been able to make various additions to the story and in particular to give Joseph's letters home, describing his journey with Keats to Rome and his friend's last illness, with greater accuracy, as at that time the original letters were not available and transcripts made by earlier writers were often inexact. Most of these letters are now in the Houghton Library at Harvard and have been published, edited by Professor H. E. Rollins, in *The Keats Circle*. I have also since had the advantage of reading several chapters of the manuscript of Joseph's reminiscences which have been preserved.

When I first wrote about Joseph Severn I knew little about Arthur, but my interest in him was aroused when the manuscript of his unpublished Memoirs came into my hands with a number of his letters. For twenty-four years Ruskin wrote almost every day to Joan Severn, and after her marriage if she was ill, to Arthur. There are thousands of these letters in the possession of the Education Trust alone, which build up a wonderful picture of their relationship. There is more Severn correspondence in the John Rylands Library in Manchester and in the Pierpont Morgan Library, New York, letters between Ruskin and the Cowper-Temples (mostly about his love for Rose La Touche and Joan's engagement to Rose's brother), and between Ruskin and Thomas Richmond, as well as letters between Lady Simon, wife of Ruskin's famous doctor friend, and Joan, written during his different illnesses. The Houghton Library at Harvard has Professor Norton's papers, which include Joan's letters to him over a period of more than thirty years, and the university libraries at Yale and Illinois also contain more relevant correspondence. The majority of the above letters are hitherto unpublished.

The two periods of Joseph Severn's life which were spent in Rome are covered by his long letters home and the middle period in London by his children's letters and Mary and Eleanor Severn's diaries.

From all this correspondence, and from family letters and albums of their drawings, I hope I have been able to build up a picture of the Severns' lives which will be of interest to some people and which shows the two great men, with whose names their own are indissolubly linked, from a somewhat different angle.

In a way I have come to feel that I have lived with them all. My favourite is Mary, Joseph's gifted daughter, who, in her early twenties, when her father's fortunes were at their lowest ebb, kept not only herself, but her family by her painting; who loved poetry, painted Queen Victoria's children, married the saturnine Charles Newton and died at only thirty-four.

But I am also very fond of Mary's 'Mama', not least for her indomitable remark when, after days of staving off writs and bailiffs, she extravagantly hired a hansom cab and sank back on the seat: 'Well, however poor I am, there are certain things I *cannot* give up — Hansoms, cold cream and violet powder.'

And who could fail to love the feminine, warm-hearted Joan, who plump and comely, at the age of sixty and far from her native Scotland, was still willing to give a display of sword-dancing, using the fire-irons for swords, and whose unselfish love for her cousin, John Ruskin, made the tragic long-drawn-out end to his life bearable?

My first thanks must be to my mother-in-law and to her sister, the late Lady Smith, grand-daughters of Joseph Severn and nieces of Arthur, who have provided such a number of letters, drawings and old photographs and by their own recollections have given me invaluable help in writing this book. I also wish to express my gratitude to Mrs Lilian Fairclough who saved the typescript of Arthur Severn's Memoirs and a number of his letters from destruction and kindly gave them to me.

For permission to read and quote from the Ruskin and Severn letters bought by the late Mr J. Howard Whitehouse and now in the Ruskin Galleries at Bembridge School, my grateful thanks are due to Mr R. G. Lloyd, Q.C., Chairman of the Education Trust, also to Mr James Dearden, the Curator, who has been unfailingly helpful in answering questions and suggesting further sources of information. For their kind assistance I wish also to thank Mr Peter Evans, of

Mackrell, Ward & Evans, solicitors to Ruskin and the Arthur Severns; the Dean of Durham and Mr Guy Severn, grandsons of Walter Severn; the late Mrs Altounyan and Miss Gnosspelius, daughter and grand-daughter of W. G. Collingwood; Mr Graham, Curator of Brantwood; the late Professor E. Robertson and Dr F. Taylor of the John Rylands Library; Miss Charlotte Lutyens and Mrs Gee of Keats House, Hampstead; Mr W. H. Bond of the Houghton Library; Mr Herbert Cahoon of the Pierpont Morgan Library; Miss Dorothy Bridgwater of Yale University Library; Mr Thomas R. Ratcliffe Jr. of the University of Illinois Library; Mr David Piper, Director of the National Portrait Gallery; and Signora Cacciatore, Curator of Keats-Shelley House, Rome. I must also express my gratitude to the staff of the London Library for their courtesy and efficiency.

For permission to quote from documents in their possession I am indebted to Dr Helen Gill Viljoen; Miss Gwen Williams, grand-daughter of Henry Severn; the Reverend I. Hutchinson; Lady Unwin, grand-daughter of Thomas Severn; the Libraries Committee of the Borough of Camden; the John Rylands Library, Manchester; the Houghton Library, Harvard University; Pierpont Morgan Library, New York; Yale University Library; and the University of Illinois Library. I am also grateful to Sir Stanley Unwin and the Ruskin Trustees for permission to quote from unpublished Ruskin letters; to Dr Joan Evans and the Clarendon Press for permission to quote from *The Diaries of John Ruskin*; to Mr Rayner Unwin and Allen & Unwin for permission to quote from *The Gulf of Years*; to Allen & Unwin for permission to quote from *Reminiscences of a Specialist*; to the Harvard University Press for permission to quote from *The Keats Circle*; to Bernard Quaritch Ltd. for permission to quote from *Letters of John Ruskin to Bernard Quaritch*; to John Murray for permission to quote from *Works and Days*; and to Mr George Leon and Routledge & Kegan Paul for permission to quote from *Ruskin, The Great Victorian*.

I also wish to thank Lady Severn; Mrs Claude Furneaux; Miss Gwen Williams; the Dean of Durham; the Committee of Keats-Shelley House, Rome; the Victoria and Albert Museum; the Libraries Committee of the Borough of Camden; Wellesley College Library, Massachusetts; the Education Trust; and the Ruskin Museum, Coniston, for allowing me to reproduce pictures or photographs in their possession; Lady Cotterell and Miss Chloe Otto for reading the proofs; and Miss June Rossdale for her continuous help in the preparation of this book and for typing and retyping the manuscript.

Keats was accompanied to Rome and attended in his last illness by Mr Severn, a young artist of the highest promise, who, I have been informed, 'almost risked his own life, and sacrificed every prospect to unwearied attendance upon his dying friend'.

Had I known these circumstances before the completion of my poem, I should have been tempted to add my feeble tribute of applause to the more solid recompense which the virtuous man finds in the recollection of his own motives. Mr Severn can dispense with a reward from 'such stuff as dreams are made of'. His conduct is a golden augury of the success of his future career: may the unextinguished Spirit of his illustrious friend animate the creations of his pencil, and plead against Oblivion for his name!

—Preface to SHELLEY's Adonais, 1821

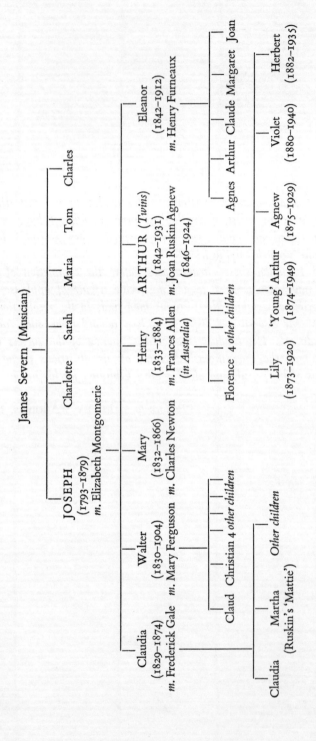

MEMBERS OF THE SEVERN FAMILY REFERRED TO IN THIS BOOK

James Severn (Musician)

JOSEPH (1793–1879)
m. Elizabeth Montgomerie

Charlotte Sarah Maria Tom Charles

Claudia (1829–1874) m. Frederick Gale
Walter (1830–1904) m. Mary Fergusson
Mary (1832–1866) m. Charles Newton
Henry (1833–1884) m. Frances Allen (in Australia)
ARTHUR (Twins) (1842–1931) m. Joan Ruskin Agnew (1846–1924)
Eleanor (1842–1912) m. Henry Furneaux

Claud Christian 4 other children

Claudia
Martha (Ruskin's 'Mattie')
Other children

Florence 4 other children

Lily (1873–1920)
'Young' Arthur (1874–1949)
Agnew (1875–1929)
Violet (1880–1940)
Herbert (1882–1935)

Agnes Arthur Claude Margaret Joan

ILLUSTRIOUS FRIENDS

CHAPTER I

ACADEMY STUDENT

1813–1819

THE STUDENTS AT THE ROYAL ACADEMY SCHOOLS were a motley crowd. Some were poorly but neatly dressed, some in threadbare coats and neckties that were none too clean. The noise was deafening when they assembled at Somerset House beneath ceilings painted by Angelica Kauffman, Cipriani and Sir Joshua Reynolds, shouting and pushing in a rush to secure a pile of the boxes on which they would perch while they were drawing. Here and there you would see a lordly fellow in Hessian boots thrusting the others aside, and taking as his right the largest pyramid of boxes and the best place to sit. These few, who gave the impression of conferring a favour on students and master alike by their presence, were the sons of Royal Academicians.[1]

Joseph Severn was not among them; he had had a hard battle even to get to the classes.

He was twenty years old, a handsome young man of slightly less than medium height, with dark curly hair and a humorous mouth. His father was a musician turned music-master, who could play five instruments. Passionately interested in pictures and delighted to find his eldest son at an early age showing signs of a precocious talent for drawing, he had set himself to develop his gift. Nevertheless, with a wife and five other children to support, it was out of the question for a music master to pay for an artistic education for his son and then to keep him, perhaps for several years, until he had established himself as a painter. So, soon after Joseph's fourteenth birthday, his father had apprenticed him to an engraver, Mr William Bond, who was unusual in demanding no premium and stipulated only that the father should give an undertaking about the board and lodging of his son. Bond was impressed by the drawings which James Severn showed him and was well pleased at gaining such a promising pupil. Joseph, too, at first was happy and the idea of drawing from oil paintings, which he had so far never attempted, filled him with excitement.

But soon he had been set to stab the copper and when he had mastered this and thought he would return to drawing, he had been quickly disillusioned. His master had told him harshly that he was employing him as an assistant in his trade, and not as a tame artist. Joseph was miserable and reproached his father bitterly for not having made clear to him what his apprenticeship involved. He

[1] *The Richmond Papers* by A. M. W. Stirling, p. 8.

I

had been 'popped into slavery', he said wretchedly, 'and doomed to stab the copper for seven long years'.

James Severn was a man with dark good looks and a violent temper. He could be hard on his children — he must never be contradicted, they must make no noise and no domestic work must be done in his presence — but when he was in a good mood, he would tell them stories and sing and act for them. They both loved and feared him. These reproaches from his son led to a terrible scene; he flew into a passion, shouting that Joseph ought to be grateful to his father for apprenticing him to an honourable trade. Joseph, for the first time in his life defying him, insisted that his only ambition was to be an artist and now he had only a few hours in the evening to practise painting. Even the finest engravings were not creative. He must have training. He must study anatomy. He must attend the Academy Schools.

After a furious tirade from James Severn about his son's ingratitude, insolence and conceit, Mrs Severn, with the serenity and sympathy which led Joseph to adore her as his 'angel-mother', calmed them both and eventually persuaded her husband to speak to Mr Bond. The engraver agreed that he should have certain holidays, on condition that he would be more assiduous in his work at other times, and Joseph divided his free time between reading and painting. He was determined to be worthy of a higher position in the world, and tried to enlarge his store of knowledge. He read history, poetry, letters and essays — he even wrestled for a short time with some books on mathematics. His enthusiasm was infinite, but his efforts to educate himself were wild and unplanned.

In his spare time he began to paint small portraits in water-colours, for which he charged half a guinea. But he felt more and more strongly that he would never make any considerable progress in his art until he had proper training and as he neared the end of his seven years' apprenticeship it became clear to Mr Bond that, if Joseph were not allowed to attend the Royal Academy classes, he would feel nothing but hatred and bitterness for his master. He had done good work for the engraver, who was anxious to be able to make use of him when he was no longer bound to him. So, almost a year before he had completed his seven years, Mr Bond capitulated, and the determined young man, now twenty years old, had his way and became a student at the Academy Schools. His delight knew no bounds.

Even the discovery that wealth and influence counted for more than talent in the Royal Academy classes failed to quench his enthusiasm. When he was studying in the Antique Class he would walk back to Hoxton after the class was ended, eat a hasty supper, and settle down to another two hours of work on Laocoon or the Dying Gladiator.

Life became easier for Joseph when his second sister, Sarah, married. She was two years his junior and more like him than the sweet, placid Charlotte who was only a year younger than himself and already married to a neighbour in Hoxton. Sarah was the cleverest of the girls — Maria was the youngest, merry and vivacious, with dark hair and blue eyes. Three years after her came Tom, who was already showing great promise as a musician. He could not only sing beautifully — they could all do that — but he won praise from his father, a severe critic in anything to do with music, for his performance both on the harpsichord and the violin. His ambition was to play the organ like his grandfather, James Severn's father, who had been organist at the church in Leadenhall Street. To all the family music had seemed as essential as food from a very early age. Little Charles, twelve years younger than Joseph and the baby of the family, was also musically gifted, but Joseph was the only one to show a talent for painting and he was his father's favourite.

After her marriage Sarah let him have a room in her house in Goswell Street; it was his first studio and he would sleep there several nights a week. He could work there in the evenings undisturbed, or sometimes they would sit together by her fire, while he confided in her his hopes and ambitions, and Sarah would listen and admire and prophesy that all his dreams would come true.

*

While Joseph was still apprenticed to Mr Bond his life was divided entirely between his home, the engraver's and the Academy Classes. But by the time that he had completed his seven years he had begun to work up a small connexion as a miniature painter and found he could raise his prices a little. The world was opening to him and he had time to make new friends.

At twenty-two, although small and still rather thin, Joseph was a strikingly handsome young man. His dark hair was naturally curly; strongly marked eyebrows arched over large brown eyes and his mouth was full under a straight nose. His manner, too, was attractive; his open face and the laughter which bubbled up so easily from the optimism and serenity which were his heritage from his mother — all these drew people to him.

Some of his new friends were fellow-students at the Academy Art Schools. There was pale, boyish George Richmond, a few years younger than Joseph, who shared his love of music. Walking home after the classes they would argue about Handel and Purcell and Mozart, and why there were no great English composers living. There was young Edwin Landseer, with whom he was set, on his first day in the Life Class, to draw the Feet of Hercules from a model. There was William Haslam, so friendly and reliable, who at twenty-one was working in his father's firm of solicitors. He had been Joseph's companion on that always-to-be-remembered evening when Mrs Siddons had emerged from her retirement to play Queen Katherine in *Henry VIII*.

Then there were three brothers whom he met with Haslam — George, John and Tom Keats. He met George, the second brother and the business man of the family, first. Their parents were dead, Joseph learned, and he worked in the office of his guardian — a Mr Abbey, wholesale tea-dealer in St Pancras Lane.

Joseph soon realized, from the way his friend spoke, what an intensely strong affection bound the three brothers together. The youngest, Tom, was very tall and thin and delicate, and John, the eldest brother, was a medical student at Guy's. Soon Joseph was friendly with all three. Or rather, he was friendly with the two younger brothers; for the eldest his feelings were too complicated to be expressed by so simple a word.

John Keats was two years younger than Joseph but he already radiated the powerful attraction of genius. He was shorter than George – in fact, he was not much over five feet tall. But he was so well made, being strong, broad-shouldered and compactly built, and moreover his bearing was so erect and manly, that one scarcely noticed his lack of inches. It was only when he was reading, or rapt in some deep reverie, that one realized that he was a small man. Then his chest would fall in, his head would bend forward 'as though weightily over-burdened', Joseph described it later, and his eyes 'seemed almost to throw a light before his face'.[1] It was these brilliant eyes which immediately attracted one's attention at a first meeting. They glowed as though with an inward light, wonderfully bright and of a curious hazel colour. It was almost as an afterthought that people who met him noted the other details of this remarkable face, the wide sensitive mouth, the forehead broad and powerful, the high cheek-bones and boldly modelled nose. 'The character and expression of Keats's features would arrest even the casual passenger in the street', wrote one of their mutual friends after his death.

John Keats made no secret of the fact that when he had passed his examination he had no intention of practising as a doctor. He could live for a year or two on his share of the money which their grandmother had left the brothers. He intended to leave Guy's when he came of age next year, and to devote himself to writing poetry. Poetry was the only thing worth the attention of superior minds, he said, and compared to it all other pursuits were mean and tame. The greatest men in the world were the poets, and to rank among them was the chief object of his ambition. His brothers did not try to dissuade him, although they knew that his decision would anger their guardian. Their admiration for their brother amounted almost to worship, and they had perfect confidence that he was born to be exalted and to exalt their name.[2]

George was the practical man of affairs of the trio. He managed their finances and neither John nor Tom questioned what he did. 'George always stood between me and any dealings with the world,'[3] John Keats was to say sadly, later on, when troubles were gathering round him, and George was far away, and Tom dead. George's common sense certainly relieved his elder brother of responsibilities and left his imagination unburdened by everyday cares. But it was tall, narrow-chested Tom who shared his life of the spirit most completely.

[1] Joseph Severn's *Reminiscences*, quoted *Life and Letters of Joseph Severn* by W. Sharp, p. 20.
[2] Henry Stephens, quoted *John Keats* by Colvin, p. 31.
[3] 31st May, 1819. *Letters of John Keats*, edited by M. Buxton Forman, p. 345.

George said that there was no man living who understood John as well as Tom did. He could understand his abnormally sensitive reactions. He realized how anything beautiful or uncommon — a sight, a sound, a scent — would pierce John Keats with a pleasure that was almost pain. It was this hyper-sensitiveness, this extra-intensity of feeling, which made him a poet and which, at the same time, left him so vulnerable to the emotional blows which were to fall on him, as one by one those he loved were to be torn from him.

Although he was a healthy, normal young man, with good spirits and fond of company, John Keats was already conscious that he had greatness within him, even though it might never be recognized by the world.

*

To Joseph his new friend's knowledge seemed infinite. Dazzled, he followed Keats, and learned to love with him his heroes — Chaucer, Spenser and Shake-speare. His untrained love of poetry grew, he loved to hear Keats linger over some phrase when he was reading aloud, savouring its beauty and betraying his pleasure with 'one of his delightful stares'.

John Keats, for his part, must have been touched by Joseph's enthusiasm and his genuine appreciation of beauty. His charm of manner made him a good companion, and he showed his pleasure and interest so naïvely in every new discovery, that Keats once burst out laughing and assured him that he was 'the most astonishingly suggestive innocent!' He was able to show Keats new beauties, too, in a world where his own judgment was less untrained. Early in their friendship he took Keats to see Titian's *Bacchus* at the National Gallery, which was mirrored later in the description of 'Bacchus and his crew' in Keats's poem, *Endymion*. After this they would often go to picture exhibitions and the sculpture galleries together. One of their favourite expeditions was to the British Museum to see the Elgin Marbles, and soon Joseph was introduced by Keats to Mr Haydon, the painter, whose efforts had led to the Marbles being bought for the nation.

What an extraordinary creature the artist was! Joseph was both fascinated and repelled. At their first meeting he felt battered by the strength and exuberance of his personality. Keats was strongly impressed by him and wrote a sonnet on their first meeting, to which Haydon replied with a promise to send it on to the young poet's hero, Wordsworth. The friendship between them grew, and so Joseph, too, came to know him better and was able to form some sort of estimate of him as a man. It seemed to Joseph that he was larger than life. His emotions seemed more tempestuous and elemental than those of a mere man — he was cast in heroic mould. As he told how he had quelled this enemy with a letter to the Press and shattered another in argument over a dinner-table, his eyes would flash beneath his great domed forehead, his belligerent chin would jut uncompromisingly and he would seem to swell with self-confidence and pride.

It was his honest conviction that he was the chosen of the Almighty, the greatest painter of all time, martyred and frustrated by malevolent enemies.

He was as fervent in his loves as in his hates, and he soon conceived a passionate admiration for Keats. Keats was dazzled by Haydon's enthusiasm and energy, and like so many others among this strange man's contemporaries, for some time he was bludgeoned into seeing his pictures through the artist's own eyes as what he intended them to be, and believed that he had already achieved the heights which he described so eloquently.

Joseph enjoyed and learned much from their conversations. The only jarring note was struck when Haydon got on to the subject of religion. He was a fanatically religious man but adopted a curious, almost proprietorial attitude towards God. He believed implicitly that God must be on his side in any dispute, however trivial, and that those who thwarted him must automatically be the agents of Satan. To Joseph, whose mother had taught him a truer Christianity, such presumption was horrifying, but he too was fascinated by Haydon's grandiose schemes, his gigantic canvases, his exuberance, his arrogance, his restless vitality.

On his twenty-first birthday, in October 1816, Keats fulfilled his intention of giving up his medical career, so that he might concentrate entirely on poetry. His first book of poems was published in the following spring and he gave a copy to Joseph jokingly inscribed, 'The Author consigns this copy to the Severn with all his Heart'. His friends waited, breathless, for the anticipated applause of the world to burst on their ears. Haydon, in his grandiose manner, wrote to Keats of one poem in the volume: 'It is a flash of lightning that will rouse men from their occupations and keep them trembling for the crash of thunder that *will* follow!'[1] But, apart from lukewarm reviews in two of the leading periodicals, the book was scarcely noticed by the outside world. Joseph did not see Keats for several months after this, for he had gone away to the country alone, to start work on a new poem called *Endymion*.

When Keats returned to London in June, Joseph would often walk across the fields to Hampstead, where the three brothers were now in lodgings in the house of a postman called Bentley. He would take one or two of his miniatures with him, so that he might have the excuse of finding backgrounds for them, for he was still so shy and modest that he lacked the confidence to arrive without some reason to explain his presence.

Through the Keats brothers he made many new friends. They were the centre of a group of young men, and a few others slightly older than themselves, such as Haydon, Leigh Hunt, Charles Wentworth Dilke, who was by profession a Civil Servant and in his leisure hours a student of English literature, Charles Brown, and Charles Cowden Clarke, son of the headmaster of the school at which the Keats brothers had been educated.

Joseph would visit all of them, and their female relatives were much taken by

[1] March 1817. *Letters of John Keats*, p. 14.

his good looks, his gaiety and his gentle manner. Of the very young men there was John Hamilton Reynolds, who was considered by Leigh Hunt to complete, with Keats and Shelley, the trio of rising young poets. He was soon to renounce his literary ambitions when he married, and to settle down as a lawyer. There was James Rice, too, another young lawyer, who, although always delicate, and often ill, was a great talker and was regarded as the wit of their circle. Charles Wells was the youngest of their friends — he was only seventeen years old at this time, and had been a contemporary of Tom's at school.

These young men formed a group of friends. They were not always in London at the same time, but some of them would see each other several times a week, dining together or going to the theatre or to dances or to Haydon's studio or the British Museum, or meeting for an evening at Reynolds's home, where his lively sisters were an attraction.

Besides the easy comradeship of youth there was another emotion which was common to them all — to the shrewd Dilke and the outspoken Brown no less than to seventeen-year-old Wells — and that was admiration for, and confidence in John Keats's genius.

Keats left London again in the autumn and Joseph's visits to Hampstead were fewer for a time. Somehow the walk was not so alluring after his day's work when the pleasure of John Keats's company lay no longer at the end of his journey. Then news came that Keats had finished *Endymion* and was back in Well Walk with the Bentleys. As soon as he could get a free day Joseph went up to Hampstead to see him, and found him alone. Tom, who had always been delicate, had produced some alarming symptoms. His cough had become worse and he had several times spat blood. George had taken him to Teignmouth, hoping that the milder climate would do him good. Keats told Joseph that he would be coming to stay in London for a little while, as he was going to act as dramatic critic for the *Champion* while Reynolds was away for a Christmas holiday. He was already busy revising and copying out his new poem for publication.

During the next few weeks Joseph dined several times with Keats — Wells often making a third, as Keats was staying with him while he was in London. Keats would insist on drinking claret, which he loved, and afterwards, when the glasses were empty, they would each choose a musical instrument to imitate, and with a great deal of laughter they would play what they called 'a concert'.[1]

On other evenings they would enjoy a different type of music, when they went together to the house of Vincent Novello, the organist at the Portuguese Embassy Chapel in South Street. This was an easy-going, cosmopolitan household, where life was ruled by music. Vincent Novello was half Italian and had been educated in France, while his wife was of German extraction. Keats was fond of music and enjoyed himself when Charles Cowden Clarke first took

---

[1] 5th January, 1818. *Letters of John Keats*, p. 74.

him to the house in Oxford Road. Charles was a constant visitor there and was later to marry Novello's daughter, Mary, who at this time was still a child. Joseph and Keats went several times together, and Joseph was enchanted by the exquisite renderings of Mozart and Haydn that he heard there in the pleasant drawing-room whose walls were papered a delicate pink and decorated with water-colours. At one end of the drawing-room was a sofa table, littered with books and prints, and at the other end was a small organ. Here Novello would sit and play, in the way that caused queues of fashionable carriages to block the traffic in South Street outside the Embassy Chapel.

There would be a pause for talk and then he would play again, or Leigh Hunt or one of the Robertson brothers would sing. Years afterwards Novello's little daughter, who was sitting so quietly in the corner, was to record her memory of John Keats, 'leaning against the side of the organ, listening with rapt attention to my father's music'. She also mentioned his 'favourite position one foot raised on his other knee'. Unlike Mrs Hunt, Mrs Novello was a practical, economical woman, and the 'feast of music' was followed by refreshments in the form of bread and cheese and what Charles Lamb called 'true Lutheran beer'.[1]

One afternoon, at the turn of the year, Joseph dressed himself with particular care, before setting off to walk to Haydon's studio in Lisson Grove.

The artist greeted him boisterously and invited him to observe the progress that he was making on his huge picture of *Christ's Entry into Jerusalem*. Then he admitted Keats and Reynolds and they all stood round the fire, chatting and gazing at the gigantic canvas opposite them. Haydon had followed the example of many artists of the Renaissance by introducing the faces of his friends and famous men of his own day in the crowd surrounding Christ. Wordsworth was already there, and Keats, too, was to have a place.

Next to arrive was Leigh Hunt. In appearance he was the romantic's ideal of of a poet – a slender figure with jet-black hair and dark soft eyes. He entered talking. Joseph had met him many times before, and was used to his flow of conversation and his love of holding the centre of the stage in any gathering, though he was not so bad when there were no ladies present. When greetings had been exchanged, Hunt began at once to pace up and down the room in front of Haydon's huge canvas, inspecting each head in turn and keeping up a continuous flow of comment, not all of it complimentary, for since he and Haydon had been living as neighbours in Lisson Grove they were frequently squabbling. Haydon never accepted criticism of any sort, and a quarrel might have developed if the door bell had not pealed at that moment.

A few minutes later Joseph felt his heart beating as a tall man followed Haydon into the room. Introductions were made. It appeared that the distinguished newcomer already knew both Hunt and Keats. As he turned to warm his back at the fire Joseph studied him eagerly. His left hand had already stolen into its favourite position, in the bosom of his waistcoat. His manner was grave

[1] Mary Cowden Clarke, *My Long Life*, vol. I, pp. 11–12.

and he answered Hunt's questions deliberately, in a deep, rough voice. His face was noble, with rather bony features and burning, deep-set eyes under a jutting brow. Wordsworth was at this time forty-eight years old and already the doyen of English letters.

The conversation at supper was monopolized at first by Leigh Hunt and Haydon, who were expatiating on the charms and advantages of a vegetarian diet. Both had recently been converted to vegetarianism by Shelley. Leigh Hunt was in rhapsodies over these vegetable banquets.

'The delicious cauliflower swimming in melted butter,' he urged, 'the peas — the beans — never profaned by animal gravy — '

The poet of the Lakes bore it for a while in patience. Then, holding up his hand, he interrupted, begging leave in his deep, grave voice to ask a question. Leigh Hunt nodded eagerly, and all leaned forward to hear what Wordsworth would say. Joseph noticed a little expression of sly humour at the corner of his austere mouth.

'If,' he said deliberately, 'by good chance in these banquets you meet with a caterpillar, do you not thank your stars for the delicious morsel of animal food?'

There was some laughter, and Hunt, rather confused, turned the conversation to other matters. Joseph, although feeling that the remark was not quite of the kind that he had promised Sarah to store in his memory to repeat to her later, could not help thinking that there was a good deal of common sense in it. Wordsworth was later proved more right than he knew. Leigh Hunt and his friends became daily thinner and paler under their new régime, but they persevered, encouraged by Haydon's appearance of ruddy-faced health. One dreadful day they detected him in the act of emerging from a chop-house. When they taxed him indignantly with treachery, he admitted with *bonhomie* that for some time past he had not felt the vegetable fare to be sufficient, so he had formed the habit of going round the corner each day after he had eaten his dinner and consuming a good beefsteak. This ended the fashion for a vegetable diet among his friends. Only Shelley continued, and that was because he felt a genuine aversion to eating meat. Leigh Hunt assured Joseph dramatically that his constitution had received a blow from which he would never recover.

When the supper was ended, chairs were pushed back and tongues were loosened. Joseph did not talk much, but a thrill of delight ran through him when he heard Haydon ask Keats to recite his classical Ode to Pan from the new poem *Endymion*, which he had just completed. Haydon knew Keats's admiration of *The Excursion*, and he realized what pleasure praise from its author would give him. Joseph felt almost as excited and nervous as though it were his own work which was to be heard. His faith in John Keats, like that of all the poet's friends, had been unsubdued by one failure and was to survive another, seemingly even more complete, to burn undimmed through years of oblivion after his death. It was a remarkable testament to Keats's personality, this unforgettable impression that he made on those who knew him.

But his friends were to receive no encouragement that night. John Keats repeated his Ode 'with natural eloquence and great pathos', wrote Joseph afterwards. 'When he had finished, we all looked to Wordsworth for praise of the young poet. After a moment's pause, he coolly remarked, "A very pretty piece of Paganism," and with this cold water thrown upon us we all broke up.'[1]

*

A few weeks later, Joseph and John Keats both dined with Leigh Hunt. Hunt had lately had to leave his pretty little white house in Hampstead, and was living as neighbour to Haydon in Lisson Grove. In the intervals of dashing off some melody on his harpsichord he would impartially recite poetry, sing in a charming tenor, or settle down to an animated discussion of Shakespeare or the iniquities of the Prince Regent. There was always company in the parlour and the talk was cultured and gay. But the observant visitor might have noticed a certain artificiality about the whole ménage – that behind the delightful façade and the light-hearted host's emphasis on the delights of the senses, behind the conversation about love and food and poetry and music, poor improvident Mrs Hunt was struggling desperately to make both ends meet, and, it was to be feared, not succeeding very well.

On this evening the only other guest besides himself and Keats was Percy Bysshe Shelley. This was the first time that Joseph had met him, although Keats and Shelley were already acquainted, and he was surprised at his youthful appearance, with his pinkish girl's skin, his aureole of golden hair and his restless blue eyes. He greeted Joseph in a gentle, courteous manner, but, as always, he could not resist the temptation to say something which would shock a stranger. As soon as they had drawn their chairs up to the supper-table he led the talk to religion. Leigh Hunt, as befitted the liberals' hero, was a self-confessed atheist. Shelley's gentle manner contrasted strangely with his high-pitched voice and flushed face as he warmed to his subject.

'As for that detestable religion, the Christian –' he cried, with an eye on Joseph, who shifted unhappily on his chair but was too shy to express his distaste for this sort of opening. Seeing, no doubt, that he was succeeding in his attempt to shock his new acquaintance, Shelley turned to Hunt and began to outline his plan for a poem which he said he intended to write, in which Christ would be shown as a mountebank, and the miracles as his tricks.

This was too much for Joseph. His indignation was so violent that it overcame his diffidence. The Hunts were astonished to hear him interrupting, in a voice which trembled with anger:

'The fact that since Christ lived all the greatest men have been Christians

[1] Joseph Severn's *Reminiscences*, quoted Sharp, op. cit., p. 33.

must alone place the Christian religion beyond the reach of such low ridicule.'

Shelley immediately denied that this was so, and each began to count on his fingers the great men who were Christians and those who were not. The argument raged all the evening, with Joseph and Shelley as the two protagonists, and Hunt skating agilely over the surface of the argument, conducting little skirmishes and withdrawals against both sides. Keats listened for the most part in silence, with an occasional smile as Joseph's enthusiasm banished his shyness still further.

When they came to Shakespeare, Shelley attempted to prove that the great poet was no Christian by quoting from *Measure for Measure*. Keats smiled again as Joseph rapidly produced counter-quotations from the speeches of Portia, Hamlet and Isabella. Hunt and Keats declared that Joseph had the best of the argument, whereupon Shelley made a sudden graceful surrender, and assured Severn that he would study the subject and later write an essay on it. Joseph was very well pleased with this ending to their argument.[1]

He was happy, too, when a few evenings later, as he was working late in his room at Goswell Street, John Keats 'burst into his lodging'. In an excited voice he told Joseph of his astonishment, after the scene with Wordsworth a few nights earlier, when the great man called on him in person and invited him to supper. Keats had accepted and was now on his way home after what he declared had been a memorable evening. From his elation it seemed clear to Joseph that Wordsworth's conduct had been very different from their last meeting. Perhaps he had afterwards been ashamed of his remark.

*

During the spring and summer of 1818, Joseph was working hard on his enlarging practice as a miniature painter, and was able now and again to make portraits of some of his friends. Thus he painted all three Keats brothers, and also Reynolds and Haslam. In January and February he walked often across the fields to Hampstead to see John Keats. One of the strongest bonds between them was their love of nature. Joseph noted colours and forms with an artist's eye, but he never ceased to be astonished by Keats's power of observation. 'Nothing seemed to escape him,' he said afterwards. 'The song of a bird and the undernote of response from covert or hedge, the rustle of some animal, the changing of the green and brown lights and furtive shadows, the motions of the wind — just how it took certain tall flowers and plants — and the wayfaring of the clouds.'

The wind was a constant pleasure to him, especially when it blew across a field of oats or barley. He would spring on to a stile or the low bough of a tree to watch every movement of what he called 'the inland sea'. 'The tide! The tide!' he would cry delightedly, and the sight of the wind stirring the surface of the field would even awaken him from the dark, withdrawn moods which

[1] Joseph Severn's *Reminiscences*, quoted Sharp, op. cit., pp. 116–17.

would sometimes cloud his happiness upon their walks. Joseph was so contented
to be with him that he never questioned or resented these moments when Keats
would scarcely answer a direct question, when his happy expression stiffened into
gloom and his eyes seemed to grow even larger, troubled and unquiet. These
moods would come upon him suddenly. One moment he would be full of
spirits, his eyes glowing with pleasure at all the little incidents of life around
them; then, with no warning, his mood would change and the gleam in his eyes
would deepen into a gloomy abstraction.

Joseph soon learned that it was useless to try to dissipate the shadow when it
had once enveloped him. Only the sudden impact of beauty could rescue him,
and the wild passage of the wind always seemed to pierce his gloom and call
him back from the shadows where his mind was wandering.

In March, John Keats went to join Tom at Teignmouth, where he had spent
the winter watched over by George. Perhaps he was not sorry to leave London,
for there had been an outbreak of quarrelling between his friends. (Haydon was
no longer on speaking terms with Hunt or with Reynolds.) In any case, he felt
that he must go, for Tom's health seemed to have benefited from the milder
climate and John felt that he should be encouraged to stay at Teignmouth.
George must return to London, because it was not long now before he was
to be married to Georgiana Wylie, and – even more final separation – he
and his bride had decided to emigrate to America, where he hoped to make a
fortune.

Joseph knew how John Keats was suffering behind his reserve at the thought
that the trio of brothers was so soon to be broken up, though he did not try to
dissuade George from his purpose, for he knew what high hopes he had of
founding a business with what capital he could take with him, and making
enough money in a short time to be able to support a family.

He did not see John Keats again until he and Tom returned to London, in the
last week of May, for the wedding. Tom Keats seemed to be stronger, so that
John felt able to accompany George and his bride to Liverpool, where they were
to embark on their ship. From there he proposed to keep travelling north and to
have a holiday. He asked Haslam and Joseph in turn to accompany him on a
walking tour, but Haslam could not leave London and Joseph dared not. In
the first place, he had no money, scarcely enough for the moderate bills of the
country inns where they would have stayed, still less to pay his fare north. In the
second place, he had made quite a good connexion as a miniature painter, and to
leave it now would mean starting laboriously again from nothing when he
returned.

But Keats felt that he must get away. He was exhausted and depressed after
his great burst of creation in the spring. *Endymion* had been published in April,
with an introduction in which Keats warned the reader to expect 'great in-
experience, immaturity, and every error denoting a feverish attempt, rather
than a deed accomplished'. While he was occupied with the corrections of

Endymion, he had found time to write two, at least, of his loveliest sonnets in Shakespearean form and another long poem, *Isabella or The Pot of Basil*.

In the end Keats went with another friend – Charles Brown. Brown was nine years older than Keats, a plump, bald, bespectacled man, with a lively cultivated mind; a man of deep loyalties, obstinate prejudices and downright frankness of speech. He was practical, cared nothing for convention, and in humour was inclined to be coarse. Joseph had met him, and liked him, at Charles Dilke's house, which was, in a sense, Brown's home too. For the two friends had built together a pleasant white house on the edge of the Heath, in one half of which lived Dilke and his family, and in the other the bachelor Brown, waited on by his Irish maid, Abigail, with whom, Joseph soon learned, her master was on the most intimate terms. The garden was their mutual property.

It was a time when the days were scarcely long enough for all Joseph had to do, with his studies at the Royal Academy Schools, commissions which were now coming to him, and work which he still did for Mr Bond. At the beginning of August Mrs Dilke began to be worried about Tom Keats's health, which seemed to have made a sudden change for the worse. Her husband wrote to John, advising him to return at once.

As it happened, he was already on his way home. The six-hundred-mile tramp through Scotland in all weathers, culminating in the climbing of Ben Nevis in a thick mist, the poor food and sitting about in damp clothing, had given him a heavy cold and he presently became feverish. The physician whom he consulted in Inverness strongly advised him to give up the idea of continuing his tramp to Edinburgh and down into Cumberland, and so, reluctantly, he left Charles Brown to walk on alone. He sailed from Cromarty in a sailing smack, and after a nine-day passage was back at Hampstead on 18th August.

Joseph heard of his return and of Tom's illness from Mrs Dilke. She described John's appearance at their house. 'He was as brown and as shabby as you can imagine,' she said. 'Scarcely any shoes left, his jacket all torn at the back, a fur cap, a great plaid, and his knapsack. I cannot tell you what he looked like.'[1] When, after the hard life he had been leading, he sank contentedly into the softness of one of Mrs Dilke's armchairs, he relaxed and quoted comically, 'Why, Bottom, thou art translated!'

Soon after Keats's return Joseph was struck down by typhus fever and nearly died. The devoted nursing of his 'angel-mother' brought him through this dangerous illness. Keats came to see him when he was convalescent, bringing Reynolds with him. But after their visit Joseph saw little of his friend that autumn. Directly he was able, he returned to the classes at the Academy and worked hard in his spare time, feeling that he must double his concentration to make up for the weeks he had lost. Only rarely did he see John Keats, but when he did he was dismayed by his friend's haggard and distraught appearance. Tom

[1] 19th August, 1818. *Letters of John Keats*, p. 212.

B

was becoming daily weaker, and by the end of October, when Joseph was about again after his illness, Keats was able to leave his brother for only a few hours at a time.

One day, when they happened to meet, Joseph urged Keats to come for a walk, but he said that he did not feel strong enough to take any unnecessary exercise. His eyes, usually so alert, were strained and anguished. His manner was lethargic. It seemed an effort even to speak. When he was just back from Scotland he had told Joseph that he intended to devote himself to study, as in his stern self-criticism he felt that he must acquire more knowledge to enable him to realize the poetry that was within him.

He may have been made firmer in his resolve by the scathing reviews of *Endymion* which appeared that autumn in two of the most powerful periodicals of the day – *Blackwood's Edinburgh Magazine* and the *Quarterly*. The former, indeed, was more a personal onslaught than a criticism. *Blackwood's* had already published a libellous attack on Leigh Hunt, and now they turned on Keats, whom they affected to regard as his disciple. The anonymous writer spoke of him as 'Johnny Keats', derided his education, and described his poem as 'drivelling idiocy'. 'We venture to make one small prophecy,' he ended, 'that his bookseller will not a second time venture £50 on anything he can write. It is a better and wiser thing to be a starved apothecary than a starved poet; so back to the shop, Mr John, back to the "plasters, pills and ointment boxes". But, for Heaven's sake, young Sangrado, be a little more sparing of soporifics in your practice than you have been in your poetry.'

All Keats's friends were furious at the pettiness and unfairness of the reviewers. But after one short outburst that he 'would write no more', he quickly determined not to allow them to influence him. 'Praise or blame has but a momentary effect,' he said, 'on the man whose love of beauty in the abstract makes him a severe critic on his own works. My own domestic criticism has given me pain without comparison beyond what *Blackwood* or the *Quarterly* could possibly inflict.'[1]

But his plan to isolate himself for a time of intensive study was made impossible by Tom's condition. His brother was so ill now that he scarcely dared to leave him. Joseph became still more alarmed about his friend after a conversation with Haslam, who told him gloomily that it was well known that anyone who spent long hours in the room of a dying consumptive was liable to be attacked, himself, by the same disease. He immediately sought out Keats and urged him to take rooms near his brother instead of sharing his bedroom. John refused point-blank.

'Poor Tom looks upon me as his only comfort,' he said.[2]

Then Joseph tried to persuade him to let him take his place by Tom's bedside sometimes, so that he might occasionally have an undisturbed night. It was

---

1 9th October, 1818. *Letters of John Keats*, p. 222.
2 14th October, 1818. Ibid., p. 230.

obvious to Joseph that he had overstrained himself on the walking tour with Brown, and had never thrown off the effects of the feverish chill which had attacked him. He was still suffering from a sore throat. He could not concentrate on a course of study as he had planned. Tom's identity 'pressed on him all day'. His only escape was into the world of poetry. 'I am obliged to write, and plunge into abstract images to ease myself of his countenance, his voice and feebleness so that I live now in a continual fever.' The poem which he had begun was *Hyperion*.

Soon he could not even write, but still he would not accept Joseph's offer to take his place by Tom's bedside. Poor Tom was now a living skeleton, torn with coughing. He had become exceedingly nervous and was terribly affected by anything which disturbed him emotionally. His brother watched over him night and day. A visit from their young sister, Fanny, upset him so much at the moment of parting that it was never repeated, and John did not even dare to tell him when the letter he was writing at his bedside was to far-off George. In November Tom had his nineteenth birthday. Slowly his strength ebbed, and with it Keats felt more and more of his own vitality being drained away.

★

Early on the morning of 1st December, Charles Brown was awakened in bed by a pressure on his hand. It was John Keats, come to tell him that poor Tom was dead. The happy trio of brothers was shattered now.

Directly he heard the news Joseph hurried up to Hampstead to persuade Keats to go with him to Cornwall for a few weeks, thinking that a change of scene might help him to recover from the blow. Keats did half agree with the idea, but the weather after Tom's death was cold and wet and the half-formed plan fell through. Brown would not let him return to the lodgings which held so many poignant memories for him. They decided to keep house together – Keats would have the front parlour and Brown the back one. At first Keats found it impossible to work, but after a week spent in seeing his young sister and visiting his friends, he began to write again. Joseph too was hard at work, with a secret excitement that would allow him no rest.

He had had no premonition that winter's day when he had hurried into Somerset House in time for the Antique Class. When the class was ended the students clustered round a notice which announced a Grand Prize to be given for Historical Painting. Joseph was at the back of the crowd and could not read it but news came from the front rank. It was for a painting in oils. What was the subject? Oh, some quotation from Spenser. The interest of most of the students evaporated when one of them read out, 'The Prize has not been awarded for twelve years, as no competitor has proved himself sufficiently worthy of it.' The crowd melted away into the street and their shouts and laughter were lost in the busy clatter of the Strand. Joseph read the notice carefully though he never thought for a moment of competing. His first experiment with oils was still unfinished.

The size of the canvas was to be 4 ft. 2 in. × 3 ft. 4 in. – an ordinary half-length. Time – there was more than a year to do it in. Subject – Joseph stiffened:

'Out of his hand she snatcht the cursed knife. . . .' Rapidly his eyes flew over the lines that followed, but he had no need to read, he knew them by heart already. The subject of the Prize Picture was to be the scene in the Cave of Despair, when Una snatches the dagger from the faint-hearted Knight. How often had he heard John Keats repeating those lines – almost chanting them – in his musical voice. Keats would repeat whole stanzas of *The Faerie Queene*, and Joseph's musician's ear had recognized their beauty, so that he had come to love the poem almost as well himself. A battered copy of it was one of his most precious possessions. He felt a sudden bound of self-confidence. It seemed almost the beckoning of Fate that this should be the subject for the Competition. Surely he would do something better than those others to whom the lines were just 'a quotation from Spenser'.

From that day forward Joseph was passionately determined to win the Prize. First of all he must accustom himself to painting in oils. He finished his first oil-painting – a picture of Hermia and Helena from *Midsummer Night's Dream* and told no one that he had begun to make studies for the figures in the Cave of Despair. At the same time he continued to accept gratefully any commissions for miniature portraits in water-colours. He could now charge up to three guineas for them, and they were the only source of money with which to pay for the canvas, brushes and paints and all the paraphernalia that he needed for the Prize Picture.

During the turn of the year he spent most of his spare time with Keats. They would go for long walks together, and often Keats would come to London to go with him to the National Gallery, or the Sculpture Galleries at the British Museum. It was on one of these days that Joseph arrived at their rendezvous – the room containing the marbles from the Parthenon, to find Keats sitting as though transfigured; his glowing eyes were wide open, but seemed as if they saw nothing of what lay in front of them. His expression was so radiant, and yet so withdrawn, that Joseph stole away, afraid to break in on his dreams. But a foppish young acquaintance was less delicate in perception. Joseph had scarcely left when a vapid youth settled himself comfortably on the seat beside Keats and showered him with a rain of fashionable inanities. At length, remembering the purpose of his visit, he unconsciously compensated Keats for the boredom of his conversation by posturing with an eye-glass in front of the marbles and, after quizzing them for a minute or two from various angles, returning to let fall the gem:

'Yes, Mr Keats, I believe we may now safely admire these works.'[1]

[1] Sharp, op. cit., p. 32.

To outward appearance John Keats had recovered from the blow of Tom's death though he could not get rid of a sore throat which troubled him. He was able to write again, he could laugh and joke, but, while he had always been a creature of moods, brilliantly talkative at one moment and the next withdrawn and aloof, Joseph quickly noticed a difference in the quality of his moods. It was not that his moments of gaiety were unnatural, but that the contrasting quietness was no longer a gentle silent abstraction, but more a sudden collapse of his eager vitality into apathy, which was more like despair than depression. Yet in spite of these changes Keats's creative powers were never more active. Before Christmas he was working on *Hyperion*. As the new Year dawned he wrote 'a little Poem called "St Agnes Eve",' and early that spring[1] he suggested that Joseph should come with him to call on a new friend of his — a Mrs Brawne — the widow who had taken Brown's house for the summer months while he had been in Scotland with Keats. Apparently she was still living in Hampstead with her three children.

Joseph had not been in their house for more than a few minutes when he realized that Keats was in love with Mrs Brawne's elder daughter, Fanny. He studied her while he was conducting a quiet conversation with her mother. She was eighteen years old, he knew, small, elegant, slight in build, and moved with natural grace. Joseph could not hear what she was saying, but she seemed to be teasing Keats. Her face was not beautiful. It was too long and narrow for beauty, though her pale complexion was lovely, her eyes very blue, and her face was soft-looking, showing no bone through the firm young flesh. She wore her light-brown hair smoothly parted in the centre. Joseph talked mostly to Mrs Brawne, but had a few minutes' conversation with her daughter. She was very lively and agreeable, but, for himself, he found the mother more charming. Fanny Brawne's was not the type of beauty that appealed to him. Her vitality and high spirits had obviously attracted Keats. He half turned and caught John's eyes on him with a curious expression in them. Fanny turned too, with a swift graceful movement, and gave Keats a teasing smile.

As they walked away together, Joseph thought it over. Her appearance was elegant, she was lively and amusing, but she seemed to him unworthy of love from such a source. He was sure she did not realize how far above other men Keats was. Still, Keats was only twenty-three, and there were many other girls in the world.

Joseph would have been astonished had his friend told him the truth — that he and Fanny Brawne were already secretly engaged. But since Tom's death Keats had become increasingly reserved about the things which really mattered to

[1] Severn says 'spring 1819' but this date has been queried and autumn 1818 suggested because of a reference in a letter from Fanny to Keats about their second meeting. I believe the phrase in this letter, mentioning Severn, refers to another, later meeting at which he was present. Autumn 1818 seems unlikely, as he was very occupied with work after his October illness and Keats was nursing Tom who died in December. Joseph knew Tom well and if he had met Fanny for the first time then, the two events would surely have remained connected in his mind.

him, and in any case, although he was Fanny's accepted suitor, he had no money for them to marry on, so it seemed more sensible to keep their engagement secret. But alas, the torment it caused him! For, being apparently an unattached young female, she continued to receive flattering attentions from other men, often in front of Keats. And being also of a lively disposition, and very young and fond of admiration, she even flirted a little with them. This was agony to him. 'He don't like anyone to look at her or to speak to her,' said Mrs Dilke. He even suffered secretly as he listened to some of the gallant compliments paid to her by Brown, and Joseph himself was the cause of a little jealousy. Fanny Brawne had to reassure him. 'You must be satisfied in knowing that I admired you much more than your friend,' she said.[1]

If Joseph had stopped to consider the matter he might have guessed how far things had gone with Keats. He might have realized how Tom's death had laid him open to love. When George was leaving for America John had said, 'My love for my brothers, from the early loss of our parents ... has grown into an affection "passing the Love of Women". I have been ill-tempered with them, I have vexed them — but the thought of them has always stifled the impression that any woman might otherwise have made upon me.'[2] And now George was three thousand miles away and Tom was dead. He was doubly defenceless against love's onslaught.

John Keats seemed to be withdrawing further from the world. As so often happens when people are in love, he could find no interest in the company and occupations which he used to enjoy. The Reynolds sisters, for instance, with whom he and his brothers had always been on the most friendly terms, were staying with Mrs Dilke that February. His only comment was, 'The Miss Reynoldses have been stopping next door lately — but all very dull.'[3] In fact, he was not only beginning to go out less into the world, but Joseph noticed that he was losing touch with many of his old friends. He stayed indoors a great deal with the object — or was it an excuse? — of ridding himself of his sore throat. Hunt got on his nerves with his too-facile ecstacies; Haslam he did not see, but occasionally wrote to, and knew that he was happily engrossed in a love affair; Charles Cowden Clarke he admitted he had not seen 'for God knows when'. He had not been to the Novellos' since December, when he and Brown had declared themselves 'devastated and excruciated with bad and repeated puns'.[4] He made efforts to see more of his little sister, but their guardian made it very difficult.

The only friends he saw much of now were Brown, with whom he was living, the Dilkes next door, the Brawnes and Joseph, who came often to the house and sometimes stayed the night in what Keats called 'his little crib'. Haydon he had not seen since, with much difficulty, he had raised £30 to lend

1 25th July, 1819. *Letters of John Keats*, p. 362.
2 Ibid., p. 152.
3 14th February, 1819. Ibid., p. 297.
4 December 1818. Ibid., p. 249.

him, which he could ill afford. Nor had he seen Reynolds for some time. Reynolds had now renounced his literary ambitions and talked of nothing but the law.

Joseph was working hard on his studies for the Prize Picture. He sent his first oil-painting, *Hermia and Helena*, to the Academy and wrote to Keats asking his permission to submit with it a miniature of his friend, which he had just finished. Keats replied: 'Of course I should never suffer any petty vanity of mine to hinder you in any wise; and therefore I should say, "Put the miniature in the exhibition" if only myself was to be hurt. But, will it not hurt you? What good can it do to any future picture? Even a large picture is lost in that canting place — what a drop of water in the ocean is a Miniature. Those who might chance to see it for the most part if they had ever heard of either of us — and know what we were and of what years — would laugh at the puff of the one and the vanity of the other. I am however in these matters a very bad judge — and would advise you to act in a way that appears to yourself the best for your interest. As your Hermia and Helena is finished, send that without the prologue of a Miniature. I shall see you soon, if you do not pay me a visit sooner — there's a Bull for you.'[1]

Both pictures were accepted, but they were badly hung and attracted no attention.

Keats described one of their days together to his brother George, sending a typical page of his London life across the ocean to the settlement in Kentucky.

'On Monday,' he wrote, 'we had to dinner Severn and Cawthorn, the bookseller and print-virtuoso; in the evening Severn went home to paint, and we other three went to the play, to see Sheil's new tragedy ycleped "Evadne". In the morning Severn and I took a turn round the Museum — there is a sphinx there of a giant size, and most voluptuous Egyptian expression, I had not seen it before.'[2]

Early in May, that year of 1819, nightingales were nesting on the Heath and even in the garden at Wentworth Place. One night Joseph went with a party of friends to the Spaniards Inn. During the evening he missed John Keats and went outside to look for him. He found him, at last, lying beneath the pine trees, and listening entranced to the song of a nightingale overhead.[3] A day or two later Keats took a chair into the garden at Wentworth Place and, sitting under the mulberry tree, wrote out, during the morning, the *Ode to a Nightingale*, 'in and out and back and forth on a couple of loose sheets of paper'. Later in the day Charles Brown saw him folding the scraps of paper carelessly away behind some books in his room and rescued them.[4] By the time John Keats left London that summer he had written four other odes which were to become immortal: *To Psyche*,

---

[1] 29th March, 1819. *Letters of John Keats*, p. 289.
[2] March 1819. Ibid., p. 311.
[3] Charles Severn to Sharp, op. cit., p. 40.
[4] Charles Brown, *Life of John Keats*, p. 54.

To Melancholy, On Indolence, and the *Ode on a Grecian Urn*, as well as the miraculous ballad which he had sent in his journal-letter to George — *La Belle Dame Sans Merci*.

Joseph was engrossed in his picture for the Prize. He had accustomed himself to the use of oils, he had made innumerable studies for the figures, and at the same time he had worked at his miniatures in order to pay for all the new materials he needed. His work seemed to eat money. The picture became a passion with him — a secret passion, as he had confided in no one at home for fear of his father's anger. All his work had to be done at Sarah's house in the room she lent him, and he would lock the door carefully when he left it.

As the summer faded he began to have bouts of despair. He had so many difficulties and not the least of these was lack of money. In the end he was forced to sell all his little treasures to pay for painting materials. Even his watch and his beloved books had to go. August passed, September drew to its close. He had no money for fuel. He sat long hours in his fireless room, painting the limbs of the figure of Despair from his own naked, shivering legs reflected in the chilly depths of the mirror.

At the beginning of October he snatched a moment from his work to visit Keats, who had just returned to London and had taken rooms in Westminster. In April the Dilkes had moved to Westminster to be nearer their son, who was going to school there, and on whom his father doted. Mrs Brawne had bought their half of the house at Hampstead and was now living there with her family.

Joseph found Keats in high spirits when he called at his lodgings in College Street. He showed Joseph several short poems and odes which he had written since they had last met. Joseph was charmed with them, but he was greatly disappointed when, having inquired 'how *Hyperion* went on', he heard that Keats had decided not to finish it. Joseph had always felt a personal interest in this poem, because it was he who had persuaded Keats to re-read *Paradise Lost*. In vain did he protest against *Hyperion* being discarded. When Keats had read a few passages to him Severn cried indignantly that it might have been written by Milton himself, and that he *must* complete it. Keats only laughed and said that he did not want to write a poem that might have been written by Milton, but one that was unmistakably written by John Keats. He seemed more interested in a new poem which he had just finished, 'about a serpent-girl named Lamia'.

Then he put his manuscripts aside and told Severn that he had decided not to write any more poetry for the moment, but that he was going to try his hand at journalism, because he must make some money. Not only did he owe money to Brown and to his publisher on his own account, but he had also had bad news from George in Kentucky. His 'mercantile speculations' had not been successful. His wife had just had a child and he needed money badly. John had to write telling him that they could neither of them get from their guardian, Mr Abbey, any of Tom's share of their inheritance, which he had left them, because their aunt had filed a suit in Chancery against them. Mr Abbey thought that she could be persuaded to withdraw it, but until this was done he could give them nothing.

Keats had hoped to raise some money from the tragedy which he and Brown had written together, with a part specially designed to suit Kean. They had sent it to Elliston, the manager of Drury Lane, but had heard that Kean was leaving England for a visit to America, so it seemed that their tragedy would have to wait and he could hope for no money from that source for some little time. Nevertheless he had promised George that he would not spare any exertion to benefit him by some means or other. 'If I cannot remit you hundreds, I will tens, and if not that ones', he had written.

His next step had been to ask Haydon to repay the £30 which he had lent him. Haydon had replied that he was unable to repay it. Keats commented that he could well understand that this might be so, but what had hurt him was that 'he did not seem to care much about it — and let me go without my money with almost nonchalance'. Severn was delighted to note his resolute bearing, but, studying his appearance, he was afraid that the months out of London had not done him as much good physically as his friends had hoped. He would try to get the position of theatrical critic for some paper, as a beginning, he thought. 'When I can afford to compose deliberate poems I will.'[1]

Joseph reluctantly admitted that he supposed it was the wisest course to pursue, and left his friend, promising to return in a few days to hear the rest of *Hyperion* and the whole of *Lamia*. But it was more than a week before he was able to get to College Street, and then it was only to find that his friend had gone. He had returned to his old home with Brown at Wentworth Place. Poor Keats! His stern resolutions for a régime of hack-writing and self-denial had melted away when he saw his love again. She was kind and he was at her mercy. She dazzled him. There was 'nothing in the world so bright and delicate'. He tore himself away and returned to Westminster for a few days, but his purpose weakened; his strength had been drained from him.

Before the end of the month he was back with Brown and living under the same roof as his 'dearest girl'. Severn followed him there the next Sunday and was distressed to see the change in him. Gone were the resolute confidence, the hopes for the future. His mind seemed in a fever. Apathy and depression alternated with moods of forced, almost violent gaiety. He told Joseph that he and Brown were working together in the mornings on a comic fairy poem, and in the evenings he was reshaping *Hyperion* into the form of a Vision. That his friend had not entirely finished with *Hyperion* was the only comfort Joseph carried away from that uneasy visit.

*

[1] 22nd September, 1819. *Letters of John Keats.*

B*

The last day of October came. It was the last day, too, for entries for the
Prize. Joseph had slept but a few hours during the last three nights; almost it was
a relief to have the picture taken from him, in a frame which he had borrowed
from a friend. Some days before, he had written a note to Keats, asking him to
call and see the finished picture. Keats replied from Hampstead:

'I am glad to hear you have finished the Picture, and am more anxious to see it
than I have time to spare: for I have been so very lax, unemployed, unmeridian'd
and objectless these two months that I even grudge indulging (and that is no
great indulgence considering the lecture is not over till 9 and the lecture room
seven miles from Wentworth Place) myself by going to Hazlitt's Lecture. If you
have hours to the amount of a brace of dozens to throw away you may sleep
nine of them here in your little Crib and chat the rest. When your Picture is up
and in a good light I shall make a point of meeting you at the Academy if you
will let me know when.'[1]

But he was not to see the picture until a few days before the verdict of the
judges was published. In the meantime Joseph had been through alternating fits
of hope and depression. During the first days of November, when his picture had
only just gone, he chided himself for his conceit in thinking that he could learn
to paint in a new medium, during one year, well enough to enter for a Prize.
Almost he regretted his effort, but after a few nights' sleep his natural buoyancy
returned, and although he could scarcely believe that he, Joseph Severn, had
dared such an ambitious attempt, he no longer regretted the amount of work he
had poured into it, and realized that in the painting of the picture he had learned
a great deal. His mind, he confided to his friends, had now relaxed to 'a certain
despairful ease'.

He broke the news to his father and to Mr Bond. The engraver seemed
scarcely interested and his father flew into one of his passions, rebuked his son
for his conceit, and reproached him for not sticking to the safe profession to which
he had been apprenticed. Joseph's mother, as always, was sympathetic and
understanding, but even she was not very hopeful. Joseph attended the classes
at the Academy every evening, and took part when the candidates each painted
an oil sketch of a given subject in the presence of the Keeper.[2] November passed
without any news. Early in December a rumour spread that the Council had
decided to award a Gold Medal for the first time for twelve years. December the
tenth was the date when the name of the victor was to be published. The name
of every competing student was whispered behind knowing hands in turn and
Joseph had the dubious satisfaction of hearing himself mentioned as 'the dark
horse that might win'.

He could persuade neither his father nor Mr Bond to come to the Academy
to see the picture where it hung with all the other entries, but a few days before
the tenth, John Keats called on him early in the morning and insisted on their

[1] *Letters of John Keats*, p. 438.
[2] *An Artist's Remembrances* — manuscript by Joseph Severn, 1852.

proceeding together to Somerset House. Although Keats admitted that he had always imagined quite a different setting for the scene, he was delighted with the picture. He protested that he had no knowlege of the technique of painting, but after careful consideration of the other canvases, he must admit that he liked it the best. He asserted stoutly that if it didn't get the Medal it would be the most honourable of the failures. Joseph knew that Keats had no expert knowledge, but his faith in his artistic intuition was so strong that he felt greatly encouraged.

At last there dawned the tenth day of December. It dragged by, hour by hour, each longer than the last, until at 8 o'clock that evening the President and Council of the Royal Academy filed solemnly into the Council Room. All the students had been invited and they were there in their best clothes. The excitement and solemnity of the occasion made the atmosphere tense. The Council lowered themselves with dignity into their chairs on the dais, which had been specially prepared for the evening; at a gracious signal the students subsided, shuffling, into theirs, and the President, Mr Benjamin West, rose slowly to his feet. He was eighty-one years old and very popular with the students because, unlike some successful painters, he was a generous friend and adviser to young artists. An expectant stillness enveloped the room in which the old voice was easily heard.

'Prizes are to be given to three students,' it said, 'and the Gold Medal for painting, so long unawarded, is to be bestowed upon a young candidate whose efforts are all the more praiseworthy in that he is entirely self-taught.'

The old man paused, and perhaps his mind went back to Pennsylvania seventy years ago, and he saw himself as a young Quaker boy, making colours from leaves and berries, and brushes with hair pulled from his cat's tail.

The silence was agonizing. Joseph's heart was jumping in his chest, as though it could bear its imprisonment no longer. The President brought his wandering thoughts back to the present and to another young man who was just beginning his artist's life. He peered downwards at the paper he held in his hand and announced briefly:

'The name of the Gold Medallist is Joseph Severn.'

Joseph's heart gave a convulsive leap and dropped rapidly into his stomach. The room rocked. Everywhere blurred white faces had turned towards him. He felt the blood rise burning to his cheeks and awoke suddenly to a friend nudging him with a sharp elbow.

He concentrated all his strength on rising to his feet and edged awkwardly past the knees to the main aisle. Once out in the open his courage flooded back, and he stepped boldly up to receive the Gold Medal from the hands of the President himself. In after days he could scarcely remember what happened after that. In memory he could feel the sudden cold weight of the medal pressing on his hand, and he could hear the old voice murmuring good wishes for his future . . . his next vivid recollection was of bounding up the narrow creaking staircase at Mason's Court. He ran into his father's room without knocking. His mother followed with a light. James Severn had gone early to bed after an outburst when he had heard where Joseph was spending the evening. He sat up in bed, blinking, his night-cap askew on his black head. 'What in heaven's name is the meaning of this intrusion?' he barked.

Joseph was panting and incoherent.

'Father! The Medal! They've given it to me!'

His father's expression changed to one of astonishment and then disbelief.

'If this is a pleasantry —' he began.

But Joseph sank down on his knees beside the bed and thrust the great Gold Medal, weighing fully half a pound, into his father's hand.[1] The physical contact seemed to carry final conviction, and James Severn flung his arms round his son's neck and kissed him.

[1] Joseph Severn's *Reminiscences*, quoted Sharp, op. cit., p. 27.

CHAPTER 2

DEPARTURE

September, 1820

IT WAS PAST MIDNIGHT when the hired carriage came jolting over the cobbles of Shoreditch. The night was overcast and cold. Joseph gazed gloomily out of the creaking window. He had been up since dawn and now he felt tired and ill. He checked in his mind the preparations he had made for the first great journey of his life.

In the morning he had visited Sir Thomas Lawrence, the new President of the Royal Academy. After a prolonged tour of Europe, painting scarcely any but crowned or coroneted heads, Sir Thomas had returned to London to find himself elected President on the very day of his arrival, in place of old Benjamin West who had just died. Joseph told him how he had won the Gold Medal the year before, and that he was leaving London now to accompany a sick friend to Rome, and would work there in the hope of winning the travelling studentship. Sir Thomas had listened kindly, and had written two letters of introduction for him: the first to the great sculptor, Canova, the other to an old German artist who was living in Rome.

Next Joseph had collected the sum of £25, owing to him for a 'miniature of a lady in a white satin bonnet and feathers'. He had made a few purchases and called on one or two friends who lived conveniently near, to tell them of his sudden departure. Then he had gathered together what he needed from Sarah's house and had said goodbye to her. She had promised tearfully to keep his room for him just as he had left it.

Now he was on his way home and the hardest moment was at hand, when he must say goodbye to his family, from whom he had never before been parted. His spirits drooped even lower as he recalled the long, bitter arguments with his father during the last three days. There had been nothing like them since before he had won the Medal. What great expectations his father had formed then, and how sadly they had lacked fulfilment. As he looked back, Joseph thought there had never been so unlucky a year. His elation had been short-lived. No new commissions had come as a result of his triumph; in fact, it had only served to rouse such envy amongst the other students that the Academy Classes had become too unpleasant for him to continue to attend.

George Keats had returned home from America. That should have been a happy occasion. But he had stayed a bare three weeks, and then he was gone, back to his wife and child waiting in Louisville, and taking with him every penny he could lay hands on. Some of Keats's friends thought that he had taken money which should by rights have been left with his brother, whose financial position was now desperate. Scarcely had George left than John Keats had collapsed. Joseph shivered now, as he remembered Brown's vivid description.

'At eleven o'clock, he came into the house in a state that looked like fierce intoxication. Such a state in him, I knew, was impossible; it therefore was the more fearful. I asked hurriedly, "What is the matter? You are fevered?" "Yes, yes," he answered, "I was severely chilled, — but now I don't feel it. Fevered! — of course, a little." He mildly and instantly yielded, a property in his nature towards any friend, to my request that he should go to bed. I entered his chamber as he leapt into bed. On entering the cold sheets, before his head was on the pillow, he slightly coughed, and I heard him say — "That is blood from my mouth." I went towards him; he was examining a single drop of blood upon the sheet. "Bring me the candle, Brown, and let me see this blood." After regarding it steadfastly he looked up in my face, with a calmness of countenance that I can never forget, and said, — "I know the colour of that blood; it is arterial blood . . . that drop of blood is my death-warrant; I must die." I ran for a surgeon; my friend was bled; and, at five in the morning, I left him after he had been some time in a quiet sleep.'[1]

For two months after that he was an invalid, his only pleasure the visits and the notes from his love next door. Then, towards the end of March, he was well enough to come to London for the first public exhibition of Haydon's picture, *Christ's Entry into Jerusalem*, which was finished at last. He was getting ready to turn out of Wentworth Place, because Brown had let his house, as usual, for the summer months, and was going on another walking tour. He half thought of accompanying Brown to Scotland on the smack for the benefit of the sea voyage. But a week or two later he had given up the idea and taken lodgings near the Leigh Hunts at Kentish Town, a village between Hampstead and London.

Joseph was lucky in getting several favourably priced commissions for miniatures that summer. At the end of June he had a brief letter from Leigh Hunt, telling him that Keats had had another haemorrhage and was moving into their house so that they might nurse him. Joseph had gone there to see him whenever he could get away from London. At first he was horrified at Keats's weakness and appearance of exhaustion. But later he seemed to rally and, in spite of his own forebodings, his friends began to hope for his recovery. Joseph wrote to Haslam in the second week of July saying: 'Poor Keats has been still nearer the next world. . . . I have seen him many times. . . . His appearance is shocking and now reminds me of poor Tom, and I have been inclined to think him in the same way. For himself — he makes sure of it, and seems prepossessed that he cannot recover — now I seem more than ever *not* to think so and I know

[1] Charles Brown, *Life of John Keats*, pp. 64–5.

you will agree with me when you see him. I shall continue to visit Keats at every opportunity — perhaps twice a week.'[1]

While Keats lay ill his new volume of poems was published. *Lamia* was in it, *Isabella, The Eve of St Agnes,* and the great unfinished fragment *Hyperion.* Joseph felt confident that this at last must bring fame to its author. Then he heard that his friend had left the Hunts and had gone to stay with Mrs Brawne at Wentworth Place. He was so busy with his miniature painting that it was hard to find time to go all the way to Hampstead. He imagined that Keats must be quite recovered, if he were paying visits.

It had been a complete shock, therefore, when Haslam had come to him a few days ago with the news that Keats was leaving for Italy at the end of the week. He had been ill ever since the end of June. Far from paying a visit to Mrs Brawne, she had taken him in, after he had flung away from Hunt's house, in a state of painful agitation, because a letter from Fanny Brawne had not been given to him by the servant until two days after its arrival, and then it had already been opened. He had talked wildly of going back to the lodgings where he had lived with his brothers, but Mrs Brawne had insisted on their right to nurse him, and since then he had been devotedly cared for by her daughter and herself at Wentworth Place.

Haslam said that the doctors had told Keats that his only chance of life lay in leaving England for the winter. Then Haslam sprang the surprise. Not one of Keats's friends could accompany him. He had written a month before to Brown, asking if he would go with him, but had had no answer. Brown was still on his walking tour in Scotland and evidently the letter had missed him. Keats had waited to hear from him but now the weather was getting colder every day, September mists were clouding the Heath, and it was obvious to everyone that if Keats were to leave England it must be very soon. His friends, unknown to Joseph, had arranged everything. There was no sign of George Keats repaying the money that he had borrowed from his brother, but Taylor, Keats's publisher, had paid him £100 for the copyright of *Endymion,* arranged a credit of £150 for his expenses in Italy, and booked his passage on a ship which was to sail for Naples in mid-September. From there he would go on to Rome. Haslam explained the position in a strained, hesitating voice. He would have gone himself if it had not been for his wife. She was expecting a baby. Then he turned to Joseph, his face grave.

'Nothing can save Keats but going to Italy. Severn, why should you not go with him?' he said. 'For otherwise he must go alone, and we shall never hear anything of him if — if he dies.'

His honest eyes pleaded with Joseph. They faced each other a moment in silence. Then Joseph spoke.

'I'll go.'

Haslam's face shone with relief and affection.

[1] *The Keats Circle,* vol. I, edited by H. E. Rollins, pp. 121–2

'But you'll be long getting ready?' he questioned anxiously. 'Keats is actually now preparing. The *Maria Crowther* sails in three days. When would you be ready?'

'In three days' time,' said Joseph decisively. 'I will set about it this very moment.'[1]

That evening, Tuesday, Haslam went out to Hampstead and told Keats the news. It was a great relief. Keats was even then preparing to leave Wentworth Place next morning, to stay with Taylor in London until his ship sailed. Now at least he would not have to travel quite alone to a strange country, where he knew no one, and where he was convinced that he was bound to die. Fanny Brawne believed the doctors, who said that the winter in Italy would cure him. But Keats himself felt that he was doomed, though for her sake he concealed his certainty. Before he left them next day he gave her his three most precious books, which he had annotated in his own hand – Spenser, Dante and Shakespeare.

On Wednesday morning Haslam confirmed with Joseph that he would abide by his decision and told him that the ship would sail on Sunday. It was only later, in the bustle of preparation for his departure, that Joseph suddenly thought that he might try for the Academy's travelling studentship, which would give him the means to live abroad for three years.[2]

*

The carriage was moving more slowly. Joseph leaned forward and saw the graceful new spire of St Leonard's Church and knew that he was home. The carriage drew up at 109 Shoreditch, about twelve doors from the church, where a narrow entrance led into Mason's Court, and his heart seemed to turn over as he thought of parting from his mother. Yet she had understood and sympathized with him in his sudden decision. It had been easy for him to explain his feelings to her. How could he leave Keats to go alone – to suffer, perhaps to die, solitary and uncared for, in a foreign land? No other friend could go. Either Joseph must accompany him or Keats must, in his own phrase, 'march up against the Battery' alone.

He climbed slowly out and plunged into the alleyway leading to Mason's Court. He felt his way across the little square of grass round which the old gabled houses clustered and shattered the stillness with a knock on the door of No. 4. Almost immediately it was opened by his mother.

As she put down her candle to help him off with his caped travelling-coat

---

[1] Joseph Severn's *Reminiscences*, quoted Sharp, op. cit., p. 48.

[2] Some modern writers have suggested that Joseph saw the journey as a chance of personal advancement. But both his father and, later, Keats gave their opinion that the Council of the Royal Academy was less likely to award a travelling scholarship to a student who had already arrived in Italy without their help. He had also to sacrifice the security of his hard-won connexions as a miniature painter in London and the companionship of his family, to whom throughout his life he remained devoted.

she thought, not for the first time, how handsome her Joe had grown – though tonight he was very pale. He gave her the miniature that he had finished a few days before, which he had collected from his room in Sarah's house. It was painted on ivory, measuring roughly four inches by five, in which small compass he had contrived a portrait of every member of his family. Tom sat with his hands on the keys of a harpsichord. Charles, Maria and Charlotte were painted full-face, Sarah, his mother and his father in profile. He handed it to her carefully for her to pack, determined that he should have at least their portraits with him on his journey. Then he gave a swift glance to her face under the crisp white muslin cap, and seemed to see a troubled look which changed the usual gentle sweetness of her expression. He kissed her on the cheek, opened the door of the parlour and went in.

He was prepared for another bitter argument, for passionate reproaches and prophecies of disaster if he insisted on rejecting his father's advice to stay in England. But he was not prepared for what he saw. On the left, by the window, Maria and Tom were putting clothes into a large trunk. Near the fire sat their father. He was sunk down in his armchair, his head bent forward, and on his face an expression of such extreme grief that Joseph checked the words of greeting on his lips and throwing himself into the armchair opposite his father buried his face in his hands.

What a wretched evening. He longed to cut short this gloomy departure and to be already on his way – on his way to Rome. But even that name seemed to have lost its enchantment, and if it had not been for the thought of Keats he would have given in, for he knew that there was a great deal of truth in his father's arguments. It was quite true that by leaving England he was giving up his hard-won connexion as a miniaturist. It was equally true that the Academy might not think it suitable to award the travelling scholarship to a student who had already got himself to Rome without its aid. But these considerations were as nothing beside his love and admiration for his friend. Since Keats would need him in Rome, to Rome he would go, and his natural optimism comforted him with the thought that no doubt commissions would be forthcoming when he got there.

He was never one to anticipate adversity. He was to annoy people all his life by never seeming to appreciate the gravity of his position, even when apparently facing ruin. Nevertheless, he thought a little grimly to himself that he would be anticipating the great adventure with more eagerness if his stomach were less queasy. He had been suffering for the last week from a liver complaint. He lifted his head from his hands as Tom touched him on the shoulder. It was time to leave.

His mother and sister had finished the packing and fastened the two heavy catches. Tom went to one end of the trunk and Joseph to the other. They strained and heaved, changed their grip and tried again, but they could do no more than shift the massive trunk a few inches along the floor. At length Joseph straightened himself, panting, and begged his father to come and help him. At first there was no reply from the chair by the fire.

Then his father stood up and turned to them a face frozen with anger. His hands were clenched, and his voice when he spoke was husky.

'If that trunk could never be lifted except with my aid, by God I would not touch it!'

He stood there with every limb stiff, as though paralysed by his rage. Only his eyes, beneath the painfully contracted brow, moved from face to face. Joseph was completely taken aback, but there was no time to waste in arguing. He must be off or the boat would sail without him. Tom went quickly out and brought the driver of the carriage in to help. Together the three of them carried the trunk to the carriage. Then the brothers went back into the house. With only a glance at his father, who was still standing, silent, by the fire, Joseph kissed Maria and left a message for Charlotte. In his hurried departure, he had not found time to pay her a last visit. Then he turned to go upstairs to say good-bye to his fourteen-year-old younger brother, Charles, who had been sent to bed some hours ago.

But as he moved towards the door, his father suddenly leaped forward and barred the way. He stood in the doorway with his arms flung wide; his face was pale and he panted as though he had been running. Joseph checked a moment and then laid a hand on his father's arm, trying to move it so that he could pass. The touch seemed to let loose the flood of fury that had been dammed up in that rigid figure. With a cry he swung his fist and hit his son a tremendous blow on the side of his head which sent him crashing to the floor. He would have sprung on him and hit him again, as he lay there, if Tom had not leaped forward and caught him round the waist, pinning him against the wall.

Mrs Severn helped Joseph to his feet, while Tom held his father prisoner. Dazed and shocked, Joseph supported himself by an arm round his mother's shoulders. He could not take his horror-struck gaze from his father. He would never, to the end of his life, forget how he looked at that moment of parting — the blazing blue eyes, the lips drawn back showing his clenched teeth, the thick black hair dishevelled, the stock awry. Mr Severn made a violent effort to free himself. He kicked and struggled with such frenzy that although Tom was a strong young man, he had to call his sister to his aid. Joseph's mother hurried him fearfully from the room. With tears pouring down her cheeks she helped him to put on his coat, but his legs were trembling so much and he felt so sick, that she had to support him for a minute before he could climb into the carriage.

Joseph's throat ached and tears rose into his eyes. How could he leave his mother in such a plight? His father had lost his senses. What if he were never to recover? What if by *his* action he had unsettled his father's reason and condemned his mother and family to a life of poverty and sorrow? Surely it was his duty, as the eldest son, to renounce his venture, to stay with his family, to be their comfort and protector.

But there was another duty calling him – his duty to his friend. Keats must sail on the *Maria Crowther*. On that journey hung his one slender chance of life. No, he could never leave Keats to face the terrible future, with no friend to cheer or comfort him.

He was so sunk in his thoughts that he scarcely noticed Tom jump up beside him, and it was not until the carriage moved forward with a jerk that he realized that he had seen the last of his home.

★

The gloom of those cold hours before the dawn, as they jolted towards the docks, seemed to symbolize the painful circumstances of his departure, and he could not prevent his mind from turning over and over every detail of the scene. He knew that his father's love for him was unbounded. He was so proud of Joseph's gifts, and delighted in his son's company. But when Joseph looked back, this proven affection served only to make the memory of the blow he had received more horrible, and when he thought of his father struggling to get at him, and his twisted face, he felt himself again overcome by nausea.

Gradually, as they rattled through the streets of London, the gloomy night merged into the chill dawn of September morning. Soon they crossed the Thames and drew up by the docks on the south side of the river. A little group was waiting for them on the wharf and as the two brothers descended from their carriage, chilled and stiff, Keats came forward to greet them. 'He was looking ill and wan and was sadly consumed away since the death of his brother Tom.'[1]

Joseph presented his brother to the other gentlemen on the wharf. Among them were the publisher, John Taylor, whose generosity had made it possible for Keats to undertake the journey, William Haslam, who had first introduced Severn to Keats, and Richard Woodhouse, a clever young solicitor, who had met the poet while acting as reader for Taylor's publishing firm. Keats led the way up the gangway to the deck of a small brigantine which lay alongside the wharf, his friends following him, and here they made the acquaintance of the captain, who led them along the deck and down a companion-way. They clambered down after him and found themselves in a small cabin with three bunks on each side. The same thought sprang to all their minds. It was *very* small. The *Maria Crowther* was a two-masted boat of only a hundred-and-thirty tons, and most of the available space was used for cargo. What would happen if Keats were seriously ill again during the voyage? This was the only cabin. Five people were to live, sleep and eat in it for the next four weeks.

Joseph was the only one of the party who had no thought for the future as he

---

[1] *An Artist's Remembrances* – manuscript by Joseph Severn.

inspected his new quarters. His liver attack seemed to be coming on again and he felt very ill. Keats led the way back to the deck, where they found a plump middle-aged lady, who dropped them a curtsy as they introduced themselves. The captain interposed to tell her which were to be her two fellow-passengers.

Mrs Pidgeon — for such she informed them was her name — gave them a comfortable smile.

They passed on, but not before Tom Severn, who was nearest to the companion-way, had overheard the lady asking the captain 'which of those two young gentlemen was the dying man?'

This news made Joseph give a wry smile. It cheered him a little to know that he was looking as ill as he felt.

Soon the vessel sheered off from the wharf and swung slowly down the river with the tide. The young men leaned over the side and talked in a desultory way, or paced up and down the deck. Haslam drew Joseph on one side and made him promise to keep a journal on the voyage and to send it to him from Naples.

The new surroundings and the voyage down the river seemed to do Keats good and he led the good-humoured attack on Joseph, who suddenly discovered that he had left his passport in his father's house. They all rallied him for his artistic vagueness but Tom and Joseph exchanged uneasy looks, their thoughts drawn unwillingly back to their home and the strange scene enacted there. Tom's face was pale above his blue coat, and he was relieved when Haslam offered to drive straight to Shoreditch and bring the passport to the boat before they sailed.

At four o'clock, after many affectionate farewells, the friends climbed into the boat which was to take them ashore. Keats asked Taylor to write to his little sister, to tell her that he was comfortably settled in his new quarters and looking forward to the voyage. Joseph had already given him the miniature of Keats which had been exhibited at the Royal Academy and asked him to have it framed and sent to Mrs Brawne for her daughter. Woodhouse took with him a lock of Keats's hair. Tom was the last to clamber over the side. Joseph embraced him and felt the tears rise to his eyes as the familiar face was gradually blurred by distance until it became unrecognizable.

*

They went silently down to the cabin, where Mrs Pidgeon was rummaging in her portmanteau. There the captain joined them and they ate a badly cooked meal, served by an untidy little cabin-boy. The captain told them that they would wait at Gravesend for another lady who was to come on board next day. Keats cracked jokes all through the meal and soon had the captain chuckling and Mrs Pidgeon delightedly protesting at his sallies. But as soon as it was finished, he excused himself on the grounds of sleepiness and climbed into his bunk. Joseph still felt ill, although he had scarcely touched the dinner, and he was tortured by nightmares all night.

Soon after midnight, as Joseph tossed and turned in his narrow berth and the others slept, a small coaster from Dundee dropped anchor off Gravesend within a stone's throw of the *Maria Crowther*, waiting for the tide. At dawn she sailed up river, carrying the sleeping Charles Brown back to London. He had hurried home from Scotland after receiving a letter telling the grievous news of Keats; he could not know that he had been so close to his friend during the night.

Next morning Joseph went ashore with the captain after breakfast to buy some provisions, apples and biscuits. He visited a chemist's, where he had several medicines made up according to Keats's written directions, and also at his request, bought a bottle of laudanum. The captain, who was a good-hearted man, tried to find a goat to provide milk for Keats during the voyage, but was unsuccessful. While they were on shore Haslam had been to the ship with Joseph's passport.

Some time after they had eaten their dinner on board they heard the splash of oars approaching and hurried up on deck. It was already dark, and Joseph noticed with anxiety that the wind was increasing. The captain leaned down to help someone up the side while the wind played with the lantern that the mate held above his head. It was a lady who stood on the deck. She was wrapped in a cloak and her face was shadowed by the hood.

She took a step and then faltered and almost fell. Keats and Captain Walsh assisted her down to the cabin. Joseph remained on deck, content to leave the doctoring to Keats, but the cold wind made him shiver and soon he followed the others down to the cabin.

The lady looked very frail. She was about eighteen years old, pretty and fair-haired, with a gentle expression and manner. Keats sat beside her, and as she grew brighter, encouraged her to talk. She was travelling to Naples to stay with her brother, who had been an officer in the Navy and was now a banker. Her name was Miss Cotterell. No, it was not a voyage for pleasure, but for her health. And then it all came out, that she was as far gone in consumption as Keats himself, that the doctors had ordered her to Italy as her only chance of life. Joseph, although deeply pitying her, was distressed to observe her excitement when she heard that Keats had similar reasons for his journey. It was an unfortunate coincidence, and his brow furrowed as he realized that she was in that morbid state when to trace the history of her illness from symptom to symptom was her keenest remaining pleasure.[1] As the evening went on Joseph resolved that he would leave Keats alone with her only when it was absolutely unavoidable.

The *Maria Crowther* sailed that night.

---

[1] Joseph Severn's *Reminiscences*, quoted Sharp, op. cit., pp. 53-4.

CHAPTER 3

SEA VOYAGE

September — October, 1820

JOSEPH SAT ON DECK. This was their third day at sea. The ship rose
and fell rhythmically with the surge of a heavy swell. He was writing an
account of their voyage for the benefit not only of Haslam, but of all
Keats's friends and of his own family too, keeping it as a diary, so that he could
send their news at once, whenever the opportunity should offer. He wrote
quickly and with scarcely any punctuation save dashes:

19th Sept. Tuesday, off Dover Castle
I arose at daybreak to see the glorious eastern gate — Keats slept till seven —
Miss C. was rather ill this morning, I prevailed on her to walk the deck with me
at ½ past 6 — she recovered much — Keats was still better this morning and Mrs
Pidgeon looked and was the picture of health — but poor me! I began to feel a
waltzing on my stomach at breakfast and soon I was going it most soundly.
Miss Cotterell followed me — then Keats who did it in the most gentlemanly
manner — and then the saucy Mrs Pidgeon who had been laughing at us — four
faces bequeathing to the mighty deep their breakfasts — here I must change to a
Minor Key. Miss C. fainted — we soon recovered her — I was very ill nothing
but laying down would do for me. Keats ascended his bed — from which he
dictated surgically like Esculapius of old basso-relievo — through him Miss C.
was recovered — we had a cup of tea each and no more — went to bed and
slept until it was time to go to bed — we could not get up again and slept in our
clothes all night — Keats the King — not even looking pale.

20th Sept. Wednesday, off Brighton
Beautiful Morning — we all breakfasted on deck and recovered as we were
could enjoy it — about 10 Keats said a storm was hatching — he was right — the
rain came on and we retired to our Cabin — it abated and once more we came
on deck — at 2 Storm came on furiously — we retired to our beds. The rolling
of our ship was death to us — towards 4 it increased and our situation was
alarming — the trunks rolled across the Cabin — the water poured in from the
skylight and we were tumbled from one side to the other of our beds — my
curiosity was raised to see the storm — and my anxiety to see Keats for I could
only speak to him when in bed — I got up and fell down on the floor from my

weakness and the rolling of the ship. Keats was very calm – the ladies were much frightened and could scarce speak – when I got up to the deck I was astounded – the waves were in Mountains and washed the ship – the watery horizon was like a Mountainous Country – but the ship's motion was beautifully to the sea, falling from one wave to the other in a very lovely manner – the sea each time crossing the deck, and one side of the ship being level with the water – this when I understood gave me perfect ease – I communicated below and it did the same – but when the dusk came the sea began to rush in from the side of our Cabin from an opening in the planks – this made us rather long-faced – for it came by pails-full – again I got out and said to Keats 'Here's pretty music for you' – with the greatest calmness he answered me – only 'Water parted from the Sea.'[1] I staggered up again and the storm was awful – Captain and Mate soon came down – for our things were squashing about in the dark – they struck a light and I succeeded in getting my desk off the ground – with clothes, books, etc. The Captain finding the hole could not be stopped tacked about from our voyage – and the sea ceased to dash against the Cabin – for we were sailing against wind and tide – but the horrible agitation continued in the ship lengthways – here were the pumps working – the sails squalling – the confused voices of the sailors – the things rattling about in every direction – and us poor devils pinn'd up in our beds like ghosts by daylight – except Keats he was himself all the time – the ladies suffered the most – but I was out of bed a dozen times to wait on them and tell them there *was* no danger – my sickness made me get into bed very soon each time – but Keats this Morning brags of my sailorship – he says could I have kept on my legs in the watery cabin I should have been a *standing* Miracle!

21st Sept.

I caught a sight of the moon about 3 o'clock this morning – and ran down to tell the glad tidings – but the surly rolling of the seas was worse than the storm – the ship trembled to it – and the sea was scarcely calmed by daylight – so that we were kept from 2 o'clock yesterday until 6 this Morning without anything – well it has done us good – we are like a Quartette of Fighting Cocks this morning. The Morning is serene we are now back again some twenty miles – waiting for a wind – but full of spirits – Keats is without even complaining and Miss Cotterell has a colour in her face – the sea has done his worst upon us. I am better than I have been for years. Farewell my dear fellow.

Jos. SEVERN – show this to my family with my love to them.

When you read this you will excuse the manner – I am quite beside myself – and have written the whole this Morning Thursday on the deck after a sleepless night and with a head full of care – you shall have a better the next time – [2]

*

[1] The title of a popular song of the moment.
[2] *Keats Circle*, vol. I, pp. 151–4.

He had scarcely finished this letter when the captain came and suggested that he and Keats might like to go ashore and stretch their legs. There was very little wind, and what there was was dead against them. The ladies were afraid to face the jump into the little rowing-boat that at one moment was level with the deck, and the next had dropped a good five feet below it. But the two young men enjoyed their scramble over the gravel of desolate Dungeness, and Joseph found an opportunity to post his letter to Haslam. They came back hungry and in high spirits, and Joseph made his companions laugh with his description of himself staring, fascinated, at the enormous waves rushing in upon the shore, until a 'miserable exciseman' appeared and demanded what he was doing. His stammered explanation that he was admiring the sea only confirmed the excise-man's worst suspicions, and Joseph moved on hurriedly.

But captain and passengers alike became less good-humoured when, after ten days at sea, they were no further than the Solent, and still waiting for a favourable wind. Miss Cotterell had been very ill as they were tacking painfully down the Channel against a head-wind. She was continually fainting, and sometimes remained unconscious for as long as five or six hours. Keats and Severn at first shared the task of nursing her, but soon Joseph was left alone to care for her, following his friend's directions, for Keats also had a relapse. Miss Cotterell craved for air. Whenever the portholes were opened Keats would have a terrible fit of coughing which would sometimes end in his spitting blood. But if Joseph were to shut out the cold air which caused his friend so much pain, Miss Cotterell would become distressed and eventually faint away.

The fourth passenger, whom the two young men had thought so good-hearted, proved to be very unsympathetic and kept herself as aloof as was possible in such crowded quarters. Once when Joseph, running from one invalid to the other, called her to help, she broke into a tirade which showed him that he need never look for aid from that quarter.

While they lay in the Solent Keats became much better, and even went ashore with Joseph to visit Dilke's sister who lived at Bedhampton. There they were welcomed with joy and Keats was resolutely cheerful. Everyone said that he seemed much better than they had expected.

Next morning on the ship Keats wrote to his friend, Charles Brown. He had waited, hoping that when he wrote he might be able to describe some definite improvement in his health. But he felt increasingly certain of his fate and feared that if he did not write now, he might later lack strength. So he shed the brittle gaiety which had sheltered his inward agony. He must unburden himself. He must write of his love; his love which was deep and full and burningly passionate — and unfulfilled. The pale ghost of Tom warned him of the danger of agitating thoughts like these. The doctors had said that excitement would do him harm.

'I wish to write on subjects that will not agitate me much — there is one I must mention and have done with it. Even if my body would recover of itself, this would prevent it. The very thing which I want to live most for will be a great occasion of my death. I cannot help it. Who can help it? Were I in health it would make me ill, and how can I bear it in my state? I dare say you will be able to guess on what subject I am harping — you know what was my greatest pain during the first part of my illness at your house. I wish for death every day and then I wish death away, for death would destroy even those pains which are better than nothing. Land and Sea, weakness and decline are great separators, but death is the great divorcer for ever. . . . I think without my mentioning it for my sake you would be a friend of Miss Brawne when I am dead. You think she has many faults — but, for my sake, think she has not one. . . . If there is anything you can do for her by word or deed I know you will do it. . . . The thought of leaving Miss Brawne is beyond everything horrible — the sense of darkness coming over me — I eternally see her figure eternally vanishing. Some of the phrases she was in the habit of using during my last nursing at Wentworth Place ring in my ears. Is there another Life? Shall I awake and find all this a dream? There must be — we cannot be created for this sort of suffering. The receiving this letter is to be one of yours. . . .'[1]

He quickly finished the letter, folded it and put it in his pocket. He did not know if he would ever send it. His spirit had failed him at last, and for the rest of the day he shunned them all and sat alone, his eyes shadowed with despair.

*

The captain had hoped to put into Portland Roads that evening, but the wind dropped again off the Dorset coast. The next day they were still becalmed, and Severn and Keats went ashore at Lulworth Cove. Here Keats seemed to have a flash of his old delight in nature's beauty, and the two young men spent the morning exploring the tunnels and caverns in the rocky chalk coast. Joseph, watching his companion anxiously, was reassured by the pleasure with which he showed him rocks and caves in the cliffs that he had climbed as a boy, 'as though they had been his birthright'.

It was with reluctance that they returned to the ship, to sit silent in the cabin, while Mrs Pidgeon sulked in a corner and Miss Cotterell lay resting in her bunk. The captain was on deck, anxiously searching the sky for promise of a wind. Keats was writing. After a while he stood up and beckoned to Joseph to follow him on deck. They stood together gazing at the star-scattered sky and Joseph, with a painter's interest, watched the shifting lights and colours on the polished surface of the sea. The chalk cliffs glimmered pale across the water.

At last Keats turned to Joseph, and said that he had a present for him. Joseph looked at him, surprised. Those curious gleaming eyes were fixed on his face. Then they dropped and John Keats began to recite in a low, tremulous undertone, which was almost a chant:

[1] 30th September (1820), off Yarmouth, Isle of Wight. *Letters of John Keats*, p. 520.

'Bright star, would I were steadfast as thou art —
Not in lone splendour hung aloft the night,
And watching, with eternal lids apart,
Like Nature's patient, sleepless Eremite,
The moving waters at their priest-like task
Of pure ablution round earth's human shores,
Or gazing on the new soft fallen mask
Of snow upon the mountains and the moors —
No — yet still steadfast, still unchangeable,
Pillow'd upon my fair love's ripening breast,
To feel for ever its soft fall and swell,
Awake for ever in a sweet unrest,
Still, still to hear her tender-taken breath,
And so live ever — or else swoon to death.'

His voice dropped even lower, so that Severn could only just hear the last phrase whispered. He waited, unwilling to shatter the beauty of the silver silence.

Then Keats drew from his pocket a well-thumbed book. It was his volume of Shakespeare's poems. He opened it and showed Severn that on a blank page, opposite the heading 'A Lover's Lament', he had written out the sonnet that he had just recited. He closed the book and pressed it gently into Joseph's hand. Then he turned quickly and went below to the cabin. When Joseph came down he was lying in his bunk and apparently asleep.[1]

Joseph was awakened by the cabin-boy, who shouted down the hatchway that the captain desired him to tell the passengers that a favourable wind had risen at last and, if it held, they would soon be seeing the last of the English coast. Joseph and Keats dressed quickly and went on deck. The wind was becoming stronger, and already the ship was rising and dipping with a lively motion. It was not long before they were both feeling qualms of sickness. There was no dinner eaten that day in the cabin. The captain stayed on deck, with an anxious eye on the rising wind, and the passengers lay, wretched, in their bunks.

It was the beginning of a storm that was to last for three days. By nightfall enormous seas were sweeping over the deck, and the motion of the ship was so violent that Joseph was several times almost thrown out of his bunk. Water rushed up and down the cabin in the darkness. Trunks bumped about the floor. Whenever the ship gave a particularly frightening lurch Mrs Pidgeon would scream, and once or twice he heard a moan from Miss Cotterell, but although he shouted several times to Keats he could hear no reply. The terrifying noises of the storm drowned his voice and seemed to batter his mind into insensibility.

[1] Severn always believed that this was the last poem written by Keats, but it had in fact been composed more than a year earlier at Shanklin and only slightly altered since. The book is now at Keats House, Hampstead.

By the hour when a grey light began to penetrate into the cabin his only thought was to cling to the edge of the bunk with cold cramped fingers, and not to be hurled into the water that dashed their belongings up and down the cabin. Several hours after daybreak he raised himself with a great effort and shouted again to Keats. There was no reply. He felt so weak and dizzy that he did not even try to climb down from his bunk. He knew that such an attempt could only end in disaster.

So the seemingly interminable day passed and night came again. He was desperately afraid that Keats might die, confined to his berth as he was, without food or assistance of any kind. The storm was as violent as ever, and the cold was intense. It seemed to Joseph that the ship must surely founder. But the dawn of another day found him still lying cold and miserable in his berth. The ship was lurching less violently. She seemed to be lifted irresistibly — then there was a pause — followed by a sickening drop. It was very uncomfortable, but at least it was a regular motion, and, as such, reassuring.

After a little while he was able to clamber down from his bunk. He held fast to the side of it and worked his way along to where Keats was lying. The water washed six inches deep round his legs. He reached up and shook Keats's shoulder and was delighted to see him turn slowly towards him and even give him a faint smile. He shouted that he was going to try to get up on deck, and Keats nodded. They had had no time to undress, so Joseph had only to put on his greatcoat, and grope his way across the cabin.

Just as he got to the foot of the companion-way a face appeared above him. It was one of the sailors, sent by the captain to see if they needed any help. Without him Joseph could not have got out on to the deck, because everything had been battened down.

★

Next day, although there was still a heavy swell, the sky was brighter. Joseph and the captain breakfasted in the cabin, with the boy set to hold the table still. They gave some tea, laced with rum, to Keats and the two ladies. Again Joseph spent most of the day on deck in his greatcoat, fascinated by the Atlantic rollers — 'each one as long as Shoreditch'.

The storm continued to abate that night, and by the morning John Keats and Mrs Pidgeon had recovered sufficiently to join the other two at breakfast. There was even some laughter when a sudden lurch sent the cabin-boy sprawling on top of the table which he was supposed to steady, and threw the coffee-pot, fortunately nearly empty, into Mrs Pidgeon's lap and the ham on to Joseph's knees. They were all impressed and secretly rather pleased, when the captain told them that at certain moments during the storm he had felt grave fears for the safety of the ship.

Soon, off Cape St Vincent, they were becalmed, and even Miss Cotterell could sit on deck in the warm sun.

During the calm weather Keats and Severn sat apart from the others and read Lord Byron's *Don Juan* aloud to each other. But when they came to the shipwreck canto Keats flung the book down, disgusted by its cynicism. The sea was oily-smooth; the two friends, leaning over the side of the ship, could see many strange fish and once, to their delight, a whale came up to blow. At the first opportunity Severn brought out his paints and made several water-colour sketches of the sea, and two of Keats.

The calm soon gave way to a steady favourable wind, and the voyage continued uneventfully until one day when several Portuguese men-of-war approached and a shot was fired across their bows. Captain Walsh, who had been shaving in the cabin, rushed up on deck. The *Maria Crowther* was hove to. A great four-decker drifted close to them and her captain shouted across the water with his speaking-trumpet. He asked in English if the little brig had seen any vessels which looked like privateers. When they replied that they had seen no vessels of any kind he signalled them to sail on. The passengers were horrified by the horde of savage, dirty sailors, who crowded the decks and clambered in the rigging which towered above the little *Maria Crowther*, and Captain Walsh was not happy until the whole fleet had disappeared below the horizon.

Later that day they reported the incident to a spick-and-span English sloop-of-war which went about smartly in pursuit of the Portuguese fleet. After this excitement the rest of their voyage passed quickly. Keats told Joseph that he was planning a poem on the story of Sabrina, and Joseph sat spellbound while he recited long passages from Milton's *Comus* in his beautiful moving voice.

This fresh burgeoning of poetic ambition encouraged Joseph to think that his friend was better and would win his way back to health. But terrible fits of coughing still tore him, and the cramped quarters and poor food were taking their toll. His hair, which had once been a bright chestnut, was now quite dark, and the curl had left it. It hung lank and straight round his thin face. Often Joseph, watching him when he thought he was unobserved, would be pained at the distraught, haunting expression of grief on his friend's face.

Gibraltar was passed, the coast of Barbary slipped over the horizon in a golden haze, and at last, after six weeks at sea, the day dawned when they were to enter the Bay of Naples.

CHAPTER 4

QUARANTINE

THEY WERE ALL UP AT SUNRISE to catch the first glimpse of the Bay, and the beauty of it exceeded anything Joseph Severn had dreamed of. The white houses, cushioned in green vineyards and just touched by the rising sun, shone tier above tier on the steeply sloping hills. Vesuvius towered over them, its crest hidden in sun-gilded smoke. The little ship glided gently through the brilliant-blue water, wafted into port by the light dawn breeze, and turning into the wind, with sails flapping, she dropped anchor near the Castell' d'Uovo.

Almost at once they were surrounded by a jostling crowd of little boats. From all corners of the harbour they came darting out, weighed down with their wares.

The group on the *Maria Crowther* leaned over the side of the ship. Wherever they looked, dark faces were upturned to them, brown hands gesticulated and delicious sun-golden fruit was held out to tempt them, while the harsh cries of brightly coloured parrots added to the uproar.

Then the discordant shouts increased in volume and bitterness as a man in some sort of uniform approached, seated in the stern of a rowing-boat. Captain Walsh stepped forward to receive him, but the official, though he stood up in his swaying boat, made no effort to come on board. When he heard that they had come from London he became very excited. He threw his hands above his head and cried that they would have to keep quarantine; there was typhus in London. Nobody must leave the ship for ten days.

It was a cruel blow, after all the discomforts of their five weeks' voyage — the crowded quarters, the bad food, the storms — to arrive at last at their destination and to be penned up on board for another ten days. Joseph was the least depressed. The deep blue of the sea and sky, the paler blue of the mountains, the vivid shifting colours of the clustering skiffs, all filled him with delight. Though he was nearly twenty-seven years old he had never before left England and he longed to capture this strange scene with his brush. Keats's worn face, too, was entranced as he gazed around him and Joseph, encouraged, was about to fetch his paints from the cabin when a naval pinnace came alongside and a young lieutenant sprang on board. The English fleet was in the Bay and the Admiral, seeing the British flag at the masthead of the *Maria Crowther*, had sent an officer to make inquiries.

Six of the sailors manning the pinnace also came on board, but the excitement soon turned to consternation when the Italian official re-appeared to shout that since the English officer and his men had broken the quarantine regulations they must remain there until the ten days were over. On the lieutenant's instructions, the pinnace went back to his ship and returned with orders that he and his men were to stay on the *Maria Crowther*, and fresh provisions, which were very welcome.

Later Miss Cotterell's brother appeared, bringing baskets of every sort of delicacy for them and armfuls of flowers which gave Keats the greatest pleasure; he was shocked by his sister's appearance and soon he voluntarily joined their captivity.

For the first day or two this led to an increased gaiety on board. While the sun shone the sea round the *Maria Crowther* was thick with little boats whose occupants had to come to make merry at the expense of the sailors from the English man-of-war. The lieutenant could speak Italian, but Cotterell, still better, could speak the Neapolitan lazzaroni-patois, and he was quick to reply to the good-natured jokes at the sailors' expense, so that the laughter was often turned back on the joker. He translated these exchanges for the benefit of those on board, and they all helped to suggest replies. Keats was by far the quickest, and seemed to enjoy the interchange as much as any of them.

But alas! the weather changed. Rain began to fall heavily. No longer did the little boats throng round the ship. The rain hissed on the empty water, dripped from the rigging and drummed maddeningly on the deck above their heads. They spent the rest of their quarantine in squalid discomfort. Seven people huddled in the one little cabin, two of them sleeping on the floor at night. Miss Cotterell wilted quickly and soon Joseph saw that her relapse was preying on Keats's nerves; he lost his good spirits and would sit with his eyes on her, marking every symptom of her decline. Joseph could hardly believe that his friend would survive this incarceration. Terrible spasms of coughing convulsed him and he grew daily weaker. It was while he was thus imprisoned that Keats wrote to Mrs Brawne:

'... The sea air has been beneficial to me about to as great an extent as squally weather and bad accommodation and provisions has done harm. So I am about as I was. Give my love to Fanny and tell her, if I were well there is enough in this Port of Naples to fill a quire of Paper — but it looks like a dream — every man who can row his boat and walk and talk seems a different being from myself. I do not feel in the world. It has been unfortunate for me that one of the passengers is a young Lady in Consumption — her imprudence has vexed me very much — the knowledge of her complaint — the flushings in her face, all her bad symptoms have preyed upon me . . . I shall feel a load off me when the Lady vanishes out of my sight . . . I dare not fix my Mind upon Fanny, I have not dared to think of her. The only comfort I have had that way has been in thinking for hours together of having the knife she gave me put in a silver case — the hair in a Locket — and the Pocket Book in a gold net. Show her this. I dare say no more. . . . O what an account I could give you of the Bay of Naples if I could once more feel myself a Citizen of this world – I feel a spirit in my Brain would lay it forth pleasantly – O what a misery it is to have an intellect in splints! My love again to Fanny – '

He sent a message to Fanny's younger sister and to her brother, a word to the Dilkes, another to Brown, and inscribed himself:

'My dear Mrs Brawne

Yours sincerely and affectionate

JOHN KEATS – '

Then his pen scribbled an anguished postscript:

'Goodbye Fanny! Glod bless you!'[1]

[1] 24th October (1820), Naples Harbour. *Letters of John Keats*, pp. 522–3.

CHAPTER 5

NAPLES TO ROME

October – November, 1820

THE TEN DAYS WERE OVER. The morning was cold and a damp fog hung over the harbour, but no weather could have depressed Joseph. In half an hour his foot would, for the first time, touch foreign soil. They were all on deck, muffled up against the weather — Mrs Pidgeon, with her false air of motherliness; Lieutenant Sullivan pacing the deck, anxious to be back in his ship; Charles Cotterell, hovering anxiously around his ill sister, who sat limply with her eyes fixed unwaveringly on the deck.

But where was Keats? He looked about to see if he was talking to the captain with whom he had struck up a great friendship, and whose kindness to the two friends had been unceasing. But Walsh was busy with one of the seamen coiling ropes. Joseph hurried aft and peered down into the cabin.

At what he saw he turned quite white and a cold horror seemed to run through his body. For a moment he stayed with a sick, empty feeling in his stomach, then he stumbled aft, and in the stern of the ship, with no one near, he sank down on the deck and covered his eyes with his hand. The sight of so much suffering was unbearable. He heard again that ghastly cough; he saw again the poor white face, the terrible pool of blood. Unnerved, bewildered and cursing his helplessness, he sat there with hot tears pouring down his cheeks, until the sudden fear that Keats would find him thus forced him to compose himself.

Eventually Keats emerged from the cabin amidst the bustle that surrounded the shore-going boat. Mr Cotterell insisted on taking them in his carriage to the hotel which he had recommended — the Villa di Londra.

Joseph was taken aback by the dirt, the noise and the smell of the city which had looked so beautiful from the sea. The streets were filthy. The wheels of their carriage passed through heaps of slush and rotting vegetables, which lay steaming on the cobbles. The stench was overpowering, but the natives did not appear to notice it. The whole population seemed to live in the streets, and the noise they made was deafening. Red-capped mariners were hawking fish, mothers nursed their babies in the gutters. Filthy beggars dragged themselves with uncanny speed along the roadway, calling attention to their deformities, and a troop of ragged children ran beside their carriage clamouring for money. At a narrow corner they were held up while a herd of cows wandered past them, and Mr Cotterell explained that in Naples they were driven to your door

44

THE KEATS BROTHERS
By Joseph Severn

(*left*) GEORGE KEATS who emigrated to America

Keats-Shelley House, Rome

(*below, left*) TOM KEATS who died of consumption three weeks after his 18th birthday

Keats-Shelley House, Rome

(*below, right*) JOHN KEATS aged 21

'This is by far the best likeness of Keats,' Joseph wrote to Buxton Forman in 1877. He always remembered the evening in the Keats brothers' lodgings in the City 'when I drew Keats's picture and Shelley read his essay on poetry.'

Victoria and Albert Museum

THE SEVERN FAMILY MINIATURE

Painted by Joseph Severn in 1820 and taken by him to Rome. His father and mother on the right, then his sisters and brothers in order of age—Charlotte, Sarah, Maria, Tom with his hands on the keys of a harpsichord, and Charles

Now at *Keats House, Hampstead*

KEATS ON HIS DEATH-BED

By Joseph Severn

'28 January—3 o'clock Mn⁹—drawn to keep awake—a deadly sweat was on him all this nig Charles Cowden Clarke told Buxton Forman was 'a marvellously correct likeness.'

Keats-Shelley House, Rome

to be milked. A masked religious took advantage of the delay to thrust a collecting box into the carriage. Joseph stole a look at his friend's white, listless face, and could have cried again as he thought how Keats, in good health, would have revelled in all the strange sights and sounds around them. To-day was his twenty-fifth birthday.

Next morning in their large airy room at the hotel, with a view of Vesuvius from its windows, both sat down to write home. Joseph continued his journal-letter to Haslam, bringing it up to date with a description of their voyage, of Keats's misery in quarantine, and of the kindness they had received from Captain Walsh and Mr Cotterell. He was too engrossed in his letter to notice Keats's expression of suffering as he wrote to Brown, the only friend who already knew so much of his love that there was no need for explanation.

'Yesterday', he wrote, 'we were let out of Quarantine, during which my health suffered more from bad air and the stifled cabin than it had done the whole voyage. The fresh air revived me a little, and I hope I am well enough this morning to write you a short calm letter; — if that can be called one, in which I am afraid to speak of what I would fainest dwell upon. As I have gone thus far into it, I must go on a little; perhaps it may relieve the load of WRETCH-EDNESS which presses upon me. The persuasion that I shall see her no more will kill me. . . . My dear Brown, I should have had her when I was in health and I should have remained well. I can bear to die — I cannot bear to leave her. O God! God! God! Everything I have in my trunks that reminds me of her goes through me like a spear. The silk lining she put in my travelling cap scalds my head. My imagination is horribly vivid about her — I see her — I hear her. There is nothing in the world of sufficient interest to divert me from her a moment. . . .'

The pen rushed on.

'. . . I am afraid to write to her — to receive a letter from her — to see her handwriting would break my heart — even to hear of her anyhow, to see her name written, would be more than I can bear. My dear Brown, what am I to do? Where can I look for consolation or ease? If I had any chance of recovery, this passion would kill me. Indeed, through the whole of my illness, both at your house and at Kentish Town, this fever has never ceased wearing me out. When you write to me, which you will do immediately, write to Rome (poste restante) — if she is well and happy, put a mark thus +; if —'

He added some other messages but could not prevent himself from returning to the one subject which filled his mind.

'. . . Is there any news of George? O, that something fortunate had ever happened to me or my brothers! — then I might hope, — but despair is forced upon me as a habit. My dear Brown, for my sake, be her advocate for ever. I cannot say a word about Naples; I do not feel at all concerned in the thousand novelties around me. I am afraid to write to her — I should like her to know that I do not forget her. Oh, Brown, I have coals of fire in my breast. It

c

surprises me that the human heart is capable of containing and bearing such misery. Was I born for this end? . . .'[1]

He finished his letter. Joseph saw him take up a volume of *Clarissa Harlowe*, but he seemed unable to concentrate on it. After frequent changes of position, he put the book down and went over to the window, where the raindrops had begun to chase each other down the panes and blurred the lights twinkling in the misty night outside. At length he turned away from his gloomy vigil over the city and began to move restlessly about the room, every now and then glancing at Severn, as though he were about to speak.

Joseph interrupted the sentence he was writing and scribbled rapidly: 'for the present I will talk to him – he is disposed to it. I will talk him to sleep for he has suffered much fatigue.'

Then he laid down his pen and tried to lead Keats on to talk. It was not easy. The truth was that Keats was aching to talk to someone about Fanny and his frustrated love. But by nature he was very reserved where his deepest feelings were concerned and with his illness, secrecy had become an obsession. Even in good health he had constantly urged Fanny to tell no one of their love. He had told her, with the prospect of a long engagement before them:

'I would rather die than share my secret with anybody's confidence.'

As his illness became more acute, he had striven even more to hide what should have been his dearest happiness. Of what use to expose a love which had no future? He had no money. He must write if he was to pay his debts. Yet the doctors told him 'not even to read poetry, much less write it'.[2]

He had kept his secret well. Of all his friends, only Charles Brown realized the intensity of his passion. There had been no possibility of concealing from Brown the constant visits of their attractive neighbour or the intimate terms that he was on with her, though Brown had not approved. But Joseph had no inkling of the depth of his feelings for Miss Brawne. Although he had met her several times he, like Reynolds, had not thought her worthy of the friend whom he idolized. He realized that Keats was strongly attracted to her, but she had always responded in such a lively way to his own laughter and good spirits that the atmosphere, when he had been with them, had never been such as might have shown him the truth.

Indeed, when poor Fanny saw the letter that Joseph had just put aside to finish later, she wrote to Keats's sister – 'From your brother I never expect a very good account, but you may imagine how lowering to the spirits it must have been when Mr Severn, who I never imagined it was possible for anything to make unhappy, who I never saw for ten minutes serious, says he was so overcome that he was obliged to relieve himself by shedding tears.'[3]

Joseph had seen little of Keats during the months immediately before their

---

[1] Naples, 1st November (1820). *Letters of John Keats*, pp. 523–4.
[2] John Keats to Fanny Brawne, February 1820. Ibid., p. 463.
[3] 4th December, 1820. *Letters of Fanny Brawne to Fanny Keats* ed. F. Edgcumbe, p. 9.

departure, because he had been painting every minute of the long summer days. So he did not realize the agony John was suffering in being parted from her, as he felt, for ever.

Gradually Keats was able to bring himself to tell Severn something of his unhappiness. The first halting words made a crack in the wall that reserve had built round his most intimate feelings. Slowly the crack widened under the urgent pressure, the words came more easily, and then the wall crumbled and a flood of frustrated longing surged round Joseph and swept him into an alien, tragic world.

John Keats cried out against the perverse fate which had allowed him to meet, love and be loved by Fanny, only to snatch the prospect of a happy union from him. But his misery and weakness made him incoherent. His frustrated love became mixed with the horror he felt at being unable to write, or even to *see* with the poetic sight that had been his. So that Joseph, even then, did not realize quite how this passion alone was consuming him, apart from the drying up of his poetic inspiration.

Keats was not able to purge himself of all his misery. He did not tell Joseph of his conviction that this passion for Fanny would kill him, that with the certain knowledge, which he felt himself in spite of the doctors, that he was going to die, every thought of her was a sword-thrust in his vitals, and thus a further impediment to any chance of recovery.

Nevertheless the confidence, incomplete though it was, relieved him. Joseph's passionate sympathy and deep emotion did much to soothe him, and he was comparatively calm when they went to bed.

'Keats went to bed much recovered,' wrote Joseph to Haslam next day. 'I took every means to remove from him a heavy grief that may tend more than anything to be fatal. He told me much, very much — and I don't know whether it was more painful for me or himself — but it had the effect of much relieving him — he went very calm to bed. . . . This morning he is still very much better. We are in good spirits and I may say hopeful fellows — at least I may say as much for Keats — he made an Italian pun today. The rain is coming down in torrents.'[1]

*

Next morning Keats received a letter from Shelley, urging him to go to Pisa. He showed it to Joseph. It was a charming letter. Shelley's generous soul had been revolted by the critics' attack, and when, in July, he heard of Keats's illness, he had at once written to invite him to Italy as his guest. Keats, although touched by his kindness, had preferred to retain his independence. Almost every literary friend of Shelley's relied on him for financial assistance, and Keats was always embarrassed lest he might think that he, too, desired to profit from his generosity. This fear had always, in his relations with Shelley, made him a little abrupt and

[1] 2nd November, 1820. *Keats Circle*, vol. I, p. 166.

even ungracious. So it was on this occasion. Although grateful for his kindness, he declined the invitation, explaining that their arrangements were already made to spend the winter in Rome.

After four days in Naples they set out on the last stage of their journey, in a small carriage. Joseph was sorry to leave Naples, where Charles Cotterell had given a farewell dinner in their honour, but Keats, with his liberal convictions, was upset by the King's betrayal of the new constitution and the apathy with which the Neapolitans themselves seemed to be facing the loss of their freedom and a resumption of the Austrian yoke. The King had fled to his Austrian friends only the day before, and Keats declared that he could no longer bear to stay in a city where men cared so little for their liberty.

The weather was delightful. The *vettura* moved slowly, so that Joseph was able to walk long stretches of the journey beside it and he was exhilarated by the pure air and the strange surroundings. They passed through mile after mile of vineyards where the vines were festooned like lovely natural garlands from tree to tree, and their green chains ran from the hill-tops down to the road in the valley and stretched away up the slope on the other side. He strode along beside the carriage, sniffing the lovely scents blown down from the hills and the briny tang of the never far-distant sea.

Keats, seated in the *vettura*, was listless and unhappy. He could not eat the coarse unpalatable food which was all they could get at the wayside inns. His only pleasure was in the wild flowers that grew everywhere about their path and whose smell became almost overpowering when they came to cross the Pontine Marches. Joseph would fill the little carriage with flowers. Keats never tired of them, and their scent and colour seemed to kindle in him a strange joy.

At last they saw before them the vast menacing wastes of the Campagna. Keats's interest quickened.

'It's like an inland sea,' he said.

Not a tree nor a house could they see in the wide monotony before them. The grass grew yellow from the cracked ground. On a hillock not far from the road a buffalo stood tense for a moment watching them, then plunged away. The dust lay thick beneath the wheels and swirled behind them in a cloud. Ahead of them, near the ruins of a solitary square tower, they saw a moving patch of crimson. As they drew nearer they found it was a cardinal in a bright red cloak. An owl, which was fastened by one leg to a stick beside him, fluttered about indignantly. Attached to the owl was a small looking-glass reflecting the sun, which attracted numerous small birds and when they came near enough the cardinal would shoot them. Two liveried footmen stood at his side and deferentially loaded the fowling-pieces. Already quite a large pile of tiny victims lay at his feet.

They passed this eccentric sportsman, and at the summit of the next hill the carriage came to a standstill. The *vetturino* pointed with his whip.

'*Ecco Roma!*'

The miles of desolate plain, the occasional massive tower, the bare rocks and, in the distance, the historic hills shrouded in mist, all combined to create an atmosphere of solitude and fallen splendour. As they gazed over the barren wastes of the Campagna, Rome seemed like an enchanted city of the dead.

They entered the city by the Lateran Gate, and almost at once they were staggered by their first view of the Colosseum. Its size and the broken grandeur of its outline impressed them deeply. They passed through the ruins of the Imperial City and turned into a series of long, narrow streets.

Soon their eyes were dazzled as they emerged into the open space of the Piazza di Spagna. Directly opposite them a magnificent flight of steps led upwards to a church with twin towers. '*Santa Trinità dei Monti*,' said the driver. Water was playing in a fountain, shaped like a stone ship, at the foot of the steps and all around stood stalls of flowers, piled high with daffodils and mimosa.

Dr Clark received them warmly in his house in the Piazza di Spagna. Keats had written to him from Naples, and the doctor had already taken rooms for them just opposite his own, in the house on the right-hand side of the Spanish Steps, which led from the Piazza to the church above.

They were on the first floor. Keats's room was at the side of the house overlooking the steps, and Joseph's faced on to the Piazza. Soon after their arrival their landlady sent out to a restaurant, or *trattoria*, for a large dish of macaroni. Keats was exhausted by the long journey and could eat nothing, but the excitement of being at last in Rome made him comparatively cheerful.

'You would never believe this could taste so good,' said Joseph with his mouth full. Then, thinking of the good English food at Mason's Court — roast beef, cabbage and pudding — he made a face and added, laughing, 'though it *looks* like a dish of large white earthworms.'[1]

---

[1] To Maria, 19th February, 1821. Keats House, Hampstead.

CHAPTER 6

NO. 26 PIAZZA DI SPAGNA

November – December, 1820

DR CLARK DID NOT CONFINE HIS KINDNESS to his patient. When he heard that Joseph knew no one in Rome he spoke to John Gibson and returned with an invitation from the young English sculptor for Severn to visit him. Joseph was delighted but apprehensive. He longed to take advantage of the introduction, yet from his experience in London of the lack of interest shown by successful artists in their poorer brothers' struggles, he feared a snub or a cold reception, which would show that Gibson had been more or less forced into extending a vague invitation to Dr Clark's friend, and thought it poor taste on his part to have taken advantage of it.

But Keats would allow no hesitation. He was gradually gaining strength after the journey, although the doctor would not yet allow him to see any of the sights of Rome, for fear that they would excite his brain too much. He divided his time between reading, learning Italian, and taking gentle walks on the Piazza. Joseph would accompany him on these strolls, but Keats was much troubled by the thought that his friend's journey to Rome might prove disastrous to him in his career.[1] He had told Joseph that he was painfully sensible of 'the great sacrifice' that he had made on his account and he had already urged him to present his letter of introduction to Canova at the earliest opportunity. Now, hearing what Dr Clark had done, he insisted that Joseph should go to John Gibson's apartment that very afternoon.

It was a short walk from the Piazza di Spagna to the Via della Fontanella where the English sculptor lived. Although only two years older than Joseph, he had already achieved considerable fame. For the last three years he had been living in Rome; he had many wealthy English patrons and it was well known that the Marquis Canova had expressed the highest opinion of his work.

The visit was a wonderful surprise to Joseph. The young sculptor welcomed him warmly and when Lord Colchester, a well-known connoisseur and collector arrived, refused to let Joseph leave but presented him to his wealthy patron and showed his work to both of them with equal attention. The two young men talked together for some time after Lord Colchester had left and before parting, Gibson begged Joseph to let him know if there was any way in which he could help him.

[1] Joseph Severn's *Reminiscences*, quoted Sharp, op. cit., pp. 55, 67, 69.

So anxious was Joseph to tell Keats about Gibson's behaviour that he almost ran back to the Piazza di Spagna. He found his friend puzzling out an Italian book.

'It was a revelation to me, Keats!' he cried, when he had described the scene at the studio. 'Making money is all that artists in London think about. But if Gibson, who is a great artist, can afford to treat a poor and unknown painter in this way, then Rome is the place for me!'

Keats was delighted. 'A first treat to humanity,' he said with his sad smile. Then his expression became more serious and he said that it was time they discussed together Severn's plans for the future. He must start at once upon a picture. No time must be lost, especially if he treasured some hope of winning the Academy's three-year pension for a travelling student. Knowing Joseph's optimistic nature, he went on to warn him against over-confidence. In the first place, the fact that he had already made his way to Rome without their help 'might have offended the pride of the Council'. In the second place, he had reason to believe that Severn's winning the Gold Medal had made him many enemies among his fellow-artists in London.

Joseph agreed ruefully, and after a moment's hesitation Keats told him what he had heard at a gathering of artists in London. He had been taken by Hilton to dine with some other artists at de Wint's house where the conversation had turned to the recent award of the Academy's Gold Medal after so many years. One of the company scornfully explained that the picture was very inferior, but that as the artist was an old fellow and had made frequent attempts for the prize, the Council had given the medal out of pity, and not for any merit. Keats awaited a flat contradiction from one of the three artists present, besides Hilton, who knew the truth. It was not forthcoming. He had then expressed his disgust at so mean a lie. He declared that he would no longer sit at the table with traducers and snobs; that he knew the winner intimately, had seen the picture and recognized its merits; that, as they well knew, Severn was a young man and the picture his first attempt for a prize of any kind. He had then risen from the table and abruptly left the party. As he described the scene to Joseph, he seemed to live it again. The generous resentment that injustice never failed to rouse in him made his eyes flash, and he seemed to increase in stature.[1]

It was a shock to Joseph to realize the malice that his triumph had aroused, but he was deeply touched by Keats's loyal championship and he made a fresh resolve to be worthy of it.

*

Things went on well enough for the first month after their arrival. Keats seemed to be getting a little stronger, and although Dr Clark would not yet allow him to visit any of the great monuments, he was able to stroll on the Piazza in the

[1] Ibid., pp. 65-6.

mild autumn weather, and even to ride about on a little pony. Joseph hired a piano for seven *scudi* a month and would play to him. Kind Dr Clark lent them some books of music and among them was a collection of Haydn's symphonies, which proved a delight to Keats. As Joseph sat playing he exclaimed, 'This Haydn is like a child, for there is no knowing what he will do next!'

He was strong enough to take an interest in their food. Like everyone living in lodgings in Rome, they had their dinner sent in to them from a *trattoria*. The dishes were brought in a large basket, lined with tin, and the food was kept hot by a little charcoal stove inside. In spite of frequent complaints, the food sent to them was so badly cooked as to be almost uneatable, although it was by no means cheap. One day Keats told Joseph that he would tolerate it no longer. He refused to say what he was going to do, but when the porter came as usual with the basket, and was beginning to set the food out on the table, Keats opened the window, which was over the Spanish Steps, and taking each dish, one after the other, emptied the contents deliberately out of it. He then quietly, but very decidedly, pointed to the basket, which the porter took away without a word.

'Now,' he said, 'you'll see, Severn, that we'll have a decent dinner.'

He was right. In less than half an hour an excellent dinner appeared. The food continued to be equally good on subsequent days, and no mention was made of the rejected dinner on their account.

About this time they made the acquaintance of a young English officer, Lieutenant Elton, who, though tall and handsome, was, like Keats, consumptive, and he joined them in their strolls. The fashionable promenade on the Pincio was their favourite place for exercise, as it was sheltered from the north wind, and at first they were always a trio, because until Keats was really better, Joseph could not bring himself to leave him, even to work. Keats had hoped that Charles Brown would follow him to Rome, but a letter from Chichester showed him that his friend at the moment had no such plans.

'I have an habitual feeling of my real life having passed,' Keats wrote to him, 'and that I am leading a posthumous existence.' Any reminder of the happiness he had known was agony to him. 'I am so weak (in mind) that I cannot bear the sight of any handwriting of a friend I love so much as I do you. Yet I ride the little horse, and, at my worst, even in quarantine, summoned up more puns, in a sort of desperation, in one week than in any year of my life. There is one thought enough to kill me; I have been well, healthy, alert, etc., walking with her, and now the knowledge of contrast, feeling for light and shade, all that information (primitive sense) necessary for a poem, are great enemies to the recovery of the stomach ... Dr Clark is very attentive to me, he says there is very little the matter with my lungs, but my stomach, he says, is very bad. . . . Severn is very well, though he leads so dull a life with me. . . . I can scarcely bid you goodbye, even in a letter. I always made an awkward bow.'[1]

[1] 30th November, 1820. *Letters of John Keats*, pp. 525–7.

Soon something made them change the direction of their walks. On their way round the Pincio they had several times noticed a lady in a magnificent carriage who was handsome, richly dressed and carried herself with a haughty air. The three young men were intrigued when they found that this was Napoleon's sister, Pauline Bonaparte, now Princess Borghese. She was a famous beauty, though no longer young, and lived in a splendid establishment apart from her husband. They had heard many stories of her private life, which was notorious, and like everyone else, they had been to see the statue Canova had made of her, nude to the waist, which was publicly on show in Rome. Keats had dismissed it as 'beautiful bad taste'.

When next the carriage passed them they all turned to gaze, and were disconcerted to find their interest more than returned. The lady's quick eye had lighted on the tall figure of Lieutenant Elton and her manner changed abruptly as her haughtiness vanished and she threw him a shamelessly coquettish glance. Every day afterwards she was on the watch for them, and her languishing glances, even though he thankfully acknowledged that they were not intended for him, so wrought upon Keats's nerves that he could not bear to stay.

Poor Keats! Something in her behaviour had pierced his indifference and brought him intolerable thoughts of beauty and desire. He had always been intensely jealous. Fanny was coquettish and fond of admiration. Even in the happy past he had reproached her for smiling on other men. What was she doing, now that he was separated from her? His nerves were so affected that they decided not to go again to the Pincio.

After this Keats and Elton would go for easy rides together — never very far, nor at a pace faster than a walk. Sometimes they would leave the city by the Porta del Popolo and ride slowly along the banks of the Tiber. These expeditions left Joseph free to go to the Vatican to study at the feet of Michelangelo and Raphael. He could make sketches of buildings and ruins, and once he risked his neck climbing to a ledge of the Colosseum to pick a wallflower, that he might show Keats how it had scented all the air.

When they sat indoors Joseph would work on a picture to submit for the Academy pension. He knew that it gave Keats pleasure to see him thus employed, for one of his constant anxieties was the thought of the sacrifice Severn had made to accompany him to Rome, and he feared lest his own misfortune should involve his friend. For Joseph's sake he would force a gaiety and humour which he did not feel, and would try to interest himself in learning Italian, and even in ideas for a poem which he would write when he felt stronger. But then some random word or thought would strike his defences from him and deliver him, powerless, to the dark enemies he was fighting.

Thus when he brought home a volume of poems by Alfieri, the first words that he read were too much his own, and he threw the book away and would read it no more.

C*

'Misera me! sollievo a me non resta
Altro che'l pianto, ed il pianto è delitto'[1]

Another evening Joseph was extolling his favourite Tasso. Keats, translated for a moment from the present, said that he 'anticipated he should become a greater poet if he were allowed to live'. But immediately he shook his head and said how cruel it was to die before he had completed anything great.

He had told Fanny Brawne a few months earlier of his sad conviction: 'I have left no immortal work behind me — nothing to make my friends proud of my memory — but . . . if I had had time I would have made myself remember'd.'[2]

When his friend's suffering were great, Joseph found that music soothed him, and he would sit at the hired piano and play until the fretted nerves were eased.

But in spite of these words of despair, on the whole he seemed calmer and even a little more hopeful, until with tragic suddenness his malady roused and sunk its claws into him again.

---

[1] 'Unhappy me! there is no solace left to me
Save weeping, and weeping is a crime.'
[2] *Letters of John Keats,* p. 468.

CHAPTER 7

JOSEPH TELLS HIS OWN STORY

To Charles Brown: *Rome, December 14, 1820*
        I fear poor Keats is at his worst. A most unlooked-for relapse
has confined him to his bed, with every chance against him. It has been so
sudden upon what I almost thought convalescence, and without any seeming cause, that I cannot calculate on the next change. I dread it, for his suffering
is so great, so continued, and his fortitude so completely gone, that any
further change must make him delirious. This is the fifth day, and I see him get
worse. . . .

Dec. 17, 4 Morning
    Not a moment can I be from him. I sit by his bed and read all day, and at
night I humour him in all his wanderings. He has just fallen asleep, the first for 8
nights, and now from mere exhaustion. I hope he will not wake until I have
written this, for I am anxious . . . to have you know this worse and worse state —
yet I dare not let him see I think it dangerous. On the morning of this attack . . .
he was going on merrily and had unusual good spirits — when in an instant a
Cough seized him, and he vomited near two Cupfuls of blood. In a moment I
got Doctor Clark, who . . . took away about 8 ounces of blood from his Arm —
it was black and thick. . . . Keats was much alarmed and dejected. O what an
awful day I had with him! — He rushed out of bed and said, 'This day shall be
my last' — and but for me most certainly it would. . . . I took every destroying
means from his reach, nor let him be from my sight one minute. The blood
broke forth again in like quantity the next morning, and the doctor thought it
expedient to take away the like quantity of blood. . . .
    This is the 9th day, and no change for the better. Five times the blood has come
up in coughing in large quantities. . . . Not a single thing will digest, the torture
he suffers all and every night and best part of the day is dreadful in the extreme.
The distended stomach keeps him in perpetual hunger . . . and this is augmented
by the little nourishment he takes to keep down the blood. Then his mind is
worse than all — despair in every shape — his imagination and memory present
every image in horror, so strong that morning and night I tremble for his
Intellect. The recollection of England — of his 'good friend Brown' — and his
happy few weeks in Mrs Brawne's care — his Sister and brother — O he will
mourn over every circumstance to me whilst I cool his burning forehead — until
I tremble . . . in concealing my tears from his staring glassy eyes. How he can

55

be Keats again from all this I have little hope, but I may see it too gloomy, since each coming night I sit up adds its dismal contents to my mind.

Dr Clark will not say so much; although there is no bounds to his attention, yet with little success 'can he administer to a mind diseased'. Yet all that can be done most kindly he does, whilst his Lady, like himself in refined feeling, prepares all that poor Keats takes, for in this wilderness of a place (for an Invalid) there is no alternative. Yesterday Dr Clark went all over Rome for a certain kind of fish, and got it — but just as I received it from Mrs C. delicately prepared, Keats was taken by the spitting of blood and is now gone back all the 9 days. This was occasioned by disobeying the Doctor's commands. Keats is required to be kept as low as possible to check the blood, so that he is weak and gloomy. Every day he raves that he will die of hunger, and I was obliged to give him more than allowed. You cannot think how dreadful this is for me — the Doctor on the one hand tells me I shall kill him to give him more than he allows — and Keats raves for more. . . . We have the best opinion of Dr C's skill — he seems to understand the case, and comes over 4 and 5 times a day. . . .

For myself I am keeping up beyond my most sanguine expectations — 8 nights I have been up, and in the days never a moment away from my patient but to run over to the Doctor — but I will confess my spirits have been sometimes quite pulled down — for these wretched Romans have no idea of comfort — here I am obliged to wash up, cook, and read to Keats all day. Added to this I have had no letters yet from my family — This is a damp to me for I never knew how dear they were to me. I think of my Mother . . . I am quite exhausted — farewell — I wish you were here my dear Brown. . . .[1]

★

Decr 24 1820 —
To John Taylor: ½ past 4 — Mor^g. —
          Keats has changed somewhat for the worse — at least his mind has much — very very much — and this leaves his state much the same and quite as hopeless. Yet the blood has ceased to come, his digestion is better, and but for a cough he must be improving, that is, as far as respects his body. But the fatal prospect of Consumption hangs before his mind's eye, and turns everything to despair and wretchedness. He will not bear the idea of living much less strive to live. I seem to lose his confidence by trying to give him this hope. . . .

The remembrance of his brother's death . . . all his own symptoms he recollects in him. . . . All that fortitude and as it were bravery of mind against bodily suffering are away from him — and the want of some kind hope to feed his voracious imagination leaves him to the wreck of ideas without purpose — imagination without philosophy. Yet this night he said to me, '. . . You know Severn I cannot believe in your book, the Bible, but I feel the horrible want of some faith — some hope — something to rest on now. There must be such a

[1] Keats Circle, I, pp. 175–9.

book — and I know that is it — but I can't believe it. I am destined to every torment in this world — even to this little comfort on my death bed. . . .' I have read to him incessantly, until no more books could be had — for they must be new to him. . . . This is the third week, and I have not left him more than two hours — he has not been out of bed the whole time. . . . He says it makes him worse to think how I should be occupied and how I am. . . . I do lament a thousand times that he ever left England. . . . For myself, I still keep up nearly as well as I did, altho' I have not got any person to relieve me. . . . Keats makes me careful of myself — he is my doctor. . . . I am rather alarmed about money. At Naples I expended nearly all my stock. Here I can get more by my Miniature Painting . . . but now I am kept from it — no one to relieve me with Keats. . . .[1]

★

To William Haslam:
      He turned to me suddenly on one occasion, and, looking fixedly at me a long while with a fiery life in his eyes, painfully large and glowing out of his hollow woe-wrought face, said, 'Severn, I bequeath to you all the joy and prosperity I have never had.' I thought he was wandering again; and soothed him gently. 'This is the last Christmas I shall ever see — that I ever want to see,' he said vehemently, an hour later, and as though no interval had elapsed; 'but you will see many, and be happy. It would be a second death for me if I knew that your goodness now was your loss hereafter.'[2]

★

Letter from Haslam received by Joseph about Dec. 24th
    . . . Why have you not kept your diary? I ask you solemnly, for no one thing on earth can give such satisfaction at home as such intimate details as you set out with. If you have discontinued it, in God's name resume it, and send it regularly to me . . . DO THIS, Severn, tho' at some sacrifice of your inherent dislike of order and of obligation to do a thing — do it, if but because I ask it. . . . Tom has several times called on me, and I understand your father has at last become tolerably reconciled.[3]

★

Jan. 11, 1821
1 o'Clock morning
(finished 3 A.M.)
To Mrs Brawne:
    I said that 'the first good news I had should be for the kind Mrs Brawne'. I am thankful and delighted to make good my promise. . . . I most certainly think I shall bring him back to England . . . half the cause of his danger has arisen from the loss of England — from the dread of never seeing it more. . . .
    In the first fortnight of this attack his memory presented to him everything

---

[1] *Keats Circle*, I, pp. 179–82.   [2] Sharp, op. cit., p. 202.   [3] Ibid., p. 72.

that was dear and delightful, even to the minutiae – and with it all the persecution and I may say villainy practised upon him – his exquisite sensibility for
everyone save his poor self – all his own means and comfort expended on others
– almost in vain. These he would contrast with his present suffering, and say
that all was brought on by them, and he was right. Now he has changed to
calmness and quietude, as singular as productive of good, for his mind was most
certainly killing him. He has now given up all thoughts, hopes, or even wish
for recovery. His mind is in a state of peace from the final leave he has taken of
this world and all his future hopes. . . .

Now, if anything will recover him, it is this absence of himself. I have
perceived for the last 3 days symptoms of recovery. Doctor Clark even thinks
so. Nature again revives in him – I mean where art was used before. Yesterday
he permitted me to carry him from his bedroom to our sitting room – to put
him clean things on, and to talk about my Painting to him. This is my good
news. . . .

For Three weeks I have never left him – I have sat up at night – I have read
to him nearly all day, and even in the night. I light the fire, make his breakfast,
and sometimes am obliged to cook – make his bed and even sweep the room.
I can have these things done, but never at the time when they ought and must be
done – so that you will see my alternative. What enrages me most is making a
fire. I blow – blow – for an hour – the smoke comes fuming out – my kettle
falls over on the burning sticks – no stove – Keats calling me to be with him –
the fire catching my hands and the door bell ringing; all these to one quite
unused and not at all capable – with the want of every proper material come
not a little galling.

But to my great surprise I am not ill, or even restless nor have I been all the
time, there is nothing but what I will do for him – there is no alternative but
what I think and provide myself against – except his death – not the loss of
him – I am not prepared to bear that – but the inhumanity, the barbarism of
these Italians. So far I have kept everything from poor Keats; but if he did know
but part of what I suffer for them and their cursed laws, it would kill him. Just
to instance one thing among many. News was brought me the other day that
our gentle landlady had reported to the Police that my friend was dying of
consumption. Now their law is that every individual thing in each room the
patient has been in, shall without reserve, even to the paper on the walls, be
destroyed by fire – This startled me not a little, for in our sitting-room where I
wanted to bring him, there is property worth about £150, besides all our own
books, etc, invaluable. Now my difficulty was to shift him to this room, and let
no one know it. This was a heavy task from the unfortunate manner of the
place – our landlady's apartments are on the same floor with ours – her servant
waits on me when it pleases her, and enters from an adjoining room.

I was determined on removing Keats, let what would be the consequence.
The change was most essential to his health and spirits, and the following

morning I set about accomplishing it. In the first place I blocked up the door so as they could not enter — then made up a bed on the Sofa and removed my friend to it. The greatest difficulty was in keeping all from him; I succeeded in this too, by making his bed and sweeping the room where it is — and going dinnerless with all the pretensions of dining, persuading him that the Servant had made his bed, and I had been dining. He half suspected this, but as he could not tell the why and the wherefore, there it ended. I got him back in the afternoon and no one save Doctor Clark knew of it.

Doctor C still attends him with his usual kindness, and shows his good heart in everything he does; the like of his lady — I cannot tell which shows us the most kindness. *I* am even a mark of their care — mince pies and numberless nice things come over to keep me alive, and but for their kindness I am afraid we should go on very gloomily. Now my dear Madam I must leave off. My eyes are beginning to be unruly, and I must write a most important letter to our President, Sir Thomas Lawrence, before I suffer myself to go to sleep. . . .

Present my respectful Compts to Miss B who I hope and trust is quite well — now that I think of her my mind is carried to your happy Wentworth Place. I would my unfortunate friend had never left it . . . he has many many times talked over the few happy days at your House . . . I hope still to see him with you again. . . .[1]

★

To William Haslam: *Jany. 15th, 1821*
Sunday night ½ past 11 —

Poor Keats has just fallen asleep — I have watched him and read to him — to his very last wink. He has been saying to me 'Severn, I can see under your quiet look, immense twisting and contending — you don't know what you are reading — you are enduring for me more than I'd have you. O! that my last hour was come — what is it puzzles you now — what is it happens?' I tell him that 'nothing happens — nothing worries me beyond his seeing — that it has been the dull day.' Getting from myself to his recovery, and then my painting, and then England, and then — but they are all lies — my heart almost leaps to deny them — for I have the veriest load of care that ever came upon these shoulders of mine. For Keats is sinking daily . . . perhaps another three weeks may lose me him for ever. — This alone would break down the most gallant spirit — I had made sure of his recovery when I set out. This is not all — I have prepared myself to bear this now . . . but Torlonia's the bankers have refused any more money — the bill is returned unaccepted, 'no effects' and I tomorrow must — aye *must* — pay the last solitary crowns for this cursed lodging place. Yet more — should our unfortunate friend die, all the furniture will be burnt — beds, sheets, curtains, and even the walls must be scraped — and these devils will come upon me for £100 or £150 — the making good. But above all this noble fellow

[1] *Keats Circle*, I, pp. 187-92.

lying on the bed is dying in horror — no kind hope smoothing down his suffering — no philosophy, no religion to support him — yet with all the most
gnawing desire for it. . . .

This is my greatest care — a care that I pray to God may soon end, for he says
in words that tear my very heartstrings — 'Miserable wretch I am — this last
cheap comfort, which every rogue and fool have, is denied me in my last
moments. Why is this? — O, I have served every one with my utmost good —
yet why is this? — I cannot understand this' — and then his chattering teeth. If
I do break down it will be under this — but I pray that some kind of comfort may
come to his lot, — that some angel of goodness will lead him through this dark
wilderness.

. . . I know not what may come with tomorrow — I am hedg'd in every way
that you look at me. If I could leave Keats for a while every day I could soon
raise money by my face painting — but he will not let me out of his sight —
he cannot bear the face of a stranger — he has made me go out twice and leave
him solus. I'd rather cut my tongue out than tell him that money I must get —
that would kill him at a word. I will not do anything that may add to his misery.
For I have tried on every point to leave him for a few hours in the day but he
won't unless he is left alone. This won't do — nor shall not for another minute
whilst he is John Keats. . . .

I read, cook, make the beds, and do all the menial offices — for no soul comes
near Keats except the Doctor and myself. Yet I do all this with a cheerful heart —
for I thank God my little but honest religion stays me up all through these trials.
I'll pray to God tonight that He may look down with mercy on my poor friend
and myself. I feel no dread of what more I am to bear but look to it with
confidence.

My hopes of being kept by the Royal Academy will be cut off unless I send a
picture by the Spring. I have written Sir T. Lawrence. . . . Dr Clark is still the
same altho' he has received notice about this bill. I have said to him that if Keats
is wanting in any possible thing now that would give him ease . . . I will be
answerable in any way he may think fit — but no, he does his everything . . .
Don't ask me for journals — every day would have been more or less like this.
Not a word at my Father's. . . .[1]

★

Now I saw that the doctor no longer had any hope, for he ordered the scanty
food of a single anchovy a day, with a morsel of bread. . . . He had no hope for
himself save a speedy death, and this now seemed denied to him, for he believed
that he might be doomed to linger on all through the spring. His despair was
more on my account, for, as he explained, his death might be a long and lingering one, attended with a slow delirious death-stage. This was in apprehension
his greatest pain, and having been foreseen had been prepared for. One day,

[1] *Keats Circle*, vol. I, pp. 195–9.

tormented by the pangs of hunger, he broke down suddenly and demanded that this 'foreseen resource' should be given him. The demand was for the phial of laudanum I had bought at his request at Gravesend. When I demurred, he said to me that he claimed it as his own and as his right, for, he added with great emotion, 'As my death is certain I only wish to save you from the long miseries of attending and beholding it. It may yet be deferred, and I can see that you will thereby be stranded through your lack of resources, and that you will ruin all your prospects. I am keeping you from your painting, and as I am sure to die, why not let me die now? I have now determined to take this laudanum, and anticipate a lingering death, while emancipating you.' Of course I was horrified, and tried in every way to explain the madness of the act, and to urge the cruelty it would evince to all his friends, and indifference to their efforts for him. Again and again I urged this, affirming my right as the principal of these friends, and assuring him that I should never be tired of him or of my ministrations, and that even on the score of my immediate prospects I was in no fear of perdition, for I expected the student's pension from the Royal Academy. This somewhat calmed him, but as I still refused to let him have the laudanum he became furious. He even supplicated me with touching pathos, and with equally touching eloquence described the manner of his death . . . but on my persistent refusal he grew more and more violent against me, and I was afraid he might die in the midst of his despairing rage. And yet in all this there was no fear of death, no want of fortitude or manliness, but only the strong feeling on my account to which he regarded himself and his dying as secondary.

So for long we contended – he for his death, and I for his life. I told Dr Clark about the bottle of laudanum and he took it away with him. This was on the second day of our sore contention, and when he learned what I had done Keats became silent and resigned, and sank into solemn seriousness. 'Twas evident that the physician was powerless to mislead the great intelligence the invalid had of his own case. Dr Clark came to see him many times a day, and it was an awful sound and sight to see Keats look round upon the Doctor when he entered, with his large increasing hazel eyes (for as his face decreased his eyes seemed to enlarge and shine with unearthly brightness), and ask in a deep pathetic tone, 'How long is this *posthumous* life of mine to last?'[1]

★

On finding me inflexible in my purpose of remaining with him, he tranquilly said that he was sure why I held up so patiently was owing to my Christian faith, and that he was disgusted with himself for ever appearing before me in such a savage guise; that he now felt convinced how much every human being required the support of religion that he might die decently. 'Here am I,' said he, 'with desperation in death that would disgrace the commonest fellow. Now, my dear Severn, I am sure, if you could get me some of the works of Jeremy Taylor

[1] Joseph Severn's *Reminiscences*, quoted Sharp, op. cit., p. 84.

to read to me, I might become *really* a Christian, and leave this world in peace.'[1]

*

Dr Clark succeeded in obtaining a copy of Jeremy Taylor's *Holy Living and Dying*, and thereafter I read daily to poor Keats, both morning and evening, from this pious work, and he received great comfort. When he became restless, and when he was willing, I prayed by him, and so a great change and calmness grew upon him, and my task was much lightened. If I had no longer any hope in the prolongation of his life, yet the gentle Christian spirit beginning to soften the rigour of his dying, relieved me more than I can well account for.

He kept continually in his hand a polished, oval, white cornelian, the gift of his widowing love, and at times it seemed his only consolation, the only thing left to him in this world clearly tangible. Many letters which he was unable to read came for him. Some he allowed me to read to him; others were too worldly — for, as he said, he had 'already journeyed far beyond them'.[2]

*

He made me go to see the place where he was to be buried, and he expressed pleasure at my description of the locality of the Pyramid of Caius Cestius, about the grass and the many flowers, particularly the innumerable violets, also about a flock of goats and sheep and a young shepherd — all these intensely interested him. Violets were his favourite flowers, and he joyed to hear how they over-spread the graves. He assured me 'that he already seemed to feel the flowers growing over him'.[3]

*

[Night after night he sat by the bedside of his dying friend and there, to keep himself awake, he drew him early one morning by the light of the candle, his eyes closed and the damp hair clinging to his brow.[4]]

*

To Maria Severn: *Feb. 11th*

He has been confined to his bed two months, during which time I have scarce ever left him, except just for a run out for a mouthful of fresh air. But no more of this letter on a subject so sad. I am writing to keep up my spirits, therefore I must not write of this. I am now trying to paint a picture for the Royal Academy. . . . This picture will be the same size as the last. I have a daily visit from the Architectural Student who is now here from the Royal Academy. His time expires in July next and he seems certain I shall succeed him. He says it depends entirely on myself. Very well does it. Then I shall continue as I did with

[1] Joseph Severn, 'On the Vicissitudes of Keats's Fame': an article published in the *Atlantic Monthly*, 1863.
[2] Sharp, op. cit., pp. 91–2.
[3] Ibid., p. 93.
[4] See drawing facing page 45.

my last picture, and do my best to be away from you three years. Three years!
O how can I bear it! . . . [1]

★

To Mrs Brawne   *12th February, 1821*
        . . . I wish many many times that he had never left you. . . . In your
care he seems to me like an infant in its mother's arms . . . his death might have
been eased by the sight of his many friends. . . . But here, with one solitary
friend . . . he has had one more pang added . . . for I have had the hardest task in
keeping from him my painful situation.
        I have kept him alive by these means week after week. He has refused all food,
but I tried him every way — I left him no excuse. Many times I have prepared his
meals six times over, and kept from him the trouble I had in doing it. I have not
been able to leave him, that is, I have not dared to do it, but when he slept. Had
he come here alone he would have plunged into the grave in secret — we should
never have known one syllable about him. This reflection alone repays me for
all I have done. It is impossible to conceive what the sufferings of this poor
fellow have been. Now he is still alive and calm. If I say more I shall say too
much. Yet at times I have hoped he would recover, but the Doctor shook his
head, and Keats would not hear that he was better — the thought of recovery is
beyond everything dreadful to him. We now dare not perceive any improvement, for the hope of death seems his only comfort. He talks of the quiet grave
as the first rest he can ever have. I can believe and feel this most truly. . . .

                                                    Feb. 14th
        Little or no change has taken place in Keats since the commencement of this,
except this beautiful one, that his mind is growing to great quietness and peace —
I find this change has its rise from the increasing weakness of his body, but it
seems like a delightful sleep to me. I have been beating about in the tempest of
his mind so long. Tonight he has talked very much to me but so easily that he
at last fell into a pleasant sleep. . . . Among the many things he has requested
of me tonight, this is the principal, that on his grave shall be this —
        'Here lies one whose name was writ in water.' . . .
        Since, a letter has come. I gave it to Keats, supposing it to be one of yours,
but it proved sadly otherwise. The glance of that letter tore him to pieces. The
effects were on him for many days — he did not read it — he could not, but
requested me to place it in his coffin. . . . I have got an English nurse to come two
hours every other day; so that I have quite recovered my health, but my nurse
after coming three times has been taken ill today — this is a little unfortunate as
Keats seems to like her. You see I cannot do anything until poor Keats is asleep:
this morning he has waked very calm — I think he seems somewhat better. He

[1] Keats House.

has taken half a pint of fresh milk, the milk here is beautiful to all the senses —
it is delicious — for three weeks he has lived on it, sometimes taking a pint and
a half a day. . . .

The Doctor has been — he thinks Keats worse. He says the expectoration is
the most dreadful he ever saw — never met an instance when a patient was so
quickly pulled down. Keats's inward grief must have been beyond any limit —
his lungs are in a dreadful state. His stomach has lost all its power — Keats says
he has fretted to death — from the first drops of blood he knew he must die.[1]

*

[During these terrible last days Joseph turned, whenever he could, to his letter
home. Whenever he felt his spirits beginning to fail he would add a few lines
and feel for a moment that he was back with his family. 'I am writing to keep up
my spirits', he had explained in the second instalment of his diary letter. 'I cannot
be merry unless I be with you,' he had written wistfully, 'yet this train of thought
always helps me to be happy.' The miniature of the family stood on the table
where he wrote, and he could raise his eyes from the paper to gain comfort from
those well-loved faces.]

*

To Maria Severn: *Feb. 19th*
          I have just got your letter. O! I have shed tears and tears of joy to
find my dear home the same, all happy and all well, I thank God for this greatest
blessing. You have written me just such a letter as I wanted. O! you cannot
know the delight it is to me. . . . These are the particulars on which I can feed
my comfort. . . . Tell father that the Marquess Canova and I had a 'pipe and pot
together' at our first meeting, that he was exceeding kind to me. The letter of
recommendation gave me a most friendly welcome — I mean our President's
letter. He has promised me his service at any time, and has already written to
His Holiness the Pope to permit me to study in any of his palaces. He seems to
think highly of my views, particularly from my receiving the Gold Medal amid
so much contest. This sets me very high here. There is great expectation from
my works. . . . Tell him that I continue to think of painting from the English
History when I return. I hope to glean all the knowledge and beauties of foreign
art, and apply them to the Annals of my own Country. This has never struck
any painter. Is it not a lucky thought? I am now thinking of my future on the
plan of Raphael's pictures in the Vatican Palace. One picture I have in mind is
the Golden Age of England, the Court of Queen Elizabeth, with portraits of all the
distinguished folk of her time, Sir W. Raleigh, Shakespeare, etc., etc. To do this
I hope to take a tour all over England, to collect the antiquities and records for
my purpose. Tell Father something tells me that he will go with me on the
tour. I know his love for all these old ruins.

---

[1] Sharp, op. cit., pp. 89–90.

My object will be to propose my plan to some English Nobleman. Father must not doubt my success in this, for there are several painters here sent out by persons of fortune.

Tell my Mother that poor Keats has lived on bread and milk for a month past. It is the only thing he can take. I get very good dinners for twopence, with my half pint of wine (for 3 half pence) afterwards. I am obliged to take great care of myself and do. I am looking very well and can assure her I am so. . . . I have every personal comfort possible, even to cabbage, altho' not my dear Mother's. I make bread and milk three times a day for Keats, for myself sometimes tea, sometimes Chocolate or Coffee. . . . Then I have pudding every day. 'Ah! still *my* Joe,' says my Mother. The puddings are beautiful, rice particularly; plum pudding, delicious, they even call it by its English name. The fact is there are so many English here (about 200) that it is almost like London. . . .[1]

*

To John Taylor:

Four days previous to his death the change in [Keats] was so great that I passed each moment in dread — not knowing what the next would have. He was calm and firm at its approaches to a most astonishing degree. He told me not to trouble for he did not think that he should be convulsed. He said, 'Did you ever see any one die,' — no — 'Well then I pity you poor Severn. What trouble and danger you have got into for me — now you must be firm for it will not last long — I shall soon be laid in the quiet grave — O! I can feel the cold earth upon me — the daisies growing over me — O for this quiet — it will be my first.' When the morning light came and still found him alive — O how bitterly he grieved — I cannot bear his cries.[2]

*

[At dawn next day Joseph again took refuge from the tragedy that was his constant companion. To escape from it for a few moments was his only hope of renewing his strength. His family, his prayers, and Keats's poor white face and enormous, glowing eyes. These were his life.]

*

To Maria Severn: *Feb. 20th*

My good-natured fire says good-morning Maria, so while my kettle is boiling I will give you a little more gossip. Now sit down and make yourself comfortable. How do you do this Morning? How are they all at home? How is Mother? Come now and sit down and hear what I have got to say. Pull off your bonnet. You know you don't see me often. . . . At some future time I have no doubt my dear Maria but here I shall be able to realize a great deal of money by my Miniatures. You see all the English here are rich, and come to buy

---

[1] Keats House.
[2] 6th March, 1821. *Keats Circle*, pp. 223-4.

pictures. They think of nothing but pictures. I should have liked Father to hear me blow up a fellow just now in Italian. I gave it him in style....[1]

*

To William Haslam: *Feb. 22nd*
                ... I have nothing to break this dreadful solitude but Letters. Day after day, night after night, here I am by our poor dying friend. My spirits, my intellect, and my health are breaking down. I can get no one to change with me — no one will relieve me. They all run away, and even if they did not, poor Keats could not do without me. I prepare every thing he eats —
        Last night I thought he was going — I could hear the phlegm in his throat — he bade me lift him up in the bed or he would die with pain. I watched him all night — at every cough I expected he would suffocate. . . . This morning by the pale daylight, the change in him frightened me — he has sunk in the last three days to a most ghastly look. I have these three nights sat up with him from the apprehension of his dying — Dr Clark has prepared me for it — but I shall be but little able to bear it — even this, my horrible situation, I cannot bear to cease by the loss of him. As regards Money my dear Haslam you will have known that the kindness of Mr Taylor sets me quite easy.
        I have at times written a favourable letter to my sister — you will see this is best — for I hope that staying by my poor friend to close his eyes in death, will not add to my other unlucky hits — for I am still quite prevented from painting — and what the consequence may be —
        Poor Keats keeps me by him, and shadows out the form of one solitary friend. He opens his eyes in great horror and doubt — but when they fall upon me they close gently and open and close until he falls into another sleep. The very thought of this keeps me by him until he dies. . . .[2]

★

Again and again, while warning me that his death was fast approaching, he besought me to take all care of myself, telling me that 'I must not look at him in his dying gasp nor breathe his passing breath, not even breathe upon him.' From time to time he gave me all his directions as to what he wanted done after his death. He told me with greater agitation than he had shown on any other subject, to put the letter which had just come from Miss Brawne (which he was unable to bring himself to read, or even to open), with any other that should arrive too late to reach him in life, inside his winding-sheet on his heart.[3]

★

To John Taylor: *March 6th*
                ... These four nights I watched him, each night expecting his death.

[1] Keats House.
[2] *Keats Circle*, vol. I, p. 220.
[3] Joseph Severn's *Reminiscences*, quoted Sharp, op. cit., p. 93.

On the fifth day the doctor prepared me for it — 23rd at 4 o'clock afternoon. The poor fellow bade me lift him up in bed — he breathed with great difficulty and seemed to lose the power of coughing up the phlegm. An immense sweat came over him so that my breath felt cold to him — 'Don't breathe on me — it comes like Ice' — He clasped my hand very fast as I held him in my arms — the mucus... gurgled in his throat — this increased — but yet he seem'd without pain. . . . At 11 he died in my arms.[1]

★

To *Charles Brown* (never posted):
>He is gone. He died with the most perfect ease. He seemed to go to
sleep. On the 23rd, Friday, at half-past four, the approach of death came on.
>'Severn — I — lift me up, for I am dying. I shall die easy. Don't be frightened! Thank God it has come.'
>I lifted him up in my arms, and the phlegm seemed boiling in his throat. This increased until eleven at night, when he gradually sank into death, so quiet, that I still thought he slept — but I cannot say more now. I am broken down beyond my strength. I cannot be left alone. I have not slept for nine days, I will say the days since —
>On Saturday a gentleman came to cast the face, hand and foot. On Sunday his body was opened; the lungs were completely gone, the doctors could not conceive how he had lived in the last two months. . . .[2]

★

On 26th February, while the sky was still dark, two carriages left the Piazza di Spagna. Day was breaking as they drew up at the foot of the Pyramid of Caius Cestius, and the mortal remains of John Keats were carried to the grave without delay. Because of the hostility towards Protestants in Rome the burial had to be over by daylight.

The English chaplain read the prayers, but Joseph Severn scarcely heard his voice. His health had suffered from the prolonged strain and since Keats's death he had been prostrated. Only by a great effort of will had he been able to rise and dress himself to accompany his friend on his last journey. William Ewing, an English sculptor who had shown him great kindness during the last days of Keats's illness, had helped him to put on his clothes and had driven with him in the carriage. Now he supported him as he stood, swaying, at the graveside. Joseph was greatly affected by the thought that he was the only one present of Keats's devoted band of English friends. In the half-light he saw that Dr Clark was there and four other gentlemen also, who by their clothes and bearing

---

[1] *Keats Circle*, p. 224. This letter was shown to Fanny Brawne, who copied it for Keats's sister with whom she had been corresponding since his departure. In her previous letter, she had told his young sister: 'Had he returned I should have been his wife and he would have lived with us.'

[2] Sharp, op. cit., p. 94.

were his countrymen. Of those present at his interment only Joseph, Dr Clark and Ewing had known Keats at all, and, of these, only Joseph had known the real Keats in the full splendour of his fine intellect and ardent imagination.

Above them towered the grey pyramid — proud tomb of a Roman, dead for eighteen hundred years. Lichen had crept over the marble and wild green plants hung from the crevices. Behind it the dark battlements of the city walls stood sentinel over the silent burial-ground, where the daisies and violets clustered in the grass and ran unchecked over the foreign graves.

The earth fell upon the coffin-lid. Beneath it Fanny Brawne's letter lay, unopened, against her lover's heart.

CHAPTER 8

LADY WESTMORLAND

1821

EVERY WINTER ROME WAS FILLED with a gay colony of distinguished English visitors. In their cumbrous travelling-coaches they came labouring over the Alps, spending a few weeks in France or Switzerland *en route*. Rich and leisured, they came to wander round the ruins, to admire the statues and pictures, to enjoy the social life which they created, and to patronize the arts. With them they brought a retinue of servants, their own cooks and cooking utensils, their own bed-linen, sometimes even their own furniture. They would rent a palace, or part of one, from some impecunious Roman noble, and there they would settle down to entertain and divert themselves.

Their mornings would be passed in visits to the picture galleries, churches or ruins, or sometimes in expeditions to Tivoli or picnics in the Campagna. Or they would visit the studio of an artist or sculptor. Every afternoon there was the fashionable rendezvous on the Pincian Hill, where they rode or drove in their coaches round the promenade, stopping every now and again, when they met a friend, to take a stroll and enjoy the lovely views over Rome.

To the west, beyond the Tiber, they could see the archangel poised on the Castle of St Angelo, and still farther away the great dome of St Peter's rose against the background of the purple hills. Then the sky would flush into a lovely Roman sunset, while from a hundred churches bells rang out the Ave Maria, signal for the crowds to melt away. There would be three or four assemblies to choose between in the evening. Every lady of fashion had at least one evening a week when she was at home to the *monde*.

The life they led was so many-sided that everyone, whether learned or frivolous, could find enjoyment. It was not surprising that so many English visitors of rank and fashion came to spend the winter in Rome.

Among these people Joseph suddenly found himself well known. The story of his devotion to an unknown young poet and the tragic death of his friend, so far from home, had spread rapidly among the English colony. And when the ladies discovered that the hero of this romantic story was a handsome young man, with easy, pleasant manners, their interest in him became even more marked.

He soon found himself with an invitation to dine out every day, but he would allow himself only an occasional acceptance, because he kept resolutely before him the necessity of winning the travelling pension from the Academy. To complete his picture soon was imperative, not only for his future as an artist, but for his very existence. The necessity of continuous work saved him from complete collapse after Keats had died. As spring matured into summer he rose at four or five o'clock and worked sometimes for as many as twelve hours a day on his picture. But, even so, he found that his countrymen did not ignore him. Seymour Kirkup, a fellow-artist with a small private income which made him independent of his work, had been introduced to him by Ewing, and he brought many distinguished visitors to Joseph's studio.

Joseph was dazzled by the position in which he found himself. The Duchess of Devonshire, who was busily directing her private excavations in the Forum, told him that when his picture for the Academy was finished he was to come immediately to her house and they would at once return together in her carriage to view it.[1]

Another evening he dined with Lord and Lady Ruthven. They were a party of fourteen, and when dinner was over, her ladyship proposed that they should all go to Mr Severn's studio to see his *Alcibiades* — for Joseph had taken as his subject the moment when Alcibiades emerged from his villa, to be assassinated by the crowd. The carriages were ordered, and the whole party drove off to No. 43 Via di San Isidoro and climbed the stone stairs to the second floor, where Joseph had been lent a studio by an English painter who was for the moment away from Rome. The picture was finished by then, but it had to wait three weeks for the paint to dry before it could be rolled up and sent to England. The ladies were in transports and vowed that he must certainly succeed. Joseph's heart was warmed by the praise and by the pretty lips that uttered it.

In spite of his many preoccupations, he had not forgotten Keats, and in his spare time he was painting a small full-length picture of him reading, as he had so often seen him at Wentworth Place when he was well, behind him the window opening on to the garden, where the old mulberry tree threw its shadow on the lawn. Soon after his death John Taylor had written to Joseph that he had been asked by several friends to write a short biography of Keats and asked him to provide him with material. Taylor had already announced his intention in the press but it was opposed by other friends of Keats. Brown in particular regarded him as 'a mere bookseller' who 'neither comprehended Keats or his poetry'. Joseph decided to send all Keats's papers to Brown which he did that summer, 'packed for safety in a box of divers things belonging to my old friend and master Mr Bond. I chose this . . . as the safest way.'[2]

★

After Keats's death, according to the provisions of the Roman law, everything

---

[1] To Sarah Severn, 6th June, 1821. Keats House.
[2] Sharp, op. cit., p. 106.

in his room had been carried out of the house and burned in the Piazza di Spagna. Even the walls were scraped and Joseph was held responsible for the expense of re-decorating and re-furnishing.

'The rooms have been entirely made new,' he wrote to his father, 'windows, doors, walls, ceilings, floors, all new.' All this he had to pay for, but had been saved by a friend from further unjust claims. 'The landladies had done the rooms in the most extravagant way, thinking that I must pay for it all, but now I have been protected by a Roman, who made them take just one-sixth their demand.'

Joseph was happy to hear from other members of his family that James Severn was now reconciled to his son's journey. He could not help boasting a little and painting his prospects in glowing colours. His father would have reason to be proud of him, he vowed; he should see that his son's decision to go to Rome had been fully justified by subsequent events.

'Oh, how happy I am I came here,' he wrote. 'Everything I do I am successful in, my miniatures are very much sought after. I have painted five and got forty guineas for them. One was a slap bang job. There are about five hundred Englishmen here now, and I can have any number to paint . . . the attention I receive from the English Nobility is most encouraging. We are hand in hand, walking in the same places, living in the same houses. . . . If the Academy keep me here or not, I shall be able to do better than ever I could in England, it is a fine thing for me to have the gold medal here. I am the first for twenty years. It is the reason for my success. The name of a Gold Medal is like Magic every-where.'[1]

Joseph's optimistic report had an unexpected result — his sister Sarah formed the idea of joining him in Rome. Joseph was not encouraging.

'Now, my dear Sarah, about your notion of coming here — it is quite impractical. A lady to come here must have £400 a year at least. . . . You must have your servants, cooks, coach — or there is nothing for a lady here. I have told you only how I live. I go out to the cookshop for my dinner — but you can't do that. . . . You can't walk about the places, you must ride. . . . Ladies come here in their own carriages with servants and everything they could want, but you must put up with anything — this a man would do but it is a very hard matter. . . . You have been too much carried away by my mention of palaces and wine, etc. The palaces are nearly all deserted — many are in ruins — for this reason, that a great part of the year in and about Rome the air is poisonous — it produces deadly fevers called malaria . . . the air becomes putrid and to sleep in it is certain death.'[2]

★

Of all Joseph's new acquaintances, there was one who, by force of character, made the others seem no more than charming shadows. The Countess of

[1] 10th April, 1821. Keats House.
[2] To Sarah Severn, 6th June, 1821. Keats House.

Westmorland was remarkable alike for her queenly beauty and her dazzling wit. 'Her ladyship is a most superior woman,' wrote Joseph to his sister, 'having all the really English nobility in her and with much learning – she is about thirty-eight and is a very noble looking lady – the charm in her manner from the many accomplishments blended down in this lady of fashion is very astonishing. She is a beautiful musician and a poetess and seems to be quite acquainted with all the great persons of the time.'

He found this great lady infinitely charming and helpful and she proclaimed for him a great future. Sir Thomas Lawrence was an old acquaintance and she flattered herself that he had some little respect for her judgment in artistic matters; she would write to him about Joseph and his picture.

Often, when he was painting, Lady Westmorland's carriage would draw up at the door, and a liveried footman would assist her ladyship to alight and escort her to the door of Joseph's studio. Sometimes she would spend as long as two hours talking with him. She brought a strange air of sophistication and distinction into his poorly furnished room, with her extravagant bonnets, her fur cloaks and costly shawls. To her Joseph confided his ambition to become a historical painter, and she encouraged him by promising her aid. More experienced men than Joseph had been fascinated by her 'wonderful talents and brilliant conversation'.[1] To Joseph she seemed a goddess, and he was lost in admiration of her extraordinary vitality, her wit and arrogance.

In July his *Alcibiades* was sent off, but by an accident it missed the messenger at Ancona, and he was in despair lest it should not reach London in time for the meeting of the Academy Council. Lady Westmorland arrived at his studio to find him in a state of depression, but she quickly talked him into good spirits. He wrote that night to his father, telling him what had happened to his picture and saying, 'Lady Westmorland writes by this post to Sir Thomas Lawrence, on my behalf, explaining the short notice I have had to send my picture and praying that the Council, should my picture not arrive in time, will consider my case at their next meeting. I cannot speak in terms too high of this lady's kindness and condescension.'[2]

But her kindness did not end there. Nor did poor Joseph's anxieties. For, when his picture had reached London, it entirely disappeared. Again Joseph despaired, and again Lady Westmorland wrote off to Sir Thomas, telling all the story of Keats's death and Joseph's hard work on his picture. At the same time she promised Joseph that, even if he did not win the pension, she would see that he got commissions for as many miniatures as he cared to paint. It must have been greatly due to her efforts that he was in fact awarded the pension, for when the picture was at last discovered, in a battered tin box in the cellars of the Royal Academy, it was found to have been badly damaged. But, before he had heard of his success, Lady Westmorland had put another proposition to him.

[1] *Journal of Hon. Henry Edward Fox*, edited by the Earl of Ilchester, p. 229.
[2] 21st July, 1821. Keats House.

Egypt was all the fashion in London that year, and in September she suggested to Joseph that he might accompany her there. She was full of preparations for the journey. She would be taking a savant to explain the mysteries of Ancient Egypt to her. It would be an excellent opportunity for Joseph to see the relics of another civilization. She had chosen him from all the artists in Rome for the honour of accompanying her.

Joseph was flattered at being thus singled out. It never occurred to him that there might be anything in his youth and good looks that could have commended him to her. To him she was a being from another world. But he kept his head, and after thinking it over, decided that he would be foolish to leave Rome just when he was beginning to do well there.

He told Lady Westmorland of his decision when she was paying one of her visits to his studio. Her brow contracted, her dark eyes became stormy. She was not accustomed to being thwarted. She was usually able to impose her will on other people by her strength of purpose and her arrogant disregard of any objections. When she failed to influence them she would resent it bitterly, and often imagined that her friends had been prompted by malicious ill-feeling against herself. Transfer to the enemy camp could be surprisingly quick, and as she loved to manage her friends' lives for them, sooner or later, in spite of her exceptional intelligence and charm, she would fall out with everyone.

She professed herself not satisfied with his refusal. His reasons appeared insufficient for missing such a favourable opportunity. Joseph saw that she was displeased, but in anything affecting his painting he would make no compromise. He told her that around Rome there were many views and landscapes of which he was anxious to make studies, so that when he returned to England they would serve as backgrounds for future pictures. Then, as he noted the impatience in Lady Westmorland's demeanour, he hurriedly added yet another reason, which was that a young artist named Catherwood, whom he had known in England, had just arrived in Rome, and that they had arranged to take rooms together.

Lady Westmorland questioned him about his friend, and when Joseph had given a favourable account of his abilities, she asked graciously if Mr Catherwood would not perhaps like to come with Mr Severn to Egypt. Joseph was taken aback.

'I — I have no doubt that Mr Catherwood would feel himself most honoured by your ladyship's suggestion. I am distressed at not being able to take advantage of your ladyship's kindness myself, but — Mr Catherwood might go without me.'

Lady Westmorland rose impulsively from the rather hard chair on which she had been sitting, and laid her gloved hand on Joseph's arm.

'My dear Mr Severn, I do not know this young man, but I would take anyone of your commending, because I feel you understand me.'[1]

To Maria Severn, 15th September, 1821. Keats House.

She paused for a moment, while she gave him a long, earnest look from her fine eyes, and then she turned and swept from the studio.

★

The following evening, at Ave Maria, Joseph and Mr Catherwood presented themselves at the Villa Negroni. They were kept waiting for some time before Lady Westmorland appeared, explaining that she had been making her toilette for the French Ambassador's ball that evening. She wore pearl ear-rings and bracelets, and several rows of magnificent pearls were twisted round her neck. Her movements were graceful and deliberate – as they always were, unless she became agitated.

Joseph presented Mr Catherwood to her. She was most charming. They talked about Egypt, and she seemed so well informed, and imparted her knowledge in such an agreeable manner, with such amusing little asides and references to contemporary personalities, that both young men were fascinated. As always, her conversation flitted unpredictably from one subject to another, and although they had begun by talking about Egypt, in a short time she was animatedly discussing the truth of the legend of the 'Masque de fer', and a few moments later was telling them how Lady Caroline Lamb and Lord Byron had met for the first time at her house in London.

As they were descending the stairs after they had taken their leave, Catherwood's admiration for this brilliant woman made him incoherent. Joseph's enthusiasm equalled his friend's, though he still held by his decision not to go to Egypt, and advised Catherwood, for the sake of his art, to stay in Rome. But his friend said that it was a wonderful opportunity, and perhaps the only one he would ever have, of going to Egypt. Travelling with a great lady, there would be such preparations made and so many servants accompanying them, that there would be no danger in the journey. Joseph argued that a knowledge of Rome was a necessary part of an artist's education. But he need not have worried about his friend.

Two days later, when they came home from a long walk round Rome, he found that Lady Westmorland had been to his studio four times that morning, and had sent her servants to the café where she knew he usually dined. The landlady was just giving them this news when her ladyship returned again.

Her appearance was most striking. Her close-fitting pélisse was black, and she wore a bonnet of black satin, surmounted by a plume of black ostrich feathers. A high triple ruff of white lace round her throat was the only light touch in her appearance.

Seeing their concern, she explained that she was in mourning for the Queen,[1] and then, with great distress, added that she must postpone her journey to Egypt until another season. She required more servants. She was in despair at not being able to go to Egypt as she had intended. She had anticipated such

[1] George IV's wife, Queen Caroline.

pleasure and proft from the journey. But she particularly requested Mr Severn to hold himself bound to accompany her next season – and, with a gracious smile, his friend Mr Catherwood also.

Joseph at once replied that nothing would give him more pleasure. She appeared satisfied and her manner became calmer. She declared that she wished Mr Severn to paint her portrait – a miniature. Again Joseph professed himself delighted and honoured.

'I have written to the Duke of Devonshire of your picture now in hand. He comes here next winter and could do much for you.'[1]

Joseph thanked her warmly and, when both young men had accepted an invitation to dine with her on Saturday, she left.

All through that nerve-racking autumn she was unfailingly kind. First there was the anxiety about the picture getting to London in time, followed by the shock of its disappearance. Then, when at last it was found – he got the news in October – there was still the question of whether the Council would consider it. Every morning he awoke worrying about his chances. Every night his last thought was of the pension. Without it he must continue to live from day to day, from picture to picture, just making enough to exist, but with no prospect of security. And what would happen to him if he were ill, or if, when his present patrons left Rome, he could find no more to take their place? But it was only when he was tired that he felt like this. Normally he remained optimistic. He refused to confine himself to miniatures only, from which he could always make a steady income. His study of 'the divine pictures of Raphael' at the Vatican had made him determined to become famous as a painter of large historical pictures.

While he was working on his picture of Keats at Wentworth Place, he received a package from Shelley, who was still at Pisa. Inside he found the first copy of *Adonais*, and with it a letter:

'Dear Sir, – I send you the elegy on poor Keats – and I wish it were better worth your acceptance. You will see by the preface that it was written before I could obtain any particular account of his last moments. . . . I have ventured to express, as I felt, the respect and admiration which your conduct towards him demands. In spite of his transcendent genius, Keats never was, nor ever will be, a popular poet; and the total neglect and obscurity in which the astonishing remnants of his mind still lie, was hardly to be dissipated by a writer, who, however he may differ from Keats in more important qualities, at least resembles him in that accidental one, a want of popularity. I have little hope, therefore, that the poem I send you will excite any attention. . . .'[2]

Joseph's eye ran rapidly over the rest of the letter, and the signature –
'Your most sincere and faithful servant,
PERCY B. SHELLEY.'

[1] To Maria Severn, 19th September, 1821. Keats House.
[2] 29th November, 1821.

Then he opened the book and turned to the preface.

'. . . He was accompanied to Rome,' he read, 'and attended in his last illness by Mr Severn, a young artist of the highest promise, who, I have been informed, "almost risked his own life, and sacrificed every prospect to unwearied attendance upon his dying friend".

'Had I known these circumstances before the completion of my poem, I should have been tempted to add my feeble tribute of applause to the more solid recompense which the virtuous man finds in the recollection of his own motives. Mr Severn can dispense with a reward from "such stuff as dreams are made of". His conduct is a golden augury of the success of his future career: may the unextinguished Spirit of his illustrious friend animate the creations of his pencil, and plead against Oblivion for his name!'

Joseph's eyes were wet with tears when at last he laid down the little book. He could not concentrate on his painting that morning. He had meant to finish a picture he was painting for Sir William Drummond, but phantoms of Keats kept rising between his brush and the canvas. He could see Keats's face when he had first known him – the eager, vital expression – the glowing eyes – the wide, mobile mouth. How he had enjoyed and savoured life. Then the face blurred and he saw him again during those last, terrible nights – ghastly white in the flickering candlelight – the hollow look of his eye-sockets where the lids drooped over his enormous eyes, the transparency of his skin, drawn tight over the high cheek-bones and nose.

Joseph felt the tears in his eyes and, striding over to the wall, chalked in large letters, where his eyes would often see them, the last words of Shelley's preface:

May the unextinguished Spirit of his illustrious friend animate the creations of his pencil, and plead against Oblivion for his name.

Then he returned to his easel and set to work with fresh determination, pausing now and again to smile to himself as he read over the words on the wall. Already he seemed to draw inspiration and comfort from them.

★

Shelley was right in not expecting an immediate stir to be made by his poem. The only violent reaction was from Joseph's family, who were horrified to find his name in the writings of that 'atheist, republican and free-liver'. Letter after letter implored him to 'break off all acquaintance with a man of such vile reputation as Shelley', and prophesied nothing but ruin and disgrace if he persisted in such a friendship.

Still no letter came from the Royal Academy. All day he kept hard at his painting. He had commissions for many miniatures among the English nobility. Lady Westmorland introduced him to everyone likely to serve him, and in such glowing terms that he was treated with respect. He had also begun a large picture of Alexander – nine feet by six – which he hoped to be able to sell when it was finished.

MARY SEVERN
Self portrait
National Portrait Gallery

MRS. SEVERN, 1851
Water colour by Mary Severn

THE TWINS ARTHUR AND ELEANOR, PLAYING CHESS, AGED TWELVE
Water colour by Mary Severn, 1854

(*below*) PHOTOGRAPH OF ARTHUR AND ELEANOR IN MIDDLE AGE IN THE SAME
WITH MARY'S PICTURE HANGING ON THE WALL BEHIND THEM

He was working at this canvas on Christmas Eve. It was the same size as the picture of *Alcibiades* which he had sent home to the Academy; there was still no news of its success or failure. When the light began to fail he put away his brushes and, taking his coat from the chair, went sadly down the stairs, his feet ringing with a hollow clatter on the stone steps. He walked slowly to the Caffè Greco, where every evening he would dine, in company with some ten or eleven other English artists. He made his way slowly through the crowded, low-arched rooms. The place was full of smoke and resounded with a strange medley of languages. It was the rendezvous of artists in Rome. Painters, sculptors and musicians of every race gathered there. Joseph found his friends and sat down, feeling tired and depressed and a little homesick. It was his second Christmas away from home. He tried to picture what his family would be doing in Mason's Court, and ate absentmindedly, not speaking to anyone.

Richard Westmacott, a young sculptor and son of a Royal Academician, whispered something to Kirkup and then ordered a large bottle of the sour white wine which they usually drank. When it came, Westmacott filled his glass and rose to his feet.

'Here's to Severn, the representative of the Royal Academy,' he said, 'and success to him!'

The toast was drunk with enthusiasm. Joseph was too dazed to reply for a minute to the shouts of congratulation, but gradually a warm wave of happiness surged through him as he realized that the travelling pension was his.[1]

He passed the next few days as in a dream. Lady Westmorland's delight – Seymour Kirkup's Christmas dinner in his honour, 'with a plum pudding that could only be equalled by my Mother's and plenty of music' – and finally the official letter announcing that the pension awarded was £130 a year for three years and £80 travelling expenses. Enclosed in the letter was the unexpected gift of a draft to cover the expenses of his journey to Rome.

His first thought was for his family, who had heard the news in London before he heard it himself. 'I never felt such Joy as I do now, in knowing the happiness you all feel,' he wrote to to his sister Maria. 'When I read that my noble father, who is the groundwork of all these fine things, "sits in his armchair and receives the congratulations of his friends," I shed tears of joy, for no one knows so well as myself, what he has felt for me.' He told her how he had heard the news and about Kirkup's Christmas dinner in his honour. 'Although I was happy, yet I longed to be in Mason's Court. . . . Now, tell Father, I will be a great painter.' And he ended by enclosing presents for them all from his new-found wealth. '£10 for Sarah to help with the rent. To my father £5 to have a new coat, for my sake, or what he pleases; and to Maria, £4 for a new pélisse and bonnet; and £1 to Charles for fiddlesticks and music.'

For three years he need have no anxieties.

[1] To Maria, 26th December, 1821. Keats House.

D

CHAPTER 9

MISS MONTGOMERIE

January, 1827 – October, 1828

JOSEPH SAT ON THE WINDOW-SILL in his studio and gazed out over Rome. He was waiting for Lady Westmorland. How often he had done this during the last few years, for her ladyship had a superb disregard for time — except as a theory to be discussed with philosophers. Sometimes she would sleep all day and expect her friends to sit up with her all night. She would not realize that even her brilliant conversation began to pall about two or three in the morning. However, Joseph had made it clear from the first that he would do anything to please her, except when it would interfere with his painting, and after several scenes she had accepted this.

Staring out over Rome, he thought of the last six years with wonder. His success had been so sudden that at times he could still scarcely believe that he, Joseph Severn, who was invited to every party in Rome, who in the season received invitations to as many as four dinners a day with carriages sent to fetch him, who talked with Dukes and even Princes and, better still, received commissions from them, was the same person as that impoverished young man who had arrived in Rome six years ago with a dying friend and no prospects.

The transition from obscurity to success had been so sudden that perhaps he was to be forgiven for his conviction that he must surely be a genius. Both his pictures and himself were in great demand. When he began to make money he bought himself new clothes, and now he was 'quite dandyish'. His complexion had darkened in the Italian sun and his figure had filled out. He held himself more erect and had more confidence in himself. He was strikingly handsome and a gay companion. His high spirits scarcely ever deserted him; he could tell a story amusingly and his infectious enjoyment of everything he did made him much in demand for parties and picnics and expeditions to places outside the city. It was no wonder that many English ladies had lost their hearts to him, and many Italians too. As for Joseph, he was only too susceptible, but always a hard core of common sense and self-interest, bred in him when he was a poor, struggling artist with his way to make, prevented him from taking the irrevocable step into matrimony.

There had been one occasion on which he had been very near to it. Two charming young English girls, nieces of Lord Elgin, had spent nearly two years in Rome with their widowed mother. He had fallen in love with the elder sister, Maria, who was twenty-three years old, very gentle and pretty. He had painted her portrait, they had sung words from *Romeo and Juliet* together, to music of his own composing, he had holidayed with them in Naples and accompanied them in their visits to the Vatican. He had felt at home with them, in a way that relieved the ache for his own home and family. For although he loved his expeditions into high society, and savoured his exchanges with titled acquaintances, it was a relief to spend a quiet evening with Maria and her mother and sister. He would take his chalks down to their lodgings and sit sketching, while Maria played the piano and her mother did beautiful embroidery.

She reminded him of his own dear sister, Maria, and he was tempted — then Lady Westmorland returned to Rome, and beside her tempestuous, impulsive brilliance, her exquisite toilettes, her air of sophisticated lady of fashion, poor Maria's attractions began to seem rather insipid, and even her uncritical adoration a little boring. Lady Westmorland cajoled, provoked, fascinated, flattered him, and his evenings were no longer spent in the homely atmosphere of Maria's family.

The matter was finally decided for him by the mother's tragic death and the sisters' departure for England almost immediately afterwards. Joseph comforted them, made all the necessary arrangements for their journey, did everything he could to spare them further anxieties, but he could not suppress a sense of escape and of relief that he was still free.

As he remarked later, with a comical smile:

'I must confess to a gay and elastic temperament which makes me suppose that marriage is not altogether my forte!'

Lady Westmorland did not contradict him.

So many things had happened since he had been awarded the pension. Although he had never been back to England he had seen quite a number of his old friends. Charles Brown had come to Florence, bringing his son — the result of his liaison with the fiery Irish maid at Wentworth Place.

Joseph had gone to stay with him there eighteen months after the award of the travelling pension, to execute a commission to copy a Raphael picture in the Pitti Gallery, and meaning to paint one more large picture before he returned to England. He was still full of plans for self-improvement. Moving in circles where everyone was well-educated, he had felt the necessity of study to bring himself to their level, and he was pleased that Brown noticed great changes in him since they had last met.

'He seems to think my improvement since I left England very great,' Joseph told his sister Sarah. He had already advised his brother, Tom, who was having some success with his musical compositions, to follow his own example. 'The greatest want I have felt,' he said, 'in the rank to which I am raised, is in the knowledge of our language and our times, and the geographical situation of places ... and soon you will feel the want of them, and as the world looks much

at these little artificial things which set men off, it is the duty we owe to ourselves to acquire them.' He advised Tom to study Italian, which would help
him in his music, and always to have a dictionary by him so that he could correct
his spelling.

'At my arrival here,' he wrote from Florence, 'I found Lord Byron and Mr
Trelawny preparing to go to Greece to fight for the poor Greeks. I have made
four small pictures of them in two days, and they were one and all delighted
with them.'

He lent his copy of *Adonais* to Byron who returned it with a note expressing
admiration for the poem; he had marked his favourite passages in ink.
Anticipating the kind of protests from home which had greeted the news
that he was acquainted with Shelley, Joseph did his best to reassure his family.
'Pray quiet yourself on the grounds of my friendship with these men. . . . You
greatly mistake to think I shall be injured by their bad principles. We never
talk but of poetry, painting and music. They are men sought after by all the
great Englishmen who come.'

Driving his moral home he added, 'I make a point never to know anyone who
is not superior to me in fortune or ability or some way or other, that I may still
be raising myself and improving ever, in my moments of pastime. *Tell Tom
this.*'[1]

He remained very modest, and attributed any success that he had to Keats.
'Poor Keats's works are here much read and admired,' he wrote loyally to
Taylor. 'I cannot but think they *will* be popular. . . . I think the great respect
shown me here is still owing to his Memory and works. You would be astonished at the interest the Nobility here have taken in my affairs — but I know it is
as the Friend of Keats.'[2] At his own expense, refusing help proffered by other
young artists in Rome, he had placed a stone on Keats's grave which bore a drawing of a Greek lyre with half the strings unstrung and an inscription suggested
by Brown: 'This Grave contains all that was Mortal of a YOUNG ENGLISH POET,
Who on His Death Bed, in the Bitterness of his Heart at the Malicious Power
of his Enemies, Desired these Words to be engraved on his Tomb Stone
"Here lies One Whose Name was writ in Water." Feb. 24 1821.'[3]

★

During that summer of 1823, living with Brown and his son in Florence,
Joseph painted nineteen pictures and made sixty drawings, many of them studies
for a large historical work *Lorenzo di Medici Rescued from Assassination by his
Friends*, which was to measure twelve feet by eighteen. From Florence they went
to Venice and returned to set up house together in Rome, where Brown nursed
Joseph through an attack of jaundice. Joseph had to send a picture to the Royal

[1] 27th June, 1823. Keats House.
[2] 5th January, 1822. *Keats Circle*, p. 269.
[3] According to Roman reckoning a new day began at 6 p.m. Thus by their usage Keats died at
5 o'clock on 24th February instead of 11 p.m. on 23rd February.

Academy within two years of receiving the pension. 'Mr Cook, an R.A., has visited me many times,' he wrote to Tom, 'and the other day in my absence he told Mr Brown that I should certainly be one of the greatest English Artists.'[1]

They were joined in their house by Ewing, a young nephew of Benjamin West's (also an artist), and Leigh Hunt's twelve-year-old son. 'We all clubbed together to make it not only reasonable, but very comfortable,' Joseph told his father. 'Mr Brown is acting manager — he directs cooking, buying and keeps our young shavers in order. Oh, what a kind, good man he is. Putting aside his delightful conversation and learning, he has such a kind open and generous heart. . . . He has managed my money affairs and now reduces all expenses.'[2] Brown advised Joseph against marriage. 'It would be in every way bad,' he said, and would interrupt his studies.

They had only disagreed on one subject. Brown still stood by the advice which he had given when Joseph had first told him, not long after Keats's death, of his resolve to become a historical painter. Brown said he would do better to stick to portraits.

'If you continue to study portraits, both in miniature and in oil, crowds will be led by vanity to your door, and you will be rich and at ease in your mind . . . Look to facts. Who has succeeded in historical painting since Sir J. Reynolds? None, save West. . . . What was Sir Thomas Lawrence's advice? Truly, it was wise. You are *now* the best miniature-painter we have. This is no compliment, you know it yourself. You need not debar yourself from the pursuit of the historical — only make portraits your sheet anchor for profit, and when your purse is swollen, sit down for a while to the other.'[3]

Brown was still of the same opinion and his advice was wise. But Joseph's success in Rome had convinced him that he was destined to be one of the great artists of his time. He did not fully appreciate his gift for miniature painting, and felt that huge pictures of historical subjects were more worthy of his talent.

Charles Brown returned to Florence in the spring but Joseph had many friends among the artists still in Rome; Gibson and he were very friendly, and planned to hold a joint exhibition of pictures and sculpture when they returned to London. Eastlake, Kirkup and Ewing were all intimate friends, and Walter Savage Landor had stayed with him for a while. Leigh Hunt had turned up in Florence, with his ailing wife and ever-increasing family. Hunt was one of the arguments that Joseph used to himself whenever he felt a weakness for the married state. After the tragic news that Shelley had been drowned in a storm off Leghorn, had come a letter from Hunt, asking for Severn's help in arranging for the interment of his ashes in Rome, which was closely followed by the

[1] Rome, 15th December, 1823. Keats House. Cook was a member of The Council of the Royal Academy.
[2] 11th January, 1824. Keats House.
[3] 13th August, 1821. In possession of author.

strange black-bearded seaman, Trelawny. It was he who had cremated Shelley's body on the seashore at Viareggio, with the white Alps towering above the beach and Elba shimmering across the sea. In the pocket of Shelley's coat was found a copy of Keats's last volume of poems, 'doubled back', said Trelawny, 'as if the reader, in the act of reading, had hastily thrust it away.'

Mrs Shelley had wished her husband to be buried beside his infant son, whose grave was in the Protestant cemetery in Rome, but the Papal Government had forbidden any further interments in the ground where Keats lay. So many of the heretics' tombs had been defaced by the Catholic population that the English residents had appealed for permission to surround them with a wall. The Papal Government refused, on the pretext that it would spoil the view, but they made a new burial-ground quite near, with a wall around it, and stationed soldiers there to protect it.

As they could not obtain permission to bury Shelley's ashes beside his son in the old cemetery, Severn and Trelawny decided that they must both be buried in the new. They found the stone recording the brief life of Shelley's son, and opened the grave beneath. To their horror there lay revealed a skeleton fully five and a half feet long. A mistake must have been made in the placing of the stone, but they dared not search any further, for, as Joseph wrote to Brown, they were 'in the presence of many *respectful* but wondering Italians'.

So, in the end, poor Shelley's ashes lay alone. But Trelawny bought a plot of ground so that when his life was over, he might lie beside his friend.

★

The bell at the front door sounded in a peremptory manner which suggested Lady Westmorland. As Joseph turned from the window, his eye ran over the canvases which leaned against the walls all round the room. To the left was *A Peasant Girl Praying to a Madonna* which Prince Leopold had bought the other day, when Lady Westmorland had brought him to the studio. His Royal Highness had ordered another picture too. Against the opposite wall stood an enormous picture, *The Vintage*, with twenty-two figures of Roman peasants painted in an Italian landscape. That had been bought by the Duke of Bedford for £150 and was waiting to be sent off to England, where it was to be hung in the next Academy Exhibition. Joseph had nine pictures in hand, all ordered by different patrons. Ironically, the only picture in his studio which had not found a purchaser was one for which poor Maria had sat as model — *Ferdinand and Miranda* he called it. Maria's face gazed up at him from the canvas with a sweet slightly insipid half-smile.

Yes, he thought, it was as well we did not marry. I have seen so many melancholy examples of marriage that (when I am not in love) I almost make up my mind to be an old fogey to the end of my days. I am so full of second thoughts that I think I shall be content to be married to my painting all my life.[1]

[1] Letters, 21st November, 1825, and 26th May, 1827. Keats House.

The bell rang again, more loudly. He gave a last, satisfied look over the evidence of his industry and hurried to open the door.

Lady Westmorland stood outside, with a footman waiting deferentially a few steps behind her. She dismissed him with a nod and entered Joseph's apartment. It was very different from the studio where she had first visited him. Now he was living in the large upper storey of a suppressed monastery in the Vicolo dei Maroniti. Here he had six or seven rooms, one of which he used for the English Academy, organized by himself as a humble imitation of the grander, State-subsidized French and Austrian Academies in Rome. The British Ambassador in Naples had contributed £100, and Sir Thomas Lawrence had sent £50 from his own pocket and a large portrait of George IV, which hung at one end of the room, where as many as twelve or fourteen artists would come in the evenings to study.

Next to this was his Painting Room, then an anteroom hung with his own pictures. These all faced north. On the sunny side he had his bedroom, a small room with a fireplace for winter nights which he called his library, and next to that, the room to which he led Lady Westmorland.

It was some thirty feet long and well proportioned, and so sunny that even in the winter, a fire was never necessary in the daytime. On the walls hung copies which he had made of pictures by Raphael, Titian and Rubens and the furniture although not new, was handsome. Two large folding windows opened on to a balcony and gave a wonderful view over Rome.

'I have come to tell you about my musical party next week,' said Lady Westmorland. 'I have decided that we two shall play Mozart's Overture to *Figaro* on the pianoforte. I have the music here and I will leave it with you.'

She laid a scroll of music, tied with ribbon, on the table beside her.

'But —'

'We shall do famously together,' she added reassuringly, as she noticed Joseph's startled expression.

'B-but I do not think — I scarcely know how — in short, I could not do it,' stammered Joseph.

He knew Lady Westmorland's parties, and saw in his imagination the enormous rooms at the Palazzo Rospigliosi — the candlelight and silken dresses, the nodding plumes — the largest room crowded with everyone of distinction in Rome, and all waiting for him, Joseph Severn, to play. No, it was too much.

'My nerves are too weak, Ma'am. I could not play with so many people watching me.'

'Pretty vanity of you,' Lady Westmorland replied playfully, rising to her feet with a laugh. 'For if we play together *I* shall be the person looked at — nobody will look at you.'[1]

[1] To Charles Severn, 1st January, 1827. Keats House.

And, indeed, her appearance would compel attention anywhere — her tall figure, her superb carriage, the head and neck set proudly on her fine shoulders. Her complexion was still lovely, and her large, expressive eyes lit up a face of great intelligence and vivacity.

She raised her hand to silence any further objections.

'I will come tomorrow morning and we will try it together on your instrument.'

She then inquired about the progress of his latest picture. Her interest in his work was so flattering and her comments so intelligent, that Joseph found himself handing her to her carriage without having made any further protest about the duet at her musical party.

As she was about to drive away, she leaned forward.

'Better still, come to the Palazzo Rospigliosi at Ave Maria, and we will try the Overture then. Your friend Mr Eastlake is coming, I believe.'

Lady Westmorland was now established in the Palazzo Rospigliosi for the winter.

Joseph gave up any hope of getting out of it, thanked her, and stood watching, divided between gloom and admiration, while the magnificent carriage, with its liveried coachman and footman, rolled off down the street.

★

Joseph and Eastlake were shown upstairs into one of the suite of small rooms where Lady Westmorland usually received. When she was entertaining large numbers of people the huge rooms below would be thrown open. The servant placed a silver candelabra on the table, closed the shutters, drew the curtains and left them. Outside the bells were ringing over the city.

They made uneasy conversation, but kept breaking off as footsteps approached the door. Half an hour passed without anyone disturbing them. Then they heard a light step outside, the door opened and there entered a lovely girl. Her eyes, as she raised them modestly to Joseph, after making him a curtsy, were an intensely brilliant blue in her small oval face. They were large and well shaped, with delicately traced eyebrows arching over them. Her mouth was small and curved, with a short upper lip and her hair clustered in curls round her face and fell in ringlets on to her shoulders. Joseph noticed that it was that rare colour — a true brown, with a touch of red in its shadows. Her skin was exceptionally fair, and the effect of its whiteness in conjunction with her dark hair and brilliant blue eyes was most striking. A narrow blue velvet ribbon was threaded through her curls.

Joseph was so enchanted with her appearance that he did not hear what she was saying, and when she paused he had to beg her to repeat herself. Her voice was low and musical, with a soft Scottish intonation.

'Lady Westmorland will not be able to receive you for some little while. She begs you to excuse her, and told me to endeavour to entertain you until she is ready.'

Both Eastlake and Joseph murmured a polite reply to this stilted little speech, though they were more than a little astonished at a young lady, whom neither of them had ever seen before, being sent to entertain two young men entirely by herself. However, she seemed to find nothing unusual in her position, and seating herself on a chair between them, she began the conversation with the greatest composure.

They were too polite to ask what they were longing to know — who she was, and what she was doing here. But Joseph set himself by dint of indirect questions to find out. Had she been long in Rome? Was her visit likely to be a long one? Until two months ago she had lived in Scotland, she said. Now she had come to live with her guardian, Lady Westmorland, and so her movements in the future depended entirely on her.

'They will incline then to be a little uncertain,' said Joseph, laughing.

The girl smiled restrainedly and turned the conversation. She was certainly an easy person to talk to, but Joseph, studying her face with quick secret glances, decided that her expression was not a happy one. He tried to put into words the impression he had from her manner. She seemed, although civil and agreeable, to be deliberately withdrawn from them. Her reserve seemed somehow a little strained, as though she were controlling her spontaneous reactions and keeping something in check.

This impression was strengthened by the way in which, when she was just in the middle of a sentence, she stopped abruptly, with a sudden, watchful look in her blue eyes. A firm footstep sounded outside the door. Lady Westmorland swept in and extended a regal hand for Joseph and Eastlake to kiss. She made no reference to their long wait, but burst immediately into a voluble description of Hortense de Beauharnais, whom she had visited at the Villa Paulina earlier in the day. Her compelling personality took command of everyone in the room from the moment she entered. She spoke rapidly, telling them how the ex-Queen of Holland could talk of nothing but herself — the romances she had written, the drawings she had made, the beauties of her villa in Switzerland, and the number of German Princes who had been to see her. Joseph's eyes turned for a moment to the girl at his side. Lady Westmorland caught his glance and stopped short.

'Ah, Miss Montgomerie has been with you. I trust she had not tired you. She had never left Scotland until a few weeks ago. I am endeavouring to educate her.' She dismissed her with a nod. 'You may go, Elizabeth.'

Miss Montgomerie curtsied to the two young men and had just reached the door when Lady Westmorland called her back.

'And for heaven's sake, child, never let me see you wear that dress again. It makes you look as white as a ghost — quite colourless.'

A wave of colour rose into Miss Montgomerie's face and vanished, to leave her skin whiter than before, but she said nothing. Her eyes rested steadily on her guardian before she turned again to the door, which Joseph had opened for her.

D*

This was only the first of many humiliations of which Joseph was the unwilling witness.[1]

★

The spring of 1827 was a gay one in Rome. The city was full of English visitors, and there were balls and receptions almost every night. Torlonia, the Roman banker, and the French Ambassador, the Prince de Laval, gave frequent parties, and foremost among the English hostesses was the Countess of Westmorland. She made a great fuss of Joseph at her own parties, and took him as her escort to many of those given by other people, where she introduced him to all the great personages.

Seeing so much of Lady Westmorland, it was inevitable that he should also see a good deal of her ward. When he called in the evening Miss Montgomerie was often sent down to entertain the visitors until her guardian was ready, but immediately Lady Westmorland arrived she expected all his attention to be concentrated on herself. When he dined at the Palazzo Rospigliosi she was sometimes there, though at other times Lady Westmorland made her take her meal in her bedroom. She did not speak much during these evenings, and often she was the butt of her guardian's witty but cruel tongue.

These occasions made Joseph acutely uncomfortable. Not only did he hate to see Miss Montgomerie humiliated, but also he did not relish these glimpses of a darker side to Lady Westmorland's character. She had been so kind to him always, and he had thought her everything that a great lady should be – gifted, witty, and magnificent in appearance and her way of living. At every crisis in his fortunes she had come to his aid. It was she who had written to the President in London when he was hoping for the Royal Academy pension, and it was she again who, on the day the pension ended, had come forward with a commission to paint six historical pictures for her, making it unnecessary for him to return to what he thought of as 'the drudgery of portrait'. It was she who had introduced him to many of his noble patrons who treated him as a gentleman. He was 'the only artist here who is on this footing with the nobility', and he was loth to throw away his advantages by quarrelling with Lady Westmorland. She had even suggested that she might get him a commission from the King of England that summer.[2]

Until now he had been proud of her regard for him, which she displayed to all the world, but now he felt almost guilty, if Miss Montgomerie were there, to see the contrast in her behaviour towards them both. Fortunately for him, Lady Westmorland's vanity was such that it never occurred to her that Joseph could feel anything but admiration for her in all her moods. He realized that Miss Montgomerie was very unhappy, but he told himself that there was nothing he could do. If he tried to speak to her ladyship about it, she would be

---

[1] Joseph Severn's *Reminiscences*, quoted Sharp, op. cit., pp. 150–1.
[2] To Tom Severn, 15th July, 1827. Keats House.

furious with him, and would only be harder on the girl. Her arrogance would permit no criticism of herself.

So he said nothing, but he made inquiries about Miss Montgomerie, in a discreet way, from some of the English ladies who came to his apartment to play with him on his pianoforte.

At first he could get only vague hints that she was the natural daughter of a Scottish baronet, who seemed very fond of her. Then, one day, from a lady who lived in Scotland, he heard a more detailed story. She was the illegitimate daughter, he discovered, of Lord Montgomerie, who, if he had lived, would have been the 13th Earl of Eglinton. Her mother, rumour said, was a friend of Lady Montgomerie, and had been seduced by Lord Montgomerie when she was staying with them. Whether this story was true or not, it was not disputed that Lady Montgomerie had shown the child great kindness.

The fact that she brought up her husband's natural daughter with her own children was thought curious by no one. Many of the oldest families were in the same position. Lady Montgomerie's marriage had been planned by her family since her childhood, and she was only sixteen years old when the ceremony took place. She was the eventual heiress of the 11th Earl of Eglinton, and by marrying her cousin, young Montgomerie, she was reuniting the family estates with the title. When Montgomerie died of consumption two years after their second son was born, his widow waited a year and then married again – a Scottish baronet, Sir Charles Lamb. Her elder son died two years later and the younger, Archie, succeeded his grandfather as 13th Earl of Eglinton when he was seven years old. Elizabeth Montgomerie had been brought up with her half-brother until he went to Eton. Then she had gone abroad, with Lady Westmorland as her guardian.

★

As the lovely Roman spring advanced, Joseph began to discover in himself feelings towards Miss Montgomerie which he knew were ill-advised. They met so constantly that a certain intimacy had grown between them, and he would often find himself thinking of those unhappy blue eyes and that attractive voice with its Scottish intonation. Her beauty disturbed him, and he fancied, too, that Miss Montgomerie was not entirely indifferent to him.[1]

He thought it over, and decided that he must check his dawning emotion. It would be wiser for him not to see too much of Miss Montgomerie. He felt glad that summer was approaching when all the English visitors would soon be leaving Rome. He was not quite certain of his strength of purpose, if Miss Montgomerie and he continued to meet so often. Perhaps it was as well that she would be leaving.

But she did not leave. In May, Lady Westmorland suddenly announced that

[1] To Tom Severn, 15th July, 1827. Keats House.

she was going to remain in Rome for ever. She took a fresh lease of the apartments in the Rospigliosi Palace, and began to refurnish most of the rooms with great extravagance and extremely good taste.

Many were the errands that Elizabeth Montgomerie was sent on, and it was surprising how often they seemed to meet, quite by chance, when Joseph had heard the arrangement made the night before. He had been right when he doubted his resolution to keep away from her. 'Women in high life are cats,' he had written to his father, but Miss Montgomerie was different from the others. She was so sweet and young and trusting, and she obviously thought of him as her one friend. For, with the departure of so many of her acquaintances, Lady Westmorland spent more of her time with Elizabeth, and when she was in a bad mood she seemed to take pleasure in insulting and humiliating her.

Joseph's feelings towards Lady Westmorland began to change that summer. He still admired her as much as ever, but he realized now that she was not the goddess he had once thought her. At the end of July she went to Naples, taking Miss Montgomerie with her, and Joseph joined them for a brief holiday. Lady Westmorland was as witty as ever; there were many English people staying there; the weather was lovely and the life was gay. But Joseph did not enjoy his holiday as he had the last one that he had spent in Naples, alone with Lady Westmorland, two years before.

He cut short his stay and returned to Rome, where he painted vehemently every daylight hour, to shut out the picture of a beautiful face, made for laughter, which yet was desperately unhappy.

Several months before, Lady Compton had asked him why he did not marry Miss Montgomerie. This Scottish lady was clever and warm-hearted, besides being very musical. She was one of those who came, when they were in Rome, to play on Joseph's pianoforte. Although her learning and inclination to pedantry had led some people to call her a 'blue', she had a woman's love of match-making and intrigue. She extracted a confession from Joseph that he found Miss Montgomerie 'the most lovely and amiable girl he ever saw', and if she had not been on the point of leaving Rome for London she would have tried to force him to a decision then. But he told her that, from a commonsense point of view, he would be foolish to marry. As a single man he could live in Rome in comfort on £150 a year and still save money. It would cost him £500 a year to live in England in the same style, even without a wife or family. He meant to save while he worked in Rome, so that he could go home a rich man. He could not afford to marry yet.

Autumn came, and the Countess of Westmorland returned to Rome for the winter. Once more the huge rooms at the Palazzo Rospigliosi were filled with people. 'She is a most queenly person and does everything with magnificence', wrote Joseph to his father. Lady Westmorland had suddenly become engrossed with politics. Her speculations were 'wild and fantastic', according to young Mr Henry Fox, great-nephew of Charles James, but he admitted that her conversation was 'always brilliant' although 'without method or consistency'.

Joseph and Elizabeth Montgomerie met frequently, but he took care not to pay her too much attention when Lady Westmorland was present. For he could not help noticing that whenever he was talking to Miss Montgomerie her ladyship would make some excuse to separate them. She would send her ward to fetch something from another room, or she would call Joseph over to look at some new book of poems or music that had arrived from England.

The circumspection that was necessary when her ladyship was with them made it seem as though he shared a secret with Miss Montgomerie. But he was anxious not to offend Lady Westmorland, and, by her behaviour that winter, she gave him good reason. He had many opportunities of seeing the lengths to which she would go to harm people who had offended her. Her restless spirit of interference was always leading her to meddle with the affairs of her friends. While she was controlling their lives — or thought that she was doing so, for she was a woman of immense vanity — no praise was too high for them, no sacrifice too great. But let them once act in a way which she did not approve — which meant contrary to her advice — and from that moment nothing they could do or say was right.

Henry Fox described her as 'a dreadful friend'. 'I never saw a manner so ladylike or a power of conversation so invariably brilliant or agreeable,' he said. '. . . Her wonderful talents and brilliant conversation make it impossible for me not to have pleasure in her society, notwithstanding the very extra-ordinary absurdities of her conduct. She is perhaps not mad, but nobody ever approached so near it with so much reason. She has fine and generous impulses, which are almost always either perverted or entirely overwhelmed by the exuberant vanity, violent temper, suspicious distrust, or ungovernable annoyance, that obscure the better feelings of her heart. It is the same with her head. Sometimes she has very just views of people's characters and actions, but when they in any way can be made to have the slightest reference to her, or when she is the least blinded by one of her vague suspicions, she instantly forgets all her former observations, and only sees them as her enemies or her friends' enemy, or her enemy's friend: for she divides the world into two classes — her friends and her enemies, which supply in her vocabulary the words good and bad.'[1]

Towards Christmas, Lady Westmorland seemed to lose something of her interest in politics and turned her enthusiasm, instead, to the Roman Catholic religion. Joseph had never lost his strong religious sense, but he remained a robust Protestant. One day at dinner, after Lady Westmorland had been talking enthusiastically about Roman Catholicism, a Lady Howard leaned across two people and said:

'So I see the Pope has made a conquest of you.'

[1] *Journal of Henry Fox*, pp. 229.

Lady Westmorland was furious.

'The vulgar, foolish woman!' she cried, and regarded her as an enemy from that day on.

A few weeks later she embarked on a bitter and more public feud. At the end of January, Laval, the French Ambassador, gave an enormous costume-ball. This was the cause of a drama which was to end only with his recall months later.

To his ball he invited Lord and Lady Blessington. They had established themselves in the Villa Negroni some months before accompanied by her dandyish French lover, Count Alfred d'Orsay. This much had been accepted by certain portions of society. But even the least squeamish were outraged when Lady Blessington married her lover to her fifteen-year-old stepdaughter, Lady Harriet, in order to make it more convenient for him to live in their house.

Many people were surprised to see the Blessingtons at the French Embassy.

'They were dressed gorgeously as Turks,' said Henry Fox drily. 'But Lady Blessington looked like one of her profession.'[1]

Lady Westmorland was furious with Laval for receiving the notorious Lady Blessington. She immediately tried to persuade the English ladies in Rome to refuse to enter his house. She talked wildly of his inviting Lady Blessington to his parties in order to degrade the English nobility and bring about a revolution in England. Having stirred up as much feeling as she could against Laval, she retired abruptly to Palo for a week, during which time she communed with God, not speaking for seven days and fasting for twenty-four hours.

It happened that the day of her departure from Rome was the first day of the Carnival, and her withdrawal was so suddenly decided upon that Joseph knew nothing about it. He called on her to discuss the details of a picture which she had commissioned and Miss Montgomerie told him that her ladyship had retired into seclusion for a week. It was only natural that they should discuss the Carnival, and when it transpired that Miss Montgomerie had not yet been to the Corso, Joseph immediately offered to escort her. She would enjoy the battles with sugar-plums and trying to recognize her acquaintances behind mask and domino, even if she did not wish to see the little horses race, riderless, down the street, driven on by the sharp spikes which at every bound fell heavily on to their bleeding sides. Miss Montgomerie did not think she would care to see the race, but accepted Joseph's offer to escort her to the Corso most gratefully.

So at noon next day, when the bell from the Capitol rang out its summons to the reign of folly, they were seated together in a carriage in the narrow, crowded street. The windows and balconies on either side were hung with brightly coloured draperies and filled with gay spectators. The two lines of carriages moved slowly past each other, while the shouting crowds on foot thrust their way between. Almost everyone, like themselves, was masked. Miss Montgomerie wore the dress of an Italian peasant girl, but her fair skin and bright hair attracted much attention. At one moment quite half a dozen masks were hanging

[1] *Journal of Henry Fox*, p. 267.

together on the back of their carriage, and chattering to them in Italian. Some of their compliments were so outspoken that Joseph hoped she did not understand them.

He had never seen her so happy, so carefree. In her excitement she forgot her troubles, and her laugh rang out again and again as they became involved in furious pitched battles, with sweetmeats for ammunition, against other carriages, until the opposite line moved on and carried their antagonists away from them.

They stayed for nearly an hour, and then Joseph invited her to come and see the sketch which he had made for Lady Westmorland's picture. It was the first time she had been in his studio. She seemed in great spirits and her gaiety became her. Her delicate, fair skin seemed to gain an extra glow from the happiness in her eyes, and her mouth had surrendered to the humour always lurking at the corners.

She pronounced the sketch quite excellent, but she teased him about the shabbiness of his cap, which was hanging on the easel. She made him put it on and told him it was a terrible colour – and it was so tattered. Why, the embroidery was in shreds. Joseph begged her, if he bought a new cap, to embroider it with something of her own devising, since she thought so poorly of his old one. Miss Montgomerie thought that, from compassion, she could scarcely refuse. Joseph felt he was really seeing her for the first time. She should always look like this.

When they met in company after that they would exchange a secret glance, and when they were separated in a crowded room each would feel the other's presence. He bought himself a new cap and sent it to her with a note.

'Miss Montgomerie – with the Cap.

Dr Miss M., – Here's the Cap – and I shall expect something pretty to be done – particularly as you rail at my purple one so – but pray come and rail again.

Yours, J. S.'[1]

Before the cap was embroidered Lady Westmorland arrived back from Palo, wilder and more ill-balanced than ever.

'God must manifest Himself more plainly!' she declared dramatically. 'I cannot fight His battle any more. There must be another incarnation. I have said "God, manifest yourself." I have done all I can do for the cause of virtue; God must complete the work.'[2]

She continued her feud with Laval, and spent much time composing letters to him. Towards the end of March she received a grossly insulting letter from Count d'Orsay. He was enraged by her crusade against the Casa Blessington, and retaliated by setting down in his letter all the unpleasant rumours that had ever been associated with her name.

She was dreadfully distressed by this letter and became so nervous and irritable

---

[1] This and all the following notes from Joseph to Miss M. in possession of author.
[2] *Journal of Henry Fox*, p. 274.

that Joseph began to wonder how much longer Miss Montgomerie would be able to support her life with her guardian. Hoping that the French Ambassador would, as a gentleman, feel compelled to have d'Orsay expelled from the Papal States, Lady Westmorland dressed herself in mourning and handed him the libellous letter in front of many witnesses at an evening assembly.

'*Cela appartient, monsieur, à la France et pas à moi,*' she said with emotion.

★

Henry Fox was on her side. He thought she should be protected from the insults of a ruffian, but the majority of the English in Rome did not support her. Many of them had suffered from her passion for interfering in the lives of other people, and they agreed among themselves that she had brought the insult on herself. Lady Westmorland spent hours at her desk, writing long, long letters about the affair to everyone she knew. Her nerves were raw and she flew into frequent passions of rage, when she would violently abuse her ward. Her only intervals of good temper came when she was well pleased with some letter that she had written. Then she would suddenly become charming, although she could still talk of nothing but the wrongs that had been done her, and her own 'angelic conduct'.

At the end of the first week in April her ladyship was *rayonnante*. She heard reports that the Governor of Rome had requested d'Orsay to leave the city. Casting aside her mourning and her martyrdom, she sallied forth in a blue silk ball-dress and lively spirits. Alas! the rumour was not justified, and the disappointment made her more unreasonable than before. She picked quarrels with everyone who had supported her, even with Henry Fox, who had almost had to fight a duel with d'Orsay over the affair.

That April was one of the hottest in living memory. Lady Westmorland, worn out by the violence of her emotions, retired to bed for two days' rest before leaving Rome for cooler air by the sea. Joseph called on her and found her in bed. Miss Montgomerie was summoned to wait on the invalid. When he was taking his leave he managed to press a note into her hand, folded into a tiny triangle. Miss Montgomerie's fingers closed round it as she curtsied, with her blue eyes on his. The great heat was making him feel dizzy, but he was shocked at the strained expression of her face. He felt he must help her, speak to her, and find out what he could do.

'They tell me that you are to go to their ball tonight,' he had written, 'now if you want a Squire I offer you my services. You may tell Lady Westmorland now, or shall I write?

Yours,
J. S.'

He returned to his studio to await an answer. He knew that, with Lady Westmorland in bed, she would be able to send one of the servants. But by the time the message came, he was feeling really ill. His head throbbed as he read her little note. She thanked him for his kindness. She would look forward with pleasure to seeing him at the ball, but she had already accepted an offer from another gentleman — she mentioned his name — to escort her there. Although he knew that he was in no condition to go dancing, Joseph felt an unreasonable irritation at her having arranged to go with someone else. He got sulkily into his bed, where, with his head aching, he lay tossing in the hot room, trying vainly to get to sleep.

By the morning his annoyance had vanished. He felt weak and ill, but he did not want her to think that he had deserted her. He sent his Italian servant round to the Palazzo Rospigliosi with another note.

'Dear Miss M., — I fear you thought me a most unfaithful knight — the truth is I should have gone only on your account, for I was ill and ill-disposed to go — and when I found you had a squire in Mr D. and feeling myself really ill, I gave up all idea of coming — I had a fever on me all night and I cannot conceive from what cause — this morning I am still ill — so believe me

still yours faithfully,

J. S.

Does Lady W. go tomorrow?'

Lady W did not not 'go tomorrow'. Rising suddenly from her bed, she abandoned the rôle of invalid and threw everybody's plans into chaos by insisting that she must leave Rome at once.

In the confusion nobody noticed that Miss Montgomerie appeared particularly melancholy that morning. Nor did they notice a sudden change in her demeanour when, as she was on the point of departure, a letter was delivered to her.

'The truth is I should have gone only on your account. . . .'

Miss Montgomerie's expression was suddenly cheerful as she climbed into the coach. Perhaps her guardian would make another change in her plans. Perhaps they would not, after all, spend very long in Florence.

*

They did not return to Rome until mid-June. Scarcely any English people had stayed in Rome for the summer. The heat was terrific, but Joseph painted doggedly all the day. He had eleven pictures on order. He wondered what was happening to Miss Montgomerie and often found himself thinking of her unhappy blue eyes. He received several letters from Lady Westmorland, each of many sheets. There were pages about her persecution and the Divine support vouchsafed to her, but no mention of her ward. He noticed that she had transferred many of her former champions into the ranks of the agents of darkness.

Immediately he heard of her return to Rome, Joseph called at the Palazzo Rospigliosi and managed to exchange a few words with Miss Montgomerie alone. She told him that she had finished the embroidery on his cap, and he begged her to bring it herself to his studio, so that she might see how much work he had done since she went away.

She had just time to murmur that she could come next day, as Lady West-morland swept tempestuously into the room. She did not look very pleased at finding them together, and spoke crossly to Miss Montgomerie before sending her away. Joseph listened to her triumphant tale of how she had had Laval turned out of Rome. He knew that the French Ambassador had been recalled while Lady Westmorland was away, but he was not certain that it was the result of her appeal to the French Court. However, Lady Westmorland had no doubt of her own triumph and enjoyed retailing it in detail.

When she had finished she insisted on driving him back to his studio, so that she might see how *The Fountain* was progressing. It was a large picture, similar to *The Vintage*, which the Duke of Bedford had bought — a country scene — a fountain in the foreground, a shepherd boy playing on his pipe while his goats were drinking, and barefooted peasant girls fetching water in pitchers; in the distance an Italian village. Joseph had been working on this picture for more than eight months. It was nearly finished, but one or two figures had yet to be painted.

When Miss Montgomerie came to his studio next day he begged her to let him include her portrait as a peasant girl carrying her pitcher to the fountain. She smilingly agreed, but then her expression altered and she said sadly that she doubted if she would be allowed to come.

'Do you mean by Lady Westmorland?' Joseph asked boldly.

She nodded silently, and then suddenly burst out that she could stand it no longer. Lady Westmorland was increasingly violent and abusive. She seemed to have some idea that Elizabeth was in league with her enemies. When she had been out of the house, even if she had only been to church, Lady Westmorland would question her suspiciously about whom she had met and what she had said to them. If they were people with whom she had quarrelled — and that, said Miss Montgomerie bitterly, meant almost everyone she knew — she would fly into a passion and would reproach her bitterly, often in front of other people, for her ingratitude. And Lady Westmorland had told people malicious stories about her — all lies, that she had invented to discredit her. She could not stand it much longer.

Her lip was trembling as Joseph took her hand in his and comforted her as best he could. He talked gently to her, telling her that she must not do anything impetuously, but that she could rely on him to help her and that she could trust him absolutely if things got any worse at the Palazzo Rospigliosi. Miss Mont-gomerie quickly regained control of herself and left, afraid to stay any longer in case her absence was noticed.

From that day they were conspirators, with Lady Westmorland as their enemy. Miss Montgomerie found herself more and more hemmed in with suspicion. Lady Westmorland seemed to sense that something was not quite right, although Joseph tried to give her no hint of his changed feelings. Her jealous scrutiny made it very difficult for them to meet, except when she sent Miss Montgomerie on some errand on foot, when she would sometimes slip up to Joseph's studio for a moment. Nothing had been said of love. Joseph particularly tried to keep their relationship on a friendly basis, but each time that he looked into her vivid eyes he found it more difficult.

They seldom had more than a minute or two alone together, but little secret notes were folded and refolded, and passed from hand to hand when they met.

'*Wednesday morning, July 9th, 1828*

Dear Miss M.,

> When will you come again,
> Or must I ask in vain?
> You're just as scarce as rain,
>   Now "per l'amor di Dio"
> And every Love profane
>   Pray let me see you.

> O how I want to trace
> Your laughing bonnie face,
> My "Fountain" has a place,
>   So pray say "Yes"
> (And "Perche no?") in case
>   I say
>   Not Yours,
>   J. S.'

She came again at last. While he painted she told him that her mind was made up. She would stay no longer with Lady Westmorland. She had a little money of her own and she would find some family in Rome who would let her live with them. She was afraid that no English family would help her, she added bitterly, because Lady Westmorland had set them all against her by the stories she told.

Joseph suggested that he should speak to a friend of his, a Miss Mackenzie, who would be staying in Rome, at any rate until next spring. It was evident that a young girl could not leave her guardian without there being some ill-natured gossip, and it would be desirable to find some respectable lady of her own nationality to look after her. From his own experience Joseph had no high opinion of the morals of the Italian ladies in Rome.

He saw that she was in earnest about leaving the Palazzo Rospigliosi, and he could not blame her. Her life there had been made wretched by Lady Westmorland, who had tormented and maligned her. It was dreadful to think of that poor young girl, so innocent and good, suffering such persecution. Lady Westmorland had, on several occasions, told him stories supposed to illustrate Elizabeth's slyness and ingratitude. He had kept silent, because to arouse her suspicions now would be fatal. She might carry her ward away to Switzerland or France, where he would be unable to help her. Occasionally he could see her alone for a moment, but most of their arrangements were made by stealthy little notes.

'Dear Miss M., — I have been thinking that as you are determined not to remain as you are with Lady Westmorland, and as you have intended to go to an Italian family here in Rome in case of extremity, I am sure my kind friend Miss Leach will receive you — she is now living with her brother (Dr Leach) at Subiaco (30 miles from Rome) and I will now write her to prepare the way — and I beg you will consider this as a recompense for my missing Miss Mackenzie which after all would only be the same as Miss Leach, who remains in Rome during the Winter.

                                      Yours very faithfully,
                                                    J. SEVERN.'

His efforts to find some suitable lady for her to live with were not very successful. August came and he could see that she was becoming desperate. It was more and more difficult for them to meet undetected. She was frightened to come to his studio even for a moment, since one day she had only just missed meeting Lady Westmorland as she was leaving. He could not bear to see her so unhappy. He made up his mind to an action which he realized might well ruin his career. He was well established as a fashionable artist in Rome, but he knew Lady Westmorland's persuasive tongue, and he had witnessed the vindictiveness with which she could use it to avenge herself on those whom she considered her enemies.

He called at the Palazzo Rospigliosi that evening. He was not left for a moment alone with Miss Montgomerie, but as Lady Westmorland rose to welcome another guest he was able to pass to Miss Montgomerie a note, asking her to call upon him the next day. It was *most important*.

He received her reply next morning. She dared not come. Lady Westmorland was watching her all the time and she was afraid of what she would do if she found out that her ward had been to his studio. But Joseph had made up his mind. He was determined to rescue her from her life of misery, whatever the obstacles. He scribbled another note on a hastily torn-off scrap of paper, and sent his Italian servant to hang about outside the Palazzo until she found a chance of speaking to Miss Montgomerie.

'I am sorry you cannot take my assurance that there is no harm — and here's an end of it — What I had to say is nothing but from my own head, but I will call at Ave Maria. Pray come to defy her.

                                                    Yours,
                                                    J. S.'

There was no reply. Once again the servant was sent round to the Palazzo.

                                                    'Wednesday, 4 o'clock.

Dear Miss M., — As it is doubtful my seeing you at Ave Maria — I say to you once more that *I have the power of insuring you 'gainst all you say* if you *yourself* have but the confidence to trust me — take courage and come early tomorrow — do believe me this once, — or I can never presume to show you respect again and fancy myself

                                                    Yours,
                                                    J. S.'

He sat in his library as the shadows lengthened. In the corner of the shelf nearest to him lay the books that Keats had read during his illness – Milton's poems, *Clarissa Harlowe*, *Holy Living and Dying*, several books in Italian, and the little volume of Shakespeare's poems which Keats had given him that night when their ship lay becalmed off the Dorset coast. He had not forgotten Keats in his new life, but he was not thinking of him now. He was angry with Miss Montgomerie. After all that he had said and done she did not trust him sufficiently to risk coming to his studio, although he had given her his word that he could protect her from the consequences if she were found out. She had not come to him. Very well then, he would not go there, as he had promised, at Ave Maria. He sat, frowning, at his bay window, as the bells chimed and night fell softly over Rome.

But he could not sleep that night. The air was sultry and oppressive. He went to bed and then got up again, to march scowling up and down his room. Soon his mood changed. She would be here in the morning. She must be planning to slip out before Lady Westmorland was awake.

He awoke early, washed and dressed, and set himself to wait for her. Half-past six. Seven o'clock. Half-past seven. Eight. She had not come. Joseph left the window and sat down at his writing desk.

'*Thursday morning* 8 o'clock.

Dear Miss M., – I purposely kept away – your want of confidence annoys me – Yet I will tell you that I have to impart something which secures *your freedom* from Lady W. for ever. Your doubts are unworthy of you, more as I have ever shown myself your true friend, and once more say, I *can* insure you against all, even from Lady W., down to the petty tatlers, but all rests in your faith of my word and power, you have no cause to doubt the one or the other, and my pride is to have them credited – I still hope to see you *here* this morning, and still to call myself

Yours,

J. S.

P.S. These are the last words *about you*, that I shall *write*, or *say*, or *read*.'

She came at last, panting a little from having run up the stone stairs, her blue eyes wide, her white brow puckered in distress. How *could* he have thought that she did not trust him? He was her only friend. Her faith in him was unbounded. But he must understand that it was very difficult – that she already had enough to bear – that if Lady Westmorland discovered that she had been to see him, she would redouble her persecution – she would tell more lies about her – she would prevent her from seeing him –

Her faltering words were silenced by Joseph's urgent voice.

'I will take you away from it all – Elizabeth.' Her hand was in his. His arm slipped round her. 'Will you marry me?'

Miss Montgomerie made him promise that their love should remain a secret until their marriage could be arranged. She was afraid that her guardian would find some way to prevent it if she knew. Joseph could not pretend to feel anything but relief at this suggestion. He too was afraid of Lady Westmorland's violent temperament. He would rather acquaint her with a *fait accompli*.

So, for a little longer, they had to dissemble, while Joseph tried to think how he could best manage the affair, with the minimum of scandal for the gossips. On one point Miss Montgomerie, usually so ready to fall in with his wishes, was adamant. Even if her guardian agreed to the marriage, she would refuse to be married from the Palazzo Rospigliosi, where she had known nothing but unhappiness. But how else could they be married in Rome? And if they went to some other town together to be married, there would undoubtedly be much unpleasant talk, especially as Lady Westmorland's malice had already put most of the English colony against her ward.

While their plans were still unsettled, things were made more difficult for them by Joseph falling ill with a sharp attack of Roman fever. Fortunately it did not last long. During all this period of worry and excitement they could scarcely ever contrive to be alone together, but little notes were still passed secretly from hand to hand.

'My Pretty Lassie, — I come tonight by invitation early, at Lady W. request — do you mean to say you have said anything to her? I hope not — You were to have written me I do not know what — I am sorry to have you sympathise with me in being ill, for I am miserably ill, and nothing but seeing you will do me good perhaps not even that — however I'd like to try.

Yours,

J. S.'

Miss Montgomerie had not said anything to her guardian, but Lady Westmorland was about to give them the opportunity for which they had been waiting.

On 24th September she removed her household to Florence for a visit of a month or two. Joseph decided to follow them to Florence. He would stay with Charles Brown, make all arrangements for their marriage, and tell Lady Westmorland only when it was too late for her to do anything to frustrate them.

'ROME, Sept. 30th, 1828.

My Dear and Better Half, — These are the last words I shall ever write you and I would that they were the last words I might speak to you in my single life, but we will begin the married one on Sunday with fun and frolic, and now — I sat me down to write you a long, loving letter and somebody has come in, and the post is going, so farewell, and believe me ever and ever

Most sincerely and devotedly yours,

J. SEVERN

On Saturday morning we shall meet, and on Sunday I hope we shall meet again never to part more.'

His letter to Charles Brown had been delayed by Brown having recently moved house, after a quarrel with Kirkup, with whom he had been living. Joseph had said nothing about his marriage but mentioned that he had been ill. In spite of having no reply he prepared to leave for Florence, and received a letter just as he was setting off. Nothing would restore his health so well as a journey, Brown wrote. 'Everybody is in strong, lively, roaring health in Florence. I give you no other news, as I expect you here. . . .' As an afterthought Brown added, 'Lady Westmorland is here: I trust that's no hindrance to your coming.'[1] Joseph smiled. He would explain to Brown, when he arrived, exactly why her presence was the reason for his journey.

One more letter he wrote to Miss Montgomerie, when he had arrived in Florence:

'My dear Eliza, – When I saw my friend Brown I could not conceal it from him, and to my delight he approves it in every respect and rejoices with me. We are going to the Clergyman, and as he thinks of Lady W. as you and I do wishes to arrange it so that she cannot interrupt our marriage. He has offered me his house, but I prefer Siena.

Ever yours,
J. S.'

All was arranged. On the Saturday Joseph called on Lady Westmorland and revealed what he had done. He told her directly that Miss Montgomerie and he were to be married at the British Consulate next day. She flew into a passionate rage, abused Miss Montgomerie, threw her benefactions in Joseph's face and rated them both for deceitfulness and ingratitude. Then, with a sudden change from violence to a control which was almost more frightening, she said that she would attend the wedding to give her ward away, but she would never, never speak to either of them again after their monstrous behaviour.

With icy demeanour she fulfilled her part in the ceremony, and left them without a word. Ironically enough, they were married in the house of her stepson, Lord Burghersh, who was British Consul in Florence, on Sunday, October 5th. The next day Joseph received a long, violent letter, full of hints and insinuations which were obviously intended to make him doubt the purity of his wife's conduct before her marriage.[2] If he had known the writer less well, what a cruel stab this would have been. It might have poisoned their marriage from the start.

He read it through to the end and then held the paper to the flame of his candle. It needed no answer. As he watched it curl and shrivel it was as though he were watching the end of his old life. Lady Westmorland with her turbulent brilliance, her uncurbed passions, her arrogance and wit, had gone for ever. In her place the lovely young Elizabeth with her straight glance, her vivid blue eyes, her honesty and laughter, faced life at his side.

[1] In possession of author.
[2] *Journal of Henry Fox*, pp. 347–8.

CHAPTER 10

HIGH NOON

1828 – 1837

THEY WERE NOT A VERY PROVIDENT COUPLE. When Joseph married he had commissions on hand for eleven pictures and his future seemed rosy. His wife had an allowance from her half-brother, Lord Eglinton, and there seemed no reason why they should not lead a very comfortable life. But Joseph's carefulness was only on the surface; in reality he was quite incapable of managing his financial affairs. He was fond of calculating how much living cost in Rome, but as he could never remember figures, and in any case always chose the ones that suited best his argument of the moment, the results were often surprising.

The first three years of their marriage were overshadowed by a fraudulent lawsuit, which cost him money he could ill afford, but brought him great support from the English colony in Rome and also from the Italians, who were delighted to see someone stand up against the corruption of justice in the Papal States. For six years before he married he had employed an Italian woman, Teresa Bartolomei, to look after his apartment and to cook for him, and had allowed her husband and child to live there with her. The husband was a porter, and Joseph had tried, when he could, to help him by recommending him to his friends. A few months after he was married he found out Teresa in some dishonesty and dismissed her. They had scarcely left the house before he received a legal document from Teresa's husband, demanding five years' wages on the plea of his having been Joseph's servant for that period.

When Joseph inquired into this false claim he found that Giovanni Bartolomei had produced several witnesses, workmen, who swore that while making a new door for the apartment in the Vicolo dei Maroniti they had overheard Joseph promise to pay Giovanni six crowns a week for his services. They even gave the date of this scene — 1st October, 1823. Joseph had no idea what he had been doing, or even where he had been, on that day five and a half years ago. He only knew that he had not been engaging Bartolomei as his servant.

Joseph and Elizabeth hunted through all his muddled papers during a sleepless night, to get a clue as to what he had been doing. Luckily they came across his passport, which showed that in October, 1823, he had been in Venice. He remembered that he had gone there with Charles Brown, and that reminded him that he had not even been living in the Vicolo dei Maroniti at that time but in the Via San Isidoro, more than a mile away. More searching produced the lease of his tenancy of the other house. With these documents in his pocket he felt that even the notorious Papal Courts of Justice could do nothing but dismiss the case at once.

He produced in court the papers which disproved the statements made by Bartolomei's witnesses. The judge then asked Joseph to come into another room and speak to him privately. He received Joseph with great politeness and shook hands with him 'in a queer ambiguous manner'. Speaking rapidly in Italian, he said that 'the whole affair of Bartolomei was nothing less than a conspiracy, and that he should forthwith give the decision in Signor Severn's favour'. Joseph was not a little surprised at the judge taking the trouble to see him privately in order to tell him that he knew him innocent, and concluded that he had been grossly prejudiced against Roman justice. Thanking him, he left the court, only to find that, the minute he had gone, the judge pronounced sentence against him. The truth was that, when shaking hands with him, the judge had expected to receive a bribe. When he found that Joseph did not give him one, he immediately called in the other parties and accepted one from them. Then he told them to change their evidence, dating it a year later, so as to correct their error in time and place. The witnesses swore devoutly to this new statement and, without giving Joseph time to prepare a second defence, the judge gave the verdict against him and sentenced him to pay four hundred and twenty-eight crowns (about £100) with costs.

Luckily it happened at a time when Joseph actually had £100 which he could have paid and this gave him the courage to refuse. Through Lord Arundell of Wardour he obtained an interview with the newly made English Cardinal Weld who listened to his story with evident pain, and undertook to have him granted the right to appeal in a new court. But the new judge confirmed the sentence in the face of Joseph's evidence.

The affair was the talk of Rome. The Roman people were delighted that such a thing should have happened to an Englishman and hoped that the scandal might lead to some reform of the widespread corruption among Papal officials. The Englishmen in Rome wanted to use it as a stick with which to beat the Papal Government. They offered to subscribe the whole sum and present it to Joseph, if he would give them the facts to publish in the newspapers of the Continent.

He refused, thinking it would be unfair to Cardinal Weld, who was supporting his cause, and also fearing that such an action might put himself and his wife in personal danger. But when Weld obtained for him an interview with the powerful Cardinal Odescalchi, the advice given to him by this Prince of the Church was 'to accept the subscription money discreetly, and when they come upon you for permission to publish the case in the European newspapers, to pretend that you had never so understood it.'

Joseph ignored this advice, and his friend Chevalier Bunsen, the Prussian Minister, spoke directly to the Pope, pointing out what harm the scandal was doing to the Roman Government. The Pope then offered to repay Joseph all the money he had spent – by now more than £150. This Joseph indignantly refused. He was determined to be vindicated in a court of law. The Secretary of State, Monsignor Tosti, arranged for him to have a new and fair trial, but at the same time he wrote to M. Kestner, the Hanoverian Minister, expressing his opinion that in the first place Joseph, instead of proving that the man had never been his servant, 'should have sworn that he had paid him the money and should have outnumbered the other side's witnesses in swearing to this'.

Even then the case was not ended. It was tried and retried until, with the aid of Cardinal Weld, Joseph won his case and the false witnesses admitted that they 'knew quite well that he did not owe the money'. It had dragged on for nearly three years, and even when he had won it, he found himself some £95 out of pocket.

He never knew where Bartolomei got the money to sustain his case, for money he had in plenty. The Severns' friends suspected that it came from Lady Westmorland, and Joseph confessed that he 'could not guess who else could have cared to spend so much money upon me, or who had it to spend in such a way'. He suspected that Cardinal Weld knew the truth, but he never questioned him.

During the anxieties of these three years Joseph and his young wife were upheld by the kindness of their own countrymen in Rome. Henry Fox was particularly helpful. Twice he lent them his lovely villa at Frascati. There, in the first summer after they were married, a daughter was born to them, whom they named Claudia, and fifteen months later, in Rome, a son, Walter. The following summer, 1831, the year that the lawsuit was at last concluded, Joseph fell ill and Henry Fox again lent them his villa which stood on a thickly wooded slope with a magnificent view over the Campagna. There were over thirty rooms, all elegantly furnished, and hundreds of English books.

They brought their own pianoforte and Joseph would play on it for hours. He recovered quickly in the healthier air and lovely surroundings, and soon he was hard at work on a large picture, *The Infant of the Apocalypse Caught up to Heaven*. Cardinal Weld had ordered it as a present for the Pope, to be placed as an altar-piece in the Cathedral Church of San Paolo fuori le Mura which was just being rebuilt.

Four months they spent at Frascati, and returned to Rome in the autumn. Writing years afterwards, Joseph said: 'When we returned to Rome we had the most complete happiness and enjoyment that it is possible for human creatures to know – prosperity, friendship, the best and most entertaining society, no end of brilliant gaieties when we wished them, our love for each other and our children, and above all we had both by this time good health to enjoy all.'[1]

He continued his work on the gigantic canvas for Cardinal Weld, who died suddenly before the picture was finished. Joseph grieved for him. It was not only

[1] Joseph Severn's *Reminiscences*, quoted Sharp, op. cit., p. 168.

that he knew he would have many anxieties before his picture was safely hung in the restored church, but also that the Cardinal had become a personal friend. He would often appear unannounced in Joseph's studio and stay there a while, watching him at work, and Joseph was often invited to dine with him. 'He performed on the French horn with great delicacy and expression, and on every occasion after dinner he requested me to play an accompaniment to him on the piano.' Poor Cardinal Weld was not for long allowed to amuse himself thus. 'This music after a while was considered to be not quite in accordance with the dignity and gravity of his high position as a Dignitary of the Roman Church, and His Eminence was invited to leave off playing on the French horn.'[1]

The years slipped happily by. More children were born. In 1832 came another daughter, Ann Mary, who was to be the most talented child in a talented family. That was the year that two great writers came to Rome. Sir Edward Bulwer Lytton was writing *Rienzi*. He told Joseph with astonishment that 'it seemed impossible to buy a Gibbon anywhere in Rome'. Joseph confessed that he owned one, but that he could not lend it to him as it was a prohibited book. He had been allowed to buy one through the kindness of Cardinal Weld, but only after giving his word that he would not lend it to anyone. In the end, after vouching for Sir Edward's discretion, he was granted permission to lend him his copy.

Walter Scott, too, arrived in Rome that year, a stricken man, worn out by six years' unceasing labour of creation. His failing mind was filled with sadness for his beloved Lady Compton, who had died in Rome two years before. When Joseph had known her she was stout and middle-aged, but Walter Scott remembered her as a child in Scotland, and still saw her as the singing angel of Raeburn's portrait. She was very musical and used often to come to Joseph's apartment to sing and play on his piano. He had got his brother, Tom, and Vincent Novello to send new music out for her from London. Scott became very distressed when he thought of her death, and it was some comfort to be able to talk about her to Severn.

Scott's daughter, Anne, told Joseph that his visits did her father good, and by their joint request he would call on them almost every day, bringing some book or picture to interest the invalid. One day he showed him the picture which he had painted of Keats reading by the open window at Wentworth Place. He was saying something about his friend's genius and his tragic death when he saw that Anne Scott had turned away, looking flushed and embarrassed. She and her father probably knew that the attack on Keats in *Blackwood's Magazine* had been written by Lockhart, Scott's son-in-law, and, like so many others who had read *Adonais* or Byron's contemptuous couplet,[2] they believed that the humiliations heaped on him by reviewers had contributed to

---

[1] Joseph Severn's *Reminiscences*, quoted Sharp, op. cit., p. 294.
[2] ''Tis strange the mind, that fiery particle,
  Should let itself be snuffed out by an article.'

his early death. Joseph stopped short in his praise of Keats. Scott was visibly distressed. He took Severn's hand and murmured falteringly, 'Yes, yes, the world finds out these things for itself at last.'

A few weeks later Walter Scott died, his body and mind worn out by the tremendous strain to which they had been subjected for six long years, while he had written and written to clear himself of debt.[1]

★

Another year, and another son was born — Henry Augustus. Joseph began to see Keats's name becoming better known. No new edition of his poems had been published in England since his death, but young Englishmen arriving in Rome would sometimes call on Joseph and introduce themselves as admirers of John Keats. Amongst them was Richard Monckton Milnes, just down from Cambridge.

Although his often-planned visit to England was every year postponed, he had so many friends and correspondents there that he was not completely out of touch with his own country. His sister, Maria, and his mother wrote to him about the family; Richard Westmacott and Charles Eastlake reported to him on the yearly Exhibitions at the Academy; and his brother Tom, who had become quite a successful composer, told him the latest musical news and sent him music.

Joseph longed to return home, but though he was still doing well in Rome he was shrewd enough to guess that he was not so well established that he could carry his fame back with him to England.

'I long to come and see you all,' he wrote to Tom. 'It will be seventeen years in October since you and I sailed down the Thames with poor Keats. I can see you now in my mind's eye, and the blue coat you had on, I can never forget you. How pale you looked at the scene we had passed and how I trembled, yet all this was for the best, for I could not expect to have done what I have done here, or certainly made so many friends who are capable of serving my family.'[2]

Joseph always loyally acknowledged his debt to Keats:

'I have gained more from poor Keats who is dead and gone than from any other source.'[3]

This made him all the more anxious to see a Memoir written of his friend — a book which would bring his poems before the world, and which would describe his life, his personality and his tragic death. It was now sixteen years since Keats's death — sixteen years in which his friends had fought over his memory. Brown asserted that George Keats had taken with him to America money which rightfully belong to his brother and which he had desperately needed. George Keats, supported by Charles Dilke, denied this charge

[1] Joseph Severn, 'On the Vicissitudes of Keats's Fame.'
[2] 9th April, 1837. Keats House.
[3] To Tom, 21st November, 1825. Keats House.

indignantly. Others supported Brown, and each faction had no name bad enough for the other.

Joseph had promised Brown his help, when he had first undertaken to write a Memoir of Keats, and also an engraving of the miniature that he had painted for the Academy Exhibition in 1819 and had given to Fanny Brawne. But it was not surprising that George Keats was definitely obstructive when he heard of Brown's projected Memoir of his brother. Even allowing for this difficulty, Brown did not seem to be working at his task with much energy. He had gone home to England with his son two years ago, so that since then Joseph could only encourage him by letter, but he continued to urge him to persevere, even threatening to write a Memoir himself if he did not finish it soon.

'If you will go on I will send you everything I can think of,' he wrote. 'If you will not, I mean to defy you and try and write his Life myself, which I am sure will make you look about you.'

'Here I have heard and heard of Keats's Life which you are doing,' he had complained when Brown was still in Italy. 'I have written and written to you about it, and now I hear nothing more, now, when the world is looking for it.'[1]

So far his protests had been unavailing, and the year 1837 was such a tragic one for him that he had little time to spare for letter-writing until it was almost ended. In the spring their new baby, a little boy of only eight months, whose christening William Wordsworth had attended, slipped down through the rail of his cot while he was sleeping and broke his neck. Joseph and his wife were heart-broken. Mrs Severn broke down completely, and in the hope of distracting her, Joseph insisted on going for an expedition which they had half-arranged before the tragedy. This was a visit to Olevano, a little town in the mountains some forty miles from Rome.

They were here when rumours were heard that cholera had broken out in Rome. There had been outbreaks in other parts of Italy, but the Romans proudly declared that 'it would not dare to enter Rome on account of the holiness of the place'. Joseph immediately decided to go to Rome and collect what they might need for a long stay. He was only just in time. The few friends he saw were in a state of alarm, and immediately after his return to Olevano he heard that cholera had broken out furiously in Rome.

Cordons were thrown at once round each of the towns near the city and no one was allowed to enter, lest they should bring the dread infection with them. Luckily he had his painting materials with him, so he was not idle. But soon his money was exhausted. He could not communicate with his bank in Rome, but the natives of Olevano proved so trusting and hospitable that the Severns suffered little inconvenience.

Their life seemed unreal by contrast with reports from Rome. They lived in the Apennine town in the midst of romantic scenery, while Joseph painted and Elizabeth sketched the children, and both rejoiced to see them thriving in the

[1] 14th March, 1834. Sharp, op. cit., p. 164.

healthy mountain air. Their only discomfort lay in being confined to the town. 'It was like the plague in Boccaccio's *Decameron*,' Joseph said.

In Rome the cholera raged. Occasionally they received a fumigated letter from the city giving terrible accounts of the death of friends and acquaintances of every class. Then they heard of 'a state of almost public anarchy. Contagion being the order of the day, all the nobles, and even the Pope himself, had bricked up their palaces, and selfishly left the rest of the city to destruction from plunder and murder. People threw the dead bodies out of windows into the streets to avoid contagion, and it was an appalling thing to see the continued falling of the corpses. The sight after sunset at the Church of San Lorenzo was the most awful that could be imagined. Carts were arriving continually, filled with naked dead bodies, which were at once on their arrival thrown into the fosse. These death-carts came in unbroken procession from sunset until two or three o'clock in the morning. . . . During a month, this rude interment was at the rate of three hundred corpses a day.'[1]

They did not return to Rome until November and it was a sad home-coming. Within their house every room brought memories of their dead baby; without, every street reminded them of friends claimed by the cholera. Joseph wrote to Brown:

'Our return to Rome seems after an absence of twenty years instead of a few months — the number of deaths, some 15 thousand, the pallid countenances all seemingly sunk in years, the vacant streets and the gloom.'

The whole life of the city was disorganized. He confided in Brown that he had been unlucky with his pictures, 'having by me some thousand pounds' worth; this is from the persons who ordered them not being able to pay me. My last commission I am now at work on.'[2]

After a moment's pause on this gloomy thought his pen dashed on to a phrase which, in slightly varying forms, was to become the motto of his family for the next twenty years: 'The future may turn up some good fortune.' Vague and charming, enthusiastic and unmethodical, God-fearing and incurably optimistic, something usually did 'turn up' for the Severns.

---

[1] Joseph Severn's *Reminiscences*, quoted Sharp, op. cit., pp. 180–2.
[2] 21st November, 1837; in possession of the author.

CHAPTER II

FAMILY LIFE

1837–1852

THE CHILDREN GREW UP TO SPEAK ITALIAN as well as they did English, and they knew the names of Raphael and Michelangelo as soon as they could talk. They lived in a romantic world, a world of crimson Cardinals and sombre friars. They heard the long-cloaked shepherds sing the old Christmas songs in Papal Rome; they knelt in the streets when the Pope passed; they played their childish games in the Ludovisi Gardens where the violets clustered thickly under the ilex trees. And when they drove outside the city they crossed the desolate Campagna, where the giant ruins of the Claudian aqueduct strode away towards Frascati.

From the first, Mary and Walter showed most talent in drawing and Claudia in music. She was seven years old when the family returned to Olevano, and her father would make her sing the Vintage songs that she had learned in the mountains. He had taught her to play duets with him too. One of their favourites was 'Figaro'. Mrs Severn loved to watch them at the piano. Joseph would be carried away by the music, gradually increasing the time from *presto* to *prestissimo*, and bursting into song, while his daughter made desperate efforts with her small childish hands to keep pace with him.[1]

They had not long returned to Rome before an old friend arrived. This was George Richmond, baby of the Academy Class that Joseph had attended while he was still an engraver's apprentice. A portrait of William Wilberforce, the great opponent of slavery, had made the artist's name in England. He brought with him his wife, with whom he had eloped to Gretna Green six years before, and their son Thomas, the only survivor of four babies born to her. She was expecting another shortly.

Joseph was delighted to meet Richmond again and they spent much time together. He took him sight-seeing, and they talked of painting and music, and their old friends at the Academy.

The Richmonds had taken a large apartment in an old palazzo, and Mrs Severn told Mrs Richmond to send her word if she needed help at any time. Young Mrs Richmond thanked her new friend gratefully and was reassured to think that there was someone she could turn to in need, as George, though a devoted husband, had a temperament that was more artistic than practical.

[1] Letter from Joseph to his daughter Claudia, 30th May, 1873, quoted in *A Victorian Artist*, unpublished manuscript by Claudia Gale.

One night Richmond was awakened from a deep sleep.

'George!' cried Mrs Richmond, 'you must go at once for Mrs Severn — my baby is going to be born!'

He decided that his wife's nerves must have been affected by the long journey across Europe. The baby was not expected for several weeks.

'Nonsense, my dear!' he replied firmly. 'Compose yourself to sleep,' and he followed his own advice.

'George!' called his poor wife some time later. 'You really must go for Mrs Severn! My baby is *here* — in the bed with me!'

'Good gracious!' exclaimed Richmond, really roused at last. 'This has made me feel quite faint!'

'Empty some cold water over your head, George,' his wife advised, thoughtful to the last.

★

Many English people arrived in Rome with letters of introduction to Joseph.

'Everywhere Joseph Severn was *persona grata*,' wrote Richmond's son long afterwards. 'His geniality charmed every member of Roman society, from high officials at the Vatican to the humblest traveller. Severn would do his utmost to render a year's sojourn in the Eternal City pleasant, and having great tact and considerable accomplishments, his house likewise became one of the centres where were to be found the foremost men and women of the day.'[1]

Henry Acland, later to be Regius Professor of Medicine at Oxford, was one of those who arrived in Rome with a letter of introduction to Joseph and became a lifelong friend of all the Severn family and of the Richmonds too. 1838, the year following the saddest in Joseph's life, opened cheerfully with new friends.

He was 'always full of anecdote' and good spirit. His charm lay partly in his enjoyment of life, and partly in his anxiety that everyone should be as happy as he. Though he wrote to Tom that his financial position was not very good and that he had many enemies, he was never depressed for more than a moment by either thought.

Elizabeth Severn, too, had a happy, impulsive temperament, which release from Lady Westmorland had unfettered. She taught her children that love of God was not incompatible with laughter. She gave them a real religion and surrounded them with gaiety and affection. Their household was run in a rather haphazard way, with more good taste than method. The food would grow cold on the table while the family was at the window admiring a sunset, and Joseph would be late for an important appointment because he was teaching Claudia a new song.

Joseph made two new friends that year, who were to help him in the future. In December, 1838, William Ewart Gladstone arrived in Rome. He was then twenty-eight years old, tall, with a pale resolute face, an upright carriage and

---

[1] Richmond Papers, pp. 42–4.

an expression somewhat severe. He introduced himself to Joseph as an admirer of Keats, and asked him many questions about the poet. He did not approve of the Papal Government. George Richmond went riding with him on one occasion and when they got outside the Papal States Gladstone flung his cap in the air and shouted 'Long Live Liberty!'[1]

Gladstone's attention was much occupied by Miss Catherine Glynne, the younger of two beautiful, tall English sisters visiting Rome, whose brothers had been at Oxford with him. Catherine was the exact opposite of William Gladstone. He was logical and austere and had schooled himself to stern habits of self-control. She was impetuous, warm-hearted, unpunctual, and unconventional, but like himself deeply religious.

In the ruins of the Colosseum he asked her to marry him, but his suit was at first unsuccessful and he returned to England. Soon afterwards Lady Glynne followed with her two daughters, and a few months later Joseph heard that William Gladstone and Miss Catherine Glynne were married.

They were to be good friends to himself and his family.

*

One last friend remained to be made, and then the first Roman chapter of his life was closed, though there was still to be a Roman epilogue.

In 1840 a delicate young man arrived, travelling with his father and mother. He approached the Severns' apartment with a letter from Henry Acland asking Joseph to be kind to young John Ruskin, who had lately won the Newdigate Prize. At their first meeting they did not exchange a word. Ruskin had climbed laboriously up the stairway, 'broad, to about the span of an English lane that would allow two carts to pass,' of the house in the Via Rasella. 'I was within eighteen or twenty steps of Mr Severn's door, when it opened, and two gentlemen came out, closed it behind them with an expression of excluding the world for evermore from that side of the house, and began to descend the stairs to meet me, holding to my left. One was a rather short, rubicund, serenely beaming person; the other, not much taller, but paler.' The first was Joseph, the second George Richmond. 'They looked hard at me as they passed, but in my usual shyness . . . I made no sign, and leaving them to descend the reverting stair in peace, climbed, at still slackening pace, the remaining steps to Mr Severn's door, and left my card and letter of introduction with the servant.'[2]

Severn had noticed the card in the young man's hand. It was obvious that he was about to call and they congratulated themselves on not having been caught. Nevertheless Joseph looked keenly at him as they passed each other on the stairs and when they were out of earshot he said to his friend, 'That young man has the face of a poet.'[3] They could not guess the fame that was so soon to come to

[1] *Richmond Papers*, p. 45.
[2] J. Ruskin, *Praeterita*, vol. 2, Chapter 2.
[3] Arthur Severn's Memoirs.

E

him, nor could they know that in his old age he would be tended by a son of Joseph's yet unborn.

But he called again and Severn was kind and helpful, as indeed he was to everyone; Joseph and George Richmond made friends with John Ruskin's parents and they all ate their Christmas dinner together.

'There is nothing in any circle that ever I saw or heard of,' wrote Ruskin, 'like what Mr Joseph Severn then was in Rome. He understood everybody, native and foreign, civil and ecclesiastic, in what was nicest in them, and never saw anything else than the nicest; or saw what other people got angry about as only a humorous part of the nature of things. It was the nature of things that the Pope should be at St Peter's, and the beggars on the Pincian steps. He forgave the Pope his papacy, reverenced the beggar's beard, and felt that alike the steps of the Pincian, and the Araceli, and the Lateran, and the Capitol, led to heaven, and everybody was going up, somehow; but might be happy where they were in the meantime. Lightly sagacious, lovingly humorous, daintily sentimental, he was in council with the cardinals today, and at picnic in Campagna with the brightest English belles tomorrow; and caught the hearts of all in the golden net of his good will and good understanding, as if life were but for him the rippling chant of his favourite song, — 'Gente, e qui l'uccellatore.'[1]

But Joseph's days in Rome were drawing to a close. Two reasons made him decide to return to England. The first was that his eldest son, Walter, was now nearly eleven years old, and his father wished him to go to an English school. The second was his conviction that Brown would never complete the Memoir of Keats unless he could see him and force him to it. Brown had been back in England now for five years.

So, with a sigh, Severn turned his back on Rome. On the evening of his last day in the city he made a melancholy pilgrimage to the grave of Keats. He had thought, in such a deserted spot, to rest in solitude a while. But, as he approached the grave, he saw, kneeling by it, hand in hand, two lovers, evidently English. He did not disturb them, but from his vantage point made a rapid sketch of the scene. His reaction was the same as that which had prompted him, during his wakeful night by the bedside of his dying friend, to draw his death-like countenance. It was not that his heart was cold, but rather that it overflowed on to the paper. His children were to be the same. At every crisis in their lives the Severns reached for paper and a pencil, and by crystallizing their emotion received comfort.

The Severn family arrived in England in March 1841, and were soon established in a charming old house in Buckingham Gate. It had oak wainscots, panelled walls and a sunny garden behind. There, in the August of the following year, their last children were born to Joseph and Elizabeth — twins, whom they named Arthur and Eleanor.

At the time of their birth Joseph's eldest child, Claudia with the beautiful

[1] From Mozart's *Magic Flute*.

voice, was thirteen. Next came Walter, one year younger, who was sent to Westminster School to be educated, as his father had always planned, as an English boy. Then came Ann Mary, who, at the age of ten, was already showing great artistic talent, and Henry, nine years old, who was entirely practical. He liked to take things to pieces to see how they worked. And now the twins.

Joseph's responsibilities, with so many children to provide for, began to weigh on him. When he first arrived in England there was all the bustle of finding and fitting into a house. Then there was the pleasure of seeing his mother again, very old now but as dear as ever, and his brothers and sisters and their children. There were many old friendships, too, that had been forged in Rome, to take up again in London, and the matter of the Keats Memoir to be investigated.

Joseph's faith in Keats's genius had never wavered during these long years when his friend's name was still comparatively unknown. He felt it his duty to see that a life of Keats was published, but when he arrived in London he found that Charles Brown was about to sail to New Zealand. Brown had made an immediate decision on hearing a lecture about the new colony. His son, Carlino, had already gone, and he was full of grandiose schemes for their future. Before he left he handed over all his material for the Life to Mr Richard Monckton-Milnes, who, seven years before, as an admirer of Keats's poetry, had sought out Joseph in Rome, when he was travelling abroad after having taken his degree at Cambridge. As an undergraduate Milnes, with his friend Arthur Hallam, had been responsible for the reprinting of *Adonais*, but the first reprint of Keats's poems in England was not until 1840, nearly twenty years after Keats's death.

Once the material was in Monckton-Milnes's hands, Joseph was satisfied that the Memoir would be produced. But he was very distressed when he heard the next year of Charles Brown's death in New Zealand. After Keats had died, Brown and Joseph had been close friends during more than ten years when they had both been living in Italy. There was news, too, that year that George Keats had died in Kentucky, of consumption like his two brothers. Joseph wrote sadly to Charles Eastlake that, with all these friends, 'his sense of youth had gone for ever'.

Now that his eldest son was at an English school, and the materials for the Life of Keats were in safe hands, Joseph turned again to his painting. But he found it difficult to sell his pictures. Soon he was pleased if he had one commissioned picture on hand, and even thought of returning to miniatures, until he found that miniature-painting, too, was out of fashion. His hopes now centred on a new form of work — fresco painting. There was a great competition to decide who should paint the frescoes in the new Houses of Parliament and Joseph submitted a cartoon to the Committee.

His anxiety was very great, so that he was overjoyed to receive a letter from Mr Gladstone, putting an end to his suspense and telling him that he had heard that his cartoon portraying 'Princess Eleanor drawing the poison from the wound of Edward in the Holy Land' would be amongst those selected.[1]

[1] 24th June, 1843. Sharp, op. cit., p. 203.

Joseph was elated by his success and concentrated all his energies and thoughts on fresco painting. But, alas, he had rejoiced too soon. His first cartoon was eventually refused and a second sketch for a subject from Spenser was also rejected after prolonged correspondence. 'While acknowledging the merit of various parts of the design,' the Commissioners wrote, they regretted that 'they were not prepared to recommend its execution in fresco'.

Fortunately the Countess of Warwick had engaged him to decorate a magnificent hall at Gatton Park, Reigate, which her son had built for her 'in imitation of a fine building in Rome'. Here he had thirteen men working under him, a pianoforte and an organ in the house, and 'a fine library, even of music'. He confessed himself in Paradise. Lady Warwick was most kind to him and invited Walter and Henry to stay there during the school holidays.

When Joseph's work was finished at Gatton Park he had to look round again. There were not many people in England who wanted large walls to be painted with frescoes. But for the first eight years in England things went fairly well. Something always 'turned up'. Mrs Severn's relations were very kind to them. Lord Eglinton continued to give his half-sister an allowance, Joseph went to Scotland to paint 'Lady Eglinton and son, now three years old',[1] and the two eldest children, Claudia and Walter, went frequently for long visits to Eglinton Castle and to Rozelle in Ayrshire, where they stayed with Lord Eglinton's aunt, Lady Jane Hamilton. Claudia was pretty and sang beautifully when the ladies showed their accomplishments in the evening. All Elizabeth's daughters inherited her air of distinction and her good taste in dress. As for Walter, he was very handsome and delighted the ladies by making clever sketches of them skating or playing croquet, though he preferred to draw stags, and Stags in the Snow at Bay was duly presented to Lord Eglinton as a birthday present.

★

Meanwhile the twins, Arthur and Eleanor, lived quietly in the house at Buckingham Gate. Eleanor's earliest memory was of their Roman nurse — her brown neck and her necklace of large coral beads. When she left them to return to Italy, an English widow, Mrs Rylands, took her place and their brother, Henry, used to help to pull the twins along in a little green wooden chaise, for there were yet no perambulators. They would go to the Mall and drink milk from the cows that were kept there, and Henry made them little boats and took them to St James's Park to sail them on the water.

The nursery windows looked over Wellington Barracks, and gazing out of them, at the age of five, Eleanor fell in love with a drummer-boy. Through the good offices of her parents' friend, Colonel Palliser, who lived with his family a few doors away, the little boy was brought to the nursery and performed with his drum, while the twins gazed at him in silent hero-worship.

[1] 21st January, 1845.

The following year, 1848, when the twins were six, was the year of the Chartist Riots. Troops were stationed all over London and the Duke of Wellington took charge. Artillery was posted in St James's Park. The Chartists gathered on Clapham Common and it looked like the beginning of a revolution. For forty-eight hours London was under military rule and Joseph and his son, Walter, were enrolled as special constables and issued with truncheons. Mrs Severn ordered half a ton of coal from Mr Chestnut, the coal-man at the end of the street, to put behind the area door and prevent it from being broken down, and the windows of the house were barricaded. The twins sat with their mother in the darkened room and heard the heavy stamp of feet passing outside. Arthur had to be restrained from climbing up on the roof 'to pour boiling water on them'. Anxiety was great until Walter appeared to tell Mama that the crowds had dispersed and there was no further danger.

The twins saw many interesting people come to visit their parents. They heard Mendelssohn play on their father's piano, they listened to Leigh Hunt discoursing on poetry. Young Dante Gabriel Rossetti arrived with a letter of introduction from his father which begged Mrs Severn to be kind to him as he was very shy.[1] And Mrs Gladstone came, as lovely and as kind as ever. With her usual carelessness and indifference about what she was wearing, she could not find her hat when she rose to leave. After the room had been turned upside down it was eventually discovered in the coal-scuttle.[2]

Walter was now eighteen years old and, having left Westminster, he was to try for a clerkship in the Privy Council Office. To Mrs Severn's dismay, he chose, a few days before he was to appear before the Council, to have a fight, which lasted for three-quarters of an hour, with a boy larger than himself. 'I remember,' wrote Eleanor, 'his coming home (he was a day boy) and I ran to the door to open it for him, knowing his knock. I was terribly frightened! There he stood with a black and bruised face quite unrecognizable. He was obliged to remain in bed for a day or two, and when he was better had to go and be seen by "My Lords" at the P.C. Office. I stood at the bottom of the stairs to see him descend resplendent in his first tail coat. Both his eyes were still black and when he entered the room they remarked on the fact. The President of the Council was old Lord Lansdowne, and he was a great friend of my mother and father. He had been at Westminster himself and, on hearing how Walter had got his black eyes, said: "A fight — and at Westminster — sit down and tell us all about it!" He was appointed to a clerkship and was in the office for forty years!'[3]

Monckton Milnes's Life of Keats was published that year and acclaimed by the critics, and Joseph painted a portrait of Milnes and another of Mr Gladstone. One of his children was already following in his footsteps for his daughter, Mary, was studying with George Richmond.

[1] A Victorian Artist by Claudia Gale.
[2] Diary of Eleanor Severn.
[3] Ibid.

CHAPTER 12

MARY

1852 – 1857

THE RICHMONDS LIVED AT NO. 10 YORK STREET, off Portman Square and the two families were great friends, the children treating each other as brothers and sisters. George Richmond was a die-hard Tory, a staunch Churchman and a man of very high ideals. But he was a stern father, and a lapse from grace by any of his ten children was immediately punished by a thrashing. In spite of this he could be 'as playful as a child when he unbent'. His children loved him and so did the young Severns.

Every Christmas the Richmonds gave a children's party at York Street but it was Joseph who made these parties such a success. His good spirits delighted the children as much as they did an older generation. His jokes and laughter banished shyness and charmed them into complete enjoyment. Little Arthur Severn and Willie Richmond used to be encouraged to wrestle. They were the same age, and at five years old they both wore short white breeches, which were black by the time the match was ended.

'Mr Joseph Severn was a great acquisition,' wrote Willie Richmond later. 'He had a time-honoured trick, beloved by the children, of manufacturing a black cat seated on the top of a door with its tail hanging down. The cat was fashioned out of a tea-canister, with gleaming tin eyes; but in order to represent its fur, an old beaver hat was required, of which he cut off the brim. In Mr Severn's excitement, however, for the success of the trick, he was not always too particular whose hat he got hold of, so that people with good hats found it necessary to hide them, for a beaver hat in those days often cost as much as four pounds!'[1]

Mary Severn was fortunate in her teacher. George Richmond would permit no slovenliness of execution and demanded extreme accuracy and patience. He worked a great deal in crayons and water-colour, and Mary could have had no better teacher in these media. He had done portraits of most of the leading men and women of his day. Newman, Charlotte Brontë, Mrs Gaskell and Lord Macaulay were among his sitters. He was very fond of Mary, not only because of her charm, which was compounded of great sweetness spiced with lively humour, but also because he saw in her unusual talent, application beyond her years and a profound belief in God.

Sometimes she would stay at York Street for a week or two, sleeping in Mr

[1] *Richmond Papers*, p. 105.

Richmond's dressing-room, which was hung round with his early drawings. When Richmond went out during these visits, his wife would give her the key of the studio and leave to bring down any drawings to copy. In return for all his kindness Mary drew portraits of the three youngest children for Mrs Richmond. She was beginning to show 'the greatest power in catching a likeness', and was particularly successful with children. Mary was nineteen when Claudia married, early in 1852.

With every year, their father had been finding it more difficult to support his family. Fortunately Walter was now working and Mr Gladstone had obtained a position for Henry in the Mint. Inspired by his friends Ruskin and Eastlake (now Sir Charles and President of the R.A.), who had both achieved success in writing about art, Joseph tried his hand with the pen. He wrote a novel about Titian in Rome, which was never published, as well as papers and essays on painting and painters. By thinking about it, he could convert a passing reference in conversation with a friend into a definite order which had only to be confirmed; so that even at his lowest ebb he saw himself as surrounded by promising possibilities which might any of them, at any moment, materialize into a splendid commission.

His wife saw what was coming. She realized that they could not go on living in Buckingham Gate, and found a cheaper house off Belgrave Road. Walter and Claudia were staying at Eglinton Castle during the move, and their mother noticed that Mr Frederick Gale, a young barrister and a well-known amateur cricketer, seemed very impatient for Claudia's return.

Claudia came back to London and all went as Mrs Severn had foreseen. Frederick Gale proposed and was accepted and they were married in the following February at St Peter's, Eaton Square.

*

Mary was now beginning to make money. As her father's commissions grew fewer, her own were becoming more frequent. She had done several portraits in water-colour or crayon for friends, and by them had been recommended to other people. Her twentieth birthday came, and that autumn she went to Ireland, to stay with a brother of Colonel Palliser, to paint his sister and her children. The Colonel came over while she was there and she painted his portrait, too. These pictures were so good that she was invited by several friends of the Pallisers to stay in their houses and to paint their children or the proud Mamas.

'I am in great spirits,' she wrote happily, 'for I see more and more "coms", in perspective. I shall soon make quite a fortune!' She sent money home to her mother, half a ten pound note in one letter, and the second half in the next. She stayed in several country houses, the owners being most friendly and helpful to her, and was able to ask ten or fifteen pounds a picture. She met Louisa, Marchioness of Waterford, the celebrated beauty and artist and they went on several painting expeditions together.[1] In spite of the pleasure she felt at working well and making enough money to keep herself, she was sometimes irked by the too great comfort and regularity of the life led by her various hosts. She felt homesick for their own haphazard happy household, with its constant interruptions of crisis or excitement.

'Last night we dined with Mrs Phipps,' she wrote to Walter. 'I sat next to Colonel Phipps who, altho' such an interesting person, full of information, was so absorbed in the discipline of his dishes, his servants, his wines and his sauces, that I could get little or nothing out of him during such an important time as dinner! I think it is such nonsense people being so particular about the waiting, etc. Surely a little orginality is delightful, now and then I long for the Denbigh Terrace irregularities; I think our way of living is after all the most interesting — at all events we have variety!'[2]

Poor Mary was to have rather too much variety when she returned from Ireland.

She was staying at Charleville, in Co. Wicklow, with Lord Monck, when she heard that Claudia had given birth to a daughter, in London. She was painting Lady Monck and her three little girls and, although the Moncks were very kind to her, she longed to be back with her own family. People's values seemed so different here. They attached importance to things which she had always disregarded or simply accepted as something natural, and in no way remarkable.

'You can have no idea,' she wrote to Mama, 'how extremely polite Lord and Lady M. are to me. Lord M. took me to the Glens and when he asked me to go he said "If I would do him the honour to accompany him." But really you can have no idea to what an extent they carry it. When they were out for a walk Lady M., though tired, insisted on remaining with me and an oldish bachelor and when we were home she said, "Now you are under *my* charge and I could not think of letting you out of my sight. What would Mrs Severn say if she heard I let you walk alone with any gentleman?" Lady M. is very proud and does not like people who are not good-looking and well-bred. She seems to think more of me because I am in some way related to the Eglintons.[3] I am sure this is one of the reasons why she likes me. The other day Mr W. was speaking *very much* against Lady E. I saw Lady M. look very uncomfortable, and looking across and not answering him. I took no notice, made a few remarks and thought no more of it. The moment we were out of the room, she came to me in way of apologizing for what Mr W. had said: "I am so sorry, so hurt that such a thing was said at my table, but the moment I had an opportunity I told Mr W. he ought not to have said it before you. But cannot you imagine I was *too* glad to

---

[1] *A Victorian Artist* by Claudia Gale.

[2] The Rectory, Clonmel, 12 December, 1852. In possession of author.

[3] Lord Eglinton was Lord Lieutenant of Ireland from February 1852 to January 1853 and again from February 1858 to July 1859.

give him the reason." I see she thinks a good deal of rank, more so than of talent. She is the daughter of the Earl of Rathdowne.'

*

Mrs Severn was relieved when Mary got back from Ireland. Mary was her great support. Claudia, newly married, could think of nothing but her husband, her house, and her new baby, though Frederick Gale had been very kind. Walter's reactions to their troubles seemed to be confined to indignation at his father's fecklessness. Whenever she spoke to him he flew into a rage about it. Henry was still working at the Mint, but he was talking about emigrating to Australia at the end of the year. There remained Arthur and Eleanor, the twins, now ten years old, who had been attending a day school. How would they educate them now? Mary must not be sacrificed for her brothers and sisters — or her father, thought Mama firmly. As for her husband, she doubted if even now he realized how serious the position was.

That evening, when the twins were in bed, Mary and her mother sat up late, adding up the bills, calculating how much could be realized by a sale of Papa's pictures and drawings if they were sent to Christie's. They had to face the fact that there was little demand now for his *genre* of painting. Mary, at twenty, was already making more money than he. His debts had been accumulating, and although Mama had so far staved off disaster, Mary realized as she went through the papers that at any moment they might be overwhelmed by an avalanche of writs. They talked late into the night, and Mama told her all that had happened while she had been away.

Eventually Mama said they had talked enough on such a sad subject. Now she must hear all about the pictures which Mary had done in Ireland, and then they must arrange one of the rooms as a proper studio. Already Mary had one commission waiting for her — a portrait of a handsome Mrs Babington — and she must have her own room to work in, where her sitters could come to her. Mary was delighted with the idea. She had been wondering how she could manage. With such an entrancing subject before them they soon forgot their troubles in the excitement of deciding what furniture, carpet and curtains would be most suitable, and after various suggestions had been reviewed they went happily to bed.

The Severns' financial affairs came to a crisis that summer. On Frederick Gale's advice Joseph left the house in Denbigh Terrace in the early hours of the morning to avoid arrest and stayed for a time with his sister Charlotte, telling her that they were moving house. Mrs Severn bustled about with immense energy directing her family. Walter moved to rooms nearby in Charlwood Street and Mama took lodgings for Mary in another house in the same street, fearing that she might lose her drawings and paints if the bailiffs came to Denbigh Terrace.

Fortunately the Severns had many friends. Lord Lansdowne was of the

E*

kindest; he lent Joseph £250, accepting an altar-piece that he had painted as security, and when their furniture was auctioned another friend, Mr Vaux, the Keeper of the Coin Department at the British Museum, bought in the most necessary pieces for them. Joseph's stock of drawings and sketches were sent to Christie's but very few sold. Sir Edwin Landseer invited Mary and Mama to his studio, made Mary show him some of her drawings, praised them and promised help; George Richmond sent a number of people to see her portraits of children and several gave her commissions.

At the worst moment in their fortunes, Mama, who never lost her sense of humour, described with great animation to Mary how at Denbigh Terrace she had had the broker in the drawing-room, Fred Gale with a disapproving relation of her own in one parlour, and a clergyman sent by George Richmond to see Mary's portraits in the other, and how she had kept them all ignorant of each other's presence as she ran between them. After this it was necessary, she explained, to consult Papa, still with his sister at Islington.

'Do let's have a spree and go to Papa's in a hansom cab,' she said. Mary objected that it would be a great expense.

'Well, I am too done up to wander about in and out of those nasty omnibuses', said Mama. 'I should never get there.'

Eleanor called a hansom. 'When we were in it,' wrote Mary in her diary, 'Mama breathed freely and said "Well, however poor I am there are certain things I *cannot* give up — Hansoms, cold cream and violet powder." '

Providentially, Mary's twenty-first birthday came only a few days later. Her lodgings were in her own name and Frederick Gale who had now collected the bills of the remaining creditors from Mama, sent Mary to a lawyer to give her affadavit that the house was hers and all in it was her own property. He then called the creditors together and told them that Joseph had no house and no property, but that his two eldest sons wished to pay what they could towards their father's debts, and that the small amount outstanding would eventually be paid.

*

So at last, with the aid of their friends, the family ship was righted. Joseph had already fled to Jersey to evade his creditors and was lucky enough to get commissions for two pictures there. Henry carried his point, obtained a position in the Australian Mint and departed, leaving the twins in tears. Lord Eglinton had been very kind to his half-sister and continued to give her an allowance. She decided that it was an ideal opportunity for Mary to study in Paris and for the twins to learn French.

Filled with enthusiasm she swept them off to France, and arranged for the twins to go to schools just outside Paris, while Mary went to work under Ary Scheffer. He was particularly pleased with a pencil drawing which she made of Eleanor sitting with folded hands and eyes downcast and held it up for his

French pupils to see, telling them to look at a drawing by a young English girl that was better than anything they could do.[1] It is a proof of Mary's charm that, even after this, she was popular with her fellow-pupils.

When Joseph got back to London he lived in Mary's little house. Soon Mama brought Arthur home, arranged for him to live with Papa and go to a day school, and then returned to Eleanor in Paris. Joseph lived quietly, painting and seeing his friends.

'Mr Joseph Severn was a jaunty, fresh-natured, irresponsible sort of being,' wrote one of them, 'leading a jocile, slip-shod, dressing-gowny artistic existence in Pimlico. Like his friend Hunt, he was not rich, but never seemed to be in actual want of anything, unless perhaps it might be a brush or a comb. . . . Mr Severn was the most buoyant of Britons, a man of cheerful yesterdays and confident tomorrows. He had a prosperous laugh and coruscated with cheerfulness. . . . Severn was especially amusing when he indulged in the melancholy looking-back vein. "Ah! Mr Locker, our youth! That was the time when Hope and Fruition went hand in hand — *altri tempi, altri tempi*. What is left to us? Vain anxieties, delusive hopes, unexpected issues!" '[2]

Before Mary returned with Mama and Eleanor to England in the spring of 1857 she had completed three important commissions, a chalk head of Lady Elgin and another of her sister, Lady Augusta Bruce, and a drawing of the little Prince Imperial — her first Royal commission.

★

While she was in Paris Mary had been reading John Ruskin's books and she longed to see his collection of Turners. Accordingly Joseph wrote to Ruskin and asked if he might bring his daughter and youngest son to the house on Denmark Hill where Ruskin lived with his parents. A charming reply came from Ruskin saying that it would 'rejoice and warm the cockles of his heart' to see his old friend again and that they must all three be sure to come to lunch at two o'clock.[3] In the end Joseph could not go, but brother and sister set off on the day named across Vauxhall Bridge to Camberwell, and thence walked up to Denmark Hill. A beautiful cedar grew just inside the gate of the Ruskin's drive. The visit made a great impression on Arthur, who had already decided to be an artist himself, and years afterwards he described it vividly.

'The bell of the lodge tolled as we walked shyly up to the front door. It was quickly opened, and in a moment, John Ruskin came to greet us, shaking our hands with both his, and hurrying my sister up to his study to look at Turners. I was ushered into the morning-room where his mother was working at some sort of tapestry; and although she was very kind, I felt a little in awe of her. Soon lunch was announced and we heard loud laughter on the stairs, — it was Ruskin

[1] *The Times*, 23rd January, 1866.
[2] Frederick Locker-Lampson, *My Confidences*, p. 324.
[3] Yale University Library.

bringing my sister down on his arm, and laughing loudly at her question as to why he made his pupils at the Working Men's College draw purple trees, — he saying: "And why shouldn't I, if I like? Purple is a very good colour and it washes well."

'After lunch, Ruskin bounded off to fetch us the plum of his Turners — the St Gothard. In a moment he was back and putting it on a chair, stood us in front of it, saying: "Now, take your time, I have to fetch something else," and off he flew again. When he had disappeared, old Mr Ruskin came in, a short, spare man with a very intelligent face, fine eyes and bushy eyebrows. . . . With an amused smile he said: "You know, I think my son John sometimes sees more in these drawings than Turner himself ever meant," when suddenly John's quick step was heard, and he vanished.

'The son came in, a little breathless, with one hand in his coat tail pocket, and said: "Well, what do you think of that drawing? Isn't it wonderful? Look at that torrent! Look at the lovely colour of those rocks and stones! People say the colour is exaggerated — No, look here!" And out of the coat tail pocket he produced a stone about the size of a small tea-cake. "I picked this stone out of that very torrent. Look how exactly the same the colour is. And now, when I wet part of it, look how true the colour is to where Turner means the stones to be wet!"

'We were much interested; though I remember wondering whether the conditions wouldn't be very different, — this stone being shown in a room, and those in the drawing in the midst of storm and spray.

'When we were getting ready to go, a gardener appeared with a large bouquet of flowers; my sister was allowed to look and admire for a moment, then it was given me to carry, with apologies for all the trouble I should have! And so ended a most delightful visit to us both, and as we silently walked away, I thought to myself: "What a kind man! How I should like to know him better and to be able to see the Turners whenever I liked!" '[1] He little guessed that in a few years' time his wish would be realized.

★

Soon after this Mary began a round of visits where business and pleasure were to be combined. First she went to Bath, to stay with Lady Jane Hamilton, the sister of her grandfather, Lord Montgomerie. Lady Jane had been ill and was taking the waters at Bath, where she had Lord Eglinton's daughter, Egidia, staying with her. As the twins were the same age as Egidia, Mary took Arthur to be a companion for her.

They stayed there for several weeks and Arthur and Egidia became great friends. When Lady Jane drove out in the afternoons they were allowed to sit together in the 'dickee' at the back of the carriage. Arthur made a kite which they smuggled into the carriage and flew from the back. It was a great success,

[1] Arthur Severn's Memoirs (unpublished).

leaping and plunging when they gathered speed. Unfortunately one afternoon attention was drawn to them when it caught in a railway bridge – they lost it and were forbidden to make another. Arthur was very taken by Egidia. Mary had painted a portrait of Lady Mary and two charming sketches of her great-niece. When no one was looking Arthur made a careful tracing of one of the sketches of his playmate, and took it back to London with him. He kept it carefully in a drawer and sometimes took it out of its wrappings to look at it, as though it was something sacred. They wrote to each other for a time, but gradually the correspondence petered out.

After a short stay in London Mary was off again, but this time Arthur could not accompany her, as he had begun the term at Westminster. He found his gift for drawing was a great asset at every school. In Paris the French boys had treated his talent with respect. A sketch which he had made in sepia of a ship with its sails filled with wind, had been passed round the classroom and each boy after inspecting it had turned to him, smiling, and bowed. At Westminister art was treated with less reverence, but he still found it a great advantage to be able to draw well. He was often let off fagging to do a portrait, and caricatures of the masters were in great demand.

In those days the boys at the school played football in Dean's Yard and in summer-time rowed on the river. They had races from Westminster to Battersea and often got in the way of the penny steamers – paddle-boats which plied from pier to pier along the Thames. Arthur loved anything to do with boats, but he often lost all sense of time when he saw something that he longed to paint. Once he lingered to look at the evening sky behind Parliament when, carrying his oar, he should have been taking his place in the second Eight. A friend, Henry Russell, called out, 'Look at that old madman,' and the name stuck. Years afterwards Arthur recalled the incident and commented: 'Boys are not supposed to look at sunsets.'

Meanwhile Mary had been to Eton to stay with a house-master, the Rev. Wharton Marriott, who wished her to do portraits of several boys who were leaving his house. This time she took Eleanor with her. While Mary was busy with her painting, Eleanor wrote long letters to Mama to keep her informed of their doings, and played with the little Marriott children.

Mama, living in the small London house with Papa and Arthur, looked forward to those lively letters from her youngest daughter, whose spelling since her stay in Paris showed a strong French influence. First she heard about Mary's sitters – two sons of Sir Charles Wood. 'Wood Majeure' often went up to Windsor to ride with the Prince of Wales. He was so handsome and gentleman-like that Eleanor found it 'quite a pleasure to talk to him'. There were descriptions of their life at Eton and prayers with the boys morning and evening. 'Sixty-six eyes upon one. Rather nervous work.'

Then she heard that young Dugdale Astley, son of Mama's friend, Sir Thomas Astley, had been to see them several times. He was a Guards officer who had fought in the Crimea, and now was stationed at Windsor. He had invited Mary and Eleanor to the Castle for a theatrical performance. Mama's optimistic heart rose at the news. She knew that Dugdale was fond of her daughter, although Mary had seemed determined not to notice it. So was Tom Richmond, but she treated him like a brother.

Mama was delighted that Mary was doing so well with her painting, but she would feel much safer about her — and about Eleanor — if she were happily married. Their father had made so little money lately. What would become of them if anything were to happen to her or to Lord Eglinton? Mary never spoke of marriage, though she must have a romantic nature — her copies of Tennyson and Keats, with passages marked and underlined, were a family joke and drew many acid comments from Walter, who preferred facts, science and Darwin.

Then startling news came from Eleanor. Mary was painting the Queen's mother, the Duchess of Kent, at Frogmore. Scarcely had the excitement of this announcement subsided in the family, when an even greater event was foreshadowed.

'Mary is very busy,' wrote Eleanor, 'so I am going to write you an eloquent letter. Mary received a command from a cabman, in the shape of Lady Augusta Bruce, which will take her to Court today at 3.30 to see the QUEEN. Fancy!!! This morning we had risen from our morning slumbers and Mary was taking her bath when lo and behold, a tap on the door and Mary the Maid brought THE summons. It ran thus:

'"H.R.H. would like you to come at 3 p.m. and the Queen will be here at 3.30 p.m. to look at H.R.H's portrait and H.R.H. would like you to be present when Her Majesty is here."

'Thus ran the elegant and acceptable epistle of Lady Augusta, and my dear sister Mary Hann is to go to Frogmore today to be present at the looking of the Queen at her August Mother's portrait. Next piece of business I have to make known is that we can't come home on Saturday because Mrs Marriott is actually going to give a party on purpose for us. By the bye, I think you will be pleased to hear that *Dugdale* came here yesterday or the day before, I forget which.'[1]

The Queen came to Frogmore, and another Royal commission was given. Mary was to do a sketch of the Prince of Wales, a fair-haired boy of sixteen, with large blue eyes, whom she had already met at Frogmore. She wrote to her mother two weeks later:

'I had such a pleasant visit from Papa today. He was really pleased with my Duchess. I want you to see the drawing, as it is one of my best.

'I must tell you about the Prince's picture. You must know that I've been sadly hurried, for he went away, and just when you know all the important touches come at the last sitting I had to hurry so over it that I almost felt inclined to give it up! And then feeling this was *the* picture of all others I wanted

---

[1] 26th October, 1857. In possession of author.

to do well made me quite nervous, but he was so kind and gave me an hour's sitting on Saturday and Monday, but had to sit with his watch in his hand because he had to go to a Funeral at eleven. . . . How I shall like you to see him — only I think you will agree with me that my picture does him so little justice and has not got his good honest look, but still, considering all, I hope it will come like. I shall ask to show it to the Queen, and if I see she likes it, I'll make a real point about his sitting in London, but how I wish I could draw him again.

'Mr Coleridge thinks my prices so much too low. He told me just now that I ought to say twenty guineas decidedly for H.R.H., but ten guineas for the Prince as it is only a sketch. The Prince and I had a long conversation about Prices. He said that that awful sketch Rose did of him cost *Seventy Guineas*. "I wish I had half the money," he said, "that they (the Royal Family) spend a year in portraits." He says it's their Mania.'[1]

The Queen was pleased with the sketch of the Prince and, hearing from Lady Augusta that Mary had done a charming little picture of the baby Prince Imperial, she requested her to paint Princess Beatrice, who was just eight months old.

Mary moved to the White Hart Hotel at Windsor, conveniently near to the Castle, and took Arthur with her as a companion. From here she wrote:

'My dear Mama, — I have just returned from the Castle. I went at 9 a.m. this morning and finished my lovely Princess, but as I did it on that "crust of bread" paper, I could not make it as like as I should like, and told the Queen (for I saw her again for so long) that I could make a drawing of the Princess *her image*, so the Queen said I might do what I liked, and leave that one as it was, for she liked it so much, and do another on white paper. I could have jumped, I was so pleased at this for I must do *one* good, just to let them see what I can do. . . . So I said I was going to stay at Windsor, and if the Queen would let me go and draw in the nursery — which was at once granted! I believe it was such a thing my asking to go up *there*, as *no* stranger, not even the ladies in waiting, ever go there — it is such a sanctum — so don't tell anyone. But fancy, there I sat, and the little Princes were *quite charmed*. I drew pictures for them and they only want me to go again. They are so handsome and so gentlemanlike. I can't tell you how I like everyone at the Castle. As for the Princesses they are the nicest girls I ever saw. They took me to their room and made me sit down and look at pictures, and when the Princess Royal regretted I could not see one at Osborne, the Princess Alice said, "O but some day she *will* see it." And they always put their arms round me and they asked why I had a Scotch accent so I told them about you, and I think they were all the nicer.'[2]

She wrote again the next day:

'. . . I couldn't go to my little Royal Baby till half-past two and when I went I found the Queen had sent to see my sketch, and said she would so much have

[1] 15th November, 1857. In possession of author.
[2] 30th December, 1857. In possession of author.

liked a different view, for I'd done the same view as the *first* one, and that she wished so much for a front face, so I at once did it over again. But the Baby had slept and was cross, so I could only do so little and I am afraid it won't be able to sit tomorrow (New Year's Day) and if so I can't finish till Saturday, but whatever I do, don't you think I am right to do all to please the Queen, and also to do a *good* portrait of this Baby? and Lady Augusta said it would lead to my doing the other children. The Queen looked at Walter's drawings but said nothing.

'Little Prince Leopold, five years old — said, "I wish you would draw a lady drawing you." And fancy the Queen sent me word, when I was in the Princesses' room, whether it would be the same to me whether I would go to the Audience Room (next her own room and where I draw) a little earlier as she would want the room at half-past three. But it was all so politely put — I can't even say it — her manners and all she says and does is so kind and nice — most people would only have said the room was wanted and I must come at another time.

'Fancy, I drew Monday and Tuesday in the Audience Room, a little room next the Queen's own, where the Queen sees all her Ministers and everyone I think. And the Queen sent a maid to say that if I wanted anything I was to go in *there*. This Audience room is hung with heads of the Royal Family by Gainsborough. I never saw such painting, it was so luminous.'[1]

Mary was allowed to take Arthur to the Castle and the housekeeper took a great fancy to him. She showed him piles of gold plates 'that almost looked like gold columns' and all the presents which had been given to her for Christmas by members of the Royal Family. She ended by pointing out Queen Victoria's worsted shawl which lay on the back of a sofa, and said laughingly that he had better try it on. She put it round his shoulders, Arthur wrote to his mother in awe, 'still with the warmth of Royalty in it.'

One last note came from Mary before she returned home:

'We are sorry we were not at your Dinner — but tho' my little sketch was most successful yet I want to make it quite right. I am to be at the Castle tomorrow at 9 a.m.

'I saw the nice Queen again. She really is pretty, for her manners, the way she bows, the way she moves is so graceful that this afternoon I thought her quite handsome, and if she would only sit in warm rooms she really would be better looking, but to me it seems as if she were frozen, quite *trembling* and no fires! Her hands were blue and shaking so she could hardly point to the pictures. I agree with you about beauty and warmth, and on the strength of it I bought some *brown* stockings.

'Arthur took a drive with his friend Lady Fanny[2], all over Windsor Park. He looked so nice in the Royal Carriage sitting by her. We are reading Southey's *Life of Nelson*!'

---

[1] 31st December, 1857. In possession of author.
[2] Lady Fanny Baillie.

CHAPTER 13

MR NEWTON

1858–1861

THEY WERE SITTING IN THE PARLOUR at 83a Eccleston Square. Mama had settled the family in the new house before she left for Hanover, where she had taken Eleanor to learn German. They were still away and Papa was in the country copying a Gainsborough—one of his now rare commissions.

Walter, Arthur and Mary, with her friend Mary Palliser, had been laughing too much and drawing caricatures all the evening. Now they were 'quite done up'.

Mary lay with her feet up on a sofa, her wide skirt spreading over on to the floor. Her dark, waving hair was drawn back from her smooth forehead into a net. Arthur lounged in an armchair by the fire, his legs, which were too long for his trousers, thrust out in front of him. Walter, now aged twenty-eight, stood by the table, an erect, handsome young man, very correctly dressed, with a fashionable short dark beard. Scraps of paper, covered with drawings, lay scattered about the floor.[1]

Mr Vaux, sitting quietly by the fire, told them that he had been talking to Newton at the Museum that afternoon. The discovery of the tomb of Mausolus, one of the Seven Wonders of the Ancient World, by an Englishman, Charles Newton, had created a sensation and the Press was full of it. Now he had just arrived back in England, bringing his discoveries with him for the British Museum. Newton was trying to find someone to make drawings of the marbles for his lectures, said Mr Vaux, and he had wondered whether to suggest Mary's name. Mary was full of enthusiasm. She had felt she was getting a little stale in her work lately. Since finishing her portraits of the older Princesses, she had exhibited several pictures at the Academy and had plenty of commissions, but somehow she felt dissatisfied and restless. It would be something quite new, and she would learn a great deal about Greek art.

Mr Vaux still seemed a little hesitant. Newton was rather a difficult fellow in some ways and had a sarcastic tongue. Mary pleaded with him. Her large grey-blue eyes shone. She had a most expressive face, and when she became excited she used her hands with more gestures than most Englishwomen. Perhaps it was her childhood spent among Italians that had taught her this, or perhaps it was the knowledge that it was with her hands that she could ultimately best express herself.

[1] This and other scenes in this chapter taken from Mary Severn's caricatures.

Mary Palliser begged to be allowed to come too. Mr Vaux at length agreed and appointed a time for the meeting.

★

Mary stood back from her easel and examined her work. Yes, she quite thought she had got the effect she wanted at last. It had not been easy. She looked across at Mary Palliser, who was drawing at her easel on the farther side of the big, cold room. With a frown of concentration she was trying on an enormous paper to reproduce one of the stone lions from Halicarnassus, which crouched, stood, and lay before her, most of them with at least one limb missing. The Artemis that Mary herself had been working on for so many hours was without a nose.

She smiled as she thought of the shock they had both had when the intimidating Mr Newton had led them into this room. She had been elated that he was going to give her a chance to show what she could do, but her heart had sunk as she looked around her. Lions' heads without bodies, lions' bodies without legs, gods without heads, goddesses with shattered arms, a headless horse with only the legs of a rider still gripping its body. For a moment it seemed a nightmare. But then, as they moved slowly round the room, she looked more into the detail of the work and was astonished by its perfection. Mary Palliser, less knowledgeable, seemed bewildered.

Mr Newton had not spoken much as he had led them round. Sometimes he stopped to point out some particular statue, or to conjecture the rightful place of some almost unrecognizable fragment. Mary glanced sideways at him. He still looked as forbidding as when Mr Vaux had first introduced them to him. Such a noble face. He was quite like a Greek god himself — the stern profile, the firm mouth, even his hair and beard seemed to grow in sculptural form. She would like to draw him. Suddenly she found his penetrating dark eyes turned on her and looked away in confusion. Her glance lighted on a female statue, and she made one of her graceful gestures, asking whom it represented. His face lit up and he leaned over to stroke the marble cheek with his long-fingered hand — like a Van Dyck's, thought Mary.

'The public don't deserve to see my Artemis,' he said in his deep voice. 'They don't appreciate her beauty.'

Mary had just restrained herself from replying that it wasn't surprising as the poor creature had no nose or mouth — only a chin, but that stern face did not encourage flippancy. She had been thankful that she had not spoken, since she had heard his caustic tongue at work on other people.

The door opened and he came in. He was tall and held himself well. He was forty years old and his body was spare and strong. With his stern face and unconscious air of distinction the whole impression given was one of austerity, until you noticed the rather grim lines of humour round the mouth and piercing eyes. He came straight over to Mary, who drew back in silence to let him see her drawing. He stood for several minutes in front of it, his elbows out, his long hands clasped in front of him. His back was turned to her so that she could not see his face. She felt her heart beating as she waited for his judgment. She would so like to do the other drawings. She *knew* that she could do them well. He turned.

'I congratulate you, Miss Severn,' he said, in a harsh voice that sounded anything but congratulatory.

Mary smiled at him in relief and pleasure. When she smiled her big eyes shone, and her expression of sweetness and friendliness was almost irresistible. Mr Newton's eyes searched her face.

'I should like you to begin work here at the same time tomorrow morning,' he said gruffly. 'Is that convenient?'

'Oh, *quite* convenient, thank you, Mr Newton.'

'Good. And your friend will accompany you?' He made a gesture towards Mary Palliser, who was still concentrating on her drawing, trying desperately to improve it before this frightening man should see it.

'Oh, yes, she would be very pleased.'

He strode over to the other easel. Again there was a silence while he gazed at Mary Palliser's lions.

'Humph. One would think these were drawings for Punch,' he grunted sardonically, and, with a brief 'Good-day' to poor Miss Palliser, he left the room.

He was not always so abrupt. He did not make friends easily, he mistrusted the other sex. But there was something peculiarly winning about Mary's simplicity of manner and her enthusiasm for learning and he found that she had read widely. He came to inspect their work every day, and sometimes he would stay to talk.

Mary loved to listen to him. He knew so much. She sat as a disciple at his feet while he talked about Greek Art, about the Athenian Empire in the days of Pericles, and the immortal work of Pheidias. As their friendship matured he talked of more personal subjects. She learned that, after he had graduated at Christ Church, he had taken the post of Assistant to the Antiquities Department at the British Museum, 'where they had classical, Oriental and Medieval objects all jumbled together in one department, and no single classical archaeologist among the officers'. He broke off to scowl over this unsatisfactory state of affairs, which was still no better. They would have to alter it soon.

After twelve years in London, he had become Vice-Consul at Mitylene, so that he could explore the islands and coasts of Asia Minor. He had found inscriptions on the island of Calymnos and then he had declined the Regius Professorship of Greek at Oxford, so that he might continue his search for fragments of a past civilization. The next year, 1856, he had discovered the Mausoleum at Halicarnassus. It had taken nearly two years to disinter the whole colossal tomb.

Mary came to look forward eagerly to these talks. Usually he stood by her easel, or paced up and down as he talked. Sometimes Mary Palliser came over from the other side of the big, draughty room, picking her way between all the unidentified fragments that lay about the floor waiting for restoration.

Sometimes they would help Mr Newton in his well-nigh impossible task of fitting them together. Mary, pointing to a fragment, would cry helpfully, 'Don't you think it looks like a horse's tail?' 'No,' would come the uncompromising reply. 'I am thinking it is undoubtedly a lion's neck!'

Another day he suddenly decided that drawing from the antique should be done from touch. Both girls had to climb on ladders, which they propped against the bigger statues, in order to feel the features with their hands.

They stood on tiptoe, looking strangely out of place beside those grey stones shaped two thousand years ago, with their wide skirts and tiny waists, and their smooth hair drawn back into little knots at the napes of their necks. Below them Mr Newton stood, as always fastidiously dressed, his beard jutting, his dark eyes alight, his long Van Dyck hands gesturing to show them what he wanted.

Another day Mary brought some clay to the Museum and thought she would try her hand at modelling one of the friezes. She looked up to find the saturnine Mr Newton standing by her side.

'Do look, Mr Newton,' she cried. 'Haven't I got on well?'

'A very tolerable mud pie,' replied Mr Newton dampingly.

She was not hurt by his cutting remarks. She was used to criticism from her brothers. She knew that he did not mean them to hurt and that they were due to his naturally sardonic turn of humour; she even wondered sometimes if they might not cover an unexpectedly sensitive nature.

Then he called one evening at Eccleston Square. He had come to talk over some work with Mary, he said. There did not seem to be anything very important in what he had to say to her, but he was soon on good terms with her family. He seemed charmed by Papa's easy geniality. He discussed Darwin with Walter, and smiled when he heard of the argument, lasting into the small hours, between Walter and Mary, which had been started by Mary incautiously asserting that Beauty was Truth. As they talked, Mary felt conscious for the first time of the idiosyncrasies of her family. She had never given them a thought before, had just accepted them as part of her happy world, but now that Mr Newton's piercing eyes were scrutinizing them, she felt afraid of what sardonic judgment might be forming in his mind.

However, he could not have disliked them, because he accepted Papa's invitation to dine with them one night. They were all on their best behaviour. Mary wore her new muslin dress and a gold net on her dark hair. To her relief, Mr Newton never once made one of his biting comments.

One morning, not long afterwards, she was drawing at the Museum. She was pleased with the last few drawings she had done. They were bold and masterly, and she had got her effects with the smallest possible amount of detail. For once she was alone. Mary Palliser, who usually worked with her (partly because she loved drawing and partly to make Mary's position more *convenable*), was away from London. Sometimes her friend, Gertrude Jekyll, 'a good creature and so willing', would accompany her, or on rarer occasions John Ruskin. Today it was Arthur who had come with her to the Museum, but he had suddenly abandoned his drawing and gone off to look for Mr Vaux; scarcely had he left when Mr Newton entered and took up his stand beside her, watching her at work. He was looking very gloomy.

After standing for a few minutes in silence, he said abruptly that he had to leave England almost immediately. He must go back to Greece. Mary was taken by surprise. She raised her startled face to his, and tears that surprised even herself brightened her grey eyes. The rather harsh lines round his mouth softened. His face blurred above her and drew suddenly nearer as he stooped and kissed her.

She smoothed her dark hair and smiled up at him. He frowned back.

'When will you marry me?' he asked abruptly.

All her happiness suddenly dropped away from her. How could she marry? Papa made so little money, and although Walter had a good position he was not very highly paid. She was the bread-winner of the family. It was the money she made from her work that enabled them to live in Eccleston Square, and to send Arthur to school, while Mama, with her allowance from Lord Eglinton, stayed in Hanover with Eleanor. She could not desert them, especially dear Mama, who relied on her so completely. She tried to explain all this to him. She was afraid he would be impatient, but he took her hands gently in his and said,

'If I believed in God I should think you were an angel.'

She did not quite realize the second half of what he said until later.

'Oh, but don't you?' she asked, distressed. 'Believe in God, I mean?'

'I believe only what I can prove to be true.'

Mary sighed. She did not want to spoil this moment she would always remember by arguing with him. All their ideas seemed to be at variance with each other. He despised her beloved Keats and Tennyson. She hated the idea of a life bounded by facts. She said she must go home. He did not try to stop her, but he raised her hand to his lips as they parted, and as she looked down at the thick curling hair on the head that was bowed over her hand, she knew that it didn't signify if his beliefs were different from hers on every subject under the sun, she would still love him, and only him, until she died.

*

He wrote to her often from Greece; letters and poems, too. Mary kept them carefully hidden away in her bedroom and would spend her evenings there, taking them all out to read. His letters were beautifully expressed. They were learned, affectionate, lover-like. Mary, sitting on the bedroom floor — her dress a dark pool round her — would glow with happiness as she read. How lovely she had looked with that gold net on her dark hair, how beautiful she was, how slender, how graceful. It was really extraordinary that he should remember the colour of her dresses, and she loved to hear in which he had most admired her.

She wrote him back long, racy letters illustrated by little drawings. She described her life, and the work she was doing, the people she met and talked with, hitting off their characters by a few words of dialogue inserted, bringing the whole atmosphere in which she lived before him, and assuring him in simple, glowing words of her love for him.

Their devotion to each other seemed to intensify rather than diminish with separation, although their letters made clear how different were their conceptions of life and art. It was a clash between the Romantic Spirit and the Classical. But whereas she did not want her Philosopher, as she called him, to change in any way, he was determined that she should learn more of the true principles of ancient Greek art, and was convinced that then she would cast aside her inferior gods. He told her frequently that it was her personality that had attracted him, and not her art. He disapproved of George Richmond's influence. He wanted her to cease portrait-painting in water-colours, and to do more work in oils.

Eager though she was to please him, this last was at the moment more than she could promise. It was by her portraits in water-colour and crayon that she was well known. She had painted the Queen's children in these media. She had exhibited at the Academy in three different years (on the last occasion *The Times* had even proclaimed with avuncular jocularity that Miss Severn deserved to be made an R.A. herself). She could get as many commissions now as she wanted, while Papa had almost none. But this criticism from one she loved so much was very disturbing.

Mama noticed it at once when she returned from Hanover with Eleanor. Mary did not concentrate on her painting as she used to. She would leave her easel suddenly, to come and sit on the floor at her mother's feet. Mama would go on with her sewing while Mary, with her palette forgotten in her hand, would talk about Greek Art and Mausolus, until they were interrupted by Eleanor dashing in to say she would be late for her music-lesson, or Claudia come to beg Mary's help with the children that afternoon.

Mr Newton had been back to England once – for a short visit when he had just been appointed British Consul in Rome. That was a few weeks before Mama's return. Although he was necessarily very busy, he had spent a good many hours at Eccleston Square. There had been many happy evenings. By this time all the Severn family were taking a proprietorial interest in everything to do with Halicarnassus, and they attended in a body the lecture which Newton gave on the Mausoleum, which was illustrated by Mary's drawings.

There were other, less formal evenings. One picture Mary remembered of him, in the drawing-room at Eccleston Square, seated by the fire, elegant and unmoved, while the Severns disputed who could draw the best caricature of him. A competition followed. Arthur's picture was entitled 'The Lecture, 14th Nov. 1859. The lecture comes off at last! Great exhibition of diagrams! Astonishment of the British Public!' and showed Mr Newton lecturing from a platform to a crowded auditorium, with a long stick ready to point to Mary's drawings, which were hung round the room.

Papa drew him in almost the same attitude as his posthumous portrait of Shelley at the Baths of Caracalla. Mr Newton was shown gazing over Rome, an unrolled scroll in one hand. Papa wrote across the top: ' "Othello's occupation gone." Mr Newton at Rome, cogitates how he can change the Castle of St Angelo into the Mausoleum of Halicarnassus.' Mary drew him in a chariot drawn by lions, behind him a signpost 'From London to Rome.'

Mr Newton remained unperturbed in the midst of their excitement. Occasionally he made some ironical comment, but for the most part he preferred to gaze into the fire, his long legs crossed, his shapely hands folded across his chest, his head bowed, until the drawings were shown to him, when he could give full vent to his talent for sarcastic criticism.

In spite of these moments, the visit had not been a very happy one. Whenever he and Mary were left alone he would urge her to marry him at once. Did she not love him? It had been agony for her to rouse his anger. But she could not desert her family, when they needed her so much. In a few days his visit had ended, and to her relief, Charles Newton's letters from Rome showed that in his heart he realized the difficulties of her position. He told her how he had wandered about the haunts of her childhood, and had been to see the house where she had once lived in Rome.

*

Eleanor was sitting to Mary. It was June 1860. Outside the sun blazed down on the dusty London streets.

'Oh, Mary, cannot we go out for a little? The room is so stuffy, and it would be lovely by the water in St James's Park.'

'I must just finish this hand,' said her sister absently, her eyes on her work.

There was a knock at the door and they both turned as the maid looked in.

'Mr Newton from Rome in the drawing-room,' she said and shut the door.

Mary's palette fell to the ground with a clatter. The brush followed it, as she threw open the door and sped down the stairs, her skirt flying out behind. Eleanor followed more slowly. From the top of the stair, she saw Mary pause for a moment at the mirror outside the drawing room, to smooth her hair with nervous fingers, before she darted through the open door into the drawing-room.

Eleanor went slowly down the stairs. She wanted to see this Mr Newton. Mary had known him while she and Mama were away, and she said he was 'a very nice person'. When she came into the drawing-room they were standing together by the window, not speaking, but gazing at each other. Mr Newton was tall and *very* distinguished-looking, thought Eleanor, as her sister introduced them to each other. Then Mama came and was introduced too, and soon afterwards Eleanor had to leave, because she had promised to spend the day with Claudia and her children.[1]

When she returned that evening, Mama told her that Mary was going next day to Bredwardine in Herefordshire, to stay with Mrs Newton, her friend's

[1] Eleanor Severn's Diary.

mother. Mr Charles Newton would be there too. Mama did not add that she
had told her daughter and Mr Newton that she saw no reason why they should
not be engaged, and though the position *was* a little difficult at the moment,
something would be sure to 'turn up'. Then Mr Newton had explained his plan.
They were reorganizing the Antiquities Department at the British Museum and
dividing it into several different branches. He would try to get the position of
Keeper of the Greek and Roman section. He would then do his utmost to get
Mr Severn appointed British Consul in Rome in his place.

Mama was all enthusiasm for this scheme. Severn spoke Italian just as well as
English, and he knew so many people in Rome. What a good idea! How kind
of Mr Newton to suggest it! One look at Mary's radiant face had been enough
to assure her mother of her happiness.

Next morning Mary left for Bredwardine, and the morning after came a
note for Papa, asking his permission for Mr Charles Newton to marry his
daughter, Mary. They were engaged at last.

Oh, those long walks in Herefordshire in summer! The hills and the orchards
and the blue sky! Heaven must be like this, thought Mary blissfully.

Two of the Severn family were missing from the usual big Christmas party
at the Richmonds'. Young Thomas Richmond looked in vain for Mary, who
was spending Christmas with old Mrs Newton in Herefordshire. Claudia was
not there either, because her little boy had died a few days before. She was left
with three little girls, and was already expecting another baby in the spring. Mr
Newton arrived back in London soon after the New Year. The first part of
his plan had been achieved. He had been appointed Keeper of the Greek and
Roman section of the Antiquities Department in the British Museum. Now he
was determined to do everything possible to ensure that Mr Severn should be
his successor in Rome.

Severn, too, left no influential friend unapproached. He was 'a candidate for
the Consulship at Rome,' he wrote, 'about to be vacated by Mr Charles
"Mausoleum" Newton (who is about to become my son-in-law).'[1] Mr Gladstone spoke in his favour and Ruskin wrote about his suitability for the post:

'What testimonial can I offer to you, that will not be a thousand-fold out-
testified by the consent of all who know you, and who knew, in those old times
of happy dwelling in the ruinous Immortality of Rome: where English and
Italians alike used always to think of Mr Severn as a gleam of living sunshine
which set at one, and melted into golden fellowship, all comfortless shadows
and separations of society or of heart. . . . As I cannot fancy anything pleasanter
for English people at Rome than to have you for Consul, so I can fancy nothing
more profitable for English people at home than that your zeal and judgment
should be on the watch for straying treasures as in these changeable times may
be obtainable of otherwise unhoped for Italian art. . . .

J. RUSKIN.'[2]

[1] To Monckton Milnes, 22nd October, 1860.
[2] Sharp, op. cit., p. 218.

Baron Bunsen, that faithful friend of Roman days, wrote from his death-bed to Lord John Russell, the Prime Minister:

'I have no hesitation in recommending to your kind notice Mr Joseph Severn, who I understand is anxious to obtain the British Consulship, now vacant, at Rome. I believe Mr Gladstone has already given him a warm testimonial, but having known Mr Severn for many years at Rome I can testify to his peculiar fitness as Consul there, for during the years he spent at Rome he made himself universally useful and popular among the English residents.... From his intimate knowledge of Italian affairs and his social relations with Romans of all classes, I should also consider him as very likely to be useful to your diplomatic agents. ... '[1]

On 30th January, Mama was reading to Eleanor when Papa walked in.

'You will be glad to hear that I'm appointed Consul at Rome!'[2]

He was full of joy. A great longing had come over him to be back in Italy. His children had been educated. The *Life of Keats* had appeared, with the hitherto unpublished poems. 'I think I shall be among the English poets after my death,' Keats had written, a few days before his twenty-third birthday. Now, nearly forty years after his death, his friend had lived to see his name among the greatest of English poets.

Joseph's four eldest children were all well settled in secure positions. Only the twins would be living at home when Mary had married. He longed to return to Rome, the city of his prosperity and his youth, with Elizabeth by his side, and to resume life *da capo* in Italy. The Consul's salary was certainly not large, but at least it was assured, and he had faced the fact that, although he loved his 'darling painting' as much as ever, fashion had outstripped him and left him far behind.

Although no one would have guessed it from his youthful appearance, he was now sixty-seven years old. He was active and upright, though rather plump; his face was youthful, his hair unflecked with grey, but this matter of his age was very worrying. There was a rule at the Foreign Office that no Consul, on his first appointment, should be more than fifty years of age. As Joseph airily remarked, he was 'just on the wrong side of it', but fortunately his extraordinarily youthful appearance had prevented the authorities from suspecting it.

Fearful lest any delay should allow them to discover his secret, Severn had a few days' instruction in his duties from Mr Newton, and set out in less than a fortnight for Rome. Mama accompanied him as far as Folkestone. They stayed there together for two days, and then Joseph crossed the Channel, pleased as a boy to be carrying despatches and a diplomatic passport. Mama must stay behind until Mary was married, and their affairs in London settled. In any case, her health had been bad lately, and it would be better for her to follow by easy stages. She could bring the twins and a few of their best pieces of furniture with her. Papa would travel light.

[1] Sharp, op. cit., p. 216.
[2] Eleanor Severn's Diary.

CHAPTER 14

BRITISH CONSUL

1861 – 1862

HOW HAPPY HE WAS TO BE BACK IN ROME, to pick up old friendships (John Gibson was still there, as he had been on Joseph's first arrival in Rome, and many more old friends), to find himself again a figure of importance, to hear the Italian rolling off his tongue as easily as though he had never been away. The clear air and the brilliant sunshine refreshed his spirit after the murkiness of London. The flower-stalls were banked high in the Piazza di Spagna, as they had been that evening when he and John Keats had driven into Rome in their little carriage forty years before. The sound of chanting voices drifted down from the church above, and he rejoiced to hear again the splash of fountains, as he wandered through the streets.

One of his first thoughts was to visit Keats's grave. He was no longer a solitary mourner, but only one of hundreds who came to stand reverently by that honoured plot. The *custode* complained that the flowers planted on Keats's grave were constantly picked by the visitors. Joseph felt only a quiet exultation as he stood in the old burial-ground, but even now he could not pass the house in the Piazza di Spagna, where Keats had died in his arms, without 'a throb at his heart'.

A man of less buoyant temperament would have been appalled at the difficulties of his position in Rome. During the time of Joseph's stay in England, the provinces of central Italy had been united under Victor Emmanuel. Only five months before Joseph arrived Garibaldi had seized the Kingdom of Naples, and the whole of southern Italy and Sicily had been annexed to the new Kingdom of Italy. At the same time Italian troops had invaded the Papal States, and only a small strip of land round Rome was left to the Pope. Had it not been for the French garrison that Napoleon III maintained in Rome, the capital would have fallen too. The Emperor himself sympathized with Italian aspirations but he needed support at home from the French Catholics.

The very air reeked of intrigue, of plot and counter-plot. The Inquisition was at work, and a man could be sent for five years to the galleys for failing to remove his hat in church. The sinister Cardinal Antonelli was Pope in all but name.

The national feeling of frustration was increased by the behaviour of the Papal Government. Not only was its rule tyrannical and corrupt, but it gave sanctuary within its domain to all the enemies of Italy, the dispossessed Italian Dukes and the ex-King of Naples who schemed and plotted across the border. Such a state of affairs could not last long, and in the city itself the longing for freedom was no less strong for being ruthlessly suppressed.

To the Papal Government everything modern was anathema. Railways, telegraphs, vaccination, modern literature, all belonged to the nineteenth century and therefore were abhorred as working against the authority of the Church. Feeling in Rome ran high and liberal conspirators took their lives in their hands when they plotted a rising in the city. In the secret strife between them and the unyielding Church party, the few voices raised for compromise went unheeded. It was in vain they argued that the Pope's spiritual authority would not be lessened, but reinforced, if he were to relinquish voluntarily his temporal power.

The official policy of England was non-intervention. At such a troubled time Joseph was the ideal man for his position. He accepted the reactionary Papal Government for what it was, fully appreciating its lack of justice (had he not suffered from it himself?) and its conception that laws made by priests were God-given, and therefore superior to those forged by man. Equally he accepted the fact that there were men whose ideal of freedom would never allow them to remain passive under tyranny. He did not align himself with either side, but even in his first days as Consul he found that his rôle could be a useful one. His facility in the Italian tongue, his knowledge of Rome, and especially his ability to joke in their own language, helped him to soften their rancour, and often to reach some agreement in small matters between the two parties.

In March, when Joseph had been a month in Rome, Charles Newton was sent there to acquire the Castellani Collection of sculptures for the British Museum. He brought young Arthur with him, as his father had taken an apartment 'large enough for *all* the Severns'. Arthur would keep his father company, and it would make Mrs Severn's journey easier if she had only Eleanor to bring with her. As soon as he got back to London Mr Newton was besieged with enquiries about his prospective father-in-law. To Mary, who was finishing a commission in the country, he wrote, with their wedding only a few weeks distant:

'He gives a most flourishing account of himself. He seems to have taken to the Consular service as kindly as he did to the uniform.

'Arnold has sent me his three lectures on Homer which I will bring with me. Darling, do not let them keep you over Sunday. I send you many kisses.'[1]

'I am well "in the saddle",' wrote Joseph to his brother, 'I have just had four rooms with divers persons in them, all with individual affairs going on, so I went from room to room, while my secretary and my son Arthur were helping....

'My appointment has caused great envy, for there is no end of people here

[1] From Travellers' Club, 7th March, 1861. In possession of author.

who were candidates. Here all is uncertainty, no one can even guess what is to transpire. The city is full of French soldiers, every monastery is now a barracks and you see monks and soldiers shouldering each other. . . .

'Cardinal Antonelli received me most graciously and assured me how acceptable my appointment was to the whole Government. Indeed I see that everything here turns on old, old associations. So in this I stand really well. . . .

'My sole care is my dear, dear wife's health. For she has too much upon her hands now I am absent, and I regret that I did not oblige her to come with me. But the approaching marriage of my daughter made it impossible.'[1]

Joseph's wedding present to his favourite daughter was a gold brooch in the form of a Greek lyre which he had had made to his own design nearly 40 years before, 'as a present to poor Miss Brawne', the strings being made of Keats's hair. He had never given it to Fanny and knowing how Mary loved Keats's poetry he realized that she would treasure it.[2]

★

After all, Mama was not able to be at Mary's wedding, on the third of May. She had been to Folkestone to recuperate after an illness, and became unwell again a few days before the wedding, so that she could not come to London. Only two of Mary's own family were in the church, for Claudia was very ill after the birth of another baby; Eleanor was a bridesmaid, with Claudia's three little girls, and Walter gave the bride away. Mr Vaux, who had introduced Mary to Charles at the British Museum, was the best man.

It now only remained for Mama to wind up the family affairs in London, and then she and Eleanor would be ready to leave England, to travel by easy stages to Marseilles, and then by boat to Civita Vecchia and on to Rome. Mama, as always, was pleasurably excited by the thought of change. By the end of June she pronounced herself quite recovered, and returned to London. Two months were needed to arrange everything. Then they said goodbye to Walter, to Claudia, who was still convalescent, and to Mary, who had just moved into her new house in Gower Street. She was painting the dining-room walls with a frieze from the Elgin Marbles, which were now under Charles's supervision.

It was a terrible wrench for her to part with Mama and Eleanor, but they consoled themselves with plans for meetings in Rome.

The travellers were still in Dunkirk when news came that Lord Eglinton had died. Mama was terribly distressed. Not only was she very fond of her half-brother, but he had always been there for her to turn to when she was in trouble, and also she could not think how she could manage without the money he allowed her. Within a few days, however, her fears on that account were temporarily allayed, when an instalment of her allowance, which was due, was paid into her account in the usual way.

[1] To Tom, 6th April, 1861. Keats House.
[2] After Mary's death her sister Eleanor gave it to Mary Palliser. It is now at Keats House, Hampstead.

Meanwhile Papa and Arthur were living in Rome. Papa had taken an apartment of five noble rooms in the enormous Palazzo Poli, looking down on the Fountain of Trevi. Below them the water rushed over the rocks where Neptune sat in stony state, and splashed down into the great marble basin. It was like living on the edge of a waterfall — the rush of the water was with them day and night.

Unfortunately Joseph's purse did not permit him to furnish the large rooms of the palazzo. 'As yet only two rooms are habitable,' he wrote to his sister in November, 'my office and my sitting-room. But the grandeur of the rooms carries the day and does not permit anything really modern, for the Palace is in the old style, so I pick up old carved things at sales. How you'd be amused to see me at dinner with Arthur, in a large saloon thirty-two feet square and twenty-eight feet high, with nothing in it but ourselves and the dinner! The first night I awoke in the night and coughed, and was frightened at the deep echo through the empty rooms, for I had left the door open!'[1]

On 13th December Mama and Eleanor arrived at Marseilles, where Mama was taken ill again. Severn was longing for his wife to join him. 'I am at a loss without her, for in the difficult things I have to do her clever Scotch head would greatly help me.'

Walter came out to Rome at the end of December, spending a few days with Eleanor and Mama on the way. It was the Season in Rome, and Walter and Arthur enjoyed what gaieties there were to the full. Joseph did not think much of them, compared to the brilliance of the Roman Season when he was a young man, but he enjoyed wearing his full-dress uniform to the Ball at the French Embassy. 'I took my two sons — I went in full uniform with my sword and hat, and it was a pleasure to me that the French soldiers presented arms to me. . . . My two boys have danced most of the flesh off their bones,' he reported, 'but by day they have drawn admirably.'[2]

Ill as she was, Mama was still full of plans for the benefit of her family. How fortunate it would be if Walter were to marry Miss Arbuthnot, an heiress whom Mary had known in Ireland, and who was luckily spending the winter in Rome. Arthur sent her all the news.

'We have been to one rather splendid Ball at the house of an American banker, and he had all the best of the Italian society and Walter immediately got introduced to half a dozen Contessas and Marchesas all covered with jewels. Walter speaks Italian so very well and everybody likes him so much.

'People in shops are delighted when he (stroking his beard) tells them, "Io sono romano, sono nato qui a Roma." I will keep Walter up to Miss Arbuthnot, and if not to Miss Leigh Smyth who is such a nice person and a most splendid rider.'

But, alas, Walter left Rome at the end of his holiday, without being engaged either to the heiress or the Amazon.

<hr/>

[1] To Maria, 19th November, 1861. Keats House.
[2] To Tom, Tuesday, 18th March, 1862. Keats House.

Joseph was finding that by the exercise of tact and patience he could do much good. He was able to rescue his secretary's brother from prison in Rome by tactful handling of the Papal authorities, and got him a position on the Naples railway through his influence with the Government of Italy. By the autumn he could point with pride to nearly forty similar cases.

Unruffled, he went to and fro between the two parties, always serene, affable, ready with a joke, mediating between bitter opponents, pleading for moderation if not understanding. His leisure moments he spent at his easel. But he was grateful that he had not returned to Rome only for his painting, 'for all the fine arts are for the moment at a standstill . . . and the artists are complaining bitterly of "no coms" '.[1]

Anxiously he waited to hear that his wife had recovered and was continuing her journey. But the news from Marseilles was not encouraging. Elizabeth wrote to her husband in March that she was still too weak to be able to turn over in bed. But she said cheerfully that she had heard of some wonderful baths near Geneva which might completely cure her. What worried her most was the expense of her illness. Their financial outlook had seemed so much more promising, if they could have lived quietly with the twins in Rome. Now her illness was costing a guinea a day and they were not even together. How ever would they find the money? Joseph could not tell her. He could only hope that 'something may turn up'.

To add to their unhappiness, he dared not leave Rome to go to her. With the unforeseen expense of his wife's illness, he must at all costs keep his position as Consul.

Mama wrote anxiously that the apartment in the Palazzo Poli sounded rather too large for them. Arthur replied:

'All you say about a *small* house is of course quite right. I laughed so much at that part of your letter when you say that a *cottage* is better than a large dirty house. I could hear you say *dirty house* quite plain, as if you had been speaking to me in your Scotch accent.'

*

Then, suddenly, the telegram came. Joseph was wakened at midnight to receive it. It was from Eleanor. Mama was dying. Would Papa come *at once*. He threw a few things into a little trunk. His poor dear Eliza, so far from him. He should never have left her behind. Surely the doctors must be mistaken. She *must* get well. He needed her so much.

He was ready to start by dawn. He took his passport to the police, for it must be signed by them or he would be turned back at Civita Vecchia. The inefficiency of the Roman administration was brought home to him then in the most painful way. For twenty-four hours he stormed, cajoled, pleaded to be allowed his passport. Nothing would hurry them. At last, almost distraught, he got it

[1] To Maria, 30th April, 1861. Keats House.

back. It had taken them a day and a half to have one signature affixed to it. He
rushed to Civita Vecchia and boarded the first boat to Marseilles.

In the Hôtel des Bains des Catalans at Marseilles Mama lay dying. Eleanor sat
at her bedside, her young face pale and haggard. She was nineteen years old.
If only Papa would come. She was alone. The doctor, the English clergyman,
and the wife of the British Consul were her only friends in Marseilles. Mary
and Charles had been there for several days only a fortnight before, but no one
had realized then how serious Mama's illness was. Now it was only a question
of how long, the doctor said. If only Papa would come in time.

The nights were so long. Eleanor scarcely dared to leave her mother. She
was so afraid that she would die alone. When Mama could speak she asked if
Papa were there, and Eleanor could only shake her head, with tears in her eyes,
and say that he was coming very soon. The tired white eyelids dropped again
over the blue eyes.

Soon she was too weak to speak. Eleanor sat by her side for hour after hour,
running to the window whenever she heard the wheels of a carriage, scanning
the sea for the boat from Italy. At her lowest moment, she took her pencil and a
scrap of paper and painfully sketched her mother's profile — her thin, sharp face
under the white cap. She sat there through the night and drew her dying
mother, just as, forty-one years before, her father had sat by Keats's bedside, in
the house in Rome, and drawn him, with the damp hair clinging to his brow.

★

Joseph arrived too late. His wife had died the day before. If the passport had
not delayed him he would have been in time — in time to speak to her, to hold
her hand, to comfort her. How cruel, thought Joseph, overcome by misery.
If he had known there was no hope he could have brought her on to Rome, to a
house of her own — and to him. But the doctors had deceived them all with false
hopes. They said that the journey to Rome might impede her recovery. Thank
God that Eleanor was with her. To die, alone, in a hotel in a foreign land — that
would have been too dreadful. If only he had insisted on her coming out to
Rome with him at the beginning. 'Then I would not have been cut off from the
last precious days of our thirty-four years of anxious life.'[1]

All his energies had been concentrated on getting to Marseilles in time to see
her, to speak words of affection and comfort. Now he had arrived too late. She
was already buried. He had not even seen her face again. He felt limp and
empty. The one purpose that had filled his whole mind, since the moment he
had received that telegram in Rome, had gone. He roused himself when
Frederick Gale, who had arrived the day before him, came to talk to him about
Eleanor. Claudia wanted him to take her back to England to live with them,
at any rate for a time, until she had got over the shock of her mother's death.

[1] To Maria, 12th June, 1862. Keats House.

She would be with her two sisters. Her mother had whispered, before she died, that this was what she wished.

Joseph agreed miserably that it would be best. Then they discussed money. He had sent his wife £60 in January, but the hotel and doctor's bills amounted to £240 and by French law there was a further fine of 1000 francs (about £40) because poor Mama had died in a hotel. Joseph nodded dumb agreement to all his son-in-law's proposals about ways to pay this debt. Then Gale said briskly that there was no point in waiting about in Marseilles. He would arrange to leave with Eleanor next day.

It was Easter Sunday. She had been dead for three days now. The whole journey had been a nightmare. He couldn't believe that it was true. All that day he spent on the boat which was carrying him back to Rome. The tranquil Mediterranean lapped placidly round him under an April sky, as he sat on deck and wrote about her. He wrote down all his memories of her. Her beauty, her humour and her ready kindliness. What a wonderful mother she had been, untiring in her care, and what a loyal, courageous wife. He wrote about her as a beautiful girl, as a young mother playing with her children among the scarlet anemones in the gardens of the Pamphili Doria, as a brave resourceful wife in times of trouble.[1]

So he sat and wrote about her, while the tears ran down his cheeks and the blue sea slipped past in a slow stream, silent as Time itself.

Fortunately when he got back to Rome there was a great deal of work for him to do. It comforted him to fill every minute of the day, and his energy, for a man of sixty-eight, was astonishing. He was generally supposed to be about fifty, and in appearance and in vigour he was certainly no more. It gave him a childish pleasure when people asked him, as they often did, about 'his father and Keats'.

A letter came to him at the beginning of May, which did much to cheer him. It was an official letter of thanks from General Durando, the Foreign Minister of Italy, writing from Turin. Joseph sent the original to Lord Russell, the British Foreign Secretary, together with an English translation.

He sent another copy to his brother, explaining, 'The Foreign Minister was thanking me for my services in liberating upwards of fifty-five of His Majesty's subjects from the Roman prisons, which you must understand I have not done officially, but solely by good-natured intercessions with the Roman Minister and trying to "fascinate them off their feet!" '

This was Joseph's way. He knew just how to handle the Roman officials. He was on the best of terms with them all, and through his personal relationship with them, he was able to get concessions which they would never have granted to him as an official.

He used his influence when the Prince of Wales and the Princess Royal came to Rome.

[1] To Tom, 2nd May, 1862. Keats House.

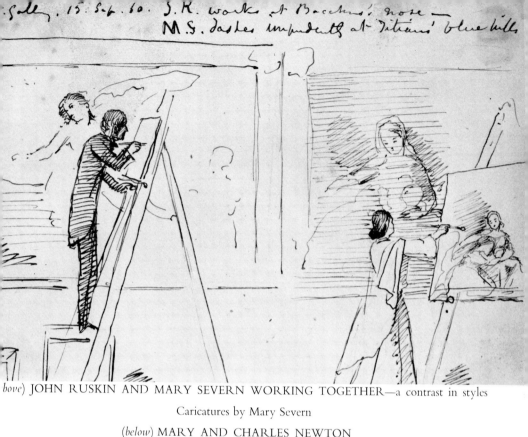

(*bove*) JOHN RUSKIN AND MARY SEVERN WORKING TOGETHER—a contrast in styles

Caricatures by Mary Severn

(*below*) MARY AND CHARLES NEWTON

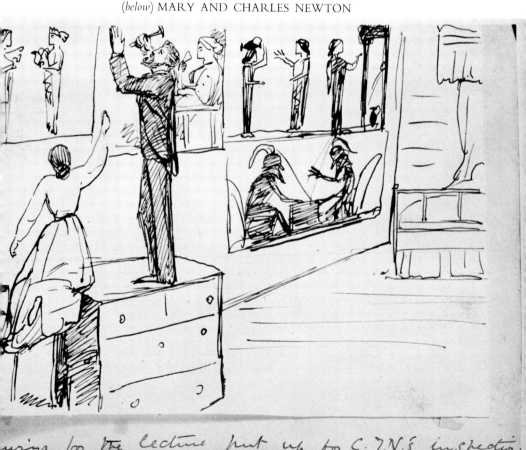

CHARLES NEWTON AND MARY AFTER THEIR MARRIAGE

'Whilst the Prince was here,' he wrote to Tom, 'the Pope ordered the English ladies who had been to visit Garibaldi to be expelled from Rome and in my visit to Cardinal Antonelli I was so fortunate as to get this hard sentence reversed. I assured him that our ladies always have a fashionable hobby and that now it happens to be this hero of Romance. And so I have saved eight ladies now here. This affair got me great credit at the Royal table.' He had dined with them and both had 'gratified him with the warmest compliments on his dear daughter Mary'.[1]

'Arthur is still with me,' Joseph wrote to his sister, 'working at painting and striving to be an artist, although we can get him a good place and he can have plenty of time for painting. Yet he is bent on the professional, though I do not think he has the "fag" in him for the purpose. Walter insists on his going to London.'

So that he might pay the debt of nearly £300, incurred by his wife's illness, Joseph had reduced his living expenses by almost half, had let a large part of his apartment and now lived in the most frugal way. Arthur went home, still determined to be a professional painter. By Easter of the next year, 1863, the debt was paid off completely.

[1] 29th November, 1862. Keats House.

F

CHAPTER 15

ARTHUR IN LONDON

1862 – 1865

ARTHUR WAS JUST TWENTY YEARS OLD when he got back to London and went to stay in Walter's lodgings. Though Walter had a good position in the Education Department of the Privy Council Office, he still painted in his spare time and a number of his friends were artists.

One of Arthur's new acquaintances was young James McNeill Whistler, who had lately come to London from Paris. He was very small, wore an eye-glass and had a thick mop of long black curly hair, with one curious white lock in it. Walter Severn's lodgings were just below Westminster Bridge, on the north bank; at high tide the river washed against the walls of the house, and Walter gave Whistler permission to paint a picture of Westminster Bridge from the bow-window of his sitting-room. He was very friendly and full of droll sayings and made no objection to Arthur watching him at work.

Whenever a visitor called Whistler was quite willing to show his canvas, propped against the table on the floor, and one day it fell on its face on a new carpet which Walter had just bought. Arthur felt acutely anxious about Whistler's sky, which was not quite dry, but the painter seemed to worry only about the carpet. Soon the younger man confided his own ambition to be a painter, and when Whistler asked what drawing he had done in Italy, showed him a water-colour of the Aventine Hill in evening sunlight. The picture was rather yellow and Arthur confided apologetically that when he painted it he had no raw umber. Whistler smiled cynically and asked, 'How can you ever expect to become a Royal Academician if you have no raw umber?'[1]

Encouraged by his interest, Arthur took his turn in the bow-window and painted the view down the river in the early morning, He was determined to be an artist, but his family were by no means happy to see him embarking on such a precarious profession; they had learned from their father's life how easily an artist's work could go out of fashion. Arthur was urged to accept sensible advice. Would it not be wiser to take some steady job and to paint, as Walter did, in his spare time? Arthur stood firm.

It was then decided that the Newtons should have Charles's old Oxford friend, John Ruskin, to dinner, so that he could examine Arthur's work and give his opinion on its merit. Ruskin had by now established himself as the

[1] Arthur Severn's Memoirs.

foremost art critic of the day; Arthur had not seen him since, as a boy, he had visited Denmark Hill with Mary.

Arthur was very nervous of this judgment. He was staying with the Newtons in Gower Street and had with him his large water-colour painted from Walter's window, the view down the river with the sun rising behind St Paul's, and Waterloo Bridge and the Shot Tower in the middle distance. He was ready early, waiting fearfully for his judge. 'At last I heard the carriage, a knock, then quick steps into the drawing-room. In came Ruskin who walked straight up to my sister, and gave her a good kiss — Newton turned away his head with a grin.' His opinion was not to be asked until after dinner. In an agony of apprehension Arthur sat through the meal, watching Ruskin, noting the brilliant blue of the penetrating eyes that shone beneath shaggy eyebrows, the slightly twisted mouth which had been bitten by a dog in his childhood, his old-fashioned courtesy and the charm and kindliness of his manner.

After dinner the picture was on view. Ruskin looked at it carefully for some time, then took Arthur by the arm 'in the kindest way' and said: 'But, Arthur what a beastly subject!' The young artist's hopes fell, but he was encouraged when the great man, pressing his arm, added 'But that little cloud you have done beautifully.'[1]

This was enough for Arthur, and even his family's doubts were allayed when, a few weeks later, the same picture was accepted for exhibition by the Royal Academy before his twenty-first birthday. From this moment they made no attempt to divert him from his chosen career.

★

Nevertheless the twins, so much younger than their brothers and sisters, remained the family problem. Eleanor was still staying with Claudia, but with the regular and rapid increase in the Gale family there would soon be no room for her there. Mary and Charles Newton were planning to leave on a long trip to the eastern Mediterranean, where Charles was to conduct important negotiations for the British Museum. Eleanor felt that she had no real home in England. Perhaps it would be better after all for her to go to Papa in Rome?

Her two sisters were not happy at the idea of her living alone with their father, with no female companion, and eventually Eleanor was sent in July to stay at Bredwardine with old Mrs Newton, while the family were discussing her future. She was not happy there. After the lively family life and the foreign travels with her mother, it was painfully dull to sit quietly in the country, miles from anywhere, the greatest excitement a visit to Hereford Cathedral. She saw the soft Herefordshire countryside through quite other eyes than Mary, for whom it held the tenderest memories. Time was flying, Eleanor sighed to her diary. She was twenty, unmarried, and as far as she could see, with no likelihood of meeting anyone who might wish to marry her. She played the piano,

[1] Arthur Severn's Memoirs.

sketched, walked, went for drives with old Mrs Newton, planted flowers in the garden, and wrote in her diary: 'It is a little *triste* for me. We do not see anybody, have no visitors, — nothing.'

Mary and Arthur came down for the twins' twenty-first birthday, but Arthur soon returned to London where, he told Eleanor, he had many new friends and was working hard, and she had to say a long good-bye to Mary, who was leaving the country in a few days' time for her journey with Charles to Greece and Turkey. Their friend, Gertrude Jekyll, was to travel with them. It had now been decided that Eleanor should go to Rome when Walter could take her, and before leaving Bredwardine Mary had a long talk with her, trying to give her the advice that Mama would have done, realizing that her father's easy-going ways might lead to his young daughter finding herself in positions that her mother would not have liked.

'Mary and Charles go on Wednesday,' wrote Eleanor in her diary. 'I shall not see them again. I cannot bear thinking of this. But they may come to Rome next winter year. . . . I long to go for many things and cannot bear the idea for others. I fear I shall have a terribly difficult position there. How careful I must be.'

★

Meanwhile Arthur, back in London, was enjoying life and had decided to grow a moustache. He did not aspire to a beard like Walter's or Newton's. At this time life for an artist in London was gay. There were many parties and a great feeling of comradeship among painters. One of the most convivial of the party-givers was Arthur Lewis, an amateur painter of talent, a lover of music, and a keen huntsman and whip. He lived in Moray Lodge, a large house on Campden Hill, and there on Saturday evenings during the winter months he gave bachelor parties which became a well-known feature of London life. A number of amateurs who called themselves 'The Moray Minstrels' would sing part-songs, glees and madrigals in the large billiard-room where the surface of the billiard table was thickly protected and on it stood pipes, cigars, jars of tobacco, tankards and bottles. At the end of the serious part of the concert, about 11 o'clock, a lavish feast of oysters was provided, and humorous songs and recitations filled up the time till midnight.

Many celebrities were present and Arthur looked forward eagerly to these 'wonderful bachelor parties' where different worlds mixed so easily together. At one of them three men talking in a group were pointed out to him as the Prince of Wales, the Duke of Sutherland and Poole, the fashionable tailor. The editor of *Punch* was usually there with many of his artistic staff — John Leech, Tenniel and Du Maurier — and Arthur caught glimpses of Millais, Frith and Augustus Egg, Holman Hunt, Anthony Trollope and Charles Keene. Amongst them moved a few peers, 'rather proud of being admitted into such intellectual society'.[1]

1 *Richmond Papers*, p. 184.

Towards the end of the evening everyone would call for Whistler. 'He was seized and stood up on a high stool, where he assumed the most irresistibly comic look, put his glass in his eye, and surveyed the multitude, who only yelled the more. When silence reigned he would begin to sing in the most curious way, suiting the action to the words with his small, thin, sensitive hands. His songs were in *argot* French, imitations of what he had heard in low *cabarets* on the Seine when he was at work there.'[1] Arthur and his friends thought Whistler's turn the best part of the evening. Sixty years later Arthur was to write nostalgically: 'To this day I remember the extraordinary noise of hundreds of empty oyster shells being emptied into pails about 11 o'clock at night.' But these enjoyable evenings were brought to an end by the marriage of the host in 1867 to Miss Kate Terry.

Before then Arthur had already found himself a member of other male societies where most of his fellows were artists. The first was the Arts Club, founded by Arthur Lewis, Tom Angel, an official in the Post Office, and Walter Severn. As well as painters there were soldiers, architects, engineers and literary men among the members. One of the most outstanding was Algernon Swinburne, at this time suddenly famous with the publication of *Atalanta in Calydon*. His appearance would have attracted attention anywhere, with his deathly white face surmounted by a great balloon of red-gold hair and his small, slim body like a boy's.

When he was in London Swinburne spent a large part of every day in the Club. He wrote his letters there and then liked to talk. Arthur was fascinated by the richness of his language, especially when he became excited or annoyed, when the words would pour out impetuously in brilliant, extravagant phrases. They became very friendly and as the poet was fond of sitting up late, Arthur often found himself the only member available to see him home.

'He had a way of drinking more than he ought, especially in the hot weather. One night when I was seeing him home, I had him tight by the arm, and got him into Oxford Street all right. As it was very late the whole place seemed deserted, but at last a hansom came along and stopped on the other side of the road. Swinburne at once began pawing the air with his foot to get in. I said: "No, you can't. It's on the other side. You must wait." At last, to my joy, a four-wheeler came along on our side and was disengaged. The cabman got off his box and helped me to get Swinburne in. He at once made himself comfortable and put his feet up on the front seat. We had not got far when it occurred to me that I did not know if it was Upper Dorset Street or Lower Dorset Street where Swinburne lodged, though I knew the number. So I thought the only thing to be done was to find his latch-key, and felt in his pocket for it. He half woke up and said: "Don't tickle me." I said: "Hang it all, I don't want to tickle you. I want your latch-key." When we got to Upper Dorset Street the key would not open the door, so we drove to Lower Dorset Street, and there I got the door

[1] Arthur Severn to E. R. and J. Pennell, *Whistler*, p. 56.

open and the cabman helped me to get him into his room on the ground floor. He wanted me to stay, but I said "Good-night" and wished that he would take more care of himself. As I left I heard something fall (I do not mean the poet) but I had had enough of it so I did not go back to see what it was. I tried to explain to the cabman that Swinburne was a sort of invalid and that he was a great man. But the cabman only smiled.'

On another evening at the Arts Club Swinburne came down into the hall as usual very late and could not find his hat. He tried on the four top-hats still hanging on the pegs and when he found that none of them would fit, he threw them furiously on the ground and jumped on them one after the other. At that moment the hall-porter appeared and Swinburne immediately demanded angrily to know where his hat was. The porter listened patiently and then said: 'Mr Swinburne, if I remember rightly, you had no hat when you came to the Club.' The owners of the four hats, who had been playing whist upstairs, now came down into the hall and were furious to find their hats ruined. They wrote to the Secretary to say that the poet must be asked to resign or they would resign themselves. Swinburne resigned at once.[1]

★

Another organization which Walter was largely instrumental in founding and in which Arthur, in spite of his youth, consequently found himself involved from the start, was the Dudley Gallery. He had sent a drawing in for a competition at the Old Water-Colour Society, but failed to become a member. Walter was disappointed and suggested that they should start an exhibition of their own. Only members could exhibit at both the Old Water-Colour society and the New, and there were few opportunities for the exhibition of drawings by artists who were members of neither. Walter's suggestion of a 'General Exhibition of Water-Colour Drawings' was canvassed with enthusiasm. A meeting was called in his lodgings to which about forty artists came, and the result was an exhibition at the Egyptian Hall in Piccadilly, which became known as 'The Dudley Gallery.' The 'Gallery' was soon forgotten and it was known simply as 'The Dudley'.

It was a success from the beginning. The expenses were kept as low as possible, the artists on the committee giving their time to their duties of receiving the pictures, selecting and finally arranging those chosen on the walls. The selection was a light-hearted business. Members of the Committee talked, joked and even sang during the examination of the work submitted to them. So successful was the exhibition in the spring months that it was decided to have another, of oil-paintings, during the winter, and the Dudley became a nursery for the older Societies.

Soon after the opening of the Dudley, Arthur joined the Artists' Rifles, known

[1] Arthur Severn's Memoirs.

at first as the Corps of Artist Volunteers. England was at that time obsessed with the fear of invasion from France. The Volunteer Movement was in full swing and almost every able-bodied young man of his acquaintance volunteered. All the best-known artists of the day were members — Millais, Morris, Burne-Jones, Holman Hunt, Val Prinsep and John Leech. Leighton was their colonel and as a gifted linguist could talk affably to the many foreigners in the Corps in their own languages.

Arthur remained a member for fourteen years, but never rose above the rank of private. Willie Richmond was soon promoted to corporal, but not all the artists showed much military aptitude. Rossetti was an aggressive recruit, wishing to be given the exact reasons for every order, and would often delay everything by arguing the point. William Morris, on the other hand, seemed unable to turn in the right direction, and when given the order 'Right turn', invariably turned left. Surprised to find himself face to face with one of his comrades, he would always politely beg his pardon before putting right his mistake.

CHAPTER 16

'THE CONSULINA'

1864 – 1865

THE BEGINNING OF ELEANOR'S LIFE IN ROME was full of interest and gaiety. With the New Year of 1864 came snow and it was bitterly cold, but this did not prevent a number of parties being given. Eleanor was taken to the opera by Italian friends, for drives on the Pincio ('saw everyone'), and along the Appian way ('to get marble'). Amongst the friends she saw most of were Emma Novello, a middle-aged woman of culture and charm, daughter of that Vincent Novello whose musical parties Joseph Severn and Keats had attended in London, and the Llanos family.

Joseph Severn had met Madame de Llanos during his early months as Consul and had been delighted to discover in her Fanny Keats, whom he had last seen as a little girl in London.

'Just now I have had a most affecting meeting with the sister, only sister, of Keats,' he had written to his brother. 'We discovered each other this morning. For a long time we remained without being able to speak, 'twas like a brother and sister who had parted in early life, meeting after 40 years. How singular that we should meet in the very place where Keats died.'[1]

Fanny Keats de Llanos was now an elderly woman, but the memory of her brother bridged the years since their last meeting. When Joseph's wife had died they had even thought of sharing a house. 'I have heard of Mrs Llanos' kind plan about your taking a house together,' Mary had written to him from London. 'I should think this would answer very well and you would be less lonely. I hear she is such a kind person.'[2] But in the end Joseph had been able to let a number of rooms in his apartment and had decided to stay on at the Palazzo Poli.

Fanny had married Llanos when he was a young liberal refugee in London, and since he had been allowed to return to Spain soon after their marriage, she had never been back to her own country. Twenty-eight years later her son-in-law, Leopold Brockmann, was appointed chief consulting engineer of the new Roman Railways which were just being built, and she and her husband decided to join the Brockmanns in Rome, bringing with them their unmarried daughter, Rosa. Eleanor and Rosa quickly became friendly, though Rosa was nine years older, and she would often call for Eleanor and take her shopping or sightseeing.

[1] 6th April, 1861. Keats House.   [2] 30th July, 1862. In possession of the Dean of Durham.

Eleanor was kept in touch with the rest of her family in England by Mary, who had now returned from her trip to Rhodes and Constantinople. Mary was very happy with Charles Newton. She led a full and interesting life, but she was worried that, so far, there was no sign of a child. She, who loved children and painted them so well, was not destined to be a mother herself.

The parties in Rome went on through the New Year and the carnival, and afterwards there were diplomatic receptions which Eleanor attended with her father. She already spoke French and German well, and now wanted to perfect her Italian. It was a wonderful life after the loneliness and despair that she had felt, cut off from her family and the world in Herefordshire. But there was one cloud in the sky and that a black one. Her sisters' misgivings about her going to live alone with her father were soon justified. Joseph's appearance was still astonishingly young. His hair was not grey, his spirits were lively and his movements quick and youthful. The Governor of Rome had to guess his age for a document. 'He actually put me at forty-five!' Joseph told his brother Tom with glee. 'What fun! I did not contradict for I never cry "stinking fish" and my well-being turns on my age. My enemies would dash me to the ground if they knew of it.'[1]

His financial position had lately improved. By rigid saving he had paid off the debt incurred by his wife's illness and soon after Eleanor's arrival he received the further appointment of Consul for the Kingdom of Italy in Rome. This added to his salary and also to his importance. 'The Governor of Rome lends me his gendarmes on every occasion,' he told his brother. On the other side, King Victor Emmanuel offered him the use of his Royal villa at Frascati for the summer of 1864 and again the following year, and orders were given that he was to be received with 'all the honours of a Cardinal'.[2]

But his easy-going disposition, and the very good-nature and tolerance that made him friendly with everyone, led to difficulties for his daughter. Whatever the straits of their life in England Mama's personality had never allowed anyone to forget that she was a lady. Now her youngest daughter was finding herself thrown together in intimacy with acquaintances of whom Mama would never have approved. Stories drifted back to London which alarmed Joseph's married daughters, and their anxiety came to a head when they heard that, for motives he said of economy, their father intended to take Eleanor to live with a wealthy Venetian countess who had offered them the hospitality of her Roman palace.

This plan was firmly quashed by Claudia and Mary, but their father seemed unable to see what all the fuss was about. He wrote to his brother Tom in February: 'You are not to believe any of the slanders you hear, particularly that I am about to be married to a Venetian Countess! 'Tis true that I was thinking to go and live at her palace on account of my daughter Eleanor, who I thought

---

[1] 22nd November, 1864. Keats House.
[2] To Walter, 2nd September, 1864. In possession of author.

would be so lonely in my big house — but the snarling world made such a row (and the house was not good air) that I gave it up and am still in my old Poli and Eleanor having many lady friends we get on very well. I take her out to all the balls, sometimes two of an evening, hoping she will soon get tired of them.'[1]

Even Tom seems to have been slightly alarmed by this airy explanation and Joseph wrote again to reassure him. 'As you touch rather seriously on my Venetian Countess, this is again to assure you that there is nothing in it, save that I esteem this lady very highly and that we are dear friends, and to me the good is great as it enables me to acquire elegance in writing and speaking Italian. Then my daughter Eleanor is delighted with her — [Oh Joseph!] — and my friends also. She is a widow of great beauty and means, *but by her husband's will she would lose everything if she were to marry* — and even *my heresy* would put me out of the question.'[2]

★

No wonder that Mary and Charles Newton should decide to pay an unexpected visit to Rome. But Emma Novello was staying at the Palazzo Poli and everything seemed quiet. They visited churches, museums and art galleries, picnic-ed and called on Mr Gibson in his studio. Mary took Eleanor to have riding lessons and ordered her a habit, and they saw much of the Llanos family.

The calm at the Palazzo Poli was disturbed one evening at dinner, when the Newtons were at their hotel, by the sudden entrance of another Italian noble-woman — this time a Principessa. Feverishly she rushed Papa into the next room, while Eleanor and Emma Novello remained seated and astonished at the table. After some while they returned, she with tears streaming down her face. 'She clasped her hands and entreated Papa to help her, etc. Then turning to me, seized my hands and said "Oh Miss S. don't, *don't say* I've been here" .... I promised not and she went away. Che scena!'[3]

A week later the Principessa re-appeared. It was late afternoon and Charles was talking with Eleanor in the big salon of the Palazzo Poli when in came the Princess, immediately followed by men laden with piles of silver and china, and announced that she had come to stay. Eleanor had perforce to help her put it away, as it could not remain in the middle of the floor 'though my anger at that woman being in the house was very great. After dinner Charles most properly got into a rage with Papa on the subject. Oh why, why, why has all this happened?' Eleanor asked her diary, 'when we might have been so happy.'

Newton's rage apparently chastened Joseph and made him more careful. The King of Italy had offered Joseph the use of his villa at Frascati that summer but he and Eleanor remained in Rome except for August, which Eleanor spent by the sea with Miss Llanos, while her father went to Albano. Emma Novello had returned to England.

[1] 16th February, 1864. Keats House.
[2] 5th April, 1864. Keats House.   [3] Eleanor's Diary.

Back in Rome in September, Joseph wrote to Walter: 'Don't be so alarmed about my ladies, for you ought to have found out that I am *the most discreet of mortals*. I am amazed at being thus reported. . . . Of course I never let anyone approach Eleanor who is not proper for her to know. Her only friends at this moment are the Llanosses and the Barberis and with one or the other she is almost every day. As consul I am obliged to know all sorts of people. . . . I can now indulge Eleanor with cabs continually. We get on charmingly, are excellent companions and I am pleased with her in everything. She begins to be "un bel pezzo di Donna" and I am proud of her beauty and great cleverness and grace'.[1]

Eleanor had indeed become a great asset to her father. Speaking German and French as well as Italian, she could translate letters and documents for him; she accompanied him to balls and receptions; she sat sketching in the Vatican while her father talked with Antonelli in another room, and the Papal Chancellor, accompanying her father when he returned, would compliment her on her drawing. She had become quite a figure in Roman society and was known as the 'Consulina', the little Consul.

She wrote to Mary: 'Papa has *cut all* the reps. The Princess de la Rocca and him are cut. He has found out she's a bore — and there is a trial pending of Prince de la Rocca having stolen or forged Lady Arnould's jewels and some cheques — so Papa is so disgusted that he has cut them all . . . so you see how much good all the rows did.

'My dear good Llanos leave on Thursday. You don't know how I shall miss them. Rosa and I are such friends — and nice Mme Llanos is so kind. The other day Rosa sent me a keepsake of a *very* handsome diamond ring. It's *so* lovely and *odd*. Black enamel with a large diamond. Fancy how kind of her! They are going to France to live in the country as Count Brockmann is to do something in the railway, and they say if I go through France next year I must go and stay with them for any length of time! I shall miss them so. Rosa used to come and take me out so often. They are *real* nice people and such perfect ladies and gentle-men . . . My very, very best love to good sweet Charles and to yourself.

Yours for ever,
NELLIO'[2]

★

Joseph was by now in a unique position. In the absence of an Ambassador he was the official representative of Britain, and at the same time the only accredited agent in Rome of the Government of Italy. ''Tis the most felicitous position, for while I have all the seeming power of an Ambassador, yet I have no etiquette to keep up, and go about my painting in the true artistic style.'[3]

Englishmen or Italians in Rome came to him for aid in trouble. With secret

[1] 2nd September, 1864. In possession of author.
[2] 11th October, 1864. In possession of author.
[3] To Tom, 29th July, 1865. Keats House.

police everywhere and an atmosphere of intense suspicion, it was easy enough to be reported for an indiscreet remark. But both factions trusted him.

When the English colony were forbidden to act a play in Lent, it was Joseph who obtained permission for the performance. When the annual Bachelors' Ball and Supper were threatened on the very day with prohibition by the Governor of Rome, Joseph, knowing what great preparations had been made, was able to get the decision revoked by giving a written guarantee of personal responsibility for what should take place. When a young Scot won a steeple-chase in the Doria colours, green and red, and, by adding the customary white belt worn by gentlemen riding against professional jockeys, combined the wicked colours of Italy, it was Joseph who persuaded the Pope to overlook the joyful demonstration of the crowd and to countermand the order for his immediate expulsion from Rome. When the Papal party, who 'did not like meetings', forbade the Archaeological Society to meet, the order was revoked when it was known that it was to take place in Signor Severn's house. 'I am trusted in everything', he said proudly.

CHAPTER 17

JOAN COMES TO DENMARK HILL

1864

WHILE ELEANOR HAD BEEN IN ROME Arthur had met again the man whose influence was to be so strong in his life, John Ruskin. In March 1864 old Mr Ruskin the wine merchant had died, an event which was to have further important repercussions on Arthur's life. In the funeral procession Arthur found himself in a carriage with his father's old friend, George Richmond, and John Simon, the celebrated surgeon. During the long, slow drive to the graveyard their conversation turned to art, and then to the way in which portrait painters are inclined to improve upon nature. John Simon mentioned particularly the case of Charles the First, whose appearance he thought had been idealized by painters, giving a weak and shifty face a look of intellect which it did not possess.

'A portrait,' he said emphatically, 'should represent the truth, and nothing but the truth.' 'Ah,' said old George Richmond, who had made portraits of more celebrities than he cared to remember, 'but the truth lovingly told.'[1]

When Mr Ruskin died, his widow, now eighty-three years old, presented a grave problem to John Ruskin. Even in the days of his unsuccessful marriage, before his wife had left him and married Millais, he had never really broken away from his parents and his home. An only child, and thought to be brilliant from a very early age, his mother and father had built their entire life round him, even taking rooms at Oxford when he was an undergraduate so that they should not lose touch with him.

Now, at the age of forty-five, he was still in many ways a child to his mother. When distinguished people came to the house, drawn by her son's reputation, she did not hesitate to rebuke him in front of them or to tell him that he was talking like a fool. Her 'sharp, decisive manner' repelled many of these visitors. At meals if she missed anything that he said, even if he was speaking to someone else, she would lean down the table and demand to have the remark repeated. 'John — John Ruskin — What was that you said?' Her son always repeated the remark gently and without complaint.[2]

Her love of contradiction also made her a very trying companion, as did her rigid Evangelical convictions. Virtue was to her always connected with

[1] Arthur Severn to A. M. W. Stirling. *Richmond Papers*, p. 49.
[2] *Memorials of Edward Burne-Jones*, by G. Burne-Jones, vol. I, p. 198.

prohibition, and her son's best-loved pictures must all be covered on the Sabbath, lest he should derive pleasure from them.

Ruskin was irked by the restrictions of life with his mother, but he felt too keenly how much he meant to her to be able to leave her for long, without a feeling of guilt which spoiled his work and sent him home to be exasperated afresh. With his father dead his responsibility to her was now still greater, but fortunately someone came into his life at this moment to whom his mother rapidly became deeply attached, thereby releasing him from the constant necessity of being at home, and who yet, by endearing herself to him also, and by easing the family relationship, made his visits far less trying.

Several young female relations had been to stay with the Ruskins before, but Mrs Ruskin had never liked any of them. After his father's death Ruskin wanted to go away for a week, but did not like to leave his mother alone. Fortunately he remembered that a young girl cousin was staying with her uncle, John Ruskin Tweddale, in his house off the Edgware Road. The girl's mother (and the uncle with whom she was staying) were old Mr Ruskin's first cousins, their father and Mr Ruskin's mother having been brother and sister. It was soon arranged that she should stay with Mrs Ruskin for the week while her son was away from home, and he drove in to London to collect her in his carriage. He had seen her only once before, when she was still a child; now she was seventeen and he thought at once how charming she was.

Joan Ruskin Agnew was a vivacious girl, with a character of singular sweetness, one of a large Scotch family, whose father, the hereditary Sheriff-Clerk of Wigtown, had died thirteen years earlier, leaving his wife with six daughters and two sons — their number being subsequently augmented to three, when another son was born after his father's death. Joan's three brothers and one of her sisters had died as children, and from an early age she learned to live with sorrow. She was not at all frightened of Mrs Ruskin, and the tyrannical old lady took a fancy to her from the first. Soon she was telling Joan to call her 'Auntie', and bidding her choose her favourite food for luncheon.

The week passed quickly for Joan. She had been brought up in a pretty old house in Wigtown, surrounded by beautiful country. She loved the big garden at Denmark Hill and dreaded her return to the noise and dirt of London streets. But when Ruskin came home she felt that she must end her stay. Mrs Ruskin, however, would not hear of it. Her clothes were sent for and her mother's permission obtained for her visit to be extended.

★

When, a year later, Joan at last returned to her own family in Scotland, her absence was felt as a keen deprivation to the odd household on Denmark Hill. She had quickly fallen into the rôle which of all others Ruskin preferred in young girls, of assistant and pupil to his part of teacher, and with his mother she was patient and kind. She never tired of reading aloud from the old lady's favourite authors, Richardson and Mrs Edgeworth, and when Ruskin sent her in the carriage to visit friends in London she would be sure to bring home some little bits of gossip to amuse them both on her return.

Ruskin had made her work to improve her handwriting so that she might catalogue his collections. She had arranged his minerals, lined drawers and made velvet covers for them. She never seemed bored in the secluded life of Denmark Hill and had become a favourite with Ruskin's friend, Carlyle, who liked to ride out from Cheyne Row and sit in the quiet garden, enjoying the fresher air and the view of the Norwood hills.

'My mother misses you much more than I thought she would,' wrote Ruskin to Joan, back with her mother in Wigtown, 'and says "she does not know how she could replace you at all; — indeed she knows she could not" ... As you know I am very remorseful about keeping you mewed up here. But ... we shall both be glad — not a little, to have you back again.'[1]

'I have got two of my school-girls staying with me ...' he wrote a fortnight later, 'two very nice ones: only you were Mama's girl, and these are mine, and Mama won't have anything to say to them, and wants you. I shall be very glad to have you back again too — though you are so much saucier than my Winnington pets, and though you never believe I mean what I say.'[2]

A week later he wrote again. 'We want you to come back, as soon as you can without breaking on any pleasant plans.'[3] But it was nearly a month before Joan returned, to a warm welcome from the old lady and her famous son. By now she had almost become the daughter that old Mrs Ruskin had never had and, in a way, Ruskin's own daughter as well. It gave him pleasure to bring her presents and he insisted on her buying new clothes. Her room was re-decorated for her, new furniture was bought, and when she went out she was sent everywhere in their carriage.

Her character fitted her exactly for a position which few girls of her age could have filled. She was by nature unselfish and was used to helping and thinking of others. She had a naturally happy and affectionate temperament, with a great capacity for enjoying the smallest things and a constant bubbling up of laughter and fun. Ruskin liked to see this spontaneous pleasure in living, a feeling that had never been allowed him in his own youth, and responded to her affectionate teasing and jokes.

She kept old Mrs Ruskin happy and her tact averted many of the scenes and rows which had been so frequent in that house before she came. Even Anne, the thin, white-haired old woman who had come as a barefoot child into the service of the Ruskin family, nobody knew how many years before, and who had been nurse to John Ruskin, would pause from endless bickering with her mistress to talk to Joan about her nurseling, to whom she was passionately

---

[1] 8th May, (1865). The Education Trust.
[2] 22nd May, 1865. Ibid.
[3] 31st May, 1865. Ibid.

devoted. The two harsh old women had conducted a running feud for years, Mrs Ruskin abusing and rebuking Anne, who would answer her with equal rudeness. If Mrs Ruskin was known to like things arranged in a certain way Anne was certain to arrange them differently. But in spite of this constant warfare it had never occurred to Mrs Ruskin to tell Anne to leave. In fact no servant of the Ruskin family had ever been turned away, and there were several ancient maids to be seen hobbling about the house apparently without any occupation. When asked by a young friend what one of these old retainers did, Mrs Ruskin drew herself up and replied, 'She, my dear, puts out the dessert.'

★

It was soon after Joan's return from Scotland that Arthur first met her. He was staying with the Newtons and went with Mary one evening to George Richmond's house, for the dress rehearsal of a play. The Richmond family were all fond of charades and theatricals as well as music.

After the first act of the play was ended there was a long pause and Arthur looked around him at the audience. His attention was immediately taken by a girl sitting alone, a few chairs away — 'a very pretty, good-natured looking girl, with very curly hair and a complexion like a rose.' As the curtain remained firmly down and she apparently had no one to talk to 'I sidled up and without introduction began to talk. She was most agreeable; not shy, and looked amused I thought, at my boldness.' Their conversation was cut short by an appeal from the actors to the unknown young lady 'to go and sing or play something until the curtain could go up'. She rose readily, without demur, and seating herself composedly at the piano launched into a series of negro spirituals in a true, lively voice. She was warmly applauded when she returned to her seat as the curtain was at last raised for the second act.

After the play had ended there were refreshments and talk, and when the guests began to collect their cloaks, Arthur, who was still at the side of his new friend, heard her carriage announced and gathered that she was a Miss Agnew. The name meant nothing to him, but he was delighted when she enquired if she could be of any help to Mrs Newton and himself by giving them a lift in her carriage. The offer was accepted, but Arthur was still unable during the short journey to Gower Street to find out who she was. As Mary, after thanking her, turned to the front door, key in hand, Arthur, lingering over his good night at the carriage, asked if she had a long way to go.

' "I live on Denmark Hill," she said.

"Oh, indeed!" said I. "Do you know Mr Ruskin — he lives there?"

"I live with Mr Ruskin and his mother." '

Arthur waved good-bye happily, ' "How splended," thought I to myself, "I can easily find an excuse to go out there." '[1]

In a few days he found it imperative to seek advice from Ruskin about the

[1] Arthur Severn's Memoirs.

painting of clouds. Arthur had not seen Ruskin since the evening at the Newtons three years before. The lodge bell tolled as he walked past the cedar tree up to the house, and this time he not only felt shy but a little guilty too.

However Ruskin was most kind, answered all his questions about clouds and invited him to stay to luncheon where he met Miss Agnew again, Ruskin introducing her as his ward. After this Arthur began to find his way out to Denmark Hill quite frequently and was kindly received.

But the pleasant new friendship was suddenly interrupted by a tragic event. In the New Year of 1866, on 2nd January, Mary Newton died.

★

Mary had been thin and pale before her trip to Rhodes, and when she returned her family thought that the holiday had done her little good. She was sleeping badly and told Claudia that she would start awake, unrefreshed by sleep, but with the sensation that she had been drawing, drawing all the night.

In London Charles made her work as hard as he did himself. In addition to her own work she made all the drawings, some of them very large, to illustrate his lectures. He was most particular about these drawings and if the slightest thing was wrong they must be done again. He was equally strict about the keeping of her household accounts and these drove Mary often to despair. He was fond of company, and when they got home from the Museum, where they had been working all day, he liked to dine out with friends or to entertain them in his own house. Mary often wished that they could have stayed quietly at home, though she never said so to Charles. He was a spare, strong, nerveless man, full of energy and fond of society. He drove her as he drove himself, but she was more delicately made.

She worked all the harder to keep the miserable thought away that perhaps she might never have a child. Then she caught measles from a little boy, whose portrait she was painting, and became very ill. As she lay in bed, with a high fever, in their house in Gower Street, she saw a maidservant fall from the top window of the opposite house and was terribly affected by the girl's scream as she fell. That evening the doctor told Charles Newton that she was suffering from brain-fever; all the next day she was unconscious, and on the day afterwards she died.

Charles Newton was stricken, but he smothered his despair beneath an icy control. On the day of Mary's death he wrote to Eleanor in Rome:

'My dear Eleanor,
          It has pleased God to take my dearest Mary back to himself.
'She died at 10 this morning, so tranquilly that she seemed to fall asleep. I leave to Arthur and Walter the task of telling your father the sad particulars of her illness.
'That your life may be as true and holy as that of your dear departed sister,

and that your death may be mourned by as many loving hearts is the prayer of
                                                    Yours affectionately,
                                                    C. T. NEWTON.'

  Arthur had returned from Paris just after Mary became ill and had stayed at
Gower Street, helping Newton to nurse her night and day. He reported that
Charles had behaved that evening just as usual. He had eaten his dinner and
opened his paper afterwards without a word about his wife. It was not until
after the funeral that his control broke. The maid asked him if she should tidy
up the studio — Mary's room, where her unfinished canvases leaned against the
walls, her palettes and brushes lay neatly in their places, her easel stood lonely,
in the middle of the room — where Mary's personality filled the air, and everything spoke of her and waited for her return. Newton turned on the poor girl in
a fury and ordered that nothing in the room was to be changed — if she touched
a single thing she should leave the house that day.

                                    ★

  Claudia wrote to her father, knowing how bitterly distressed he would be by
the sudden loss of the daughter of whose talent he had been so proud. 'When I
last saw Mary she was as happy as a human being could be. She has often said
she was afraid she was too happy. . . . Not having been allowed to be with dearest
Mary has been so sad to me. All I have done was to make a lovely cross of
evergreens and red berries, symbol of our Happy Faith, and a chaplet of sweet-
scented leaves and bunches of violets, symbol of Eternal Life, to make her look
bright as long as we could see her above this earth. The cross I made *for us all.*
Tell dearest Eleanor the chaplet I made for her. I thought of her all the time I
was at my sad work and did so long for her to have been working with me. As
poor Charles said in his letter to me, "Dearest Mary was so fond of flowers."
He looked at them as they were on the coffin and never took his eyes off them as
they were lowered into the ground.'
  Claudia was now living at Mitcham, where the air was thought to be better
for her, and Newton went out there to see her, as in her delicate state of health
she had not been allowed to come to Gower Street during Mary's illness.
  'I feel more for poor Charles than for anyone,' she wrote to Eleanor, 'for she
was *all* to him, and to think of his lonely room is too dreadful. He came here
and I feel it did us both good, we talked of nothing else but dearest Mary and he
felt he could open his grief to me when he could not to others. . . . Arthur has
been such a good boy. He is to live with Charles at any rate for the first year. I
hope he will do all he can for Charles, it will be an object in his life, and having
dearest Mary before him, as he must have, living in the same house and as he
says, poor boy, all her work things are about just as she left them. . . . I do so feel
for you, for I know you have lost your best friend.'[1]

                    [1] 17th January, 1866. In possession of author.

To Joseph and Eleanor in Rome the shock was terrible and unexpected. It was nearly four years now since Mama had died in Eleanor's arms in the little hotel bedroom in Marseilles. Now Mary was dead too. Mary the loving, Mary the clever, the good, the gay, the gifted. To Eleanor she had been the dearest of them all since Mama's death, dearer even than Arthur, her twin. To Joseph she had been the favourite child. He referred to her always as 'my gifted daughter'. The complimentary notices in *The Times* and other papers he read with pride, and was comforted a little by news of the Queen's sympathy in a note sent by Lady Augusta, 'so kind and full of feeling'.

But his distress made him ill. He became crippled with rheumatism and for two months was in great pain and could only creep about, his spirits quenched, his laughter stilled. Poor Eleanor was ill, too. Her world seemed ever more insecure. Since Mama died Mary had become part-mother to her as well as sister. Now she was gone, and Claudia in increasingly poor health and pre-occupied by the care of her many children. Her father was crippled and ill. If he had to give up his consul-ship, what would become of them both?

'My dearest Child,' wrote her elder brother, Walter, 'I received your letter to-day so evidently written in great distress of mind and now I feel for you more than ever. . . . It is quite extraordinary how much more reconciled I am to our loss. In the first place our darling sister was *so good* that we can have *no doubts* about her having left this for a far better and happier existence. . . . I quite saw that she would in a short time have taken an important place in London Society and however satisfactory this might have been in a worldly sense, it would not have been the best preparation for the other world, beset as such a position must be with all kinds of temptations and allurements.

'Her greatest pleasure was in doing good to others. There was only one cloud to throw a little gloom over her happiness. She was constantly regretting that her kind and devoted husband had not the same views about the Christian Religion as she had herself. He has told me, however, that if either exercised any influence over the other — there was much more influence exercised by her over him, and to please her he used to go to Church. Since her illness and death I have every reason to believe that the great wish of her life has been granted. Her dear Charles has found Faith and with it consolation. . . . I can't tell you how happy I feel about this change in Charles N. You know that many of my friends, especially men in the P.C.O. are sceptics. . . . At one time I myself had slight, I am glad to say *very slight* doubts, but during the last year or so I have become, more than I ever was, a firm believer in our beautiful Christian Religion . . .' (Walter did not mention here that during the last year he had become much attached to a very devout Scottish girl to whom he was shortly to announce his engagement, Mary Dalrymple Fergusson, sister of Sir James Fergusson of Kilkerran in Ayrshire.) 'If my surmises are correct about C. N. I believe beloved Mary would willingly have sacrificed her life to save a soul so precious to her. Cheer up, my dear Eleanor, and do not let Papa be too much cast down. He must remember how much depends on his keeping his health.'[1]

The little household in their grief were unalarmed by the rumours which were now flying about Rome. There was talk of an attack on the city — a rising in Venice — the French troops were to be withdrawn — Garibaldi would attack — the Pope would treat with the King. Joseph sat, uncaring and sad, in the Palazzo Poli, with the sound of the Trevi fountain filling the high rooms with the rush and splash of water.

At the end of the year he was left alone, when Eleanor went home to be a bridesmaid at Walter's wedding. Time seemed to stand still for a while when Eleanor had left. Claudia had intended to visit her father when Eleanor came home, but she was not well enough to make the journey.

The struggles and fevers of the Papal power in its death-throes made little impression on Joseph Severn. He did his best to help those who appealed to him, but he could not share their excitement, their hopes and fears. Under the terms of their Convention with the Government of Italy, the French troops evacuated Rome in December. But the powerful Catholic party in France compelled the Emperor to keep a force of twenty thousand men at Toulon, ready to sail for Italy if Rome were attacked.

In the summer Joseph went to Tolfa, where he could take baths for his rheumatism. There was no longer any semblance of law in the country outside Rome. The villagers and all the local landowners were being terrorized by bands of brigands. Joseph evaded them by passing himself off as a simple *pittore*; they did not bother with such small fry. The baths relieved him a little, and soon he was able to move more freely and with less pain.

On 23rd October the long-looked-for rising broke out in Rome, and Garibaldi crossed the frontier at the head of seven thousand volunteers. Eight hundred rebels in the city, armed with a few revolvers and bombs, captured one of of the gates and advanced on the Capitol. For three days there was fierce fighting, but by the end of the third day the last struggle was overcome in the slums of Trastevere district and order was restored. Joseph took the opportunity to get three days' work on his new picture, which was destined for the Ashburton collection.

The Papal Government was triumphant, but it was also panic-stricken. It knew that its troops could put up no effective resistance to Garibaldi, who had already captured Monte Rotondo and was advancing towards Rome. The Irish and English monks rushed to claim Mr Severn's protection, and in case the city was taken, he engaged to give sanctuary to a Cardinal and twenty-two nuns in his own house.

But the Catholics in France forced the Emperor to act. The French troops sailed from Toulon, landed at Civita Vecchia, marched inland, and met and defeated Garibaldi's volunteers at Mentana. It was clear that Rome would never be taken while the French were ready to protect the Pope. The uneasy stale-

[1] 25th January, 1866. In possession of author.

mate continued. The French troops withdrew, but only to Civita Vecchia. Everyone knew that it was the strength of France alone that prevented the fall of the Temporal Power.

Joseph's position was a difficult one. Everything savouring of Liberalism was anathema in Rome. English residents became increasingly uneasy, and when an English priest was attacked in the street many of them fled. Within the city a feeling of approaching, unprecedented change was in the air. It led to growing disorder and crime, but Joseph remained unaffected by the pervading fears. He loved Rome. It was his true home. His only fear was lest it should be plundered by a victorious army. Apart from that he felt no apprehension.

When the Romans were rioting in the streets outside his window, when shouts of 'Viva il Re!' mingled with jeers and cat-calls at the Papal troops, Joseph sat, unperturbed, at his easel, puzzling over his Marriage at Cana and how he should give the effect of water changing into wine. While Papalists looked with dread towards the day when France should again withdraw her troops, and while Liberals plotted, with the fear of the Inquisition chilling their blood, Joseph went serenely about his consular work, and painted and entertained his friends. There were still old friends with whom he could talk about tempi passati, and there were still a few visitors who came to his studio to see his pictures. But they were not carelessly munificent like those noble patrons who had thronged to Rome when Joseph was a young man. Since his return to Italy he had sold only two pictures. Yet with each visitor his hopes rose anew. Something always seemed to turn up, and meanwhile he would spend only what was absolutely necessary, so that he would be able to save some money for Eleanor, and to send five or ten pounds at intervals to his sister Maria.

His consular duties kept him very busy. After the fiasco at Mentana, the Italian Government sent him 3000 francs for the wounded Garibaldi prisoners. 'Each man on leaving the hospital receives from me 40 francs,'[1] he told his sister. The victory of the Papal forces (for the Pope's troops spread the story that they had already defeated Garibaldi's men before the French soldiers had arrived on the scene) had given a triumphant impetus to the reactionaries among the Papalists.

'I am fighting with the Inquisition,' Joseph wrote, 'which from day to day is taking away the many privileges I have gained from the Papal Ministers. But Mr Odo Russell says that he is sure I have an extraordinary influence over the said Ministers, and that they have at times been induced to grant me more than was convenient or in order, so that now the Inquisition has stepped in to correct this mistake . . . 'Tis a great matter my speaking Italian so fluently.'[2]

Although the sulphur baths at Tolfa the summer before had relieved the pain of his rheumatism, and reduced the swellings on his hands and feet, the trouble kept recurring, and then he found it difficult to sign so many letters, and painful

[1] To Maria, 26th December, 1867. Keats House.
[2] To Tom, 25th March, 1868. Keats House.

even to move. If his secretary had not been so efficient and devoted, he might have been ousted from the Consulate as unfit for his duties. But Frantz had never forgotten Joseph's kindness in negotiating his brother's release from a Roman prison. Now this brother joined him, and together, when Joseph was ill, they stood between him and the outside world, and by stratagem and subterfuge protected him from prying eyes.

'I fear I shall never get rid of this rheumatism,' he said ruefully. 'It sticks to one like a creditor.'

But he still looked amazingly young, and no one could have guessed that he was seventy-five years old.

CHAPTER 18

THE WILD ROSE

MEANWHILE LIFE HAD NOT BEEN UNEVENTFUL for Joseph's family in England. Arthur was doing well with his painting and was falling in love with Joan Agnew. Though his path was not an easy one for he was hovering on the fringe of uneasily complicated emotional relationships.

John Ruskin had for several years been passionately attached to a young girl, Rose La Touche, whose mother, an admirer of his work, had persuaded him to advise on the education of her three children when Rose, the youngest, was only eleven years old. Ruskin could never resist the rôle of leader, teacher and guide, and though he was willing to pursue it with young men who were practising art or interested in social problems, he was happiest with admiring young girls, ruling them with a strong but capricious hand, imbuing them with his own fads and enthusiasms, setting them to work at drawing or botanizing or reading, or learning Italian so that they might have the pleasure of reading Dante in the original.

This he did with the girls at the school at Winnington, where he had his 'pets', some of whom would visit him at Denmark Hill and be put to work there arranging his minerals or cataloguing his prints and be scolded or praised or flirted with. It was the relationship, half-instructive, half-flirtatious, which he most enjoyed, and he was to have dozens of these young female disciples during his lifetime.

But his feelings for Rose La Touche soon became deeper, more intense and more obsessive than any other love in his life, and on her seventeenth birthday, the month after Mary Severn's death, he asked her to marry him.

Rose said that 'she could not answer yet', but told him to ask her again in two years' time, and promised that whatever happened she would give him a definite answer on her twenty-first birthday. The La Touche parents were startled by Ruskin's proposal to their daughter. He was forty-seven, thirty years older than Rose, and — which weighed even more heavily with them — they thought him an unbeliever. Mrs La Touche was a strong Anglican, and her husband, who had been Master of the Kildare Hounds, and had had in his youth no other interest but sport, had been converted and baptized by the Evangelist, Spurgeon, and had since become fanatical in the Baptist faith. The idea that his daughter should marry a man who had publicly questioned some of his Christian beliefs was obnoxious to him, and seemed even more important as an obstacle than the great disparity in their ages.

With Mrs La Touche Ruskin's position was very different. She was a hand-some woman with strong intellectual interests, frustrated by the narrow Irish society in which she had to live, where hunting and racing were thought the most important things in life and were the sole subjects of conversation. With Lady Drogheda, Lady Cloncurry and some other friends, she had tried to start a society of intellectuals whose members were to be known by names taken from the classics, Stella, Lycidas, and Alethea (this being Mrs La Touche), but it had been killed by ridicule. Her uncongenial surroundings led Mrs La Touche to value and seek to enlarge all her contacts with a wider and more intellectual world, and it was with this object that she had first written to Ruskin and persuaded him to come to see her and her children in London.

When in Ireland her greatest pleasures were gardening and painting – she liked best to do studies of her flowers – but she was also an excellent linguist and widely read. She was five years Ruskin's junior, still a pretty woman, and their friendship had become very intimate. He said that she was 'certainly the ablest and I think the best woman I have ever known'. She delighted in his friendship and had given Ruskin reason to believe that her feeling for him was something warmer. She took it for granted that his tenderness for her daughter was no more than another proof of his deep affection for herself. The realization that Rose was first in his heart was a shock and a terrible personal blow to her. She regarded her daughter as a child, and thought it quite impossible that she should return his love. She and her husband quickly decided that they must keep them apart, so that Rose would have the opportunity to form some more suitable attachment.

Rose La Touche was a strange, unworldly, almost unearthly, creature. Her mother found her less lovable and less easy than her elder daughter, but she was undoubtedly very gifted. She read widely, wrote poetry 'at railroad speed', and her intelligence and delicate elusiveness fascinated Ruskin. She was tall, very slender and very fair, with 'deep blue eyes, flaxen hair and exquisitely chiselled features', and had run wild for a large part of her life in Ireland, where she would be out of the house from daybreak to dusk, galloping across the fields on her cream-coloured pony, with her huge dog, Bruno, at her heels.

Her mother called her 'The Wild Rose'. 'All day long she is in and out, let the weather be what it may, and not one single thing that girls do does she do – except a *little* music when she pleases. She has the run of all the cottages and cabins about, and gets fed from the labourers' dinners, and is an exception to every rule and custom of society.'[1] She was very highly strung and had suffered when she was fourteen from a nervous illness brought on, her mother thought, by excitement at being admitted to her First Communion. She had been at first unconscious, then completely lost her memory; she had to be kept in bed for weeks, and remained in a very weak state for nearly two years.

Ruskin's proposal had been, not refused, but postponed. While Mrs La Touche

[1] *Reminiscences of a Specialist* by Greville MacDonald, p. 103.

still thought, or at any rate said, that Rose was far too young to feel anything more than a child's love for Ruskin, he was convinced that she loved him as he did her, and that she was only prevented from realizing it fully by regard for her parents and by religious scruples. Mrs La Touche, on the other hand, persisted in telling their friends that they were being kept apart as much as possible solely in order to save Ruskin from pain.

In this situation Joan Agnew now became involved. She had been very friendly with Rose, who had been a frequent visitor to Denmark Hill, and as confidante of Ruskin she had been in touch with the whole affair. In March 1866, a month after Ruskin's proposal, Joan went to stay with the La Touche family at their house, Harristown, in County Kildare, and Rose's brother, three years older than she, began to pay her marked attention. Like his father before his conversion, all Percy La Touche's interests were centred in sport. He was an amateur steeplechase jockey, rode well to hounds, and spent every day out of doors. He had no interest in reading or painting or music or indeed, in anything that did not consist of exercise or skill in the open air. But he was manly and strong and had the assurance that goes with physical good health, and the knowledge that he excelled at the sports which he most enjoyed, and that one day he would inherit the big house where he had been brought up.

Nothing for the moment, however, came of Percy's apparent admiration for Joan, as her visit was cut short by a letter from Ruskin telling her that she was to go with him on a visit to the Continent. As usual he was travelling with a party – he never liked to go alone on these expeditions. Even when he was working hard on architectural drawings or measurements he liked to have congenial company to come back to, leisurely meals and someone to listen while he related the progress of his work or expounded his ideas.

On this occasion he planned to go first to Paris and then on to Milan and Venice with his old friends, Sir Walter and Lady Trevelyan. Lady Trevelyan had not been well and it was thought that the warm Italian spring would do her good. With them, he told Joan, he intended to take herself and Constance Hilliard, Lady Trevelyan's niece, who was a few years younger than Joan. This was thrilling news for Joan, who had never yet crossed the Channel, and she made haste to write to Mrs Ruskin, for she realized that she could not have gone if the old lady had clung to her:

'My dearest Aunt,
        . . . I must first try . . . to make you understand the great joy and delight and surprise too, I had from Mr Ruskin's letter which came yesterday telling me that *I* – only think Aunt dear! that Joan of all people in the world – was to be allowed to go abroad and see things I have so longed for, but never expected to have any such longings gratified – and now all words leave me that ought properly to express the gratitude I feel to both you and my cousin for ever thinking of or arranging such a thing for me. . . .'

Rosie and she had driven to a beautiful waterfall among the Wicklow mountains the day before and Rose had told her how she and Mr Ruskin and some others had gone there one day, and 'she took great pleasure in telling me of the dangerous part "St. C."[1] insisted on going over, to try her skill in climbing; but she was determined (even at the risk of her neck being broken) not to be beaten.'[2]

So Joan made her first trip abroad, but it was a short one because poor Lady Trevelyan died suddenly on the way. Sir Walter went home to England and Ruskin was left with the two girls. The rumours of war in Italy were too persistent for him to ignore, so they confined their sightseeing to France and Switzerland. Rose had been forbidden by her parents to write to Ruskin and she ostensibly obeyed them, but still sent oblique messages through the letters she was allowed to write to Joan.[3]

Soon after their return to England Joan went back to visit Harristown and Percy La Touche asked her to marry him. This caused consternation to his parents. Although they had previously been very fond of her (Mrs La Touche had called herself Joan's 'Vice-Mother'), her relationship to Ruskin and the affection between them made the idea of her marrying Percy most unwelcome to them. Now thoroughly alarmed by Ruskin's love for their daughter, their energies were directed towards detaching Rose completely from his influence, and this would clearly not be easy if their son were to marry his ward. All the relationships became increasingly strained and unhappy; Joan did her best to remain calm and to support Ruskin in his frequent moods of melancholy, when any post might bring a worrying or ambiguous letter from one of the family at Harristown.

Though the La Touche parents had not openly declared their opposition to their son's marriage to Joan, they had made it quite clear that they would never allow their younger daughter to become engaged to Ruskin. 'I . . . make all my friends suffer with me,' wrote Ruskin apologetically to Richmond, 'but I am weak with pain and cannot but cry. Your letter is wise — but men dying of thirst cannot think whether the water they see may be bitter or sweet — and strange as it may seem to you I have twenty times more fear of the mistake of Maroh for Elim[4] in Joan's love than in mine. From the present feel of it, all *cannot but* be well if she keeps her health — the youth has honour and principle and has solemnly asked her and to all purpose of heart been accepted and knows it. But for the issue, finally, I am deeply anxious — I mean *after* marriage. I think the parents were wrong in permitting here — then in refusing me'.[5]

Ruskin, unable to write directly to Rose, who had been forbidden to receive letters from him, persuaded his friend, Mrs Cowper, to intercede for him when she could. Rose was very fond of Mrs Cowper, herself a deeply religious woman,

[1] Rose's childhood name for Ruskin, 'St Crumpet'.
[2] Harristown. 17th April, (1866). Education Trust.
[3] John Ruskin to Mrs Cowper from Interlaken, 30th May, 1866. Pierpont Morgan Library, New York.
[4] Bitter for Sweet.
[5] Undated (March 1867). Pierpont Morgan Library.

nd to her expressed her fears about Ruskin's loss of faith. She was becoming
more and more engrossed by her religion — the same form of stern Evangelism
which through his mother had ruled Ruskin's childhood and against which as a
man he had rebelled. She seemed to feel this as great a barrier to their love as
her parents' opposition. Her attitude infuriated Ruskin.

'Rose is a very dear and noble child,' he wrote to Mrs Cowper, 'but you must
not think that all conditions are to be of her making. If our faiths are to be
reconciled, it seems to me quite reasonable to expect that an Irish girl of nineteen who cannot spell, reads nothing but hymn books and novels, and enjoys
nothing so much as playing with her dog, should be brought finally into the
faith of a man whom Carlyle and Froude call their friend and whom many very
noble persons call their teacher, as that he should be brought into hers. . . . Rosie
must come out from her country and kindred for me — like Ruth or Rebekah —
or she is not worthy of the love I bear her. . . . If she can join herself to my life
and its purpose and be happy, it is well; but I am not to be made a grotesque
chimney-piece ornament — a disfigurement — of the drawing-room at
Harristown.'[1]

Arthur's appearances at Denmark Hill were pleasant to Joan. The company
of an uncomplicated, fun-loving and admiring young man was a welcome
chance to relax and forget her worries.

At the end of May (1867) Joan left for Scotland, where her sister was to be
married later in the summer, and soon afterwards Ruskin, having delivered two
important lectures, went off, depressed and bitterly unhappy about Rose, to
Keswick, where he delayed for a month before paying a visit to his cousins at
Wigtown. He wandered desolate about Skiddaw. 'I could not bear to go far
from that Irish sea and have another sea between me and sorrow.' He spent
his time in climbing, walking and collecting specimens of rock and ferns,
accompanied only by his valet, whose duty it was to carry the specimens of
minerals, and his gardener, Downs, who collected the plants. He carried with
him his most precious letters from Rose pressed between two thin sheets of
gold.

The emotional strain under which he had been living had now seriously
affected his health. He was alarmed by fits of giddiness and a feeling as though
a mist had formed before his eyes and enveloped his mind, so that he could not
work. His life continued to be centred on letters from Harristown, and he wrote
everyday to Joan and expected her to do the same to him. His affectionate
relationship with Joan was by now very important to him. In her, though she
was so young, he confided all his hopes and fears, and she comforted him with
her simplicity, affection and admiration.

Having grown up an only child, not even allowed to see much of his cousins,
who had not risen in the world as his parents had, Ruskin, though the centre
of his parents' lives, had been starved of family affection. In Joan whose nature

[1] Denmark Hill. 26th March (1867). Pierpont Morgan Library.

was loving, sympathetic and cheerful he found what he had lacked. At time she was like a daughter to him, grateful for the care that he delighted to take for her, obedient and cheerful and sometimes teasing, reduced to tears if he was unkind — at others the relationship seemed reversed and it was he who would be 'her poor boy' and turn to her for comfort and mothering. He delighted in the pet names and baby-talk that he had never known, in his own austere childhood Joan was 'Doanie', 'Pussy', 'Fernie', 'Wee amie', or 'piggie', and soon he was writing that they would have to be careful or they would not be able to speak in anything but baby language.

When there was no news of Rose from either Joan or Connie Hilliard, to whom she also sometimes wrote, Ruskin fell into black depression. 'They *canno* understand, I suppose,' he wrote to Mrs Cowper, 'that a man of my age car suffer for love like a youth. But who would not for *such* a love — she is so different from other creatures that nothing else can in any wise break the steady sense of *utter want*.'[1]

Just before he was due to leave the Lake District for Wigtown, Ruskin at last received a letter from Joan with a message for him from Rose. '. . . And so, here comes in the letter with the rose and the crumb, besides, of pure manna,' he wrote . . . 'I am so *very* thankful for these crumbs, for I thought she had been put under some new forbidding even to name me — and that you were trying to keep it from me as long as you could . . . Forgive this short note — because if it was ever so long, it couldn't thank you enough — or her. . . .

'1 o'clock.

I've been to church, and put a sovereign which I had been saving to buy minerals with, into the offertory plate. And I'm so happy. Though it's an East Wind again. If only it would carry me with it — westwards.'[2]

After a week's stay in Scotland Ruskin left, a few days before Kate Agnew's wedding, and returned to Keswick where he toyed with the idea of buying a house on Lake Windermere, but continual rain soon turned him against it.

Still feeling unwell he returned to London, where he found Joan 'sad about Percy's faultful ways'.[3] In an effort to improve his health Ruskin moved to a doctor's home in Norwood for a month, where the régime allowed him to drive out when he wished, and almost every day went out with Joan, to hear a concert at the Crystal Palace, or for long walks across the fields to the hills of Croydon.

Returning from one of these walks on 12th September, Joan found a letter from Percy La Touche in which he brusquely broke off their engagement, without a word of explanation or regret. The time of their engagement had not been a happy one for her, but the brutal way in which he had ended it wounded her gentle, affectionate nature. Sadly she returned his letters.

[1] 18th June, 1867. Education Trust.
[2] Keswick, 7th July, 1867. Education Trust.
[3] 24th August, 1867. *John Ruskin's Diaries*, edited Joan Evans and J. H. Whitehouse.

CHAPTER 19

TWO SUITORS

1867 – 1868

ARTHUR KNEW NOTHING OF JOAN'S BROKEN ENGAGEMENT. He was busy with his painting and had made several long journeys abroad with a friend, Hercules Brabazon Brabazon, an amateur musician and artist. Brabazon was twenty years older than Arthur, a wealthy land-owner, tall and shy, who devoted all his time to painting, music and travel. The journey which Arthur made with him to Algeria was the first of many which they were to make together, Brabazon paying Arthur's expenses.

Arthur's own career was now flourishing, for at the Exhibition at the Dudley Gallery, he had achieved a triumph. Fascinated, as he had been since childhood, with the effects of light on moving water, he had sent in seven drawings, of which the largest was of waves seen by moonlight. One of Mary's last suggestions before her illness had been a title for it, taken from Keats's sonnet:

'The moving waters at their priestlike task
Of pure ablution round earth's human shores.'

Arthur's pictures were all accepted and he was advised by the Committee to put a higher price on the largest. Two sketches by Mary, painted at Scutari and Rhodes, were favourably noticed, but Arthur's picture *Waves Breaking by Moonlight* was praised by all the critics and pronounced one of the outstanding works at the Exhibition. All his seven pictures were sold on the first day of the Exhibition, and this immediate success silenced any self-doubts that he may have had and determined him irrevocably to make painting his profession.

A few days after the private view Arthur received a letter from the Duchess of Sutherland, saying that she had heard so much about his painting of waves breaking by moonlight, but was too much of an invalid to be able to go to the Gallery to see it. Could it be sent for her to see at Stafford House? The Committee were pleased at the attention that the picture was attracting and readily gave their permission for it to be removed on the Saturday evening, on the understanding that it would be returned before the public were admitted on Monday. This was done and the Duchess liked the picture so much that she asked Arthur if he would paint a replica of it for her. After getting permission from the purchaser who had bought the original at the private view, Arthur was able to copy the painting and was invited to lunch with the Duchess to see where it was hung.

She was very kind to him and must have been charmed herself by the talkative, gay, rather naïve young man, for a few weeks later he was invited to lunch again with her, this time at her country house on the Thames, where, to his surprise, he found she had taken his painting with her. On this occasion he was again the only guest, but conversation was more difficult as a piper marched round the house during the meal playing the bagpipes.

A few days later he was at a party in the House of Commons given by Lord Charles Russell when he was told that Mr Gladstone wished to speak to him. Gladstone told him that he had seen his picture at Stafford House, had much admired it and wished to ask him some questions about breaking waves. He listened very closely to Arthur's answers. 'Gladstone was always a good listener if he thought people could tell him anything he did not know,' Arthur wrote later. 'In this respect he was like John Ruskin, who was the best listener I have ever known.'[1]

★

During this time Arthur had been seeing Joan Agnew whenever he could and she became very friendly with his twin, Eleanor. When Ruskin first became aware of Arthur's admiration for Joan he invited him to take a walk in the garden at Denmark Hill, and finding a shady spot, stretched himself on the gravel path, leaning his elbow on the grass at the side.

'Now, tell me,' he said, 'what you like about Miss Agnew — what is it you see in her?'

Thus challenged Arthur was confused and scarcely knew how to reply, but he did his best to be detached and coherent, and Ruskin appeared pleased and amused when he ended his speech — 'And then she is more the Titianesque type than Fra Angelico, and I like that.'[2]

Soon afterwards he felt emboldened to confess to Ruskin that he had fallen in love with his ward, and though not exactly receiving encouragement he was told that he would be allowed to continue to see her, but that he must not make any mention of marriage. To Ruskin, who had literally been counting the days off in his diary until Rose would be twenty-one, when he believed she would decide to marry him in spite of her parents' opposition, the terms that he proposed to Arthur seemed generous. In the meantime Ruskin decided to make Joan's future secure by settling some capital on her.

At the New Year of 1868 Joan went to stay with Eleanor at Newton's house in Gower Street, and then with Connie Hilliard at Cowley Rectory. As always now when she was away, Ruskin wrote to her every day.

'There *is* a little letter for you;[3] but I read it and it was so slight and frivolous that it could not have given you pleasure, and might have given you pain. I

---

[1] Arthur Severn's Memoirs.
[2] Ibid.
[3] From Mrs La Touche.

keep it for you. On *no* account write any more. And remember that no one, except in mockery, can be called a vice-mother who wilfully hurts your *real* vice-father.... It is very bad for me to be without you just now — I have no one to tell me when I make bad faces, and the sense of my mother's loneliness weighs on me all day long like a guilt in my own employments....[1] 'I am very much pleased with your long and excellent account of the Newtonian spheres and I am rejoiced to hear you are so happy. ... I must force myself into the habit of living alone, now; (for you're sure to be married to somebody before you know where you are) — '[2]

Her cousin was more than ever depressed since Christmas, when Rose La Touche had promised faithfully to write to him and no letter had come. Unknown to him, she had again been seriously ill and now Lily Armstrong, who had been one of Ruskin's 'pets' at Winnington, wrote to him that when she visited Rose in a nursing-home she had found her strapped to the bed to prevent her from becoming violent. Arthur had ventured to speak again to Ruskin to see how long he was expected to keep to the instructions given him about Joan, and had been told that if, at the end of three years, he was still of the same mind, her guardian would make no objection to his proposing to her. Until then he could see her — but not too often — and was put on his honour not to write to her when they were apart.

Arthur was too much in awe of the older man to protest, although he said later that if he had then known him better he would have returned to the charge in a year's time and might have got his permission to speak. But Ruskin was a famous and wealthy man, while Arthur was a young artist with his way to make. He had to be content with this limited licence. On Joan's birthday, however, he sent her a drawing with which he had taken great pains — a small watercolour of a sunset at sea, with breaking waves and two dogs on the seashore.

It is not every artist-suitor who has his work automatically submitted to the greatest art-critic of the day.

'I have been mightily interested in the little drawing you have sent to Joanna,' wrote Ruskin. 'If you could simply enlarge every touch in it by a scale of a foot to the inch, it would be a quite magnificent drawing — the light in the sky is perfect — and the horizon line worthy almost of "the Master" himself.' After this praise he went on to detailed criticism about such waves being impossible on a level shore.

'You should never let yourself, even in the *least* sketch for any purpose of play, relax the habit of accurate memory and true thought — otherwise you blunt your sensibilities as well as waste your time. ... Joanna is delighted of course — I don't know what I shall do to keep her in order — she gets frightfully spoiled.'[3]

[1] 3rd January, 1868. Education Trust.
[2] 7th and 8th January, 1868. Education Trust.
[3] 5th March, 1868. In possession of author.

Arthur could not know that Ruskin, behind his calm façade, was tortured with frustration, and writing wildly to friends of his who were also friends of the La Touche family, trying desperately to find some way to make Rose his own in the face of her parents' opposition. By now he regarded the mother, who had been so intimate a friend, as an implacable enemy, but he would have been less tormented if Rose had not been so incalculable. A highly strung girl, full of mysticism bordering on religious mania, she was being pulled in one direction by her emotions and in the opposite by her sense of duty, strengthened by the dictates of an evangelical conscience. To her parents she owed obedience – and they bade her forget Ruskin; but on the last day of April she suddenly broke the barrier between them.

'Oh φῐάη, φίλη,[1] I have a letter from her,' wrote Ruskin rapturously to Mrs Cowper, 'saying "say what you will to me". Be thankful for me, and pray God may make me worthy of her always, and able to be her peace.'[2] In answer to his reply Rose wrote him a long, affectionate letter and Ruskin told Mrs Cowper next day, 'She is mine and nothing can come between us any more.'[3]

Arthur was fortunate to have chosen this day to write to Ruskin, and if the older man's love had continued to prosper he might well have found his period of waiting shortened. 'I was very glad to have your letter last night,' wrote Ruskin, 'and to know that you had been so happy. I was quite sure that I could trust you in all points of honour. I hope I may also trust you in those of prudence. Perhaps, fond as I am of my little pussy myself, I a little under-rate her attractive powers as compared with that of other girls; and I *partly* have let you see so much of her, because I thought you would get tired of her. If you do not, and as time goes on, and you see thoroughly what she is, and is not, and you still prefer her to other girls, the matter will take a different aspect to my mind; young people who like each other should be allowed to see and judge of each other in simplicity, under due knightly laws of courtesy, without the petty, provoking, or it may be agonizing, doubts as to what either they themselves, or those to whom they owe obedience, precisely mean.'[4]

Ruskin's resumed correspondence with Rose was not unalloyed pleasure. She was, as always, incalculable. When she was well and happy she would write him long, affectionate letters full of bright intelligence and teasing humour. But in times of mental stress she could withdraw coldly and write him harsh sermons, 'lecturing me as if she were the Archangel Michael and the Blessed Virgin in one'.

Mrs La Touche was away from home. 'Another lovely letter yesterday,' wrote Ruskin to Mrs Cowper, 'but very difficult to answer – for she keeps blaming me for not having trusted her, and I can't tell her what her mother was writing of her.' He asked Mrs Cowper to try to persuade her to be more humble.

---

[1] One of Ruskin's names for Mrs Cowper, meaning 'love'.
[2] 30th April, 1868. Pierpont Morgan Library.
[3] *Ruskin, the Great Victorian*, by Derrick Leon, p. 398.
[4] 5th May, 1868. In possession of author.

RUSKIN'S FORMER WIFE, EFFIE
She posed as a model for this picture
by Millais in 1853, while she was still
married to Ruskin, and told her
mother, 'It is exactly like.' She had
been happily married to Millais for
14 years when she wrote the virulent
letter to Mrs. La Touche about her
former husband which was shown to
Rose.

Detail from *The Order of Release*

ROSE LA TOUCHE IN 1874, THE
YEAR BEFORE HER DEATH

Drawing by John Ruskin

(*below*)
JOAN SEVERN AND
CONSTANCE HILLIARD AT THE
HARBOUR BELOW
BRANTWOOD IN THE EARLY
SEVENTIES. ARTHUR'S BOAT IN
THE BACKGROUND

'Try to make her believe in the possibility of her having been wrong, even when she most desired to be right – and please suggest to her that what people say of the guidance of men by the wisdom of maidens, does not in every word apply to maidens who are never allowed to speak to their lovers – and who have the misfortune to have lovers of fifty when they are just out of their teens.

'The agony they have made the poor little thing suffer, too! – and she keeps telling me how much they love her!'

He wrote to Rose that he could not discuss her parents with her, and that she was not to think of any serious matters but to rest in his quiet and constant love and get well as fast as she could. But he dreaded Mrs La Touche's reaction when she returned, and asked Mrs Cowper, if she saw her, to soothe her by 'saying that I will never take her daughter's affection from her, if she will not only give up plaguing us, and I don't mean to press for marriage in the least. If they had but the common sense to let us alone! Perhaps Rosie and I might quarrel to their perfect satisfaction – on a point of divinity – before a month was out!'[1]

A few days later Ruskin left for Dublin to deliver a lecture with which he had taken particular pains because he thought Rose would be present. Just before he left London he had had another 'lovely letter' from Rose – 'full of all sacredest love and truth'.[2] But by then her mother had come home and a note arrived on the morning of the lecture: 'I am forbidden by my father and mother to write to you or receive a letter.'

The blow was crushing. Enigmatic as ever, Rose had enclosed two rose leaves. This was a trick she had played on him before. In his bewilderment Ruskin almost decided to cancel his lecture, though the demand for tickets had been so great that they had had to change from the theatre of the Royal College of Science to a larger Concert Hall, and an audience of two thousand crowded the building long before the hour appointed.

'However, I tried to fancy the difference between getting a note with two rose leaves in it and getting none,' he wrote to Mrs Cowper, 'and so I did my lecture as well as I could. . . . At the end of it, while I was talking to the people behind me a man came up with a rather large white paper parcel, which he said he was to give into my own hand. I took it ungraciously thinking it some troublesome person and carried it carefully home. When at last I opened it, I found a large cluster of the Erba della Madonna in bloom, which was always considered as *my* plant, at Harristown – enclosed in two vine-leaves.'[3]

He was cut off from letters again, he wrote next day. Could it be a punishment 'for not liking to be unjustly scolded, even by her?' He had received a letter from Mrs Cowper that morning, enclosing an affectionate one from Rose, though she feared it was wrong of her to send it to him against the wishes of Rose's parents.

[1] 6th May, 1868. Pierpont Morgan Library.
[2] 11th May, 1868, Pierpont Morgan Library.
[3] 14th May, 1868. Leon, op. cit., p. 401.

G

'You are *too* naughty in talking of its being "wrong" to send me this letter,' wrote Ruskin angrily, 'and not saying a word of the great wrong. What — are these people to let their son throw off that innocent and true girl, Joanna, as if she were a moth to be brushed out of their way — and then is the mother after winning her entire trust to go writing lie after lie (to her) about Rose — and at last to throw her away as her son did, in a single ghastly letter, and you think the authority of this woman is a sacred thing! and that the Father, who has never commanded his son to do so much truth or justice as to write to Joan to ask her pardon — who is utterly impotent to command *any good* whatever to his only son — is *his* authority sacred, to make his other child cruel to the man who loves her so that he will bear *anything* for her?' His life was 'deadened in all usefulness' because Rose couldn't write to him.

He hinted to Mrs Cowper that Mrs La Touche was spurred by jealousy. 'This wicked woman's commands are obeyed by her husband, for whom *I* saved her, and by her child, whom she prayed me not to love, because if I did, "I should take her mother away from her".'[1]

Ruskin remained in Ireland for another week. He was staying within twenty miles of Rose and climbed the spurs of the Wicklow hills to look across the plain to where she was. 'I have debated often with myself whether or not to take the train to Salles and walk round and round Harristown on the chance of meeting her on a walk. But I felt that if I succeeded I might only give her pain and that the coming away again would be too terrible for me.'[2]

★

From Dublin he went for a few days to Winnington, the girls' school which he often visited, as a refuge from the problems of the world outside and wrote from here to Joan: 'How little all the pleasantness and brightness of affection which I receive here, makes up to me for the want of the perfect rest which I have in your constant and simple regard. There are many here who care deeply for me — but I am always afraid of hurting them — or of not saying the right thing to them. . . . But with you I am always now at rest — being sure that you know how I value you — and that whatever I say or don't say to you — you won't mind, and besides all the help that I get from your knowledge of all my little ways and inner thoughts. So I am rather sulky just now even with my best pets.'[3]

Back at Denmark Hill, miserable and lonely, he wrote to her in Scotland and every day: 'Longing for my Doanie to sing to me and play me my game of chess. Many things are troubling me all at once and I've no Doanie to comfort me. . . . Send me a letter — however short, *every* day. I can't do without one at breakfast.'[4] The reliance that he placed on this girl of twenty-two was shown

---

[1] Dublin, 14th May, 1868. Pierpont Morgan Library.
[2] 25th May, 1868. Pierpont Morgan Library.
[3] Winnington, Friday morning. *Works of John Ruskin*, vol. 36, p. 549.
[4] 2nd, 3rd, 5th June, 1868. Education Trust.

most clearly when she received a letter from him begging her to come
back.

'I have your long, sweet letter which *is* a great comfort to me already, – but
you must be of more. I have let you be as happy as I could, as long as I could, but
there is something very dark happening and I want you here; and that speedily
... the loneliness and necessity of being more or less cheerful to my mother are
too heavy upon me; and you must come back for a little while. Leave by the
earliest *convenient* train after you get this and send me word by telegram what
train you will come by, that I may meet you at the station. '[1]

Joan left her mother and sister and returned at once. The violent ebb and flow
of Ruskin's hopes of marriage with Rose had now been almost finally frozen.
Mrs La Touche, deciding at last that it was useless to continue the pretence that
the love was on Ruskin's side only, had consulted a solicitor. Ruskin's first
marriage had never been consummated and having left him his wife had obtained an annulment of the marriage, after submitting to a medical examination,
on the grounds of her husband's impotence.

Unfortunately the solicitor advised Mrs La Touche very badly, as was shown
when Ruskin himself later took Counsel's opinion on the same matter. Ruskin's
case was that they had had a mutual agreement that the marriage should not be
consummated, but he had refused to defend himself, going abroad, and leaving
everything to his father to settle. The fact that his wife was shown by a medical
examination to be *virgo intacta*, was considered by the Ecclesiastical Court, which
at that time adjudicated in cases of divorce, to be sufficient proof of his impotence. His wife had obtained her freedom and had subsequently married
Millais.

The solicitor advised Mrs La Touche that no clergyman, if he was aware that
a man was impotent, 'not . . . on hearsay conjecture, but by some known Public
Proof, such as a previous divorce upon this ground', could consent to marry
him, as the marriage would not be a legal one, but only the semblance of a
marriage. If, on the other hand, the man were to marry for a second time and it
was found that he was not really impotent, the divorce would be automatically
annulled and his previous marriage would be held good. 'In the case submitted,' wrote the solicitor, 'the parties would either contract a marriage that
would be a nullity – or else, if the lady *should* have children, they would
necessarily be illegitimate.'[2]

Mrs La Touche, in her passionate determination to prevent a marriage
between Ruskin and her daughter, imparted the solicitor's advice to the bewildered girl, ignorant and highly-strung, who had already suffered two mental
breakdowns, and the consequences were fatal both to her and to her tormented
lover. In letters to him and to mutual friends, Rose accused him harshly of
terrible sins and he, ignorant at first of the reason for her sudden accusations,

[1] Denmark Hill. 6th June, 1868. Education Trust.
[2] Leon, op. cit., p. 403.

wrote frantically to his friends, seeking their help to find explanations for her behaviour, and sinking into a wild darkness of spirit.

★

A further tragedy had struck the La Touche family with the death of Rose's elder sister, Emily, her mother's favourite and also a close friend of Joan's. 'I can't help being selfish and thinking what a daughter and friend she would have been to me,' wrote Mrs La Touche to the MacDonalds, telling them of her bereavement. 'Rose is quite different. She is a wonderful creature, but not *home-like* at all. She is full of genius and angularities. Genius, when it is young, and particularly when it is female, is a very prickly flower.'

Ruskin had confided everything to George MacDonald, the writer and poet, who had originally been introduced to him by Mrs La Touche and had since become a close friend. MacDonald and his wife considered that he had been badly treated. 'We had been feeling all this and a great deal more for you,' Mrs MacDonald replied to Mrs La Touche. 'But as friends of Mr Ruskin and Joan Agnew, we did not think it possible to write to you as we used, or that you would care to hear from us.'[1]

A few weeks later MacDonald wrote a long letter to Mrs La Touche, which he sent for Ruskin to read before dispatching it, but Ruskin declined to let it go. 'I will not send it,' he said, 'for this reason mainly — that it clearly manifests your knowledge of what as far as regards her you must never conceive yourself to know. For I hold that when a woman cares for a man to the point of wholly trusting him, and committing herself by writing — he is bound, however afterwards she may betray *him*, never to betray *her*. And though it is necessary for me to tell you the facts that you may . . . counsel me, yet you must hold them in utter fidelity to her. . . . Besides, when I wrote to you of this first, she was by various efforts keeping R. and me separate, when it was not R.'s will that it should be so: and I wish you to show your sense of her folly and cruelty in this, because I thought you could help me. But *now*, R. *herself* has left me — past hope. You can help me no longer — you can only add to anger and pain.'[2]

Joan was Ruskin's only comfort during that dreary summer of misunderstandings and frustration. Eleanor Severn heard with resentment of Arthur being told to wait three years before he could talk about love or marriage to Joan, and impulsively wrote to Joan herself urging the unfairness of this arrangement to her twin. Ruskin, writhing in the torments of frustrated love, was in no mood to sympathize, and Eleanor's bold bid for her twin's happiness brought him only a letter of rebuke:

'My dear Arthur,

I have no time, this week, to speak or write to you at any length on this matter. It is a somewhat difficult one — for on the one hand, you must not

[1] 2nd July, 1868, Leon, op. cit., p. 412.
[2] 21st July, 1868, Denmark Hill. Ibid.

do Joanna the wrong of allowing her to become an occasion of breach — or discontentment, between you and your twin-sister: neither on the other hand, ought you to allow your sister to interfere in a discourteous ~~and clandestine~~ *
manner with an arrangement so gravely affecting your happiness, and the dignity of the girl whom for the present you regard. . . . But as things are — I believe I should do both you and Eleanor an injustice, if I allowed her petulance to be the immediate cause of the interruption of all relations between Jonnna and you. For the present, I simply ignore Eleanor's letters — I wish you to meet Joanna at the Richmonds as if nothing had happened: and I have desired Joanna to forget everything but the play — and . . . to conquer the very natural pro-vocation which might otherwise have made her so far visit your sister's fault upon your head — as to disturb the comfort of the evening. There is so little happiness in the world that I grudge the loss of an evening. (I myself shall look back all my life with sorrow to the loss of — half an hour !)

'Afterwards, we will determine what is best. I have no doubt that you will agree with me as to what is right, and will fearlessly do it: — and for the present, rest content with my assurance that I will do nothing without your concurrence in its expediency — and that I will not allow anything that has happened to alter my own feelings of interest in you and regard for you.

Believe me faithfully yours,

J. RUSKIN.

'*I have drawn my pen through *this* word for Eleanor has erred partly through frankness and impulsiveness. But I meant that she ought first to have spoken to *you*, and then written to me, not to Joanna.'[1]

However, Arthur continued to see Joan, as often as he could without incur-ring her guardian's displeasure, until she went north in August for the birth of of her sister's baby. Then, keeping to his agreement, he did not write to her. Ruskin left home a few days afterwards for Abbeville, and wrote to her as usual every day. He was trying to immerse himself so constantly in work that he would have little time to think or to feel. 'My work is an opiate,' he said. Forgetting the difference in their ages, he urged Joan, too, to find her happiness in work: 'I think the happiness you have felt . . . in your mathematical drawing, your illumination, your flower painting, and your more tedious writing from my dictation, or more playful unpacking and dusting of minerals and books — and perhaps most of all, in the new ideas given you by the study of history, may show you . . . in what directions the safest, if not the highest happiness lies; and we will both hope henceforward to make our days less dependent either on other persons, or on future hopes.'[2]

'My dear, it was not tiring of work, but wanting to play — that used to be your misfortune — nor need you mind having a treacherous memory. . . . It requires no memory to dust books, to weed gardens, to plan furnishings, to

---

[1] 1st July, 1868. In possession of author.
[2] 22nd September, 1868. Education Trust.

paint flowers, to illuminate, to cook, to sew, or to write from Cuzzie's dictation. All that we ought to do – we always can. What we can't – we oughtn't. Ever your loving Cuzzie Piggie,

J. R.[1]

★

Ruskin was making immensely detailed architectural drawings of the buildings of Abbeville. Apart from the visits of several assistants, whom he put to drawing other buildings, and of his gardener, Downs, brought over to observe how the French grew their melons, his life was quiet and retired, and he began to feel better and to believe that if he could continue this existence he would find some sort of happiness, even without hope of Rose. He wanted Joan to share it.

'I won't be taken out of this quiet life any more as long as it does me good,' he wrote, 'and I won't see people – and I won't let you go out often to tire yourself – but I must get you to fall into our old pleasant ways – and live with old Greeks and Jews – and not with Ps nor As[2] nor any disturbing letters.

'And I believe the Proper P or A if he is to come at all – will come when you are properly helping P. A. – Pa.'[3]

It did not occur to him that this was an unnatural programme for a lively young girl of twenty-two. Joan seemed to have recovered from the hurt of her broken engagement the year before, though the enforced estrangement from Rose, with whom she had been so intimate, still gave her pain. 'I hope we shall have a much pleasanter autumn than last,' Ruskin wrote. 'It may easily be that! . . . and I trust no letter that comes to me wee *amie* this autumn will be other than some sweet message of love to her from one or other of her many *true* friends.'[4]

After a few days in Paris, where he saw his American friend Professor Norton, and met Longfellow, Ruskin returned home to Denmark Hill and at first his new calm continued. 'Whenever you can come I shall rejoice to have you,' he wrote to Joan, 'but I am well now into tranquil work, and am in no direct need of you. Tomorrow, I shall write you a quite *proper* letter, beginning "my dear Joanna", with Auntie's various messages . . . but today, I for myself tell you, for your friends' sakes and your own, to do exactly what is pleasant and free.'[5]

He knew that his mother would be jealous and disapproving of the complete intimacy with which he wrote to Joan, and so frequently sent two letters in an envelope, one of which had been shown to old Mrs Ruskin and could equally be handed round the family circle in Scotland. These letters included no reference to 'dearest wee pussie' or 'cuzzie piggies' but began "My dear Joanna' and ended 'Ever your affectionate Cousin, J. Ruskin.'

---

[1] Saturday, 26th September, 1868. Education Trust.
[2] Percys nor Arthurs.
[3] 27th September, 1868. Education Trust.
[4] 9th October, 1868. Education Trust.
[5] 22nd October, 1868. Education Trust.

Soon he began to be more urgent about her return: 'Come away, now, Pussie, as fast as you can. We want you.'[1]

Throughout all the dramas and misunderstandings Mrs Cowper had remained a true friend both to Ruskin and to Rose, in correspondence with both of them and helping whenever she felt she could. Towards the end of the year, however, her latest letter to Rose was returned, unopened, by Mrs La Touche, accompanied by an offensive letter, which also contained a note to Joan, asking her never to write to Rose or to herself again.[2] So uncontrolled were these letters that Mrs Cowper, remembering that Mrs La Touche had been worrying about Rose's illness and that during the past year she had also lost her elder and favourite daughter, destroyed them, without passing on the one addressed to Joan. With her usual kindness she asked Ruskin to bring Joan with him on a short visit to Broadlands and she and her mother-in-law, Lady Palmerston, showed her particular attention.[3]

A few days after their return Mrs La Touche, evidently overcome by remorse, wrote to Mrs Cowper to apologize for her previous letter.

'Since I dispatched my letter ... I have much regretted what must have appeared to you its discourteous language, and I have felt that not only an explanation, but an apology, was due to you. ... After Rose had sent her first letter to Joan last Wednesday, she was seized with one of the attacks of violent pain which the slightest agitation now causes. Her doctor at once saw that she had been subjected to fresh excitement, and said it was vain to hope for any progress as long as there was a possibility of renewed agitation. I wrote as I did by his express orders.

'I send you a copy of a legal opinion taken on the supposed case of a man divorced on the plea of "incurable impotency" ... and I ask you if it is pardonable that he should have offered marriage to any woman upon earth.'[4]

A few days later she wrote again, 'Will you, in justice to me – tell Joan I wrote to her? ... There were none but loving and kind words in the note you did not give her. ... No one feels more deeply than I do, the wrong that she has been done her. She knows that I *never* thought my boy worthy of her, and *he* knows how bitterly ashamed of him I have been, and how grieved, both at what he did and at the way he did it.'[5]

Ruskin's interpretation of Mrs La Touche's behaviour to Joan over her broken engagement was stern: 'You perhaps do not know,' he had written to George MacDonald some months earlier, 'that Percy La Touche was engaged to my cousin six months ago, and broke off the engagement in so dastardly a way that I cannot, in looking back to all things, believe that it was wholly his own doing – but the mother's, *through* his weakness. ... The mother got (Rose), after she

[1] 5th November, 1868. Education Trust.
[2] (First week December 1868.) Leon, op. cit., p. 414.
[3] Ruskin to Mrs Cowper, 8th December, (1868). Pierpont Morgan Library.
[4] 11th December, 1868. Leon, op. cit., p. 415.
[5] December 1868. Ibid., p. 416.

had stayed staunch and true for these last two years, at last into her power, through — as far as I can trace — the influence of an evangelical friend on Rose, and the child gave me up. The mother wrote lie after lie about her for some time after that to my cousin — but at last, in the vilest and cruellest way, abandoned my cousin also.'[1]

Scarcely had Arthur, unconscious of these dramas, seen Joan on her return to London, than news came that his father was very ill and he had to leave in haste for Rome.

[1] 7th March, 1868, Leon, op. cit., p. 395.

CHAPTER 20

JOURNEYS AND EVENTS

1869 – 1870

JOSEPH SEVERN WAS SEVENTY-FIVE YEARS OLD. Claudia wished to go to him, but she was an invalid now, with seven children, and rarely left the house. After anxious family conferences, Eleanor and Arthur set off together and completed the long journey without a stop, arriving just after Christmas (1868). They found their father still very weak but in good spirits and overjoyed to see them. He had been seriously ill for six weeks, but had been nursed with devotion by his two secretaries, 'who have been like my sons'.

For some time before his illness he had been suffering from recurrent attacks of rheumatism which affected his knees and fingers, so that sometimes he could not play his piano and even painting was painful. But he was still full of optimistic plans. An old picture which he had bought for £2 10s., with the idea of cleaning and retouching it during his convalescence, was said by a knowledgeable friend to be by Coreggio and of great value. 'It seems that I have great skill in these matters and so as the old pictures cost a song when in their dirt, I shall go on and pick up all I can, as I may form a valuable collection.'

His optimism was still unquenchable, his spirits as resilient as a young man's. His one worry was how to provide for Eleanor, in case she did not marry, and by two months after Christmas he had at last scraped together £100 with which to buy fifty shares in a scheme to bring the famous water, Acqua Marcia, from a mountain lake to Rome. Now he felt he would be sure of £150 a year 'whatever befalls'.

The spring was lovely in Rome. Arthur had brought out several finished pictures to show his father and they spent happy hours discussing their painting.

'You know that I have got my dear twins with me,' Joseph wrote to his sister, 'and you can imagine how pleasant it is for me . . . but 'tis singular they don't in the least resemble each other. We make a nice trio, very jolly.'[1]

Arthur was surrounded by fine subjects for his painting, and Eleanor set out to make her father's home less shabby. 'My twins are well and very pleasant,' wrote Joseph to his brother. 'Arthur is drawing and Eleanor sewing covers to my chairs with her machine.' In the same letter he asked 'a great favour of you and which you granted me once before — *to get me the mask of Keats* somewhere in Trafalgar Square, and have it *slightly* packed so as to come to me in the

[1] 22nd February, 1869. Keats House.

despatch bag without injury. . . . Mr Story, the sculptor, has done a beautiful bust of Shelley and will now do one of Keats.'[1]

In the early summer Arthur left his father and Eleanor for a painting tour of Germany with Brabazon. On the way back to Munich at the end of June they stopped in Verona, where Arthur had heard that Ruskin was staying. He had been working there for nearly two months, having taken, after his usual habit, two painter protégés with him, on this occasion Arthur Burgess and John Bunney. When Arthur found him he was hard at work with an assistant, measuring tombs and making a careful drawing of one of the stone griffins outside the Cathedral.[2]

Ruskin seemed pleased to see Arthur and immediately invited him to dinner. Arthur made several attempts to bring the conversation round to Joan, but Ruskin 'answered in rather a sad way' and let the subject drop. When this had happened several times Arthur saw that he would get no encouragement and gave it up.

It was with great sadness that Joseph saw the twins leave him in the autumn, but nothing could keep his spirits subdued for long: 'Sorry I am that I am to be alone . . .' he wrote to Tom, 'as I am very dull . . . *in the evenings*, but my friends begin to tumble in and so I shall be kept alive. Here's a charming English lady takes me out in her carriage two or three times a week, she has just come back.' He added a wistful postscript. 'We have a beautiful October – when shall I ever be able to come to England again?'[3]

He rarely went out after dark. The disorders in the Holy City were becoming worse, and anarchy spreading right up to the city walls. A suburban train was attacked and pillaged by brigands, and seventeen murders were committed or attempted in Rome within three months. The Pope chose this moment to canonize twenty-one new saints. 'If His holiness had given orders for the construction of twenty-one more trains, or for the execution of twenty-one notorious assassins, or for the release of twenty-one unjustly imprisoned citizens,' said Joseph, 'or even for the banishment of twenty-one mischief-pandering Princes of the Church, his action would have been more to the point.'[4]

★

Arthur lost no time in calling at Denmark Hill when he and Eleanor got back to London. Ruskin, too, had just returned from Italy, and had been elected Slade Professor of Art at Oxford, but Arthur's hopes of seeing Joan were not realized. She had spent July and August in Scotland with her sister, who was expecting a second child, and just before Arthur's return in October news came

---

[1] 21st April, 1869, Keats House.
[2] Athur Severn's Memoirs.
[3] 20th October, 1869. Keats House.
[4] Joseph Severn's *Reminiscences*, quoted Sharp, p. 277.

that Kate was very ill, and she left again immediately for Scotland and did not return until the New Year (1870). Kate died in November and she stayed with her distraught brother-in-law, helping to care for his two motherless babies.

'I do not doubt but that you feel as if you never could be happy any more', Ruskin wrote to her. 'But there is much in life yet for you, and we ought not to think ourselves less happy than other creatures because for so long, we have had a sister so dear that her loss makes the world a blank. I declare to you Joanie dear — I know it — if only I had ever been happy with — for a few, ever so few years, I would not feel so bitterly as I do now.'[1]

Everything for Ruskin still came back to Rose. Since her mother's letters to Mrs Cowper the previous December he had had no word from her, nor had he attempted to communicate with her directly. But that autumn, after his return from Italy, he heard from Mrs Cowper that Rose had unexpectedly written to her again, and that she was obviously very unhappy at home.

'It is impossible to help writing to you,' she had said. 'I try not to . . . but I cannot help thinking of you and longing to talk to you. . . . Mama grows harder to me and I shut up, for what I *do* say she misunderstands. I should not mind her disagreeing with me in everything, if she only seemed to love me — but I don't want to grow hard — only it seems as if I *must*, or else feel it all and be so unhappy.'[2]

Mrs Cowper wrote to Ruskin that Percy La Touche had become engaged to Lady Annette Scott, daughter of Lord Clonmell. 'Indeed I fear that poor little Joan is still foolish enough to be troubled by that piece of news,' he replied; 'though when I think how I should feel, if I heard that someone else was going to be married, I don't wonder.'[3]

He missed Joan and her calming effect on his mother and himself. 'Auntie is so far well,' he wrote to her, 'but has had pain in her side; she reads wonderfully — and has taken to lecturing me from my own books — as if I entirely disobeyed everything that was in them!'[4]

Joan arrived back at Denmark Hill on 3rd January, 1870, which was Rose's twenty-first birthday — the date to which Ruskin had once counted the days. It was the moment when he had long believed that she would feel free to make her own decision, independently of her parents, and proclaim her firm intention to become his wife. Joan's return helped him to get through the weary day and mitigated its bitterness a little, but it was a sad homecoming and continued so. 'Joan is a real angel,' wrote Ruskin to Mrs Cowper. 'She keeps as cheerful and sweet as ever while I am by, to keep from hurting me — then I see the poor face get sad in a minute or two, when it's by itself.'[5]

★

[1] Thursday, 19th (November, 1869). Education Trust.
[2] Leon, op. cit., p. 477.
[3] 24th October (1869). Pierpont Morgan Library.
[4] Tuesday (November, 1869). Education Trust.
[5] Denmark Hill, 4th January, 1870. Pierpont Morgan Library.

Four days after Joan's return Ruskin met Rose accidentally, and she refused to speak to him. The encounter took place in the new rooms of the Royal Academy which had just moved to Burlington House.[1] 'I went into the rooms of the Royal Academy yesterday about noon,' wrote Ruskin to Mrs Cowper, 'and the first person I saw was R.

'She tried to go away as soon as she saw me — so that I had no time to think — I caught her — but she broke away so that I could not say more than ten words — uselessly.

'She then changed her mind about going, and remained in the rooms apparently quite cheerful and undisturbed. Having looked at her well, I went up to her side again and said "I think you have dropped your pocket-book" — offering her her letter of engagement between the gold plates. She said, "No." I said again, "No?" enquiringly. She repeated the word. I put the letter back in my breast and left the rooms.

'She is usually as quick as lightning but I am not sure that she saw clearly what it was I offered her. She might have thought it was only an endeavour to give her a letter.

'I am so brisé that I can hardly move or think today.'[2]

The encounter affected him so painfully that he was ill for a week and unable to work, just at the moment when he was painstakingly preparing his inaugural lecture for Oxford and wanted his mind to be clear and strong.

'Three years ago a brother and sister were engaged,' he wrote to a friend. 'One to my good little cousin Joanna. The other to me. Joanna's engagement was sudden, but to her very vital and precious. Mine was after service of seven years. . . . Today Joanna's lover is being married far away. *She* is with me, her favourite sister just dead, and last Friday . . . my mistress passed me and would not speak. The way she was taken from me was singularly horrible. Her mother was jealous of her with me, and having sought to break the engagement by every other means in her power, and from the love she bore me changed into an incarnate Hate, brought the child, who was utterly holy and pure, into such communication with all those who speak or know any evil of me, as to cause her love to perish in the bitterest pain.'[3]

Poor Joan, already exhausted and miserable after nursing her sister, seeing her die and comforting the stricken husband, had returned to Ruskin's grief and now an even more personal blow. It was Mrs Cowper, ever kind, who realized that the accumulation of what Joan was being asked to bear was too much for any girl of her age, and pressed her to leave Denmark Hill for a visit to Broadlands, where she could have a rest from all responsibilities. William Cowper's mother, Lady Palmerston, had died the year before and his step-father having made Broadlands over to him, he had now taken the name of Cowper-Temple.

---

[1] Not, as has hitherto been thought, in the street.
[2] Denmark Hill, 8th January, 1870. Pierpont Morgan Library.
[3] 12th January, 1870. Leon, op. cit., 478.

At Broadlands Joan was surrounded by people who were devoted admirers of Ruskin, and their kindness acted like balm on her bruised heart.

Perhaps on Mrs Cowper-Temple's advice, Joan went back to Scotland soon after her visit, and stayed there with her brother-in-law for the next two months, helping him with the children and the house, and doing her best to comfort him with her quiet cheerfulness. About the same time Ruskin wrote a bitter letter to Rose, reproaching her for her cruel behaviour, not only to himself but to Joan, and questioning the value of a religion which allowed her to be influenced to do what she knew herself was neither kind nor right. Rose first sent an indignant reply, addressed to Mrs Cowper-Temple, asking her to send it on only if she wished. Mrs Cowper-Temple decided not to do so.

Rose had concluded her letter with a verse:

> 'This is my prayer, if Thou dost send
> Blessing or pain to him and me,
> Give me the pain — but bless my friend,
> Whom I have loved eternally.'[1]

★

Ruskin was occupied with his first lectures as Slade Professor of Art at Oxford; the audience for this inaugural lecture was so large that it had to be given in the Sheldonian instead of the Museum as planned. He went back and forth between Denmark Hill and Oxford, where he stayed with the Aclands. Towards the end of February he returned to London on a sunny, warm day and quite unexpectedly found a letter from Rose waiting for him on his study table, in which she promised that she would never withdraw herself from him again.

'If my love is any sunshine to you take it — and keep it,' Rose had written to him.

'She has come back to me. She will not leave me any more,' he wrote joyfully to Mrs Cowper-Temple. But he could not see her yet or even write.[2]

'You have every right to know that the great darkness has ended for me,' he wrote to George MacDonald. 'R. has come back to me, and nothing now can take her from me — in heart — though if fate will have it so, I may never see her — but she is mine, now. No one must know this, however, as it would cause her infinite grief and pain with her people.'[3]

Ruskin wrote to Joan daily, and was soon asking when she would be coming back from Scotland, questions which before long turned to urgings. He told her that he had just been making a new will 'and I've left you my great Turner of the Lake of Geneva, Doanie dear — but I'm sure you like having me better, so I hope you won't have to for ever so long.'[4] His other Turners were to be

---

[1] In this year Rose published a little volume of devotional verse and prose, entitled *Clouds and Light*.
[2] Denmark Hill, 23rd February, 1870. Pierpont Morgan Library.
[3] Denmark Hill, 11th March, 1870. Leon, op. cit., p. 481.
[4] Denmark Hill, 25th March, 1870. Education Trust.

divided between Mrs Cowper-Temple, his American friend, Professor Norton, and herself. Norton was to have all his books and manuscripts but to give Joan any that she wanted. 'I shall be very, very thankful to have my Pussie back. For now — tho I am fond of many people in a way — and heartily desire to make them happy, I don't really *love* anybody except Rosie and my Pussie.'[1]

As soon as she returned he set off for the Continent, taking her with him, also Connie Hilliard and her mother, their maid, his man-servant, Crawley, and the indispensable Downs. Ruskin always preferred to travel in a party of his own choosing — and usually one that he paid for. They were away for three months and on their return Joan left again almost immediately for Scotland.

---

[1] 16th April, 1870. Education Trust.

CHAPTER 21

TWO MARRIAGES AND
A RAPPROCHEMENT

1870–1871

A S THINGS HAD FALLEN OUT Joan had been away from London almost all the time since Arthur had returned from Rome in October. While she was abroad with Ruskin and the Hilliards in that summer of 1870 Arthur's twin was married to Henry Furneaux, an Oxford don — a Fellow of Corpus Christi. He was some years older than she, a great classical scholar and a charming and witty companion.

He gave up his Fellowship on his marriage and was appointed to the living of Lower Heyford, which was in the gift of his college, a village of grey stone cottages in the Cherwell valley. He was a man of some fortune and immediately began to make plans for the construction of walled gardens and greenhouses, new coach-houses and stables. Charles Newton had given her a fine trousseau from a leading dressmaker for her marriage. Some of the bonnets, she reflected ruefully when she settled into her new home, were perhaps a shade too smart for church in an Oxfordshire village.

*

Autumn came and with it the end of the three years that Ruskin had told Arthur he must wait. The young man wrote to him, reminding him of his promise. 'My dear Mr Severn,' Ruskin answered formally, 'I am glad to receive your letter, for, whatever may be the issue, it is an honour to any girl to be remembered during three years of absence — and preferred after deliberate comparison with others.

'Joanna is at present in Scotland — she will probably return about the 10th or 12th of October — you shall then have free permission to come here as often as you wish — if you can obtain her's. In the meantime, can you dine with me any day after Monday this week, and talk the matter over?'[1]

'Arthur Severn dines here, I hope, tonight,' he wrote to Joan in Scotland. 'I shall only *now* ask if he really is sure that he will always take as much care of my pussy as I should myself — (not easy) — and if he will, — why I suppose I must give him leave to try and get her.

[1] Denmark Hill, 25th September, 1870. In possession of author.

'But "one never knows". Men are such horrid creatures – I think there should be nothing but beautiful Rosies and Joanies and Connies in the world.'[1]

Arthur left the big house at Denmark Hill elated, having won Ruskin's permission to see as much as he liked of Joan and to talk freely to her. But before she arrived in London she wrote a letter to Ruskin which he was to preserve all his life, put away in an envelope marked by him 'Joan, very precious'.

'My darling Coz,

   . . . Of course I am wondering very much whether Arthur *did* dine with you last night – and what the result was of any talk you had with him . . . I consider *you* unspeakably dear and good about the whole matter – whatever the consequences may be – "one never knows"! – truly. This much I *do* know, that there never could be anyone to come up to my di Pa – or take the same care of me *he* has always done – and be to me what he has always *been* – and it is a great grief to me that I never have any way of showing you this thoroughly. Di Pa I wonder if you know how much Pussy loves you? and how grateful she is? and how she can never repay you except by just being always your own wee Pussy – and she must always be this? – for her chief happiness in life depends upon it. Whatever happens – or "turns up" this at least must be certain.

'Then I am continually thinking of all *you* have on your mind – and heart? – and I shall be oh! *so* thankful when things are settled – one way or another – no I don't mean "or another" I mean the *one way* that is best, and happiest for my di Pa.'[2]

Joan arrived back at Denmark Hill on 11th October. Lily Armstrong was also staying there and it was arranged that Arthur should join them in Ruskin's box at the theatre on the evening of the 14th.

Arthur took immense trouble with his dress that evening and spoiled a number of white ties before he was eventually satisfied with his appearance. Ruskin had omitted to tell him the number of his box, so Arthur took with him a pair of opera glasses with which to scan the boxes from the back of the dress circle. The play was *Kenilworth*, with Mrs Rousby as Amy Robsart. 'I had a good look round, but to my disappointment saw no one answering to Miss Agnew or Ruskin anywhere. But there was a pretty-looking girl in black, leaning out of a box, and I thought I would have a look at her (through my glasses) in the meantime before going round to the boxes.' To his astonishment he saw in a moment that this was Miss Agnew herself – he had never thought of her wearing black.

'I lost no time in going round – and found Ruskin, Miss Armstrong (a pretty Irish girl) Miss Aitken (a niece of Thomas Carlyle) and – Miss Agnew!'[3] The meeting was made easier by the necessity of listening to the play, and conversation (not that Arthur ever had much difficulty with that) by having the acting and the story to discuss. The girls were all lively and Ruskin at his most

---

[1] Denmark Hill, Wednesday, 28th September, 1870. Education Trust.
[2] Thursday, 1st (October 1870). Education Trust.
[3] Arthur Severn's Memoirs.

charming. Arthur sat a little behind Miss Agnew and watched her as the play proceeded. Her wonderfully delicate skin showed to perfection against the black dress, her thick reddish-brown curly hair was carefully arranged, and the peak that it grew into on her forehead was even more definite than he had remembered. She was very pretty. An added attraction for Arthur was her soft Scottish accent which reminded him of his mother's voice.

Before the party separated it was arranged that Arthur should come out to Denmark Hill the following Friday afternoon. He had told Ruskin that his friend, Brabazon, would like to see his Turners, and Ruskin wrote two days later to suggest that they should both come to dinner — 'Not that I will promise to be at home; but the Turners will be there at any rate, and with warning, perhaps Miss Armstrong and Joanna may be there to take off the covers — but come to dinner if you can'.[1] Brabazon could not manage it, but another young man took his place — Harry Acland, one of Henry Acland's seven sons.

After this Arthur and Joan met frequently. Lily Armstrong who was still staying at Denmark Hill, had an admirer called Mr Edwardes who made a convenient fourth for dinners or for excursions to the Richmonds' or other mutual friends. Then Connie Hilliard came to join the party for a few days, bringing her first grown-up evening dress, which Ruskin had given her. It was immediately decided that an opportunity must be made as soon as possible for her to wear it in public, and before the evening ended it was all arranged. A party was to be given at Denmark Hill such as had never been given in the Ruskins' house before — a *Dance*.

A night was chosen (8th November) when Ruskin had an engagement. Mrs Hilliard was persuaded to come as chaperone and to help Joan in her duties as hostess. Connie appeared in the full glory of her first décolleté dress, and the party was already a great success when Ruskin returned. He had spent the earlier part of the evening in a rather different atmosphere at the Metaphysical Society, where in company with the Deans of Westminster and Canterbury, the Bishop of Worcester, the Chancellor of the Exchequer, Archbishop Manning and the Principals of various university colleges, he had heard Huxley reading a paper entitled, 'Has a Frog a Soul? and if so, of what Nature is that Soul?'

Ruskin was working on a course of lectures, *The Elements of Sculpture*, which he was to deliver at Oxford at the end of the month, and in these few weeks he rarely went out during the day — except occasionally to the British Museum to consult Newton or to visit Mr Vaux, the Severns' old friend and Keeper of the Coin Room, as he intended to illustrate his lectures with Greek coins rather than with broken fragments of statues. In the evenings he liked sometimes to take the girls to the theatre, when Arthur and Mr Edwardes usually made up the party. Old Mrs Ruskin did not approve of the theatre and her permission had always to be obtained before her son could take his party to a play. This task had for

<hr>

[1] Denmark Hill, 16th October, 1870. In possession of author.

some time now been delegated to Joan, whose diplomacy almost always ensured that permission was granted.

Mrs Ruskin had long been very lame from a broken leg (or 'limb', as she preferred to call it) which had not set properly, and by now she could scarcely walk at all. Her eyesight was also failing and she was nearly blind. But the dictatorial old lady was still very much mistress of the house. 'She knows where everything is and should be, and considers that she takes care of Joan, and not Joan of her.'[1]

Ruskin's preoccupation with his approaching lectures left the carriage free almost every day for the girls to use, and they could drive into London and pay calls or visit picture exhibitions. Sometimes Arthur would dine at Denmark Hill and after dinner they would all sing, with Joan at the piano.

The day before Ruskin left for Oxford to deliver his lectures Joan, Lily and Arthur went to stay with Eleanor and her husband at Heyford, and it was there that all was finally settled between Arthur and Joan. They felt happy and care-free – only Joan could not help worrying a little about her cousin. They met him in Oxford after his second lecture, and Ruskin was introduced to Eleanor's husband. Afterwards he went back to Abingdon, where he was staying, and wrote to her: 'Mr Furneaux looked very nice, but you know I don't like people who marry people. I wish Arfie would let things go on just as they are.'[2]

But Arthur was to be put off no longer, and their engagement was announced. His father's old friend, George Richmond, at whose house he and Joan had first met, wrote him a charming letter of congratulation:

'I should be ashamed of myself if I could hear of any good, or ill happening to a Severn without warm interest, for I have known you all from infancy and have followed your several fortunes with affectionate interest, but when I hear that Arthur! is to be married to Joan! then I cannot but exclaim, he is indeed a lucky fellow, for you have won the affection of a fair lady who, whether in sunshine, shade or shower will I believe be as true as gold. One whose "outward semblance" lovely and attractive as that is, is as nothing to the warm and generous and noble nature that dwells in it, and may well make a man very happy to call his own. Dear Arthur I heartily congratulate you, and wish you and my dear friend Joan many many happy years of married life.'[3]

Once the marriage was a certainty Ruskin behaved with his usual generosity, saying that he would give them the remainder of the lease of the house on Herne Hill, which he had lived in as a child, and which he had lately planned to fit up to take some of his collections. His own hopes of marriage with Rose now seemed finally to have ended. Mrs La Touche had found out that there had been a rapprochement between them and in a last desperate attempt to separate them had written to Ruskin's former wife, now married to Millais. Effie Millais, after

---

[1] *Octavia Hill* by E. S. Maurice, p. 164.
[2] Abingdon, 27th (November, 1870) Education Trust.
[3] 10 York Street. 30th November, 1870. In possession of author.

fourteen years of happy married life with her second husband, replied to Mrs La Touche with a virulent letter.

She was a worldly woman, and having, as Ruskin's wife, enjoyed buying expensive clothes and having her own carriage, and particularly being invited to parties in grand houses — a pleasure which he did not share, though he humoured her in it — she had really suffered from the social ostracism which was the aftermath of the scandal caused by the suit which she had brought against her husband. This had continued for a time, even after her marriage to Millais. The idea that Ruskin might be about to remarry and that the whole scandal would be brought up again, just when her second husband had established himself as a successful and highly paid artist, when they had lately moved into a large house in a fashionable area of London, when they had won their way to acceptance in the social world, was enough to make Effie Millais violent in self-justification, and it followed, in denunciation of Ruskin.

'I think his conduct can only be excused on the score of madness,' she wrote to Mrs La Touche. 'His wickedness in trying his dreadful influence over your daughter is terrible to think of.' She described Ruskin's conduct to herself as impure, discreditable and dishonourable. His mind was inhuman and he was utterly incapable of making a woman happy. 'He is quite unnatural and in that one thing all the rest is embraced.'[1]

Armed with this letter, Mrs La Touche was now able to present Ruskin to her daughter as a monster of mysterious depravity. Rose was made to swear to her father that she would have no more correspondence with him, and her friends undertook never to mention his name to her again. Mrs La Touche wrote a letter of warm thanks to Effie Millais, but Rose, although shocked and terrified by the heavy burden of guilt which she must believe that Ruskin bore, in her heart could not think that his influence over herself had been an evil one. In her diary, a short time before, she had reviewed her mental and spiritual life, and in many entries had acknowledged the debt she owed to him. 'I think it was Mr Ruskin's teaching when I was about twelve that made me first take to looking after the poor. . . . Mr Ruskin taught me that which was good. . . . The letters Mr Ruskin wrote me only helped me, and did me no harm, whatever others may say.'[2]

Until the Oxford term began Ruskin was at home, but he felt lonely, and complained 'Joan's always away now, somewhere',[3] though he refused Eleanor's invitation to join them all at Heyford in February, being 'afraid he'd be pounced on by other people'. He was preparing three lectures on *Landscapes* for Oxford, and had just published the first of a series of monthly letters addressed to the Workmen and Labourers of Great Britain, which he called *Fors Clavigera*. In these letters he was to criticize the times they lived in, to castigate commercialism

---

1 *The Order of Release*, by Admiral Sir William James, pp. 254–6.
2 *Works*, vol. 35, p. lxxxii.
3 To Mrs Cowper-Temple, 10th January, 1871. *Works*, vol. 37, p. 27.

as the cause of poverty and crime, and to call on individuals by reforming their own lives, to help to put right the evils of the modern world.

It marked a change of purpose in his life. His mother, in passionate gratitude for the gift of a son at the age of thirty-eight, had dedicated him to the service of God. She had always intended him to be a minister, and it was many years before she was reconciled to the idea of his being a layman. Yet Ruskin was in truth a spiritual teacher all his life. During that part of his life which was now ending he had preached the gospel of beauty. His early books were full of vivid eloquent descriptions of the beauties of mountains, clouds, and sky. He saw in them a reflection of God and had tried to open other men's eyes so that they, too, could feel the same rapturous response to natural beauty. The artist he saw as a priest-like figure, whose duty it was to interpret Nature — and thus God — to his fellow men. 'All great art is praise,' he had written.

This had been his message, and with it he had deeply influenced his generation. Charlotte Brontë wrote that his book, *Modern Painters*, had given her a new sense — sight. But as he grew older he had become increasingly aware of evil in the world, and a sense of personal responsibility for the well-being of his fellow-men had grown upon him. He saw around him the results of the Industrial Revolution, blighting the countryside, covering it with a rash of ugly, jerry-built houses and polluting the air with coal-dust, while in the cities the artisan was becoming a mindless slave of the new machines.

Ruskin burned with rage as he contemplated the brutalities of a society which called itself Christian, and he had set his hand to no less a task than to remake England and to convert his countrymen to his own kind of Christianity. He wanted to create a society where art and industry, beauty and commerce, would be interdependent, in which every workman would receive a fair wage and be certain of employment, and art should be enjoyed by all.

It was this mission that he felt was threatened by the emotional strain of his relations with Rose La Touche and his battle with her parents for her mind. 'No other man in England ... has in him the divine rage against iniquity, falsity and baseness that Ruskin has, and that every man ought to have',[1] his friend, Carlyle, wrote to Emerson in America.

Arthur and Joan were to be married in April. Most of the time before then Ruskin spent at Oxford delivering his lectures. 'This seems to put an end, abruptly, to all Denmark Hill life',[2] he wrote to Norton.

He still wrote every day to Joan and complained if he had to pass a day without a letter from her. Fortunately old Mrs Ruskin, now in her ninetieth year, had taken a great fancy to Arthur and looked forward to his visits. Every evening he passed at Denmark Hill he was invited to go upstairs and sit by her bed. 'She was most agreeable, and appeared to me much better-looking and gentler and sweeter than when I had been a little frightened of her as a boy. She never

---

[1] *Correspondence of Carlyle & Emerson*, vol. 2, p. 352.
[2] 23rd February, 1871. *Letters of John Ruskin to C. E. Norton.*

lectured me, often tipped me, getting her purse from under the pillow without any difficulty and nearly always talking of her early days. Just before my marriage she gave me a considerable sum of money, but it was only to be spent on our bedroom furniture, and that was to be mahogany.'[1] Ruskin was very pleased. 'It is immensely nice Auntie's and Arfie's going on with each other like that!'[2]

That spring he was elected to an Honorary Fellowship of Corpus Christi College. Until then, when working at Oxford, he had stayed either with the Aclands at their house in Broad Street, or outside the city, at Abingdon. During a visit to examine some illuminated manuscripts he had asked a tutor of the College if it would be possible for him to obtain rooms in Corpus. Now the President and Fellows had elected him to an Honorary Fellowship and he was to have the rooms on the first floor looking out over the meadows which, until his marriage to Eleanor, had been occupied by Henry Furneaux. Members of the Senior Common Room would have been surprised at the words in which the professor of Art imparted this news to his cousin, saying that he had 'leave from great big peepsie today, to have my little room all to selfie — and to have Wattie to fit it up and dow — so *ats* all *ite*'.[3]

Ruskin was sad at Joan's approaching marriage, and his melancholy increased when, on returning home on the last day of March he found his old nurse, Anne, had died. To him, with his nostalgia for childhood, this was a great blow. She had nursed him since his birth and had adored him and his father. Only his mother had never been able to get on with her, and they had carried on a running feud for as long as Ruskin could remember — she was, said old Mrs Ruskin, possessed by the Devil. Anne was buried near her old master. Mrs Ruskin's verdict was uncompromising: 'She always persecuted me. But one must hope there are intermediate kinds of places where people get better.'[4]

His depression was increased by bad weather, to which he was abnormally sensitive. Just as his reactions to the beauties of nature were extraordinarily intense, so ugliness had a far more shattering effect on him than on most people.

They were married on 20th April at St Matthew's Church on Denmark Hill. The service took place in the morning and Ruskin gave the bride away. Arthur thought that the Professor 'looked quite the bridegroom himself; a new bright blue stock, very light grey trousers, an almost fashionable frock coat, with a rose in his buttonhole — and quite gay in his manner'.[5]

After the ceremony the guests returned to Ruskin's home for an old-fashioned wedding breakfast. At the end of the meal the Professor made an eloquent speech, in which he alluded to the bridegroom's father and the death of Keats, and moved one old man to tears.

[1] Arthur Severn's Memoirs.
[2] 27th February, 1871. Education Trust.
[3] 23rd March, 1871. Education Trust.
[4] *John Ruskin's Diary.* 31st March, 1871.
[5] Arthur Severn's Memoirs.

Mrs Ruskin was not able to come downstairs, but entered into the excitement and was visited not only by the bride and groom, but by many of the wedding-guests. At last the time came to leave and off they went in a flurry of good wishes, in a carriage drawn by two grey horses. At Euston old Downs appeared — the Ruskins' gardener with whom Joan had always been a favourite — and presented her with a bouquet. The young people at last got to the train and were locked by the guard into their carriage, bound for Yorkshire, where the first week of the honeymoon was to be spent with Ruskin's old friend, the Rev. W. Kingsley. They intended to go on to Scotland to visit Joan's family afterwards and had been persuaded that Yorkshire would be conveniently on the way.

Their host was a very talented man, an artist who knew a great deal about Turner and owned several of his drawings, a musician and mathematician, whose principal interest was astronomy; there was a telescope in almost every room of the house. Arthur had expected in April to find spring. When he complained that it still seemed to be winter in Yorkshire — Joan suggested hopefully that the primroses must be out. Soon afterwards they found their host at a window with a large telescope, examining the fells some four miles distant. 'No,' he said regretfully, 'I am afraid there are only one or two out as yet, so it is not worth your going to see them.'[1]

They stayed at South Kilvington with Kingsley for a week, where Ruskin continued to write regularly every day. Joan was one of those people, full of warmth and sympathy, who always seem to be at hand when illness or tragedy occurs, ready to nurse the invalid or comfort the bereaved. Only a few days after their arrival in Yorkshire their host's mother died.

'We have been of great service helping and cheering him,' she wrote to old Mrs Ruskin. 'Arthur has been busy painting all day. He is so very dear and charming and we are more happy than I can say — indeed, I think I am the very happiest and luckiest girl to have got such a husband. We speak of you very often.'[2]

She was certainly not left to enjoy her husband's company untroubled. Apart from feeling that she must write frequently to Mrs Ruskin, worried as she was by the thought of how lonely the old lady must be in the big Denmark Hill house, she had also to expect reproaches from the son if she did not write to him every day.

'... Me was fitened dedful for no ettie — no ettie — no ettie — no ettie — Sat-day — Sun-day — Mon-day — Two's day — so fitened. At last me got wee ettie at Dr Ac's. Today — here — no ettie again — me so misby — thisby — misby — poo — poo —poo, oos own Donie

St C.

'That's a very poking first page for my poos moos — only it must be nice to be missed. Oh me miss oo — more than tongue can tell.'[3]

---

[1] Arthur Severn's Memoirs.
[2] 24th April, 1871. Education Trust.
[3] Wednesday, 25th April, 1871. Education Trust.

A letter from Joan cheered him a little: 'I was very glad of your affectionate letter yesterday, and as you know its quite impossible for me ever to believe that anybody cares for me except you. You don't mean to say that Arfie could ever be the least bit fond of me? I'm just a fusty old critical father-in-law — you know he *can't* possibly, he only fancies he does in his honeymoon.'[1]

After a week with Mr Kingsley the young couple moved on to the Tennant Arms at Hawnsby, and then to rooms in a pretty little cottage near Rievaulx Abbey. Joan was perfectly happy. She would sit with Arthur while he worked, and sometimes herself painted the wild flowers which by this time abounded everywhere.

'Arthur has been working very hard — and carefully. I often sit beside him while he paints and read aloud — we brought Mrs Gaskell's "Cranford" which has afforded us the greatest pleasure and amusement.'[2] She loved the wild countryside and the picturesque ruins of the great abbey, but when rain drove them indoors, their clothes soaked through, Arthur, who was no lover of the country, except as providing subjects for his painting, found Yorkshire village life a little slow.

While Joan was away Ruskin, who had seemed to regard the rupture with Rose the year before as final, had heard that her friends were very anxious about her health. 'I wrote a wee line to R. on Sat. morning — telling her to get well,'[3] he told Joan, and a few days later, 'I had both your letters — but not Arfie's yet. It is very dear and sweet of him wanting to help me about R. — I don't think anything can be done, now, without losing some of my influence at Oxford. Had it not been for my Pussie I should have gone away to a cave last October and never come out unless R. had come to fetch me — but I couldn't spoil my pussie's love-time; — so also now, I am tied fast by the duty of keeping my power at Oxford, and for my greater plans. Rosie must . . . leave everything she does wrong for God to put right — as usual.'[4]

Rose answered his letter, but to Mrs Cowper-Temple. 'I didn't write yesterday,' Ruskin wrote to Joan. 'Much on poo Di Pa's mind. R. got my letter and wrote to φιλη — saying she had "been made so happy" — and would try to get well and not to die. φιλη sent me the letter. And what with the pity of it, and the nonsense, I wasn't able to write.'[5]

After a month in Yorkshire Joan and Arthur went on to Scotland towards the end of May so that she could introduce Arthur to her family and friends. But they had barely arrived before Joan developed rheumatic fever — 'all owing to that confounded climate in Yorkshire,' said Arthur, 'sitting out in the evening with me when I was sketching'. She was in bed for some time and it was a month before she was well enough to travel.

---

[1] Thursday, 27th April, 1871. Education Trust.
[2] 15th May, 1871. Education Trust.
[3] 10th May, 1871. Education Trust.
[4] Denmark Hill, Saturday, May 1871. Education Trust.
[5] From Denmark Hill (early June 1871). Education Trust.

CHAPTER 22

ILLNESS AT MATLOCK

June - July, 1871

A S JOAN'S ILLNESS HAD PREVENTED THE FULFILMENT OF THE PLAN for them all to meet at Abingdon, Ruskin now proposed that he should meet them in Derbyshire.

He did not tell Joan that he had at last heard of the opinion given to Mrs La Touche by her solicitor, that he was not in a position to contract a legal marriage, and that he had been challenged by Mr La Touche to deny it. After consultation with William Cowper-Temple, he had decided to put all the relevant documents about his divorce in the hands of a lawyer and obtain written Counsel's opinion. The Cowper-Temples were determined to lay the truth clearly before Rose, thinking it grossly unfair to Ruskin that such serious accusations should have been made, without his having had any chance of refuting them — or even, for some time, of knowing what they were.

'Yesterday evening I made search at once,' he wrote to Mr Cowper-Temple, 'and found the documents which I send you herewith; you may like to see my Father's account of this matter.'[1]

Enclosed was a letter, dated 23rd May, 1854, from the lawyer who had handled the divorce case to Ruskin's father, in which Ruskin had marked the passage: 'I consider our wisest course still to be as passive as possible, the correspondence on the other side leaving your Son in an advantageous position. I do not wonder at Mrs Ruskin being shocked at the observation made by the Woman to her. I hear the people in Scotland and at the West End are also shocked at her conduct. . . . Certainly if your Son can get freed from her . . . you ought all most gratefully to thank Providence for so much to be desired release.'[2]

Also enclosed were two letters from John James Ruskin to old friends, giving his own account of his son's marriage. His son had proposed marriage to Miss Gray, 'to which . . . we consented, though disliking the restless undomestic character of the Girl and although I was also aware that her Father was just then ruined by Railroad Speculation. I did not go to the Marriage but I told my Son that out of Respect for him I would settle £10,000 on her. The marriage took place in Mr Gray's House in Perth. It was only after settlements were signed that Mr Gray told the young couple . . . that he was a ruined man — his House

---

[1] Waterloo Day, 1871. Pierpont Morgan Library.
[2] Pierpont Morgan Library.

and Furniture not being his own. I had told my son all this before, but he only deemed it more his duty to proceed.'

John James Ruskin had received anonymous letters from Perth, warning him that the Grays only wanted his son's money. His son had now found himself married, without his parents' full approval and with the prospect of having to support a large family at Perth, and had work in hand which required extensive travel. 'His wife had apparently a perfect horror of having children until, to use her own expression She had sown her wild oats. They mutually agreed to act monk and nun for a few years till they could settle in one place.' By that time, according to his father, Ruskin had discovered she was totally unfit as companion in his pursuits or mother to his children. 'She was devoid of all truth and moral principle. She was never one day quiet or satisfied without the House being full of Company or going to Plays and concerts nightly.' His son had had to steal out of his own house to his old home to be able to study or write.[1]

She had wanted to make him 'a mere man of the Town' and had been recklessly extravagant, spending £15,000 in six years and complained of being short of money, though she and her father had at first protested that the thousand pounds a year which the elder Ruskin had given her as an allowance was most liberal. When she left his son, 'with the artfulness and falsehood inherent in her character, she told the world that those men whom she had forced on my son, destroying his domestic Quiet, were brought by him and left with her for improper ends'.

His son had never spoken on the subject but 'went quietly on his intended Swiss tour while she got her acquaintances to believe and propagate the most outrageous falsehoods which my son will not condescend to notice. . . . Reports are that she will marry Millais whom you saw her with at Edinburgh. She left, home in April and got the marriage dissolved no doubt for this purpose.'[2]

Ruskin had given his own version of the case the previous autumn. 'The Decree of Divorce was passed against me because I had never fulfilled a husband's duty to my wife, and it was assumed necessarily in my declining to give any answer to the charge that I was impotent.

'I believed until two years ago that this was all that had taken place. I never inquired into the matter at all. I only was able to retain my own life and power by . . . coming from it as I would from any pestiferous room — and as far as I could, forgetting it in intense work. My father and his lawyer managed the suit, and only asked me a few necessary questions. I am in Law unmarried and in my conduct to my wife — I boldly say and believe — guiltless, though foolish.

'I never would seduce a pure woman and I never would associate with an impure one.'[3]

Ruskin's solicitor had some difficulty in finding the divorce Decree, as the

[1] To Alexander Leith, 14th December, 1854. Pierpont Morgan Library.

[2] To J. Collins, 28th December, 1854, Pierpont Morgan Library.

[3] 20th September, 1870. Pierpont Morgan Library.

case had been heard before one of the Ecclesiastical Courts which had been swept away by the Divorce Act of 1857, and no proper provision appeared to have been made for the custody of their records. Having found it at last, he showed it first to Ruskin's cousin, Richardson, who was also a lawyer, and they both told Ruskin that they were convinced of its validity. However, it was decided to submit it to Counsel for an opinion.

Matlock Spa had been chosen for the meeting between Ruskin and the Severns – the New Bath Hotel, were Ruskin had stayed with his parents as a child. It was an old building with low doors and ceilings and narrow, twisting stairs. He had looked forward to showing Joan and Arthur the places near by which he remembered visiting with his father as a boy – the pretty village, the caves where he had begun his study of minerals, and the deep Speedwell mine at Castleton. But he could not conceal his anxiety from Joan, and after only one day in their company he began to complain of a bilious attack and stayed in bed.

On the day of their arrival he had written to William Cowper-Temple:

'It would indeed destroy both health and usefulness, if I allowed hopes to return such as I had once. I wish that they could return – if they were allowed – but I have been too often and too sorely betrayed to trust, or hope, more; and even if all should be determined favourable, as regards the legal question, I shall only request that with the Bishop's aid and influence, you would undeceive Rose as to the points of unjust evil speaking against me. I am very weary of life, and will not ask her to come to me. If she wants to come, she must say so to me:

'. . . However much a man may love a woman, he cannot be twice left to die (if he chooses) and then be asked to prove that he is not a villain! – and yet obey the whistle as he did once.'[1]

Worry about the outcome of his consultations with the lawyers and what the effect of their opinion might be on Rose, began to make him increasingly ill. He no longer planned to accompany Joan and Arthur on sketching expeditions or walks. He could only lie in bed, feeling increasingly sick and feverish.

The Divorce Decree, given by a lawyer and the Bishop of Winchester, was sent to Mr Tristram at the Temple and with it the note written by Ruskin. 'You are requested to advise whether the Sentence could now be impeached in any way by anyone.'

'You say she is probably too ill to decide at once,' he wrote to Cowper-Temple. '*I* am too ill also, and I hope – too wise. I am not going to offer – still less to urge – marriage now. But I insist on free intercourse – face to face. She never understands my letters.'[2]

But the strain of waiting and worrying had become too great for him, and the day before they were due to leave, Ruskin was prostrated with continual vomiting which became so violent that Joan, Arthur and his valet, Crawley, became seriously alarmed. The local doctor, too, took fright and it was decided

---

[1] 1st July, 1871. Pierpont Morgan Library.
[2] 7th July, 1871. Pierpont Morgan Library.

to telegraph to Ruskin's old friend, Dr Acland, at Oxford. Acland came immediately. His patient had at first refused to remain in bed, but was soon so exhausted that he had perforce to give way to persuasion.

Besides Crawley, Joan and Arthur, Albert Goodwin was also in their party at the hotel – he was one of the artists employed by Ruskin to paint special subjects for him. Ruskin was a very difficult patient and at one time they feared that he would not live through the day. Joan had not only to direct the nursing of her cousin, but had also to wire and write daily to his mother. 'Your Son's chief anxiety is, that *you* should not be alarmed about him, or be made unnecessarily anxious. Therefore, I must beg you my dearest Aunt for *his sake*, and your own, not to alarm yourself. At his own request Dr Acland is to be here tonight and he has implicit faith in him as a medical man (and friend). . . . Of course I shall write again tomorrow, and telegraph if necessary.'[1]

Poor Mrs Ruskin, now ninety years old and bed-ridden, could not go to her son, and as she was accustomed to receiving a daily letter from him, leapt to the conclusion, when none arrived, that he must be dead. But Joan wrote regularly to give her the latest news. 'Dr Acland says I am to tell you from him that it is "a violent attack of exhausting and long-continued vomiting, the result of which *is*, great prostration, and for several days will require extreme care and perfect quiet." '[2] What Joan did not mention to her aunt was the high fever that her son was in, which led to delirious dreams, remembered quite clearly when he had recovered as being of great beauty – 'I have never heard such divine singing before or since.' When his illness was at its worst he said to Acland, 'I feel I should get better if only I could lie down in Coniston Water.'

They had felt bound to send for Acland again because Ruskin seemed to be getting weaker all the time, but refused to obey the local doctor, who was trying to carry out the orders left by Acland on his first visit. They found this Dr Holland sitting on the bed in the dressing-room next to Ruskin's bedroom, his coat off and sweat running down his face. 'I can do nothing with him,' he said. 'He will do nothing I want. You had better get Dr Acland again as soon as you can.'

They telegraphed immediately to Acland in London, where he was staying, and at least two hours before expected he walked into the hotel, accompanied by another eminent, though elderly medical man, Dr Stokes of Dublin. The telegram had reached him at a Medical Council where he was sitting next to Stokes, and his neighbour had volunteered to go with him. To get to Matlock more quickly Dr Acland had pulled the alarm cord and stopped the express, which would otherwise have carried them on to Derby, and had then left the train with Dr Stokes, having first courteously presented the guard with his visiting card.[3]

[1] Monday, 10th July, 1871. Education Trust.
[2] Tuesday (11th July, 1871). Education Trust.
[3] Arthur Severn's Memoirs.

Next day Ruskin's condition was improved, but it was several days before he was out of danger. They were told by the two eminent doctors before they left that Ruskin must be very carefully nursed. He must have complete rest and be kept on a very light diet. This presented great difficulties to those caring for him. Meat, pepper, anything highly seasoned, and spirits were all forbidden to the patient. But they were exactly what he insisted on having. Joan was the only one who could coax him into behaving properly, but she could not be with him all the time. He sent Goodwin out to a cookshop for a slice of cold beef and Arthur came into his room, at eleven o'clock, when he should have been sleeping, to find him shaking the pepper-pot violently over it. When it was taken away from him he had a long drink of brandy and water.

In spite of this behaviour he began to get better, and Joan was given some relief when his old friend, Mrs Cowper-Temple, arrived to help with the nursing. Her charm and beauty cheered all Ruskin's anxious friends. Mrs Simon and Charles Newton were other welcome visitors.

Joan wrote daily to his mother: 'Your son has got a globe of fish on a little table by his bedside which is a great delight to him — and I am able here to get him fresh grapes — he does not eat them but enjoys having them to *look at*. He has just asked me to go and get him some fresh ones as yesterday's are rather withered.'[1]

Joan first knew he was really better when he asked her to go and search for some mountain thyme as the smell of it would be refreshing. Soon after this, when Mrs Cowper-Temple was resting, Joan and Arthur, seeing that Ruskin was dozing, decided that he was well enough to be left alone for a few minutes. It was a fine day and they thought they would take a stroll outside the hotel. As they emerged they heard the sound of music and found a young woman singing in a small sweet voice with a man accompanying her on the harp. They listened a minute, and then strolled on, but presently became aware that the singing had suddenly stopped, and on looking back saw the young woman advance towards the hotel with her apron held out. 'As she looked up, we saw a window slowly opened, then a small hand come slowly out with white sleeve to follow, then something white dropped into the apron — and the window went slowly down. My wife gave a sudden start, saying: "Good gracious! That must be the Coz!" "Impossible, Joan!" I said, but she was off like a swallow to his room. I followed with more dignity. When in the room I found Joan standing over the bed, saying: "Is it possible? Have you dared to get up?" Head a little more under clothes. "Cuzzie darling, have you really been up?" Head quite under clothes. "My prettiest of lambs, how could you do such a wicked thing?" Head half way down the bed!

'Some time later, we found out that, hearing the singing and liking it, he had got up (this was the first time for a month!) opened a wardrobe and found a waistcoat and in a pocket of it half a sovereign which he carefully wrapped up

[1] Tuesday (July, 1871.) Education Trust.

in paper; then moved the toilet table, opened the window, dropped the money into the apron and put everything straight before we could get to his room! Pretty good this, for a man so weak that we thought anything of the kind absolutely impossible!'[1]

The relief of the improvement in Ruskin's condition resulted in high spirits in his friends. One beautiful Sunday morning, with the sun shining, four of them walked in the garden of the hotel and eventually came to a halt by the large goldfish pond, covered thickly with water-lilies. The party consisted of Charles Newton, as usual elegantly dressed, Albert Goodwin, Arthur and a Mr Graves, who was also staying in the hotel, a poet, who would return from long walks garlanded with wild flowers. A discussion began as to what weight the leaves of the water-lilies would carry. At last one of them threw a sovereign which remained poised on a large leaf some way from the bank. Arthur volunteered to retrieve it if they would form a chain to support him and scrambled down the steep bank, and as he leaned over the pool to reach the coin, felt the chain beginning to give a little, and giving a sudden extra pull, into the water he went head first, dragging the others after him. When he got his head above the lilies he laughed to see the immaculate Newton spluttering and gasping in the water. 'No one could have recognized the discoverer of the Tomb of Masolus, and Keeper of Greek and Roman Antiquities at the British Museum, in that struggling figure. The getting out was not so easy, as the sides of the pond were curved and slimy.' Newton, who had brought little luggage with him, had to go to bed until his clothes were dried. Arthur went quickly to tell Joan the joke and it was whispered to Ruskin who; weak as he was, was seen to laugh.[2]

★

As soon as his illness had abated and he was able to read again, Ruskin considered Counsel's opinion which his cousin, Richardson, had forwarded to him. Mr Tristram reiterated the facts of the case which had led to the Divorce Decree: Ruskin had not brought to the attention of the Court an alleged arrangement that the marriage was not to be consummated; his wife had stated that Ruskin had proposed that it should not be consummated until she was twenty-five; she had at first assented but later withdrew her consent. 'The facts that A slept with B for six years without attempting to have connection ... and that she was proved to be at the end of it a *virgo intacta* are cogent evidence that A was impotent quo ad B, whatever his ambition may now be or might have been in regard to other females, and was quite sufficient to warrant the sentence....

'Having regard to all the circumstances of this Case I cannot conceive that any Court would ever directly or indirectly give a decision which would in effect reverse this sentence.'[3]

[1] Arthur Severn's Memoirs.
[2] Ibid.
[3] Counsel's Opinion, 19th July, 1871. Pierpont Morgan Library.

Richardson added the comment: 'For all practical purposes you are free to marry again.'

Ruskin forwarded this legal opinion at once to Mr Cowper-Temple for his support. 'By today's post,' he wrote, 'I have written straight and simply to R. herself telling her all is ascertained and safe, and that you and Philé,[1] and her aunt, and others, if she chooses, will tell her that I deserve her trust.'[2]

'I am afraid it is some time since you have received a letter from me,' Arthur wrote to old Mrs Ruskin, 'it is only because I am often busy all day with my painting and have Joan to write all the letters. In fact I tell her that it is one of the reasons why I married. . . .

'Joan is very well and happy, but is a little tired of being away so long – I have not quite made up my mind whether the *Husband* ought to give way to the Wife, or the Wife to the Husband, perhaps it is time now I should know!'[3]

While he was writing to Mrs Ruskin, Joan was comforting the invalid, whose hopes had been shattered by a cold and unsympathetic reply from Rose: 'It came upon me as I was recovering, as if it meant to throw me back into the grave.'

Joan wrote to Mrs Cowper-Temple, who had returned home:

'R's answer to his letter is so unaccountably strange, without a spark of kind feeling – and using expressions with regard to him utterly unworthy and untrue. I feel so very angry and bitterly grieved that she – Rose whom I so loved – could have been guilty of such a thing – not a word in her whole letter to redeem her from the utmost blame. . . . I am almost thankful it is at an end. . . . Her final treatment of him is so heartless and wicked that I suppose it is less hard for him to bear, though I was full of dread. . . . You must not think me too hard upon R. Indeed I'm not – it grieves my heart so.'[4]

With this letter another was enclosed for William Cowper-Temple, which began in Ruskin's own hand. He was making a great effort to keep his life going – described his own impressions of his illness, told his friend that he had finished the August number of *Fors Clavigera*, and announced his first gift, of a thousand pounds, to his newly formed St George's Company, asking Cowper-Temple to be one of two Trustees. Doctor Acland's brother, Sir Thomas, was to be the other, and they were to hold money contributed by himself and he hoped later by other like-minded people, to buy land in England 'which shall not be built upon, but cultivated by Englishmen with their own hands, and such help of force as they can find in wind and wave. . . . We will have no steam-engines upon it, and no rail-roads; we will have no untended or unthought-of creatures on it; none wretched, but the sick; none idle but the dead'. So he had described his vision of a new England, which would not be dominated by materialism or machines, in the May number of *Fors*, and had pledged himself to start the fund

[1] Mrs Cowper-Temple.
[2] 23rd July, 1871. Pierpont Morgan Library.
[3] 27th July, 1871. Education Trust.
[4] 27th July (1871). Pierpont Morgan Library.

with a tenth of all he had, and a tithe of what he should earn hereafter. Then he dropped his pen, exhausted, and Joan continued the letter, writing at his dictation about Rose.

'I sent her a very civil letter to which she sent an answer which for folly, insolence and selfishness beat everything I yet have known produced by the accursed sect of Religion she has been brought up in. I made Joanna re-enclose her the letter, writing only, on a scrap of paper with — (Joanna writing that is to say, not *I*) "My cousin and I have read the enclosed. You shall have the rest of your letters as soon as he returns home — and your mother shall have hers." So the letter went back, and the young lady shall never read written — nor hear spoken — word of mine more. I am entirely satisfied in being quit of her — for I feel she would have been a hindrance to me ... in doing what I am more and more convinced that I shall be permitted to do *rightly*, only on condition of putting all my strength into it.'[1]

As soon as Ruskin was well enough to sit up with a shawl wrapped round his shoulders, he had sent Arthur and Goodwin out daily to explore the mines and caverns in the neighbourhood, mapping out their route and telling them what they were to look for. His carriage and pair would be brought round to the door and the two young men would be driven off, taking their painting material with them. When they got back in the evening they would have to show their sketches to him.

Soon he was well enough to travel, and Joan told his mother that his return to health seemed to have banished his gloomy obsession with the evil of dark skies and 'plague wind', and his depression when the sky was overcast.

'We are all looking forward with the greatest pleasure to being with you tomorrow!' she wrote. 'It seems almost too good to be true after the sad delay we have had owing to your son's illness — which now, strange to say is hardly a matter of regret! since it has had the wonderful effect of making him pleased with things in general. You know he used to growl so! — and now he seems so pleased — and instead of thinking that the streams and country are everywhere polluted, he sees that there is still much to be admired and loved, and in both his looks and conversation the old sad despondency seems to have vanished, and I have real and earnest hopes that both in health and spirits he will be so improved for the future — that even when there's a dense fog, and candles have to be lighted in the study, he'll accommodate himself to circumstances without a complaint!'[2]

---

[1] 27th July, 1871. Pierpont Morgan Library.
[2] Matlock, Sunday. July 1871. Education Trust.

CHAPTER 23

THE END OF DENMARK HILL

August, 1871 – April, 1872

OLD MRS RUSKIN WAS OVERJOYED AT HER SON'S RETURN, but it was clear to them all that her strength was failing. Her son, too, felt 'great fear of relapse into illness' and spent the month of August quietly at home, revising two books for publication and sitting with his mother for a little while in the evenings.

He wrote to thank Acland for his care during his illness, and sent him a cheque for five thousand pounds for Oxford University to endow a mastership of Drawing.

'I am now going to attend to my health as the principal thing, until I can lie down in Coniston Water.'[1]

By a curious coincidence within a few days of his return to Denmark Hill he received a letter from an old acquaintance, W. J. Linton, the poet and wood-engraver, now living in America. Linton told him that he was looking for a purchaser for his house, Brantwood, on the eastern shore of Coniston Water, with sixteen acres of heather and copse.

Arthur and Joan had moved into their house at Herne Hill. They were only half a mile from the Ruskins' home on Denmark Hill, so that Joan was able to go every day to the larger house, where she would sit by Mrs Ruskin's bedside. Ruskin told them immediately about Linton's letter and said that after his strong yearning when he was ill to lie in Coniston Water, he had decided to buy Linton's property himself.

The Severns were staggered. Did he even know the position of the house? they asked. 'Yes, I know it is opposite the "Old Man",' said Ruskin. 'Just the part I like, and I have known the lake since I was a boy.'[2] The purchase, for fifteen hundred pounds, was arranged at once, and Ruskin, who was feeling better after his month at home, went north to see his new property.

From Coniston he sent Joan a drawing of the front of the house, which looked westwards across the lake to the heights of the mountain known as the 'Old Man'. It was a simple, white, two-storied building of rough stone and the centre of the three windows had been built out into a bow by Linton. This and the one to the right of it lit the library, and the left-hand window, which was rather

---

[1] 5th August, 1871. *Works*, vol. 22, p. xviii.
[2] Arthur Severn's Memoirs.

JOAN AGNEW ABOUT THE TIME OF HER
MARRIAGE TO ARTHUR SEVERN IN 1871
Water-colour sketch by John Ruskin
Now in Wellesley College Library, Massachusetts

JOSEPH SEVERN IN HIS CONSULAR UNIFORM AND WEARING THE CROWN OF ITALY GIVEN HIM BY KING VICTOR EMMANUEL

This self portrait was begun early in 1876 when he was just 83 years old

JOAN AND HER THREE ELDEST CHILDREN IN 18

larger, the drawing-room. The dining-room was dark, looking north across the yard outside the front door into the side of the hill.

'The view from the house is finer than I expected,' he wrote to Joan, 'the house itself dilapidated and rather dismal. I want my Doanie to come and see it directly with Arfie . . . and tell me what she thinks.'[1]

The surroundings delighted him — 'such rocks and heather — which I didn't expect'. He rowed for miles on the lake, he scrambled up the bed of a little stream on his own land, cut wood in his own copses and gathered some nuts which he sent in a box to Joan.

The weather was beautiful and the air on the hillside exhilarating. 'I feel as if I had two legs again, instead of two stumps only.' He was full of plans. 'The house is built on the rock itself — and in a recess of the hillside — which rises *too* steeply behind the house. A bridge twelve feet long would reach the hillock from my roof — and I'm sorry to say, the spring which I am so proud of has been allowed to soak its way down exactly there. The first thing I've to do is to cut a trench in the rock to carry away this drainage — it is just like a dripping well at Matlock, behind the house. For the house itself! — well, there *is* a house, certainly, and it has rooms in it, but I believe in reality, nearly as much will have to be done as if it were a shell of bricks and mortar'.[2] He hoped that it might be ready for him to occupy in November, but returning at the beginning of October, after a visit to Scotland, he found that little progress had been made and had to be content to accept the offer of Tom Richmond at Windermere, to keep an eye on the work, and return himself to London.

He had intended to give a series of lectures at Oxford during the autumn term, but his mother seemed so frail that he dared not be away from her for long and decided to cancel the course, only leaving home for a few days occasionally to stay at Oxford with the Aclands, arranging the furnishing of his rooms at Corpus and planning the organization of the Drawing School. The University had already accepted his gift of five thousand pounds to endow a Master of Drawing; now he was designing mahogany cabinets for the School, in which he intended to display drawings, engravings and coloured prints, chosen for their educational value. It cost him about four hundred pounds to fit up the room and he eventually spent another two thousand on buying specimens for the collection, as well as adding to it nearly three hundred of his own drawings and some of his most precious Turners and illuminated manuscripts. He did not mean the Ruskin Drawing School and Art Collection to train professional artists, but to encourage 'gentlemen and scholars' in proficiency and understanding. He hoped to widen their education in such a way that they would leave Oxford capable of enlightened patronage and appreciation of the arts.

By the end of November old Mrs Ruskin was very weak and rarely conscious

[1] 12th September, 1871. *Works*, vol. 37, p. 35.
[2] 14th September, 1871. Education Trust.

H

of what was going on about her, and on 2nd December, as Joan was dressing to go to church, an agitated note was brought to her from Ruskin:
'My dearest dearest Joanie,
                You had better not go to church today but come down here alone. I am anxious.

Love to Arthur always,
Your loving J. R.'[1]

She went immediately, but Mrs Ruskin lingered on for another three days, and died at last on 5th December, with one hand in her son's and the other in Joan's.[2]

Joan, who had been devoted to the old lady, was very distressed, but roused herself to comfort Ruskin. 'Joan is a preciousest creature in any real need,' he wrote to Dr Acland, — 'very precious at all times.'

Ruskin decided immediately to sell the house at Denmark Hill. Brantwood would be his home. He now had his new rooms to live in when he was at Oxford, and arranged with Joan and Arthur that when he came to London he would stay with them in the house on Herne Hill. He fought depression, as usual, by flinging himself into work. He had lectures to give at Oxford in the spring term, and began immediately dictating the first to Joan.

The past few years had seen Ruskin's gradual change from one interested primarily in aesthetics — the art critic, the lover of landscape and architecture, the champion of the Pre-Raphaelites — to the social reformer, who sought to put right the ills of society. With his regular monthly letters addressed to the work-men of Britain, and with the Guild of St George which he had just founded, he hoped to overcome the tyranny of money and to open all men's eyes to beauties which commercial interests were rapidly defiling. As a first example of how things should be ordered he obtained permission to sweep certain streets and crossings between the British Museum and St Giles's, where Eleanor had been married. 'In going to the British Museum in this weather I stick to the ground, and slip back half of every step,' he had written to a friend in November. '*I want to show what a clean street is.*'[3]

Downs, his faithful head gardener, was put in charge, and a number of boys were engaged to work under him.

At first this experiment went well. Ruskin wielded a broom himself at the beginning, and later drove parties round in his carriage 'to show a bit of our London streets kept as clean as the deck of a ship of the line'. The boys were interested in their job and worked hard. People left their houses to watch their street being cleaned and parties of distinguished outsiders came to observe the work.

---

[1] Education Trust.
[2] Letter of Joan Severn to C. E. Norton, 16th July, 1886. Houghton Library.
[3] *Works*, vol. 37, p. 43.

'I had, a grand "field" or rather pavement day,' Ruskin wrote to Joan, 'and find my three boys will be able to do a great deal. Two members of the Board of Works, the District Surveyor and the Police Inspector all came to St Andrew's Street to see how the work went on. There was a sensation in the quarter as you may suppose. . . . Then I went to see my Tea shop! Immensely nice – I'm going to give Harriet China saucers to hold her samples in and have a Real Tea Plant from Kew to show in the window.'[1]

The tea-shop was another of Ruskin's social experiments. He planned to have a shop where only the purest tea would be sold, and where it could be bought in packets as small as poor customers wished to buy, without any extra profit being made on the subdivision. He had just found suitable premises in Paddington Street, near his Marylebone property, where he subsidized Octavia Hill in a scheme for slum reclamation, and proposed to put two old servants of his mother's in to run it, but it was not ready to open for another two years.

In the meantime interest in the road-sweeping inevitably faded. Downs complained that people living in the street threw everything into it for them to clear away and seemed to think the whole thing rather a joke. The boys had worked well at first, but now when he went to see how they were getting on he often could not find them, and would eventually discover them playing pitch and toss. At the end of the year Ruskin gave up the experiment – but he had set the parish authorities a good example.

Ruskin was lecturing at Oxford during the Easter term, but his old nursery at Herne Hill was refurnished for his use when he came to London. It was at the top of the house, with an iron gate at the window which had been fitted years ago to prevent his falling.

An unexpected result of the sale of the Denmark Hill house was the sudden appearance of a number of gardeners in the small garden at Herne Hill. Joan and Arthur were amazed as they trooped in, one after the other, but it was soon explained that Ruskin now had no use for the seven under-gardeners who had been employed at the old house, and had therefore sent them on to work at Herne Hill, until they should have found new places elsewhere. As no limit was put on this arrangement, it was naturally a long time before they all found other employment.

Busy in Oxford, with ten lectures to give on the relation of art to natural science, Ruskin left all the arrangements about the move from Denmark Hill to Joan, only making a few personal decisions, such as selling his largest Turner, of the Venice Rialto, which was too big for Brantwood and for which he got four thousand pounds. The move entailed much hard work for Joan, and she was happy to have a holiday in March when she and Arthur went to stay with Eleanor and Henry Furneaux at Heyford and spent a day in Oxford with Ruskin, being shown round his galleries, hearing him lecture, and lunching with him afterwards in his new rooms.

[1] Denmark Hill, January 1872. Education Trust.

Arthur was surprised to find them so ugly. 'As regards colour, he was singularly insensitive about it in a room. His own rooms at Oxford were atrocious in colour; mahogany bookcases against a buff-coloured wall; bright heavy mahogany chairs with magenta coloured leather over the seats and a carpet of the worst taste, with banner-screens of rose-coloured silk hanging from the mahogany stands. But all these things were of the best work and would have lasted eighty years without so much as the loss of a castor. . . . The Professor had been brought up with this kind of furniture; but it did surprise me that, with his eye for colour and as Professor of Art, he could live amongst these discordant tones in his rooms at Corpus; and yet, in some of his architectural studies nothing can be more beautiful or subtle than they are in colour.'[1]

The furniture and decoration of Brantwood were to be very similar but Ruskin had one imaginative idea which was much admired. This was a wallpaper which he had specially made for the drawing-room and study, copied from a greyish-white damask robe in a picture at the National Gallery. By the end of March he had spent his last night in his old home and was so sad at leaving it for the last time that Joan drove with him in the carriage to the station and stood waving on the platform until the Oxford train had disappeared from sight.

'Dearest Pussie,' he wrote from Corpus, 'it was very sweet seeing your bright face as far as I could today. I got quite comfortably down and my rooms are nice and I am very well.'[2]

Thomas Richmond was supervising the work at Brantwood and trying to arrange for a twenty-year lease of the field and lake shore below the garden. The negotiations were by no means easy, for Ruskin would brook no kind of conditions being attached by the owner, a Major Harrison who owned most of the land surrounding Ruskin's property.

'If I choose to grow thistles six feet high all over the ground – I will. And I'll build my boathouse as I like or not at all – and the moles shall be un/mole/ested . . . and any other than so – Major Harrison may keep land and lake to himself.'[3] His own employees must have been puzzled, too, by some of the instructions sent to them through Richmond. No tree must be cut, no weeds pulled up, except in the carriage drive and on the lawn. Iron fencing was certainly not to be put in the hedges. He submitted to lime being put on the field in front of the house with a very bad grace, but his men were not to shoot rabbits or anything else, and the shore and the ruined boat-house were to be left altogether alone.

[1] Arthur Severn's Memoirs.
[2] Corpus Christi College, 28th March, 1872. Education Trust.
[3] 7th April, 1872. Pierpont Morgan Library.

CHAPTER 24

ROMAN TWILIGHT

THESE CHANGES MADE A SPLENDID EXCUSE for Ruskin to make one of the journeys to the Continent which he so much enjoyed. 'Where *do* you think we're all going?' he wrote to Richmond in a letter which his friend marked *The last letter that came from D.H.* 'To Rome – to let old Mr Severn see his daughter-in-law! I can't pitch into Michael Angelo properly, till I've been and seen him and I want to see Assisi. So its all harmonious and Connie's wild with expectation of balls and midnight flirting in the Coliseum with, I suppose, a lover in every arch. . . . I think seeing the old papa with Joan *will* be worth going for. Then we're coming "home" to Brantwood and Tom. Joan has never seen Brantwood you know.'[1]

In mid-April he set out, accompanied by just such a company as best pleased him. Joan and Arthur were with him, the young painter Albert Goodwin, Connie Hilliard and her mother, and his valet, Crawley. The party went first to Paris for one night, moving on next day to Geneva. On arrival Ruskin insisted on driving immediately up the Salève, so that they should have a view of Mont Blanc in the evening sunlight.

The expedition was a great success. The effect of the light on the great mountain impressed them all immensely, and Ruskin was delighted at their pleasure. Arthur and Goodwin made sketches as the sun was setting and Ruskin in the rôle of benevolent judge, said 'I think Arthur has beaten Master Albert this time.' Next day Arthur spent on a water-colour sketch of the rushing water of the lake as it poured into the narrows and became the Rhône; there were beautiful colours and shadows in the foam and quiet eddies. Ruskin, who had always been fascinated by water, and could spend hours watching the changing effects of a hurrying stream, showed great interest in Arthur's attempt, and Joan was happy to see them so much in accord.

But in spite of his enjoyment of the new scenes, the opportunities for painting and the comfort of their lodgings, Arthur found this method of travel a little irksome after the carefree bachelor journeys that he had made with Brabazon. To begin with, Ruskin attached great importance to dinner. Although he was not himself a big eater, he liked the meal to be of many courses, to last a long time and never to be neglected. Only very occasionally could the two young artists escape what they felt to be the tyranny of the dinner hour. 'When one is in a strange and beautiful place, and anxious to be at work, to have to sit at a

1 Pierpont Morgan Library.

long and tedious meal making conversation, I felt to be cruel waste of time. Oddly enough, the Professor, with all his love of work, couldn't see this.'[1]

Another restriction which Arthur found a trial was Ruskin's aversion to the smell of tobacco; he had had to agree to give up smoking before they left London.

From Geneva they went on to Annecy and Chambery, with Ruskin in good spirits, as he always was when the Alps were close at hand, and teaching Connie Hilliard the rules of perspective during the train journey, then to Genoa, Sestri and Pisa.

All the party were looking forward to visiting the next town on their itinerary — Pisa — for the Professor, as most of them now called him, had spoken to them with the enthusiasm of the Campo Santo and the Baptistery and above all his favourite little Chapel of the Spina. As usual Ruskin had reserved the best rooms in the hotel for his party, and they were bowed to them by the landlord as if they were royalty. Ruskin's impatience to show them these beloved buildings could not be denied, and he soon collected them in the hall and after counting them to see that none was missing, led them across the bridge over the river to see first the exquisite Chapel of the Thorn.

'Off he went,' wrote Arthur, 'we following like children. He was well in front all the way, too eager to keep at our pace, until at last we got to the Chapel. I saw his pace slacken, his face fall, then flush crimson with rage. We all undertood the cause in a moment — the place was under restoration! Dust and noise and hammering; beautiful bits of Gothic carving lying about; and apparently no one of any responsibility to ask questions of. We all hesitated whether to advance or not. I heard the Professor panting with rage as he looked at the scene; then suddenly, with long strides he walked into the building and began shaking his small fist in the face of the nearest workman. The man looked up in amazement, called to some of the other workmen to stop their hammering and when silence reigned they all stood looking at this strange figure, shaking his fist at them and quivering with anger. It was indeed a curious sight: Ruskin's tall, spare figure in blue frock coat with blue stock and stick-ups and his face now livid with anger — and the open-mouthed simplicity of these workers as they all stared at him in astonishment. — "What do you mean by spoiling this beautiful place? Are you aware that the Austrians never did so much harm in Italy as you men are now doing with your chisels and mallets?" As there was no foreman or architect present, we thought it better to get him away. I explained to one of the men what it all meant; he shrugged his shoulders and said they were only acting under orders.

'We all came away with a miserable feeling of disappointment, chiefly on the Professor's account. When we got to the hotel the little fat landlord met us with a beaming face and low bows: — in a moment I heard the Professor beginning again! Shaking his fist, this time in the landlord's face, saying what he had seen

[1] Arthur Severn's Memoirs.

over the way, asking what the landlord meant by allowing such a thing to happen just opposite his hotel! How could his hotel prosper, etc., etc? To which the astonished landlord kept bowing lower and lower with his hand on his heart, and saying, as he backed from him: "Ma signore! Non e culpa mea! Signore! Eccellenza sua — sensi — ma ec-cel-len-za!" We again had to close round and assure the landlord that he needn't be afraid, and that we would not leave the hotel that very minute, and that "il Signor Rooskin" was the kindest of men.'[1]

They were soon joined in Pisa by Ruskin's friend from New England, Professor Norton. To him Ruskin poured out his rage and disgust at the vandalism which he had witnessed. He then had the idea that he should himself settle down in Pisa and become Curator of the Spina Chapel — an idea reluctantly abandoned only after the many difficulties had been repeatedly pointed out to him.[2]

He made several drawings for his School at Oxford. By now he had all the party drawing. Joan was put to do careful drawings of a cross in the Baptistery and another on an old tomb in the cathedral of the town which they next visited, Lucca.[3] This Cathedral was another building which Ruskin had long loved and he and the two young artists were soon at work on it. It was here that Arthur first discovered what a good head Ruskin had for heights. 'He stood calmly in the top storey of the façade, examining the marble of the columns, and almost walking round them. There was no protection of any kind and the least giddiness would have precipitated him down into the piazza — a drop of about seventy or eighty feet. Though anxious to hear his views on the marble. I couldn't follow, but remained cowering under an arch.'[4]

At Lucca, too, Ruskin found another beautiful building — the Chapel of the Rose — destroyed since his last visit, and this confirmed him in his determination to record by drawings the appearance of such exquisite examples of architecture, before they were either spoiled by restoration or completely destroyed. In his enthusiasm he rose often before four in the morning, working 'to save a few things I shall never see again'.

From Lucca they drove on to Florence. Again Arthur felt the difference between this and his other painting tours. A magnificent suite of apartments had been reserved for them in the Hotel d'Arno. The sitting-room was enormous and elaborately decorated, with golden cupids tumbling about huge gilt mirrors. Arthur and Goodwin felt awkward at coming into this grandiose room for luncheon in their working clothes. They both made careful drawings of the Ponte Vecchio and other subjects and Arthur, still with the same enthusiasm for water and the night, studied moonlight effects from a boat on the Arno.

Ruskin was loath to leave Florence for their next stopping-place — Rome —

[1] Arthur Severn's Memoirs.
[2] Ruskin to Joan Severn, 26th September, 1882. Houghton Library.
[3] These drawings are now in Pierpont Morgan Library.
[4] Arthur Severn's Memoirs.

which he had never liked. He did not care for its churches or its ruins, and was taking his party there chiefly so that Joseph Severn might meet his daughter-in-law, whom he had never yet seen. On the 11th of May the Professor tore himself away from Florence in a bad temper, writing in his diary: 'Setting out for Rome, to my disgust.' The entry for the following day read: 'Rome. Pouring rain, rooms horrible, and place more repulsive to me than ever', and the day after: 'Quarrelling with everything and everybody'. In spite of his ill humour the rest of the party were thrilled to be in Rome, though none so much as Arthur.

*

His father, now seventy-nine years old, had just ceased to be British Consul. In July the previous year, soon after Eleanor's marriage, the long-threatened conflict had broken out between France and Prussia. The French troops which had kept the Papal Government in power were recalled from Italy to defend the motherland and the French Empire tottered to its fall. News of the collapse at Sedan had reached Rome on 3rd September and on 11th September Italian troops crossed the frontier with the Papal States, to occupy Rome and make her the capital of United Italy.

Soon afterwards Joseph Severn had received a dispatch from the Foreign Office. As the Legation was now removing to Rome, Lord Granville did not feel justified in continuing the office of Consul, but intended to name Mr Severn for a pension 'adequate to the services he has rendered'.

The Times commented in London: 'It seems a pity the abolition of the Consulate could not have been deferred during Mr Severn's lifetime. His services have been sufficiently important to merit great consideration. The office he has filled during a time of considerable difficulty has been one requiring great tact and discretion, for notwithstanding that we have had an unaccredited Minister in the person of Mr Odo Russell, duties have necessarily devolved on Mr Severn beyond those usually attached to the consular office, which duties he has performed to the satisfaction of both his own and the Papal Government. In how much estimation he was held by the Ministers of His Holiness is shown by his having been able to obtain the release of a number of political prisoners, so great that on the entry of the Italians he received a complete ovation from them.'[1]

For some time before his retirement much of Joseph's work had been done by his devoted secretary, Frantz, and the brother whom Joseph had saved from a Roman prison. His rheumatism kept recurring and then he had found it difficult to sign letters and painful even to move.

Professional diplomats such as Odo Russell, nephew of the Foreign Secretary, had never had much of an opinion of Joseph, and it is true that he could hardly have been more unlike a professional diplomat. His good nature and occasional impulsiveness had earned him several reprimands from the Foreign Office, but though he had at first been stigmatized by Russell as 'a good-natured goose,

1 The Times, 8th November, 1871.

utterly unfit and unqualified for his post',[1] he nevertheless, throughout his eleven years as Consul, managed to do many kindnesses and to help a great many Italians as well as his own compatriots.

Joseph received honourable recognition of his work from King Victor Emmanuel, who made him Officer of the Order of the Crown of Italy, and his official pension of eighty pounds had been supplemented by a further sixty pounds from the Civil List. It was not much to live on, but in Rome he managed fairly well. He was still living over the Fountain of Trevi and it was there that Arthur took Joan to meet him.

He shared his apartment now with a Dr Valeriani and his wife. The Signora kept house, the doctor defended him against his enemy, the rheumatism which lurked, waiting for a traitorous draught, or a damp day, to cripple him, and the faithful Betta, his servant since he had returned to Rome, tended him devotedly.

With Joan's warmth and sympathy and Joseph's easy friendliness, the meeting was an immediate success. He was proud of his youngest son and his new daughter, and at once decided that he must do a portrait of her in coloured chalks. Painting was no fatigue to him, he said, whereas doing nothing was.

The sittings for this portrait and the visits of members of Ruskin's party gave the old man great pleasure. Ruskin had hired two carriages for their stay, each pulled by a pair of fine black horses, so they were able to get about easily, and while Ruskin took Mrs Hilliard and her daughter to draw the Arch of Janus, or went shopping with them to buy shawls and a Roman dress for Connie, Arthur could show Joan round the City which he knew so well.

'It is a great pleasure being in Rome with my husband, and making the acquaintance of my father-in-law', Joan wrote to Professor Norton who had returned to America. 'Coz, I am sorry to say, is much out of humour with everything, or rather, triumphant at having his bad opinion of things in Rome confirmed. I am very tired, as we have been in a constant whirl seeing things....'[2]

They would gladly have stayed in Rome much longer, but after ten days Ruskin was becoming so restive that they had no choice but to agree to move on to northern Italy, which he loved. There had already been one scene between Ruskin and Arthur in the Vatican sculpture gallery. Arthur had called the attention of the party to the view across the Campagna towards the Alban Hills, with the mountains in the distance. Ruskin suddenly flew into a passion, said the mountains were mole hills, and that the view wasn't worth looking at.[3]

After this everyone agreed with Ruskin that it was time for them to be making their way towards the north. Joseph said a sad goodbye to Arthur and Joan and they drove off northwards, bound eventually for Venice. The old man was left to his painting, and his little company of friends.

Still sometimes a visitor would seek him out, leaving the Trevi Fountain,

---

[1] *The Roman Question: Extracts from dispatches of Odo Russell,* by Noel Blakeston, p. xxix.
[2] 13th May, 1872. Houghton Library.
[3] Arthur Severn's Memoirs.

H*

with its rocky Neptune wet with spray, and climbing the steps of the Scala Dante in the huge Palazzo Poli. He would turn along a dim carpetless gallery and pull the bell which hung by an unpretentious door and it would sound sweet and faint, like a muted echo from another century.

The old servant, Betta, would open the door and admit him to the little lobby, half hall, half sitting-room, its walls hung with engravings, and then, after some delay, he would be shown into the studio and the old man would greet him.

The visitor would say that he was an admirer of Keats and lead him on to talk about his friend. It was not difficult. The days of his youth were now more real to him than the mists of middle age and his thoughts turned often to his father and his angel-mother and life at Mason's Court, to the days when John Keats had just renounced the calling of a surgeon, when the hopes of his friends ran high, and Joseph was admitted to the friendship of three devoted brothers.

So he would talk and the visitor would listen and sometimes prompt him with a question. Perhaps he would show the book of Shakespeare's Poems that had belonged to Keats, with the sonnet 'Bright Star' that he had written in it. The visitor would hear how, on that far-off night when the *Maria Crowther* slept becalmed, Keats had pressed the book into this old man's hand, and perhaps if he was very lucky, Severn would tear a corner from some old letter and give it to him. Then he would own a precious scrap of paper on which the words had been traced, more than fifty years before, by the hand of Keats.

The shutters veiled the sun from the lofty room in the Palazzo Poli. Letters were scattered about on the marble floor, and paints and brushes. In the half-dark the old voice talked of dead men and forgotten days, until it seemed that in this strange untidy room, Time had no power.

But there were still those in England who could share his memories. When his visitors left he would turn back to his desk. In the dusky room, with its tall windows darkened to thwart the searching sun, he would sit and write to his sister Maria and his brother Tom. In the still air the words and thoughts of so many letters in the past, and of letters not yet written, rose and mingled in the timeless shadows.

'Walter writes me that the great preacher – Stopford Brooke – preached a sermon on the subject of my friendship for Keats in the church in York street, St James's Square, and I hope to get a copy of it, for I am gratified (not so much personally) as it shows that friendship still holds society together, and that mine is noticed after half a century!'[1]

'I am calling up all my recollections of Keats in notes to the beautiful poem of *Adonais* by Shelley, in which he mentions me. All this I had done when someone stole all my papers and left me to do it all over again. 'Tis true I receive many admirers of Keats, both American and English, and someone with an overflowing love carried off all my papers. . . .

[1] 1st July, 1873. Keats House.

'The picture I am preparing is of Keats, Shelley and myself, when I drew Keats's picture and Shelley read his essay on poetry.'

'I would not allow my good friends, The Doctor and his ladies, to keep my 81st birthday, for 'tis sad that all my old friends are dead and gone and I cannot bear to rejoice without 'em. Yet as good luck would have it, just then arrived young Willie Richmond and his wife – he is like my son, for his Father and I have been like brothers – and so the dinner was got up and was very pleasant. With two young Italian ladies we were eight in all, and Dr Valeriani was very joyous, and I was pronounced to be a fine specimen of Roman Antiquities. But 'tis enough that I am "bobbish" and am painting to my heart's delight. I dread the cold winter and the long drear evenings, when I can do nothing but keep the fire warm, for I am a very chilly body.'

'I am sorry to say my painting languishes, as I can't shake off a certain apathy or idleness (call it what you will). My pictures unfinished stand round me like starving children and reproach me with cruelty, but I hope to pick up as the Spring advances.

'You will be surprised and amused when I tell you that Walter has sold the letter of Keats's to Sir Charles Dilke for £5. As for the two letters of the brothers, I don't think they are of any value. I have four letters of Keats and many MSS. of which I give a scrap sometimes to his admirers as a great favour.'

'I begin to feel the loneliness of having lived too long.'[1]

[1] 10th August, 1873; 7th December, 1874; 21st March, 23rd April, 1875; 18th May, 1876. Keats House.

CHAPTER 25

FALSE DAWN

June – September, 1872

RUSKIN'S PARTY HAD GONE ON TO NORTHERN ITALY when they left Rome—to Assisi, Florence, Verona and Venice. Here they arrived at night and Ruskin's old friend Rawdon Brown met them in his gondola. None of the party except Ruskin had been to Venice before, and there was excited talk when they landed at Danieli's Hotel as to who would be out first in the morning. Ruskin made them all promise that they would be punctual for breakfast at nine o'clock. As Arthur could speak Italian he quietly ordered a gondola for himself at five in the morning and by breakfast time he had already sketched the fleet of Venetian fishing boats in the early sunlight.

Goodwin had not been out so early but had had a general look at St Mark's and the Piazza. These did not seem to have impressed him very favourably, as when Ruskin pressed him to give his opinion of them he answered after a pause, 'Well, Professor, if you really don't mind what I say, my first impression of the Church and those domes above and the flagstaffs was that it all looked very like a travelling show.' Ruskin burst into a roar of laughter in which they all joined.[1]

It was while they were in Venice that Rose broke into Ruskin's life again. During their travels he had been so overjoyed to revisit places that he loved, so pleased to be able to show them to the young people for the first time, so worried by former beauties that he had found destroyed, working so hard to record by his drawing the appearance of buildings now threatened by demolition or restoration, that Rose, for the first time in years, had receded a little in his mind. Besides, their last *rapprochement* had ended in his illness at Matlock and he had regarded that separation as final.

Now he heard from his friend MacDonald that Rose was in London and wanted to see him. She had been writing to MacDonald from Harristown since the spring, pouring out her heart in a series of incoherent letters full of suffering and despair. She felt it was her duty to obey her parents and all they asked of her was that she should be well and happy – she could be neither. She complained of continual pain in her head and side, and an empty life, 'simply hour after hour of spare time', racked with guilt at the contrast between the luxury of her own home and the terrible poverty of her father's tenants. Did Mr Mac-Donald believe that God ever put one in a position where it was impossible to

[1] Arthur Severn's Memoirs.

do His will? And how could one keep oneself from being tortured with disquiet when this was so? If only she could have kept the *friend* who had brought such pain and torture and division among so many hearts. If there had never been anything but friendship between them how much might have been spared.

MacDonald had answered these letters kindly, in consultation with Mrs Cowper-Temple, and when, her parents deeply anxious about her health and the doctors thinking that a change of surroundings might help her, she was allowed to come to England to stay with the Cowper-Temples, she saw a great deal of the MacDonalds, too. She talked to them about Ruskin and they all felt that a great part of her suffering was caused by the stories that she had been told about him, which had become exaggerated in an already hysterical brain and had poisoned all her feeling for him.

Unfortunately the trouble was aggravated when she left Mrs Cowper-Temple for a short while to stay with her aunt at Tunbridge Wells. Ruskin, two years ago, had appealed to this aunt to intercede for him, and had answered frankly questions he had then been asked. Her aunt now saw fit to show these private letters to Rose, who already in an unbalanced state of mind and haunted by the memory of Ruskin's former wife's accusations, read into his words a confession of terrible and mysterious sins.

Again her faith was shaken, but between them Mrs Cowper-Temple and the MacDonalds had now half-persuaded her that she might be doing Ruskin less than justice, and she had agreed to meet him if he so wished. Her friends thought this was the only way of lightening the load of anxiety and despair which lay so heavily on her. She had written to MacDonald: 'I know that to receive and love Christ, to repent and be as a little child would blot out the past indeed – but *has* he repented? Does he even believe in Christ, and Eternity? I who have loved (do love him) am powerless to alter him, or lighten my own suffering.'[1]

Now, on the last day of June, Ruskin received a letter from MacDonald urging him to come home at once. At first he tried to preserve the calm which he had found abroad, and mindful of his many disappointments, he telegraphed that he would not move 'unless in certainty of seeing her'. But he could not stop there. He wrote the next day, and again three days later, in case his first letter should miscarry.

He was becoming increasingly agitated by the revival of all these old hopes and troubles, and he now had no Joan to confide in, for she and Arthur had gone home, leaving him with Mrs Hilliard and Connie, who when he was nervous often irritated him. 'I have been moping about and doing no good,' he wrote to Joan, 'and want to be at home with Arfie and you. I believe Arfie has a true regard for me – and mean to trust it, and make the most I can of it. We should have been happier, on the whole, had we come abroad, as we originally intended, by ourselves, though we should not have had quite so much play – but Connie has learned much – and *I* have learned the difference between your

[1] 18th June, 1872. Leon, op. cit., p. 489.

quiet affection and the restless and irritable feeling which torments instead of comforts.'[1]

He could not concentrate on his work in Venice and wrote to MacDonald again: 'Kindly set down, without fail (by return of post if you can), in the plainest English you know – the precise things R. says of me – or has heard said of me. I am very weary of justifying myself.'[2]

'You speak of explanations:' wrote MacDonald, '*not one of these reached her*. Mr C. T. wrote to her father, probably: you sent letters to her aunt. The former was never mentioned to her; the latter she has only seen within the last fortnight or so, and they were interpreted to her, in her girlish ignorance, by the lurid light of Mrs M's letters to her mother, as confirming the worst things in the latter. Surrounded with false and devilish representations . . . hearing no defence of you, or anything you said to rebut the charges.'[3]

The letters from London and from Venice flew back and forth, crossing each other in the post, the London letters urging Ruskin's immediate return and warning him of the dangerous state of Rose's mind and health, Ruskin's seeking to pin down what he had been accused of and to be assured that if he gave up all his plans and came home it would not be to another rebuttal. Nevertheless he left Venice two weeks before he had intended to, and urged on by letters and telegrams at every halting place from the MacDonalds and Mrs Cowper-Temple quickened his rate of progress in response to their pleas of 'if he knew all', until he ended by dashing home from Geneva at top speed, 'half killing the poor girl and her mother whom I had charge of'.

Meanwhile Rose had been waiting in London, in increasing uneasiness and apprehension, against the wishes of her parents – torn once again between her eagerness to see Ruskin and to believe the good that his friends spoke of him, and her parents' wish for her to return to Ireland immediately. 'I shall try and wait three days – and yet I cannot bear the idea that you are sending for him after his apparent unwillingness. . . . My father and my mother want me to come home on Monday and I feel I ought to obey them . . . for they . . . are the divinely appointed guardians to whom I must give heed.'[4]

Ruskin breakfasted in Paris on the morning of 26th July and arriving at Herne Hill at half-past seven that evening, was furious to find no word from any of the friends who had been so urgent about his return. But it was soothing to be welcomed so warmly by Joan and Arthur, and comforting to go to bed in his old nursery at the top of the house, and to be woken next day by 'soft morning light through the window bars'. The morning brought him a note from the Mac-Donalds inviting him to their house in Hammersmith on the afternoon of the following day, a Sunday. Rose would be there.

[1] Tuesday afternoon, July 1872. Education Trust.
[2] 5th July, 1872. Leon op. cit., p. 491.
[3] Undated. Ibid., p. 492.
[4] 16th July, 1872. Ibid., p. 493.

How could he get through the hours until this promised time? All his reluctance had now vanished, and he was on fire to see her again and consumed by bitter anxiety. Saturday passed at last—a large part of it spent in driving down to the Royal Academy and seeing the year's pictures. Sunday dawned, and with his dislike of dark weather it seemed a good omen that he should be dressing in bright sunshine. Until it was time to go to the MacDonalds Ruskin forced himself to work.

His feelings had been divided. Partly he longed to see her again, partly he dreaded becoming involved once more in a situation which had already brought him so much suffering. But at the first sight of her his misgivings vanished, his heart melted and all reproaches were forgotten. Rose, thinner than ever, looked pathetically fragile and emaciated; her cheeks were flushed, her deep blue eyes seemed enormous, and her delicate face under the smooth golden hair was illumined by a tender smile, like the smile of a trusting child. She was no longer well enough to sit at the table for meals, and could scarcely bring herself to eat — her dinner one day of her visit was only three green peas, and the next, one strawberry and half a biscuit.

The MacDonalds left Ruskin alone with Rose that afternoon, and again during the afternoons of the next two days. All grievances and misunderstandings melted away; Ruskin was ecstatically happy and spent blissful hours making a drawing of the 'delicately chiselled beauty' of her face. To the MacDonalds his position seemed poignant and futile, to have found his love again when she seemed already beyond any possibility of marriage.

'A pretty note from Mrs MacDonald came last night saying how sorry you both were for me,' wrote Ruskin, 'but . . . I have had three days of heaven, which I would . . . have very thankfully bought with all the rest of my life . . . I thought before I saw her, that she could never undo the evil she has done — but she brought me back into life, and put the past away as if it had not been — with the first full look of her eyes. . . . But think what it was to have her taught daily horror of me — for years and years, in silence. I had prepared myself to hear that she was dead — and had died in indignation with me. I know now that she is ill — but she is at peace with me, and I may help to save her. I think you may be *very* happy in having done all this, for us both.'[1]

★

After a short visit to her parents in Ireland Rose came back to stay for a few days with the Cowper-Temples at Broadlands and Ruskin spent a whole day 'from morn till even' with her there. They walked together through the garden, down to the river, and she told him that she was happy to be with him. They crossed the river in a little boat and wandered together through the fields, and Ruskin could not help his hopes reviving in the new atmosphere of kindliness and peace. He had prayed that morning for her to be given to him, as he had not been able

[1] Herne Hill, 11th August, 1872. MacDonald, op. cit., pp. 120-1.

to pray for ten years past. 'Seven hours afterwards, she was standing in the same room beside me, mine. Not yet quite with her own consent; but with her utter confession — and promise never more to give me grief, except in death, and I believe that for neither of us shall it be grief — even then. For the faction of this world has past, for me, in winning her — and death cannot conquer me more'.[1]

He accompanied Rose in the train to London and during the journey gave her a drawing that he had made of a branch of olive.

Next day he wrote to Mrs Cowper-Temple, who had made it all possible:

'I have no words today — I should come and lie at your feet all day long, if I could, trying to thank you with my eyes. Nothing can come now that I cannot bear.'[2]

But this mood did not last. Rose had gone on to stay with some relations of Mrs Cowper-Temple near Crewe, and two days later Ruskin wrote again:

'Oh me, dearest Isola — we are poor weak things — I thought my one day at Broadlands might have lasted me a century, and now I am quite sick with pining for one hour — one minute more. Why did you let her go away? I was too timid and feeble — but I did not know what hold I had. If only I had seen what I saw yesterday — her letter to Mrs MacDonald after she had first seen me (28th July) — she would never have gone home — except to mine. And though I know and am wholly sure that unless some fearful tragic thing happen, she *must* come to me — still, this pleasant year is flying fast — another month of pain and all the sweet summer days will be ended. *Can't* you get her back again for me — I was so foolish and wrong to let her go. . . . Ah, get her back for me, and give me yet some days with bright morning and calm sunset, in *this* year — I am too old to wait — think!'

As he wrote, a letter arrived from Rose, summoning him to come to her the next day, where she was staying near Crewe.

'Ten o'clock — Your letter and William's and two from Her. And I shall see her, God helping me, and keep her — at least save her from all fear. . . . The little lovely thing — doesn't she see that I *do* love God best — in the form I see him . . . I would leave life for her, if I might — but neither lie for her, nor fail in any duty I had upon me, for her. She *is* second — if only she would forgive me for loving secondly too well!'[3]

Ruskin answered Rose's summons the next day, Sunday, and they went to church together, he rejoicing to stand beside her and to hold her prayer-book. But afterwards Rose, with one of her swift changes of mood, suddenly became cold towards him and he returned to London in misery.

Between them the Cowper-Temples and the MacDonalds had been able to disentangle the truth from the web of mysterious hints and insinuations about

[1] 15th August, 1872. Leon, op. cit., p. 495.
[2] Morning, 15th August, 1872. Pierpont Morgan Library.
[3] Saturday, 18th August, 1872 (should be Saturday 17th). Pierpont Morgan Library.

Ruskin, which had horrified Rose and made her bitterly unhappy, but now she felt unable to cope with the reality of his love for her. In vain she had urged that he must love God more than herself — the strength of his feeling frightened her. Ill and frail, and constantly torn between her feelings for him and what she felt to be her duty to God and her parents, she could not surrender to his love. Now, when she had caused him to be sent for, when the dark suspicions had been dissipated, when the time had come for her to commit herself, she finally withdrew in fear. Mrs Cowper-Temple had some idea of what was happening and tried to warn him.

'Your letter is wise and kind,' wrote Ruskin, 'yet how can I entirely trust your judgment? It must have been mainly formed since Wednesday? You had as much hope as I, then? Had you not? You did not then think her a basilisk. . . . In your house, I vowed loyalty to her, to the death, and she let me kiss her. I cannot break my oath. I do not think she can ever give it back to me. Basilisk or not, I must serve her, obey her — live and die for her, now.'[1]

Rose wrote to Mrs MacDonald: 'It has not ended as you wished and hoped. . . . His last word to me were a blessing. I felt too dumb with pain to answer him, yet God knows if any heart had power to bless another, mine used that power for him — though I could only yield him up to greater love than mine. I cannot be to him what he wishes, or return the vehement love which he gave me, which petrified and frightened me. . . . When we come "face to face" in that Kingdom where love will be perfected — and yet there will be no marrying or giving in marriage — we shall understand one another.'[2]

★

Joan grew anxious as Ruskin lingered in London at the Euston Square Hotel, waiting to hear from Rose, who had returned to her family in Ireland. He did not yet fully understand that she had finally rejected him, even as a friend.

'Dearest Joanie,' he wrote, 'I am very thankful for her letter and would come out to Herne Hill if I could talk at present, but I am not in humour for talking. We will all go down to Coniston on Tuesday, please God, and we will see everything and have some happy days and arrange the house and talk to our hearts content — as far as talking can give content. I *may* any day have good news from Ireland, which would put everything right. . . . Don't be the least frightened about me; but glad for me; that I have got my full life back — through whatever pain. No word from Ireland, nor sign yet. . . .'[3]

Later that day he heard from Rose at Harristown and again the following day, but her letters did nothing to cheer him, and it was with a heavy heart that he travelled north with Joan and Arthur, to stay in Coniston village until he could move into his new home. The weather increased his depression — day after

[1] Monday (19th August, 1872). Pierpont Morgan Library.
[2] MacDonald, op. cit., p. 121.
[3] Thursday, 22nd August, 1872.

day of mist and pouring rain and he had been there only a week when a letter came from Rose, which made it clear to him at last that she would have no more to do with him. His cup of bitterness was full when two days later, as he and Joan were about to enter Coniston Church for morning service, he was handed the last letter that he had written to Rose, which she had returned unopened. He was so shattered by this final blow that he turned away from the church door and Joan doing the same, they walked sadly back together to the inn where they were staying.

Bitterly Ruskin wrote to MacDonald, 'She is mad – and it is an experience to me of what "possession" means . . . nor have I any just cause to be angry with her, but only to be grieved for us both – and angry enough with the people who have driven her to this.' Then he could no longer restrain his pain and anger. 'Would you kindly write to her saying nothing more than that you are requested to direct her to send the drawing I gave her (in the railway carriage coming up from Broadlands) back to me, carefully packed, as I made it for Oxford, not for her.'[1]

The return of his drawing of the olive branch became almost an obession with him for the next few days, and he wrote again to MacDonald: 'Say I will draw her some bella donna with monk's hood: and that I could make a more delicate drawing of hemlock, but knew she would prefer Christian to Greek poisons.'

Then his feelings changed again from anger to despair and disillusionment: 'I would take it bravely, only first there is the deadly fact whether it is the Devil that makes me feel . . . that she is not worth my fidelity to her, and that the fidelity itself is worthless for it is only because she is pretty. If she hadn't a straight nose and red lips, what should I care for her? . . . My only fault had been letting her see I still hope. I got the returned letter at the church door last Sunday, and walked home again. Even Joanie couldn't go in. When the thing one meant to pray for turns out not worth prayer, what is one to do?'[2] Ruskin's invariable anodyne for suffering was to immerse himself in work.

'Fallen and wicked and lost in all thought;' he wrote in his diary, 'must recover by work.'

---

[1] 8th September, 1872. Leon, op. cit., p. 497.
[2] 9th September, 1872. Ibid., p. 498.

CHAPTER 26

BRANTWOOD

September, 1872 – May, 1873

ARTHUR AND JOAN MOVED FROM THE CONISTON HOTEL into Brantwood with Ruskin on 12th September. There was much to be done; all the furniture and hangings which had come from Denmark Hill and the new furniture and hangings, supplied by the same decorators and almost indistinguishable from the old, to be sorted and arranged.

The view from the windows of Brantwood compensated for any ugliness within. All the principal rooms faced west; below them the ground sloped steeply from the house to the lake shore, with the road between, and beyond lay the whole width of Coniston Water with the mountain, the Old Man, rising into the clouds on the further shore. Ruskin had had a little octagonal turret added to the bedroom at the south-west corner of the house, with latticed windows from which he could look down the full length of the lake.

Though he left most of the arrangement of the house to Joan, Ruskin took great trouble with his study. A round table at which he would write was put in the bow window. The specially made paper covered the walls, but not much of it was to be seen by the time that his book cases, mineral cabinets designed by himself, and a secretaire with sliding cases for pictures had been brought into the room — still less when a large early Turner of the Lake of Geneva was placed over the fireplace, and the rest of the walls were closely hung with smaller Turner water-colours.

On 13th September he wrote the heading BRANTWOOD in his diary for the first time. 'Morning dark, cloudy, with gusty wind. Slept quietly last night in my turret-room. Blue sky now breaking over the moors under the Old Man.'

There was plenty for Joan to do; organizing the house for her cousin brought out all her energy and practical ability. The landscape was just the kind that Arthur preferred for his painting, and the lake was a constant joy to him. He had always loved boats and sailing and here was the opportunity to indulge in his hobby and combine it with his painting — all close at hand. Ruskin worked on the preparation of lectures on Botticelli and the Florentine Schools of Engraving which he was to deliver at Oxford during the autumn term, and also on his monthly *Fors*.

When he was not writing his new home gave him plenty of occupation. He had plans for the diversion of the little stream which ran through his property, cutting winding paths through his woods, planting bulbs, terracing the steep hill-side to make a garden, and building a new boathouse and harbour at the lake-side below the house. Lily Armstrong and Connie Hilliard's brother, Laurie, soon joined the party. Laurence Hilliard — or Lollie, as he became known to them, was a bright gifted boy of seventeen who planned to be an artist and could make and rig beautiful models of sailing ships. Arthur was now twenty-five and the two got on very well together.

Meanwhile Mrs Cowper-Temple was in Ireland, and Ruskin heard from her that Rose had had a complete breakdown.

'I knew perfectly well that there was a mental derangement at the root of it all,' he replied, 'which does not make the thing less sad; but it prevents it from being cruel and monstrous. . . .

'I wish you would . . . tell me what *sort* of "anguish" the mother is in. Is she furious as well as anguished, still? What sort of terms does she keep with *you*? I can't fancy.

'I am thankful for any report — either of death or life.'[1]

In her answer Mrs Cowper-Temple tried to comfort him by saying that everything is bearable but *Remorse*.

'Now I *have* that also, to bear,' wrote Ruskin wretchedly in an incoherent reply. '*I* failed in faith and perseverance, long before *she* gave way. I shall always feel that had I deserved her, I should have got her. . . . I shall never more come to Broadlands. . . .

'Do you notice how intensely *selfish* all *insanity* is? Very curious? "Troubled — between fear of hearing of me, and fear lest *she* should be misjudged." Is a baser or more wicked state of mind — supposing it *sane* — conceivable?'[2]

Mrs Cowper-Temple wrote back unhappily and Ruskin hastened to reassure her:

'The good that you may be sure you have done me, remember, is in my having known, actually, for one whole day, the *perfect* joy of love. For I think, to be *quite* perfect, it must still have *some* doubt. . . . I don't think any *quite* accepted and beloved lover could have the Kingly and Servantly joy together, as I had it in that ferry boat of yours, when she went into it herself, and stood at the stern and let me stop it in mid-stream and look her full in the face for a long minute, before she said "now go on". The beautiful place — the entire peace — nothing but birds and squirrels near — the trust, which I had then, in all things being finally well — yet the noble fear mixed with the enchantment — her remaining still above me, not mine, and yet mine.

'And this after ten years of various pain — and thirst. And this with such a creature to love. For you know, Isola,[3] people may think her pretty or not pretty, as their taste may be, but she is a *rare* creature, and that kind of beauty

---

[1] Brantwood, 28th September, 1872. Pierpont Morgan Library.
[2] Brantwood, 2nd October, 1872. Pierpont Morgan Library.
[3] Isola Bella — another of Ruskin's names for Mrs Cowper-Temple.

happening to be *exactly* the kind I like, and my whole life being a worship of beauty – fancy how it intensified the whole.'

He could grant that every lover thinks his mistress perfection, but he felt there was a difference between an instinctive, groundless preference and his own deliberate admiration of Rose 'as I admire a thin figure in a Perugino fresco, saying "it is the loveliest figure I know after my thirty years study of art". Well, suppose the Perugino – better than Pygmalion's statue, holier, longer sought – *had* left the canvas, come into the garden, walked down to the riverside with me, looked happy, *been* happy (for she *was*, and said she was) – in being with me.

'Wasn't it a day, to have got for me? – all your getting. . . . That day is worth being born and living seventy years of pain for. . . . Mad, or dead, she is still mine, now.'[1]

Arthur and Joan left Brantwood for Scotland at the end of October and Ruskin drove south with Laurie Hilliard to deliver his lectures at Oxford. He was further depressed as he was leaving to have news of business troubles from his cousin, George Richardson, which he sent on at once to Joan.

'I was so deeply interested in George's letters,' she replied at once. 'Poor fellow! What a terribly anxious time he must have had.

'I'm so glad di Pa that Arfie's an Artist, tho' I sometimes lament that you don't know him and his good points a tenth part as well as I do – for I'm quite sure there's no other man living that you could have allowed me to marry who would have been such a precious husband to me, and I *do* wish he would sometimes be less diffident in telling you what an angel of goodness he thinks you – and how grateful and loving he is at least to you, for everything. But no doubt I'm boring you – but when husbands and wives *are* nice they're a wonderful comfort to each other . . . and when you get Clochette[2] she'll I hope be the cumfy of oos ife di Pa – and the sweetest of wee ife – but perhaps you'll insist on her being tall – and of course as slim as the poker!'[3]

*

Joan, happy in her marriage and most feminine of women, was overjoyed to know that she would have a baby in the New Year, and Ruskin wrote to her more cheerfully after a short visit to London where he had seen Charles Newton at the British Museum:

'Darling Pussy-Mussky,

I saw Newton at musey isterday.

He says – first thing (no – not quite) – How is Mrs Arthur? She's all right – says I. Is the event near? – says he. I'm afraid so – says I.

Tell her, of all things, not to have twins – says he.

---

[1] Brantwood, 4th October (1872). Pierpont Morgan Library.

[2] Joan's playful name for an imaginary bride for Ruskin, with whom he would find perfect happiness.

[3] Physgill House, Saturday (November 1872). Education Trust.

Darling Pussky — I wish you were twins yourself and could always be one here and one there.'[1]

Arthur and Joan were soon back in their house at Herne Hill, and Ruskin often came up from Oxford to spend the night with them in his old home. In spite of her marriage he continued to write to Joan daily and counted on a daily letter from her. When he was with them he expected her to act as his secretary, copying out documents and writing letters for him.

Their first dinner-party at Herne Hill nearly ended in disaster. Ruskin, up from Oxford for the night, was their principal guest. As they were going into dinner and Arthur was half-way down the stairs with the most important lady on his arm, their little Yorkshire maid rushed up the stairs towards them calling that the kitchen chimney was on fire. The procession to dinner broke up in confusion, Arthur and a General who had been behind him dashing down into the basement where, groping their way through a fog of smoke, they found the cook holding a blackened leg of lamb under the hot water tap. Whatever had caused the blinding smoke, the chimney appeared now to be clear, so they retreated upstairs to better air, where they found several scared ladies on the drawing-room landing and heard voices at the top of the house.

There they discovered Ruskin, who having heard that the correct thing to do in such a case was to put a wet blanket over the chimney-pot, had hurried up-stairs, dragged a blanket off a bed and held it under a tap on the top landing. He had been surprised to find how difficult it was to wet a blanket in a short time, but nothing daunted had then tried, with the blanket in his arms, to get out of a very small window on the roof. From this position Joan and his valet, Crawley, had only just managed to extricate him.

Eventually the party re-assembled in the drawing-room, several looking rather grubby. Dinner was then announced for the second time. 'Luckily,' said Arthur airily, 'there had been things in saucepans unspoiled by the soot, and when I listened to the merry flow of conversation, quite unlike the ordinary talk on such occasions, I felt that, after all, the chimney catching fire had turned out to be rather a help to our first important dinner-party.'[2]

The Severns remained in their house at Herne Hill, but Ruskin returned to Brantwood at the end of December. It rained almost every day, but he seemed to find a quiet content in arranging his collections and walking on the hills.

'I'm cataloguing my books — and finishing my coins,' he wrote to Joan, 'and really it's a sort of ideal life now, so quiet and far away — and yet with so many pretty things about me, and lake and mountains outside and my Joanie and Arfie lovin me all the while (Is Oo quite *soo* Arfie likes me? One nevvy knows).'[3]

He busied himself with plans to make Brantwood 'more and more perfect' and wandered about the countryside accompanied by his cook's dog, which had taken a great fancy to him.

[1] 6th November, 1872. Education Trust.   [2] Arthur Severn's Memoirs.
[3] Brantwood, 1873 (January). Education Trust.

Georgie Burne-Jones and her six-year-old daughter paid a ten-day visit to Brantwood in January. She had thought nothing but love for his parents could have reconciled Ruskin to the 'heavy dullness' of his old home at Denmark Hill, and was astonished to find at Brantwood the same heavy furniture and dark colours and decided that Brantwood was, if anything, the duller of the two.'[1] Ruskin was not very pleased at the few criticisms that she voiced. He wrote to Joan about some re-arrangement of pictures and china in what he called 'our pretty drawing-room': 'Georgie put me in a passion by finding fault with the carpet the moment she came in, which I didn't get over while she stayed!'[2]

Joan prepared happily for the birth of her child. She had only one anxiety. How would her cousin — alone at Brantwood — manage without her daily letter? With her unselfish nature and after all the troubles she had shared with him, the 26-year-old girl realized how much he still depended on her. 'I believe I am really more anxious about Joanie than I know,' he had just written to Tom Richmond, 'and it will be a great relief to me when this affair of hers is well over. It is not merely the danger, but I can't bear the poor dear little thing to have the pain. She has been very happy and well lately, and is my chief treasure in life now.'[3]

'I need not I hope say, my darling,' he wrote to Joan, 'that though I am not anxious, knowing your general good health, and the care that you have wisely taken, I do not write my foolish jesting letters without a very solemn sense of the approach to you of one of those periods of life which are intended to make us look with closer trust to Him in whom we live, and move, and have our Being.'[4]

His nervousness about Joan increased as the expected date of the birth drew nearer. 'I can't make out from your letter,' he wrote to Arthur, 'if Joan was really thinking of getting up to go to the Simons' — I shall be anxious till to-morrow's letter. I think she oughtn't to go out, this weather. I don't myself but I'm old and crazy.

'There's nothing "odd" in Rose's behaviour — any more than in consumption, or cancer, or brain-fever or any other mortal disease. But there's a great deal that is profoundly tragic in it.

'Tell Joan . . . it's absurd in her to go out at night and bad for the child.'[5]

A few days before the birth was expected Joan wrote her cousin a letter which he put aside in a fresh envelope with a photograph of her, and kept so all his life, marking it on the outside *My beautiful Joan — photographs and letter.*

'I've just been thinking what a horrid bore it will be soon when I'm not able to write to you for a time! though you may be sure the instant I am allowed to hold a pencil I shall use it for your benefit. . . . I've everything in the greatest

[1] G. Burne-Jones, op. cit., vol. 11, p. 32.
[2] 28th January, 1873. Education Trust.
[3] Brantwood (January 1873). Pierpont Morgan Library.
[4] Brantwood, Tuesday (28th January, 1873). Education Trust.
[5] Brantwood, Wednesday (February 1873). In possession of Rev. I. Hutchinson.

order and perfect readiness, and I'm very well and very happy – and you're to love me *all the same* di Pa and me'll be so dood! – and I'll never let *it* come near you, or bore you, or do anything unless it can amuse, or help, or comfort my best Cuzzie-Pa, but I think D.V. when it's able to say "*di Pa*" quite prettily it *may* be allowed to give you a kiss.

'I'm greatly amused with the remarks some people make on the subject – they all conclude as a matter of course that I would prefer a boy to a girl! – and that without doubt we'd call him "John Ruskin" and can't understand why I insist that I never would call a child of mine by that name unless *you* specially wished it – and I don't know that I would even then. To me, and Arfie too, there is and never will be, but one John Ruskin – and I don't think . . . that any other human being is quite worthy of it.'[1]

On 10th February Ruskin went to London, staying at the Bath Hotel, for a meeting of the Metaphysical Society. Even at such a moment Joan seemed to do her best to make things as easy as possible for him, and had her baby next day when he was already in London – a little girl.

'My darling,' he wrote to her at once, 'I'm so very thankful, I send you my love. I know you must be quiet. That love I hope never disquiets you.' But he could not restrain himself and wrote twice during the following day: 'Me's been so fitened knowing that my wee amie was going to have such dedful pain. But Arfie says you were so brave and good. Will oo always ove oos poo Donie just the same? Me fitened – di ma? Is oo velly much peased? Pease no be peased too mut.'[2]

Ruskin settled back into his routine of work at Brantwood, varied by rowing on the lake, long walks up the hills and helping with the work on his harbour – leaning out of the boat and rolling stones out of the calm lake, with the reflections of the opposite shore 'absurdly real,' and the peak of Helvellyn silver-white to the north. The beauty of his surroundings soothed him and the ache of his longing for Rose became a little numbed. 'I have a great sealed well of feeling, under the ice still – thank heaven and you,' he wrote to Mrs Cowper-Temple, 'for nature and her true children, and for my work.'[3]

He interrupted this quiet life only to go to Oxford for his lectures, when he would pay a brief visit to Herne Hill to see Joan and Arthur before returning to Brantwood. The baby was to be named Lily, after Lily Armstrong, who had been one of Ruskin's 'especial pets' at Winnington, and had since become an intimate friend both of Joan and Rose.

After lecturing at Oxford in mid-March he came to Herne Hill for two days, and stood as god-father to little Lily Severn. 'As a matter of feeling, I should even now have liked Rose better than Lily,' he wrote, 'but I dread the evil star.'[4]

[1] (February 1873). Education Trust.
[2] 12th February, 1873. Education Trust.
[3] Brantwood, Sunday, 2nd March, 1873. Pierpont Morgan Library.
[4] Oxford, Saturday morning (15th March, 1873). Education Trust.

From Oxford he returned to Brantwood and the daily letters continued to arrive at Herne Hill.

'What "French Revolution" are you reading – Carlyle's?' he asked Arthur. 'If so, I don't quite understand you thinking them such monsters; I have always fancied C. Newton was right in saying I was very like Robespierre. I fancy I should only have cut the *old* women's heads off – not the young ones.... Lily's[1] going to be married as I suppose you know by this time. She told me a month ago, but in confidence. I've been rather sulky, ever since. .... I really don't know what to do now – it's such a bother going looking for Clochette – and I don't feel as if I should much like her, after all.'[2]

He was impatient for the Severns to join him at Brantwood, but Joan was still unwell. Lily Armstrong was staying with them at Herne Hill when Joan had the news of her mother's death in Scotland and for a few days was very ill. She had to give up nursing the baby, and followed Ruskin's advice to 'get a stout wet nurse'.[3]

To Lily, in gratitude for her kindness in nursing Joan he sent a cheque and Arthur in high spirits described its arrival:
'My dearest Mr Ruskin,
          'Hurrah! Hurrah! Hurrah! for Lily's Hundred Guineas!! A Princely gift! There is something very "Je ne sais quoi-ish" about a hundred guineas!

'It is quite amusing to see the two girls looking at each other ... and wondering how in the world they were to find words to express their thanks, for Joanie and I feel quite as pleased as Lily herself! When they asked me what they were to say, I could only poke the fire like a maniac and tell them to settle it amongst themselves!'[4]

Joan, though still feeling rather weak, was soon able to go out and see the spring flowers in her garden. Ruskin urged that they should all come to him soon after 17th May when he would be returning from Oxford for the summer. The change of air would do her good, the construction of the new harbour would be far enough advanced for Arthur to be able to bring a boat into it, and they would both enjoy the beauty of spring on the lake. Joan was afraid that a very small baby at close quarters in a small house would be irritating for him. 'My dear, I don't care about twenty babies if only you and Arfie can come after 17th May,' he answered. 'The baby doesn't the least worry me by squalling and I'm only sorry for its loving Mamma.' In the end, after many more letters, Joan promised that they would come at the beginning of July. Until then he was kept company by the artist Alfred Hunt with his wife and pretty little daughter, Venice, who was Ruskin's god-daughter, just eight years old.

[1] Lily Armstrong.
[2] In possession of author. Brantwood. March (1873).
[3] 2nd April, (1873). Education Trust.
[4] In possession of author.

'My visitors are greatly pleasing to me,' he wrote to Joan. . . . 'Venice enjoys dabbling nearly as much as I do, and fell head foremost into the lake yesterday, but I pulled her out by the waist . . . being luckily near her and quick with my hand.

'Mr and Mrs Hunt are very nice. . . . And we get on very smoothly.

'The relief to me is very great, for when I am alone the shadow of past and future is always heavy on me, but somehow the human presences take it away.

'But they're none of them as much astonished at Brantwood as I expected. It's only my own Pussie who really peciates Brantwood.'[1]

The carriage was ordered to meet the Severns at Ulverstone. The little road crossed a stream near the southernmost end of Coniston Water and wound its way along the eastern shore. To their right the wooded hillside rose steeply to the heathery moors above and on their left through the trees gleamed the still, sunlit water of the lake. It was the first time that either of them had seen the lake country in early summer and its beauty astonished them. The predominating colour was an intense green — green ferns everywhere, sprouting from the base of hedges and stone walls, and the green of moss and grass brilliant between the slim grey stems of trees. Ahead of them, as the narrow lane twisted in and out, bringing the carriage sometimes to the verge of the lake and then retreating to leafy shadow, they could see the mountains, and as they drove the Old Man seemed all the time to grow in size.

Ruskin met them on the road, so that they could walk the last quarter of a mile together. He was sad that they had not come earlier — they had missed so much. 'The beauty of the spring is over, and now it is green summer,' he said. 'Very nice; but another thing;' and they had missed the daffodils and bluebells in the thick woods which grew down the steep hillside to the very back of the house.

They turned a corner and there on the hill ahead it stood, a little turned away from them, its windows gazing out across the lake and nearer to them, the lodge, quite half as large as the house itself, which Ruskin had just built for Crawley and his family.

As they looked again at the white house above them, neither Arthur nor Joan realized how much it was to mean in their own lives.

---

[1] Whit-Sunday 1873. Education Trust.

CHAPTER 27

'THE CHILD-ANGEL'

June, 1873 – May, 1874

THEIR LIFE AT BRANTWOOD THAT SUMMER WAS IDYLLIC. The baby thrived. Arthur painted and sailed on the lake, climbed the hills with Joan and helped Ruskin to make paths through his woods and clear the banks of the stream which ran down through them. Ruskin rose, as usual, at dawn, and worked for two and a half hours before breakfast at nine o'clock. He liked to saunter through his woods, billhook in hand, to work in the little woodland garden which he was making, or sail along the lake with Arthur and wander back through the heather and foxgloves which grew among the grey rocks on its banks, to gather currants with Joan in the kitchen garden for their dinner.

Joan busied herself with running the house and making new additions to the garden in which her cousin was not so much interested. She had thrown off the effects of her illness and had never felt better.

Ruskin, as always, had a great number of different projects in hand at the same time. The restless activity of his brain never allowed him to relax. When tired of one subject he turned at once to study another. He was working on two long essays — one on Walter Scott and the other an analysis of Carlyle's book on Frederick the Great — for new issues of *Fors Clavigera*, as well as preparing his lectures for the Michaelmas term at Oxford, revising his Botticelli lectures for publication, correcting the proofs of his Bird lectures which were being published as *Love's Meinie*, writing an introduction to a new edition of *The Stones of Venice*, painting trees, studying old French, reading the New Testament in Greek, and making drawings to illustrate his forthcoming lectures on Tuscan art.

As always now, his time was divided between trying to show people the beauties of the world they lived in — the miracle of a leaf, a bird's feather, or a lichened rock — and inveighing against the injustices and suffering inflicted by man on man.

The Hunts, after leaving Brantwood, had taken rooms in Coniston for the summer, where their other daughter, Violet, had joined them. They often rowed over to Brantwood and Ruskin would take the girls for walks, or later to gather nuts in the woods. Sometimes he would play hide-and seek with them, when the children would politely agree to spare his feelings by not finding him too quickly, though their sharp eyes had seen him immediately, 'lying spread

231

out on a rock near the waterfall, looking like a grey trout that had somehow got on the bank'.[1]

Among the neighbours Ruskin made friends with the Miss Beevers, who lived at the Thwaite at the head of the lake, and the Marshalls, a family living in a large house called Monk Coniston. There were several other houses standing between Brantwood and the village of Coniston, which was at the north-western end of the lake, nearly three miles by road round the lake head, but less than a mile by water. To the south of Brantwood there were no buildings until the other end of Coniston Water.

Several friends travelling in the Lake District called on them during the summer, and in August Mrs Cowper-Temple and her husband came to stay for a few days. They dutifully admired the treasures of the house – the manuscripts, the collections of coins and minerals, and above all the pictures. Disappointingly, the weather was not good for their stay. But Ruskin, anxious to share with them all the joys of his new kingdom, drove them with Joan up the steep hill to Monk Coniston Tarn, so that they could admire the famous view.

There had originally been three small pieces of water high in the hills, but the Marshalls, by making a dam, had joined them into one small lake of irregular shape. Unfortunately a cold mist had veiled the hills. Ruskin, much distressed, began to describe the beauties that lay invisible before them, and as he warmed to his subject it was almost as though his guests could see all that he described so eloquently.

The Cowper-Temples were still in touch with Rose, who had been to stay with them at Broadlands just before they came north. Ruskin refused an invitation to visit them. 'Quiet end of life in faithfulness to R. would be best for myself and others. She has been so cruel to me that I cannot be rightly faithful to her; this is the real root of all that is worst in my present days. I cannot rest, even with my cold glass idol – it is flawed.

'But I think the best way of looking at the whole business is to remember that the happier life might have led me away from what I had to do.'[2]

Connie Hilliard, Dora Livesey (another of his 'pets' from Winnington) and other friends came in the autumn, and they continued on the surface to be a happy party. Joan's cheerfulness had its usual good effect on Ruskin's melancholy. He enjoyed their long walks together, picnics on the hillside, working on the harbour with Arthur, and a day when the whole party sailed across the lake and went blackberrying on the farther shore. He even enjoyed the afternoon when he and Arthur managed to capsize the boat. But the nights were not so easy for him. After a game of chess and an evening of singing or music he would find himself unable to sleep, or would at length fall asleep only to have nightmare-ish dreams. Sometimes he would lie awake for hours, weary and sad, oppressed by the feeling of work undone, and he complained of feeling dizzy or headachy

[1] Violet Hunt, *Works*, vol. 23, p. xxv.
[2] Brantwood, 4th September, 1873. Pierpont Morgan Library.

when he woke. As always when he was over-tired or emotionally upset, his stomach was affected. This he put down to unwise eating – a pear or crystallized orange peel at dinner. He felt a sensation of nervous hurry, of working against time; he knew that it made him exhausted and irritable, but he could not relax. 'Death coming nearer makes rest so dear bought', he wrote in his diary.

The Severns stayed on at Brantwood when he left for Oxford, and did not return to their own home at Herne Hill until the end of November, where Ruskin joined them soon after the end of the Oxford term. It had not been a happy one. He was feeling depressed and unwell and his lectures had not been well attended. In his letters to Mrs Cowper-Temple he still wrote of Rose, and she tried to soften his resentment by explaining to him that Rose, with her intense spirituality, was not like other girls – more like a child-angel.

'I am *not* unjust to her,' he wrote. 'I have but one word of eternal blessing for her – one thought of eternal love – though she slay me.

'But the purpose of God is that angels should love as angels, and children as children, but maidens as neither or these. And it is because she loves only as these, that now *she* cannot help me, though angels – and children, may. And that she does love only as these, you yourself have been most earnest that I should know. I know it too well.'

Of Rose's return to Broadlands in the summer he wrote, 'R. *could* not have gone but that she is yet a child. For it was there – on the same day last year – that I had the only hour of perfect peace in love that life has ever given me. She gave herself to me for the time, without shadow – even caressed my arm a little as we walked.'[1]

Ruskin spent the Christmas vacation with Joan and Arthur. He continued to feel restless and unwell, but a visit to Margate for sea air was cut short and afterwards he remained at Herne Hill, going to the circus, the pantomime and several theatres, and making an occasional sortie to Oxford. Arthur had another picture in the new Exhibition at the Dudley, and Ruskin told Joan that he thought it 'quite the best at the exhibition'. He had now set Arthur to paint a sign which was to hang outside his new venture, the tea shop in Paddington.

In the shop window he arranged some pretty blue and white Nankin china bowls which he had bought in Siena, and Arthur was given a long board, painted gold, on which, at Ruskin's request, he inscribed in bright violet-coloured letters, *Ruskin's Shop for the Supply of Pure Tea*. The enterprise was not a financial success and after a time it was abandoned. Ruskin used it once or twice when he wished to change into evening dress in London without going all the way back to Herne Hill. He said he was afraid of going to the Athenaeum by himself, in case the servants might not know him.[2]

*

[1] Undated letter (December 1873). Pierpont Morgan Library.
[2] Arthur Severn's Memoirs.

By the beginning of the year, Rose had become so ill, mentally and physically, that it was thought that she must be put unreservedly in the care of a doctor, away from her own home, and on arrival in London she sent a message to Joan asking her to come to see her. Joan, with her ready sympathy and warm heart, immediately agreed. She was shocked by Rose's appearance; all past sorrows were forgotten, and they parted as close friends once more. A few days later Rose wrote to Mrs MacDonald from Broadlands: 'I have never felt so ill – even being here does me no good, and I am almost glad to be going thoroughly into a doctor's hands in a few days . . . and be entirely under his treatment for as long as he likes.'[1]

On her return from Broadlands she stayed near the Crystal Palace and Joan took the opportunity of seeing her almost daily while she was there. She was still not allowed to see Ruskin or to correspond with him, but she began to send him little messages through Joan. Joan delivered the messages and told him how ill Rose was. He knew that he could get no work done in London, with her so near, so he returned to Brantwood, spending a week at Oxford on the way.

But the fleeting calm of the summer had left him. The lake was veiled in rain and fog. The 'black east wind' blew. He could not sleep. He fought hard against the gloom and distress which threatened to overcome him, and 'the old deadly anger against Mr La Touche'.[2] He felt that if Rose's parents had not forbidden their marriage, and if they had not poisoned and shocked her mind by the hideous things they had told her of him, she would never have declined into this fatal illness. Yet he must overcome these bitter thoughts and force himself to work. He was 'not beaten yet, but wonder-struck at the cruelty of all things'.

Joan from London sent him daily news of Rose.

'I'm so thankful to hear of Arfie's working in the garden with Downs and that you miss me, both,' he wrote to her. 'All else – of R's bettering – is new life to me. I am so helped by the blessing of hearing daily of her.'[3]

But try as he would, he could not get his three lectures on geology done, and at length had to send a message to Oxford that he could not deliver them during the Lent Term.

'There'll be rather a row at Oxford today,' he wrote to Joan. 'It's the first time I've broken down in promised lectures. . . . I could not do it this time, and it is as well Rose should know a little of the mischief she does in a definite way. I suppose she never has really got it into her stupid little head that she has done me any.'[4]

Although he had found it impossible to deliver his lectures he kept hard at his other work, seeking strength from his habit of opening the Bible every

[1] 3rd February, 1874. Leon, op. cit., p. 499.
[2] *John Ruskin's Diary*, 23rd February, 1874.
[3] Brantwood (28th February, 1874). Education Trust.
[4] Brantwood (8th March, 1874). Education Trust.

morning and taking what he found as his text for the day. Even that consolation sometimes turned to bitterness.

'Text. "Rejoicing in hope." It's all very well, but what hope have I, but for others?'[1]

Joan's letters were his only comfort. 'Your letter today is perfect in sweetness and fitness; exactly what I wanted. . . .

'Yes, it is bad for me to be alone – yet only alone can I do my work; only alone, or if it could be, as it used to be, with my own Joanie, all to myself. Don't cry out, dear, that you're just the same. You love me as much or more; – but you can't unpack my minerals for me and dress Bibsie and talk to Arfie, all at once – you needn't think it – nor need I. . . .

'Now, I have no hope, no future, no Father, no Mother, no Rose – and only the third part of a Joan. I oughtn't to have so much – but believe I have that.

'It is curious that my work for my geological lectures required me first of all, or nearly so, to complete the map I left unfinished, breaking off, at Harristown, to watch Rose at play on the Lawn. She threw up her mallet at me – calling to me to come down. I would not, for I said I must finish my map. I did not go down – but I did not finish my map. *That* one will never be touched more – but I must make another. . . .'[2]

He could not always keep up the pretence to himself that some good was coming out of his unhappiness and occasionally relieved his feelings by lashing out at Joan. Anything less than complete acceptance of his rebukes or reproaches he would not allow.

'My letters must never "drive you wild",' he wrote, 'nor must you "resent" them. . . . When you often say that you love me so that you don't know fot to do, remember always this is to be *done* – to keep your temper when I am unreasonable. I do not often put you seriously to trial.

'Remember, my dear, that the pain – indignation and acute sorrow – which I wear continually, like red hot armour, through all my jesting or working, can only be conquered by efforts made, perhaps every hour of the day, to keep myself from being "driven wild" for your sake, as much as my own. And if ever I am a little wild you should be more than usually gentle and tender. . . . My darling wee Doanie if this letter is a little cruel, forgive it. I have so much, much, pain.'[3]

Arthur, too, had been seeing Rose and had played several games of chess with her. He found her 'rather beautiful to look at – a most refined face – hair cut rather short'. The doctors so far did not seem able to effect any improvement in her health.

'Thanks for lovely description of game at chess,' wrote Ruskin to Arthur. 'It is so *exactly* like her.

[1] *John Ruskin's Diary*, 9th March, 1874.
[2] Brantwood, Tuesday, 10th (March 1874). Education Trust (part of this letter in *John Ruskin* by Joan Evans).
[3] Brantwood, (March 1874). Education Trust.

'I am quite sure you are fatally right in your conception of her mind . . . but I am comforted at least in your not thinking her an *utter* fool – nor mad – and in your thinking her pretty.

'The worst of it is that exactly what you describe her – is exactly what *I* love. I never thought her for a moment comparable to Dora or half a dozen others. But then I reverence and don't care a bit for Dora, and I don't in the least reverence – but am dying for – Rose.'[1]

To distract his mind from his troubles Ruskin decided, as often before in the same case, to make a long working journey through Italy. But before coming to London he stopped in Oxford to inaugurate a scheme which he had been planning for some time. He had a great dislike of organized games, and had often tried to persuade his friends among the undergraduates that football, rowing and cricket were a waste of time and energy, which could be put to more useful purposes. As a practical example he now gathered together a group of Balliol men to a breakfast party in the Common Room at Corpus, whence they adjourned to Ruskin's rooms and listened to an eloquent exposition of his plan.

They were to set to work on a lane near Ferry Hincksey which was now a rutted, muddy track, and were to transform it by their efforts into a smooth, well-drained road, with wild flowers growing on its banks. This was not only to improve the road for those who lived in the row of cottages on its verge, and its appearance for the passer-by, but would also show his pupils 'the pleasures of *useful* muscular work'. Henry Acland had already obtained the permission of the owner, Mr Harcourt, for the work to be done, and Ruskin's persuasive ardour was such that the volunteers left the meeting full of enthusiasm, having agreed to start work on the road at the beginning of the following term, under the supervision of the ubiquitous Downs.

Ruskin then left for the Continent accompanied only by his valet, Crawley, and a Swiss courier, Klein, with instructions to Joan to keep his letters carefully, as they would be a desultory diary for his own future reference. All their letters to each other were to be strictly numbered. From Paris, two days later, he wrote that she could always read any letter that came for him during his absence. 'There is no possible case in which you need not read and it is at least one little compensatory good for not having you with me, that I can have such a *secretary*.'[2]

There had been no question of the Severns travelling with him this time, as Joan was expecting a second baby later in the summer. In any case her presence at Herne Hill was very welcome to him, as she was seeing Rose constantly and could send him the latest news of her. Mrs La Touche now appeared in England and Joan met her again at Tunbridge Wells, where Rose was staying with her aunt and having treatment from a well-known doctor. Joan drove Mrs La Touche home with her, and they had a long talk about Rose, who had been

---

[1] Brantwood (March 1874). In possession of author.
[2] Hotel Meurice, 1st April, 1874. Education Trust.

ARTHUR SEVERN READING.
A drawing by Laurence Hilliard
Education Trust, Bembridge School

NTWOOD FROM THE LAKE
ing the corner turret and the dining
with seven Gothic windows added
.ıskin; Arthur and his boat in the fore-
d, 1881.

By Laurence Hilliard
Education Trust, Brentwood

THE SEVERNS' HOUSE AT HERNE HILL WITH YOUNG ARTHUR AND AGNEW. THE T
WINDOW IS RUSKIN'S OLD NURSERY Water colour, 1883, by Arthur Severn

RUSKIN'S OLD NURSERY AT HERNE HILL, ALWAYS KEPT READY AS HIS ROOM
Water colour by Arthur Severn, 1883
Ruskin Museum, Goniston

left behind with her aunt. Mrs La Touche was at her wits' end as to what to do for her daughter. During her talk with Joan she even said that she had been wondering whether it might help her after all to be allowed to hear from Ruskin again, and wondered what his reaction would be to such a suggestion. Joan kept her cousin faithfully informed.

'I have today your long letter from Tunbridge,' he wrote to her from Palermo. 'Anything more comic than your carrying Lacerta[1] away to Herne Hill and leaving R. and Grumpie, has not occurred in the range of history with which I am acquainted. I am greatly amused also at their wondering what I should do under the circumstances – they had better try me.'[2]

By 4th May Ruskin was back in Rome, where he settled for a month, working on a copy of a Botticelli figure in the Sistine Chapel.

On Whit-Sunday he wrote to Joan that he was glad to hear that Arthur had gone to look at Brantwood. 'You will have often to go and look after it a little for me, for if I keep my health, I shall be little there. . . . I never sit down by the fireside in the evening at Brantwood without the intense feeling that R. should be opposite.'[3]

Joan was not the only one to send him news of Rose. Mrs Cowper-Temple still wrote whenever she had anything cheering to tell him. 'I have just written to him,' she told Joan, 'and ventured to send a little nice letter that I got from Rosie. It is all past *hope*, but I think there is something softening in his desolation in the thought that in her unearthly way she cares for him always.'[4]

Before leaving Rome Ruskin called on Joseph Severn in his old rooms, and stood at his window looking down into the flurry of water in the Trevi Fountain. He found the old man better than he had expected and sat talking with him for some time. Painting was still Joseph's greatest interest, and he routed round his studio to find pictures to show to Ruskin, some of them painted years ago, when he was a young man. Ruskin talked about his own work and Joseph's interest was so enthusiastic that Ruskin promised to bring some examples to show to him. True to his word, he sorted out the finished drawings that he had made since coming to Italy, and took the folio round to the Palazzo Poli on the last day of his stay in Rome.

The old man spent a happy hour with him looking over the drawings and discussing them. Then Ruskin said good-bye and returned to his hotel to prepare for his departure the next morning. They never met again.

---

[1] Mrs. La Touche.
[2] St George's Day, 1874. Education Trust.
[3] Education Trust.
[4] (May 1874), John Rylands Library, Manchester.

I

CHAPTER 28

THE HAWTHORN BLOSSOMS FALL

June, 1874 – June, 1875

ARTHUR'S ELDEST SISTER, CLAUDIA GALE, died at the end of May. She had been an invalid, and bed-ridden, for some time. Her husband's grief showed itself in a strange way. Cricket had always been his first interest in life, and he was a prominent member of the Surrey side. Claudia had never been interested in sport. Now as a last tribute, he arranged for her to be carried to her grave by members of the Surrey Eleven, and was with difficulty restrained from placing a cricket bat on her coffin.

A few weeks later Joan's little nephew died in Wigtown and she began to worry about what she should do if Rose were to die while Ruskin was away. She knew that even now, it would be a shattering blow to him. 'I had a very perplexing argument with myself about Rose — I began wondering if ever anything happened to her suddenly — and *you* away abroad, what should I do? And it made me so utterly miserable and wretched — with all her whims, and naughtinesses I believe it would nevertheless half break my heart to lose her — and then it would be worse still how such a thing would affect you? — and I can't think how I could ever be the teller of such news. If ever I live to see such a thing happen — and if you've ever thought it out Di Pa — do tell me what you would like best? Remember I have no reason whatever to be especially alarmed. I had a sweet little note from her this morning and even if she is never well again, I believe with care she may live many years yet.'[1]

Joan's anxiety about Rose diminished as the birth of her own second child drew nearer and engrossed her mind. Arthur took over from her some of the work of writing to her cousin.

'I am very glad of your letter and that Joanie is resting,' Ruskin wrote to him from Assisi, where he was studying Giotto's frescoes and writing in the Sacristan's cell of the Franciscan monastery. 'Do not let her exert herself now in writing to me, and send any chat you can at your own leisure.

'I have been meaning to tell you what I thought when your father showed me his sketches on my last visit — very early ones, made when he was much younger than you. He had then a most true and tender genius for landscape — his skies are very deeply and strangely beautiful, his sentiment entirely poetical

---

[1] Herne Hill, 29th June (1874). Education Trust.

and natural at the same time. Had he gone on earnestly — he might have cut the Stanfields and Hardings all up to nothing.

'But he let himself be tempted away by a more ambitious and quite false feeling about figures. He got into an unlucky school — a sort of Sir Thomas Lawrentian, Raffaelesque, Contadinesque — I think it is one of the saddest examples of the venomously destructive power of Raphael I have ever seen. But I now write to you of it, because it makes me nervous about your little wavery tendency to portraiture, which I was much inclined to encourage . . . at one time. The Arno sunlight, and the sea which the Academy very properly wouldn't have but which nevertheless was a really very powerful and impressive impertinence, make me, together with what I saw of your Father's work, very anxious that you should fasten on landscape till you beat it, and have made the public understand that you can paint light better than anybody else.'[1]

Ruskin was allowed to erect scaffolding so that he might study Giotto's work more closely, but he did not devote his time exclusively to painting during his stay in Assisi. In the quiet of the old monastery he recovered the faith in Christianity which had wavered as his admiration for the great worldly, irreligious painters had grown. Now he realized that religion in Giotto 'had solemnized and developed every faculty of his heart and hand', and the atmosphere of the holy place worked powerfully on his imagination. He felt he was in reality a brother of the third order of St Francis and that his true work at the moment was not painting, but preaching the reformation of society in the monthly editions of Fors, and that he must begin a 'steady explanation of what the St George's Company have to do.'

He lay awake at night thinking what he could do for England. He worked on two numbers of Fors, one of them his Sermon to Landlords, and two separate courses of lectures. But even these activities were not enough to keep his brain fully occupied. Each time he returned to Italy he found old buildings that he loved destroyed, beautiful views spoiled, and paintings clumsily restored. Every time that he discovered another loss he felt a furious indignation with those responsible, and a feverish determination to make records of as many things as possible before vandals could ruin their beauty for ever.

He had moved on to Lucca, on his way to Florence, when, on 16th August, he was relieved and thankful to get a telegram from Arthur telling him that a son had been born to Joan. He telegraphed at once to Herne Hill, 'Long life and peace to him.'

'What games the two Arfies will have at Brantwood!' he wrote. Joan was not well again after the little boy's birth.

'Dearest Arfie,' wrote Ruskin, 'I have always thought the gift I gave you in Joanie had its human measure of drawback and counterbalance in some of her relatives and I have always much admired the way you put up with some of them . . . and the way in which you appreciated what was really sweet and dear

[1] 4th July, 1874. Education Trust.

in her mother and sister, though not exactly either of them West End wits. . . .
I shall look with some anxiety for the next report of Joan.'[1]

After the end of August Joan began to feel better, though not well enough to
see Rose before she left for Ireland. But on the train journey Rose wrote to her,
her despairing heart full, as she neared the station where Ruskin had come to
visit her, during her short halt on just such a journey back to Ireland two years
before. After their blissful day at Broadlands he had followed her to Cheshire,
where she was staying with the Leycesters, Mrs Cowper-Temple's nephew and
niece, and had stood beside her in the church sharing her prayer-book. Afterwards he had been harshly dismissed and returned in misery to London, while
she continued her journey home to Harristown.

> '9 p.m. in the train
> 4th Sept.

'My Dearest Joanie, We are nearing that abominable station Crewe which I
have every reason to hate and I'm tired. I wonder if you and the small child are
asleep and what Arthur is doing. I wish I had seen him again.

'I wonder what Some People[2] are about just now. Joanie do you think I shall
ever see him again?

'I sometimes wonder if you and your Arthur have thought at the bottom of
your hearts that we weren't meant always to be so far apart — or not?

'I wonder if you and Mama had any talks when she was at Herne Hill and if
they'd ever give *real* permission to my having just a bit of a letter from him now
and again.

'I cannot help coming out with this.

'Somehow a blight seems to have got at the very stalk of my life and I shall
never grow out of it.

'Do you think he has forgiven me for my behaviour two years ago? I sometimes feel I would give so much to know Arthur's opinion about it all. I believe
his opinion on all matters small and great would be just. I have one of your notes
in my jacket for company but I am so sorry not to have seen you at all.

'Good night dearest Joanie. Sweet sleep to the whole family.

> Rose.'[3]

Joan had begun to write to Ruskin, now in Florence, when the letter from
Rose arrived. 'Arthur has been reading me some of your last *Fors* – oh di Pa
how dedfully you do pitch into peepies! . . .

'Rosie sent her maid out to inquire after me and the boy – and she says she has
stood the teeth operation *so well* (Mr Woodhouse did it) and that she's quite
sure there's no disease either in her stomach or her breast — but gave me broad
hints that it was because she hadn't *you* that she was ill! . . . Oh dear I wonder if

---

[1] Florence, 23rd August (1874). In possession of Rev. I. Hutchinson.
[2] Rose and Ruskin referred to each other, to friends, as 'some people'.
[3] Education Trust.

things will ever come right between you and R! She'll never be well unless —
and if they *did*, it's too late now to do, I fear!

'This instant as I had been interrupted by Arfie's entrance — the postman's
knock! — and the enclosed is brought to me, and I feel I must send it and A.
thinks I'd better. His opinion, is, that if you both love each other enough to
marry, *you ought to*, and *she* ought to leave father and mother, and cleave to *you*!'[1]

Such a dramatic decision was not taken, but after Ruskin had received another
letter from Rose, this time forwarded by 'Mamie' — Mrs Hilliard — she began
to write to him direct again, and he to reply. A pale autumnal shaft of sunlight seemed to play upon them now, lightening a little the gloom which had
settled on Ruskin's mind.

'I climbed or sauntered from green to green and shade to shade,' he wrote to
Joan from Lucca, 'till I had got up about twelve hundred feet, and then lay
down under a rock among the cyclamens, to read all the letters I had in my pocket.

> Two from Joanie,
> Two from Mamie,
> One — but in three pieces written at different times — from Rosie,
> And this one, enclosed.

'It would have been difficult I think to find anyone else this autumn morning
who carried three letters at his breast written from three such loves — Joanie,
Mamie and poor wee Rosie, after all that's come and gone, writing — "It's tea-
time — I shd. like to pour out your tea."

'Dear wee mamie, pease be sure of one thing — that even if I get wee Rosie, I
shall always be the same to my Doanie. Time was, when I would not have said
so — when R. would have been all in all to me. But the seven years of our
Denmark Hill life become more and more sacred to me as time goes on. If Rosie
ever comes to me I do not think she will complain of being too little loved; but
she cannot remember with me the bedside in the little room. And, since the
little room has been empty, Doanie has been to me a mother and sister in one —
wee Doanie-amie.'[2]

A few days later Joan wrote to him that Mrs La Touche had said that his
letters to Rose were 'quite excellent and exactly what is good for her, but the
good I suppose takes time to grow'. Some had been shown by Rose to her
mother of her own accord.

Ruskin wrote playfully and in good spirits from Chambéry about his social
experiment — the tea shop. 'I've been thinking of taking up that tea business in
an exemplary and profitable manner — to show that I'm a business man! How
do you think some peepies[3] would like being a Mrs Grocer? — Carrying on
business afterwards as a widow—"Mrs R.R. Tea Importer." Christian Humility
does not usually contemplate that sort of thing.'[4]

[1] Herne Hill, 5th September (1874). Education Trust.
[2] Tuesday, 27th September, 1874. Education Trust.
[3] 'Some people' i.e. Rose.
[4] 4th October, 1874. Education Trust.

Ruskin, slowly making his way home for the Oxford term via Chamonix, Geneva and Paris, continued to hear from Rose, and Joan wrote that Mrs La Touche (always referred to in their correspondence as 'Lacerta') was sending her 'such nice letters' from Ireland.

'Neither Lacerta nor the Master will oppose your seeing R. I believe as much as you like. Indeed in a letter from L. this morning she wishes very much Rosie would go and stay with a very nice Dr at Kensington and "some people could see her there as much as some people and other people pleased". . . . But she does *so* oppose every definite plan.'

Joan had just returned from Mr Woodhouse, the dentist to whom she, Ruskin and Rose all went. 'I was put to much discomfort! He is looking forward with great joy to seeing you. We talked a little about R. who goes to him again beginning of November. He thinks her very clever and charming — and is much interested! — and asked if it was to be Platonic or otherwise. I told him that was not yet certain. He fears you'll find her a *worry* if it's the "otherwise"! But I told him you were prepared for all that . . . I proposed to Lacerta you and R. should be allowed to meet *here* as much as you liked and she seems readily to assent to this — but all this you needn't inform R. about.'[1]

Ruskin had been writing Aphorisms during his trip and sending the best to Joan to keep. 'I've sent Rosie a pretty new proverb, I think, this morning. "A Living Wife is better than a dead World." ' Rose, in her letters to him, showed flashes of her old, teasing playfulness.

'I *can't* help telling you,' he wrote to Joan, 'but oh dear, for your life don't let on I did — *one* little postscript in a letter I have in my pocket. It had a pease blossom in it, and "Sweet P stands for disagreeable Professor." Isn't that *herself-*ish — the old self, I mean, not the self-ish self.'[2]

A golden light indeed seemed to play round his journey home. (In Paris: 'All my letters, lying in *wait* for me here, were lovely — Rosie's celestial.') But it was to prove only a short, fitful gleam of sunshine before the night fell.

After a tiresome journey with a gale in the Channel, he eventually arrived at Herne Hill on 22nd October in time for breakfast, and drove into London to see Rose at mid-day. She was staying at Edward's Hotel. She was painfully thin and very excitable, but was well enough next day to go for a little walk with him, as far as Mrs Cowper-Temple's house in Curzon Street. Again on the following day he was able to sit with her for a while in her hotel before going on to the Dudley Galleries with Mr Hilliard, Connie, Joan and Arthur. The next day, he called on his beloved Carlyle before leaving for Oxford, still buoyed up by the happiness of seeing Rose again, although she was so ill, and the prospect of further meetings whenever he could get to London.

'I've had a perfect day of usefulness and niceness,' he wrote to Joan, 'all founded on the sense of R's being given me as a gift from Heaven — on

[1] Monday 5th October (1874). Education Trust.
[2] Chamonix, 15th October, evening (1874). Education Trust.

condition of my doing all I could for everybody.'[1] But his new-found happiness did not prevent him from correcting Joan, just as his mother might have done. 'My darling, I'm a little oppressed with the sense of untidiness increasing on you at Herne Hill. When I came away to Carlyle's, everything in *his* room was in its place to a hair breadth — and the oldest things looking as good as new. Oh my pussie — mind what you're about, now. All happiness of life will depend on the next year or two.'[2]

Even in his recovered hope for his own happiness Ruskin would not neglect what he regarded as the work he had been set to do in the world. The undergraduates who had been working on the road at Hincksey were rewarded by invitations to breakfast and to talks in his rooms at Corpus, where they would listen spellbound to the eloquent exposition of his views on the reorganization of society.

A walk out to Hincksey to laugh at the amateur roadmen had become a fashionable amusement at Oxford, but Ruskin did not mind the ridicule, the facetious letters in the papers or even the cartoon in the window of the shop in Broad Street. He admitted later that the road which his pupils made was about the worst in the three kingdoms, and gave the credit for any level patches to the versatile Downs, but he had supporters as well as critics in the press, and he had succeeded in his purpose of showing a body of undergraduates the dignity and achievement of manual labour.

★

In addition to the digging he had a course of lectures to give, but whenever he could possibly get away he left for London, sometimes just for the day, to visit Rose, who was now living in a doctor's house in Westbourne Terrace and having treatment there.

'Here I am at my green table as if I had just been to the village instead of to London,' Ruskin wrote to Joan from Oxford after one of these visits. 'I had rather a nice time of it. She was a little on her stuck-up side, but gave me one of her little "twitches" — to my little finger under a book. Then proposed a walk to Mrs Cowper's. . . . We caught her just going out — she looked radiantly at us, and the very footman, pleased . . . and together to Mr Woodhouse's, for something she had left there — and into the waiting-room together, talking over the books.

'My goodness — if I had been told, once, that would ever be. Then I took her back and left her politely, and to Carlyle's. . . .

'I should like you to write to Lacerta that Dr Reynolds, and I and Mr White-head, are all now in accord as to what is needful for R's health — that we will all do what we can, but that she is tormented by the sense of disobedience to her

---

[1] Corpus Christi College, 27th October (1874). Education Trust.
[2] Oxford, Monday (26th October, 1874) Education Trust.

father's fixed will or wish. Now he has kept her from me till – if I save her at all – it is only as a wreck that she can ever come to me. . . .

'The child is fearfully ill – and what hope there is of recovering her to any strength of mind or body depends on there being more peace between her parents and me. If they refuse it, her fate – whatever it may be – will be their causing, not mine. . . .

'But now I offer them, for her sake, whatever peace they choose to have with me – not hollow, but entire and true, on my part.

'And if they will believe it – much as I love her (and though now I never will marry any other woman if she won't come to me) – still, unless she changes much, I most assuredly will not marry her. I must be sure she is fit to join my life without destroying its usefulness before I take her, and so I wrote to her, on the first renewal of intercourse . . . You may send this letter itself to them, if you will.'[1]

In spite of these words of stern resolution Ruskin could not prevent himself from going to London at every opportunity, if only to have tea with Rose. 'You're so dreadfully faithful!' Arthur had said to him, feeling that he had been treated very ill by her. As soon as a lecture was finished Ruskin would make for the London train. His diary told the tale.

'Nov. 13th. Friday. . . . Yesterday got first letter from Lacerta after eight years of anger. Very thankfully. Gave lecture, nervously and not well; but found all right at Westbourne Park. Had game of chess, and some music and gladness.

'Nov. 14th. Saturday (HERNE HILL) How wonderful it all is! . . . To Carlyle, and talk about Knox. Then to Westbourne Terrace; take R to tea with Lucy. Dine with R and she sings a word or two of hymn with me.

'November 15th Sunday. . . . Wrote till ½ past 12. Then to Westbourne; lunched with R and took her to church in the rain. Back to quiet little afternoon tea; read lessons and psalms for the day to her.'

Back he went to Oxford on Monday, but after delivering a lecture on Giotto, left immediately again for London and called on Rose before a dinner of the Metaphysical Society. To Oxford again next morning early; on Thursday, a visit to the diggings at Hincksey and on Friday a lecture on Brunelleschi. 'After lecture lunched with Acland. Then to Leamington Park; saw R on sofa; to Woodhouse; back to R and had game of chess, but tiresome Dr Murphy there.' Next day, Saturday – 'Tea with R but she ill and restless.'

The strain was telling on him and one night he had a dreadful dream of his mother insane, and calling out wildly that she would tear the flesh off her arm. In his diary Ruskin recorded his restless night and the 'terrible dream, the consequence of much sad thought restrained'.[2] The dream showed him the shape of his fears for Rose, which he had attempted to suppress, though, as usual, he tried to attribute his depression to unwise eating. He must return to Oxford

---

[1] Corpus Christi College, 31st October, 5½ p.m. (1874). Education Trust.
[2] 22nd November, 1874.

next evening, but could not resist dining with Rose first, though he had to grope his way there in a bitter cold black fog, and afterwards catch the slow train to Oxford which took three hours. He was partly reassured by a 'sweet letter' from her and by the company of Joan, who came down to hear him lecture, but reports from Westbourne Terrace were not all good.

His last lecture, delivered on Carlyle's eightieth birthday, was quite spoiled, he felt, and he left for London immediately afterwards. The next evening he spent with Rose and the following one as well, when at last he received a message from her parents, who, despairing of her recovery, gave their sanction to anything he could do for their daughter. 'Had leave to nurse her,' he wrote in his diary ' — the dream of life too sorrowfully fulfilled.'[1]

He had to return to Oxford the next day, but the term was now over, and he was cheered by the news that Rose had gone to stay near Herne Hill to be close to Joan and Arthur. His mind revolved hopefully round ways of restoring her to health. The idea of Rose in his old home at Herne Hill lightened his spirits, and he dared to hope that given peace and rest and sheltered in his love, her mind might grow calm and her body be restored to health.

'How wonderful it all is!' he wrote to Joan. 'Fancy Rosie reading up there in in the old room — my cousin Mary's once! I am so thankful she's near you. If you can, get her father to leave her there for the present. . . . If Rosie stays I'll come home on Monday from Cowley and not go back to Oxford. I have only social engagements not duties there now — and then I can talk quietly with you. My notion is set mainly now on getting her a little cottage in Somersetshire on Sir Thomas Acland's estate, who is a perfect darling. . . . Oh me, I wish I could take my poor Rosie's pain for her — I've a sad note this morning, quite reasonable and tender and sweet, but saying the pain is so great and it must be.'

A letter from her mother disturbed him further, telling him of things that Rose was supposed to have said about him to her parents, and claiming that stories she told of her father were untrue. 'I've such an odd letter from Lacerta too — with horrid things in it of poor R — I don't know now whether mother or daughter lies most pathetically or dismally or damnably.'[2]

Rose was to return to Ireland for Christmas. Ruskin visited her where she was staying, near the Crystal Palace, and noted with gratitude that she was glad to see him, but the following day he had to go to Eton to lecture on Botticelli. On his way home he called on his surgeon friend, John Simon, and arranged for him to come out to Herne Hill to see Rose that evening before she left. She was in a teasing mood and hiding in Joan's back drawing-room when he arrived. Simon came by seven o'clock and she was well enough to have a little talk with him before she had to leave. But she knew herself that she was no better and despaired of her own recovery. 'My only hope is for the time when I shall have

[1] 6th December, 1874.
[2] Corpus Christi College (December, 1874). Education Trust.

I*

"shuffled off this mortal coil",' she wrote miserably to Mrs MacDonald when she got home to Harristown, '– but that may be a long way off.'[1]

*

It was not to be so long as poor Rose thought. Soon after her return home she had a terrible relapse into madness, and when she was once again removed to London in the New Year the doctors said that there was now no hope for her life. Ruskin got the news at Brantwood where he was already deeply depressed, having caught a chill on the journey there. The weather was very bad, dark and foggy, with cold winds and rain. His digestion was upset and — which worried him more — he had fits of dizziness, when flashes of light zig-zagged before his eyes, and he could not see to read the largest print.

Mrs Cowper-Temple, as always, was quick with sympathy and offers of help, fearing that he was lonely at Brantwood and inviting him to join them at Broadlands immediately. He thanked her but would not come. He was ashamed of the trouble that he had given both her and her husband, 'all turning to no good'. He had been reading the 24th chapter of Ezekiel that morning: 'Behold, I take away from thee the desire of thine eyes with a stroke; yet neither shalt thou mourn nor weep, neither shall thy tears run down.' He admitted ruefully that his exceptional sensitivity to the sight of beauty made things even harder for him. 'The worst of me is that the Desire of my *Eyes* is so much to me! Ever so much more than the desire of my mind. . . . So that the dim chance of those fine things in the next world does me no good, and though I've known some really nice girls, in my time, in this world, who wouldn't perhaps have been so hard on me as some people, none of them had a thin waist and a straight nose quite to my fancy.'[2]

From Brantwood he drove back to Oxford and then on to Herne Hill, continuing to feel weak and ill and desperately sad. Very occasionally Rose still had a brief moment when her mind was clear. 'Poor Rose is entirely broken — like her lover,' Ruskin wrote wretchedly to George MacDonald, 'and what good there may be for either of us must be where Heaven is — but I don't know that much of the Universe — and of Time.'[3]

'Of course she was out of her mind in the end,' he wrote years later. 'One evening in London she was raving violently till far into the night; they could not quiet her. At last they let me into her room. She was sitting up in bed; I got her to lie back on the pillow, and lay her head in my arms as I knelt beside it.

'They left us, and she asked me if she should say a hymn, and I said yes, and she said, "Jesus, lover of my soul" to the end, and then fell back tired and went to sleep. And I left her.'[4]

[1] 17th December, 1874. Leon, op. cit., p. 499.
[2] 16th January, 1875. *Works*, vol. 37, p. 153.
[3] 25th February, 1875, Leon, op. cit., p. 500.
[4] *John Ruskin's Letters to Francesca* edited L. G. Swett, p. 118.

Doggedly Ruskin continued with his work. From Oxford he wrote to Joan after his tragic evening with Rose:

'I'm perhaps a little better, but so intensely melancholy I don't know what to do. In my botany I've come on some of the old things I used to tell Downs to get for the greenhouse, and they bring me back to the sweet Sunday afternoons — with George so happy on the lawn, peaches on the walls, my Joanie so enjoying gathering them, Auntie upstairs, Lucy in the Pantry. Anne waiting on the stairs to say something unpleasant and see if she couldn't get me my waistcoat or my stock or my coat, or something. And I — the Evil spirit of it all, it seems to me now. . . .

'I could tear my flesh from my bones, when I think how I left my poor father and mother for nothing but my own whims.' Then his present anxiety broke through his memories of the past. 'And you will nurse me, if I fall ill? as you did at Matlock?'[1]

In his despair and depression he thought of abandoning all his work, even of giving up his Professorship. 'Di Ma, if me fall ill, and give up Felyship and come away to live in the nursery and be nursed out of people's way, won't Arfie and you tire of me?'

It was not the weakness or biliousness which alarmed him, but the symptoms which he felt of an overworked brain — and he was frightened that they might foretell another breakdown. His worst fears were allayed by a consultation with Acland and he spent a more cheerful Sunday in London, finding Carlyle well and having 'a pleasant chat with Walter Severn', before going north with Joan to Brantwood for a gloomy Easter.

Back at Oxford for the summer term Ruskin tried to forget himself in work. But his mind kept yearning for happier times in the past.

'I got down here in lovely weather,' he wrote to Joan, 'over meadows quite disgustingly yellow with buttercups — as if all the poached eggs in England had been smashed over them. It is curious that I feel the summer in my rooms here quite horrible. I want my old hayfield at Denmark Hill — my mother; you at eighteen, and Lacerta and Wisie[2] and Rosie coming out in the afternoon — and Anne to say something disagreeable — and George coming out to dinner.

'I enclose you some letters. When you get parcels of letters like these, spare time to look over them — and treat them as you would if I were dead . . . I was wilful — foolish — boundlessly idiotic — in marrying Effie . . . Perhaps I was idiotic because my father and mother were first cousins.'[3]

The young men at Oxford cheered him a little, and the feeling that he was influencing a new generation to see the world rightly, but even with them there were disappointments. 'I'm a little downcast about my Hincksey work,' he wrote to Joan. 'All the excitement about it is over and there is not one man for six there were last year.'

[1] Corpus Christi College (March 1875). Education Trust.
[2] Rose's sister, Emily. [3] Corpus Christi College, 15th May, 1875. Education Trust.

Ruskin kept coming up to Herne Hill from Oxford, heavy with the dread of hearing more tragic news of Rose. He went with Arthur to the exhibition at the Royal Academy several times, and set himself to write his annual *Academy Notes* — a criticism of the year's pictures — before he left London. Driving slowly back to Oxford he stayed at Aylesbury, and wrote from there to Joan:

'To-morrow, write to Oxford. I shall post there if I can — the old dusty roads are so dicious. And I walked along the hard London one last night, till I came to an old milestone saying it was "41 miles to London" — it looked quite awful to be so far away. One fancied oneself with a bundle and 6d in pocket and nothing in the bank.'[1]

Next morning he drove through Thame — 'an exquisite village; a true summer thundercloud and silver tracery above, with softest pure air.' But as the coach approached Oxford a change came over the sky. 'The north west black wind came up, filled the country with mist like burning manure; . . . carded down the clouds into one blackness; changed the soft air into a malignant chill.'[2] It was so dark that when he reached his rooms and drew up the blinds he could not read the titles of the books in his book-case. The darkness everywhere was symbolic of the crushing news that awaited him. Rose was dead — had died two days before.

'Of course I have been prepared for this,' he wrote brokenly to Joan. 'But it makes me giddy in the head at first. . . . Don't write about it to me; but about anything else and tell me all you can hear, when I see you'.[3]

Still he was resolved not to break under this final blow to his dearest hopes, and doggedly determined not to let it stop his work. A few days later he received Princess Alice in the new Ruskin Drawing School, with her son, Prince Leopold, one of the Professor's most ardent followers. The royal party remained in Oxford for several days, being joined there by the Prince of Wales, and Ruskin had to see a good deal of them, though after the first formal meeting of the Trustees, with Prince Leopold in the chair, he told Joan that he had got out of the dinner-party for eleven that evening: 'I really cannot face the Prince of Wales and Dean of Christ Church together.'

Underneath his courteous exterior he felt numb with grief.

'My dearest,' he wrote to Joan, 'with all the prepared thought that has been so long fixed in me, I find this thing more terrible than I knew, in the way it seems to possess and shadow me all through and through. . . . It's a horrible feeling this dead grief — wrapping one all around like clay . . . I had set aside this morning to write such a pretty description of hawthorn that was in my head for my botany. I got it partly done, too, in spite of fate. But it will always be associated with hawthorn now — for I had that lovely sunny walk in the buttercup fields under the hawthorn hedge . . . the day she died.'[4]

[1] 27th May, 1875. Education Trust.
[2] *John Ruskin's Diary*; entry made the following day, 29th May, 1875.
[3] 28th May, 1875. Education Trust.
[4] Friday (June 4th) 1875. Education Trust.

'I ... was away into the meadows to see buttercup and clover and bean blossom,' he wrote to Carlyle, 'when the news came that the little story of my wild Rose was ended, and the hawthorn blossoms, this year, would fall — over her.'[1]

[1] 4th June, 1875. *Works*, vol. 37, p. 168.

CHAPTER 29

MESSAGE FROM ST URSULA

EVERY DAY RUSKIN WROTE TO JOAN and every day he must still receive a letter from her.

'I wonder, when Nina Colé asked about me, what you answered? That I was going to parties . . . and did not care?

'For I don't tell you, Pussie, how much I do care and am not sure how far you guess. . . . But I hope you did not let Nina think that "it was the best thing that could have happened to me", as I suppose many of my friends would say.'[1]

With the Trustees' meeting over he was able to go away for a few days — to the Spread Eagle Hotel at Thame — and took Rose's letters with him.

'I have been to church!' he reported to Joan, 'and have come home again full of old thoughts, of some people's bonnets and ways. Her letters are inexpressibly touching now — I am arranging and dating them. The perpetual cry to have it believed that she was ill! The beautiful under mind, through all the misery and warped sense!'[2]

The term ended and Ruskin drove over early in the morning to Heyford, breakfasted with Eleanor and Henry Furneaux, whose third child, Claude, had been christened the day before in the village church, and carried Joan and Arthur away to drive with him by stages to Brantwood, where they remained during the summer.

Joan was expecting her third baby in the autumn.

Friends came — among them two pupils from Oxford, Wedderburn and Collingwood, Ellis, the bookseller, Burgess and Coventry Patmore. The latter found Ruskin's manners courteous and obliging to an almost embarrassing degree, but noticed that a little scratch or contradiction would put him out strangely. Nevertheless, no one could be kinder and he thought the Severns 'a delightfully pleasant, lively and unaffected couple. My whole day, every day . . . has been filled with healthy, active amusement — rowing in the morning, walking up the mountains in the afternoon; and talking, laughing, and listening to nice unlearned music in the evenings.'[3]

Ruskin joined in all these activities, called on his friend Miss Susie Beever to admire her garden, and made a miraculously detailed drawing of moss on a rock above a stream, which necessitated his sitting half the day on a chair in the

[1] Corpus Christi College, Oxford (June 1875). Education Trust.
[2] Thame, 13th June, 1875. Education Trust.
[3] *Works*, vol. 23, p. xxvii.

water with his feet on a stool; but nothing served to allay his constant sense of loss.

With an increasing sensation of pressure – of vital work that must be done in the little time left to him, he drew up a list of what he had already planned: a history of fifteenth-century Florentine art in six volumes, for which he had already collected the material; a life of Walter Scott with an analysis of modern epic art, in seven volumes; a life of Xenophon, with an analysis of the principles of education, in ten volumes; a commentary on Hesiod and analysis of the principles of Political Economy, in nine volumes, and a general description of the geology and botany of the Alps, in twenty-four volumes.[1] This list, made in July, soon after his arrival at Brantwood, was only partly ironic, and did not include his lectures as Slade Professor, his attempt to reform the whole social life of the country by his monthly sermons in Fors, or the work involved in answering the hundreds of letters which he received from people asking for his guidance.

It was a relief when Mrs Cowper-Temple wrote again, inviting him to stay with them at Broadlands. The thought of being taken care of was very comforting to him, 'in the midst of the weary sense of teaching and having all things and creatures depending on one',[2] and he agreed to go there early in October before returning to Oxford, on condition that he would be allowed to stay quietly in his own room in the evenings, instead of coming down to their late dinner.

Joan went home at the end of August to prepare for the birth of her child, and Ruskin and Arthur, left alone, posted into Yorkshire, where they spent several days together, drawing and painting.

Ruskin admired the speed with which Arthur could complete a drawing. 'He is really doing quite splendid work,' he wrote to Joan. 'I am entirely taken aback by his rapidity and technical knowledge in these rock subjects; he did in half-an-hour this afternoon as much as I could have done in a day, and better, in all essential ways.' They parted at Bolton, having greatly enjoyed their time together.

Ruskin arrived at Broadlands early in October, bringing with him some of his Turners, the courier, Klein, (arranged for by Joan because Crawley's wife, who had been behaving very wildly at Brantwood, had finally to be put under restraint), and his faithful gardener, Downs. Cossetted by Mrs Cowper-Temple, he settled more happily into life at Broadlands than he had hoped. But even so he felt a pang whenever he came upon some place in the grounds which he had last seen with Rose by his side, during that blissful day of perfect happiness three summers ago.

'I can't get over that Harristown feeling yet,' he confessed to Joan. 'I seem to have been everywhere on that one long day's walk. I thought I was out of the

---

[1] Works, vol. 26, p. 96.
[2] 10th August, 1875, Ibid., vol. 37, p. 173.

way of it this evening, and just came to the very gap in the hedge where we scrambled through.'[1]

On 15th October Joan's third baby was born — another son. Lily Severn was now two years old and little Arthur one. Ruskin sent Joan a present — a minutely detailed painting of a feather from a hen's wing, in a little painted frame surrounded by seed pearls, making a locket. 'How loyally and sweetly brave you are, in this chief holy War of Womanhood,' he wrote, but he continued to be anxious about her. 'A black day, and fashionable company and φίλη unwell, make me fain to be in my little nursery with hourly news of Joan.

'I never felt her extreme preciousness to me more.'[2]

Arthur reassured him, and a quick visit to London at the end of the month showed Ruskin Joan and baby well (he was to be named Agnew, after Joan's family). Ruskin spent most of November at Oxford, delivering his lectures on Sir Joshua Reynolds, while Joan and Arthur remained happily at Herne Hill with their three children. Arthur had several commissions and his painting of Bolton Abbey had been favourably noticed. In December Ruskin returned to Broadlands for a further ten days, and wrote that he was taking part in spiritualist séances. Joan, knowing his mind so well, felt uneasy at the news.

The Cowper-Temples sometimes had religious conferences at Broadlands, when George MacDonald or some other religious thinker would talk to the assembled guests. The devout Mrs Cowper-Temple, like many intelligent people at that time, particularly among the Pre-Raphaelites, was very interested in spiritualism. She had already persuaded Ruskin to attend one séance some years before, when his father had just died, but he had not been convinced by it. Now, with the loss of Rose weighing on him, he was in a mood to welcome any attempt to prove the survival of the soul after death. Mrs Cowper-Temple had a friend staying who was a medium, and much time during the ten days of Ruskin's visit was spent in séances or earnest talk. Mrs Cowper-Temple believed absolutely that it was possible to penetrate the veil which separates us from the spirit world, and Ruskin, too, was soon convinced that the medium had seen Rose standing beside him.

'Heard from Mrs Ackworth,' he wrote in his diary, 'in the drawing-room where I was once so happy, the most overwhelming evidence of the other state of the world that has ever come to me.'[3]

To Joan he wrote: 'I'm hearing such tremendous things about spirits that I'm utterly stunned. . . . It's horribly uncomfortable and yet comforting.'[4]

George MacDonald arrived just before Ruskin left Broadlands, and had a talk with him. 'There is a Mrs A. here,' he told his wife. 'I don't take to her much, but Ruskin is very much interested. . . . She has seen and described, without

---

[1] Thursday (7th October, 1875). Education Trust.
[2] Monday evening (18th October, 1875). In possession of Rev. I. Hutchinson.
[3] 14th December, 1875.
[4] Broadlands. Wednesday (December 1875). Yale University Library.

ever having seen her, Rose whispering to Mr Ruskin. He is convinced.'[1]

The excitement of these discoveries left Ruskin bewildered, happy but unfit for work, and after spending Christmas with the Hilliards he wrote crossly to Joan, who had expressed her anxiety: 'I have not been able to write nicely lately, because I was so utterly paralysed by your thinking that all that happened at Broadlands was imposture.'[2]

'At Broadlands,' he wrote to Norton, 'either the most horrible lies were told me, without conceivable motive, or the ghost of R. was seen often beside Mrs Cowper-Temple, or me.'

He took it as a sign that, 'just after the shade of Rose was asserted to have been seen beside Mrs T. and beside me ... I should recover the most precious of the letters she ever wrote me, which, returned to her when we parted, she had nevertheless kept.'[3]

He enclosed this treasured letter between the two very fine plates of gold which he had had made for it and carried it always in a silken envelope against his heart. Rose's other letters he put together in a box made of rosewood, which he took with him wherever he went.

★

One of Ruskin's happiest childhood memories was of tours with his parents in a carriage. He loathed railways and had built himself a coach in which he planned to ride with the Severns from London to the north of England 'in the old fashioned way'. He had made it quite clear to Joan that 'the new Brougham' was not to be used in London. 'It's for posting and country; and not only the railways and trams, but the reckless and rude driving which is now universal among the lower orders, make it mere panic to me to drive in town or to hear of your doing so. We'll have a nice wee posting and stopping at Inns.' Arthur described the brougham as 'a regular posting carriage, with good strong wheels, a place behind for the luggage, and cunning drawers inside for all kinds of things we might want on the journey'.

They left London on 20th April. Postillions were found for most of the stages, and their departure from the various inns where they stayed en route drew astonished crowds to stare at them.

On their way they visited great houses, abbeys and cathedrals. Arthur and Ruskin sketched together, and they all enjoyed the views which Turner had immortalized. Ruskin had taken a portable chess-board with him and while they drove across the moors he and Arthur played games of chess. The only things to detract from their enjoyment were the rheumatism from which Arthur had been suffering for the past few weeks, and the weather, which at first was

---

[1] George MacDonald and His Wife, Greville MacDonald, p. 472.
[2] 1st January, 1876. Education Trust.
[3] 1st February, 1876, Ibid., vol. 37, p. 190.

cold and wet, and had its customary depressing effect on Ruskin; but later it improved and when, in just over a fortnight, they ended their journey at Brantwood, he was in better spirits than for many years.

Miss Thackeray and her brother-in-law, Leslie Stephen, came to stay in a nearby farm-house in July and proved charming neighbours. Ruskin called on them in the costume which he wore indifferently in London, Switzerland, Coniston or Venice — tall hat, old-fashioned frock coat and a bright blue cravat which emphasized the brilliant colour of his eyes. (He had an aversion to black clothing, especially on women.) He welcomed them with old-fashioned courtesy and invited them to call on him at Brantwood the next day. It was quite close, he said: 'A dash of the oars and you are there.' So they, too, took to this delightful method of travel, and rowed over the lake in an old punt.

Tea was the great meal at Brantwood. Joan sat behind a silver urn and dispensed fine wheaten bread, Scotch scones, trout fresh from the lake, and home-grown strawberries, while outside the window the sunset turned the lake to liquid fire. All the while Ruskin talked in the delightful, copious, playfully dictatorial way that was his alone. One subject led unexpectedly to another, his lively fancy decorating his knowledge. Every so often he would spring from his chair, still talking, and unlocking a drawer, would bring precious stones or glowing minerals for his guests to handle, while he pointed to the beauty of reflection or marble vein; another drawer would yield golden coins, or a bookcase would be opened and priceless illuminated manuscripts expounded. All this learning was combined with a peculiar sweetness of manner and expression. It was thus that the fascination of the man was most clearly seen and his genius felt. Many people disagreed with him or disliked his opinions, but no one who met him personally could resist his charm.

In August Ruskin left them at Brantwood with Connie Hilliard and 'Lollie', her brother, who had lately become Ruskin's secretary. In spite of this appointment Ruskin still relied on Joan to make all arrangements for him. Before he set off for Venice with his new Irish valet, Baxter,[1] he gave her his power of attorney, and a day or two after his arrival he was writing crossly: 'You must really get into the way of managing things without reference to me, when I'm abroad.'[2]

Arthur was suffering again from rheumatism and Ruskin suggested that they should join him, 'have a wee peepie at Venice and spend the winter at the Baths of Lucca'. But the Severns, who in October had returned to Herne Hill, stayed there with their three babies.

Meanwhile Ruskin in Venice was engrossed in his new enthusiasm for the work of Carpaccio, and in particular for the series of paintings from the life of St Ursula: but he was also working on his *Guide to the Principal Pictures in the Academy*, and a new edition of *The Stones of Venice*, as well as writing his monthly

---

[1] Crawley's wife had been removed to an asylum and Ruskin had given him fresh employment in his Drawing Schools at Oxford.   [2] Venice, 12th September (1876). Education Trust.

edition of *Fors*, and sketching on the Grand Canal and the islands of the Lagoon.

Round him a group of friends and pupils soon gathered. But his love for Venice and his interest in his pupils' work were rapidly exceeded by his obsession with the picture, *The Dream of St Ursula*, which he was copying with immense care. By a mixture of money, charm and persistence he had the picture removed from the wall and taken into a room apart, where he could copy it. 'Fancy having St Ursula right down on the floor in a good light and leave to lock myself in with her!' he wrote to Joan soon after he arrived in Venice. '. . . There she lies, so real, that when the room's quite quiet, I get afraid of waking her. . . . Suppose there *is* a real St Ursula, di ma, taking care of somebody else, asleep, for me.'[1]

Gradually, as he spent so many hours alone with the picture of the girl saint sleeping in her bedroom, he began to identify her with Rose, and the two girls became merged in his imagination.

Since the glorious revelation of Rose's presence the previous Christmas at Broadlands, doubt had set in again. Once more she seemed to have eluded him, and as Christmas approached he prayed again for a new sign from her. In the morning post on 24th December came a letter from Joan, enclosing one to her from Mrs La Touche. He read it and his heart softened. 'I thought I would forgive poor Lacerta,' he wrote in his diary, 'not so much because Rosie wanted it, as because I pitied, or couldn't refuse, poor Lacerta's baby talk with Joan, and her use of Rosie's old name St Crumpet.'

A few hours later, returning to his room after walking home from the Academy in crashing rain, he found there a pot of dianthus — exactly like the one on the window-sill of St Ursula's bedroom in Carpaccio's picture. It was sent by an Irish friend in Venice, Lady Castletown, who knew that he was copying the picture and sent him St Ursula's flower 'with her love'.

'Irish fortune, kindness, and wit, all used by St Ursula, to make me understand, thoroughly,' he wrote. He saw it as a message, not only from St Ursula, but also from Rose, the two now mingled in his brain. He felt that the arrival of the flower a few hours after he had read Mrs La Touche's letter was meant to convey a message to him. 'I received it as a direct command from St Ursula. . . . So I forgave Lacerta, and wrote accordingly to Joan.'

The December number of *Fors* began abruptly: 'Last night, St Ursula sent me her dianthus "out of her bedroom window, with her love" . . . (with a little personal message besides, of great importance to me) by the hands of an Irish friend now staying here.'[2]

This certainty of a message from another world buoyed him up for several days, but then again his feelings began to fluctuate, and after the excitement depression followed. He dreamed of signs from Rose and woke 'confused and vague', but there were more cheerful days when his work went well and good news came from home.

---

[1] Venice, 19th (September 1876). Education Trust.   [2] *Works*, vol. 29, p. 30.

'I am in a humour to give you much more credit than I did for Joan's portrait,' Ruskin wrote to Arthur. '. . . Joanie has sent me a lovely letter today, full of good sense . . . and your nice time at Mr Gale's. Oh me — and Martha[1] has such a figure, has she? N.B. Can't see St Ursula's a bit — all under the bed clothes — mere angles of drapery — no good at all. Poor di Pa.'[2]

Still in Venice Ruskin wrote to Joan that if she didn't object, and if she and Arthur really *liked* having him in his old nursery, he would give up his rooms in Corpus and not live at Oxford any more, only go there to give his lectures.

A week later he had changed his mind, though he still meant to move his best things to London. 'I don't mean to give up my Corpus rooms or disfurnish them. My Father's Portrait shall always stay there and my bookcases, as they are, with my useful books. But I shall never more think of influencing Oxford life; the fact . . . that not a single tutor helped me in the push I made to give the men rational motive in that Hincksey work, entirely disgusted me; and ever since that week after the 26th of May, when I had to go and dine at the Deanery, there has been a horror on the place to me . . . I shall keep my Professorship and go down for needful work, but will bring whatever I can find nice room for — Hunts, Raphael portrait etc. etc. to Herne Hill, and make myself a little nest there. (And di ma, oo mustn't tell nobody me's upstairs oo know?)'[3]

Eleanor and Henry Furneaux, with his brother, Alan, spent a few days in Venice with Ruskin after a fortnight with Joseph Severn in Rome.

It had seemed strange to Eleanor to see the Italian flag flying over the Castle of St Angelo, and soldiers walking the streets of Rome in Italian uniform. She had taken her husband and his brother to the Protestant cemetery 'to see Keats's new tomb and Shelley's. It all looked lovely, with camelia trees out and azaleas all over the place.'

She found her father looking wonderfully well for a man of 84, though very crippled, and he was well cared for. The faithful Betta was still with him, and nearly smothered Eleanor with kisses when they first arrived. Doctor Valeriani was a charming man. The only drawback, Eleanor found, to staying with her father was the enormous amount which Signora Valeriani expected them to eat. While she was there she bought her father a new carpet for his room and sorted through a mass of papers, destroying many of them. She also gave him a Plutarch in six volumes which he read again and again, as he found that he forgot the beginning as he read on. His hands were now too crippled for him to play his piano, but he could still paint. He told Eleanor that his younger brother, Charles, had sent him a Festive March and a Duet of his own composition, which Italian friends had played to him.

'How I should like to pop in on you when you are in the Orchestra,' he had written to Charles. 'But alas! — this can *never* be any more, for not only that I

---

[1] Martha Gale.
[2] In possession of author.
[3] Venice, 29th April, 1877. Education Trust.

have no longer strength to travel, but if I had the expense would be beyond my scanty means — scanty, but here in Rome I am very comfortable and have enough. My painting still flourishes and sometimes I am so lucky as to sell a picture, and now I have done one which my friends tell me is the best work I I have ever done — it is from Keats's poem of the Pot of Basil. Also I am putting the last touches to a *ten* years' work, done during the intervals of my illness and Consulate, it is the *Marriage of Cana*, wherein I have represented the scene as under a vine arbour and as the water pours out I show it changing into wine.'[1]

[1] Easter Sunday 1877. Keats House.

CHAPTER 30

THE LONG DREAM

WHEN RUSKIN ARRIVED HOME FROM VENICE in mid-June he stayed with Joan and Arthur for a month at Herne Hill, seeing old friends and going with them to the Royal Academy and to the exhibition at the newly opened Grosvenor Gallery — a visit which was to have dramatic consequences. Then he went on to Brantwood, having arranged for them to follow later.

He was anxious about sudden spells of dizziness which had begun when he was overworking in Venice; he felt unwell, and was at first unable to begin work on the many projects which he had planned. But soon he could write in his diary, 'Joanie came in evening and all was bright.' Then Arthur joined them at Brantwood for a while, and the children with their nurse took over the lodge which had been built for Crawley's family. They were quiet, restful days, with only an occasional visit from a friend, but Ruskin still worried about his health.

In September Arthur left them to go abroad. He had planned a long painting trip through Italy and Switzerland, but it was cut short by Joan becoming seriously ill. Telegrams were sent from Brantwood and eventually reached him on Lake Maggiore, when he turned for home at once. Ruskin was deeply affected by Joan's illness and when she was at her worst would not leave her, even at night. 'It was a period of profoundest emotion to me,' he wrote afterwards, and when she was pronounced out of danger he gave thanks to God in his diary for the 'priceless relief' of her recovery, and presented a handsome cheque to the doctor. 'I've had a terrible fright,' he told his friend Ellis, 'and feel now stunned a little, and giddy, and can't remember dates.'[1]

He seemed fairly well when Joan and Arthur left to go home to London, but she was anxious about him. He was staying on at Brantwood, until he went to Oxford in November for another course of lectures. She wrote to him, as always, every day, and he to her. His flirting with his 'pets' had always been a joke between Joan and himself — but now she did not feel quite happy about it. In London he was seen with Frances Graham, or Sara Anderson or any one of a number of his girl disciples with licence to tease him. He liked to have them to stay at Brantwood, too, and the demonstrative affection that he showed them made her fear that people might begin to criticize.

'Yes di ma,' he wrote to her from Brantwood, 'peepies all quite right about me flirting. It *isn't* right. — But then, di ma, it *isn't* all *my* fault! Now just ask

[1] 20th September, 1877. *The Life of Ruskin* by E. T. Cook, vol. II, p. 396.

Diddie or Francie if they think it is! You know, one can't pretend one doesn't like kissing if one does — And really, the root of all my naughtiness is my not being naughty any other way!'[1]

He seemed to enjoy teasing Joan about his 'pets'. When she told him some story in a letter of the workings of little Arthur's conscience, he replied: 'How sweet that is of little dragon, having such a conscience. Innate, di ma. How thankful you should be, when oos di pa has no conchy ponchy to speak of at all.'

Ruskin was still thinking, and sometimes even talking, of St Ursula and Rose as though they were one person, from whom he received private messages and signs, but he mastered the confusion of his mind to give a very successful course at Oxford in November. He had not felt able to trust himself to deliver lectures, so the course was described as 'Readings in *Modern Painters*'. His reading from his own work was magnificent, and when he became interested in a subject he departed from the text with great eloquence and earnestness and talked of Christian principles and immortal life. The last lecture was as well attended as the first, when even the corridors were crowded and Mrs Liddell, Mrs Acland and Eleanor Furneaux had all been unable to get in.

A few days before Christmas he arrived at Herne Hill with a bad cold, which became so severe that the doctor kept him in his room for a week, where his boredom and depression were slightly mitigated by being waited on by Sarah, the Severns' maid, who was very pretty.

On his first day downstairs he had 'a delicious evening' with Joanie, when they told each other ghost stories. 'I had such a nice dinner all alone with Joanie,' he told Susie Beever, 'and Sarah waiting. Joanie coughed and startled me. I accused her of having a cold. To defend herself she said (the mockery), perhaps she oughtn't to kiss me. I said, "Couldn't Sarah try first, and see if any harm comes of it?" (Sarah highly amused.) For goodness' sake don't tell Kate.'[2]

Soon he was allowed out and celebrated by taking Frances Graham, 'my new pet', to the circus. 'And my pet said the only drawback to it all, was that she couldn't sit on both sides of me.'

★

By his fifty-ninth birthday, on 8th February, Ruskin was back at Brantwood alone, and his mind kept sliding off into dreams which were difficult to distinguish from reality. He heard from Heyford, where the Severns were staying with Eleanor and her husband, of more successes for Arthur — two pictures had been accepted for the Paris Exhibition, 'one a portrait life size in watercolours of Joan.' 'I am profoundly happy in your success,' Ruskin replied, 'having very truly now a father's feeling towards you both . . . though of course the personal claim of pride in you is less than "the Governor's". . . . How happy he will be.'[3]

[1] Brantwood, 24th (October 1877). Education Trust.
[2] *Hortus Inclusus*, p. 122. Kate was the parlour-maid at Brantwood.
[3] Brantwood, 13th February, 1878. In possession of author.

Ruskin's imagination was still obsessed with Rose and St Ursula. The girl saint, sleeping quietly in her room, had become to him a picture of his sweet, elusive Rose, whom for so many years he had hoped to make his own, now at last at rest — or did she only sleep?

The snow lay deep on the ground as he talked to his friend, Susie Beever, about Rose. Though she was already sixty-eight years old when Ruskin came to live at Coniston, she had become one of his most intimate friends and listened with eager sympathy. After his visit he sent her one of his drawngs of Rose, brought, like so many of his letters, by boat across the lake.

'And so this sweet face is our darling,' she replied. 'And now we see what her *eyes* were like! lovely! and the eyebrows lovely too. . . . To me, that was a most happy visit! . . . You were so tired when you were here, that I fear you would be doubly so, when your reached your Brantwood — what a happy thing for me, and for many, that you ever saw it advertised and bought it. How much you have made me know, that I never should have done. . . . You make me so hungry to know more.'[1]

Susie Beever had noticed his exhaustion. When he got back to Brantwood he sat down and wrote to Arthur, almost as though he might have no further opportunity. It was a short letter: 'Dearest Arfie, This is the last letter I write tonight or today! — to thank you for all your care of my own and your own Joanie, to wish you both — and your children — all good — now and ever.'[2]

Strange nightmares, alternating with joyful dreams of messages from another world, prevented him from sleeping at night, and during the day his mind grappled with a thousand problems, but seemed less and less able to fix itself on any one. In his excited state his thoughts jostled uneasily together — and political anxieties were over-shadowed by longing for his sleeping Rose.

On 21st February he finished the first draft of his Turner Catalogue and it was hurried off to the printers. The same day he wrote an incoherent note to Mac-Donald, calling him by his Christian name, which he had never done before, and telling him of a heavenly dream which now seemed to be no dream but the truth. MacDonald, who had been so true a friend to him and Rose, should be the first to hear: 'We've got married — after all after all — but such a surprise!'[3]

In a distorted way his mind seemed to be aware of the danger that threatened him. He had a terrible premonition that the Devil planned to seize him unawares that night. Greatly agitated he retired to his room at eleven o'clock, resolved not to succumb but to give him battle. It seemed to him that to be successful he must fight naked, so although it was a bitterly cold night, he threw off all his clothes, and to keep awake paced up and down his bedroom in a state of increasing excitement. Thus he remained, marching about his little room, armed with a poker, until the dawn began at last to break. Not believing that the night

---

[1] 18th February, 1878. In possession of Rev. I. Hutchinson.
[2] 17th February, 1878. In possession of author.
[3] 21st February, 1878. Leon, op. cit., p. 510.

could have passed without the terrible encounter to which he had nerved himself, he went towards the window to see if the faint light truly heralded the dawn when, as he raised his hand, a large black cat sprang forth from behind a mirror. In a moment Ruskin had decided that this must be the dreaded enemy whom he had awaited, and throwing himself at it, he grabbed it with both hands and hurled it with all his strength on the floor. He waited, panting, to see if the devil would take another form—then victorious but exhausted, and his body numb with cold, he fell senseless across his bed.

There he was found later in the morning in a state of wild delirium. Laurence Hilliard sent for Joan and Arthur at once and when they arrived the doctor pronounced him dangerously ill. John Simon, old friend of his parents and President of the Royal College of Surgeons, came hurrying from London to be greeted by Joan and Arthur with infinite relief. Ruskin was still delirious and often violent, and had to be held down in his bed to prevent him hurting himself. His valet, Baxter, could not be with him all the time and male nurses had to be brought in to help. After a while Mr Simon decreed that Joan should not go into his room more than was absolutely necessary. Her cousin did not recognize her — nor anyone else — and the violence of his movements and his unintelligible shouts distressed her beyond measure.

For a fortnight Mr Simon remained at Brantwood. Dr Acland also appeared, uninvited and heralded only by a telegram from Didcot station announcing that he was on his way. He begged Joan on his arrival 'to forgive him, if he did wrong in coming, but he could not help it.' Acland and Simon, although both dear friends of Ruskin, could not abide each other. Simon and Dr Parsons were in charge of the case and did not welcome Acland's presence. Moreover every bed in the house was full, with the extra nurses who had to be accommodated: he did not stay long and a later offer to return was refused by Joan as 'quite unnecessary'.

★

Word had leaked out of Ruskin's illness and bulletins were issued daily, which were repeated in Italy and in America. An appeal was made for prayers in all churches. Mrs Cowper-Temple wrote to Joan: 'If the illness should come from a Spiritual cause Prayers may be the special remedy. It would touch you to read the warm answers to our appeal — I send a few of them. From Inverness to South Hampshire prayers have been put up by the churches for him and if we are not permitted to witness the result, we must believe that it will be great in the Spiritual sphere.'[1]

Letters poured in from friends and admirers. Joan and Arthur were almost overwhelmed. People who had been working for Ruskin wrote to them for guidance, and they had to decide what should be done. Stacy Marks wrote to Arthur about the sale at which Ruskin had told him to buy a number of

[1] Tuesday (March 1878). John Rylands Library.

Bewick's drawings of birds which were coming up for auction. Knowing how much Ruskin had wanted them, Arthur advised Marks to go ahead as planned, which he did, paying out the money himself.

After a fortnight outbreaks of violence had become rare, and Simon felt that he could leave Ruskin in Dr Parsons's charge, though he was ready to return at once if sent for. Joan wrote daily to Mr Simon or his wife, giving details of her cousin's progress and even sat in his room taking down the words that she could distinguish in his constant muttering. Amongst the senseless jumble the words 'Rosy Posy' constantly occurred. Sometimes now he would have brief moments when his speech was quite clear, but his brain was still clouded.

'You can never know what you have been to us for the last fortnight, in this terrible time,' Joan wrote to Mr Simon. '. . . The house is most desolate without you. . . . Thank God, our poor darling here has been wonderfully quiet today – talking of course, but quietly. "Everything white! Everything black!" – repeated, was the theme for some time.'

One of the chief problems was prevailing on the patient to take food. 'Now we're in the kingdom of darkness – and everything brought out of the kingdom of light, can't be touched. . . . Now it's reversed and unless it's prepared *in* the kingdom of darkness it won't do, and must be poison, (but if at A's suggestion it's made in *both*) then it becomes diagonal, and *will* do.'[1]

By now, when Ruskin had been ill for over a fortnight, money had become another problem, and Arthur went off to London, planning to take the solicitor to Ruskin's bank to arrange about getting enough money for current household expenses. While he was there the Simons offered to put him up, but he preferred to stay at Herne Hill, so that he could see the children, whom they had had to leave so suddenly. Joan was left in charge of her cousin.

'Alas! he refused to eat anything at breakfast,' she wrote to Mrs Simon. 'He is very quiet – and apparently unconscious. About 11 I tried to get him to take a little essence of chicken, as a jelly. He kept his teeth closed – but at last sucked some through them . . . I greatly dread his refusing food entirely.'

Mrs Simon had inquired about what would happen about Ruskin's fortune, if he was incapable of administering it himself.

'Unfortunately my Uncle is only the Coz's nearest relation by his father's side,' wrote Joan, ' – a cousin once removed. You know dear old Auntie always kept her relations well in the background, but two of her sister's sons are still living[2] though I fancy the Coz has forgotten their existence – but of course *they* are legally his nearest heirs.

'. . . The Coz always seemed to think because he liked *me* better than any of his relations, that the world would of course recognize me as his child! Poor Darling – if I had been, I couldn't love him more!'[3]

---

[1] 10th–11th March (1878). John Rylands Library.
[2] George Richardson had died the year before.
[3] Wednesday (13th March, 1878). John Rylands Library.

Next day Ruskin was quiet all morning, talking at intervals. Joan arranged some white violets and primroses in a saucer for Laurie to put on his table, and gave him a few violets to put in his hand.

'He said "Thank you", but took no notice of them. When Laurie said "How are you?" — he answered "I'm killed".... All yesterday afternoon he seemed to be afraid of cannon balls hitting him.... He has sent for me several times to-day, which I think is a good sign — to tell him "what it all means etc" — and when I arrive he reproves me for "treachery" and plotting with the Queen to have him shot. It is most painful,' Joan told Mr Simon and added with inexplicable optimism, 'but the symptoms are surely good.'[1]

Her cousin had still to be fed with everything, like a child, and showed no signs of recognizing his surroundings.

'I hope to have Arthur back tomorrow,' Joan wrote to Mrs Simon. 'Now that I have neither him, nor *your* good husband, I feel as if such a load of responsibility rested upon me — and I cannot help being *very anxious*, in dread of excitement after this state of calm.' But that night she had a joyful moment. 'As I bent over him, he looked at me with his old sweet expression — it was wonderful to see the way he seemed to gather it together — and said oh so tenderly: "*My Doanie*" (his most pet name for me) three times. My heart lept with joy, like the pain of breaking — then he wandered off about the Queen ... but oh me! I ran to my room — and trust he may never know such tears and prayers as there came for him! — my own darling Coz!'[2]

Arthur came back safely, having made temporary arrangements about the money for household expenses but with great pain in his back. He could scarcely move and had to go straight to bed. Dr Parsons diagnosed an acute attack of sciatica. He could do nothing for himself and Joan found herself dividing her time entirely between the two invalids.

That evening, after painting poor Arthur's back with iodine, Joan went into Ruskin's room and kissed him. She could see that he knew her. 'Then I'm not dead?' he said. 'You are my own Joanie and I am still living!' Joan told him he had been very ill and he asked her why she had vanished, because that was one of the things that had made him think he was dead. He did not like it when people had kept cramming his mouth with nasty things. He was trying to think what had happened, but Joan said he mustn't think at all until he was quite better.

During the conversation he took his soup and toast from her and even fed himself a little. 'I thought there were bullets and balls fired at me, and then that my Empress had my head cut off.' Joan spoke soothingly to him: 'Now you mustn't talk any more. All that was a dream — people do have such strange dreams when they're ill.' Then he drew up the clothes and lay down peacefully, and said good-night and shut his eyes. But the improvement did not last. He

1 Thursday, 14th March (1878). John Rylands Library.
2 Sunday (17th March, 1878). John Rylands Library.

slept for only two hours, and when Joan went into his room in the morning his eyes were fixed steadily on the roof of his bed and he was apparently giving a lecture, in a continuous, monotonous voice, about Joan and the importance of drawing level lines. However he quietened when she stroked his forehead and talked soothingly to him. Then she brought him a few little single daffodils with their own leaves and left them on his mantel-piece. He remained quiet with his eyes fixed thoughtfully on the flowers.

Then his illness took a new and even more painful turn. On 27th March Joan tried to give Simon some idea of the new phase over the past few days.

'While I write I am down in the depths after a good cry. It is so difficult *not to mind* when he speaks in a calm deliberate voice, accusing me of the most dreadful things — saying he *knows* I am the cause of all this — and *through me* he has been poisoned; or that he is lying dead in his coffin, as he holds my hand, and that I only *think* he is living, and that I have set everybody against him, and that I have killed him to get his house and property — it breaks my heart! and I implore him not to say such things. Then he says — "Why cry now? It's too late — too late! You and the Simons have plotted together against me, to destroy me, and prevent my disposing of my own property as I think fit — all that you may get it for yourselves etc." This is his strain today.... He won't take any food.... I don't think I *could* live through it, if it were not for the sudden changes for good that come, and give me strength.'

During the last two days he had shown more consciousness, had asked the male nurse to hand him a Prout drawing to look at — '*That* one, hanging beside my dear Father's portrait. You know my Father is in Heaven, where I shall soon be' — and had asked how long he had been ill and what the doctors called his illness. Then he asked Joan anxiously what would become of his Turners, and was pleased when she told him that people were crowding into the Bond Street galleries to see them. 'But I have made no provision for them.' Joan told him that everything should be as he wished, but that he must first get well.

'"I can never get well," he said, "while you are under the orders of that wicked Queen — you should obey only the laws of Heaven." I said I would, and then tried to get him to take a little soup . . . but he said poison had been sent from Windsor in it. I said, "Oh but Prince Leopold loves you, so he wouldn't allow such a thing and is so anxious to see you better and telegraphed to ask after you." This delighted him, so I said that any poisoned food the Queen *might* send from Windsor, Prince Leopold would send its antidote.'

Later that day he suddenly asked her if Dr Parsons was the same doctor who had attended her when she was so ill, and when she said he was and that he might trust him after that sad time, Ruskin suddenly said, 'Oh my Joanie, do you remember how I lay in such distress beside your bed — and then went to meet the doctor in the dark and rain, and gave him a cheque as a present when you were better?'

'All this was so true, I could hardly bear it. *He* was so much to *me* then, and now *I* am no comfort to *him*! . . . I called him by my pet Baby-talk name of Di Pa (meaning Dear Papa) and he instantly answered me in the same strain, calling *me* Dautie meaning Daughter! My poor Arthur is still in bed. I do hope he will soon be better — he is as patient and good as can be.'[1]

Next morning force had to be used to get Ruskin to drink a little milk, but later, just before lunch, Baxter came down to Joan and said the master had promised to take his dinner if *she* would give it him. 'You may be sure I lost no time.' He was sitting up in his armchair, well wrapped, and took some chicken jelly, toast, pudding and an orange. 'Each thing I tasted first before giving it him. I bathed his forehead and blew on it, and kissed it several times, but remained *silent*. He looked eagerly at me several times and at last said, "I wonder which is the dream. *You* standing there feeding me — or Jackson holding me down so cruelly in bed?" I answered they were both realities, "but Jackson only prevents you getting out of bed, in case you get cold, as you have been *very ill*." '

Then she ran into her own room and brought him some fresh daffodils and a sprig of Japanese prunus from a tree in the garden at Herne Hill which Ruskin had given her. 'He pressed it twice to his forehead closing his eyes, and said "Do you remember the dancing on the lawn that night when Manning was made Pope?" I thought, or pretended to, and said, "No, I cannot remember that at all, but Manning has been much grieved by your illness." "Ah," he said, "soon people will do nothing but curse me." I answered sternly, "Coz, how dare you say such wicked things?" . . . My *severity* did good, I'm sure. It was very hard, but I made up my mind after the terrible abuse he gave me yesterday to try this new tack. Then I stroked his hair, and kissed him, and said I must go to *my* dinner now.'

That night it snowed and all next day. Arthur was still unable to leave his bed, and Ruskin asked Joan, 'How will you ever bear the shame my madness will bring upon you?' and told her often that he would not recover. He continued to appear more reasonable, but terribly depressed, and thought he had been guilty of dreadful sins. 'Unfortunately the Coz has taken a violent dislike to Dr Parsons . . . his presence at once excites the Coz into an abusive phase.' He was eating quite well, as long as Joan would feed him, 'though he is in a state of great depression, and thinks he will die and never get to heaven. To-day he told me how his illness began, and how he paced up and down his room thinking he was defending St George, and battered the door when he first lost his reason, with the poker, and then asked *how* they found him. He is as sweet as can be to me now, and for this my heart is unboundedly thankful. . . . Arthur is a shade better but still in bed.'[2]

Next day her cousin seemed much better and begged Joan to let him read Miss Edgeworth's *Moral Tales*. 'Surely it can't be bad for him if it dispels other terrible thoughts? He spoke so sweetly to me — with *very* few vagaries! — and

[1] Wednesday, 27th March (1878). John Rylands Library.
[2] To Mrs Simon. 1st April (1878). John Rylands Library.

said he now saw clearly all the mistakes of his past life, how he had wasted his Father's money, and that he believed the best thing he could do was to give up his Oxford Professorship, and study birds quietly here – and he was so rejoiced to hear we *had* got the Bewicks for him.'

Joan felt that her darling Coz had become entirely himself again. 'He came into Arthur's room, and talked *as clearly* on every subject, and with the same lovely expression of thoughts as ever. It was like a bit of heaven to us, and this illness seems to have cleared away all "vagaries"! Only he said he would now put aside all public work, and we must think of him as a "withered leaf" or "rag". His one great desire is, as quickly as possible, to take steps for making over his Turners to us that we may, without troubling *him*, be able to secure for the rest of his life "a comfortable maintenance". All of this came of himself – and he is *most earnest* about it, lest anything sudden should happen to him. He says *this snap* has brought him to his senses – and do tell Mr Simon it might have been *him*, instead of the Coz, who spoke – every word being what he already has said to us about the Coz's money matters.'

After twelve hours of clear reason dark depression settled on him again. 'Arfie hobbled up and is now sitting with him – he has a horror of seeing the men who held him in bed, no wonder! – and his room had such horrible associations I got him into the next one, that Mr Simon had. He implored us to leave him alone, and we did, but were on the alert, and at *two* he went to Laurie's room, saying he had watered his fire, as the flickering on the ceiling of the flames disturbed him but that the room had got so cold, he wondered if Laurie could get it lighted again. L. lighted it and sat with him for the rest of the night, till I went in at seven this morning as it was evident that poor Coz was becoming depressed, and slept little. . . . Today I am rather a wreck not having hardly slept at all – it is anxious work and I shall be very thankful to God when the strain is quite over.'[1]

It was now nearly six weeks since Joan and Arthur had answered the urgent call to Brantwood. The constant worry and strain, combined with Arthur's illness, were telling on Joan, and she needed rest. Arthur wrote in her place to Mr Simon:

'Fancy what a blessed afternoon that must have been to us when he came in to my bedroom and read to me and looked at the sunset, and put the glass in such a way that I could see it from my bed! Then I got up and we looked at it together and I never heard him speak better – every colour and cloud form, and complex reflection in water he noticed, in fact was quite J.R. of old, only a little more calm and sad.

'We find these changes trying, requiring our utmost tact and judgment to know what is best to do.

'The day after this sunset he was not so well – sad all day, and in bed, and as Joan did not seem well in the morning, I got up and sat with him all day until

---

[1] To Mrs Simon. Thursday, 4th April (1878). John Rylands Library.

eleven at night. I could see he was getting more tired and at ten he was certainly not himself – and would not take his sleeping draught. However, later on I got up and got him to take it at 1.30 a.m. All this was two days ago. You see now that we are looking after him ourselves (all the men servants away) it keeps us very anxious.

'Yesterday he was so sweet and well all day, and went to bed *still* well, and allowed me to go in and give him his sedative. He went down to his study! We couldn't prevent him, nor did we try. He was quite calm, and good about not doing anything – and evidently pleased at finding his study *just the same*. He had tea there, all alone, and after, when Joan went in, he *would write a letter* to you – with a cheque for some money you are to keep for us, and part for yourself I believe – I hope you will do as he wishes – it will please him.

'I managed to get out of doors yesterday, and had a chair put in the sun! I am a little better – really I feel *quite well*, and have felt so all along, only can't move about the least quickly. I am longing for you to *come here again*. We want you more *now* than before. Your being here for a little would be so good for the Coz and Joan. Poor Joanie is very nervous, and starts at the slightest thing! but is much better when she is not disturbed in her sleep. Two nights, when he wouldn't take his medicine, and got up, and pushed things against his door etc – kept us in a very high strung state as you may suppose, and Joan showed very considerable signs of nervousness and fatigue next day. But I am able to get him to take his sleeping stuff now, and you can't think how much better he is next day. We find if he *fails* in going to sleep he becomes a wreck. . . .

'My only consolation in being laid up myself is that it makes a kind of sympathy with the Coz, and it is easy for him to come in and see me, and prevents his thinking he is the only *ill one*.'[1]

Of that day Ruskin wrote in his diary later: 'On the 7th of April. . . . I got first down into my study, after illness such as I never thought to know. Joanie brought me through it.'

---

[1] Sunday, 7th April (1878). John Rylands Library.

CHAPTER 31

END OF A LONG LIFE

October, 1878 – August, 1879

WHILE JOAN AND ARTHUR HAD BEEN ENGROSSED with Ruskin's illness, Arthur's father, too, had been very ill. Joseph Severn was now eighty-five years old and since Eleanor's visit with her husband twelve months before, in April 1877, had been leading the same quiet life in his old rooms overlooking the Trevi Fountain, lovingly tended by the faithful Betta and Dr Valeriani. His sight was still good, his hand steady and painting even now his 'darling occupation'. He told his sister, Maria, in the autumn, that he had just completed a portrait of Keats, life-size, for everybody asked if he had a portrait of him, 'and it seems to me very like the dear fellow'. His rheumatism had much improved. He drove out in a cab with the doctor several days a week, and on a fine day he would sometimes take a walk for half an hour.

Three years earlier he had received a letter from a Mr Buxton Forman, which had been the first of many, asking for information about Shelley for a new, complete edition of his works which Forman was editing. Joseph had given away his letter from Shelley and the one which Keats had received on landing in Italy had been stolen. But Forman, who had found great difficulty in collecting the original texts of Shelley's poems, particularly that of *Adonais*, which he had been 'wholly baffled in obtaining,' was delighted to be lent Joseph's copy, given to him by Shelley when it was first published.

In return Forman sent Joseph each volume as it appeared. He was delighted to receive them and even more interested when the editor told him that he intended to bring out a new edition of the works of Keats and would welcome the old man's help. Forman had written to Madame de Llanos in Madrid, but Fanny Keats had been only seventeen when her brother left England and had previously been so much separated from him by her guardian that she knew little about his friends. She sent Forman's query on to Joseph, who was able to identify the 'Ladies' mentioned in Houghton's Life as 'the Miss Reynolds.'

His answer produced another letter from Forman, asking many more questions about Keats's life in London and Rome. It also gave great news.

'Your letter is a joy to me,' wrote Joseph. 'That you have received 37 letters of Keats to Fanny Brawne astonishes me with delight, for they must be even superior to his poetry and will be a boon to the world quite unlooked for – I will maintain your secret and now I proceed to answer all your questions. . . .'

At the end of his letter he added a postscript. 'Pray command me, but excuse my great age of 84 years, my memory is good except in names and I can go back for three generations.'[1]

Six more letters he wrote to Forman in the next three months, answering innumerable questions, dredging up from the depths of his memory details of his life more than fifty-five years before, and supplying Forman with material which he could have found nowhere else.

'I have thought well over the questions you have put to me. Most certainly "the Miss" mentioned at the 252 page of Lord Houghton's life *cannot possibly be Fanny Brawne* for Keats seemed *never* to have words in reference to her, such was the depth of his passion. . . . Wentworth Place was a few detach'd houses or Villas with gardens and, I think when Charles Dilke left, Mrs Brawne and her son and daughter took possession of it; when I visited Keats (which was often) he always took me in to see them next door . . . the house was double and had side entrances.'

During his last illness in Rome 'Keats had a beautiful white Cornelian, oval and large' which he kept always in his hands, 'shifting it from hand to hand but never putting it down . . . no doubt 'twas a gift from F.B.'

He advised Buxton Forman about Keats portraits, too. He thought the best was a sketch which he had done 'in the presence of Shelley'. He had given it to Keats, who had given it to Leigh Hunt, who had sold it to a Mr Foster, M.P., of Manchester Square — 'this *is by far the best likeness of Keats*'. Mrs Cowden Clarke eventually found this drawing in the John Forster Collection in the South Kensington Museum and the miniature of Keats, which Joseph had given to Fanny Brawne when they left for Italy, was traced to Sir Charles Dilke, grandson of Keats's friend, who also had two duplicates which Joseph had painted later; the one in the National Portrait Gallery was a bad copy of the original by Hilton. The small full-length portrait of Keats reading, in the same Gallery, was painted after his death, 'being my attempt to remember poor Keats, happy in his room'.

No good portrait of Fanny Brawne was known, but Joseph told Forman that one of the two figures in Titian's picture, *Sacred and Profane Love* in the Borghese Palace, was very like her: ' 'Tis the *Lady in White* in Titian's picture which I consider so like F.B. and not the nude for shame ! !'

He was proud when Mr Forman wrote that the new edition would be dedicated to him, and was impatient for its publication. 'Your book I am most anxious to see,' he wrote, 'and hope 'tis nearly got together for I think of it day and night.' He wrote to his sister Maria, too, telling her how his memory had been 'fairly taxed' but had just come up to the mark. 'The work is dedicated to me and so 'twas my duty to aid all I could on this account, added to which my regard for the memory of the Poet and my joy at these thirty-seven letters which I am told are of a beauty beyond his poems. . . . I expect you will see Keats's new

[1] 26th September, 1877. *Letters of Joseph Severn to H. B. Forman.*

K

work in the papers, for Mr Buxton Forman tells me there has never been any-thing like it.'[1]

The first volume to be published was a small one, consisting only of the letters to Fanny Brawne, with a dedication to Joseph Severn and an Introduction by the editor. In it an engraving of Joseph's drawing of Keats on his death-bed was seen for the first time by the public. The book arrived in the spring — the thirty-seven letters which survived of all that Keats had written to Fanny Brawne. Sir Charles Dilke had already burned those that he had been able to buy.

Joseph opened the book unsuspectingly, with delighted anticipation, but such a searing agony of soul had risen from its pages, such a vivid resurrection of his tortured friend, that the shock had shattered him. He collapsed and at one moment the doctor held out no hope for his recovery. But his robust body refused to give way. Walter, as the eldest son, had been called to Rome, being told that his father was gravely ill — conscious, though partly paralysed — but by the middle of March he seemed to have rallied.

Walter sat at Joseph's writing-table, looking down on the fountain, from which his father had penned so many letters home to England, and wrote to Eleanor at Heyford:

'My dearest Eleanor,

      'Your charming letter came after mine to you had gone, so I must write again. As Papa was not so well yesterday I did not think he could attend to it, so instead of reading it I constantly referred to your letter. In this way I got him to think about it so much that this morning (he is always more lively in the morning) he *asked me* to read it, and I thoroughly enjoyed doing so, sitting on the end of his bed, while he sat up on the side of the bed with his feet on the ground, and propped up behind with lots of cushions. We had our breakfast together as usual, and he repeated several times that he was better today. His perpetual cough is not so irritating — you would be surprised how well he looks this morning — quite himself, and he stopped me several times while reading your letter to tell me about the carpet you had made for his room when you were here, and various other kind and clever things you had done.

'He does not seem to approve much of your destroying all the official de-spatches, but I *strongly approve* of all you did. I daresay you know the kind of look the dear old Pater puts on when he does not want to express approval of a thing, which he really knows quite well was done for his good! Everyone is most kind and he is well attended to and looked after. Betta even sleeps on a mattress in the room.

'Papa made his Will and took the Com[n]. a few days before I arrived. Frantz and the doctor are the Trustees. Papa has left all the Keats MSS. to the doctor and all the money remaining from the Italian Consulship, about £150, to Betta. He leaves certain pictures and medals to each of his children and *all else to me*. I

---

[1] 9th December, 1877. Keats House.

only hope this means that I shall not have to *pay a good deal* instead of *receiving anything*. I could not help feeling a little sorry about the Keats MSS. but the thing is *done* and so I have not even hinted that I was displeased, but on the contrary have already talked to the doctor about the disposal of them to Sir Charles Dilke and what he ought to get. Papa thinks about £50, but the doctor evidently reckons on much more.'[1]

Joseph's heart, which had faltered, made a gallant rally and by the end of the summer he was walking about again, with the aid of a stick.

★

And now there was great excitement in the Severn family. Joseph's second son, Henry, was returning with his family from the Antipodes. When they had last seen him he was a boy of twenty-one setting out in a sailing-ship for Australia, with a job waiting for him in the newly founded Mint in Sydney. Now, after nearly twenty-four years, he was returning to England with his wife and five children.

The Henry Severns went straight to Herne Hill, where Arthur and Joan were awaiting them, and when Walter arrived with his wife, Mary, whose brother, Sir James Fergusson had, as Governor-General of New Zealand, been unfailingly helpful to Henry, the three brothers were together again for the first time in more than twenty years. This meeting was followed by a gathering of all the family. Joseph was well enough by then to write proudly to his sister from Rome that with Arthur's and Eleanor's children, and the Gales and Walter's family, a grand total of 'twenty-three children and grand-children showed up and there was all kind of rejoicing'. But he was sad that he was so far away himself. 'I have not yet seen my son, as he is trying to be well settled before he comes to Rome. . . . Keats MSS. begin to sell high to my great surprise — what I thought worth £10 goes for £100 — I have given them all to the Doctor as I could not give him money.'[2]

A letter of welcome came for Henry on the day of his arrival, from Ruskin, who shortly afterwards followed his letter in person. The family were drawn up to receive him as David the coachman reined in at the door. The children were fascinated by the old-fashioned coach, with its countless pockets for his books and notes and treasures. Henry's eldest daughter, Florence, then fifteen years old, had always thought of Ruskin as inexpressibly old and wise, and she was awed and nervous at the idea of meeting him. He greeted everyone warmly and his manner was kind and gentle, so that she began to feel reassured. His clothes surprised her — check trousers, double-breasted check waistcoat, blue frock coat with velvet collar, and large blue stock. But she soon forgot the peculiarities of his dress in the fascination of observing the piercing blue eyes under their heavy eye-brows and his radiant smile.

---

[1] In possession of the author.
[2] 15th March, 1879. Keats House.

Ruskin did not stay long in London and Arthur went with him to Brantwood towards the end of the month. It was arranged that when Joan joined them in the first week of November Florence Severn should go too, to stay until Christmas, Ruskin saying that he would supervise her studies. He had already made her father free of his collection of minerals at Herne Hill. 'Joan has told me of your finding some interest in the mineral cases at Herne Hill. The whole mass of them is utterly at your service; I have more minerals in my cabinets than I will ever look at or use, and the boxes full at Herne Hill are now to me — a provocation, and to Arfie an encumbrance. If you will only ballast a ship with them it will be the greatest relief to both of us . . . I hope soon to see you and my new Grand-cousins — or *cousines* — at Brantwood.'[1]

Brantwood was strange to Arthur's niece, used to a very different life in the Southern hemisphere. At the school in Auckland one of her fellow-pupils had been Alice Christian from Pitcairn Island, a descendent of the *Bounty* mutineer, and now she was to do her lessons with the famed John Ruskin and dreaded the bad impression that her total ignorance of art must make on him. She need not have worried — she had two assets which endeared her to him at once, she was a pretty girl and she had a beautiful singing voice.

At first, though everything was so strange, she enjoyed herself. She was surprised to find that the Professor invariably rose at daybreak and that he seemed to have done most of his literary work before the rest of the household was awake. She did not usually meet him until family breakfast, though soon, fired by his teaching, she began to get up much earlier herself and go up on the moor to gather mosses, or to see the sun rise on Fairfield and Helvellyn. After breakfast she would work for several hours with Ruskin in his study. Sometimes she studied Roman History with him, sometimes Literature or Botany. Italian he taught her by writing a short Italian quotation, usually from Dante, at the top of the page; below it he would list each word separately in a column with a space beside it for her to put its meaning. At the foot of the page she must write a literary translation of the whole sentence. Ruskin took great trouble with these lessons, as he did with all his teaching.

The afternoon was almost always spent out of doors. She sailed on the lake with Arthur or rowed with Laurie and Connie Hilliard, or they would go for long rambles of five or six miles up and down the hills. Frequently friends came to lunch or tea, or the Brantwood party would call on their neighbours by boat.

Everyone changed for dinner (Ruskin liked all the ladies to dress up) and afterwards foregathered in the drawing-room with its yellow brocaded chairs and the Turner pictures neatly covered to protect them from the light. Joan or Florrie would play and sing for a time while the others worked, some sewing, others drawing or playing chess. Then Ruskin would read aloud to them for an hour or more, until ten or eleven o'clock when they dispersed to bed. This reading aloud was a great feature of life at Brantwood. If Ruskin were not well

[1] Hawarden, 14th October, 1878. In possession of Miss G. Williams.

Joan or Connie would read in his place, while the others sketched or embroidered. When Florrie was ill and had to stay in bed, Ruskin came up and read to the assembled household in her bedroom. Unfortunately at the time when Florrie was staying there, he was reading the story of *Sir Charles Grandison*. The poor girl was extremely bored by the book, but there was no escaping the reading. On one occasion, recorded guiltily in her diary, she fell asleep and she came to hate Sir Charles as if he had been a personal enemy.

At times the fifteen-year-old girl became irked by this regular routine. She had led an exciting life so far, and on the voyage home had been proposed to by a young man on the ship — she had even received a letter from him since their arrival (alas, he had now left England) signed 'Yours till death'. It was not surprising that she found the regular life of Brantwood unexciting, and added to this was home-sickness for her own family. It was not so bad while Arthur was there — he was so gay and amusing and reminded her of her father, to whom she was devoted, but about a week after her arrival he left for London and then she found herself bored and irritable. She thought that Connie was jealous of her voice, and that Laurie Hilliard's manners compared very ill with Uncle Arthur's.

Joan took her to task for her sulkiness. She could not bear any one not to appreciate the Coz as much as she did herself. There was 'a tiff' which Joan ended by saying crossly, 'Don't you know that many a young girl in England would give ten years of her life to be in your place?' Florrie made matters no better by bursting into tears and sobbing that *she* would give ten years of *her* life 'to be in London with Father and Mother and the others'.

*

Arthur had gone to London to act for Ruskin in the libel action which Whistler was bringing against him. This arose from a criticism of Whistler's pictures which he had published in *Fors* the year before, after he had visited the exhibition at the Grosvenor Gallery, then newly opened by Sir Coutts Lindsay, on his return from Venice, and before his terrible illness of the spring. There, among highly finished canvases from the Pre-Raphaelites, now celebrated and successful artists, hung seven impressionist pictures by Whistler, who had lately taken to giving all his pictures sub-titles — a portrait of Irving as Philip II of Spain was described as *Arrangement in Black*, and Old Battersea Bridge as *Nocturne in Blue and Gold*. Only one was for sale. Entitled *Nocturne in Black and Gold — The Falling Rocket*, it had previously been shown at the Dudley, where it was little noticed, and was now priced at two hundred guineas.

Coming straight from his concentrated study of Carpaccio's work in Venice, Ruskin had been outraged by the high price demanded for what he regarded as a daub that could have been dashed off in a few minutes. He knew what hours of work had gone to the painting of each picture of the Italian masters and that this was true also of other artists, whose work was represented in the same exhibition. 'For Mr Whistler's own sake, no less than for the protection of the purchaser,' Ruskin had written, 'Sir Coutts Lindsay ought not to have admitted works into the gallery in which the ill educated conceit of the artist so nearly approaches the aspect of wilful imposture. I have seen, and heard, much of cockney impudence before now: but never expected to hear a coxcomb ask two hundred guineas for flinging a pot of paint in the public's face.'[1]

Whistler was not the man to take such remarks lying down. Although himself possessing a tongue like a knife and a natural insolence which eventually alienated almost all his friends, he resented bitterly any criticism of himself. He announced that he would bring a libel action against Ruskin. Ruskin had accepted the challenge with alacrity and wrote to Burne-Jones: 'It's mere nuts and nectar to me the notion of having to answer for myself in court. . . . *I've* heard nothing of the matter yet, and am only afraid the fellow will be better advised.'[2]

All this had taken place during the summer of the previous year. Now, in November 1878, the case was to be heard; but Ruskin, after his long and serious illness, was advised by his doctors on no account to be present at the trial, which could only lead to dangerous excitement. Ruskin wrote to Arthur before the trial began:

'The Professor of Medicine might just as well be brought into court for denouncing an apothecary who watered his drugs, as the Professor of Art for denouncing an ill finished picture.

'I should like you to express to whichever of our Counsel listens best, the *one main* difference between me and other economists — that I say, all economy begins in requiring and teaching every craftsman to give as *much* work as he can for his money, and all modern economists say you must show him how to give as *little* as he can for his money. . . . All sums spent on bad workmen are so much lost to good ones.'[3]

Whistler's counsel urged that Ruskin's criticism had been unfair and had done the artist's professional reputation injury, which entitled him to damages. Defence counsel pleaded that Ruskin had devoted his life to writing about art, and that nobody in all these years had attacked him or sought to restrain his censure by legal action. It would be an evil day for art in this country if he were to be prevented from voicing legitimate criticism and all critics were to be reduced to a dead level of adulation. Arthur found himself in a very difficult position. He had known Whistler ever since his return from Rome as a young man, when he had watched him painting Westminster Bridge from the window of Walter's lodgings, and he admired his work. He thought Ruskin's words about flinging a pot of paint in the face of the public ill-judged, and that these 'Impressions' of Whistler's were very beautiful and true in colour, though he considered that he had asked a very high price for so little work. But he also felt

---

[1] *Fors Clavigera*, Letter 79.
[2] *Works*, vol. 37, p. 225.
[3] In possession of author.

that Ruskin's criticism was no harsher than many others, and certainly not more
so than remarks about other painters which he had heard Whistler make himself.

Before Arthur left Brantwood Ruskin had asked him 'if he knew Frith well
enough to ask him to bear witness'. Arthur replied that he did and obtained
Frith's agreement to be called as a witness. This had pleased Ruskin, as Frith was
known to dislike him, and he felt that the artist's testimony in his favour would
carry more weight than the word of a friend.

Edward Burne-Jones was also a witness for the defence, and felt himself in an
even more delicate position than Arthur. He, too, was a friend of Whistler,
and the article complained of was largely a comparison of his own work and
Whistler's to his own advantage. Nevertheless he said truthfully in court that
he felt good workmanship was essential to a good picture and regretted the
want of finish in *Nocturne in Black and Gold*. 'You are a friend of Mr Whistler,
Mr Burne-Jones, I believe?' asked the judge. 'I was,' Burne-Jones replied
ruefully, 'I don't suppose he will ever speak to me again after today.'[1]

On the morning of the trial Arthur, on Ruskin's instructions, took the Titian
portrait of Doge Andrea Gritti from the house at Herne Hill to the Law Courts,
to be exhibited to the jury as an example of good workmanship. It was a large
picture and Arthur had to transport it on the top of a four-wheeled cab. The
case had aroused great interest and the court was packed.

Tom Taylor, *The Times* art critic and another friend of the Severn brothers,
joined Frith and Burne-Jones in supporting Ruskin; William Rossetti, W. A.
Wills and Albert Moore praised the *Nocturnes*. Ruskin was at a great disadvant-
age in not being able to give evidence himself, while Whistler gave a brilliant
exhibition in the box and scored repeatedly off the Attorney-General, who was
appearing for Ruskin.

'Can you tell me,' the Attorney-General asked him in cross-examination,
'how long it took you to knock off that Nocturne?'

'I was two days at work on it.'

'The labour of two days, then, is that for which you ask two hundred
guineas?'

'No,' came the answer; 'I ask it for the knowledge of a life time.'

Eventually the judge ruled that Ruskin's words had in fact been libellous – the
question of damages was left to the jury. After an hour's deliberation they
awarded damages of one farthing to Whistler. Both contestants were left un-
satisfied and owing several hundred pounds for their costs. Arthur returned
immediately to Brantwood, arriving in a snowstorm, and described the trial to
Ruskin and Joan with great *verve* – there was nothing he liked better than re-
counting a story, embellishing it and bringing out the unexpected. There had
been several humorous incidents. *The Falling Rocket* had been produced in court
upside down. One of the *Nocturnes* had been held up for Whistler to identify
and in being passed over the heads of several people, so that he could see it more

[1] *Time Remembered* by Frances Horner, p. 57.

closely, had slipped and a corner of the frame struck the bald head of an elderly gentleman below. There was a roar of laughter which increased as the picture, as it approached its creator, showed signs of falling out of its frame. 'Is that your work?' Counsel had asked.

'Well, it was once,' replied Whistler, fixing his eye-glass in his eye, 'but it won't be much longer if it goes on in that way.'

Arthur had sat next to Ruskin's solicitor in court, with the volumes of *Modern Painters* in front of him, in which he found passages for Ruskin's counsel when they were needed. He told the story that a member of the jury, looking at the Titian and remarking the dark colouring and the gold embroidery of the Doge's cap and cloak, mistook it for Whistler's *Nocturne* and was heard to say 'A horrid thing! I entirely agree with Ruskin!' Whenever Arthur and Whistler met during the course of the trial, Arthur had felt uncomfortable and embarrassed, but the older man had been unexpectedly courteous, evidently understanding his position.[1]

Though Ruskin had kept up a façade of jauntiness about the action, insisting that Whistler could not be considered a serious antagonist, it had nevertheless preyed on his mind as the date of the trial approached. Dr Parsons had been called to see him several times and one day Florence Severn had had a frightening experience which she now retailed to Arthur. She had been in the Professor's study helping him to sort out some minerals when he suddenly led her to the window and asked her in an excited voice if she did not admire the beauty of the view. There was a thick mist outside and she replied, astonished, that she could not see it. Ruskin became very excited. 'Not see it!' he cried wildly, 'It's that damned glass!' and with a blow of his hand he smashed the window pane.

Florence was very happy to see Arthur. He had brought her some albums of music and letters from her family. Joan had given her a new brown velvet dress, she told him, made for her by the local dressmakers, sisters of Jonathan Bell the builder. Every one admired her singing, and she noticed signs of Connie Hilliard being jealous of Arthur's affection and the time he spent with her. The principal drawback remained the readings from the interminable *Charles Grandison* in the evenings, which were only made tolerable by the mulled port handed round in cold weather when they ended.

While Arthur was there she sailed with him every day. The weather made little difference to life at Brantwood. They sailed or sculled across the lake even in heavy snow storms, to spend the day with Miss Beever or the Marshalls, sometimes walking home or being sent back in a carriage by their hosts, and they re-rigged Arthur's boat when there was an inch and a half of ice in the harbour. But alas, he stayed only a week. When he had gone they went tobogganing with the Marshalls, and one afternoon they hired a brougham, drove up to the Tarns and skated in the moonlight. Florence was fascinated. 'Ice to me is the most beautiful thing I've seen in this New World,' she wrote in her diary. 'Oh

[1] Arthur Severn's Memoirs.

I wish Arfie was home.' Ruskin did not skate but was very fond of sliding on ice, so they made a slide on the fishpond in the wood.[1]

The bitterly cold weather continued, day after day. Ruskin was delighted by it. As soon as he had heard the result of the libel action he had written to Dean Liddell, resigning his Art-Professorship and emphasizing that the cause of his resignation was not ill-health, 'but because the Professor-ship is a farce, if it has no right to condemn as well as to praise'.[2] He now felt quite free to concentrate on his studies of nature and the severe weather gave him a splendid opportunity to investigate the phenomena of snow and ice formation. He settled down to his work all the more happily for the pleasure given him by his admirers and friends who had raised by subscription £400 to pay the whole sum of his costs in the libel action. Whistler was not so fortunate. A similar effort by his friends came to nothing and his financial affairs, which were already in hopeless confusion, brought him a few months later to the bankruptcy court.

★

The girls were always expected to have some sewing or work to do in the evenings when they were not singing or playing the piano. During her stay Florence trimmed a hat for her aunt, knitted a shawl from Shetland wool given to her by Miss Beever, for Uncle Walter's wife, Aunt Mary, and made caps for the housemaid and muslin curtains for Joan.

As Christmas approached Florence left Brantwood to rejoin her family in London. Ruskin was sad to see her go. He liked always to have a pretty girl about the house, preferably one with a good voice who would sing to him in the evenings, and who would be a companion in his walks, a willing pupil with whom he could maintain a semi-professorial, semi-flirtatious relationship. This would not always end when they left his house but would be continued by letter. One of the things which had struck Florence most strongly about him was his kindness to anyone who came to him in trouble or difficulty—not only to his friends but to total strangers who wrote to him for advice. She had seen while she was at Brantwood how carefully he would consider their problems, how he would reply, often at great length, and continue to correspond with them as long as they seemed to need his help. With all his friends, too, he kept in constant touch by letter, even when he had not seen them personally for some time, entering wholeheartedly into their triumphs or troubles and speaking frankly of his own.

As a result, perhaps, of this vast correspondence which he maintained, he placed far more importance than most people on the letters that he received. In the same way that, when they were apart, he relied on Joan to write to him constantly and reproached her if she missed a day or if her letter seemed to be written carelessly or in a hurry, so he expected the girls whom he befriended to

[1] Florence Severn's Diary.
[2] 28th November, 1878. *Works*, vol. 29, p. xxv.

K*

write him playful, flirtatious letters, and if they did not come up to his expectations would complain about them to his other 'pets'.

'My dear Flossy,' he wrote, 'We were all very sorry to let you go yesterday; and the evening was dull beyond anything you could fancy. It was lucky for one thing, you were gone, for I was so cross, (because I wasn't pleased with my letter, when I got it!) that there was no speaking to me.

'I'm not much better this morning — so that on the whole, perhaps, it's as well you don't see a Professor so out of temper. Meantime I hope you will enjoy your first Christmas; (as I know you haven't got such a thing in those precious Cols.) and I'm always your affectionate though cross — what am I, by the way? — a sort of Cross-cousin isn't it?'[1]

Joan and Arthur remained at Herne Hill after Christmas. Henry's lectures had gone off well and now he hoped to find some business position so that he could settle down with his family in England. Ruskin felt incapable of much effort that spring, and stayed quietly at Brantwood, husbanding his strength and trying to avoid occupations that irritated or excited him. Frederick Gale's two youngest daughters came to stay with him in March and their visit was a great success. Though neither of them could sing as well as their mother, they were described by their host as 'really immensely nice', and sat down obediently to study the Prophecies of Habakkuk. Martha Gale, the prettiest of Claudia's daughters, had just the sort of looks that Ruskin most admired. She was tall and slender, with a tiny waist and a rather austere but perfect profile. She was soon teasing him in the way he liked, and had become 'Mattie' and one of his 'pets'.

News came of Joan in London at a party — 'There was Joan', Ruskin was told, 'looking like all the jollities of earth and heaven.'[2]

At Easter Mattie was given the privilege of christening Ruskin's new rowing-boat, which was to be kept for his own personal use. It had been largely designed by himself, with the help of Laurie Hilliard, and built by the local carpenter, William Bell. It was painted in his favourite colour, a brilliant blue, and decorated with a wavy white pattern round the gunwale. On Easter Saturday she was christened the *Jumping Jenny*, after Nanty Ewart's boat in *Redgauntlet*, and was launched ceremoniously, with a wreath of daffodils hung round her bows, while Mattie recited a verse written by Ruskin for the occasion:

> 'Waves give place to thee!
> Heaven send grace to thee!
> And Fortune to ferry
> Kind folk, and merry!'

She soon became known to the Brantwood coterie as *The Jump*.

Ruskin had been so struck by the beauty of Florence Severn's voice that he arranged to have it tested by his friend, Mary Wakefield, who was an authority

---

[1] Brantwood, 22nd December, 1878. In possession of Miss G. Williams.
[2] 3rd March, 1879. Education Trust.

on Folk Music, and then offered to pay for her training at the Brussels Conservatoire. Henry was overjoyed. He had just been commissioned by a London company to go to India to report on the working of the Wynaad Gold Mines in Madras and it was decided that his wife should take Florence to Brussels while he was away.

The decision brought happiness to Joseph, too, in Rome. Having made a remarkable recovery from his illness he had written to his sister in May: 'My son, Henry, has not been able to come and see me! He is now trying to establish himself in something like business for his family.' He had been happy to be able to send fifty pounds to his brother, Tom, who was now completely crippled and almost bed-ridden. 'You'll be amused to hear,' he added, 'that the MSS of Keats have risen in price from £10 to £110. I have given them to my good Doctor as I can't give him *cash*, for his kind attention is very great. . . . I get but few visitors, now and then, and am a little lonely, never speak any English — but continue to drink tea in the morning.'[1]

One last pleasure was in store for him. At the end of May he wrote to Eleanor: 'It may be in the *hurry* that you do not know that Henry is on his way to India (Madras) and he takes a 2 days' *snatch of* me, "strada facendo" — he has a commission from a company in London to examine certain gold mines, and will return for his wife and children to meet 'em in Rome and stay with me 3 months. So my longing to see him will at last be satisfied, which I was afraid would not be before my death. . . . Yesterday I had Harry's letter. . . . His Family is now in Brussels learning French. . . . How I desire the warm summer to set me up perhaps, so Dr V. says, and that I have a fine constitution and may live many years. I am quite prepared to die rather than suffer the discrepancies of age, but all about me are kind, Betta particularly. I never go out but with the Dr in a Calle but it is some time that I have not dared to encounter the cold and damp. I have just been looking at your Photo of your baby which delights me and I think with the aid of a strong lens to paint it.'[2]

This was the last letter that Eleanor had from her father. His wish to see his son again, after so many years, was at length fulfilled. Henry spent two days with him in Rome and then left on his journey to India, promising to stay three months in Rome on his way home, and to bring all his children to meet their grandfather. But two months after Henry's departure, on 3rd August, 1879, Joseph died. He was buried next day in the new Protestant cemetery.

★

To the last moment of his eighty-six years of life, his devotion to John Keats had continued to repay him a thousand-fold. In the days of Joseph's prosperity Keats's name was scarcely known, though his friends had never for a moment forgotten him, or ceased to believe that one day his true worth would be recognized. In all the crises of his long life, Keats, though dead, was yet most powerful.

[1] 16th May, 1879. Keats House.
[2] 31st May, 1879. In possession of author.

It was as Keats's friend that he had first been sought out by Englishmen of rank and influence, though it was his own happy charm that had warmed their feeling into friendship. It was their influence that had won him the Consulship in Rome, and the addition to his pension when he retired.

Even then his benefits were not ended. Though his painting was out of fashion, he could sell a portrait of Keats; and though there was no market for his novels, his article on 'The Vicissitudes of Keats's Fame' was published in *The Atlantic Monthly* and quoted in book after book. The manuscripts and letters among his papers went to pay his doctor. His last picture was of Keats.

For some time before his death Severn had not been able to see visitors or to leave the house. By the busy Roman world, humming with the energy of a young, proud country, he was forgotten. His last links with that modern world had been broken the year before, when in one short winter had died a King and a Pope: Victor Emmanuel, first King of United Italy, and Pius IX, whose weak nature had been dominated by the sinister Antonelli.

Joseph's former secretary, now Vice-Consul, failed to inform the British Embassy of his death but soon the news reached England. There was a leading article in *The Times* and letters were written asking why the British Ambassador had not attended the funeral, saying that it was shameful that England had not done more honour to him, and through him to one of the greatest of her poets. The Ambassador blamed Frantz. He would certainly have wished to be present at the funeral 'to testify the high esteem and respect to which Mr Severn was so justly entitled.'

Joseph's children felt strongly that he should have been buried, as he had always wished, near his friend, John Keats, and his own son who had died as a baby in Rome. But interments had been forbidden in that burial ground for many years. Walter wrote to Sir Vincent Eyre, and on his advice he and Arthur applied formally, through the British Ambassador, for permission to transfer their father's body from the new cemetery to the old. Their request was supported by a number of influential friends, including Gladstone and Monckton Milnes, now Lord Houghton. After some negotiations their petition was granted, and two years after their father's death Arthur and Walter made the journey to Rome, when Joseph's body was moved from the new, unfriendly cemetery and buried beside John Keats. Tennyson, Rossetti, Lord Houghton, all suggested inscriptions for his tomb. In the end the words proposed by Houghton were cut into the stone.

To the memory of Joseph Severn, Devoted Friend and Death-bed Companion of John Keats, whom he lived to see numbered among the Immortal Poets of England. An Artist eminent for his Representations of Italian Life and Nature. British Consul at Rome from 1861 to 1872: And Officer of the Crown of Italy. In recognition of his services to Freedom and Humanity.

He lies, among his friends, in the sunny field where violets riot over the graves, and the shadow of the Pyramid chases the hours silently across the grass.

CHAPTER 32

NEW FACES

August, 1880 – December, 1882

JOAN'S FOURTH BABY WAS BORN AT THE END OF AUGUST. Ruskin had gone to northern France earlier in the month, taking with him Mrs Hilliard, Laurie and his younger sister, Ethel, as well as his Irish valet, Baxter. Arthur telegraphed the news to them at Amiens. Joan had had a daughter – the sister that Lily had longed for – and as arranged long before the birth, Miss Susie Beever was to be the baby's god-mother. Susannah was already decided upon as one of her names, but what should the other be?

'Why not Susan Rose,' wrote Ruskin. 'Or, as Lily would have it – Susan Violet?' Phoebe, too, he suggested – 'very pastoral and Brantwoody.'

Arthur was delighted by the new addition to the family; he was devoted to his elder daughter Lily, now seven years old, and refused an invitation from Ruskin to join the party in France and to bring Martha Gale with him.

Ruskin sent a letter to Joan, carefully timed to reach her on his mother's birthday. 'I had a sweet evening walk in old places which she knew well, last night, and I hope she's very happy in seeing how you have done all you could for her child, as you did for her. I should not have been walking now among the vines of Beauvais, but for you.'[1]

The twelve months since Joseph Severn's death last August had been happy ones for Joan and Arthur. Ruskin had stayed with them in London in the autumn, and had been painted by Herkomer in his little room at the top of the house, once his nursery. Herkomer, who was just 30 years old and specialized in water-colour portraits, had learned to play the zither as a boy in Bavaria, and at the end of every sitting Ruskin would bring him down to the drawing-room and make him play to them.[2] During this visit Ruskin had also sat to the sculptor, Boehm, for a bust, which was presented by public subscription to Oxford University.

At the beginning of the New Year Arthur and Joan had joined him at Brantwood, bringing their children with them. He seemed much older since his last illness, but on the surface life at Brantwood had returned to its old rhythm.

Ruskin wrote a new *Fors* in January; he could not live without working, but tried to confine his activities to subjects which would not excite his brain. He

[1] 1st September, 1880. *Works*, vol. 37, p. 323.
[2] Arthur Severn's Memoirs.

arranged and re-arranged his Turners, and began family prayers for the whole household at which, remembering St Francis and his own stay at Assisi, he liked the family pets to be present.

Joan enjoyed managing the house. She was one of those women whose greatest pleasure is to make a home comfortable, to see that everyone has plenty of good food, that jams are made, fruit bottled and linen properly cared for, that the vegetable garden is productive, and the flowers in spring and summer a joy to the eye, with plenty to pick and bring into the house. She had been overjoyed, too, to find that she was having another child. With her cousin apparently so much better, Joan had bloomed as a happy wife and mother.

In the evening, while Ruskin read Scott's *The Antiquary*, Arthur sketched Joan and the Hilliards, sitting round the drawing-room busy with their work. He spent much time sailing on the lake and painted outside whenever the weather permitted, ending by getting a chill and a bad cough which kept him awake at night. There was no room in that small house for him to paint indoors. The weather at Coniston was raw and damp, and Joan became worried about his health. When he showed signs of wanting to get back to London she encouraged him, thinking that it would be warmer there and less damp.

Arthur was pleased to be back in London, but immediately got another chill, perhaps from the journey. It was difficult for Joan to leave the children at Brantwood, and Dr Parsons was in any case not anxious for her to travel more than necessary, so Eleanor was sent for and came to nurse her brother and they were soon joined by Ruskin, who came to London to give a lecture on Snakes at the London Institution.

Arthur was not allowed out to go to the lecture, but Eleanor accompanied Ruskin. The hall was packed and several old friends were waiting to enter with him — Leighton, William Morris and as special guests, the great ballerina, Taglioni, with her grand-daughter, Princess Troubetskoi.

One of the listeners described the lecture afterwards and Ruskin's effect on his audience. 'As the theme developed, and his interest in it gained, and as he felt — for he must have felt — that he held us in the hollow of his hand — the fascination increased, and the power and beauty that justified it. I have heard with great delight... Tennyson read some of his poems. ... But he reached no effect that was quite so much of an enchantment as did John Ruskin, with his voice more and more wonderful and tender, that March afternoon in Finsbury.'[1]

Ruskin was himself to have a surprise during the afternoon. What he described as 'one of the chief *éclats* in the lecture' was to be the unfolding of the skin of an enormous boa constrictor. The hall was so full that a few people had found places for themselves behind the lecturer, below his diagrams. This had happened before and Ruskin was prepared for it, so in order to avoid their being muffled in the skin when it was unfolded, he had arranged with Burgess and George Allen, who were to hold the two ends, that he would climb on to the

[1] E. T. Cook, op. cit., vol. II, p. 438.

table holding the centre of the skin, which would thus be held up in a great crescent. This was where the Severn brothers had prepared a surprise for him. Henry had only just returned from his mission to India, and Ruskin had no idea that he was back.

'In due time,' he told Joan, 'I jumped on to the table (it's rather high!) apparently much to the satisfaction of the audience, and pulled out the middle of the skin with me, when turning round to give directions, instead of Allen and Burgess — behold at two ends of the skin, for heraldic supporters, Walter! and Henry!! I couldn't believe my eyes for a moment, but recovered myself, and nodding to Henry, went on with my talk — finishing by a *jump* down from the high table — pretty well for sixty-one, at least Eleanor says so — (I didn't ask Taglioni!) . . . Arfie received Eleanor and me at supper — quite himself though he still only gets sleep by snatches.'[1]

The lecture had been so successful that Ruskin was asked to repeat it a week later. In the meantime he went to see the latest exhibition at the Dudley and took Henry to the British Museum. He was 'a little over-excited with Harry's wonderful stories and handfuls of samples', he told Joan. In many ways Henry had more in common with Ruskin than either of his brothers. He had brought home hundreds of stones of different kinds which he had found while tunnelling for gold in Madras, and they spent happy hours sorting through them.

Ruskin admired Arthur's gifts, and Walter's facility for quick sketching.

'You Severns,' Ruskin told Henry, 'would have carried the world away with you by this time — like the three brothers in a German Fairytale — if you hadn't every one of you a little flaw in you somewhere that brings you up short.'[2]

Two old friends had come to visit him before he returned to Joan at Coniston. Carlyle, whom he had long regarded with reverence and affection, had always enjoyed the drive out to Herne Hill, and announced that he was coming for tea and would bring the historian, Froude, with him. Arthur knew that their drive gate was not easy to open, so gave orders that it should be opened beforehand, so that Carlyle, who was now very old and frail, should not be kept waiting in his carriage. To his horror, on looking out of the window that afternoon he saw the gate firmly shut, with Froude trying hard to open it from outside while Ruskin pulled at it from within. Arthur could do nothing to help as he was not yet allowed by the doctors to leave the house, but eventually the two *savants* discovered that the gate had to be lifted and to his relief the carriage drove up to the front door.

Eleanor was still with him and together they welcomed the visitors. Arthur immediately noticed how infirm Carlyle had become, and regretted that he had not arranged to have tea in the dining-room on the ground floor instead of in the drawing-room above. 'However the great man got upstairs all right and I warned Ruskin to take him to the sofa where he could sit in safety. Carlyle could

---

[1] Herne Hill, 24th (March 1880). *Works*, vol. 37, p. 312.
[2] Undated. In possession of Miss G. Williams.

not hold his cup of tea and Ruskin knelt at his feet holding it to his lips. Carlyle seemed to enjoy his tea and took two cups, and I thought Ruskin rather clever in the way he managed it. Froude sat talking to my sister. When the visit was over we helped Carlyle downstairs and he got into his carriage without much difficulty. A little fairhaired maid we had, helped to make him comfortable in the carriage in the most patronizing way, putting his rug over him and tucking it well under his knees, then presenting him with his gloves. Carlyle gave her a gracious smile as the carriage drove away. I had a feeling he liked that part of the proceedings as much as any incident of the afternoon. He probably was amused at her innocent and patronizing air for she had no notion who he was. I felt proud at having entertained the three great men.'[1]

★

Joan was engrossed by her new baby and Arthur now planned to go to France with his friend Brabazon. Ruskin had heard so much about him from Arthur that he was anxious to see him at work, and arranged to join them at Amiens. Before crossing the Channel, however, he spent a quiet week at Canterbury with the Gales. Claudia's children had all gone, on their mother's death, to live at Canterbury with their father's unmarried sister. Ruskin enjoyed his stay with them. The Gale daughters, and especially his favourite, Martha, were all eager to do lessons with him, or to accompany him on walks or visits to the great cathedral. The evenings were spent in the way he most liked – he would read aloud and the girls would play the piano or sing glees to him.

He felt much refreshed when he left this quiet retreat to catch the mail boat at Dover. Arthur met him at Amiens and they immediately began a happy exploration of the town. Ruskin and the tall, shy Brabazon got on well together and another young artist, Ditchfield, completed the party. Arthur and Brabazon painted every day on the banks of the Somme, while Ruskin worked at the Cathedral, which he called 'the Parthenon of Gothic Architecture'. He had begun work on a new book, to be named *The Bible of Amiens,* and sub-titled *Our Fathers have Told Us: Sketches of the History of Christendom for Boys and Girls who have been held at its fonts.*

Joan thought, when Ruskin returned to Herne Hill, that he did not seem well. He kept putting off his return to Brantwood, until after a month's stay, during which he corrected the proofs for the first Part of *The Bible of Amiens,* he persuaded her to go north with him at the beginning of December. He knew that he had been over-taxing his strength and ought to avoid excitement and restrict his work to quiet study of botany and mineralogy. 'Much beaten and tired,' he wrote in his diary, 'and must positively take to the rocks and grass again for a while.'[2] Joan spent a miserable Christmas, not only worried about her cousin, but also in great fear for little Lily who had been taken ill with

[1] Arthur Severn's Memoirs.
[2] 26th December, 1880.

measles, followed by complications, and for some days the doctors feared for her life.

Mrs Henry Severn and her children had returned from Brussels, where Florence had completed her training at the Conservatoire, and they were all at Herne Hill with Arthur for Christmas. Henry had gone back to Madras, where he had been put in charge of the Wynaad Gold Mines.

Ruskin seemed a little better in the New Year (1881) in spite of what he described in his diary as 'grotesque, terrible, inevitable dreams'. But the depression which accompanied them deepened, alternating with moods of excitement and intense irritability. Another symptom of the approach of a breakdown was a reckless extravagance which Joan found difficult to check. He had long admired Sir Walter Scott, and was writing about his work in a series of essays on Fiction in the *Nineteenth Century*. He had already bought the manuscripts of several of his novels and now heard from his bookseller friend, 'Papa' Ellis, that the manuscript of *Guy Mannering*, which had just been sold at auction, had not been bought for him because Ellis thought the price too high.

'I've been speechless with indignation since you let go that *Guy Mannering* MS.' wrote Ruskin. He was *really* angry with Ellis for being so much of a Papa. The manuscript of *St Ronan's* was for sale now and he must not lose that too. 'What on Earth do you go missing chance after chance like that for! ... Seriously, my dear Ellis, I do want you to secure every Scott manuscript that comes into the market. *Carte blanche* as to price – I can trust *your* honour; and you may trust, believe me, my solvency.'[1]

Since the New Year he had been thinking about Rose every evening, as he read passages from the Bible in preparation for family prayers next day. 'Gradually I . . . got in my own evening thoughts into a steady try if I couldn't get Rosie's ghost at least alive by me, if not the body of her.'[2] The continuing strain was too great for him, and when there was added the shock of news of Carlyle's death, once more his brain gave way and he passed into 'terrific delirium'.

Once again he was violent and out of his mind. Once again Arthur and Joan were called upon to care for him. Once again there were painful times when he would recognize them for a moment, raising their hopes that he was himself again, only to slip away into a private, terrifying world of dreams, more vivid to him than the real world that surrounded him. During this attack, as before, Joan reported every development to Mrs Simon for her husband's advice, but more demands were made on Arthur this time as Joan had a badly sprained ankle and had to retire to bed. One morning when Ruskin had become violent during the night and had broken his bedroom window, Arthur brought him to Joan's room, where he soon became '*almost* himself – and said he was tired – so Arthur with my permission got him to lie down on the sofa beside me (I being

[1] *Works*, vol. 37, pp. 342–3.
[2] *Letters of John Ruskin to C. E. Norton*, vol. 2, p. 169.

in bed) — and wrapped him up — and he fell fast asleep — how I thanked God for that! He woke much refreshed, in about half an hour — wandering a *very* little — calling me "mama" — and himself "a little donkey boy!" — but quite calm and sweet.'[1]

After a month he had apparently quite recovered and Arthur left England again in April with Brabazon for another painting tour, travelling through France to Avignon and working in Provence, before going on to Monaco and then to Switzerland. He was a good correspondent and wrote lively letters to Joan at Brantwood full, like all Severn letters, of little sketches and caricatures.

★

Ruskin's recovery from his last attack had by no means been as complete as from previous ones. He was more restless and irritable and although he could still write affectionately to Arthur, 'I was very thankful for everything that you both have been and are, and must always be to me,'[2] yet the suspicion of his friends, which was such a trying element in his periods of acute mental illness, seemed this time not to have vanished with his recovery. Joan and Arthur, who returned to Brantwood in August, tried to ignore it, and Ruskin did not realize it himself. 'I've the house full of people, Joan's well and in good feather,' he wrote to Professor Norton, 'and I'm just what I always was, except a little crosser when I'm bothered and a little merrier when I'm not.'[3]

Sara Anderson and Alec Wedderburn were at Brantwood, too, that August, helping with Ruskin's work, and two young sisters came to stay towards the end of the month, Rosalind and Peggy Webling. The former was just such a girl as Ruskin admired — slim and graceful and daring, as Rose had been. The soft rain of the lake country was falling as they drove in the carriage to Brantwood and Ruskin met them at the door when they arrived, coming out to greet them with arms outstretched. He swept them into the house, across the square old-fashioned hall and straight upstairs to the little turret bedroom which he had built to command the view of the length of Coniston Lake. They all looked across the water, 'sun-hazy in the light of the afternoon', and then Ruskin showed the girls very carefully how to open and close the lattice windows without pinching their fingers.

Soon Joan and Arthur left to visit friends, but the Webling sisters remained at Brantwood. The mornings they spent working with Ruskin in the study, the afternoons in the woods or on the lake. On wet days he let them look through his folios of early Turner drawings or play with his mineral specimens, arranging little nuggets of gold to make serpents with uncut rubies for their eyes.

Often they went on the lake in the *Jumping Jenny*, the Professor's own boat, and learned to row. Rosalind, the more fearless of the sisters, was soon able to jump into the boat as she pushed it off from the bank. In the woods she would

[1] To Mrs Simon. 9th March, 1881. In possession of Dr Helen Gill Viljoen.
[2] 2nd April (1881). In possession of author.
[3] 29th August, 1881. C. E. Norton, op. cit., p. 171.

climb lightly and swiftly along a fallen oak that bridged a stream, while he, with her sister on the bank, warned her to be careful, half amused, half alarmed, but delighting in what he called her 'squirrelling grace'.[1] It was the same combination of fearlessness and grace which he had so admired in Rose, springing from rock to rock as they climbed the hills in Ireland when she was still a child.

The sisters had left before Joan and Arthur returned, at the same time as Laurie Hilliard. Ruskin had spent the last few days arranging and looking through his old diaries with Wedderburn and the revival of past emotions had agitated him. They all noticed that he seemed very excitable and Joan's heart sank.

He was full of projects for all kinds of writing and for improvements at Brantwood. He had lately built a big dining-room at the end of the house, with gothic windows looking down the lake and a large bow-window facing west towards the Old Man. He was planning further additions to the house, which would involve digging back into the hillside, and had begun a large-scale scheme to drain the boggy moor above. He was also employing several artists to travel all over Europe drawing details of churches and cathedrals for him. Less and less did he seem able to bear any criticism or opposition to his plans. There were several sharp exchanges with Joan, when she tried to restrain him from too much work and sudden inexplicable changes of plan, exchanges which ended in increased excitement in her cousin and tears and headaches for Joan.

After a short while Joan decided to go back to London, as she felt her presence was making him worse and the scenes preyed on her nerves. She knew that she must keep herself strong for whatever she had to face in the future. Arthur remained at Coniston, staying for a time with their friends, the Marshalls.

Laurence Hilliard wrote to Professor Norton in New England in answer to inquiries about Ruskin's health.

'I am sorry I cannot give you a very satisfactory account. . . . He seems more and more to find a difficulty in keeping to any one settled train of thought or work, and it is sad to see him entering almost daily upon new schemes which one cannot feel will ever be carried out.

'So far as he will allow us, we try to help him, but the influence of any one of those around him is now very small, and has been so ever since the last illness. I hope that this mistrust of his friends may some day wear off.'[2]

Joan tried to keep her own letters to quiet, uncontroversial topics, but even so could not avoid provoking his annoyance.

'This is the first letter since you went to London that has said a word about my books, or anything that people were saying of them. If you were a little more interested in either the Scott papers, or the history of Amiens . . . which are at present my true work, — you would not immediately think me out of my wits because I tell you some truths either about Lacerta or yourself, which are not subjects of my usual talk to you. I usually treat you as a loving child or

[1] *A Sketch of John Ruskin* by Peggy Webling, pp. 20–2.
[2] 15th October, 1881. C. E. Norton, op. cit., vol. II, p. 171

loving pet. But you are now on the point of forgetting that I cannot always be amused by the ballet, or the Rogues' March or the Christy Minstrels. . . . Try to recover some of the feeling you used to have when I taught you your drawing — and let me see that even as the mother of a family you can be interested in my present work. . . . It is at least one little comfort to me in this time of extraordinary health — to see how much better you get on without *me*, than I without *you*. . . . You will probably answer, eagerly, that you *do* care about the Scott papers, and my books. How is it then, that you never ask whether I am getting on with them?'[1]

Even in the heavy depression which he uneasily felt growing on him, Ruskin could still find interest in observing wild life. Collingwood caught an adder when he was cutting heather on the moor with Ruskin, who took it to the greenhouse, where he arranged 'lodgings' for it so that he might study it at leisure.

During the same week they found a wounded buzzard. 'The rest of us were not very ready to go near the beak and talons of the fierce-looking and, as we supposed, desperate bird. Mr Ruskin quietly took it up in his arms, felt it over to find the hurt, and carried it, quite unresistingly, out of the way of dogs and passers-by, to a place where it might die in solitude or recover in safety.'[2] No wild creature was ever killed on his estate. He was gentle to all animals. If his cat leaped on to his table when he was writing he would wait for her to move before he resumed his work, and once Arthur lost sight of him in a crowded railway station to find him eventually, at a lonely part of the long platform, on his knees beside a calf 'in a bag with its face just showing and its eyes wild with fear at the noise. The Professor, kneeling in the dust, was giving it what comfort he could.'[3]

At the end of that week Ruskin sank into a state of complete lethargy.

'My cold is certainly better,' he wrote to Joan, 'but the fit of languor that is on me, following the excited state in which you left me, makes me more anxious than ever before about my mental power, and more afraid of anything that may draw me back into exertion.' He begged her to send him an account, 'as accurate as may be, of the two instances in which you believe there was clear indication of failure of mind in me, before you went away'. At times he felt that if he could only understand his illness he might be able to avert another attack. 'Please tell me all about that tebby webby excited time dectly. It wasn't mere Webb*b*ly was it? How was it — *when* was it — me can't quite memby.'[4]

But he was not always so conciliatory. 'The one serious thing I can say is that, as long as we are both well enough — you to enjoy your children and take care of them, and I to write my promised books — we should "let well alone". When we cannot talk without you getting neuralgia and my getting cross, we

[1] Sunday (October 1881). Education Trust.
[2] *The Life and Work of John Ruskin* by W. G. Collingwood, vol. II, p. 206.
[3] Arthur Severn's Memoirs.
[4] 3rd November, 1881. Education Trust.

should hold our tongues . . . . You say I am not answerable for doubts or suspicions. Who is, then? or whom were you thinking of?'[1] It annoyed him to
think that Joan had been frightened of him in his excited state. 'All I've to say is
that if you're not frightened of me *now*, you'd better come back again. I didn't
see that Diddie was — and if Arthur, or Lollie, or Collingwood are, they can go
away if they like.'

Arthur judged him better by the end of November and came to join Joan
and the children at Herne Hill. Ruskin missed their games of chess, but Arthur
had been getting bored, and in any case had to come to London to arrange
about several of his pictures which were to be hung in an exhibition at the
Grosvenor Gallery. Joan was happy to have her husband and children once more
together under one roof, but she worried about her cousin. Although his
behaviour was quiet he was sunk in gloom. 'I cannot understand the way the
sadness and languor come and go like clouds,' he wrote to her. 'But then — I
don't understand the clouds — how much less the mists in one's own heart.'

He complained of the weather — fog and rain — he hadn't seen the sun in the
morning for at least two months: 'I really think I shall have to give up Brantwood after all.'[2] To increase his depression, he had now begun to worry about
all the money that he found he had spent, and more that he owed. 'To crown
it all, I've [been] sent £800 worth of books from Quaritch, and £500 worth in
Mary Queen of Scots missal from Ellis — which accounts together £1300. The
Trustees will have to pay with St George's money.'[3]

Joan could not bear to think of him, unhappy and depressed, and agreed to
come to Brantwood for Christmas. Ruskin was overjoyed:
'Di wee Ma,

How *does* oo tink me's to sist till the 22nd! Oos velly cooel. I
really am a little doubtful of the rightness of bringing you so far just to go
back again after Christmas — but I can't think about it today, it is so dark and
misby.'

So Joan left her husband and children in London, and made the long train
journey north to her cousin. Her visit cheered him, and when she had gone he
began to think that his depression and lack of energy might be cured by a change
of scene. He had left Brantwood only once, for a short stay by the sea, since his
recovery from his illness the previous spring, and early in February he decided
to visit London. He had a good pretext in that he had promised to take the chair
for Frederick Gale, who was giving a lecture on Modern English Sports. This
public appearance was a success and, much heartened, he believed that he was
now out of danger. 'No — I won't believe any stories about over-work,' he
wrote. 'It's impossible. . . . I can't buy any Romances just now,' he wrote
virtuously to Mr Quaritch, 'I'm out at elbows.'

[1] 9th November (1881). Education Trust.
[2] 2nd December, 1881. Education Trust.
[3] 8th December (1881). Education Trust.

Then unfortunately he caught a cold which left him with a bad cough, preventing him from sleeping, and ended in another very severe mental breakdown. He had to be nursed in the Severns' house and the eminent doctor, Sir William Gull, attended him. Joan had every confidence in him, but her cousin's violence terrified her, and she was anguished by not being able to help him — to be with him and yet unable to comfort him, or even to make any contact, was acutely painful to her.

Arthur did all he could to help her, but when after more than two weeks Ruskin seemed no better, he began to worry about Joan. Her ready smile had gone, her face was pale and drawn. She could not sleep for fear that her cousin might be needing her, and she trembled and jumped at the slightest sound. The doctors said that she was suffering from nervous exhaustion and Arthur decided that for the sake of her own health she must get away. He sent her off to the care of his twin in Oxfordshire. But before she left she insisted that there must be someone in the house whom her cousin was fond of, besides Arthur, so that he could always see a loved face if at any time he became fully conscious of his surroundings. Sara Anderson and Martha Gale came to help Arthur and the nurses.

Collingwood, who had been living at Brantwood and acting as secretary, wrote to Professor Norton:

'Please forgive my opening your letter . . . because Mr Ruskin is away from home, and unwell, as he has been for months; but now worse, so far as I can gather. It has been so difficult to approach him on any subject but the most commonplace. . . . His illnesses have mixed most of his oldest and best friends with delirious dreams and unkind hallucinations. That is why, and that's the only reason why you don't hear from him. When I came to live here last summer I found him dreadfully altered. . . . As soon as ever he is a little better, and I can summon up the courage, he shall have your note. . . . I'm under orders to save him all correspondence.'[1]

★

In the quiet, grey stone village in the valley, where the lane went no further than the rectory and the old church, Joan was able to rest. Eleanor and Henry Furneaux were very kind to her; Arthur sent her daily telegrams and their niece, Martha, wrote when there was any news of 'poor Coz'. Still for some time he was no better mentally, though he was eating well, chiefly turtle or oysters.

'Poor Coz!' Joan wrote to Mrs Simon, 'when he began to get ill he said very solemnly "you know when people are insane they always turn against those whom they love most when they're well".'[2]

This attack, like the others, passed and Ruskin seemed to make an astonishing

---

[1] Norton, op. cit., vol. II, pp. 173–4.
[2] Lower Heyford, Sunday (March 1882). John Rylands Library.

and complete recovery. During his illness Joan had realized that she was having another baby — it was due in the autumn and it was arranged that she should go quietly to Brantwood with the children for the summer months, while Ruskin remained at Herne Hill with Arthur. By now it was clear that Ruskin would always be liable to these attacks, which would temporarily incapacitate him, and that even when his mind was not seriously deranged he might go through weeks or months when his brain and judgment would be clouded and he would need help and constant care. They might have to spend a great deal of time at Brantwood in the future. So far, when the children had been there for holidays, they had been accommodated in the lodge. Ruskin was anxious that they should all be comfortable. The new building at the back, as large as the original house, would contain a number of extra bedrooms and a school-room, and he planned later to build a studio for Arthur.

To pay for these buildings and his debts he decided to sell some pictures. 'We must be very economical and really begin directly,' he wrote to Joan, with her children and Collingwood at Brantwood. Would she mind his selling most of the Turners now in the drawing-room, if they filled the spaces with some from his bed-room? 'I don't like the feel of being the least cramped at elbows — but me'll be *ever* so economical after this.'[1] He gave her a list of ten Turners and told her to send these to London, as well as 'all the sketches in my long new table facing the fire'.

He also decided to sell Meissonier's picture of Napoleon at the head of his army — a smaller version of the picture in the Louvre. Arthur paid a short visit to Brantwood and took it back to London with him. Joan had been with her cousin when he had bought it more than twenty years earlier, and used to describe how he had examined it carefully with a magnifying glass and had been astonished at its finish. He had given one thousand guineas for it. Now he was tired of the picture; he told Arthur that it looked like a coloured photograph and asked him to arrange for it to be sold at Christie's.

Arthur went to the sale with instructions to bid up to two thousand pounds. The bidding opened at one thousand and rose, by hundreds, until Arthur nodded for the last time at two thousand. But it went on without him, until at last there were only two dealers left bidding against each other — a Frenchman and young Wallace, son of the man from whom Ruskin had bought it. The Frenchman gave up, with a gasp, when the English dealer bid six thousand guineas. Arthur was told that it was the highest price ever paid for such a small picture.

'I mean to be quite tebby economical with *this* money when I get it,' Ruskin wrote to Joan. 'I *can't* think what ever I did with that Marylebone money — it went like snow off a dyke.'[2]

He took Christie's cheque himself to his man of business and found old Mr Tarrant just beginning his lunch. 'I insisted on his going on. He said Grace before

[1] Herne Hill, May 1882. Education Trust.
[2] 6th–7th June, 1882. Education Trust.

meat in the form of a loud "Hallelujah" when he heard I was coming to *buy* stock instead of sell !'[1]

★

Arthur had many friends in London, but he was careful to come in during the evening for a game of chess with Ruskin, knowing how much the older man enjoyed it. Ruskin, himself, began to go about much more. 'London is really beginning to understand that I'm alive again,' he wrote to Joan. He surprised her by going with Arthur to a dinner given by Mr Quaritch to 'the African traveller, Captain Burton', and though he nearly turned back as they went over Westminster Bridge and had to to be over-persuaded by Arthur to go on, when he got there he enjoyed himself — sat between a Member of Parliament and the Editor of the *Daily Telegraph*, and even made a speech.

Frederick Gale took him to the cricket match between England and Australia —('I rather enjoyed my crickety-wicket yesterday though the English got beat all to nothing; but it was very pretty to see the play, whichever won — and a fine quiet day, and Frederick Gale sitting beside me to gossip about it').[2]

His 'pet', Frances Graham, took him one evening to the first performance in England of the Wagner opera, *The Meistersinger*. This was not a success. He scolded her all the time and longed for Mozart and Rossini. 'In the interval he stood up looking very tall, stretched himself and said, "Oh, that someone would sing Annie Laurie to me." ' Frances was embarrassed by this wish having been made public before several of her musical friends.[3]

Mrs Burne-Jones arranged an evening for him which he enjoyed far better — 'the most delicious performance of *Don Giovanni* I ever was at'. Afterwards they drove back together in the moonlight to the Grange at Fulham, where he slept in Ned Burne-Jones's dressing-room, surrounded by piles of his sketch books, and at breakfast he was happy to see William Morris again. Arthur, too, took him to a concert, before leaving London to see Joan and the children at Brantwood. There he found the roof off most of the house and the whole family living in the lodge.

'How snuggy you must be all in the lodge together,' Mrs La Touche wrote to Joan. (She had written earlier in the year, asking if Ruskin would forgive her; he had told Joan to say that he *had* forgiven her six years before, on that Christmas day in Venice when he felt that he had received a direct message from Rose and St Ursula. Since then she and Joan had corresponded frequently.) 'How delightful about the Meissonier. . . . Of course all that money will be instantly spent, but no doubt well spent, and the new building will be lovely.'[4] Ruskin was still not quite a reformed character about casual expenditure. After getting

---

[1] *Works*, vol. 37, p. 403.
[2] 11th June, 1882. Education Trust.
[3] Frances Horner, op. cit., p. 54.
[4] Harristown, Thursday (June 1882). John Rylands Library.

his money, he wrote, didn't Joan think 'with the odds and ends of it over' he might buy himself a new grand piano and a silk dress for Rosalind Webling 'and then me'd be twite economical for ever so long'.

He was feeling so much better, he told Joan, that he had been to Sheffield to talk to the Mayor and Corporation about the St George's Museum which he was making there and left them 'more eager about it now than I am myself!'[1]

Joan could not help begging him not to do too much, though she feared he might resent it, as he had her admonitions the previous autumn. 'I am sure you need not be afraid of warning me, at any time or about anything,' he replied, 'as long as there is not any special subject on which we chance to be at issue. I would not take any warnings last autumn, because we were at issue whether the house should go on, or not — and I thought you fancied me ill only because I had changed my mind about it. But *now*, I only wish I had you here to watch me — and tell me when I *am* tired. . . . But the fact is, that though I have been going about so much, I have been extremely cautious, all this while, *writing* absolutely nothing, except necessary letters — so that all book excitement is withdrawn, and keeping off all subjects of sad thought. In spite of which I am always so sad when I am alone that for the first time in my life, I have sought company as a distraction.'[2]

The doctors had advised a change of air and foreign travel to complete Ruskin's recovery, which had been remarkable. He was flattered to hear from Sir William Gull, acknowledging receipt of his fee, that the eminent doctor preferred to keep the cheque as an autograph. He felt no desire to go abroad, but Sir William was adamant, so in mid-August he set out for a four-month tour, accompanied by Collingwood and Baxter, re-assuring Joan before he left — 'Don't be fitened that I should ever be extravagant any more.'

Arthur took the opportunity to make a short painting visit to Venice and Joan wrote enthusiastically of her delight in 'the new house' before her return to London in September to await the birth of her fifth child.

'I am rather happy about the Coz at present,' she wrote to Professor Norton, 'and thank Heaven, when these terrible attacks are got over, they do not leave him shattered either mentally or bodily, as one would expect — and when he recovers one *is* so thankful to forget all the horror and distress. Sir William Gull saw him frequently all through last Spring's illness, and assured us he *might* never have another attack, or he might — but he did not dread any softening of the brain, or actual disease — in short they seem to be a sort of D.T. of the brain, from *overwork* instead of drink. . . . My ankle is still useless — and daily I expect a No. 5!'[3]

★

---

[1] 21st July (1882). Education Trust.
[2] Saturday (July 1882). Education Trust. Part published, *Works*, vol. 37, p. 404.
[3] Herne Hill, 30th September, 1882. Houghton Library.

Arthur telegraphed to Ruskin at Lucca to tell him of the baby's safe arrival, and he wrote at once to express his joy that mother and son were well, 'but it's a great bore it being a boy'. He returned to spend a happy Christmas with them at Herne Hill.

Ruskin's strength seemed to have revived miraculously during his tour. Immediately after his return he gave a lecture on Cistercian Architecture at the London Institution and everyone remarked on the revived vigour of his mind. He seemed ready and able to take part again in public life, and let it be known that with his return to health he would be willing to resume the duties of Slade Professor at Oxford. William Richmond, who had succeeded him, immediately resigned, and soon after the New Year Ruskin was reinstated.

While in Florence with Collingwood he had met a young American, Francesca Alexander, who lived in Italy with her parents. Her father was an artist, of a distinguished Boston family, and Ruskin found that the daughter, although untaught, drew with beautiful simplicity. Her mother was equally sympathetic. 'I never knew such vivid goodness and innocence in any living creatures,' he had written in his diary. Francesca had grown up in seclusion in the Italian countryside and from the peasants she had gleaned a collection of local ballads and songs which she had translated into English and illustrated with drawings in pen and ink. Ruskin was enchanted by them and immediately decided to publish her work in England. Soon he was calling her 'Sorella' and her mother 'Mammina', and when he left Florence he carried with him more than a hundred of her drawings for which he had engaged to pay her six hundred pounds. (She had refused to accept the thousand which he offered.) On his return to London he had to sell stock to enable him to pay for Francesca's book; he had bought it for St George's Guild and planned to publish it as *Roadside Songs of Tuscany*.

No sooner was he back than he called on Kate Greenaway, who had just sent him a copy of her latest book. He had been corresponding with her for some time about her drawings and now, from the first moment of their meeting, a warm friendship sprang up between them. She was quite unlike his usual 'pets'. In feminine beauty he had always admired a tall, very slim, willowy figure – fair girls whose features were classical and whose movements were quick and graceful. Kate Greenaway had none of these attributes. She was thirty-seven years old, small and dark and very plainly dressed, with a quiet, reserved manner concealing a certain shrewdness. But he was captivated by her drawings of an enchanted children's world, the figures charmingly grouped and delicately coloured, and she, in turn, regarded him as a prophet. She told friends that there seemed to be a 'holiness' about his words and ideas.

CHAPTER 33

FAREWELL TO OXFORD

1883 – *Spring*, 1885

JOAN WAS BEGINNING TO LEARN AGAIN NOT TO WORRY all the time about her cousin. Happy in his recovery, she and Arthur were living contentedly with their children at Herne Hill. From Brantwood he sent word that she was to choose furnishings for the new rooms whenever she liked: 'My pocky-wock will stand it just as well at one time as another. I hope to make a heap by the new *Modern Painters* which is quite done and will be out soon'.[1] That spring he began a new course of lectures at Oxford.

'The undergraduates cheered no end, and Baxter said the people going away who couldn't get in were like a church coming out,' he told Joan after the first lecture, and he had to repeat it the following day. It was the first of a series on contemporary artists to be called *The Art of England* and was about the work of Rossetti and Holman Hunt. He planned to give the next after Easter on Burne-Jones, and another on Leighton and Watts.

After a few days at Oxford he came on to Herne Hill and in answer to anxious inquiries from Professor Norton wrote that there was no sign of the symptoms of illness that he had felt in former springs. 'But it is curious that I really look back to all those illnesses... with a kind of regret to have come back to the world. Life and Death were so wonderful, mingled together like that — the hope and fear, the scenic majesty of delusion so awful — sometimes so beautiful. In this little room, where the quite prosy sunshine is resting quietly on my prosy table — last year, at this very time, I saw the stars rushing at each other — and thought the lamps of London were gliding through the night into a World Collision.'[2]

Encouraged by the success of his lectures and feeling renewed confidence in his power to work, Ruskin left London for Brantwood on Good Friday. Joan wrote to him next day, heading her letter 'Bad Saturday 1893', and telling him that Arfie and she had never enjoyed one of his visits more. 'But oh dear it was too tebby that deserted room! And I shut my eyes, and knelt down on the rug by my still Di Pa's fire, and prayed for his safety, and health and happiness — and was a little bit comforted, and with our Rosie's face looking down at me I felt as if her protective spirit might be near us both.'[3]

[1] March (1883). Education Trust.
[2] *Works*, vol. 37, p. 442.
[3] Education Trust.

They had arranged to join him almost at once, but the visit was postponed when Baxter's children at the lodge caught whooping-cough. Ruskin became most impatient with Joan. He was anxious for them to come as soon as possible and they *must* bring Kate Greenaway with them. Joan's protests about her children were brushed aside. She must leave them at Herne Hill to come later. 'Please write and ask if Kate has had it — if so — you and she come on Tuesday anyhow.'[1]

They did come, leaving Arthur, who could not remember having had the disease, with the children in London, and taking their tickets to Ulverstone as directed by Ruskin, though it involved a drive of fifteen miles in the carriage — 'I can't have Kate seeing Windermere before Coniston.'

Kate Greenaway's visit was a great success. She was a little dazed on arrival by having been rushed up there at short notice. Her life at home was quiet and hard-working, and her habits regular. It was most unusual for her to do anything on the spur of the moment without previous methodical planning.

At Brantwood she found herself plunged into a new and exhilarating atmosphere. She already venerated Ruskin. She felt honoured to be taken into his study after breakfast and shown drawings and missals, manuscripts and precious stones from his collections, and she concentrated hard to remember all that he told her about them. She learned more from him in walks up the hillside in the afternoon, and sat in the stern of the *Jumping Jenny* while he rowed across the lake.

'Then it is dinner-time; then he reads us something nice or talks in the most beautiful manner,' she wrote home blissfully. 'Words can hardly say the sort of man he is — perfect — simply.... Everything is confused. I never know day or date. I'm always looking at books or pictures. I am absorbed into a new world altogether.... Such wild wide stretches of country and then such mountains — such mossy trees and stones — such a lake — such a shore — such pictures — such books — my mind ... entirely content and satisfied.'[2]

★

Although apparently completely recovered after the series of brain storms from which he had suffered, Ruskin did not feel strong enough to live in his own rooms when he went to Oxford, but stayed with Macdonald, his drawing-master, in Woodstock Road. Henry and Eleanor Furneaux had a house near by. At Heyford Furneaux had found himself missing his university life and friends, and not long after his marriage had engaged a curate to help in the parish and bought a house at Oxford in Banbury Road. Since then they had spent six months of every year at Heyford Rectory and the other six in Oxford.

One evening during Ruskin's stay the Macdonalds gave a small dance for their undergraduate son. Young Henry Newbolt, who had been among the

---

[1] 5th April (1883). Education Trust.
[2] *Kate Greenaway* by Spielmann and Layard, p. 113.

enthusiastic audience at Ruskin's lectures, suddenly noticed the Professor, looking very frail, watching them from the doorway. As Newbolt and his partner were leaving the room at the end of the dance, Ruskin laid his hand on the young man's arm and begged them 'almost pathetically' to go back and dance one more Highland Scottische for him. They petitioned their hostess and in a moment the music began again. 'As we pranced round the room we saw John Ruskin beating time to our step with his head thrown back and his eyes half closed in a kind of ecstasy.'[1] Ruskin's Scottish blood meant a great deal to him. He loved the songs and ballads of Scotland and often begged Joan to do a sword dance, which she would perform with great verve, using the fire-irons for swords.

After three successful lectures in May, which had each to be repeated to a second audience, Ruskin came to London and gave another, to an audience of two hundred in a private house, on the work of Kate Greenaway and Francesca Alexander. His choice of artists and the high praise which he gave to them both occasioned some comment. Next month Joan went with him to Brantwood, taking the children and leaving Arthur in London.

There was great excitement as the time approached for the arrival of Professor Norton from America. He was one of Ruskin's most intimate friends and he had not been in Europe for ten years. Now he was coming to Brantwood and bringing his son, Eliot, with him. Joan was almost as fond of Norton as Ruskin was, and wrote delightedly, 'The Coz and I are counting the hours till we can welcome you! He is in excellent health, and shyly confessed he had to change a certain article of clothing today – known as a pair – they being much too tight! So be prepared for a beard, moustache, and a little corpulence! . . . Ever your loving and delighted Joan R. Severn with 5 chicks of her own to introduce to you!'[2]

They stayed for a week, and Ruskin was very happy to have his old friend there with him, to show him new treasures and talk of old times. Norton found that Ruskin had changed greatly in the ten years since their last meeting. 'I had left him in 1873 a man in vigorous middle life, young for his years, erect in figure, alert in action, full of vitality, with smooth face and untired eyes; I found him an old man, with look even older than his years, with bent form, with the beard of a patriarch, with habitual expression of weariness, with the general air and gait of age. . . . But there were hours when the old gaiety of mood took possession of him with its irresistible charm. He had become, indeed, more positive, more absolute in manner, more irritable, but the essential sweetness prevailed.

'Given his circumstances, no ordering of life could have been more happy for him than that at Brantwood. He was the object of the most loving and watchful sympathy and care. His cousin, Mrs Severn, was at the head of his household,

---

[1] *My World as in My Time* by Henry Newbolt, p. 114.
[2] Brantwood, 22nd June (1883). Houghton Library.

and the best of daughters could not have been more dear and devoted to him. Her children kept the atmosphere of the home fresh and bright; the home itself was delightful, beautiful within with innumerable treasures of art, and surrounded without by all the beauties of one of the fairest scenes of the English lake country. A pleasanter home, or one more lovely in its surroundings and more appropriate for him, could not have been desired.'[1]

Norton left, happy in the thought of his friend's idyllic surroundings; he had seen the sunny side of Brantwood. His visit was in June when the Lake country wears its fairest face – he saw nothing of the fogs and snow of winter. Ruskin himself was well, and Joan, always cheerful whenever it was humanly possible to be so, was thankful for her cousin's well-being and happy to see an old friend and to have her children playing round her. Norton had not experienced the hard times when Brantwood's master veered between moods of gloom and intense irritability, when the children had to be sent away, the doctors called and the whole house was filled with uncertainty and foreboding, while he slipped away into a land of fantasy where horrid and fearful dreams were lit by flashes of unearthly beauty.

The Nortons' departure left rather a blank at Brantwood, but other visitors soon arrived in the shape of Mrs La Touche and the 'Master', as her husband was always called by their friends, who were staying in Coniston at the Waterhead Hotel. A note from Brantwood was waiting for them when they arrived, and the next day they walked round the lake and were given an enthusiastic welcome.

'The Professor was delightful,' wrote Mrs La Touche to a friend in Ireland, 'carried off the "Master" and showed him enchanting things, all Francesca's wonderful drawings, and his garden and his wood, his building and draining, etc. etc., while Joan showed me the children and the new rooms etc.... The kindliness of these lake-dwellers is striking.... Our servants went over to see Brantwood and its treasures, and the Professor and Joan received them and showed them everything.... People pay their visits in the course of a mountain-walk or after a hard row on the lake, so that dressing for the occasion is never thought of.'[2]

★

In August Joan and Arthur went to stay in Ireland, leaving the children at Brantwood. It was Joan's first visit to Harristown since the time when she was engaged to Percy La Touche, and it brought back memories of the slim, quicksilver figure of Rose. The La Touche parents had now been completely accepted again as intimate friends both by Ruskin and by Joan – especially Mrs La Touche, whose charm and cleverness had endeared her so much to them both before tragic events had separated them. Now all was forgiven, if not

---

[1] Norton, op. cit., vol. II, p. 165.
[2] Coniston, 20th July, 1883. *Letters of a Noble Woman* edited by M. F. Young, pp. 92–4.

forgotten, and Ruskin called her 'Lacerta' again (or 'Lacy' for short), and liked her using Rose's old name for him – 'St. C.' – and sent her little presents, as he did to all his friends.

'Your di ma is delightful,' Mrs La Touche wrote to Ruskin, 'and her brightness is not *much* dimmed by our having just sent off Arthur to Galway. The Master said everything he could think of about bad weather, bad hotels, bad food, etc., to discourage him from going and keep him with us; but I told him the Master was an old Philistine, and must not be minded when Atlantic waves and cliffs of Moher were asking to be looked at. So now he is gone, with endless written directions and cautions from Joan in his pocket, and last words in his ears, about possible damp beds, prowling Invincibles, slippery cliffs, and other perils.'[1]

Arthur journeyed across Ireland to the west coast, spending the first two nights at a large, ramshackle hotel at Galway where the only other visitors were a number of wild young Irishmen celebrating after the races, and then some days at a hotel in a small spa called Lisdoonvana, where the visitors included nine priests who had come to drink the medicinal waters. One of them Arthur observed on several occasions the centre of a group of earnest young men, and was later surprised to find that they had come from some distance to consult him about likely winners at a race-meeting.

Farther along the coast at Kilkee he painted every day. Great breakers crashed on to the rocks below the cliff, 'the water emerald green and the foam as white as snow – because the sea on the west coast is perfectly clean'. The grass at the top of the cliffs was quite flat, and on this green lawn a vast design had been cut in the turf representing a skull and crossbones and crossed swords, with a notice threatening death to a man who had turned King's Evidence in a Fenian murder case. Arthur's artist's eye noticed that it was 'quite a good design and most neatly cut', but it gave him a disagreeable sensation when at the end of the day, he had to pass it on his way back to the inn.

★

Although Joan enjoyed her stay at Harristown, she was, as always, made to feel slightly guilty at not being with her cousin. 'It's very lovely your being *there*,' he wrote, 'but me do wish oo was *here* too.'

Joan returned to him and the children at the end of August, but Arthur went south. Professor Norton and his son were coming to Brantwood again for a few days before leaving for America. 'You cannot think what bliss it is the thought of you and Eliot coming back here so soon,' she wrote to him. 'I don't know who's the wildest with joy! – the only regret being that alas Arthur (the old one) is not here.'

She had consulted Norton on his previous visit about a subject that worried

[1] Saturday (August 1883). Education Trust.

her — what would happen to her cousin's old diaries on his death. She knew that there were in them many intimate revelations about his private life, his unhappy marriage and his thwarted love for Rose, and she could not bear the idea that they might be exposed to public curiosity. After her discussion with Professor Norton she had picked a good moment and talked the matter over with her cousin. Now she could tell Norton what the result had been.

'The Coz said, "I'm going to let Charles put his name in all my diaries he cares to have, for I want him to have them if I die — as he will I hope write my life." ' She had tried to persuade him to let his friend take at least the earlier ones with him when he returned to America, but he said that he might have to refer to some of them for his books. 'I did not like to press the point. I do hope it will all be as you wish — and as I wish.'[1]

They had another talk during Norton's second visit. She told him that her cousin had often spoken to her of his intention of leaving the house and everything in it 'just as they are', in trust to her and her children, and his private manuscripts to Norton. Now there was some suggestion that Wedderburn should control the copyrights of Ruskin's works. She had always understood, she told Norton, that the copyrights 'were to be a free possession to us and our heirs — to produce funds for the keeping up of Brantwood (as a first charge) and then for the payment of annuities — and as they died off to fall into the Brantwood fund ... I feel my position is delicate and difficult but knowing your influence with the Coz and friendship for me too — I think it well to trouble you with all this. ... I told Mr W. frankly I disapproved of his being the possessor with complete control of copyrights — he is clever, and our friend, but also a keen man of the world.'[2]

Norton sympathized with her concern. He had the highest opinion of her character and her unselfish care for her cousin, and did his best to give her good advice. She stayed on at Brantwood when Ruskin left for Oxford. The children's new governess, Miss McClelland — 'Clennie' — who was even prettier than her predecessor, was away, and Joan was kept busy looking after the children and doing much secretarial work for her cousin as well.

With the improvement in his health it was no longer thought necessary to have secretaries living in the house. Laurie Hilliard had retired from his position when his father died, to devote more time to painting, and was living with his mother in a small house on the way to Coniston village; Collingwood was about to be married. When Ruskin was at Brantwood Sara Anderson often came to work for him there, but at the moment she too was in London. 'Please di ma stay at Brantwood as long as ever you can enjoy it,' wrote Ruskin affectionately from Oxford. 'It's so good for oo — and if you were at Herne Hill I should be misby here and torn in two.'[3]

[1] Brantwood (3rd September, 1883). Houghton Library.
[2] 10th September, 1883. Houghton Library.
[3] (October) 1883. Education Trust.

RUSKIN, JOAN SEVERN AND
HENRY ACLAND,

Photographed at Brantwood by Angie
Acland August 1st, 1893

RUSKIN AND JOAN SEVERN IN
THE *JUMPING JENNY* ON THE
LAKE. ARTHUR'S SAILING BOAT
IN THE BACKGROUND

THE GREAT FROST OF 1895

Ruskin, Joan Severn, Arthur, Lily and the Brantwood Staff on the ice on Coniston Lake in February.

Life seemed much brighter to Joan. Arthur came back to Brantwood at the end of October and they had a happy month there together with the children, reassured by the letters she received from Oxford.

At the end of the Oxford term Ruskin stayed for a few days at their house in London, where he entertained Arthur's niece, his favourite, Martha Gale, to dinner, and then spent a night without Baxter in attendance, with Stacy Marks and his daughters. 'The girls are in great feather at the idea of valeting me,' he told Joan. Next day he bought a doll for Kate Greenaway's little girl model, who at tea insisted on removing the mob cap in which she was posing and putting it on Ruskin's head. Kate said it made him look exactly like the wolf in Red Riding Hood. Then he came on to Brantwood, but before Christmas the Severn family left and he found himself sad and lonely without them.

It happened that Sara Anderson, who now usually attended to his correspondence, was also away. Collingwood had been married earlier in the month, and he and his bride moved into their new house, on the other side of Windermere, a few days before Christmas. They had only a week together there before Ruskin had successfully urged their coming to stay with him at Brantwood, and set Collingwood to work with specially luminous water-colours on large pictures of sunsets, to illustrate the lecture which he was preparing, *The Storm Cloud of the Nineteenth Century*. Arthur sent news from London of a very good critique given to his latest picture – a study of moonlight – and in February Ruskin went to Herne Hill, leaving the Collingwoods free to return to their interrupted honeymoon.

In his lecture Ruskin gave vigorous expression to his conviction that since his youth the heavens had darkened, fouled by smoke belching from the factory chimneys which had proliferated in England and industrial Europe. For years he had made notes on sunrise and sunset almost every day, had measured the intensity of the blue in the sky, and had studied the shape and movement of the clouds. Now he saw in the ominous Storm Cloud, 'made of dead men's souls', a symbol of the moral darkness of the modern world.

He spent several weeks with the Severns in London before returning by himself to Brantwood. The remarkable improvement in his health now seemed to be faltering. He began to feel 'a very steady gloom' gaining on him and, as in every spring, begged Joan to come to Brantwood. She responded at once and spent a fortnight with him, leaving the children in London, and when she returned to them at the beginning of April, promised Ruskin that they would all come back together in mid-May. Her cousin soon followed her to London, but after a few days spent in seeing the new exhibitions of pictures and going to the theatre, he returned to Brantwood. Before he left Joan was horrified to see definite signs of the old symptoms of over-excitement. It was during an evening which he was spending alone with her and the children's pretty governess, Clennie. Ruskin suddenly noticed the fear in their faces and it shocked him. Joan could not go to Brantwood as soon as she had promised. She began to have frequent bleeding

L

from the nose which was difficult to staunch, and the doctors said she was run down and must rest.

Ruskin was not very sympathetic. He longed to check the feeling of increasing isolation which was growing on him, and to regain security by having Joan near him and by the sympathetic companionship of his young favourites. 'I am sure there is no cause for anxiety about that bleeding but it shows you have been over-taxing yourself and need quiet. Suppose you come down here to chaperone Ada[1] — leaving the children to Alice and the nice new maid — and fetch Clennie to take care of you.'[2]

But the doctor would not allow her to travel until the end of the month. She came then, bringing her children with her but leaving Arthur to follow later. That summer was very hot, and although sometimes there was a strong wind, little rain fell. Brantwood was full of visitors who succeeded each other as guests, or came across the lake from Coniston village — Georgie Burne-Jones and her daughter, Martha Gale and Ada Dundas, Diddie Anderson, Professor Norton with three female members of his family, Mrs La Touche, Jowett (the Vice-Chancellor of Oxford), the artist, Henry Holiday, and his wife, the Colling-woods and Wedderburns.

Arthur spent several weeks in July sailing with friends on a yacht called the *Silver Star*, and came back in August, very brown and well. He and Joan were both naturally gregarious and enjoyed the daily gathering of friends, though Joan was still not very strong.

They had just made a tennis lawn in a glade above the house, which had entailed a great deal of work, mostly done by the young people who were to use it. Ruskin had been the engineer. Although he did not like tennis he was always glad to see people digging. When it was levelled they could look on one side over the lake which lay far below them, and on the other up the dark wooded hillside. Arthur had become very fond of the game, and divided his time largely between sailing on the lake and playing with tremendous energy on the new tennis lawn. Lily was now eleven years old and she, young Arthur and Agnew loved to sail with their father, and spent many happy hours that summer building a hut in the woods. In the evenings Ruskin read aloud from *Rob Roy*, four candles placed on a table beside him as the light waned. Arthur played chess or made sketches of the others listening to the reading, and then there was music before they all went to bed.

Every evening Ruskin liked to listen to Joan singing, usually Scotch songs which were his favourites. He would stand behind the piano and gaze into the face of the singer. 'My wife did not mind this,' Arthur remembered in later years. 'She used to look up at him and add a few singing words about his going to bed and sleeping well, in which he would join. This was always in the *Spinning Song* which came as a wind up for the evening. He would look in this way

---

[1] Ada Dundas.
[2] 8th May, 1884. Education Trust.

from the back of the piano into the face of any attractive singer, and it never seemed to occur to him that by so doing they would be made shy or get confused.'

The Severns' Scotch governess, Clennie – a very pretty, dark girl from the Isle of Skye, was embarrassed one evening when he did this while she was at the piano. She stumbled over the notes and when she had finished Ruskin remarked crossly that she had not played at all well. Arthur was irritated by his lack of sensitivity. 'How can you expect her to play well with you standing there looking into her face?' he asked. Ruskin was furious.

'No one dared contradict him on any subject without his flying into a passion,' Arthur wrote later. 'What he liked was absolute obedience, and in return he would pet and flatter. His ideal was a "kind feudal system" – everyone round to be willing to help, to obey and to love him. To all such he would be kind and helpful, but woe betide the man or woman who ventured to differ or put him right. A pretty girl could do it a little and it amused him, but hardly any other kind of human being. I did so more than any other man, standing well up to him now and then, but it required courage, and I think he took it better from me than he did from other people. Of course I was very careful to be on the right side, and this is not very difficult when dealing with an overwrought and excited brain, as his often was.' On this occasion Ruskin left the room in a rage but later, after a little coaxing from Joan, returned and said good night in the usual way.[1]

★

It was just the life that Ruskin liked best now, surrounded by congenial people who all knew his ways and delighted to conform to them – with Joan always ready to help him re-hang the Turner drawings on his bedroom walls or re-arrange his collection of coins. But he felt an increasing depression, found it difficult to sleep in the heat, and as the summer went on startled Joan with outbursts of anger which left her distressed and himself frightened about his health. Then, towards the end of September, the glorious sunny weather ended. At last they had rain and a wild wind that whipped up white horses on the lake and Ruskin left for Oxford.

Joan and Arthur soon returned to London. The news from Oxford was not reassuring. The latest course of lectures which Ruskin had planned to give he had called *The Pleasures of England*, his intention being to trace the history of England, seen from his own religious standpoint, and illustrated by the arts of the various centuries. His friends saw with concern that he was restless and excited, and Joan although still not well, paid a short visit to Oxford and returned unhappy to London. Ruskin's servant, Baxter, informed her of any change in his master's condition and as in all her cousin's illnesses she kept in close touch with John Simon for advice.

After her visit Simon went down to Oxford himself for a night and told her

[1] Arthur Severn's Memoirs.

that 'there did not seem as much amiss as Baxter's words . . . had led me to fear; but of course it is needful to have a watchful eye on his health, and . . . I rejoice to know that Arthur can find occasion to be at Oxford.' Ruskin was doing, and planned to do in the next few weeks, far more than suited his strength, 'but I fear nothing short of another break-down will lead him to see how strict he ought to be with himself'.

Ruskin was staying at Balliol with Jowett, who tried to persuade his guest to rest as much as possible. But now he was becoming increasingly restless and irritable, and also showed signs of suspecting everybody about him, including his servant, who wrote to Joan, 'Just before he went out I caught him staring so very suspiciously at me, as much as to say You think I am off, but I am not.' His suspicions and crossness extended to Joan and Arthur as well. Joan was given instructions to send him immediately a number of pictures, including several which were hanging on the walls of their house at Herne Hill and which he had often said he wanted them to keep.

'I am so very sorry I can't "reprieve" — as you call it — the "pics",' he wrote. 'I want them all immediately here. . . . I had noticed lately that Arthur was beginning to "think" . . . that I had given the Lewises.[1] I had been giving too easily and too much. . . . And observe finally this, that I watched all this time patiently to see if having all these pictures — so much admired — beside him would do Arfie any good. He has never learned a single thing nor even attempted to learn, from *one* of them.'

Joan took Baxter's advice to write cheerful letters to Ruskin without showing any suspicions about him, but even her normal solicitude could infuriate him in these moods. 'Will you be so good as to mind your own business, just now, as far as you can — and *read* my letters and enjoy them — when I've time to write any — and make yourself easy.'[2]

But he had periods when he would be quite himself and Baxter still hoped that the symptoms might die away and a serious illness be avoided. After Ruskin had given his fifth lecture Baxter bravely suggested that he might take a week's rest somewhere a few miles outside Oxford, 'so that he would not be tormented with Callers. But he bawled out "All his work lay in Oxford and he would stay there", so I had to keep quiet.'

The lectures of the Slade Professor had been well attended; the applause was as loud as ever, but it was not his old eloquence that drew the crowds. The lecture room was now largely filled with undergraduates who had come to hear what he would say next, and to enjoy his eccentricities and too vehement language. This last lecture had alarmed his friends. It was supposedly on the subject of Protestantism and having first shown the audience his copy of Carpaccio's *St Ursula*, 'as a type of Catholic witness', he demanded what should be the types to represent the spirit of Protestantism, and proceeded to untie two

---

[1] Pictures by J. F. Lewis, R.A.
[2] 16th November, 1884. Education Trust.

pictures which lay on the table in front of him in an atmosphere of mounting excitement. These, he promised, would show the two aspects of that spirit – the earnest and the hypocritical. The first, when he held it up, proved to be a drawing of a pig by Bewick, and the second a drawing of Mr Stiggins with shabby gloves and a concertina. The undergraduates burst into roars of laughter, but other members of the audience caught their breath in astonishment. The matter was reported in the London press and at least one paper had a leader protesting against 'this academic farce'.

He had already announced the subjects of the next two lectures – *The Pleasures of Sense* (*Science*) and *of Nonsense* (*Atheism*), and had told his friends that he intended to denounce the scientists, and particularly their plan to establish a physiological laboratory, which would involve the practice of vivisection – an idea which was repugnant to him. His friends feared that the strain of such controversial thoughts, combined with the excitement of the crowded lecture-room, might lead to a disaster, and much against his will, he was persuaded by Acland, Jowett and Macdonald to postpone the last two lectures of the series, and to substitute readings from his earlier works, on *Birds* and *Landscape*.

'Lovely weather,' he wrote to Joan, '. . . but people worry me frightfully by saying I look ill or look tired – or was out of temper or the like. Of all the absurd things to say to one, just in mid-business, its the absurdest. But there's no doing good lectures when people bother like that.'[1] In a second letter to her, written on the same day, he said tartly, 'I hope you will soon begin writing livelier letters than any I have had lately.'

The removal of controversial topics from his lectures made Ruskin less excitable, but he was still sleeping badly and felt 'horribly languid and wretched'. He cheered up a little when Joan came down at his request to see him at the end of term before he left Oxford. She came in spite of having a heavy cold, and was pleased to find his manner quite calm again. He seemed to have hovered on the verge of a break-down, but mercifully to have avoided it.

Back at Brantwood, Ruskin wrestled with depression and resolved that he would 'never stir out of quiet work more'. He told Joan that he did not think he could come to London or do anything but vegetate this spring. 'I am so seriously frightened at the feeling of collapse, and the sense of despondency is so terrible.'

He was worried, too, about his finances. As always after one of his periods of over-excitement, he found that he had spent a great deal of money with nothing to show for it. 'I am utterly aghast . . . to see what I have let slip since I went up in October. . . . There's cheque after cheque for cash.' Allen had just sent him £150, making £1650 from the sale of his books during the year. 'If that holds, I ought to be able to live on it, somehow? But what I've been doing with my money this year I can't make out, no how! I've spent £200 in small cash and

[1] 25th November, 1884. Education Trust.

don't recollect buying anything but an umbrella! Di wee ma, I really think
oo'll have to manage my money for me.'[1]

Arthur's habit of exaggerating or embroidering his stories to make a better
effect had lately come under fire from Ruskin. 'Arfie had better mind what he's
about, when he's talking,' he wrote censoriously to Joan. 'He is getting into his
Father's habit of beautiful comic varnishing, but his Father did it definitely and
pointedly — Arthur is beginning never to see facts but with pantomime ver-
milion on the edges.'[2]

There was something in Ruskin's criticism. Facts were never sacred to Arthur.
They existed as a basis on which he could build an amusing or dramatic tale.
'In telling a story,' he wrote as an old man, 'I always try to throw in my broad
effects and not lose myself in a sea of details. To me there is nothing more tiresome than a story-teller who stops in the middle to think about a date to be
exact — or a name.' No one could have accused Arthur of this failing, and when
in writing his reminiscences he occasionally ventured on a date it was almost
invariably inaccurate.

It had been clear to Joan for some time, and now become clear to Ruskin, too,
that for him to continue his work at Oxford, in an atmosphere of excitement
and controversy, would be fatal to his health. In the spring the resolution was
passed to establish a physiological laboratory at Oxford, endowing vivisection.
Ruskin had fought against this proposal which he loathed, not only because of
cruelty to the animals, but also as being contrary to the Franciscan doctrine of
the brotherhood of all living creatures. He immediately resigned from the
Slade Professorship. He had already been infuriated by the University's refusal
to build a new room at the Ruskin Drawing School and to buy two Turner
drawings which would have completed the collection which he had given. He
had intended to bequeath to the Bodleian Library his books, his Titian portrait
of the Doge, and the best of his own Turner drawings, but his annoyance with
the University authorities had already led him the previous summer to revoke
this bequest.

He never returned to Oxford, and two years after his resignation he withdrew
many of the pictures which he had lent to the drawing school.

[1] Brantwood. December 1884. Education Trust.
[2] 14th January, 1885. Education Trust.

CHAPTER 34

THE QUARREL WITH JOAN

1885 - 1887

IT WAS TIME FOR YOUNG ARTHUR AND AGNEW SEVERN to go off to boarding school. It almost broke Joan's tender heart to see the little boys in their first long trousers, complete with Eton jackets and top hats. The only comfort was that they were going to Mr Churchill's school at Reigate, and Mrs Churchill was her old friend, Connie Hilliard, who had been bridesmaid at her wedding; but even so the wrench of parting was very painful. Arthur took these things more lightly.

Ruskin stayed with them for a few weeks in the summer and went on to Orpington where George Allen lived, whom, when he had decided to become his own publisher, he had set up in business at a week's notice and with no previous experience. A shed in the garden was his warehouse, and public and booksellers alike could obtain copies of Ruskin's books only from him, at a fixed price and paying cash. This step had been taken because Ruskin disapproved of the system then in force whereby the price of a book would vary from shop to shop, each bookseller trying to undercut the other and many ruining themselves in the process. It was conceived as part of his plan to reform modern business methods, as well as other aspects of modern life, through his letters in *Fors Clavigera*, in which he preached fixed prices, profits openly declared, payments by cash and no advertising. Three years before he had modified his original plan to the extent of giving the booksellers a fixed discount, large enough to allow them 'a living wage', to cover the cost of retailing the books, and his experiment had proved surprisingly successful.

At the beginning of July Joan took the three younger children to Brantwood and Arthur went off to stay with a friend at Barmouth who owned a 10-ton yawl. He was passionately fond of sailing boats. This was one of the few sporting interests which he shared with Ruskin, who liked rowing, particularly in stormy weather, and had even tried to design a new kind of oar.

But he and Arthur had several sharp arguments about other recreations. As in the old days when he had put the undergraduates to work on road-making at Hincksey, and at Broadlands set Mrs Cowper-Temple and the Recorder of London to collect wood and bind it into bundles of faggots for the poor, Ruskin still believed that all recreation should be useful. In vain Arthur argued that for people who worked hard, 'the pleasure of a game of lawn tennis or racquets, or football was refreshing to the mind'. Ruskin had already advised the young ladies at Somerville College 'to stop their lawn tennis and clean the floors and carry up coals' instead, and now he thought it was time to teach Arthur's children this valuable lesson.

'I am going to make those children of yours do some nice useful work,' he announced. 'They are to come up into the woods with me and Jane Anne, and as I chop the branches into lengths of firewood, they can tie them up in bundles, and we shall all be very happy.' Jane Anne was the little daughter of the farmer who lived on the fells above Brantwood, and she liked to accompany Ruskin when he was working in the woods. Lily and young Arthur and Agnew were at first delighted with the new game. But after four or five days of the same work they wanted to go fishing or to build their hut, and left Ruskin puzzled at the habits of the young.[1]

★

At first Joan's visit to Brantwood was happy and peaceful. It was lovely weather. Ruskin was writing his autobiography — a little every morning — which he planned to publish gradually in separate chapters. Mrs La Touche had come to stay, bringing Rose's niece, named for her, the child of the elder daughter, Emily, who had died so young; Diddie Anderson had come north with Joan, and soon Kate Greenaway joined them too. Gradually Joan, who had been through it so often before, began to feel a cloud creeping over them.

'He evidently got rather excited in the autobiography,' she wrote to Norton, 'and I think puzzled what to say, and what not! — then he got off his sleep, more and more, and new ideas poured into his poor brain, and less and less could *he* realize the danger. New projects were daily developed — people asked to come — and daily a sort of bell ringing all out of tune with Kate Greenaway and Mrs La Touche here — both contrary, and exciting elements.' In the end Joan implored them both to leave. Ruskin was furious. Mrs La Touche, though not understanding the necessity, did leave, but Kate, urged to stay by her host, remained in the house.

'I'm sure you know how anxious I always am and in dread of a breakdown,' Joan wrote to Professor Norton, 'and the worst of it is, the more danger *I* see, the less *he* is aware of it — and any apparent concern of mine only irritates him! . . . If I looked serious, it bored him — and if I forced myself to be cheery, it was not with much success!'[2]

Up to the last moment Joan was anxiously hoping that a crash might be averted, as it had been at Oxford the previous winter, but it was not to be, and by the time that Arthur returned from his sailing holiday Ruskin was out of his mind. Nurses had to be found and the governess had to be sent off with Lily and the two boys, 'on the very day they arrived for their holidays', to stay with

---

[1] Arthur Severn's Memoirs.
[2] 22nd August (1885). Houghton Library.

their neighbours, the Marshalls. They could not be allowed to remain in the house.

It soon became clear to Joan and Arthur that this was the most serious illness that Ruskin had had, and it was nearly three weeks before he showed any sign of improvement. Long before this the news had got into the papers; they were deluged with telegrams and letters and the house was besieged by reporters, so that daily bulletins had to be issued. Joan was kept so busy that a month of the school holidays had passed before she could see her sons.

Ruskin's recovery when it came was rapid, but he remained very depressed. 'He still needs my tender care,' Joan wrote to Professor Norton at the beginning of September, 'and writing and receiving letters and all work sternly prohibited. He is full of sweetness to me — and *faithful promises* never again to disobey my advice etc. etc. — and I tell him *we'll see*! — but that I *must* be a dragon whether he rebels or not, if he's to be saved from these terrible attacks. . . . He really ought to live the life almost of an invalid, and be freed from work, and society, and all that can excite, irritate or tire him. And I'm sure I'm ready with heart and soul, to guard him from all this — if only he will let me! — for you know how infinitely precious he is to me, apart from any of his public greatness or authorship.'[1]

As always when the whirlwind had died away, Ruskin emerged, remorseful, humble, grateful and anxious to make amends for the trouble and suffering which he felt he had inflicted on his friends. No sooner was he a little stronger than he sent for his lawyer from London, waited for him with the greatest impatience, and insisted on a deed of gift being drawn up immediately, which made over all his property at Coniston to Arthur and Joan and their heirs. Diddie Anderson was brought in to witness it, and noticed 'his intense thankfulness' when it was completed.

Joan continued to guard him from himself. He found it very hard not to work, and she insisted on writing his letters for him to save him the exertion. 'It's a *rich reward* after our anxiety and nursing to have him so wonderfully restored to us — and *if only* he continues as he is, in submitting himself to my Dragonizing — but as regards *work* — or St George's Guilds — I think *they* must go to sleep.'[2]

By the end of October she felt that he was well enough for her to go for a few days to London. The lease of their house at Herne Hill, which Ruskin had given to Joan, was due to expire the following year. Now Arthur had bought a new lease for twenty-one years.

★

All the family spent Christmas at Brantwood, but everyone seemed to be ill. The weather was cold and damp. Ruskin had a bad cold about three weeks

[1] 2nd September, 1885. Houghton Library.
[2] 24th September, 1885. Houghton Library.

L*

before Christmas, bringing with it a restlessness that made Joan anxious. Her advice was disregarded and she felt worried and miserable. Arthur and Lily had been south to collect the two older boys from school. Joan caught Ruskin's cold, Arthur caught it from her; little Arthur, Lily and the baby, Herbert, all had colds and Joan's eventually ended in pleurisy. When she had recovered and the holidays were ended, she went to Herne Hill for a day or two, leaving Arthur at Brantwood.

Daily letters followed her from Ruskin, addressed to 'My dear, dearest and dearestest and sweetest Di Ma,' but often complaining. The servants were annoying him — he had 'nearly turned them all off in a bunch and ordered a fresh lot from London.' Joan dared not stay away long, but by the spring he was happily employed in writing *Praeterita*, his autobiography. He now seemed calm and well and she and Arthur felt able to return to London.

'We are still here mixing in the giddy throng of a London season,' Joan wrote happily to Professor Norton in June, 'and the blessed Coz keeps so well that we are not hurrying back to him just yet, for I fancy it is good for him to be alone sometimes — and after nearly ten months at Brantwood there is much to be done here, and friends to see! . . . Arthur has had great success this year (at his Royal Institute)[1] with his pictures — especially a very big *Sunset at Sea*! . . . and the reviews have been excellent.'[2]

Barely a week after this happy letter they were suddenly called away by a telegram from Brantwood. 'I was quite unprepared for it,' wrote Joan, 'which makes the shock and distress of it all the greater. I was at H.H. and came off at a moment's notice — and have now got everything into good working order — and a trained man nurse. The present phase is *most trying*, and consists in the vilest abuse of Arthur and me — every crime we are accused of, including plots to murder him, but this will soon pass I trust. . . . But it is really too terribly trying while it lasts — and it's not a thing one "*gets used to*" from past experience. We know of no particular cause for this illness,' she ended sadly.

On the whole her cousin seemed quieter during this attack and Joan was encouraged to hope that it might pass more quickly. But her presence seemed to make him more excited, so that the doctor advised her to keep out of his room as much as possible. There were outbursts of violence, during one of which he sprained his wrist struggling with his male nurses. Then he would be quite quiet and ask Joan to come to his room. He would be delighted to see her and at first seem almost himself, then would say in a reasonable, calm voice that he knew every thought that passed through her mind by the baa-ing of the lambs in the field before the house, or give her a message for the Queen, adding that he would know if she had delivered it properly if she played a little tune on the piano when she got downstairs.

---

[1] In the previous year the Dudley Gallery and the Institute of Painters in Water Colours had combined and had since become known as the Royal Institute, etc.

[2] 22nd June, 1886. Houghton Library.

For a month he remained out of his mind, but by the beginning of August seemed better. He came downstairs, showed little sign of depression or weakness, and soon was able to go for drives in the carriage with Joan. But he remained appallingly irritable, complained that the servants thought themselves his masters and that he had been 'fearfully ill-managed' during his illness. Arthur went away on a yachting trip with friends and Joan found herself the principal target of his spleen. The fact that in all other ways he now seemed quite normal made his abuse even more difficult to stomach. She wrote to Professor Norton that he was very irritable, 'especially *against me* for having done *everything wrong* and caused all these illnesses! He seemed in all else *so himself* it nearly made a devil of me — but I've triumphed and my conduct is Saint like!'[1]

Fortunately she had Diddie Anderson in the house with her and Laurence Hilliard, of whom she was very fond. Collingwood, too, came almost every day, and one or other of them would act as companion to her cousin so that she might get some rest. Soon he felt well enough to think of going to the sea for a change of air. Plans were formed to see that he would have friends with him all the time, rooms were booked, preparations for the journey made, servants given permission to go on holiday — and at the last moment Ruskin changed his mind and decided not to go — 'offering most pathetically,' wrote Joan, 'to live on bread and water if he *might* stay — which has ended in real turtle soup, oysters, grouse and other dainties, at which he expresses *no* surprise'.

Arthur returned from his yachting holiday to find that Ruskin had finally decided to go to Heysham for a few days, where first Joan, and then Arthur and Alec Wedderburn followed him. He still refused to take any advice and announced that he had invited Froude and his daughter to stay at Brantwood the following week, although Joan had begged him to keep as quiet as possible for a while.

The Froudes were pleasant visitors, 'but apparently,' Joan told Professor Norton, 'the excitement of having visitors at all isn't good for the Coz — and he's restless and irritable, and looks ill, and makes me anxious, and won't listen to my advice about anything — and so I'm rather miserable. . . . He certainly didn't enjoy Froude's visit, and was always either disagreeing with him or put out with him because he didn't advise the things he wanted him to — so that it was a trying experience. . . . But of course the poor Coz gets less and less able for society and exertion of either brain or body.'[2]

Arthur had another brush with Ruskin on the day that the Froudes left. He had taken the governess, Miss McClelland, and Agnes Greig, another girl who was visiting them, to play tennis on the new lawn. He was playing against them both — two very pretty girls, the first a dark beauty and their neighbour, Agnes, very fair. All were enjoying themselves, when Ruskin approached slowly by the path from the woods. In the ordinary way he would have passed on to the

---

[1] 6th August, 1886. Houghton Library.
[2] 7th October, 1886. Houghton Library.

house without a pause, contemptuous of such games, but attracted by the sight of the two exceptionally pretty girls, so contrasted in colouring, running about the lawn, he stopped and applied himself with the same intense concentration to watching their movements that he would have used to observe every detail of a picture, a carving or a sunset.

Not unnaturally this close observation distracted the two girls from the game. Miss McClelland was by nature shy and reserved. She had never been able to accustom herself to Ruskin's ways and had often annoyed him by her immediate withdrawal and awkwardness when he teased her. He liked pretty girls to respond with playfulness and to tease him in their turn. Eventually Arthur, who saw that the game was being spoiled, told him that he was making the girls feel shy and asked him to go away. Ruskin then enquired in a semi-humourous, semi-contemptuous manner, why the balls kept catching in what he could only suppose to be a salmon-trout net, and why one of the young ladies had been nearly struck in the eye by a ball which the net had failed to catch. This witticism failing to conciliate Arthur, and the girls remaining bashful and embarrassed, he went crossly on to the house and his tea, fulminating about Arthur 'warning him off his own tennis ground'.

Some days later, when his annoyance had worn off a little, he composed a rhyme while he was dressing, which he read aloud to them that evening, remembering that Miss McClelland came from Skye and Agnes from the banks of the Lune, near Lancaster:

> In the Isle of Skye
> The girls are shy
> And out of tune
> At the Crook of Lune.
> And — they can't tell why —
> But balls go awry,
> And they can't play tennis—
> Not Aggie nor Clennies —
> With the Stones of Venice
> A-standin' by.

This unpleasantness, like others, blew over, but it was only a surface symptom of a more deep-seated *malaise*. Even for Joan, with her gentle, affectionate nature, her love of mothering, and her boundless devotion to her cousin, it was difficult to live with him in this mood. For Arthur it was maddening. He was by nature easy-going, but it was exasperating to be taken up on everything he said, to be brusquely contradicted if he gave an opinion which did not agree with Ruskin's and to hear her cousin being rude to Joan, knowing that it would only make things worse and distress her more if he were to defend her.

'Life is rather difficult and trying here at present,' Joan wrote miserably to Professor Norton. '... The poor Coz hardly sleeps at all — declares himself to be in splendid health and is at intervals very sweet and like himself — but as a rule *most* irritable and unreasonable — and won't have the slightest contradiction or advice and says and does all sorts of harsh and wrong things — and if anyone dares to oppose him he becomes furious. I feel it *might* be better if we left him — and yet as we do not consider him quite responsible, he might if left to himself do something seriously wrong'.

The constant strain had its effect on her, and after Christmas she took the older children to London, partly so that they could visit the dentist and make other preparations for school, partly so that she could have a short rest from anxiety. They dared not leave Ruskin for long alone, so Arthur remained at Brantwood most of the time with the younger children. Her cousin was still in a quarrelsome mood, but he wrote affectionate letters daily to Joan. 'I'm keeping pretty well, considering my Doanie's so far away, and Arfie's very good to me.'

By the beginning of March Ruskin seemed much calmer. Another instalment of his autobiography had been published and he had many more chapters planned. He had for some time taken a great interest in the teaching at the village school and had had special sets of handbells made which he encouraged the children to play, without much success, also a large, hollow globe in which a child could sit and see a representation of the heavens. It could be moved to show the changing positions of the stars. This had been placed in the school playground at Coniston, and had soon succumbed to the attentions of the children, aided by the Lakeland weather.

In spite of these failures Ruskin's interest in the education of the village children persisted, and on Saturday afternoons about a dozen of the older girls were invited to play on the Brantwood lawn. The games were limited to those approved by their host — throwing and catching balls and playing at shuttlecock — and they would afterwards be given lessons in scripture, Shakespeare or botany, which were followed by a hearty tea in his study.

Jane Anne, the farmer's daughter who liked to accompany him in his woodchopping, pleased him by saying that they would be lost without their lessons, afterwards remarking to a friend, 'He's a foony man is Meester Rooskin, boot he likes oos to tak a good tea.'

Arthur left for London, travelling with Laurence Hilliard, who was going on a yachting-cum-painting cruise in the Aegean. Although so keen on sailing Laurence had never before had the opportunity of going on a long yachting trip. 'I watched the white steam of Arfie and Lollie's train from the wood, with all good wishes,' wrote Ruskin pathetically,[1] but he was soon consoled by Joan's return, and she was delighted to find him '*so* well — no irritation against anybody or anything. . . . We are quite alone together! — a sort of honeymoon couple — and it is *very gratifying* to be told I look *just 18*! The great joy in my heart I suppose shines in my face — and then one's figure!' she exclaimed to

[1] 8th March, 1887. Education Trust.

Norton. She had put on a lot of weight during the past few years and had now been on a diet for twelve months, during which time she claimed to have lost three stone.

After a month at Brantwood she returned to Arthur in London. Her cousin was 'woeful at losing her,' but was cheered by a visit from a young admirer, nineteen-year-old Sydney Cockerell, who had corresponded with Ruskin about a collection of shells and ventured to suggest that he might call on him during the Easter week-end. Ruskin, being alone, was pleased to show his treasures to his young admirer, made him play at shuttlecock with the girls from the village school before tea on the Saturday, invited him to lunch on Easter Sunday, and lent him the *Jumping Jenny* to row on the lake. His kindness warmed Cockerell's feelings to hero-worship, and he left full of happiness at the end of his visit, cherishing an invitation to return next month and to bring with him his sister, who was a year younger than himself.

★

A week later tragic news came of a desperate loss to the Brantwood *coterie*. 'I cannot let anyone else tell you our terrible news but myself,' wrote Mrs Hilliard in a note which she sent round by hand to Ruskin. 'We had two telegrams from Dardanelles yesterday afternoon. The first said "Laurence exceedingly ill — apparently acute pleurisy". The second said that all was over — I cannot write and you will understand how hard it is to believe.'[1]

The shock of this news threw Ruskin into intense melancholy, and soon afterwards Joan again received a call from Brantwood and with Arthur left London at once. They found Ruskin in a very excitable and aggressive state — a frame of mind when he would brook no denial of his wishes, however unreasonable, and suspected everyone about him of conspiring against him. Nevertheless there was so far no sign of delusions and Dr Parsons still hoped, Joan wrote to Mrs Simon, that the attack might pass off. 'Things could hardly be worse than they are! at least not more trying or difficult.'[2]

As always at these times of excitability Ruskin was full of plans, and wrote off to young Cockerell urging him and his sister (whom he had never seen) to come and stay for as long as they liked. 'I never was better . . .' he wrote optimistically, 'am hitting straight out now with the left — and they don't like it! Olive's turret is ready for her now — and will remain, D.V. till she chooses to watch there — as long as she likes.'[3] With this letter Joan had enclosed a note. She had not met Cockerell, as she had been in London during his Easter visit to Coniston, but she asked him not to act upon her cousin's suggestion as he was not himself.

Among her most difficult tasks when he was in this condition was to try to prevent him spending his money with reckless abandon. He had already an-

[1] (13th April, 1887). Education Trust.
[2] Brantwood, 5th May, 1887. John Rylands Library.
[3] 12th May, 1887. *Friends of a Life Time* edited by Viola Meynell, p. 36.

nounced to his servants that he would immediately double all their wages. This was not serious as they simply refused to take the extra money, but in this state he would order early copies of the Bible, books in manuscript and first editions, without any thought of their cost.

There was a terrible scene when Joan reasoned with him about his wild extravagance, but immediately afterwards he seemed to repent and to become calmer. Joan wrote hopefully to the Simons that there had been a decided change for the better that afternoon: 'Peace is now declared between us — after a fearful and stormy interview!'[1] But the improvement did not last. His manner and behaviour were becoming so eccentric that Joan tried to prevent his having the school-girls from Coniston to spend their Saturday afternoon with him at Brantwood. He had already announced to the parents of one of them that he intended to adopt her. This led to a final, appalling scene at a moment when Arthur was out, when Ruskin reproached Joan bitterly, proclaimed that he *would* be master in his own house, hurled accusations at her and showed such signs of becoming violent that she ran upstairs, terrified, and locked herself in her room.

When Arthur came home and found her collapsed on her bed they discovered that Ruskin had left the house and removed himself to the Waterhead Hotel, taking some of his favourite Turners with him. The prolonged anxiety and strain, culminating in such violence and rage, prostrated Joan, and the doctor said that she was suffering from shock and must remain in bed and as quiet as possible. Meanwhile Ruskin had sent for a friend and disciple, Albert Fleming, who lived near Ambleside and ran a linen weaving industry there, according to the principles of St George's Guild, of which he was a member. Fleming came to the Master immediately, listened attentively to his tirade against Joan and Arthur, and at once constituted himself Ruskin's champion.

'I knew you would do all you could for me,' Ruskin wrote to Fleming from the hotel, 'but there is nothing whatever to be done — except to get the Severns out of my house — which Joan being ill — of her own rage and shame mostly I believe — I can't yet effect by police force. I am perfectly "comfortable" in my rooms here — have lived in inns all my life and am really more at home in them than at home! I have long borne the misery of seeing Joan spoiled into folly and ingratitude by her —— of a husband — but have been accustomed to bear everything — of evil from men or clouds — as the nature of them. The Severns *must* go back to their own affairs — in a week or so — and D.V. I shall go back to mine.'[2]

But even Fleming was not immune from Ruskin's reproaches. 'It is entirely wonderful and dreadful to me that *you* leave me,' he wrote to his supporter. 'Or that after what I said to you, you so much as open one of Arthur Severn's letters.

[1] Monday, 13th (May) 1887. John Rylands Library.
[2] Waterhead, Whit-Monday (30th May) 1887. Yale University Library.

'I have not a friend left now — but who qualifies and temporizes — more or less deceives *me* — and believes — Doctor Parsons! and the common rumour of the wicked and foolish world.'[1]

The day after writing this letter he moved into lodgings kept by his old parlour-maid, Kate Raven, where Fleming visited him, bringing with him a friend and neighbour, Mrs Julia Firth, a subscriber to St George's Guild who was already doing some translating for Ruskin. Fleming proposed that she should take Joan's place and run the household at Brantwood for him. She was an ardent disciple of Ruskin's and misunderstood the situation as completely as her friend Fleming.

As soon as Joan was well enough to travel she and Arthur left Brantwood and returned to their children in London. In the meantime Ruskin had been writing to women friends begging them to come to stay with him. Sympathetic though Albert Fleming was, he could not supply the feminine solicitude on which Ruskin was so dependent. Diddie Anderson had been away when he had quarrelled with Joan, and he suspected that she might take her side. His old friend, Edward Burne-Jones, wrote anxiously to Arthur: 'Send me a line about you all — for I am miserable about you. What is happening . . . is Joan ill? Oldie[2] has written twice to me — one letter this morning from Waterhead hôtel — so I know something unhappy is going on. . . . He wanted Georgie to go — its impossible — she is too weak and unwell to travel — nor would it help at all. It might comfort Joan — but even in that way might only aggravate things. I feel very wretched about it — and so sorry for you all as no word can say. Is Joan ill? No wonder if she is poor dear thing.'

As soon as Joan and Arthur had left, Ruskin returned to Brantwood, bringing Mrs Firth with him, and immediately wrote again to Sydney Cockerell: 'Dearest Cockerell, Come as soon as ever you can; but could not Olive come sooner? I have got a kind and good chaperone for her, and for my Coniston pets, — Mrs Firth of Ambleside, who will keep my servants in order for me, and leave Olive as free as the lake waves and moorland winds.'

But Mrs Firth was quite unable to cope with Ruskin, to cheer or soothe him, and he missed Joan in every part of the house and garden. Only the next day he wrote her a sorrowful letter: 'I could have wept tears of blood for you, in seeing the beauty of the place, yesterday evening and today, all lost to Doanie and me. Your room shall stay as you have left it. . . . Perhaps later in the year you might like to come down with Baby and Violet. . . . Send me word how you are as soon as you can.'[3] Yet on the same day he wrote another, furious letter, accusing her of being responsible for rumours in the newspapers about the state of his health. 'I meant to have written kindly again today, but a paragraph which I find has been inserted in all the papers — false and cunning to a point which I

---

[1] (4th June, 1887). Yale University Library.
[2] Burne-Jones's name for Ruskin.
[3] Brantwood (8th June, 1887). Education Trust.

had not conceived possible – renders it vain for me to express any feelings of the old days at Brantwood more.'

Joan, relieved of the strain of constant watching and fear, slowly began to recover her health. She was comforted by their friend, Harvey Goodwin, the Bishop of Carlisle. He was a man deeply interested in Church legislation, education and missionary work and as he had often to be in London to attend the House of Lords and important meetings, he had taken a house in Harley Street where he spent some months every year. By good fortune he was in London when Joan returned, miserable, from Brantwood, and as he knew and admired both her cousin and herself, she was able to pour out her heart to him and to receive comfort.

A few days after receiving the furious letter from Ruskin she had another, sad note: 'Write to me, if you care to write of yourself or of your children. Speak no more of the unpardonable past, till you wish – as much as I – that it should be as though it had never been.'[1] She wrote a kind, non-committal reply which provoked an immediate response.

'The comfort your letter is to me this morning you cannot measure. You never have really known how I have loved you and the desolation of all sweetness to me in garden or wood, for want of you, has been the saddest thing I have ever known in all this life. But that you are out again, watching the children in the daisies, and have had your dear Bishop to see you – and could keep him for two hours – is such a comfort.'

He began to write again to her almost every day, but he was clearly in a state of deep depression. 'The sweetness to me of having you to care again a little about my room and me – and the desolateness of me, without you – there are no words for.' He wrote that he had heard from Francesca – 'her only hope for me is that you will return to me. I think you have arranged all the things in your room very beautifully. But the sadness of entering it now – '

He was pathetically grateful for her letters – 'So many and many thanks for the letters, as in old days, and for keeping affairs in order for me still. I will do everything I can to save you farther trouble. My days are very desolate now for I am ever your loving Di Pa. What lovely brooches those are you have sent the maids.'

He confessed himself heartbroken. 'The love you send me at the end of your letter is worth more than worlds to me,' he wrote, 'and believe me in anything I'm trying to get done about Brantwood I am only thinking now of how to quit you of trouble about it and have you mistress of it.'[2]

Joan now seemed to have recovered and Arthur felt able to leave her at Herne Hill for a short time while he went away to the sea to paint. He had not been gone long, however, before Joan made up her mind that she must return to Brantwood. She realized that there would be unpleasantness to face –

---

[1] Sunday (12th June, 1887). Education Trust.
[2] 26th June, 1887. Education Trust.

awkwardness with the servants and neighbours. She was under no illusions as to how much stir had been made in the small society round Coniston by the accusations which Ruskin had made against herself and Arthur, which had been given wide circulation by Albert Fleming, and she had felt keenly the humiliation of their departure from Brantwood. But news came to her from a distraught household that their master was 'in a fearfully depressed state — refusing food, and having painful delusions of not having a farthing and that he and the servants must all starve'. So she pocketed her pride and once more left her children to hurry to her cousin's side. Sara Anderson went with her.

Ruskin greeted her tenderly and treated her with sweetness and affection, showing himself full of remorse for his cruelty. Joan soon coaxed him into eating. When they arrived he was suffering from delusions, but after a week these disappeared. He remained in bed for a while but soon cheered up a little. Joan had to cope with the results of some of his previous actions as best she could; he seemed to have lost all will to do anything, and her energies were concentrated on saving him from worries and preventing him from slipping into a a hopeless mood of despair. Sara found him one day 'sitting at his study table with his head between his hands, and groaning, "Oh, why didn't Albert see that I was mad?"'[1]

★

Soon after Joan returned a letter came from young Sydney Cockerell for Ruskin, saying that his fortnight's holiday would begin during the following week and that he and his sister looked forward to staying at Brantwood as Ruskin had suggested. Joan felt very sorry for the young pair, who had clearly been counting on two weeks with Ruskin in his home, but her cousin was still in bed and too low in spirits to want to see anyone. She wrote that unhappily he was ill and it was out of the question for them to stay at Brantwood, but if they would care to come as his guests to rooms kept by his retired parlour-maid, she would do everything she could to make their holiday a pleasant one. The Cockerells did not like to accept this suggestion, feeling that Mrs Severn must have enough to do already, but they came to the lodging at Coniston where Sydney had stayed at Easter.

The day after their arrival they had tea at Brantwood with Joan and Sara Anderson, both of whom they were meeting for the first time. They learned that Mr Ruskin was too melancholy to see anyone and returned to their lodgings laden with flowers from the garden, and with the promise of the loan of Ruskin's boat for the two weeks of their stay. The brother and sister spent hours on the lake reading Shakespeare aloud to each other, climbed the Old Man before dawn to see the sun rise, and returned often to Brantwood where they were very kindly received. But Ruskin was still not well enough to see them when they left for London.

[1] Sara Anderson to Joan Severn, 13th December, 1891. Letter in possession of Dr H. G. Viljoen.

Another visitor was Professor Norton's son, Eliot. During his mood of irritability and suspicion, Ruskin had sent word to his old friend, demanding the immediate return of all his drawings that were in Norton's possession. The son had brought them over from America and arrived with them at Brantwood. This, too, Joan was able to smooth over. She propped them up on her cousin's bed and after some time he heaved a deep sigh and said he should never have sent for them. Joan said quietly that Professor Norton would miss them and feel the blank spaces on his walls. Eliot could easily take them back. Ruskin seemed relieved and agreed at once.[1]

By the time that Arthur arrived at the beginning of the school holidays, bringing young Arthur and Agnew with him, Ruskin was better and able to get out a little. He seemed pleased to have them there. The boys caught two pike on the first day of the holidays and Connie Hilliard, now Mrs Churchill, came with her children to stay at a little farm close by. That was a great pleasure, Joan told Professor Norton, 'but oh dear — the loss of poor Laurie is always present to me — one of the saddest trials of my life to have lost him!'

Her cousin could do no work. The greatest exertion he was capable of was to re-arrange his drawings, with Joan moving them round for him. She spent most of the day with him, while Arthur took the two boys fishing or sailing. For Joan the great thing was that her cousin was better. 'I try to forget the past,' she wrote to Norton, 'and to leave the future in God's hands, while I have the joys of this little "heaven on earth" time.'

---

[1] Joan Severn to C. E. Norton. 18th July, 1887. Houghton Library.

CHAPTER 35

VOLUNTARY EXILE

August, 1887 – May, 1888

THE SHOCK THAT RUSKIN HAD SUSTAINED when he came to himself and found that he had quarrelled with Joan, had insulted her and Arthur and made her ill, had turned him against Brantwood. After he had left the house in a rage and established himself at the Waterhead Hotel, he would look across the water in his calmer moments and wonder if Joan would ever be well and happy again. And when he returned to the house even his precious Turners had failed to cheer him with Joan away.

'My Splügen[1] gave me no pleasure over at the Waterhead,' he told her, 'nor all the Turners in the house when I was there alone.'[2] He felt that he would never get over his depression in these surroundings, where everything reminded him of his madness, and seemed to reproach him for having wilfully spoiled the happy days of the Lakeland summer. He thought wistfully of the busy, useful travels in France which had restored his health before, and persuaded Joan that he should go again – get right away from Brantwood and the unhappiness which now seemed to him to cling about it like a shroud.

Arthur and Joan accompanied him on the journey south to Herne Hill, and from there Arthur posted with him to Folkestone, where he left him with Baxter, apparently in control of himself, but undecided as to when he should cross the Channel.

Arthur remained in London where he had work to do, while Joan collected their younger children and took them back with her to Brantwood, and set about getting everything straight again in the house and garden. It was arranged with Baxter that if he had difficulty with his master he should telegraph immediately to Arthur. Ruskin had asked them to give no one his address and to forward no letters. He wanted complete rest, with no correspondence to trouble him. Joan was to deal with everything. He would not even take a cheque book – he was so frightened that he would fall again into habits of thoughtless extravagance.

The news from Baxter was not good. Within a fortnight he was writing to Joan: 'The Master has been awful lately and the Hotel servants and everyone

[1] Turner's drawing of the Splügen Pass, presented to Ruskin by friends and admirers after his illness in 1878.
[2] 21st October (1887). Education Trust.

sees he is a good bit queer. . . . I had to get in a hairdresser for him to smarten him up as I do not cut his hair fashionable enough – so he just got the first cut or two when the Master jumped up and damned him for his modern style of cutting, ordered him to leave the room and bawled to me to pay him and send him off. He is having two new top coats made and five waistcoats. The tailor was not to tell me but I seen them this afternoon when he brought them to fit on – one is to come down to his feet almost, so as the waves can dash against him without wetting him. . . . He is on his very high horse at present. You may all fervently thank God he is not there.'[1]

The worst of the news was that Baxter himself was not feeling well and wished Mrs Severn to find someone to replace him. In spite of the worrying picture that Baxter gave of her cousin, she felt that after what had happened that summer she must leave him to himself, if it were at all possible. She had been deeply pained by hearing a report, on her return to Brantwood, which she believed to have originated with Albert Fleming, that she and Arthur 'had spirited him off into an asylum'.

John Simon had sent Ruskin the name of a good doctor in Folkestone, and the next letter from Baxter said that he seemed 'quite cool and almost himself'. He had agreed to his servant going back to his wife at Brantwood; he was to return as soon as he was well. 'I quite agree with your determination not to interfere with the Master until it is absolutely necessary,' wrote Baxter. Ruskin had ordered him to send off a model boat 'addressed to Baby – not Baby Severn, only Baby – so that the Boys may be able to sail it before they go back to school'.[2]

Ruskin unfortunately did not remain 'cool' but was next day reported to be 'often at the Boiling point', and had told Baxter that he would write to Lord Mount Temple[3] to send him 'a good servant who will hold his tongue and do as he is bid. . . . I will certainly stay with him if I possibly can, but on no account will I leave him alone unless he got what I consider a respectable servant. . . . I consider Fleming's conduct most infamous. He really ought to be Horse-whipped!'[4]

'I should certainly not advise you to come here at present,' he wrote next day. 'I am sure the Master would make your life not worth living. . . . This morning he is up to his games again – and his face like scarlet.' He had sworn at one of the porters and had then given him a bottle of sherry and sent two bottles of champagne to the maids. 'I question if he will get better, at all – it seems to hang on him so. I do feel so sorry to think he should go on so, for everyone takes notice of him and then he goes out and gets into such tempers at things and people which he has nothing at all to do with. . . . I will telegraph for Mr Severn at once – it looks very like it at present.'

[1] Paris Hotel, Folkestone, 30th August (1887). Education Trust.
[2] Ruskin always called Herbert Severn his Baby.
[3] Mr Cowper-Temple, who had been made a peer in 1880.
[4] Folkestone, 1st September, 1887. Education Trust.

Joan and Arthur held to their resolve not to interfere with Ruskin unless it became absolutely necessary. They knew how Albert Fleming and his friends would seize on any action which they could construe as their taking advantage of him. 'I have just got my Master dressed,' wrote Baxter miserably. 'He is very bad – this morning he struck me for the first time and his face was awful red but he has cooled down since a little and wanted to know when I wanted to go home. I told him I was in no hurry and at least I would not go until he was suited. "I am certainly not suited now," with such a look at me. . . . I quite expect squalls today.'[1]

Arthur had joined Joan and the children at Brantwood for the end of the school holidays, but it was becoming clear that Baxter could not hold out much longer. 'My Master seems to go on just about the same – better and then worse again, swearing and bullying everyone in turn. . . . I am sorry to say I feel very unwell myself. I have not any strength left and can't sleep. . . . There is no chance of a breakdown that I can see – of course he is mad half his time, he is really not fit to be at large. . . . Madam, I implore of you and Mr Severn to get him another Man at once for I feel I can't hold out any longer – the cruel insults I can never forget. I acknowledge I am thoroughly crushed and beat.'[2]

The Severns were most unwilling to interfere. Joan still smarted from her cousin's wounding treatment of her when she had last tried to control him, and feared that he might turn on them again, and thus they would do more harm than good. Although they were willing to be responsible if the position became intolerable, they felt that they could not assume an authority over Ruskin which they did not possess, and which might lead to violent and public expressions of resentment.

'I am sorry to hear that you are feeling so unwell,' she wrote to Baxter, 'and unable to go on in your trying position. Of course if you are not well, I suppose your Master will not mind your coming home, and the hotel people will be able to do for him until he finds someone else. . . . Mr Severn thinks that if you have to leave, the Mistress of the Hotel should be told to write at once to us, in case the Master seemed becoming a little too eccentric for her servants or her hotel.'

Baxter was not so cautious in his opinions. 'During the afternoon,' he replied next day, 'the Master has engaged the chambermaid for good to be his parlour-maid. She is now on the hotel books as his private waitress and to serve him only, bedroom and board charged accordingly, the same as I am. He got a cold yesterday – he would ride on the Box and act so silly – I can't tell you how grieved I am at everything. It is quite time that you and Mr. Severn his appointed guardians ought to adopt stringent measures for my dear Master's own sake and reputation – for he is simply the laughing-stock of the people about and yet he seems in a way to know what he is about. I do feel crushed, and of course they see he is the goose who lays the golden eggs and say there is not much the

---

[1] 4th September, 1887. Education Trust.
[2] Folkestone, 10th September, 1887. Education Trust.

matter with him. Mr Severn ought to come at once and bring a keeper for him and take him away from here at once.'[1]

★

Still Joan and Arthur did not interfere, except to find a man to take Baxter's place. 'Appointed guardians' they were not. Ruskin corresponded daily with Joan, made a brief excursion to London and wrote for more money. Sunday drives had cost £5 and he had bought several beautiful model boats. Then he had to pay board wages to his newly engaged parlour-maid, and as she only had black dresses (Ruskin could not bear black clothing) he was giving her what he described to Joan as 'a sober green dress and a sober blue one. . . . So I've only 2 fives left and some change, so you must send me some mo Di Ma, but I'm getting anxy about fot's to become of me — for I'm living at a 'normous rate.'[2]

Joan had barely dispatched twenty-five pounds to him when she heard that he had left Folkestone. He was going to London for a time, and had sent Alice off to Brantwood 'to be made a housemaid of'. Poor Alice had been instructed to find her way to Coniston as best she could, and to telegraph to Joan if she got lost. Joan received this unexpected addition to the household with her usual kindness and wrote to her cousin that he would see Alice there when he returned. But it was because he thought of going to Abbeville, not Brantwood, that he had sent her, he replied. 'All my thoughts and plans for Brantwood are founded on the idea of my not being there. . . . I can't imagine living at Brantwood now — but as a burden to everybody.' He felt that a lodging of his own, 'where Doanie could direct what was done for me if I fell ill, would be the rightest and safest thing'. In the meantime he had this strong yearning to go to Abbeville. 'I shall be more at peace there than elsewhere.'

After his visit to London Ruskin returned to the sea, but not to Folkestone — instead he went to a hotel at near by Sandgate and also took some lodgings two minutes walk from the hotel, close to the sea, so that he could sit at the window and watch the waves. 'He does not yet seem inclined to return here — and that I cannot much wonder at,' Joan wrote to Norton from Brantwood. 'For in his last time of excitement he did many things he must regret, and made rash promises — in one case of adopting a girl (*not* Jane Anne) as his daughter — and will be glad to let these follies be forgotten. And here he seems so easily excited, with his own surroundings and everything to do as he likes with — that I am sure humdrum Hotel life is better for him — for a time at least.'[3]

But life in Ruskin's hotel was anything but humdrum. His letters to Joan became increasingly wild and full of incomprehensible orders. Joan wrote to Sir John Simon:[4] 'I am again very anxious about the precious Coz. He seems in a

[1] 11th September, 1887. Education Trust.
[2] 4th October (1887). Education Trust.
[3] (November 1887). Houghton Library.
[4] John Simon had been knighted in that year.

very excited state, and though Dr Bowles sees him daily it would be a great relief if you communicated with Dr B. about the poor Coz as he is a new patient. . . . Arthur and I are going in any case the end of next week to join him, and fear if we went sooner it might create a disturbance — but we're ready to go any moment if the symptoms are serious.'[1]

Joan felt that she must conserve her resources so that she would be strong when her cousin needed her. If he had a complete collapse, she wrote to Lady Simon, he would need all her tenderest care and highest spirits to cheer him. 'That stage is easier to bear,' she said, 'than showers of abuse — and to see him doing foolish things without any power to prevent them.' Dr Bowles's report to Sir John was not reassuring. His patient had had little sleep for a week and had been very excitable. He had been smashing glasses, plates, fire-irons 'and anything that does not appear to him to be in good taste. Two nights ago he shied the candle-sticks at his man's head and he generally gives him a very lively time of it at night. To me he is always delightful and I had no difficulty in soothing and calming him.'[2]

When Arthur and Joan arrived at Sandgate to stay for a week in the lodgings overlooking the sea, he was quieter and the danger seemed to be passing. But Joan was distressed to hear from Lady Simon that she had received an abusive letter from him. 'Of course I had no idea the Coz *had* written to you, last week when he was in that very excited state,' she wrote immediately. '. . . The contents of your letter made both Arthur and me *boil* with indignation. We're quite used now to all sorts of insults — but to you — or Sir John! — his truest, best and dearest friends — well, it's hard to bear, even tho' we know he'd *never* say such things if he *were* himself — and the one thing *is* to be merciful and take *no* notice. We find he quite forgets, and never even asks, when he's better, what effect such letters had!

'I used to try and comply with all his folly, but now *silence* is always best. He wrote to me — utterly absurd things — ordering them instantly to be published, *not* in the *Pall Mall*, but in either *St James's Gazette* or the *World*, and Lily was to write things to be copied by one of the peasant children . . . and he was at once going to get the Queen . . . to make special shillings of purest silver to repay her, as the common ones weren't good enough! His mother's portrait was to be brought to London and endless other things — none of which he has asked about since we came.

'He is quite wonderfully better, and any outsider would think him *quite* himself. . . . In these excited states he seems now to have a devouring wish for publicity — and to have everything he says, writes, or does, put into print! and a feverish desire to have everything copied — by the last person whom one would wish to see what he writes. I think Dr B. quite takes in the situation and he could not be in better hands. . . .

---

[1] Brantwood, 2nd December, 1887. John Rylands Library.
[2] 6th December, 1887. John Rylands Library.

'My poor Coz! — *he* seems quite happy, and most comfortable in all ways — nice pretty rooms, and excellent food. He stays on here (he says) till he can come to us at Herne Hill in January'.[1]

★

During his short visit to London after his week of over-excitement Ruskin had become acquainted with another young girl. One of his reasons for staying at Morley's Hotel, in Trafalgar Square, was its proximity to the National Gallery, and he was looking at the pictures there one day when an attendant approached and told him that a lady had been inquiring for him. Ruskin followed the man and was led up to a young girl, quite unknown to him, who was copying a Turner picture. When she saw him she appeared confused and embarrassed and said that the attendant had made a mistake. Ruskin went on to the room where the Turner water-colours were hung and some while afterwards the girl followed him and explained that she had not meant to be rude but that she had heard that he had been in the Gallery, and had only asked the attendant if Mr Ruskin was still there because she admired his books and had wanted to see their author in the flesh. She had never intended the man to ask him to come over to her.

The misunderstanding was quickly put right and Ruskin consented to look at the copy she was making, which was nearly finished. He praised it, told her that she had great feeling for Turner and after some further talk, offered to give her tuition, provided she gave up the classes which she had been attending and learned to work instead according to the principles which he had always taught. Her name was Kathleen Olander.

He gave her his address at Sandgate and told her to write to him there. This she did, and when Joan and Arthur had left, he made another short visit to London, met her by appointment at the National Gallery, and set her to copy one of Turner's little water-colour sketches. Before they parted she put into his hand a letter, written beforehand, telling how she longed to be an artist. Her father was an engineer who worked for the Great Western Railway and the family lived at Acton.

The parents were delighted when they heard of his offer and Ruskin wrote to the father before he left London, saying that he would think it a privilege to take some part in his daughter's training. To Kathleen herself he suggested, when he got back to Sandgate, that perhaps her father would bring her and her sister to take a little Christmas holiday there with him, in the lodgings just vacated by the Severns with the bow window looking over the sea. She longed to go, but her father refused the invitation without consulting her.[2]

Arthur and Joan had gone on from Sandgate to their two boys at school at Reigate and then, after a short stay in London, returned with them to join their

[1] Devonshire Terrace, Sandgate. Thursday (December 1887). John Rylands Library.
[2] *The Gulf of Years*, edited by Rayner Unwin, p. 15–20.

other children at Brantwood for Christmas. Her cousin wrote to her from
Sandgate that he was thankful they were happy there. 'It is different from when
I used to look across to it from the Waterhead, wondering if you would ever be
well, or happy with your children again. And certainly the place is no good
to *me* any more — since I can't climb . . . nor pull in rough water.'[1]

He had been unable to keep his good resolutions about not spending money.
In November he had written to the book-seller, Quaritch, whose customer he had
been for many years, 'Please send me all those jolly little books here to look at. I
shall keep some of course'; and during his stay in London he had visited Quaritch's shop in Piccadilly. 'I could not sleep last night, after the excitement of
seeing those MSS,'[2] he wrote the next morning. He had carried away two of
them and wrote for another to be sent to him at Sandgate to look over. He had
already sent a cheque for £40 and in the first week of January told Quaritch
that he had written to Mrs Severn 'who keeps my accounts for me this year, as
I can't be bothered with a cheque book away from home', to send another.

The Christmas holidays at Brantwood were uneventful, and uninterrupted
by any crisis at Sandgate. Ruskin's only intervention in the normal Brantwood
life was to have Downs sent to him bringing some atlases he wanted, but he
was apologetic even about this. 'You may leave Joan in security that she shall
not be plagued with looking for things any more,' he wrote to Arthur, but
spoiled the reassurance by immediately asking for some notes of Leslie's on *The
Old Temeraire* which would be found loose in one of the many drawers in his
study. 'I don't think its possible that I can want anything more till next Christmas — if ever,' he finished, but his words carried no conviction.

Arthur took the two older boys back to their school and remained in London,
where Joan was to join him a few days later. Ruskin had felt lonely at Sandgate
and invited young Sydney Cockerell to bring his sister to stay with him for a
week-end by the sea. In his usual style he wrote to 'Darling Olive', though he
had never met her, and on their arrival kissed her warmly. He had hung some of
his favourite pictures in the lodgings where they stayed, in the same rooms
which Joan and Arthur had occupied, and enchanted the two young people
with his old-fashioned courtesy and his fascinating conversation. They took all
their meals with him at the hotel, where he showed them some of his treasures,
among them a beautifully illuminated Book of Hours.

After dinner he produced a new chapter of his autobiography which he had
just finished, and read it aloud to them with all his old power, 'responding with
glance and voice to each tiny demonstration of his spell-bound listeners, as
though they were an instrument on which he was playing'.[3] They left him to
return home, enchanted and uplifted.

[1] 27th December, 1887. Education Trust.

[2] 22nd December, 1887. *Letters of John Ruskin to Bernard Quaritch*, edited by C. Q. Wrentmore,
p. 105.

[3] *Friends of a Life-Time*, p. 43.

Olive sought to cheer him by sending a careful drawing of a peacock's feather in her next letter. This pleased him. 'But what a naughty girl to waste it on a bit of love-letter — however is it to be kept or shown rightly?' he asked.

Arthur and Joan brought Lily with them for a week's visit to the lodgings when the school holidays were over and she had her fifteenth birthday while they were there. Ruskin still seemed very sad, but cheered up a little with Joan to himself, when Arthur took Lily across the Channel and they stayed at Boulogne for a night. 'Her first trip abroad!' Joan wrote to Lady Simon, 'and the Coz and I are to meet them at Folkestone, and pretend they've been gone for months!'[1]

When the Severns had left, the only thing he seemed able to summon the energy for was to write letters to various girl disciples. 'Illness always has hold on me, more or less, now.' He feared, if he lived, he would become a burden to those who loved him, he told Kate Greenaway, and to another of his 'pets', now married, he wrote that he had no books that he cared to read and that he was tired of pictures and minerals and the sky and the sea. 'But every morning I get some little love-letter from a Joanie or a Mousie which makes me think I had better try and keep awake a little longer.'

The letters which Joan received at Herne Hill began to make her anxious, and eventually he wrote urging her to bring Kate Greenaway down with her immediately. Kate was very anxious to go to him. Like many of Ruskin's young disciples and 'pets' she felt that her relationship with him was unique — that she was the only person who really understood him and could help him. Reluctantly, and against her better judgment, Joan agreed and Kate, delighted at the prospect of being of help to her beloved and revered friend, accompanied her to Sandgate. Here they found Ruskin in a very excitable state.

Kate had never had to deal with him in this condition, though she had been at Brantwood when he was in a state of complete collapse. This man, head-strong and unpredictable in his actions, easily excited or irritated into a passion by a harmless word, was a stranger to her, but she would not leave Joan to cope with him and soothe him as she had succeeded in doing so many times before, and thus avoid a further plunge of his mind into complete insanity. She clung obstinately to the fact that he had begged her to come — he must want her to be there, and though his violence shocked her, she insisted on remaining with him. If Joan could be of help to him why, so could she.

This was the period of his illnesses which Joan most dreaded — when he could appear quite reasonable at times, and at others would do or say the most out-rageous things, mostly associated with reckless spending of money or with rash promises or presents to girls. When he was in this state it was almost im-possible for her to restrain him from actions which he would later deeply regret, yet he was not ill in the sense that he could be put in the charge of a doctor or a nurse. If the attack continued to grow in intensity that would come later. If it

[1] 9th February (1888). John Rylands Library.

waned he would probably fall into despair and hopeless depression which Joan knew better than anyone how to combat.

After a week of this Joan felt the only solution was to go home herself, when Kate would also have to leave. 'I have been here since last Thursday with the Coz,' she wrote to Lady Simon, 'and I hesitated to write because he has been in an excited state, and each day I've hoped it might pass off and I still hope it will. He would ask me to bring Kate Greenaway on a visit, and her influence and presence have I fear not soothed and comforted, or helped the position of things. And of course she's been miserable — and Heaven knows so have I — but as she won't leave as long as I am here, I'm determined to take her back today — and when we're gone, I hope he'll get better. . . . The Coz has set his heart on our going abroad with him in April — it makes me rather quake lest he should get ill, while we're away, and yet I believe the thorough change *might* do him good.'[1]

Among his other girl correspondents Ruskin had lately been writing frequently to Kathleen Olander, instructing her (as he had Connie Hilliard so many years before and more recently, Kate Greenaway) in the mysteries of perspective and giving her a Bible, which she had asked for, after he had offered to lend or give her any of his books that she wished to read, to save her from going to a public library. He had also arranged for her to meet his favourite god-daughter, Connie Oldham, who had puzzled her by hinting that she should not take Ruskin's attentions too seriously.

Kathleen Olander did not take the hint. She was already dreaming of a life when she could be constantly with the Master, perhaps as his secretary, or as she later suggested, his adopted daughter. She was not even daunted when he unexpectedly sent her a number of registered letters for her to forward to various people, quite unknown to her, one of whom was Cardinal Manning, and was annoyed when he found that she had done nothing with them. She was puzzled and confused by his instructions, and dismayed by the loss of religious faith which he revealed in his letters. She was herself in what he described as a state of religious enthusiasm, and replied with letter-sermons which sought again to draw him into the fold.

When Ruskin was in these states of excitement he invariably wrote abusive or unreasonable letters, and the doctor had arranged that all his letters should be sent to Joan, who would suppress any that would give pain or cause embarrassment. Her cousin occasionally managed to evade this control. He had evidently found someone who would post his letters to Kathleen, and this was his reason for sending her letters to forward for him, though she could not know it.

To add to their troubles Ruskin had now embarked on a spending orgy with Quaritch. Joan wrote to Quaritch when she forwarded a letter from Ruskin, ordering rare books and manuscripts to be sent to him on approval.

[1] Sandgate, 7th March (1888). John Rylands Library.

'All my cousin's letters by the Dr.'s orders come at present enclosed to me and so I send one on to you — trusting to your friendship and discretion in answering — only I may warn you that neither he, nor St G's guild have any longer sums of money to buy costly books with — and if he does when he's well feel able to buy the £63 one — he certainly has not the money to buy others. But when these attacks alas! come on he loses all control and understanding of his money matters — so please temporize with him as a friend.'[1] Ruskin signed himself to the book-seller 'Your lovingest J. R.'

Arthur found Joan sad and pre-occupied when she returned to him. Her cousin's last instructions to her were that she was to go immediately to Brantwood to do a number of commissions for him there, but she felt it was essential for her to stay close at hand in case he became worse. 'Of course the poor Coz was both cruel and foolish in having K. G. on a visit,' she wrote to Lady Simon, 'but I believe she pestered him into it, and is herself so foolish in the matter — and quite asserts she has a right to expect all sorts of favours from him after the way he has gone on with her — and perhaps she is right, but oh the sorrow and perplexity of it all. . . . The Coz has been taking on new girl acquaintances, and got very angry with me for showing how I objected to it. It is all inexpressibly sad'.[2]

★

With the worry about her cousin, Joan was anything but her usual cheerful self at Herne Hill, and she would not go about with Arthur or see anyone. The news got worse, her cousin became violent and Dr Bowles had to get a trained attendant for his patient. Joan travelled back and forth between London and Sandgate. Dr Bowles did not think she should remain there for any length of time until Ruskin's health improved. The hotel management refused to keep Ruskin in the hotel, so Joan had him moved into the lodgings, where the landlady was sympathetic and he could be properly nursed.

All through March he was busily ordering rare books and manuscripts from Quaritch, while Joan tried vainly to limit his purchases, knowing how much they would worry him when he recovered. 'The German Historical Bible,' wrote Ruskin from his lodgings to the book-seller, '. . . I believe you priced £400 — but I buy it for St George at the price you named whatever it was, and want it sent down here as soon as ever you can. The other, which you sent down with the Shakespeare — price £63, is one of the best 12th century Psalters I ever saw, and cheap to me at the money.' Three days later he was sending a cheque for £80 written on a fly-leaf and ordering more books. Joan sent on this letter, too, to Quaritch with a covering note of her own: 'I thought it had better to go to you as you are aware *he is not himself* yet — and you must please just keep the cheque for a time and not cash it. Indeed his Bankers have orders not to cash his cheques at present. . . .

[1] (8th March, 1888). *Quaritch*, p. 108.
[2] Sunday (March 1888). John Rylands Library.

'I told my cousin a little while ago that if he spends at the rate of £12,000 a year when he has only £4,000 to spend he must get into difficulties – and the result last year of his extravagance was a collapse for a month when I had to nurse him through the most painful delusions of thinking he hadn't a sixpence – and was starving to death. If his new edition of M.P.'s[1] pays him well enough to enable him to buy some manuscripts no one would rejoice more at his pleasure than I.'[2]

In the meantime Ruskin complained, 'I have been fearfully annoyed since I came here by doctors and servants – my present man Edwin obeys *any* orders but mine! . . . I am getting the reins in hand again, however – and hope to be up in Piccadilly myself, before long.'

Joan continued to send on his letters to Quaritch, enclosing notes from herself. 'I am glad to say my cousin is better – tho' still alas! far from being himself – I send on enclosed knowing you will act discreetly. . . . Do not let him know I have written – he is so suspicious of everything and everybody.' 'I am delighted with the Psalter,' her cousin had written, 'but there is foul play going on somewhere, and I never know if my letters will go safe. . . . Send me your whole catalogue of MSS now on sale.'[3]

Gradually the attack died away. The letters to Quaritch ceased, and Joan was able to spend some days with him, and try yet again to smooth over all the difficulties and complications in which he had become involved. He seemed almost normal, but he would not hear of going to Brantwood, though he particularly wished Joan to go as soon as she left him, to look out some old poems which only she could find.

Arthur took her place at Sandgate. 'He says the Coz *seems very well*,' Joan wrote to Lady Simon. 'I fear he has taken a dislike to Dr Bowles, as he always does to all his Doctors who have attended him when he's ill. Of course he doesn't admit yet that he *has been ill* this time – but he was *very bad indeed*. . . . There were terrible tangles and tiresomenesses, and the usual cheque squanderings, with great violence – and delusions too. . . . I was very thankful he was well enough for me to come here – as it was such a joy to see Violet and Baby! after a 2 months' absence.'[4]

Soon Arthur felt Ruskin was well enough for him to leave him and rejoin his family at Brantwood for a fortnight before going back to London. Ruskin had given Joan a great deal of work to do there, and she heard from him that he had gone to London to see his dentist, meaning to return to Sandgate next day, but had changed his mind and decided to stay. He was 'greatly enjoying his old haunts and seeing people', and had given up the idea of them all going abroad together in the summer. Rumours about his health had penetrated to London from

---

[1] *Modern Painters.*
[2] 23rd March, 1888. *Quaritch*, p. 113.
[3] 28th March, 1888. Ibid., p. 116.
[4] 7th April (1888). John Rylands Library.

Sandgate. 'It is necessary that my friends should once more see me in London
— as I am.'

He had met Kathleen Olander again, at her suggestion, in the National
Gallery, and they had talked together as they walked round the rooms. A few
days later they had another meeting — this time at the South Kensington
Museum, where Kathleen was copying a picture by Thomas Faed, a commission
for which she was to be paid three pounds. Ruskin had always disliked the
original. Kathleen excused herself by calling it a necessary evil, but Ruskin led
her to Turner's picture of Hornby Castle, which he had long admired, and
commissioned her to copy it for him for the sum of twenty guineas.[1]

His daily letters to Joan were on the whole affectionate, but sometimes she
would receive two, written on the same day, entirely different in mood. He was
so thankful to think of her at Brantwood with her children, 'and people will
understand more and more why I gave it you — that you might be happy there
while your Di Pa could still send you love — and get it back again — and you
could forget the woeful times, and the place become your own in peace'. Yet
on the same day he accused her of having separated him from the creatures he
loved. He seemed devoted and anxious to make her happy, but in the same
breath forbade her to interfere in any way with his affairs.[2]

The day after Arthur got back to London he dined with Ruskin at his hotel
and spent most of the next day with him. Their first call was at the exhibition
of the Institute of Painters in Water-Colours in Piccadilly.

'I had a lovely time with Arfie at the Institute,' Ruskin wrote to Joan, ' — two
hours, looking at every picture, and I thought Arfie's much more tender and
refined than ever before.' Then they went to see the Panorama of Niagara,
which delighted him, and afterwards on to the South Kensington Museum,
where he showed Arthur the ruby and the uncut diamond which had cost him
a thousand pounds, both of which he had lately given to the Museum to join
many other gifts over the years. This, as Arthur well knew, was only one of
many institutions to benefit from his generosity and his knowledge — he had
already presented complete collections of minerals, carefully arranged and
catalogued, not only to his own museum at Sheffield, but to other museums and
schools.

He said he felt better and thought of trying the experiment of living in
London for a while. Then, after a long inspection of all the birds' nests in the
Museum, they separated, Arthur feeling uneasy at Ruskin's new plan. But
wherever he lived Joan would worry about him; even when he seemed quite
well she was still anxious. 'I live now in a daily dread of the cloud coming over
us,' she said.[3]

It was very difficult to say what would be best for them all. Wherever he and

[1] *The Gulf of Years*, pp. 41, 47.
[2] Joan Severn to Lady Simon, 25th April (1888). John Rylands Library.
[3] To C. E. Norton, 9th April, 1888. Houghton Library.

Joan might be living she was liable to be called away at any moment, leaving him and the children for an indefinite time, even if she did not beg him to go with her. He could not have left her to cope alone with the terrible attacks which her cousin had suffered, although again and again it had meant giving up all the obligations of his own life, leaving commissions half-finished, prospective clients unseen, meetings unattended, while he interviewed doctors, comforted Joan or tried to calm her cousin and avert some threatened collapse. It was hard to know how it would all end.

JOAN SEVERN AND RUSKIN

RUSKIN'S BEDROOM AT BRANTWOOD WHERE HE DIED
Water colour painted by Arthur for Joan in April 1900 after Ruskin's death.
The pictures are all by Turner except for the two top ones above the fireplace:
the upper is a water colour of Conway Castle painted by Ruskin's father and
the second W. H. Hunt's *Grapes and Peaches*.

ARTHUR PAINTING IN THE WOODS ABOVE BRANT WOOD

CHAPTER 36

SUMMER JOURNEY

1888

A RTHUR AND RUSKIN WERE ENSCONCED IN THE OLD INN at Abbeville, the *Tête de Bœuf*. After his first burst of satisfaction at being in London again, dark depression had settled on Ruskin and he had returned to Sandgate, weighed down by an all-pervading sorrow and haunted by fears of insolvency. His bodily health was good, but nothing seemed to make a rift in the thick curtain of gloom which enfolded his mind. Joan had elicited a promise from him that he would come back to Brantwood, though not at once, which delighted her as she was 'anxious to dispel all the sad association with this dear place'. But at last, as he showed no signs of improvement, she persuaded Arthur to take him to France to see if the change of scene might lift the cloud. Ruskin, too, remembered how his journey abroad six years before had sent him home with renewed energy and able once more to work.

Before leaving Sandgate he wrote to Quaritch, asking him to let Joan know if he heard of anyone who would like to buy the German Bible from him: 'I have been more extravagant than I ought to be.' Then, accompanied by his servant, Baxter, who had now returned to his post, they crossed to Boulogne and journeyed on to Abbeville which Ruskin had once written about so eloquently.

Quaritch had replied by return of post that he would pay Ruskin £400 for the Bible, and Joan was able to tell her cousin and get his agreement before he left. She wrote next day to the bookseller, arranging to bring the precious book to his shop herself: 'My poor cousin alas! tho' he had immense pleasure in it at first, told me "he couldn't lately bear the sight of it – it made him so miserable the thought of his extravagance in buying it, when he couldn't the least afford it".'[1]

At Abbeville Ruskin remained silent and sunk in gloom and Arthur found things very slow. After ten days alone with him, Ruskin still showed no sign of feeling any better or happier in France than he had in England, and Arthur began to wonder if it was worth exiling himself to no purpose.

The correspondence between Kathleen Olander and Ruskin had been stopped by her parents when they heard about the twenty-guinea commission; they regarded the sum as suspiciously large. They had subsequently relented,

---

[1] 11th June, 1888. *Quaritch*, p. 118.

influenced perhaps by her obvious unhappiness and by her complaint that they had made her lose a great chance of progress in her chosen career. Just before he left for France Ruskin had resumed his correspondence with her in the midst of his deep melancholy.

She was intrigued by the frequent references to Joan in his letters and by his evident devotion to her. 'You ask me to tell you about Mrs Severn,' he wrote from Abbeville, 'but you can't be told about her, except by her own sweet face — she has been life and strength to me these twenty years, and now I am become — too often — in my fits of illness — only a torment to her. Here is just a little scrap of letter of her's — for you to begin to get an idea of her by.'[1]

After this he sent several of Joan's letters on to her to read, as he had earlier done with some from Francesca. Kathleen, youthful and earnest, disapproved of them as too petty and childish to be written to such a man. She was scornful of the baby talk which Ruskin so much enjoyed, and would have been surprised to see his own letters to his cousin.

Joan at home was hoping that Ruskin would return in better health to Brantwood. One of her cousin's most trying habits when he was not quite himself was to invite, or beg Joan to invite, various friends or acquaintances — usually girls — to stay at Brantwood, when he was not there himself.

'The Coz is better and more cheerful and does not show so much anxiety about money,' Arthur wrote to her. '*I do hope you have got Miss Warren to go* — please do. I am sure she has been long enough there — the Coz never mentions her or thinks anything about her being there or not — he never mentions anyone. If he writes to you as if he were in the depths, just remember that, and think him better. I much prefer him rather down — it is such a bore when he rides his high horse!' He thought of returning towards the end of the month. He could take Ruskin with him to Salisbury and Stourbridge, and leave him at an inn for a week while he went on a visit to friends the other side of the New Forest, where he wanted to paint.

'As being in France seems to be so little extra pleasure to him, it seems he might as well be in England. But if he thinks he would like to go on staying here a little, and I think I can leave him for a time, I will.' He sent messages to their pretty governess, Clennie, who was leaving them and going back to Scotland. Both he and Joan were very fond of her and Ruskin, when he had got over his *pique* at her shyness with him, had also become attached to her and admired her beauty, which was very striking.

'The Portrait will have to be finished when she comes to pay us a visit some day! *Mind* you do not say a thing to the Coz about her going for good — there is no occasion to mention it at all. . . . The Coz seemed pleased with your letter about the play and supper party — and I am sure he *ought* — but I never think he has much real heart, and I am afraid he will sink into a kind of stupid state. . . .

'I am keeping abroad as long as I can stand it — to be of service to you —

[1] *The Gulf of Years*, p. 53.

besides I feel we had such a nice time at Brantwood. But between ourselves I am dreadfully bored sometimes. . . . Just read through your long letter! All right – I will stay on for the present, I only thought of going if he seemed much better – or of returning with him.'[1]

Help was on the way for Arthur in the shape of young Sydney Cockerell and a friend of the same age, Detmar Blow, who had landed at Dieppe, armed with a copy of Ruskin's *Bible of Amiens*, intending to study the architecture which he had described. Their quest led them to the cobbled streets of Abbeville and by a coincidence to the *Tête de Bœuf*. There were few other visitors in the hotel and they were astonished, as they sat alone at breakfast the next morning, to see Ruskin and Arthur Severn enter and seat themselves at a round table at the other end of the room. Cockerell's first thrill of pleasure at meeting his hero at the very beginning of his fortnight's holiday, in circumstances so favourable for daily intercourse, quickly turned to doubt whether he should make any sign of recognition, as they had unwittingly discovered Ruskin's retreat. His doubts were soon put at rest when Ruskin presently rose from his table and approached them with a smile, introducing Arthur to them and being introduced in turn to young Detmar Blow, who was training to become an architect and could scarcely believe his good fortune in so unexpectedly meeting the great man. In no time they had become a party of four.

Immediately after the meal Arthur and Detmar Blow went off to sketch, and Ruskin led Cockerell through the narrow, crooked streets, showing him his favourite corners of the old town – a carved wooden stairway entwined by a green vine, a picturesque group of houses, a view across the river which he had often drawn. Occasionally he pointed out places where beautiful buildings had disappeared and sunk again into a gloomy mood. But the appearance of the two young men had certainly made him less sad and for the next week, while Arthur and Detmar drew the west front of St Wulfran's Church from an empty house opposite, Ruskin and Cockerell continued their exploration of the town.

All four made an expedition one day to the battlefield of Creçy – but it was not a success. It rained, the horse's harness broke and had to be mended with string and, worst blow of all, the windmill from which Edward III was said to have watched the battle had been destroyed during the previous year. The circular foundations of chalk were all that remained. Ruskin was much downcast.[2]

Next day Cockerell heard that he could have an extra week's holiday and it was decided that they should all move on together. Arthur and the two young men packed their luggage and went to Amiens for a night to see the Cathedral, but Ruskin refused to accompany them – he feared that his many acquaintances in the town would pester him and he did not feel equal to company. He and Baxter followed the next day, met them at the railway station, and they all

[1] Tuesday (20th June, 1888). Education Trust.
[2] Arthur Severn's Memoirs.

travelled on together to Beauvais. Here the weather improved. The sun shone and Ruskin's spirits suddenly rose. 'Carlyle (Sydney Cockerell) carries my umbrella for me as if he were attending the Emperor of Japan,' he wrote to Joan, and 'Detmar is as good as gold.'

Next day he wrote cheerfully again, praising Arthur's work. 'He has been doing some beautiful sketches on the river at Abbeville – with more tree drawing than I've seen him do before – and two sunsets here behind the Cathedral – of which I shall let him have no peace till he paints one big. Also I really admit that I am the least tiny bit better today than when I crossed.'[1]

He began to draw again and in the evening, instead of playing cards, he read a French play aloud to his young friends, translating as he read. Joan had written to say how proud she felt at his praise of Arthur's sketches, and he answered with a suggestion that they might do a picture together. He particularly admired the sunset that Arthur had painted, and was reminded of one of his own sketches which had been reproduced in *Modern Painters* under the title *Light in the West – Beauvais*. 'Now this sunset of Arthur's is ... brighter and more stormy than mine – but as, next year, I hope there will be a good deal of talk about *M.P.*[2], suppose ... that the Institute were to elect me an Hon. Member like the Old Water-colour – and that Arfie and I sent in a blazer called *Light in the West – Beauvais*, Arfie doing the sunset and I the Cathedral?'

★

Arthur was delighted to find Ruskin so happy in the companionship of the two young men. He felt now that he could leave him with a clear conscience. He had been sorely tempted for some time, since he received an invitation from his friend, Froude, to join a yachting trip to Norway and Ireland on Lord Ducie's yacht, *Monarch, R.Y.S.*, and it had been very hard for him not to accept at once. Before he left, he told Joan, he did all he could to ensure that everything would go well after his departure.

'I showed the Coz where the Bank was, and told him all about the way to get the money and everything. I do hope he won't be silly, and make presents to girls. I gave Cockerell and Blow strong hints of his tendencies in that direction, and they are both very nice simple innocent young men. I would *not notice* anything about girls he says to you – as I am sure you have had trouble enough. ... He always makes presents or gives money – and then because the people are very civil, thinks he has made a conquest.'[3]

Arthur would have been less happy had he known that the very next day Ruskin would be writing to Joan to suggest that she should invite Kathleen Olander to stay at Brantwood, though he would not be there himself. 'I'm obliged to be rather cautious,' he told Kathleen, 'because I'm afraid she's just

---

[1] Beauvais, 8th July (1888). *Works*, vol. 37, p. 605.
[2] The new edition of *Modern Painters*.
[3] 14th July, 1888. Education Trust.

the least bit more jealous of *you* than she is of my pets in general, but it will be all right when once you're there – and I want you to paint some moss on rocks! and some clear pools in the streams.'[1] He had already asked Kathleen about it and been told that her parents would be pleased for her to go. On the same day he wrote to her father and suggested that before she went to Brantwood, he might bring his daughter to Beauvais for a week. None of these plans came to anything.

Cockerell stayed with Ruskin until the end of his holiday – he afterwards said that they were perhaps the happiest seven days of his whole life. Ruskin's magnetism for the young remained, and it was the only company which he could now in any way enjoy; but even with them gloom would sometimes overcome him. One evening he told Cockerell sadly that after his last illness he had suffered great pain because of his ingratitude 'to dear friends'. He did not mention Joan's name, but quoted

> 'And to be wroth with one we love
> Doth work like madness in the brain.'

He told the young man that in his melancholy moods he was so conscious of the utter failure of his life that he lost all hope of ever again being with the saintly Rose – 'the girl he loved'.[2]

Reluctantly Cockerell had to return home, but Detmar Blow was free of obligations and delighted to accompany Ruskin and Baxter on a further journey to Paris and on over 'the old road', to Dijon, the Jura, Geneva and Sallenches. The reports of Ruskin's health from Detmar Blow and Baxter were not all good. He had been 'fearfully enraged' with a photographer at Beauvais and was 'put out very much' at Joan knowing that he was going to Paris. In one of his fits of suspicion he forbade Detmar Blow to write to anyone except his father.

Quaritch also incurred his displeasure. Ruskin had lately told Joan to enquire, and had himself asked, what the bookseller would give him for the original manuscripts of *St Ronan's Well* and *Peveril of the Peak* by Walter Scott. But before there was time to answer Ruskin had received the cheque for the German Bible, and found that Quaritch had sent him only half the money, as a first instalment, meaning to pay the rest later. This infuriated Ruskin, who immediately wrote a letter addressed to 'The Book Keeper' of Quaritch's firm: 'Kindly inform Mr Quaritch . . . that I have no further occasion for his catalogues.' This was followed a week later by a broadside: 'As Mr Quaritch deputes you to manage his most private business, will you kindly notify to that Gentleman that I hold the Toggenburg MS. to be mine, not his.' He could write to the Berlin Library if he wished, saying that the book was not his to sell, but Professor Ruskin, to whom it belonged, would sell it to Berlin for a thousand gold pieces, and if they refused he would sell it to the British Museum, and if *they* refused

---

[1] 15th July, 1888. *The Gulf of Years*, p. 55.
[2] *Friends of a Life-Time*, p. 54.

Professor Ruskin meant to keep it himself. 'My legal ground of claim is that Mr Q. agreed to pay £400 by the middle of July – not 280 ... by the 10th.' If Quaritch disputed the ownership Ruskin would take him to court.[1]

★

At the Hotel Meurice in Paris Ruskin's behaviour alarmed his young companion, but Baxter still hoped to avoid a breakdown. 'I do believe if he keeps on the move he will be all right yet,' he wrote to Joan, but added, 'He was very full of Gussie, Jane Anne and Maggie Borns[2] last night. . . . The Master has given it to Allen something awful – he read it all over to me – a sheet of foolscap. I think if Mr Allen ever had any doubts about his sanity they will be removed now.'[3]

Ruskin sent daily scraps of diary to Joan. He seemed to get better after leaving Paris. In Sallenches he wrote another chapter of his autobiography and talked of 'life given back to me.' He would go on to Chamonix, 'wearying sadly for letters', he said, ' – much more than at Paris. I behaved so shockingly there that I was afraid every letter would be a scolding!'[4]

At Chamonix he wrote that he was 'entirely well – so far as I know – some little stomach symptoms plaguing me again a little', and again 'I dreamed more than I like last night'.[5] He finished the Epilogue for the new edition of *Modern Painters* and then the travellers went on down into Italy, to stay with Francesca Alexander and her mother at Bassano, Ruskin carrying with him the rosewood box containing Rose's precious letters, which still went everywhere with him.

As he journeyed across Europe he had been in correspondence with Kathleen Olander. She had sent him a book of daily texts which he now used with the one given him long ago by Rose (through which he believed that she sent him guidance) and earnest messages of her affection and loyalty. When Ruskin wrote jokingly that she could never come near Paris – it was too wicked a place for Irish girls – or even girls with Irish names, he corrected himself quickly – she replied at once that there was no place so wicked that she would not meet him in it. When he wrote from Dijon that he was being fearfully teased by everyone he knew, she answered 'Kathleen will never tease you', and that she had wanted him dreadfully since their last meeting in the South Kensington Museum. He planned to have a necklace made for her in Venice, he told her, of seven fine chains of the purest gold. She must send the measurement – 'just above the shoulders'.[6]

Ten days later he was writing to Joan from the foot of the Simplon Pass that he felt 'horribly alone' and far away with no letters having come. He couldn't understand at all how his money had gone. 'I wish you would ask Mr Lees if

---

[1] 26th July, 1888. *Quaritch*, p. 124.
[2] All Coniston school-children and among his 'pets'.
[3] 7th August, 1888. Education Trust.
[4] Madonna's Birthday (8th September) 1888. John Rylands Library.
[5] 16th, 18th September, 1888. University of Illinois Library.
[6] 9th September, 1888. *The Gulf of Years*, p. 67.

he would mind lending me £500 till the end of the year . . . the hotel bills are fearful.'[1]

Ruskin was engaged in writing the chapter in his autobiography which told of the beginning of his love for Rose, and reading and re-reading her letters to him. Since long before her death she had been an obsession to him. Even so many years afterwards he could still reproach himself bitterly to Francesca for his own part in their unhappy story, and torture himself with wondering if he could have done anything to save her. While these thoughts were freshened in his brain by re-reading her letters and writing of those happy days when he had first loved her, this other young girl, Kathleen Olander, had come into his life.

They had met in all only four times, but she wrote sermons in her letters as Rose had done, she sent him hymns which she had copied out for him, again like Rose; her parents, like Rose's, had forbidden them to meet or correspond – though they had later relented. The slip in his letter when he spoke of her as an Irish girl – though he had quickly changed it to a reference to her name – had shown how inter-mingled in his brain the two girls had become, just as St Ursula in Carpaccio's picture had become mixed with Rose in his mind in Venice, before his first bad breakdown.

On his way to Milan he wrote to Joan that he was 'in one of my worst downs – Italy being infinitely sad to me'. The deadly melancholy was creeping over him. He found himself so much feebler, he wrote from Milan, 'and a languor on me such as I have not had since Abbeville – and scarcely there. . . . My Doanie, me *is* so sorry I left the Jura where I was so well and happy.'[2]

His letters to Kathleen Olander, though still playful, became more excited and finally, in a letter from Milan, he wrote that he had been getting ill again but that her two letters were new life to him. 'That little postscript to the second letter . . . sends me quite wild with joy – for now, because you can be to me all I need, so can I be to you.' If she had held back he would have tried to be what she wished to her, but 'it could only have been torment as well as joy – not health and peace, as with God's blessing it will be now'. In his mind the romance with Rose was repeating itself – but with a happy ending. It was only love that he wanted, to keep him sane. 'I am as pure – except in thought – as you are – but it is *terrible* for any creature of my temper to have no wife – one cannot but go mad.'[3] His letter to Joan next morning was full of the old excitement, though he made no reference to Kathleen Olander: 'And now I'm going to make *Praeterita* as sweet as honey, now that Rosie has come into it, and you're coming! My Doanie, we will make oo so pitty, and so dood – and say how much me loves oo and always did.'[4]

At the Alexanders' summer villa at Bassano he was surrounded by affection

[1] Wednesday, 19th September, 1888. University of Illinois Library.
[2] 23rd September, 1888. University of Illinois Library.
[3] 25th September, 1888. *The Gulf of Years*, pp. 77–8.
[4] Verona, 26th September, 1888. University of Illinois Library.

and confessed himself among the kindest people in the world, 'but oh, di ma, they have the energy of American rivers, — endless'. He could no longer compete with society. 'I am so sick at heart to be so far from you. . . . It is impossible to say how kind these people all are to me, but they take me to see gardens and picture galleries, when the ladies of the garden and directors of the gallery come out to do me honour and show me everything — and there's scarcely ever anything I care to see. My own Brantwood-Strawberry-hill is worth any quantity of Italian gardens and the pictures above my bed worth any quantity of Italian galleries and I don't know what to say nor how to answer and am in misery.'

'I want to come home again dreadfully but don't know how to manage it,' he wrote to her next day. 'Oh my Doanie — if you could get me out of this, as you got me out of Sandgate! — I'd never go far away from you again.'[1]

The next day he received a letter from Kathleen Olander. She had taken fright at the word 'wife' in his excited letter from Milan. 'I have your grievous letter of the 1st,' he wrote back sadly. 'I will be to you always what you bid — and love you always as you choose. . . . The sin would be in my letting you — or in your consent — sacrifice your youth to my old age.'[2]

In her fright Kathleen had consulted her mother and had reluctantly been made to give up to her parents all Ruskin's letters. They wrote forbidding him to have anything more to do with their daughter.

The following day he brought himself to leave his kind friends Francesca and her mother, and went on to Venice. As always after a period of excitement he had sunk back into melancholy. 'I feel it absolutely necessary to come to some close of the sort of life I was leading,' he wrote to Joan as he was leaving, 'and mammina is so excitable that I'm terrified she'll telegraph or do something to frighten my own Di wee ma. Heaven knows I should love to have her here, but I must come home to her — and there shall be no more wanderings from under her wing.'[3]

*

Nothing now seemed to lighten his despondency. Detmar Blow had turned out to be the kindest and most considerate companion. Ruskin knew that he had never been to Venice before, but he could not bring himself to introduce him to anyone. Those who saw him thought he looked frail and that his talk was vague. He stayed only ten days — the excitement of all the old associations in Venice was too much for him. 'I can only write you from here the sort of sighs and whines I used to send from Abbeville,' he wrote to Joan. 'I was an infinite fool not to hold on at Beauvais where I was so well and busy. . . . But oh my di wee ma I hope you feel how much I always love you now — whether happy or unhappy. If happy — it is to you I come to exult — if unhappy to you for help.'[4]

[1] Bassano, 2nd–3rd October (1888). University of Illinois Library.
[2] *The Gulf of Years*, pp. 81–2.
[3] Bassano, Friday, 5th (October), 1888. John Rylands Library.
[4] Venice, Sunday, 7th October, 1888. University of Illinois Library.

Throughout the tour his mood had fluctuated between terrible despondency and excitement, when he had suffered from occasional delusions and odd, unreasonable fancies. Now he seemed fixed deep in depression. The little party moved on from Venice to Switzerland, where the mountain villages which he had once loved almost to ecstasy evoked no response from his often clouded brain. Joan wrote to him from Brantwood every day, bright cheerful letters such as he most liked; his own letters showed the melancholy which he was powerless to banish.

'Oh my Doanie my Doanie — if only I can see your sweet face again — and be yet the source of some happiness to you. I hate sending this, but I *am* in one of my low fits — that's a fact — and its no use trying to hide it. . . . There's nothing to answer to such a letter as this. I know with what loving comfy you would answer, if you could.'[1]

During his short time of excitement he had written to Paris and engaged lodgings for the winter for 400 francs a month — 'lovely rooms in the Parisian old-fashioned style'. Now he worried about having to pay the landlord and found that he could concentrate on nothing. 'I cannot employ myself any more than . . . when Arfie had the burden of me at Abbeville. . . . This letter leaves at three o'clock and then I've the whole long afternoon with nothing to do but think!'

He had left behind him in England a number of bills, incurred during his excited state at Sandgate, when he had been recklessly extravagant. Joan told him that she had obeyed his instructions to raise money by selling a book of early Florentine drawings, and that Sidney Colvin had bought it for the British Museum. 'I shall be very thankful to pay my debt to Mr Lees,' he wrote to her, 'but I will keep the full balance at the bankers for a little while. . . . I am trying to make up my mind this afternoon to start for the north — but it is such a puzzled and sad sapless little mind.'[2]

He planned to go to Berne 'and be the least bit nearer you', he wrote. 'I can't bear leaving the mountains yet it seems doing me no good to stay. . . . They are so lovely in the autumn colour and light — but I do want my Doanie more than all the lights and colours in the world — only I should only make her misby if I came to her.'[3]

The daily letters arrived at Brantwood, now from Merligen on the Lake of Thun, with their sad yearnings. In this mood he could see his life only as a gigantic failure and feared to return to her lest he should make her unhappy again. Joan would try to reassure and comfort him.

'I have to-day your precious Sat[y] and Monday letters. . . . My Doanie, everything you say to me and tell me is too lovely and I am trying to think the best of myself — and hope all for you that it is still left in oos poo Di Pa to be to

[1] Milan, 18th October, 1888. University of Illinois Library.
[2] Fluelen, 26th October (1888). John Rylands Library.
[3] 28th, 30th October, 1888. University of Illinois Library.

M*

you. (I should like to write a little diary for you only – and translate pretty plays for you only – and buy all the pretty things in Paris for you only – and then take Arfie and Lily to Pau with us ... and – my mind wanders on from wish to wish.) ... The one pleasure of the day is my Doanie's word, and imagined look, and yet to-day I don't know how to tell you where to write or when to look for me. But the rain has come – and the snow is low on the hills.'[1]

He and Detmar and the faithful Baxter lingered at Thun for another three weeks and then moved to Berne, but Ruskin remained bowed down with an inescapable conviction of guilt, in which all that he had done in his life seemed 'ruinously and unpardonably wrong'. At Berne he was so much worse that his companions decided to make for home without delay. They managed to get him as far as Paris, and from the Meurice Hotel telegraphed to Joan to come immediately. Joan responded to the call at once, and with a heavy heart found her cousin in the grip of fearful depression, suffering from morbid and painful illusions and subject to attacks of violent trembling.

After five days in the hotel, with no sign of any improvement in his condition, she felt that it would be better to take him back to England, where she could nurse him more easily and where his own doctors could see him. So the painful journey was made and for three weeks they remained at Herne Hill, with no change for the better in her cousin's health.

It was a sad Christmas away from the children, and immediately afterwards Joan decided to take him to Brantwood. But after ten days there she wrote to Professor Norton that she was anxious that the illness might be settling into a permanent form.

However, by the time that the holidays ended and the three older children had gone off to school, he had 'recovered wonderfully. We have quite long intervals ... when he is apparently his sweet self again.' This attack had alarmed her more than the others, she told Norton, it had lasted so long without a change. Now the trembling had quite gone. Her younger daughter, Violet, had been ill, Arthur had sprained his left wrist severely, but Joan was happy because her beloved Coz was better.

---

[1] Saturday, 3rd November, 1888. John Rylands Library.

CHAPTER 37

SUNSET AT CONISTON

1889 - *January*, 1900

SPRING CAME TO CONISTON. Daffodils flowered round the little harbour where the *Jumping Jenny* lay, while Arthur's sailing-boat, *Lily of Brantwood*, bobbed at her moorings, and soon Joan's gentians bloomed brilliant blue in the border running down to the lake. The first buds to open she cut and put in the bow-window of her cousin's study, with three early roses. After months of nursing, she loved to think of little things that could give him pleasure, now that he was convalescent. He was well enough to write a few letters, but only to his closest friends. One day he spent going through the drawer in which he kept all Kate Greenaway's drawings. It had not been unlocked for such a long time, he wrote to her, and now it had sent 'balm and rose and lily sweetness all through the old study'. He hoped she might come and do some drawing at Brantwood, 'and poor Joanie will be so thankful to have somebody to look after me a little, as well as her'.

To Francesca he wrote in a less happy moment, still torturing himself about the old tragedy, and asking if she thought he was answerable for Rosie's death. Francesca's reply was comforting – 'I know you would have saved her if you could,' she wrote. 'If any were to blame they were those who parted her from you; and I do not blame even them as I did once, for believe me, *Fratello*, that I do not say it to comfort you but because I feel sure it is true. She would never have lived long! The beautiful face that hangs before me in the little silver frame ... was never made for this world.'[1]

He even began to work again on *Praeterita*. Old letters and journals were collected together, with the help of Collingwood and Diddie Anderson, and the titles of the chapters chosen. In vain Joan tried to make him rest. 'He has been writing again,' she told Professor Norton, '... *Praeterita*. ... My life now is full of increasing anxiety about *him* – and one might as well prevent the sea coming in ... as keep him from *working*. In defiance of all entreaties, he drowns one's reasoning with his own, and anger at any thwarting of his wishes is worse than anything.'[2]

Trying to keep his effort as small as possible, she would write at his dictation. Three chapters of the third volume of *Praeterita* were already done. Nine more

---

[1] May 1889. Education Trust.
[2] 14th May, 1889. Houghton Library.

343

had been planned. But he felt his strength ebbing and determined to write, while he still could, a chapter about Joan, which would make up for some of the suffering he had caused her.

Out of his tragedy he wrought one last thing of beauty, the chapter entitled *Joanna's Care*. In it the effort and the heartbreak were hidden, and the happy innocence of the days when Joan came to live with a mother and son in the house on Denmark Hill were brought to life again.

'Just read your number of *Praeterita*,' Froude wrote to Joan. 'I thought it not only absolutely true as regards you, but as in itself the most beautiful of the series which have yet appeared — calm, mellow, charming, without a trace of excitement, with all sorts of lovely thoughts flitting about like the blue moths on a summer evening.'[1]

In desperate hope of keeping him well Joan took her cousin to Seascale on the coast for a change and sea air. Collingwood and Baxter came with them, but Joan's advice to relax went unheeded. 'In his bedroom at Seascale, morning after morning, he still worked, or tried to work,' wrote Collingwood. '. . . But now he seemed lost among the papers scattered on his table; he could not fix his mind upon them, and turned from one subject to another in despair; and yet patient, and kindly to those with him whose help he could no longer use, and who dared not show . . . how heart-breaking it was.'[2]

Driving with Joan about the countryside in the afternoon now gave Ruskin no pleasure, and an attempt to sketch had to be abandoned. On their return to Brantwood, his condition again gave rise to acute anxiety. Professor Norton was the latest of his intimate friends to be the recipient of abusive letters, though by the time Joan heard of it her cousin seemed to have made a sudden recovery. She wrote on his behalf, sending apologies to his old friend, about whom he had just written so affectionately in *Praeterita*. 'I am sure he feels the remorse and pain the matter merits, only we must bear and forgive, knowing that he was *not himself* when he wrote those letters . . . just as when he nearly breaks *my* heart with torture and reproaches. . . . Yes, I thank you gratefully for grasping in some measure what I have continually to endure . . . in these terrible attacks and yet, just now, he is as tender and sweet and dear as ever at his best time.'[3]

Arthur had spent a large part of the summer in London. He was one of a group of artists who had been invited each to design a page in an illuminated album, which was to be presented to his father's old friend, William Gladstone, for his Golden Wedding.[4] A great meeting of friends and supporters gathered at the National Liberal Club on 26th July, and after the book had been given to

---

[1] 12th July (1889). In possession of Dr H. G. Viljoen.
[2] Collingwood, op. cit., vol. II, p. 243.
[3] 11th July, 1889. Houghton Library.
[4] It is interesting to note that Arthur's niece, Margaret Birkenhead, was one of the contributors to the *Golden Book of Roses* given by their children to Sir Winston and Lady Churchill for their Golden Wedding in 1958.

the great man and his wife, the artists were presented to him in turn. He questioned each of them about his design and was evidently delighted with the album. He was now eighty years old, but after the ceremony made an eloquent speech, speaking without apparent effort, and received an ovation from his audience.

★

Meanwhile Ruskin's condition had worsened again, and in August he suffered another terribly severe attack, from which for a long time he showed no sign of recovering. For months he had no idea where he was, and did not recognize anyone about him.

'I am sorry to hear the Professor is still very bad,' wrote Stacy Marks to Joan at the beginning of September, 'and that he has such a strange fancy of being under the impression that you are only a heap of stones — you of all people whose *heart* is the utmost antithesis of anything so hard.'[1]

Her cousin still lay in bed as autumn passed into winter. Sometimes he recognized her, but he was very feeble. 'His condition seems never now to improve and if there are even a few days of betterness he lapses off again . . . into a state of blankness,' she told Professor Norton. 'He looks comfortable and placid — and eats and sleeps well . . . but mentally he seems to get weaker.'[2]

One of Joan's most comforting correspondents now was Kate Greenaway, who wrote constantly and entered into all her hopes and fears. When after more than three months of unremitting care, Joan planned to go with Arthur for a little while to London, Kate wrote encouragingly to her: 'I think you are so wise to go away sometimes to live your own life as much as you can, and with Mackay and Baxter there, all must go right — and besides, the little changes help you to bear the terrible times when they come.'[3] And in February she sent Joan a Valentine which she had drawn for him.

Arthur and Joan went in the spring to the official opening of the Ruskin Museum at Sheffield, where, in a large house supplied by the Corporation, there were displayed the pictures, books, casts, coins and minerals which Ruskin had bought for his St George's Guild. But it was useless for them to try to explain to him where they had been. He had 'little glimmers of consciousness in which he *almost seems* to be himself and then lapses in a vague blank state again', Joan told Professor Norton. 'Even in this sad condition, I feel that to lose him would be heartbreaking.'[4]

From the moment of their sad homecoming to Brantwood she would never leave him, even for a few days, unless Diddie Anderson could be in charge. On

---

[1] 4th September, 1889. In possession of Dr H. G. Viljoen.
[2] 7th November, 1889. Houghton Library.
[3] 20th November, 1889. Education Trust.
[4] 26th April (1890). Houghton Library.

occasions when it was necessary for her to go to London on family business or to visit the two older boys who were now at Westminster, and Diddie could not be at Brantwood, Arthur would remain there while she was away. Lily, too, was at school in London, and Kate Greenaway was very kind in having her often to her house.

Ruskin remained silent and seemingly without any desire to do anything. He would go out, but only if taken. Joan did not despair, and soon she was writing to Norton that he could 'sustain pleasant little chats at times — and is as sweet and dear to us all as can be'.[1]

Their old friend, Henry Holiday, paid a few days' visit that summer and was taken by Joan to see her cousin when he was in one of his brighter moods. She warned that he must not be tired with too much talk, and said she would come in when she thought he should rest. Holiday was struck by Ruskin's 'peculiarly gentle' manner after his illness. He seemed to enjoy the talk and when Joan appeared, suggesting that Holiday should come to Arthur's studio, he took hold of his guest's wrist and said he could not spare him. The change that Holiday noticed most was a 'softening of the aggressive side' of his nature. Arthur looked in after a few minutes (probably at Joan's instigation) and said he would be in the studio whenever Holiday liked to come and have a cigarette. This suggestion would have infuriated Ruskin only a short time ago, for he had always felt a great aversion to smoking, but in his new-found gentle calm it only brought a smile.

By Christmas, sixteen months after his collapse on his return from Seascale, he was going out regularly for two walks a day, either with one of the Severns or with Baxter. If the weather kept him indoors he would play battledore and shuttlecock with Joan and the children, and he liked to play games of chess or cards or tiddly-winks in the evening with the family. 'He enjoys being talked to and hearing what goes on and looks at simple books... and now and then the papers,' Joan told Professor Norton. 'He looks his old self — eyes as blue as ever, doesn't get over-excited or difficult, but is easy and pleasant to manage.' Baxter was excellent; it had not been necessary to have a trained mental attendant in the house for several months. 'The Coz shuns pen and ink and paper as a child the fire who has been burnt — and a good thing too.'[2]

Their friend, Harvey Goodwin, the Bishop of Carlisle, who had comforted Joan when she was ill and unhappy after the break with her cousin, came with his wife to stay at Brantwood for a service in Coniston Church. He was now seventy-three years old and had been Bishop of the diocese for twenty-two years. He had stayed at Brantwood often in happier times.

When they arrived the Bishop did not look well, but after a short rest he seemed quite himself at dinner. The service at Coniston was next day and they were to leave early the following morning. Ruskin sent a message that he would

---

[1] 23rd September. Houghton Library.
[2] 27th December, 1890. Houghton Library.

very much like to take leave of them, and the departing guests came to his room in the morning, but when they had said goodbye the Bishop noticed a look come over Ruskin's face as though he had expected something more. Quickly understanding what was passing in his mind, the Bishop raised his hands over him saying 'The Lord bless you and keep you. The Lord lift up the light of His countenance upon you, and give you peace, both now and ever more. Amen.'[1] From Brantwood the Bishop went on to visit the Archbishop at York, and there, exactly a week later, he died.

★

So the months passed at Brantwood, with Joan engrossed by the care of her beloved Coz — though her heart was large enough to take him in without excluding anyone else.

Since Ruskin's latest illness his secretary, Collingwood, had returned with his family to live nearby, at a house only a mile from Brantwood on the road to the village, and had embarked on a biography of his employer. When the first volume was finished Sydney Cockerell, who had helped him with it, came to stay at Lanehead, the Collingwoods' home, to read the proofs over Easter. They dined at Brantwood and Cockerell was full of emotion at seeing his hero again. He was more feeble, more bent, he thought, his beard longer and whiter, his smile subdued. But he took the young man's hand and spoke a little in a very low voice about their days together at Beauvais. Joan soon produced a chess board, and after a game with Cockerell, Ruskin yielded his place to Arthur, and sat listening in silence, while Joan played and sang to them. Then she took him away to bed.

'It is a sort of calm drifting of life,' Joan wrote of her cousin to Professor Norton. It never occurred to her that anyone might find her beloved Coz frightening. He took his meals alone in his study and Violet, now aged twelve, 'always takes him his bread and cheese and butter nicely cut into mouthfuls at luncheon — and Herbert' (not ten years old as she wrote) 'an orange nicely cut up, and a small liqueur glass . . . of cherry brandy'.[2] So much did she love her cousin that she could not imagine that for a child to wait, alone, on a silent old man with a long white beard and something unusual and incalculable in his presence might be a frightening ordeal.

Arthur's one-man exhibition in October at the galleries of the Fine Art Society was a great success. In all he showed eighty-eight pictures which he had painted in widely separated places — many at Brantwood or nearby, a number at sea — others painted at Amiens and Venice, and several London river-scenes. Almost all of them showed effects of light on water — whether sea-waves, lake or river — or of sunsets, moonlight or dawn. Ruskin had intended to write an

[1] *Harvey Goodwin, Bishop of Carlisle* by H. D. Rawnsley, pp. 325–6.
[2] 5th February, 1892. Houghton Library.

Introduction to the catalogue, but he was no longer capable of it, so that Arthur was called upon to write something himself, which he was not unwilling to do as, like his father, he was under the impression that he could write well if he chose.

'I am sorry that for this exhibition of mine, I cannot get Ruskin to write something,' he began, 'but it is out of the question in his present state of health. If he had been well enough, I am sure he would have written me a preface, and a very interesting one too! as he would have been able to have some nice hits at some of us painters who go out of our way to paint atmospheric effects in London and elsewhere, produced by fog and smoke and gloom, and which suggest what he considers mere squalor and the smoke which he hates. . . . With Ruskin, I have always noticed, a great deal depends on association of ideas in his mind in looking at a scene in nature. A hayfield at Coniston in the early morning dew, with blue sky above, or a rock covered with beautiful moss, is to him a subject to enjoy and paint if possible. He once offered me a carriage and pair to drive, I don't know how many miles, and fifty guineas when the work was done, if I would draw a particular rock with velvety moss growing about it. . . . Had I done a London subject, equally well, he wouldn't have cared a straw. . . .

'In my small way I think I may claim to be the first artist who seriously took up the beautiful effect produced upon buildings and sky in London by smoke and fog. So also was I the first to see that breaking waves could be made a subject by themselves, without the necessity of adventitious aids of rocks, or wrecks, or fishermen hauling up impossible pieces of mast.'

The Exhibition had very good notices and the sales of the pictures amounted to well over seven hundred pounds.

Ruskin's old friend, Henry Acland, came to stay with them that summer, bringing his daughter, Angie, with him. He was now seventy-eight years of age — four years older than Ruskin — and had been made a baronet three years before. Angie Acland was a skilled photographer, and during their visit she took several photographs of the two old men together. They had been friends for more than fifty years.

Lily Severn was now grown up, twenty years old. She was not as pretty as her mother, but had a beautiful, slender figure, refused to be stiffly corseted as most women were at that time, dressed well, in somewhat unusual colours. She played the piano, loved riding and like her father, enjoyed parties and meeting people. Joan left Brantwood so seldom now that Arthur fell into the habit of taking his elder daughter about with him, first in London, then on a long summer journey round Italy, where they stayed with the Alexanders in Florence. He found Lily a good companion, bright, interested in new places, and appreciative of his stories. 'Here comes Lily — white and eager,' he once remarked as she entered a room. Arthur remained very youthful in appearance, with a trim figure and thick dark hair; he was full of energy. He would not allow Lily to call him 'Papa' — on these expeditions she always addressed him as 'George darling'.

Lily was a year older than young Arthur, who had to be specially coached to pass into Oxford and went up after Agnew, who was a year his junior. Both were keen athletes, and Arthur was to achieve the distinction of staying up at Oxford for four years without passing a single examination. He was small, had great charm and a sad, low voice and although unacademic played football and cricket for his college, coxed an eight in the bumping races, rode in point-to-points and was elected to innumerable clubs. Agnew was taller and handsome, with a strong resemblance to his mother. He was at Christ Church, she told Professor Norton in one of her letters, '*not* I'm thankful to say among the rowdy lot'.[1] Violet played the piano quite well, liked riding better than anything else, and was not very good at her lessons. 'Herbert seems to have more brain than the others.'

The Severn children, and particularly Lily, had a rather exaggerated way of talking, which was partly derived from their father's way of telling a story with more regard for effect than for facts. Together they would play up to each other, and gradually Arthur, who in his youth had been easy-going and natural, though always full of high spirits, came to adopt the character of the artist with a fiery temperament and a tyrant in the home. No one still could be more charming or tell a more amusing story than he, but slowly he began to grow into the part.

It may have been that sub-consciously he resented the way in which the whole household revolved round Ruskin, and thus enjoyed drawing attention to himself by a display of temperament. Eleanor Furneaux's children, when they visited Brantwood, found the atmosphere uncomfortable, in spite of an affectionate welcome. Her eldest daughter, Agnes, who was delicate but gifted both musically and artistically, had always been a favourite with Ruskin and held her brothers and sisters spellbound on her return from a visit to Brantwood with stories of her stay.

After one appalling family scene all except Uncle Arthur had retired to Aunt Joan's room to talk over how awful he had been. In the middle of their discussion Arthur burst in, shouting, 'I won't have you *seething* in vulgar bedrooms!' and after loud reproaches to Joan, stormed out again, leaving her lying on the sofa apparently about to faint. Lily rushed out and returned with smelling salts, which instead of holding to her mother's nose she emptied into her mouth. Aunt Joan was heard, through gulping and coughing, to cry out in a dramatic voice, 'They've poured hell-fire down my throat!'

There was no doubt that the family enjoyed these scenes. On another occasion during Agnes Furneaux's visit Violet's stomach made a slight rumble at breakfast and her father turned on her: 'For God's sake, Violet, don't make a noise

[1] 6th December, 1894. Houghton Library.

like a governess at family prayers!' Violet immediately dissolved in tears and was led sorrowfully from the room by her mother.

★

In spite of Joan's devotion to her cousin there were still a few who, through malice or ignorance, misunderstood the position. She had never forgiven Albert Fleming for his part in the episode when Ruskin had left Brantwood after quarrelling with her, or for the rumours for which she believed him responsible, that she and Arthur had had her cousin locked up somewhere secretly, when he had gone away to Folkestone and then Sandgate, asking that no one should be told of his whereabouts.

Two women, aunt and niece, who wrote together under the pseudonym 'Michael Field', came to stay with Fleming and were regaled with the story of Joan's perfidy, which the younger recorded in her diary. Foolish old Ruskin was a modern King Lear, he told them. He had made over Brantwood by deed of gift to the Severns. Joan had quarrelled with him and left the house, but when he became ill, had returned with nurses and had ruled absolutely ever since. They had hoped to see Ruskin, with whom the aunt some years before had exchanged a number of letters when she had subscribed to the Guild of St George, but a note from Joan said that this was not possible and ended, 'We were rather startled by receiving your names on Mr Albert Fleming's card, as our friendship with him ceased some years ago.'

This was taken by the two women as proof of the truth of Fleming's story and they decided to make another attempt to see Ruskin, rowed over the lake, called at Brantwood, and were told that Mrs Severn was out and that Mr Ruskin could only be seen by appointment made through her. They discovered from the maid that he had gone for a walk, followed and found him on the road beside the shore, with Baxter in attendance. They spoke to him, but he only repeated Albert Fleming's name after them and did not remember having corresponded with the aunt.

The novelist's imagination took over when the niece described the scene in a letter to a friend next day. 'Oh, child, one feels that he has no heart to raise his voice, any more than the dying, who are hopeless, will trouble to speak – he looks as if freedom had been murdered in him. . . . Every day he goes this tread-mill walk; no young people charm him with soft voice; he is never taken for a drive or row; he is relegated to his study – no friend is allowed near him, lest he should be persuaded to revoke the deed of gift that has bound him to hell. . . .' Even poor Baxter was included in the diatribe, being described as 'little coarse Baxter, a horrible Sancho'.[1]

By the beginning of the last illness, which had left him incapable of any further work, Ruskin had dispersed the whole of the £200,000 which he had inherited from his parents, except for what was represented by his collections

---

[1] *Works and Days*: Journal of Michael Field, pp. 169–224.

at Brantwood. He had gradually disposed of the capital in gifts to institutions, to relations, to people who wrote to him asking for help, to St George's Guild, and in paying artist-assistants to travel round Europe making faithful records of places and buildings likely to be destroyed. Fortunately his scheme of employing George Allen to publish his books and sell them direct to the public, without going through a publisher, had prospered. And ironically, as he retired from the world himself, his books became more and more widely read; cheaper editions of his early books were re-issued, and his work was translated into many foreign languages. His social teaching, which had at first made little practical impact, now exerted a strong influence on all interested in educational reform, social justice, or the preservation of natural beauty. Ruskin Societies were founded, institutions were named after him, and while the prophet lived in seclusion at Brantwood, speaking rarely more than a few monosyllables and writing not at all, his books sold more and more widely.

The money earned annually by the sale of his books was now his only income, and a large part of that was mortgaged by generous pensions and annuities to people who had worked for him, or their dependants, and regular contributions to various institutions in which he had been interested. Nevertheless, his system of publishing and selling his own books had, after the first few years of loss, brought him in far higher royalties than he would otherwise have earned; they now amounted to a steady two to three thousand pounds a year.

Joan usually wrote any necessary letters for her cousin – if he was well enough, at his dictation, but very occasionally he would make a tremendous effort to write himself. When Miss Susie Beever, his old friend, lay dying at the Thwaite, just across the lake, he wrote her an affectionate note of eight lines in a faltering hand. It took him three hours to complete it. He wrote once, too, in his own hand to another old friend, Lady Simon, and whenever Joan was away for a few days, to her.

In the New Year of 1895 there came the famous frost which lasted through January and February and into March. The Thames was frozen over and on Joan's birthday, 4th March, Arthur and she walked on the ice from the harbour to Coniston Bank, half a mile up the lake, while Lily and Walter Severn's daughter, Christian, who was staying with them, skated about a long way from the shore. Later the household, including Ruskin, posed in a group on the ice for a photograph. When darkness fell they let off fireworks, and Christian skated round at speed carrying a red Bengal Fire above her head.

The birthday celebrations were scarcely over when Arthur received a letter from the Secretary of the Royal Institute of Painters in Water-Colours which gave fresh reason for rejoicing. The Queen had bought one of his pictures in the show – *Ice on the Thames: Chelsea*. This was a study of the river at Chelsea with boats and buildings seen indistinctly through the wintry mist, and the setting sun reflected on the floating blocks of ice. Arthur and Joan were proud of the Queen having bought his work and elated to read in the papers that 'there was always a crowd before Mr Arthur Severn's picture of the ice-bound Thames, which has been purchased by Her Majesty The Queen'.[1]

★

Joan made one of her rare excursions to London that May, but she did not stay long. On his daily walks Ruskin was sometimes upset by being accosted by admirers or curious strangers. She returned to Brantwood at once after receiving a pathetic note in his own hand:

'Dearest Joanie,

Please come back quickly. Find I can't write letters now, and I don't like anything that's going on. all kinds of bothers — but the weather's nice come back to stop the plaguing trippers from everywhere.

Ever your affect. Di Pa. J. Ruskin.'[2]

When Arthur was lent a yacht of 132 tons in August, she felt she could not leave her cousin, so he took Lily, the governess and young Arthur for a cruise round the west coast of Scotland, leaving Joan at Brantwood. Her days were full. She had two households and servants to arrange for, as well as the affairs of her husband and children. Yet she managed to spend a large part of every day with her cousin. She always went in to see him in the morning before his breakfast, sat in his study with him for an hour afterwards, reading to him or talking before his morning walk. She often — and *always* on Sundays — walked with him in the afternoons, and after his tea at five o'clock would sit with him 'or rest beside him' until dinner-time. He had dinner in his study and came into the drawing-room afterwards for a cup of tea and a game of chess. Then, after a glass of port and usually some music, he went to bed.

Ruskin was particularly vulnerable to vulgar curiosity. He still liked to take a little walk whenever the weather permitted, but for a long time he had not been able to manage the paths which climbed the steep slope behind the house. The only walks that were possible for him lay along the road which ran past Brantwood along the eastern shore of the lake. One of his favourite expeditions, always accompanied by the faithful Baxter, took him half a mile southwards along the road where, just half way between Brantwood and Fir Island, the mountain stream Beck Leven ran into the lake. A seat was made there so that he could sit with the sound of running water in his ears and look out across the lake.

When he bought Brantwood the land had consisted of only the ten-acre wood on the hill behind the house and six acres of moorland above. The property was surrounded on all sides by the estate of Major Benson Harrison, who lived at Coniston Bank and had leased to him the fields which ran down to the lake in front of Brantwood. For the past few years Harrison, who suffered from rheumatism, had let his own house and had been living at Leamington Spa. Now they heard rumours that he intended to sell part of his estate and that the rest,

---

[1] *Westminster Budget*, 15th March, 1895.
[2] 22nd May, 1895. Education Trust.

with the house itself, was to be turned into a hotel. If this plan had come to pass Ruskin's outings would have become impossible. The country lane, which was now usually deserted, would have been full of curious sightseers anxious to meet the great man. Joan was horrified. Even if her cousin sat out in front of the house he would be easily seen from the road, which was only a few yards below. After long negotiations she eventually managed to buy the whole Harrison estate, and also a sheep farm on the fells above Brantwood – in all about 500 acres. They now felt quite secure.

As Ruskin's eye-sight became worse Joan told Professor Norton that she read a good deal to him, 'and he daily becomes more precious to me'.[1] They still occasionally had old friends to stay, who would be taken to see Ruskin, if he was in one of his brighter moods. Walter Crane was one of them, and said that he had 'rather a shock' when he first saw him with Joan in the garden. He 'looked the shadow of his former self – the real, living man with all his energy and force had gone, and only the shadow remained. He was carefully dressed and scrupulously neat, having gloves on, which, seeing a visitor approach, he began to pull off rather absently, when Mrs Severn said, "Never mind the gloves", and I took his hand, but, alas! he had nothing but monosyllables, and soon went away supported on the arm of his constant attendant.'[2]

Crane sailed with Arthur, admired his drawings of scenes round Brantwood, and played tennis and bowls with him and his sons. The tennis lawn in the wood had now been converted into a bowling green. Ruskin had never allowed the oaks and hazels in his woods to be cut periodically to the ground, as was the usual custom, to be used for charcoal. He had let all his trees grow, only pruning the dead wood and weaker shoots, and the slender saplings had sprouted, tall and thin, until they resembled the trees in a Botticelli picture. On the lake side of the green lawn one saw the water gleaming between their grey columns. A new place had been levelled to make a tennis lawn in the field below the house, just beyond the wall which bordered the road. Arthur was a keen player and liked to win. His voice raised high in protest or loud expletives could be heard by road-users from far off.

Crane noted 'the curious contrast between the extreme quiet and retirement in which Ruskin existed and the active life of the household with the varied interests and pursuits of the young people'. He saw Ruskin once more during his visit, when Joan took him into his study. Ruskin had a benign expression and with his long flowing beard looked like a prophet, but when Crane spoke of subjects he thought might interest him 'he only said "yes" or "no", or smiled or bowed his head'.

Occasionally there were moments when Ruskin would seem aware of things about him, but they never now lasted very long.

Eleanor Furneaux's young daughter, Margaret, found him very frightening

[1] 27th November, 1896. Houghton Library.
[2] *An Artist's Reminiscences* by Walter Crane, p. 448.

when she stayed at Brantwood. Ruskin was not in one of his clearer moods, which were becoming rarer every month, and at the time had an obsession — as he often did — with one word, and when he spoke would say almost nothing else. On this occasion the word was Damn. He spent most of the time in his room. When Margaret saw him, in house or garden, he was usually sitting quietly with Aunt Joan beside him, hand-in-hand, but she was frightened by the glistening blue eyes under the shaggy eye-brows. Her aunt would talk to him in a coaxing voice and always in their private baby-talk. Margaret saw her kneeling beside him. 'What would Di-Pa like for din-din?' A long pause and then she heard the reply in a low voice: 'A damn on toast'.

When Aunt Joan was not with him his devoted servant, Baxter, was always at hand. Margaret, being not quite grown up, was sent to bed earlier than the others. Her room was at the top of the narrow staircase on the right. On the left, almost opposite her door, was Ruskin's bedroom. Every evening of her stay she lay in her room and heard Ruskin climbing the stairs on his way to bed, accompanied by Baxter. He climbed slowly, and the heavy tread on each step was followed by a pause and a muttered Damn. 'Damn — Damn — Damn — Damn', and encouraging words from Baxter. Margaret lay rigid with fear as the footsteps, with their monotonous, muttered accompaniment, passed her door and he retreated with his attendant into the room opposite her own. She never slept well while she was there.[1]

★

With the three boys away, Arthur and Agnew at Oxford and Herbert, like Violet, at school, only Lily was at home, and when her father went away she very often accompanied him, so that Joan was sometimes left for several weeks at a time alone in the house with Ruskin, save for the servants. She never minded this. She loved working in the garden and driving herself in her own carriage and pair to call on her friends in the neighbourhood, when she was not with her cousin, but she could not disguise from herself the fact that he was growing feebler.

On a short visit to London — the first for a long time — she and Arthur dined with Burne-Jones. 'They were very nice, both of them — and unchanged, which is a lovely thing in friends,' Edward Burne-Jones told his wife. Edward asked anxiously for the latest news of Ruskin, and Joan told him sadly how he had wanted to write to his old favourite, Mary Gladstone, when her father died, and had sat an hour or more with his pen in hand, but could get no further than 'Dear Mary, I am grieved at the death of your father — '[2]

Soon afterwards came news of Edward Burne-Jones's death. 'That's my dear brother Ned,' Ruskin said one evening, stopping on his way to bed to look long at a photograph of Philip Burne-Jones's portrait of his father. His old friend died

[1] Margaret Countess of Birkenhead to author.
[2] 1st June, 1898. G. Burne-Jones, op. cit., vol. II, p. 342.

next day. His own eightieth birthday was approaching. 'O, take care of your-self my dear,' wrote Lady Burne-Jones to Joan, 'for you are the key-stone of the arch.'[1]

In February 1899, on Ruskin's eightieth birthday, flowers, letters and tele-grams of congratulation poured in from all over the world. Deputations arrived at Brantwood, the principal one presenting an illuminated address on vellum from the many Ruskin and kindred societies which had lately been formed, signed by the Prince of Wales and officers of most of the learned and artistic Societies of Great Britain. Ruskin was well enough to see the members of the small deputation which made the presentation to him, but he could utter only a few broken words in reply.

And now they could see his strength ebbing. He was no longer strong enough for his daily walks. When it was very warm he would occasionally go out in a bath-chair and be wheeled to a favourite spot, from which he could look across the water of the lake to Helvellyn in the distance. But soon even this was too much for him, and he no longer came downstairs, but spent his days between his bedroom and the little room next door with the turret which he had built on when he first came to Brantwood to command the view down the lake. The walls were hung with his favourite Turner water-colours, but they no longer gave him the same exquisite pleasure as in days gone by. 'My Turners,' he said to Joan, 'seem to have lost something of their radiance.'[2] Only the changing beauty of the sky and the shifting light on lake and hills still held him, and he would sit for hours at the window in the turret room, gazing silently at the world outside.

The faithful Sydney Cockerell found him there with a little book on his knee, his hands encased in fur mittens. He was not sure that he was recognized. Did he remember Detmar Blow? No. 'He looked tranquil, rather wistful, shrunken, but very little changed in face since I last saw him in 1892 — his hair still dark and very thick . . . his beard still with a trace of brown. It was like interviewing a ghost, but very wonderful.'[3]

Ten weeks after Cockerell's visit the end came. Joan and Arthur were at Brantwood with him. It was mid-January and several of the servants were ill with influenza. On the morning of the 18th Ruskin seemed particularly well but when Joan went in as usual after tea to read to him he had a sore throat and admitted that he felt pains 'all over'. Baxter immediately helped his master to bed, while Joan sent for Dr Parsons and then sat by her cousin's bed-side, singing one of his favourite songs. When the doctor arrived he found that Ruskin had a high temperature. He diagnosed influenza and told Joan that unless his strength could be kept up the illness might be very grave.

That evening Ruskin ate a good dinner, of sole and pheasant and champagne,

[1] 2nd December, 1898. In possession of Dr H. G. Viljoen.
[2] *Works*, vol. 35, xliv.
[3] 7th November, 1899. *Friends of a Life Time*, p. 61.

and seemed much better next day. But on the following morning, Saturday, there was a sudden marked deterioration and the doctor was alarmed. Ruskin became unconscious, his breathing slowly lessened in strength until in the afternoon, with Joan holding his hand and Baxter and Dr Parsons standing by, it gradually faded away.

Later, when the first shock was over, Lily persuaded her mother to look at the sunset from the window of the little turret room, as her cousin had so often done. 'The brilliant, gorgeous light illumined the hills with splendour; and the spectators felt as if Heaven's gate itself had been flung open to receive the teacher into everlasting peace.'[1]

---

[1] Joan Severn's description

CHAPTER 38

AFTERMATH

NOW THAT THE LONG DREADED MOMENT HAD COME FOR JOAN she was not able to rest. Immediately pressure was brought on her to agree to her cousin being buried in Westminster Abbey. Letters were written to *The Times*, a memorial signed by many distinguished men was presented to the Dean and Chapter – the Chapter was unanimous in agreeing with it and a grave in Poets' Corner, close to that of Tennyson, was suggested. But Joan refused the offer. Her cousin had told her that if he died at Brantwood he would like to rest at Coniston, and she was determined to do as he had wished.

As soon as her refusal became known various friends protested, and George Allen, who was responsible for the sale of Ruskin's books, wrote urging her to change her mind. 'The occasion of his funeral calls for more public obsequies than those at Coniston,' he wrote. He hoped public opinion would be allowed its way. The Dean was writing that evening asking Joan to waive her objections; the position of the grave in Poets' Corner had been settled. 'Even the undertakers have been consulted and there is no difficulty whatever.'[1]

Joan steadfastly refused to change her mind. To the last she would do what her 'beloved Coz' had wished. So Ruskin was buried in the quiet churchyard at Coniston, next to the grave of his old friend Susie Beever. 'Why should we wear black for the guests of God?' he had once written to her. He had always hated black. Now his coffin was covered with a pall given by the Ruskin Linen Industry at Keswick; on the natural linen were embroidered the words, *Unto this Last* and the initials J. R., surrounded by a border of wild roses. It was lined with crimson silk. His grave was heaped high with flowers – from royalty and scholars, from famous artists and the village tailor. Two wreaths were much remarked upon; one of olive sent by the artist, Watts, from a tree in his garden which had been cut only three times before – for Tennyson, Leighton and Burne-Jones – and the other a cross of red roses from Joan.

There was a Service in Westminster Abbey at the same time as the funeral service at Coniston. Georgie Burne-Jones was there and wrote to Joan that sunshine had streamed in on the pillars – there were as many men as women among the congregation, both young and old. Joan had been to him what no one else in the world could be, she said, 'the joy of his good days and the comfort of his evil ones'.[2]

---

[1] 23rd January, 1900. In possession of Dr H. G. Viljoen.
[2] February 1900. In possession of Dr H. G. Viljoen.

Lady Mount Temple, now very old and infirm, sent a dictated letter from Torquay: 'Oh! how I feel for you – his sister, his friend, his child.'

Sydney Cockerell wrote, too, with condolences, and added that if she was in a position to part with the St Louis Psalter, which he had so much admired on his last visit to Brantwood, and had a mind to do so, he could find her a purchaser for £1000. He would not have mentioned it so soon, but remembered 'when Mr Morris died we were in some trouble about obtaining ready money to pay the heavy duties – and you may be in the same position'.[1] He offered his help and advice if she wished to dispose of any other books.

Joan had little time for letter-writing. Everything was made more difficult by several of the servants being ill, and after the funeral Arthur also went to bed with influenza, which was of a severe type. But she found time to write to Professor Norton who, as one of Ruskin's oldest and most intimate friends, must have priority. 'I still feel almost too bewildered by the sorrow and desolation of my Darling's death to write – even to you. . . . Mercifully I must make efforts – for my husband is now very ill with influenza . . . and still some of the servants. *His* end was perfect peace and for *him* just what I have always prayed for! – and I cannot wish him back tho' it is so heart-breaking for *me*, to be without him, and he no longer my chief care and thought.'[2]

Soon after writing this letter Joan, too, became ill, and even when she recovered there was still too much illness in the house for them to have lawyers to stay there. Ruskin's solicitors wrote from London to say that Arthur and she, with Mr Barker, a partner in the firm, were the executors. Joan felt quite exhausted by the illness, coming immediately after the shock of her cousin's death, and Arthur, too, felt the need of a complete change after his bad bout of influenza, so they decided before trying to tackle all the problems which loomed ahead, to take a holiday abroad. They spent some time in Cannes and then travelled on to Florence, only returning to England in mid-April, having had nearly two months away, both feeling much stronger and able to face the many important decisions which must be taken.

*

For a short while they stayed in London, saw the solicitors, and had an official meeting with George Allen and Alec Wedderburn about Ruskin's publishing business which produced and sold all his works. He had left Brantwood to Arthur and Joan 'and to the survivor of them and their heirs for ever for their very own', begging them never to sell any part of it, or allow building on it, and to keep the whole property 'in decent order and good repair in like manner as I have done'.

Joan and Professor Norton were given full authority to publish or destroy any

---

[1] 31st January, 1900. In possession of Dr H. G. Viljoen.
[2] 31st January, 1900. Houghton Library.

of his diaries, unpublished manuscripts or private papers. Joan and Alec Wedderburn were to have control of the copyrights and everything connected with his books, whether already published or in the course of publication, but they were to continue to publish any further editions through George Allen. Alec Wedderburn was to receive £100 a year for general supervision of the sale of Ruskin's books, and one-third of the net profit of any volumes revised or edited by him. From the remaining profit one thousand pounds a year was to be paid to Joan and Arthur, or whoever succeeded them at Brantwood, for the upkeep of the house and estate. The residue was to be used by Joan and Wedderburn to carry on the sale of his works, and when the copyrights expired any money left in their hands was to go to Joan or whoever she appointed in her will.

The position of Joan and Arthur was not clear. The phrase in the will which left Brantwood and its contents to them *and to their heirs for ever* was said by the lawyers to make it impossible for them to take any decision about the house and its contents, unless it could be decided that they had the power of willing them to someone after them. Otherwise, there could later be claims from any number of their relations. After a great many legal arguments, the case was brought before a Judge in Chancery in the summer, postponed until after the long vacation and eventually a decision was given, nearly a year after Ruskin's death. Joan and Arthur were each to have £500 a year from the income derived from Ruskin's books for the upkeep of Brantwood. The surplus income from the books was to accumulate in a fund which it was hoped would eventually yield £1000 a year for the upkeep of Brantwood when the copyrights had expired. In the meantime the Severns were to have the yearly interest in the sum thus accumulated.

Joan had been relieved of much anxiety by Professor Norton coming to England in the summer. She relied on him to advise her what should be destroyed and what kept among her cousin's papers. One decision they made immediately. Ruskin's letters from Rose and his to her, which he had preserved so carefully in the rosewood box, should never be read by anyone else. Together they carried them up to his little woodland garden on the hill above the house and solemnly burned them. To please Joan, as soon as they had returned to Brantwood Arthur had made a careful sketch in water-colour of Ruskin's bedroom, just as it was during his lifetime, with the bed made up, the sheets turned down, and the Turners glowing on the walls.

Just after Norton had left them and gone on to London Joan received 'a most *unpleasant* letter' from Ruskin's Richardson cousins. They had heard that the Severns had sold, or were planning to sell, some of Ruskin's many Turners; they were taking Counsel's opinion and intended to dispute the will. Professor Norton warned her not to write to Miss Richardson herself, but to leave it all to her solicitors. He enclosed a letter for her to forward to them, in which he wrote that as long as thirty years ago, when Ruskin had first made a will, he had told him that it was not his intention to bequeath his possessions or property to his relatives. 'He anticipated that his relatives would be annoyed at his Will and might try to break it, and in a letter to me, whom he had made his executor . . . he bade me resist any attempt that might be made to break the Will, and to do so to the last point, and even to sell his Turners if need be to meet the costs of resistance.'[1] After this the Richardsons were evidently advised to proceed no further.

★

Arthur went to London during the summer, but Joan stayed all the time at Brantwood. Although her cousin was dead her days were still largely devoted to him. 'I went to his little woodland garden to-day,' she wrote to Norton, 'and over that sad little spot a wild rose is covering a rustic trellis — just what *he* and *she* would have liked . . . and soon Baxter and I are going to the grave to plant his favourite little *erba della Madonna* and that lovely little alpine from the walls of Thurland. . . . He literally rests in the shadow at sunset of the Old Man he loved.'[2]

At Norton's suggestion she and Collingwood packed some of Ruskin's drawings for him to take back to Boston with him, where he thought he could sell them well. Arthur put provisional prices on them. Their affairs had still to be settled and the cheque which Norton sent them in August for £175, for the first drawings that he had sold, was welcome. This was followed by two more, for £180 and £75. Amongst the drawings he had taken were a number, unpriced, which they asked him to keep as a gift from them both.

More vexatious was the news, revealed to them by George Allen soon after Ruskin's death, that although in the will her cousin had expressly left all his manuscripts to her, Allen in fact had the manuscripts of most of the books in his possession. His name was not mentioned in the will, save for the request that the executors should continue to publish Ruskin's books through him. But he 'said that the Master had given them to him, and produced a letter in support of his statement which spoke of two volumes being given. When her cousin was alive Joan had on several occasions asked him where the manuscripts were, and he had told her he was not sure, 'but he supposed they would turn up somewhere'. Collingwood, too, said that Ruskin had told him that he thought the manuscripts of his best known works had been destroyed. The letters about the two volumes being given to Allen had been written, Joan knew, when her cousin was 'far from well'. But the Severns were advised not to dispute Allen's claim — their solicitor thought that a judge would decide against them, 'saying "If Ruskin gave two volumes why not the others?" '[3]

Wedderburn — now a Q.C. — who had edited many of Ruskin's books which had been re-issued during the years when he was himself incapable of work, approached Joan and Arthur with a scheme which he and George Allen had concocted together, to publish a complete Library edition of Ruskin's works. They had their plans ready. 'The complete work would consist of 30 volumes

---

[1] 25th June, 1900. In possession of Dr H. G. Viljoen.
[2] 19th June, 1900. Houghton Library.
[3] Joan Severn to C. E. Norton. 6th November, 1902. Houghton Library.

costing £1 each — limited to 2000' sets, the cost being £60,000,' Joan told Professor Norton. Half this would cover their total expenses. The other half, when all the books were sold, 'would represent a profit of £10,000 to Allen, £10,000 to Alec Q.C! (as he's to have one third of the profits on all the books he edits) and £10,000 to the Brantwood Fund.' The plan was complete in every detail. Wedderburn even brought with him a sample page which they had had printed.

Joan 'ventured to hint it was a large amount of profit for Allen, but Q.C. said "I assure you Allen thinks himself very badly paid." I did not venture to hint *his* share was a big one! . . . He insisted on seeing every letter and bit of manuscript given to me by the beloved Coz — and took them to look over . . . and was evidently surprised to find there were still so many! I hope you will not disapprove of what I have done — or what *he* proposes to do. The contrast was terrible from having *you* to look over things — but I do trust it's all right, and for the best, and as the beloved Coz would have liked.'[1]

Joan and Arthur had to advise about the various memorials to Ruskin which were proposed. Arthur was a member of the committee formed to arrange for a memorial in Poets' Corner of the Abbey. The Dean and Chapter had assigned to them the space immediately above the bust of Sir Walter Scott, and the committee decided that the memorial should take the form of a bronze medallion. The sculptor was selected, and it only remained to decide whether the likeness of Ruskin should show him clean-shaven or with the beard which he had grown after his first serious mental illness in 1878, and which had later grown to patriarchal proportions.

It was eventually decided that the bas-relief should show Ruskin when he was clean-shaven, and Joan unveiled it on his birthday, two years after his death. By that time she had already unveiled another memorial — a monolith on the crest of Friar's Crag above Derwentwater. This ceremony was held in a driving storm of wind and rain — or as the local paper called it, 'boisterous weather'. Ruskin's old friend, Canon Rawnsley, who was in charge of the proceedings, thought it better to move the audience a little down the hill for the speeches. Even here the creak of the swaying trees and the howl of the wind through their foliage made speech-making difficult. Nevertheless Joan and the Canon did their best against the roar of the storm, and the monolith with its medallion portrait of Ruskin was then unveiled.

She had also helped to arrange a Memorial Exhibition of his sketches with many personal relics at Coniston Institute. This had brought more than 10,000 visitors to the village, and ended in a permanent Ruskin Museum being made, largely from material which she and Arthur had presented. She had also caused a monument, designed by Collingwood, to be erected on her cousin's grave, and helped Arthur with the selection for an exhibition of Ruskin's drawings at the Old Water-Colour Society in London.

[1] 28th October, 1900. Houghton Library.

This was followed by another one-man Exhibition of Arthur's work at the Fine Art Society, where he again sold a large number of paintings.

Joan continued to rely completely on Professor Norton. So many of her cousin's friends were now dead. Acland and Burne-Jones had died before him, and the year after his death saw the end not only of Lady Simon and Lady Mount Temple, but also of Kate Greenaway – the last bringing further perplexites.

Joan consulted Norton about every decision for the literary executors. 'As regards the Kate Greenaway *Life* that Mr Spielmann is going to do – I suppose if I over look all the letters chosen . . . it will do?' Norton was ready with advice. He was very fond of Joan and asked her to send him a portrait of herself. She sat to Collingwood's wife, who was a distinguished miniaturist, and sent the result to him, but he thought it only quite like her.

'I should like to have your husband try a sketch some day,' he wrote, 'and see whether he could give to the face the sweetness, and the force, the mingling of all dear womanly tenderness with quick intelligence and strength of character which belong to the original. . . . As to the new edition Allen seems to me grasping as usual. Between him and Wedderburn not much, I fear, will be left for you. You ought to have some entirely trustworthy and capable confidential adviser who should . . . maintain and protect your interests. A strong and efficient man is needed to deal with two such hard and gripe-all characters, who have such advantage of position over you. You have been too yielding as regards Wedderburn, and have submitted to too much from him. . . . As to the K. G. biography, of course Spielmann is likely to make the most of the Coz's letters to her and admiration of her work. Spielmann seems to me . . . a poor sort of . . . penny-a-liner.' She should insist on seeing any of Ruskin's letters which he wished to include in his book. 'To go back . . . to Allen. He speaks of having MSS of the Coz as yet unprinted. Before he prints them I will insist on seeing them, if necessary. He is not to be trusted.'[1]

Joan did not take such a gloomy view of their prospects. She had every confidence in their solicitor and was quite satisfied with the selection of E. T. Cook to co-operate with Wedderburn in editing Ruskin's *Works*. 'If you hear of Ruskin Manuscripts going to America I wish you to know it has nothing to do with us,' she wrote. 'Allen had them all – except fragmentary late things. . . . Mackrell said it was no use trying to dispute the matter. I hear he sold *The Seven Lamps* for £1000 and *Modern Painters* for £5000 last week . . . to America.'[2]

She worried about Ruskin's letters being quoted in various books which were being published and told Norton that she had seen Kate Greenaway's biographer. They both knew only too well how easily his way of writing to people could be misunderstood – as it sometimes had been by his correspondents. 'The tiresome point is the letters, on K. G.'s side especially to J. R., savour of much

[1] 17th January, 1902. In possession of Dr H. G. Viljoen.
[2] 25th April, 1902. Houghton Library.

deeper feeling than ordinary friendship, and of course his letters to her are very affectionate, beginning "Darling Kate" etc. Now do you think it will be wise to let the world think it was only an ordinary affectionate friendship – and suppress the idea it meant anything else? – or what? When John Greenaway and Spielmann pressed the question – I said I must consult you!'[1]

Arthur, like his father, had never had any head for business and all these business arrangements and discussions bored him. He took his younger daughter, Violet, for a trip to Italy in the spring and then decided to go for a longer journey. Joan was too involved in all the arrangements about the new edition of her cousin's books to think of leaving England, so when Arthur sailed for Calcutta in the autumn, on a P. & O. liner, he was accompanied by Lily. They both loved the sea and the voyage was a wonderful chance for Arthur to do water-colours of changing seas and sky. They sailed in November and were to be away until the following April.

During their absence Joan busied herself putting things in order at Brantwood. Since her cousin's death life seemed to have been full of interruptions. Wedderburn had persuaded her to write to Norton, asking if he could see letters written by Ruskin to him, as he must have all the material at hand before they started the new Library edition. Joan passed on the request, though she said it seemed to her that private letters would hardly be available for such a purpose. Wedderburn also wanted Ruskin's diaries, but she would not let him have them until she had consulted Norton. She felt it was a sacred trust to guard her cousin's name. 'I have been annoyed lately at numbers of (some foolish) letters from J R being sold by his old pets. Have you decided about yours – which will have the best of him in them?' she asked.

Another irritation was for everyone to think that she and Arthur had got the money, when they read that Ruskin manuscripts had been sold for large sums. 'So many people seem to think *we* are the people benefited by the sale of these manuscripts, tho' we don't get a farthing. But I *am* proud they *are* of such value, for the beloved Coz's sake who wrote them.'[2]

★

In India Arthur and Lily attended the Durbar at Delhi and Lily was dangerously ill with enteric fever and spent eight weeks in bed. Joan was horrified at her daughter's appearance when they returned to Brantwood and immediately threw herself into nursing her. This was an occupation far more pleasant to her than all the work that she had been doing while they were away.

She had found that the new edition of her cousin's books involved a great deal of work for herself. At the editor's request she had been through hundreds of letters, from her private knowledge dating them or explaining obscure references, had answered innumerable questions, and read through the proofs. The

---

[1] 24th July, 1902. Houghton Library.
[2] 6th November, 1902. Houghton Library.

only person who could help her in all this was Sara Anderson, who came whenever she could, but she had an invalid father in London and often could not leave him.

The first volume of the new edition came out three years after Ruskin's death, but brought no immediate profit to Joan and Arthur. They were finding their financial position difficult. Any surplus money from the book business was being used to finance the new edition, and they had a great many expenses. There were now two houses to keep up, a large number of pensioners of the Ruskin family to be cared for, and all their children to support. Agnew had married a very delicate girl who was often ill. Young Arthur had come down from Oxford without a degree, and his sole and passionate interest in life appeared to be fishing. (Towards the end of his four years at Exeter College, he had entered for a casting competition nearby, which he won. His father heard that he was competing, appeared by his side after his winning cast and turning to the crowd, appealed to them: 'My son has been four years at Oxford, and what has it done for him? *Simply* taught him to throw a fly!') His only other interest was hunting, an enthusiasm which Lily shared. Having tried in vain to make him a Civil Servant, his parents were now paying for him to learn about breeding trout. The two girls were unmarried and the youngest of the family, Herbert, was training to be an engineer.

Arthur had done well from his London exhibition but they had only a limited amount of capital between them, and they could only make ends meet by selling things. Professor Norton continued to dispose of drawings in America for them. He inquired about Scott manuscripts, but Joan replied: 'We now only possess *The Fortunes of Nigel* (for which the Coz paid £600 at Christie's about 40 years ago!) – and the Abbotsford Scott Letter – and we would not like to part with them. The Coz sold *St Ronan's Well* some years before he died, and we were tempted, when we were rather hard up. There always seem such heavy expenses here – and with Pensioners – beside Herne Hill, and the family! – and you helped us greatly by the American sale of J. R. drawings, *Libers* etc. . . . Of course we *shall* always keep a full and characteristic collection of everything the Coz had – Pictures, Manuscripts, minerals etc. books and all else, but as regards parting with *some* of the things here sometimes, it has been necessary to carry out the beloved Coz's wishes in keeping up this place, *as it has been* – with all his servants, and Pensioners elsewhere. In short the £1000 a year provided goes in no time for them, and the actual repairs etc, without food, coal etc – and we are bound to keep on Herne Hill for another 4½ years – and keeping Herbert in Manchester – Arthur at Fish Culture, and Agnew with a wife. . . .'[1]

Although Arthur loved the sea he was not really a countryman. Unlike Joan, he had no interest in gardening or country things except as subjects for a picture. He liked Brantwood in the summer, when they had relations and friends to

[1] 19th and 26th June, 1903. Houghton Library.

stay, and could play tennis and sail on the lake, and he enjoyed gatherings of neighbours when he shone as a raconteur. As a family they excelled at quick talk across the table, and visitors were delighted by Joan's high-pitched protest, 'Arthur!' which was always beautifully timed. She sat at one end of the table, stout now but still handsome, her skin beautiful, her thick, curly hair springing up from the strongly marked peak on her forehead, and a charming expression of warm-hearted intelligence shining in her face. 'Pa', as Arthur was called in the home, sat at the other end, his hair as dark and thick as on the day of their marriage, his bright blue eyes and youthful face and manner making him seem still a young man. He always shone in company and with his humour and infectious high spirits it was almost impossible to believe that he was sixty. In this he was like his father, who had been taken for a man of fifty when he was nearly seventy years old.

Brantwood in the winter did not appeal to Arthur, and he had usually managed to spend a good deal of it in London or abroad, preferably in Italy where he felt at home. Although he was appointed a magistrate in December 1903, he was never really happy in the rôle of country gentleman. He much preferred the more bohemian company of fellow artists, though he was always meticulously dressed. He loved to strike up an acquaintance with people he met on his travels, and his new friends would find him a delightful and amusing companion. At home he played the part of the brilliant artist – spoiled and wilful.

Joan's faith in Professor Norton received a severe jolt when Alec Wedderburn came to her in a furious temper, to say that he had heard that Norton was publishing some of Ruskin's letters to him in the *Atlantic Monthly*. Joan could not believe that her friend and adviser would do such a thing without a word to her, his colleague as literary executor. 'I do hope there is some misunderstanding about it, and that you will write and silence my anxiety?' she wrote. 'Of course if Wedderburn is right, it would put us all in a most serious position with regard to our pledge in the Circular about the publication of the new Complete Library Edition.

'I may mention that the Coz's old friends the Mount Temples, the Simons, La Touches and others, all gave or left me their letters to keep absolutely for myself, and to destroy what I pleased, but I would not dream of publishing *any* without consulting *you* and having your approval – and none certainly till after the present new edition is completed – *if* then!'[1]

To her dismay Norton confirmed that a selection of Ruskin's letters to him were being published in the *Atlantic Monthly*, and that they would afterwards appear as a book. 'Apart from any Legal Considerations, I cannot help being hurt at your never telling me . . .' she wrote reproachfully, 'considering our great intimacy, and my devotion to you as a friend – (whom, of all others, the Coz thought it would be possible for me to work with, and confide in,

[1] 11th March, 1904. Houghton Library.

N

without any friction!) It certainly *was* a shock to hear of your intention, without ever consulting me.' It hardly seemed fair as Co-Trustee.

Joan's fears were fully justified when Norton sent her the two volumes of Ruskin letters. He had included several things, both in the letters and in what he had written himself, which she would gladly have seen altered. 'I am sorry for the introduction of poor Rose. I suppose it couldn't be helped, but newspapers make so much of it — and it is a great pain to her poor Mother, who has lately lost her Husband, and has some trying sorrows besides. I thought when we made the little sacrifice in my beloved Deepie's[1] little garden here, that we agreed to burn *all* letters bearing on that sad subject — and I have done so, and destroyed many since, to myself and other people. Then our Beloved so varied in his Religious view — and to my mind was *not* a sceptic. And in later days I don't think the Parents *were* blamed for their bringing up of him. During the seven years I lived with his mother I loved her dearly — and we got on so happily together and she showed me a tender, soft side of her nature outsiders never gave her credit for. Her real passionate devotion to her son was extraordinary considering how hard she could sometimes seem to him! They never really quite understood each other.'[2]

★

Arthur had another exhibition of his work in June 1906, five years after his previous one — this time at the Leicester Galleries.

Again he had good notices, and the pictures sold brought him £550. But this was in no way sufficient for their many expenses. Joan was determined to keep Brantwood exactly as it had been in her cousin's life-time, as he had 'earnestly prayed' in his will. Not a servant had been dismissed. Not a pensioner went unpaid. The garden was beautifully kept, the hospitality lavish.

They still had to pay out for all their children. Young Arthur, now thirty-three years old, had needed money to help him establish his Fish Hatchery at Bibury, though it was, Joan told Professor Norton proudly, 'quite a success'. Lily, a year older than he, had not married though she was always in love with someone, and spent a great deal of time with young Arthur at Bibury, where they hunted throughout the winter with the Heythrop. She was very short-sighted. Margaret, Eleanor Furneaux's daughter, now married to a young barrister, F. E. Smith, was staying with friends nearby, and was surprised to have Arthur and Lily pointed out to her at the Meet by her host: 'See that couple over there? Avoid them like the plague. If you have a fall she's certain to jump on you.'

Agnew and his wife had no children. Violet was at home and the youngest child, Herbert, was working at Barrow in the drawing-office of an engineering firm, and studying for further examinations. His spare time he devoted to playing the violin. When they were at home he and Lily spent much time in the

---

[1] Di Pa's.
[2] Brantwood, 20th December, 1904. Houghton Library.

lodge, where one of the turret rooms had been furnished as a room for her. Herbert would play the violin and Lily accompany him on the piano. All in all, they were an expensive family.

Joan enlisted Professor Norton's help again to sell a silver patera which her cousin had given years ago to Arthur. It had been found in a tomb. 'Coz said if we ever parted with it the B.M. ought to have first offer, and it should fetch not less than £250.' Charles Newton's successor at the Museum had seen and admired it, but had no funds available at the moment. Did Norton know an American millionaire who might like it for the Boston Museum?

The selling of treasures continued slowly. Now the extended lease of Herne Hill, which Arthur had bought 21 years before, was due to expire. 'I suppose they will pull it down before long,' wrote Joan sadly, 'and build horrid little houses like those with which it is now surrounded — and all the old associations and beauty of the place, be swept away!'[1]

In its place they bought the lease of 9 Warwick Square, a large, tall house in a leafy square not far from Victoria Station. Arthur's twin, Eleanor, whose husband had died soon after Ruskin, sold their home in Oxford and took the house next door. That was the year that George Allen died, but according to Ruskin's agreement with him the publishing business would still be carried on by his family — two sons and a daughter.

The move to Warwick Square meant a terrible turning out of drawers and cupboards, and Joan was glad to be able to call on Sara Anderson to help. Diddie was devoted to Joan and was very methodical. Throughout the preparation of the various volumes of the new edition she had been most helpful. 'I send in separate parcel,' she wrote to Joan, 'an envelope full of letters from you and Deepie to each other, to go in old dining room drawers. There is a drawer with letters from *you to him*, as you know.' Alec Wedderburn had just asked Diddie when she would next be at Brantwood. It was difficult for her to get away from home at the moment, but if there was something to be done which Joan would dislike, she would try to go. 'Now if it's to "verify" the Deepie's letters to you before printing,' she wrote to Joan, 'I think it would bore you horribly, and you would want to read *all* the letters as you opened each year's packet, and you would be interrupted and have to leave them unarranged lying on the stool or table with a duster over them! And if Alec did it, well there are certainly things in many of the letters that are not meant for his eye, and yet which it is not in any way necessary to destroy.'[2]

Diddie had been so close to them all for so long that Joan felt no compunction about her seeing anything. 'I have now read all your Vice-Mother's letters and burnt all those relating to the terrible Rosie times,' she wrote to Joan. 'All the others are readable by anyone, so now we have a weight off our minds. I have done up Rosie's own letters to you and sealed them, and put "for Joan only"

[1] 8th October, 1907. Houghton Library.
[2] 7th May, 1906. Education Trust.

outside. All the other letters I am arranging so that I hope you will be able to see quite easily what you have. ... Do search your mind for anything else that requires looking over ... and don't let us have scandals turning up after our lamented demises.'[1]

[1] 12th May, 1906. Education Trust.

CHAPTER 39

MARIE CORELLI

'Pa's' charm for the ladies had long been a joke in his family, and he was encouraged in his rôle of the autocratic wilful genius by the way in which it was willingly accepted, even encouraged, by the opposite sex. His latest conquest was an uneasy one for his family, for she was not a woman to admire in silence or to be content with flirtatious letters like some of his younger acquaintances. Marie Corelli was at the height of her fame when she first came to Brantwood with her friend and companion, Bertha Vyver, in the summer of 1906.

She was fifty-one years old, a tiny, plump little figure, dressed like a girl, her head crowned with a mass of golden hair. Incomprehensibly now, her novels sold in thousands. Mark Twain admired them, fashionable clerics preached sermons about their Christian message, Mr Gladstone had called on her personally to express his interest, Queen Victoria sent for each new book as it was published, and they were translated into almost every European language. Melodramatic romances, fairy tales with a strong moral flavour, they were conjured up by a feverish imagination which coloured everything for her and which also gave her a unique conception of herself.

Her girlish mannerisms were no affectation, nor were the youthful dresses and picture hats. In her world of fantasy she was the heroine, perpetually youthful, 'for ever fair', brilliant in intellect, beauty and virtue and beloved by all — except for a dastardly few consisting of those who disagreed with her. The critics had never written favourably about her work, and for more than ten years she had carried on a vituperative warfare with them in the press and had refused to send any of her books for review. But her sales seemed to increase with every novel that she published and her name was a household word. That year 100,000 copies of her books were sold at a moment when two other popular novelists, Rudyard Kipling and Conan Doyle, sold only 55,000 between them.

It was no wonder that there was excitement at Brantwood when Joan opened a letter one morning and found that it was from the celebrated novelist. She was staying, she said, at the Waterhead Hotel with her friend Miss Vyver, and begged permission to see Brantwood, home of the great Ruskin. An invitation was sent immediately and Baxter was dispatched in a boat to fetch the ladies a mile across the water.

Arthur went down to the little harbour to meet them. Miss Corelli was very small and fair, with innocent, grey-blue eyes. Her companion was stout and

motherly and rather silent. Marie Corelli conversed in the most charming manner as he led them uphill through the gardens, showing a bright interest in everything and admiring Joan's azaleas and the blackberry bushes which she had
trained to grow over a rough stone wall. After a tour of the house the guests
departed again by water, having accepted an invitation to dine that evening.
Baxter amused Joan and Arthur by his Irish enthusiasm for Miss Corelli. He had
lost his heart to the charming little lady during the voyage, he said, and later
confessed to Joan that he had talked so much about her that evening that his
wife 'had taken the poker to him — the only time she had ever been jealous in
twenty-five years of married life'.[1]

Marie Corelli was as charming as ever at dinner. She referred to Brantwood
as 'the pilgrim shrine', and showed great interest in Arthur's painting. They all
parted on friendly terms, Miss Corelli extending a warm invitation to Arthur
and Joan to visit her at Stratford-on-Avon. No one guessed that for the first
time in her life she had fallen in love.

★

The invitation was renewed a little later, when Joan was still at Brantwood
and Arthur in London. He went to stay for a few days at Mason Croft, the house
which Marie Corelli had bought in Stratford-on-Avon a few years before,
which had become a place of pilgrimage only slightly less sacred than the birthplace of Shakespeare. Visitors would lie in wait to catch a glimpse of the famous
novelist in her little chaise pulled by two Shetland ponies, with a man-servant
perched up behind, or gliding down the Avon, parasol in hand, in the gondola
brought from Venice and propelled by an Italian gondolier.

Increasingly she had come to regard herself as the greatest living authority on
Shakespeare and made an annual pilgrimage to his grave. She had constituted
herself his champion, getting herself embroiled in tremendous battles with the
Trustees of Shakespeare's Birthplace over the preservation of buildings in the
town, which ended in a law-suit, and with the Memorial Theatre Committee
over what she described as its mismanagement of the Festival. So closely had
she managed to identify her name with Shakespeare's that bemused tourists
sometimes left Stratford with the idea that she was a member of his family.

She liked to receive distinguished visitors at Mason Croft and laid herself out
to make Arthur's stay pleasant and entertaining. This visit was the first of many.
Soon she showed him the manuscript of a short book which she was just
finishing, and consulted him flatteringly about its illustrations. The title was to
be *The Devil's Motor: A Fantasy*. It was a strange vision of the Devil riding
through the sky 'in a huge Car', and rushing crowds from the countryside into
cities, where they have no room to breathe, no time to think, and forget that
God exists. Finally he sweeps them all into Hell. 'Take back Thy planet, O great
God,' he cries, 'cleansed of a pygmy race! Create a new Humanity! — for this is

---

[1] Arthur Severn's Memoirs.

past!' Marie and her publisher wanted illustrations for it, and she showed Arthur one that had been sent for her approval.

Arthur thought the drawing careful but very dull – it ought to be much more sensational, considering the subject, he said. As it happened a flat, brown paper parcel had just arrived for him from his colourman that morning. He caught it up and quickly dashed off on it an idea of what he thought should be done. He drew 'a half-naked devil apparently in a car full of fire, with vast wings lit by the glare, and in front two great eyes like search-lights. The car was high up in the air; down below was Westminster in pale dawn, with the towers of the Parliament house reflected in the river'.[1]

Marie was enthusiastic and admiring, and when her publisher came next day to talk about the book, he agreed that it was exactly what they wanted.

After some persuasion Arthur agreed to do a number of drawings as illustrations for the book. He had other work to finish first, but Marie immediately embarked on the building of a studio for him in the garden of Mason Croft. She liked to think of them both at work so near to each other – she in her little study writing immortal prose, and he, the great artist, painting in ideal surroundings, his genius unfettered and untroubled by family worries and interruptions – his career fostered, his fame furthered by his devoted friend. In her imagination Joan had become the rich, unloved wife, she the pure, beautiful woman who understood his genius, a creative artist like himself, burning with passionate, unselfish love for him.

Some time before, she had bought from the school next door an enormous room, which stood between them, and had connected it to her own house, making it into a Music Room with huge French windows leading into the garden. Here her grand piano stood on a dais. Before becoming a writer she had trained to be a professional pianist. Her lack of height was never so noticeable when she was seated, and she was fond of wearing dresses with long trains which, when she rose from the piano, she would sweep forward to hang over the edge of the dais, making her appear much taller than she really was. In her vast music room Arthur would sit by the log fire after dinner, while Marie played to him – Wagner, or her own improvisations.

Marie and her friend, Miss Vyver, paid another visit in the summer to Brantwood. This time they stayed in the house for five days.[2] 'Such happy days!' wrote Marie in the visitors' book.

The illustrations for *The Devil's Motor* were finished, and were to be beautifully reproduced in colour for the book. Only two included the Devil. The other four were studies in Arthur's usual style, among them a group of trees with a wintry sun sinking behind them, and a silvery lake in moonlight.

When he had finished the drawings Marie would have been miserable if there had been nothing to bring Arthur (whom she had now christened 'Pendennis')

[1] Arthur Severn's Memoirs.
[2] 3rd–8th June, 1909.

to Mason Croft. Fortunately (or perhaps Fortune was nudged) he was commissioned almost at once to do twenty-five drawings, as illustrations for a book
on Shakespeare — drawings of places near Stratford-on-Avon, which the poet
might have known. Another reason for him to make frequent visits to Stratford-
on-Avon had been established. Marie had Arthur's original drawing for *The
Devil's Motor* framed. It hung in her study, with the marks on each end, showing
where the seals had come on the parcel.

*

It was natural to Marie to pour out her feelings on paper, and when Arthur was
away she would write page after page, supposedly addressed to him, in her
journal.[1] 'If I — I, who am writing this record, love you, it is indeed nothing to
you, and should be nothing. . . . The wind rouses me to exhilaration and excita-
tion — the sea fills me with vague melancholy; but both wind and sea are unconscious of their effect upon my soul, and you — you, my one love in this
world and the next, are equally unconscious of the thoughts you awaken in
me. . . . I am conscious of joy when you are near me and of desolation when I
see you not at all. . . . It is Nature alone that has set this pulse of love thrilling in
my blood. . . . In the years I have spent on earth I have attained a few of the
things which the majority of people consider most worth winning, — wealth is
one of these things, and also the poor fact of a certain renown. . . . They seem the
idlest trifles compared with one glance from you, — one smile on your lips, —
one fleeting expression on that beloved face. . . . If you lived no longer I too
should cease to be. . . . But this is my secret. . . . My friends and acquaintances
know nothing of it, — if they could guess . . . they would hold up their
hands in pious horror and feign the usual ridiculous amazement that anyone
should love where love is, by the world's estimate and law, forbidden.'

Again Marie and Bertha came to stay at Brantwood the next summer — this
time for over a fortnight.[2] Joan found Marie a great trial, and with her gift for
mimicry could not resist a few imitations of her girlish, gushing behaviour
with Arthur. Marie, on her side, was equally irked by Joan, who had become
in her eyes the tiresome impediment to a great love. Nevertheless her comment
in the visitors' book at her departure was suitably ecstatic (no one else ever wrote
comments in the book): 'A dream of sunshine — fair scenes and sweet blossoms
— Emblems of the kind hearts that alone make the world worth living in.'

Her private admonitions to Arthur in her journal were more astringent: 'We
harm ourselves infinitely by imagining duties and ties to this or to that person,
when such ties and duties hamper the soul in its wider and nobler attainment,
and many a lonely heart has sacrificed its rightful heritage of love on account of
some trifling home obstacle which in the long run shall prove but cold comfort.
The road should widen as we pass onward . . . and those who would force us to

---

[1] This was published after her death, ostensibly as a work of imagination, entitled *Open Confession*.
[2] 30th May–16th June, 1910.

walk in one cramped path of routine should be broken away from and left with all possible speed.'

To make sure of Arthur's company later that summer, she professed herself fascinated by his talk about the sea. She longed to enjoy the true pleasure of sailing. Arthur, who loved every moment he could spend on the sea, told her he knew of just the boat — a schooner of 150 tons belonging to a friend of his — an admirable sea-boat and very comfortable. It was the *Silver Star*, which he had often sailed before. Marie had soon decided to charter it, and of course Arthur must come too, to arrange everything and decide where they should go. They spent a month sailing round the west coast of Scotland; the famous authoress fortunately proved to be a good sailor, and Arthur took the opportunity to make many sketches.

The Devil's Motor was published and Arthur showed nine of the drawings which he had made for illustrations in his one-man exhibition the next year[1] — his second at the Leicester Galleries. He also showed 51 water-colours and charged slightly higher prices than at the previous show. About the same number of pictures was sold and altogether he made £690. It was at this exhibition that Marie made a scene which embarrassed Arthur's family. On the morning of the private view his niece, Margaret, and her husband, F. E. Smith, now a Member of Parliament and a K.C., came into the gallery and bought a picture. A red tab was fixed to the frame. Later in the day Margaret came in again. The room was crowded and Marie Corelli was there, dressed in pastel shades, her dress trimmed with girlish ribbons and gauzes floating round her. They had scarcely met before, but she bore down on Margaret, threw her arms round her neck and exclaimed in loud, heart-rending tones, 'You've taken *my* picture. Pendennis *promised* I could have it. He painted it for *me*. You *must* let me have it!'

Margaret tried to explain that her husband had chosen it, but Marie only raised her voice even louder and then burst into tears. To Margaret's embarrassment everybody present abandoned any pretence of looking at the pictures and gathered round them, staring. Eventually she managed to extricate herself from Marie's arms, and feeling that anything was better than prolonging such a scene, 'Oh for goodness sake *have* the picture,' she said and left the gallery. It was an unfortunate day for her, as when she told her husband that evening what she had done, he was very cross and said that she should not have given in to blackmail. He had particularly liked that picture.[2]

Later in the year Marie published another novel, *The Life Everlasting*, which showed how much her romance had changed her view of life. Her books had until now been full of suffering, disillusioned women, subdued by tyrannical men, whose coarse natures prevented them from understanding feminine delicacy. In her new book she gave an ecstatic picture of perfect love. 'Soul

---

[1] March 1911.
[2] Margaret Countess of Birkenhead to author.

rushes to soul,' she wrote, 'heart leaps to heart ... the immortal soul-spark strikes its kindred fire across a waste of worlds until they meet in the compelling flash of that God's Message called Love.' The pure, exquisite woman finds her perfect mate. 'Like two notes of a perfect chord we mould our lives on the keyboard of the Infinite, and we know that the music will become fuller and sweeter as the eternal seasons roll on.'

Marie still kept up the pretence of being a family friend. When Joan came to London she would often be greeted by flowers from Marie — always a florist's arrangement, the flowers stiffened by wire or in a basket with enormous bows of ribbon attached. Joan could not bear them. 'I don't know *what* to do with them,' she would complain. Her imitation of Marie's voice and mannerisms was by now perfect, and it was difficult for her nieces to keep a straight face when Marie addressed their uncle, as she often did, with her slight Cockney accent: 'Ow, Pen*dennis*!' or after drinking tea, dabbed her lips daintily with the end of her coloured chiffon scarf.

A large oil painting by Arthur, *A Misty Sunset on the Italian Riviera*, was presented to the Birmingham Art Gallery that year by an anonymous admirer of the Gallery, and in June Arthur attended the regatta at Stratford-on-Avon in Marie Corelli's gondola. She had some time before presented a Challenge Vase for the senior race and this year had also given several extra prizes. 'The appearance of Miss Marie Corelli on the classic stream,' wrote the *Stratford Herald*, 'was the signal for a continuous round of applause as the gondolier propelled the distinguished novelist to the island by the winning post, where Miss Corelli — who was accompanied by Mr Arthur Severn, R.I., and Miss Vyver — had the pleasure of witnessing several exciting finishes.' Later she distributed the prizes in the Bancroft gardens, 'having a pleasant word for each of the successful competitors', and was loudly cheered, 'bowing her acknowledgements to the large ring of spectators'.[1]

When Arthur stayed with her at Mason Croft she would send him every morning in her car wherever he wished to paint, and it would return again in the evening to pick him up, when his work was finished. She consulted his comfort in everything, and delighted to humble herself playfully before him. She would call him the Master and herself the Studio-boy, and would even submit to being cut short in the full flow of her conversation, when Arthur, exasperated, would bark 'Oh shut up!' She had never allowed anyone to speak to her like that before, but she cherished his brusqueness as a sign of male domination.

'Why should women seek to be equals with men when their very existence depends on their ability to be lost like melted jewels in the wine of life?' she demanded in her journal. 'These war cries are screamed by women who not only have never loved, but who have never been loved. . . . I speak of actual and real Love, of course; the casual animal impulses have little to do with the positive Divine Passion which uplifts, transfigures and transforms.'

[1] 28th June, 1912.

Arthur may have found her intensity cloying, but he was never with her for very long at a time, and it is astonishing how little harm a man sees in flattery when it is directed exclusively at himself. Marie, for her part, was revelling in the great romance of her life — a transcendent love between two geniuses, as she saw it, tragically held apart by convention, but perhaps all the more beautiful for that reason.

'It is altogether away from the canons of respectability, but nevertheless true, that the great passions of men have ever been roused by women who are not their wives, and who, moreover, never wish to be their wives,' she confided to her journal. 'I would not be a fetter on your life. I could not see you frittering away your mind in the discussion of domestic happenings. . . . I would not have you bound to me by Law and State and Church. I love to know that you are free to come and go to the nest of my heart as you will. . . . If our love were of the sensual or sexual type, criminally degrading to both of us, restraint of selfishness might not be so easy — but we do not drag our jewels in the mire!'

What could be more perfect than their after-dinner walks in the moonlit garden of Mason Croft, or the evenings in the lofty Music Room, with Arthur at ease in an armchair by the fire, while she played the piano for him? 'The other evening I was playing the melody of an old song,' she wrote, '. . . and you turned towards me with a look in your eyes that well compensated me for many solitary hours! — for in that brief moment I saw your very soul, the angel of you, flash out recognition, and my own soul sprang up in swift response.'

When she came again to Brantwood — this time without the dignified Miss Vyver — she was very possessive with him. She wanted to take him away from the others for walks in the woods and sulked when he retired to his studio or talked to anyone else. Joan's patience was sorely tried, and Arthur did not enjoy her visit. 'To-day I have so longed for one word, one glance from you!' she exclaimed in her journal '. . . Do you know — can you guess — this corroding mental suffering which makes me unlike myself?' She comforted herself by remembering a moment when they had found themselves 'soul to soul' in the woods, and 'merged in each other's thoughts became suddenly rapt into nature, as though we were no more than fine essences drawn out of her bosom to mingle together and float towards the sun'.

These problems were overshadowed soon afterwards by the coming of war, and Marie threw herself into writing patriotic articles and pointing out the terrible danger of leaving so many people of German extraction at large in the country.

*

Without their having realized it, the Severns' financial position had been changing, and now the onset of war accelerated the process. George Allen had turned out to be a good man of business, as well as a fine engraver, but his children were not so capable. By Ruskin's agreement with George Allen they continued to publish his books after their father's death, and for some time, while the thirty-nine heavy volumes of the Library Edition were being published, there was a steady demand for them. But gradually this demand decreased, and the Allens no longer confined themselves to Ruskin's work, but turned to publishing other books as well. Here their lack of business ability was fatal. Though they produced beautiful books, they often unconsciously sold them for less than they had cost to make. Eventually in 1911 they amalgamated with another publishing business which was also in financial difficulties, and three years later, in January 1914, the joint company was declared bankrupt.

After a short time a new company was formed which bought the assets of Allen's business. But the remaining stock of Ruskin's books, as well as all the blocks for the illustrations, were the property of the Ruskin Literary Trustees — then Joan, Wedderburn and the solicitor — and the new company was entitled only to a commission on the sales. There was still a demand for a few of Ruskin's books, and as the existing stocks of these particular volumes melted away, there was anxious discussion among the Trustees as to whether they should find the money to replace them. The price of paper had soared owing to war shortages, and to do so would have consumed most of the money made by those volumes which they had just sold. By the judge's decision after Ruskin's death, the first thousand pounds made by the sale of his books in every year was to be paid to Joan and Arthur to enable them to keep up Brantwood as he had directed in his will, but they had found that even this had never been sufficient for the purpose. It was a large house and there were many servants. Now everything cost more, and the Trustees decided not to pay for any volumes to be reprinted until the war was ended. By that time Ruskin's reputation had suffered the eclipse which so often comes after death to men whose names have been venerated in their life time. There was no question of 'the first thousand pounds' derived from the sale of his books in the year; they did not sell at all.

Joan and Arthur still had their house in Warwick Square, as well as Brantwood. Neither Lily nor Violet had married. Joan still had her gardeners and her carriage — she would never have a car. They made no attempt to change their way of life.

Thus it was that they began to sell more and more treasures. They got Collingwood to make a copy of Titian's *Doge* which Arthur had taken to court to show the jury in the Whistler libel case what was meant by 'sound workmanship'.[1] They sold the original, and hung Collingwood's copy in its place on the dining-room wall.

No improvement in their circumstances came with the end of the war. New writers and critics had arisen, new forms of art were admired, new social problems faced society. No one now read Ruskin's books, and Arthur's painting, which had remained popular until the beginning of the war, was thought hopelessly old-fashioned. Like his father, when he too had outlived his vogue as an

---

[1] This picture is now in the National Gallery and attributed to Catena.

artist, he made several attempts to write. He had begun a Life of Ruskin years before, but had never got very far with it. Since then he had begun his reminiscences, but somehow he never seemed to finish them.

When Lily died of typhoid soon after the war it was a terrible blow to him. She had been his favourite child – the most like him, sociable and fond of company. Violet was different, shy, simple and retiring, unable to cope with the outside world, but she remained her mother's favourite. Young Arthur and his father had never got on well. Now he lived all the time at Bibury and scarcely ever left his trout farm – his father could not understand anyone liking such a life.

Joan was often disappointed by the price they got, when they decided to sell some treasure from Brantwood. In 1921 she wished to dispose of the manuscript of Scott's *Fortunes of Nigel*. She knew that Ruskin had given six hundred guineas for it, and hoped to get that amount and perhaps a little more. But this proved impossible. Anything to do with Keats or Shelley was in great demand, she was told, not so the great Victorian authors; Scott, Ruskin and Carlyle were all out of fashion.

Joan and Arthur celebrated their Golden Wedding in 1923. Arthur remained astonishingly youthful in appearance. He was eighty-one that year but he looked far younger. He was always very dapper and was a familiar figure at picture exhibitions, clad in a black overcoat with an astrakhan collar. He still had a thick head of hair, which he wore rather long.

The romantic friendship with Marie Corelli had only recently come to an abrupt end. Since the book that she wrote after the beginning of her love for Arthur, *The Life Everlasting*, she had published five more novels, but none of them had enjoyed the success of her earlier work, and now she was regarded as a relic of the old, far-off, pre-war world. She had always needed adulation to help her to maintain her fantasy of herself as the perfect woman. Bertha Vyver was still there to support and comfort her with unquestioning devotion, but her other admirers had melted away. She was now even more resentful of any criticism and Arthur's brusqueness was no longer seen as a tribute. When he concealed his boredom with her more intense rhapsodies by interrupting with a joke, she felt that he failed to show a proper appreciation of her superiority over other women. She was by now acutely sensitive to any threat to the conception of 'Marie Corelli', the personality which she, an illegitimate child who had begun life as Minnie Mackay, had created for herself – a woman beautiful, brilliant and admired by all.

The end had come one evening at Mason Croft, when Arthur had been more than usually irritated by her effusions. He had always been fond of walking about outside in the evening, and studying the effects of moonlight or a cloudy sky. In the past he noticed with surprise how to Ruskin 'Nature ceased to exist when the sun went down. ... I don't suppose he ever went out walking by moonlight in his life. All he knew about the night was going to the theatre in a shut brougham.'[1] On this particular evening Marie accompanied him on a stroll in the garden and kept up a flow of high-souled chatter which got on his nerves. An owl hooted in the trees. 'Ow, Pen,' she said, 'just *listen* to the aowls!'

'Aowls!' he repeated crossly. 'For God's sake, woman, say "owls", if it's "owls" you mean.'

Thus was the thread of magic snapped.

She turned at once to her journal and her pen dashed over the paper in page after page of hysterical invective. He had joined the ranks of her enemies and no virtues were left to him.

Arthur had never really understood the intensity of her feeling, or the power of her imagination, and he was surprised to have an angrily sarcastic, would-be wounding letter in reply to one from him. He had no idea of the existence of her journal.

[1] Arthur Severn's Memoirs.

CHAPTER 40

SIC TRANSIT

1924 — 1931

IN JUNE 1924 JOAN DIED, as she would have wished, at 'beloved Brantwood' and was laid to rest beside her cousin and her daughter, Lily, in Coniston churchyard. On the plain stone cross which Arthur placed on her grave she was described as 'the trusted cousin and helper of John Ruskin' — an epitaph which she would have preferred to any other.

Arthur spent more and more time in London, at Warwick Square. He had never been so fond of Brantwood as Joan, and now that he was over eighty and could no longer enjoy the sailing, he preferred to be in London, where he had friends and picture galleries to visit. His twin, Eleanor, had died just before the war, but two of her daughters were in London, and another niece, Katie Milroy, daughter of Joan's sister, lived in the corner house opposite him in Warwick Square.

In old age Arthur resembled his father in youthfulness and charm. But his father had always been sunny-tempered, he had never shouted at people as Arthur was prone to do. Nor had Arthur the strong affection for his children that Joseph had, perhaps because, with the exception of Lily, who had died, they were all so unlike him. He had never understood his two elder sons' passion for sport, or Herbert's enthusiasm for engineering.

He resembled his father, too, in his ignorance of money; like Joseph he was always confident that 'something would turn up', and never in his life had he planned or schemed about it. Perhaps it would have been better for him if he had been forced to worry more. Fate, by making him an adjunct to Ruskin and involving him irrevocably in the Brantwood cult, had probably treated him cruelly as an artist. The very facility which had brought him success so early, at his first exhibition, was a danger to his artistic development, and with personal popularity and a comfortable life, in which he could indulge his love of sailing and travel without worrying about the future, had combined to prevent his gifts reaching their full fruition.

But even in his old age the Severn charm worked for him, as it had for his father. Neither of them ever had to face the cruel loneliness that so often mars the end of a long life. Arthur began now to be troubled by rheumatism, and he was quite unused to arranging anything to do with a household. To his aid came a woman who had once stayed with them in the old days at Brantwood. Drawn

to him, as Marie Corelli and many others had been, she took over supervision
of his household, managed all day-to-day arrangements for him, and eventually
moved into his house to care for him. Violet very rarely came to London. She
lived at Brantwood and spent a great deal of her time rowing on the lake. She
was looked after by one of the gardeners and his wife, who lived in the house
with their large family of children. The other gardener, Joe Wilkinson, who as
a young man had lived in Coniston and rowed across the lake every day to
work, had moved with his family into the lodge when Baxter died; he, too,
remained.

Arthur was quite unable to manage his financial affairs. He lived from day to
day, and when he found himself hard up he sold something, not taking any
trouble to get a good price. A cheque proffered was always accepted, though
sometimes with mild regret: 'I hoped the missal would have fetched more. . . .
I will look out some drawings and send them.' His rare visits to Brantwood
became a search for further treasures to dispose of, to pay the bills which seemed
incessant. He had all the expenses, too, of his house in London, which had by
the terms of his lease to be painted outside every three years, and kept in good
repair, and he had to pay the wages of the gardeners at Brantwood.

Quickly Brantwood deteriorated. When Ruskin first bought it he had complained of damp, due to the hill rising so steeply from the back of the house to
the peaty moor above, where water gathered and seeped down the slope. Now
that only a small part of it was lived in and there were no fires in the un-
occupied rooms, the damp began to penetrate the house again. It stood, too, exposed to the full force of the south-western gales and the heavy rain-storms
which in that mountain country sometimes raise the level of the lake by as much
as eighteen inches in a single day. Windows began to let the rain drive through,
and water leaked through the roof into buckets and saucepans placed below.
Arthur got only £4 each for nine large drawings by Ruskin, because the buyer
said that they were stained by damp.

Friends urged him to complete his Memoirs and he did so as best he could.
Like his father when he, too, had sat down in old age to write his reminiscences,
he was hopelessly inaccurate in his dates and self-contradictory in his statements.
He was also lacking in an instinct of what would be interesting to others. He
would devote several pages to retailing a humorous story which someone had
told him, but would tantalizingly give no proper description of people or
occasions at which he had been present. One of his friends approached several
publishers for him, but with no success. The same man, who was a trustee of the
Guild of St George, tried unsuccessfully to negotiate the sale of Brantwood to the
Guild. It was in fact doubtful whether Arthur was in a position to dispose of it —
he could not in any case have done so without the consent of the Trustees.

Agnew, who was one of the executors of his mother's will, and a Trustee of
the Ruskin Literary Trust, protested that his father had no right even to sell any
drawings from Brantwood. Arthur replied furiously that this was nonsense.

Though admitting that he was not quite clear what his son's powers were as Trustee, 'Brantwood belongs to me,' he said, 'and I have a perfect right to sell what I choose.' He told friends that he would like Brantwood to become the property of the nation, but nothing came of the idea. For the last few months of his life he was an invalid and seldom left his house, though he still liked to see visitors, sitting up in a chair in his bedroom looking over the Square gardens. He died there on 23rd February, 1931, six months before his ninetieth birthday, without even leaving a will.

★

His son Agnew had died two years before him. There remained only 'young' Arthur, aloof in his Bibury trout farm, Herbert, who assumed the responsibility of settling the estate, and Violet, who could not be persuaded to come south for her father's funeral service at St Gabriel's Warwick Square, when Bishop Wild, husband of Christian Severn, officiated. It was rumoured among her relations that Violet was rowing about on Coniston Water at the time and nobody had been able to reach her. Arthur was buried beside Joan in Coniston churchyard.

Young Arthur was not at all interested in Brantwood, Ruskin, Keats or anything, indeed, except fishing. Herbert, the youngest of the family, had gone to work in Canada when he was twenty-eight and had spent some years there. He was equally uninterested. Both were unmarried. With the consent of the Trustees, now Eleanor Furneaux's elder son and a son of Henry Severn's, they decided to sell Brantwood and also the house in Warwick Square. Violet went to live in a small house in Coniston village, accompanied by the gardener and his family who had lived at Brantwood with her.

Most of Ruskin's library, including twenty-seven volumes of his own diaries and notebooks, hundreds of letters to his father, and manuscripts of a few of his later books, together with a large number of Kate Greenaway's letters and drawings, had been sold at Sotheby's by the Trustees seven months before Arthur's death. Now there was a sale of the final portion of the library, including three large parcels which contained many hundreds of his letters to Joan (sold for only £6), and some of Arthur's papers, among them a number of letters written to Joseph Severn by friends in London, when he and Keats had just arrived in Rome and after the poet's death, and some of the manuscripts of Joseph's reminiscences.

Almost everything in the house in Warwick Square and Brantwood was dispersed at various sales throughout the summer. It was the period of the great Depression and not a good time for selling anything. Ruskin's Botticelli *Madonna and Child* realized only three hundred pounds, Turner's self-portrait in oils at the age of twenty, which used to hang in the dining-room at Brantwood, sold for nine. Ruskin's own reputation was at its lowest ebb.

The personal relics of the great man were sold for pathetic sums, most of them with Joan's carefully written labels still attached. His gold repeater watch, a twenty-first birthday present, which he had always worn on a long gold chain round his neck, was bought for ten guineas, but a lace handkerchief, one of his blue stocks and his stockinet night cap fetched only a pound between them. Another lot was a gold whistle, labelled by Joan: 'Given to Aunt Ruskin by her son J R when she broke a thigh, so as to save ringing the bell.' Someone gave twenty-five shillings for it.

Arthur had had some good furniture (mostly French) and china in his house in Warwick Square. There was a sale there, but the best things were sold at Sotheby's and a few pieces of furniture which Ruskin had used personally were brought to London, to be included in the same sale. They might as well have been left at Brantwood. His armchair, in which he sat when he wrote, went for five pounds, and his dressing-table for two pounds five shillings. It was no longer fashionable to be interested in Ruskin.

The saddest spectacle still remained – the three-day sale at Brantwood itself. Here mismanagement added to the usual pathos when the once-loved contents of a home are exposed before indifferent eyes. For some reason – perhaps because the rooms on the ground floor of the house were judged to be too small – the sale was held in the garden, and for most of the time it rained. It was well known that the most valuable contents of the house had been sold in London, but many local people came, and furnishings and domestic utensils went for more than their actual value, as souvenirs. A few local dealers and a number of tourists were there, in spite of the weather, but only one London firm was represented. They were bidding for American clients, and most of the more important lots were bought by them. What remained of the letters, which over the years had been so carefully preserved by Joan, docketed, and tied into neat parcels by her and Sara Anderson, were brought from the drawers in the old dining-room, with odd bits of manuscript, and sold just as they were in the rain for trifling sums, the outside letters of the packets spattered with the rain which fell on drawings, manuscripts and letters alike. So careless and ignorant were those concerned that a number of papers were rescued by collectors, when about to be thrown on to the bonfire of rubbish after the sale was over.

The paths which Ruskin had made up the hillside behind the house had long since been overgrown, and the course of his little stream was choked with stones. The garden in the heart of the wood, which he had tended himself, was lost in weeds, and no boats lay in the harbour below the house. The tennis lawn had reverted to rough field and nettles had invaded Joan's garden.

Everything that they had made with such care and thought had crumbled in decay; but around their little domain still the wider beauty reigned – the beauty of cloud and sun and sky, which Arthur had painted and in which Ruskin had seen the hand of God.

Ruskin, Joan and Arthur – they have all gone, but the brilliant colours of the sunset still stain the waters of the lake, and the Old Man towers to the sky on the further shore, his slopes gilded by the rising sun, as when Ruskin watched the dawn from his study window before the household was awake: 'Morning breaks . . . along those Coniston Fells, and the level mists, motionless, and grey beneath the rose of the moorlands, veil the lower woods, and the sleeping village, and the long lawns by the lakeshore.'

BIBLIOGRAPHY

Unpublished material:

Arthur Severn's Memoirs.

Joseph Severn's Letters to his family from Rome: Keats House, Hampstead.

Severn and Ruskin Letters: Ruskin Galleries, Bembridge.

Severn and Ruskin Letters: John Rylands Library, Manchester and Pierpont Morgan Library, New York.

Joan Severn's Letters to Professor C. E. Norton: Houghton Library, Harvard University.

Ruskin Letters: Yale University Library and Illinois University Library.

Severn Letters: originals with the Author, Dr. H. G. Viljoen, The Dean of Durham, Miss Gwen Williams and The Rev. I. Hutchinson.

The Diaries of Mary, Eleanor and Florence Severn.

A Victorian Artist — Unpublished Memoir of Mary Severn by Claudia Gale.

ABBOTT and CAMPBELL : *Life and Letters of Benjamin Jowett:* Murray, 1857.
ADAMI, MARIE : *Fanny Keats:* Murray, 1937.
ATLAY, J.B. : *Henry Acland:* Smith Elder, 1903.
BELL, QUENTIN : *Ruskin:* Oliver & Boyd, 1963.
BENSON, A.C. : *Ruskin: A Study in Personality:* Smith Elder, 1911.
BIGLAND, EILEEN : *Marie Corelli:* Jarrolds, 1953.
BLAKESTON, NOEL : *The Roman Question: Extracts from Despatches of Odo Russell:* Shenval Press, 1962.
BLUNDEN, EDMUND : *Leigh Hunt:* Cobden-Sanderson, 1930.
BROWN, CHARLES ARMITAGE : *Life of John Keats:* Oxford University Press, 1937.
BURNE-JONES, G. : *Memorials of Edward Burne-Jones:* Macmillan, 1904.
BUXTON FORMAN, H. (ed.) : *Letters of John Keats to Fanny Brawne:* Reeves & Turner, 1878.
BUXTON FORMAN, MAURICE (ed.) : *Letters of John Keats:* Oxford University Press, 1935.
CLARK, SIR KENNETH : *Ruskin at Oxford:* Clarendon Press, 1947.
CLARK, SIR KENNETH : *Ruskin Today:* Murray, 1964.
CLARKE, MARY COWDEN : *My Long Life:* T. Fisher Unwin, 1896.
CLARKE, CHARLES and MARY COWDEN : *Recollections of Writers:* Sampson Low, 1892.
COLLINGWOOD, W.G. : *The Life and Work of John Ruskin:* Methuen, 1893.
COLLINGWOOD, W.G. *Ruskin Relics:* Isbister, 1903.
COLVIN SIDNEY : *John Keats:* Macmillan, 1918.
COOK, E.T. : *The Life of Ruskin:* Allen, 1911.
COOK, E.T. and WEDDERBURN A. (ed.) : *The Works of John Ruskin* (39 Vols.): Allen, 1903–1911.
CORELLI, MARIE : *Open Confession:* Hutchinson, 1925.

Correspondence of Thomas Carlyle and Ralph Waldo Emerson: Chatto & Windus, 1885.

CRANE, WALTER : *An Artist's Reminiscences:* Methuen, 1907.

DILKE, CHARLES WENTWORTH : *Papers of A Critic:* Murray, 1875.

EATON's *Rome in the 19th Century:* 1820.

EDGCUMBE, F. (ed.): *Letters of Fanny Brawne to Fanny Keats:* Oxford University Press, 1936.

EVANS, B. IFOR : 'Keats and Joseph Severn': *London Mercury,* August 1934.

EVANS, JOAN, and WHITEHOUSE J.H. (ed.): *Diaries of John Ruskin:* Clarendon Press, 1956–9.

EVANS, JOAN : *John Ruskin:* Jonathan Cape, 1954.

GITTINGS, ROBERT : *John Keats: The Living Year:* Heinemann, 1954.

HEWLETT, DOROTHY : *Life of John Keats:* Hurst & Blackett, 1948.

HOLIDAY, HENRY : *Reminiscences of My Life:* Heinemann, 1914.

HORNER, FRANCES : *Time Remembered:* Heinemann, 1933.

Hortus Inclusus, Letters from John Ruskin to the Ladies of the Thwaite, Coniston: Allen, 1887.

ILCHESTER, THE EARL OF (ed.): *Journal of Hon. Henry Edward Fox:* Butterworth, 1923.

JAMES, ADMIRAL SIR WILLIAM : *The Order of Release:* Murray, 1947.

KING, BOLTON : *History of Italian Unity:* Nisbet, 1899.

KITCHIN, DEAN : *Ruskin in Oxford:* Murray, 1904.

LEON, DERRICK : *Ruskin the Great Victorian:* Routledge & Kegan Paul, 1949.

Letters of John Ruskin to Charles Eliot Norton, Houghton Mifflin, 1905.

Letters of Joseph Severn to H. Buxton Forman: Privately printed, 1933.

LOCKER-LAMPSON, FREDERICK : *My Confidences:* Smith Elder, 1896.

LUTYENS, MARY : *Effie in Venice:* Murray, 1965.

MACDONALD, GREVILLE : *Reminiscences of a Specialist:* Allen & Unwin, 1932.

MACDONALD, GREVILLE : *George MacDonald and his Wife:* Allen & Unwin, 1924.

MARKS, HENRY STACY, R.A. : *Pen and Pencil Sketches:* Chatto & Windus, 1894.

MATTHEWS, HENRY : *The Diary of an Invalid:* Murray, 1822.

MEYNELL, VIOLA (ed.): *Friends of a Lifetime: Letters to SCC:* Cape, 1940.

MEYNELL, VIOLA (ed.): *The Best of Friends—Further letters to Sydney Carlyle Cockerell:* Hart-Davis, 1956.

MILLS, J. SAXON : *Life and Letters of Sir Hubert Herkomer:* Hutchinson, 1923.

MILNES, RICHARD MONCKTON : *Life, Letters and Literary Remains of John Keats:* Moxon, 1848.

MOORE, T. and D.C. STURGE (ed.): *Works and Days from the Journal of Michael Field:* Murray, 1933.

NEWBOLT, HENRY : *My World as in My Time:* Faber & Faber, 1932.

QUENNELL, PETER : *John Ruskin, The Portrait of a Prophet:* Collins, 1949.

RAWNSLEY, THE REV. H.D. : *Harvey Goodwin, Bishop of Carlisle:* Murray, 1896.

Ruskin and the English Lakes: Glasgow, 1901.

RICHARDSON, JOANNA : *Fanny Brawne:* Thames & Hudson, 1952.

RITCHIE, ANNE : *Records of Tennyson, Ruskin and Browning:* Macmillan, 1892.

ROBERTSON, GRAHAM : *Time Was:* Hamilton, 1931.

ROLLINS, H.E. (ed.): *The Keats Circle:* Harvard University Press, 1948.

ROSENBERG, JOHN D. : *The Darkening Glass:* Routledge & Kegan Paul, 1963.

SCOTT, WILLIAM STUART : *Marie Corelli:* Hutchinson, 1955.

SHARP, WILLIAM : *Life and Letters of Joseph Severn:* Sampson Low, Marston, 1892.

SPIELMANN and LAYARD: *Kate Greenaway:* A. & C. Black, 1905.

STIRLING, A.M.W. (ed.): *The Richmond Papers:* Heinemann, 1926.

SWETT, LUCIA GREY: *John Ruskin's Letters to Francesca:* Lothrop Lee & Shephard, 1931.

TAYLOR, T. (ed.): *Autobiography and Memoirs of B. R. Haydon:* Davies, 1926.

UNWIN, RAYNER (ed.): *The Gulf of Years: Letters from John Ruskin to Kathleen Olander:* Allen & Unwin, 1953.

UNWIN, SIR STANLEY: *The Truth about a Publisher:* Allen & Unwin, 1960.

VYVER, BERTHA: *Memoirs of Marie Corelli:* Alston Rivers, 1930.

WARD, AILEEN: *John Keats:* Secker & Warburg, 1963.

WHITEHOUSE, J. HOWARD: *Ruskin and Brantwood:* Ruskin Society, 1937.

WHITEHOUSE, J. HOWARD: *Vindication of Ruskin:* Allen & Unwin, 1950.

WILENSKI, R.H.: *John Ruskin:* Faber & Faber, 1933.

WRENTMORE, C.Q. (ed.): *Letters of John Ruskin to Bernard Quaritch:* Quaritch, 1953.

YOUNG, M.F. (ed.): *Letters of a Noble Woman* (Mrs La Touche): Allen, 1908.

INDEX